ACCOUNTING
principles and applications

PARTS ONE AND TWO

FOURTH EDITION

Horace R. Brock,
Ph.D., C.P.A.
Professor of Accounting
College of Business Administration
North Texas State University
Denton, Texas

Charles E. Palmer,
D.C.S., C.P.A.
Chairman of the Board
Strayer College
Washington, D.C.

AMERICAN INSTITUTE OF BANKING

AMERICAN BANKERS ASSOCIATION

Gregg Division/McGraw-Hill Book Company

New York   Atlanta   Dallas   St. Louis   San Francisco
Auckland   Bogotá   Guatemala   Hamburg   Johannesburg   Lisbon   London
Madrid   Mexico   Montreal   New Delhi   Panama   Paris   San Juan
São Paulo   Singapore   Sydney   Tokyo   Toronto

Sponsoring Editor: Sherry Cohen
Editing Supervisor: Elissa Pinto
Production Supervisor: Laurence Charnow
Design Supervisor: Karen T. Miño
Art Supervisor: George T. Resch

Library of Congress Cataloging in Publication Data

Brock, Horace R.
  Accounting: principles and applications.

  Includes index.
  1. Accounting. I. Palmer, Charles Earl,
date   joint author. II. Title.
[HF5635.B85452   1981b]   657   80-16707
ISBN 0-07-008091-7

Special edition prepared for the
American Bankers Association
ISBN 0-07-008086-0

**Accounting: Principles and Applications
Parts One and Two, Fourth Edition**

Copyright © 1981, 1974 by McGraw-Hill, Inc.
All rights reserved. Copyright © 1969, 1963 by
McGraw-Hill, Inc., as *College Accounting—
Theory/Practice.* All rights reserved. Printed in
the United States of America. No part of this
publication may be reproduced, stored in a
retrieval system, or transmitted, in any form or
by any means, electronic, mechanical,
photocopying, recording, or otherwise, without
the prior written permission of the publisher.

1 2 3 4 5 6 7 8 9 0   DODO   8 7 6 5 4 3 2 1

CONTENTS

Preface   ix

PART ONE
ACCOUNTING: basic principles

The Accounting Cycle

UNIT 1   Analyzing Business Transactions   2

Accounting Begins With Analysis • Starting a New Business • Purchasing Business Property for Cash • Purchasing Property on Credit • Paying a Creditor • Preparing the Balance Sheet • The Fundamental Accounting Equation • Effects of Revenue and Expenses • Selling Services for Cash • Selling Services on Credit • Collecting Receivables • Paying Expenses • The Income Statement • The Balance Sheet • The Importance of the Statements

UNIT 2   Setting Up Accounts   19

Accounts for Assets, Liabilities, and Owner's Equity • Recording Payment to a Creditor • Accounts for Revenue and Expenses • The Rules of Debit and Credit • The Double-Entry System • Chart of Accounts • Permanent and Temporary Accounts

UNIT 3   Basic Accounting Records   38

The General Journal • The General Ledger

UNIT 4   The Trial Balance and Worksheet   52

The Trial Balance • Finding the Balance of an Account • Preparing the Trial Balance • Purpose of the Trial Balance • The Worksheet • The Income Statement and the Balance Sheet

UNIT 5   Closing the Books for the Period   68

The Revenue and Expense Summary Account • Transferring Revenue Balances • Transferring Expense Balances • Transferring Net Income or Net Loss to Owner's Equity • Ruling the Ledger Accounts • The Postclosing Trial Balance • Using Dollar Signs • Finding and Correcting Errors

BUSINESS PROJECT 1
Service Business Accounting Cycle   83

Chart of Accounts • Preparing the Ledger • Recording the Daily Transactions • Completing the Cycle

Special Journals and Subsidiary Ledgers

UNIT 6   Accounting for Cash Receipts   87

General Journal Entries for Cash Receipts • The Single-Column Cash Receipts Journal • Posting From the Single-Column Cash Receipts Journal • The Multicolumn Cash Receipts Journal • Posting From the Multicolumn Cash Receipts Journal • Advantages of the Cash Receipts Journal • Balance Ledger Form for the General Ledger Accounts • Recording Sales Taxes • Recording Cash Discounts on Sales • Recording Other Cash Receipts • Safeguarding Receipts • Need for Internal Control Over Business Operations • General Principles of Internal Control • Internal Control Over Cash Receipts • Control of Cash Receipts in a Small Business • The Cash Receipts Journal

UNIT 7   Accounting for Cash Payments   107

General Journal Entries for Cash Payments • The Single-Column Cash Payments Journal • Posting From the Single-Column Cash Payments Journal • The Multicolumn Cash Payments Journal • Posting From the Multicolumn Cash Payments Journal • Advantages of the Cash Payments Journal • Recording Other Cash Payments • Internal Control Over Cash Payments • The Voucher System for Control of Liabilities and Payments of Cash • The Petty Cash Fund • Internal Control of Petty Cash

UNIT 8 Banking Procedures and Reconciliations — 129

Cash Controls • The Deposit Slip • Preparing the Deposit • Making Payments by Check • The Bank Statement • Bank Reconciliation—Modern Cleaning Shop • Bank Reconciliation—Extended Illustration

UNIT 9 The Sales Journal — 149

General Journal Entries for Credit Sales • Recording Entries in the Sales Journal • Posting From the Sales Journal • Advantages of the Sales Journal • Recording Sales Tax • Recording Sales Returns and Allowances • Returns and Allowances Involving Sales Tax • List Price and Trade Discounts • Use of Credit

UNIT 10 The Accounts Receivable Ledger — 169

Recording Credit Sales • The Need for More Information • Accounts for Individual Credit Customers • Revising the Sales Journal • Revising the Cash Receipts Journal • Recording Sales Returns and Allowances • Posting Sales Returns and Allowances • Sales Returns and Allowances Journal • Daily Routine • Subsidiary Ledger Account Balances • End-of-Month Routine • Proving the Subsidiary Ledger • Accounts Receivable From Credit Card Company Sales

UNIT 11 The Purchases Journal — 191

Studying New Plans • Recording Merchandise Purchases in the General Journal • Recording Entries in the Purchases Journal • Posting From the Purchases Journal • Advantages of the Purchases Journal • Recording Freight In • Purchases Returns and Allowances • Internal Control of Purchases • Purchases by Use of Credit Cards

UNIT 12 The Accounts Payable Ledger — 205

Recording Procedures for Purchases • The Need for More Information • Accounts With Individual Creditors • Recording a Purchase • Posting a Purchase to the Creditor's Account • Recording a Cash Payment to a Creditor • Posting a Payment to the Creditor's Account • Recording a Purchase Return or Allowance • Posting a Purchase Return or Allowance • Daily Routine • Subsidiary Ledger Account Balances • End-of-Month Routine • Proving the Subsidiary Ledger • Accounts Payable Resulting From Credit Card Purchases

UNIT 13 The Combined Journal — 221

Designing a Combined Journal • Recording Transactions in the Combined Journal • Daily Postings From the Combined Journal • Proving the Combined Journal • End-of-Month Postings From the Combined Journal • Typical Uses

UNIT 14 The Voucher System — 231

Internal Control in a Medium-Sized Business • The Payment Voucher • Preparing and Approving the Voucher • The Voucher Register • Posting From the Voucher Register • The Check Register • Paying an Invoice Less Discount • Posting From the Check Register • Proving the Accounts Payable Balance • Transactions Requiring Special Treatment • Recording Purchase Discounts Lost • Other Cash Control Procedures

Payroll Records and Procedures

UNIT 15 Payroll Computations, Records, and Payment — 252

Objectives of Payroll Work • Illustrative Case—The Kent Novelty Company • Determining Gross Pay for Hourly Workers • Deductions From Gross Pay Required by Law • Deductions From Gross Pay Not Required by Law • Determining Gross Pay for Salaried Workers • Deductions From Gross Pay • Recording Gross Pay and Deductions for Hourly Workers • Payroll Register • The Accounting Entry for Payroll • Paying the Payroll • Recording Gross Pay and Deductions for Salaried Workers • Individual Earnings Records • Completing January Payrolls • Proving the Individual Earnings Records • Recording the Liability for Unpaid Wages

UNIT 16 Payroll Taxes — 279

Changes in Tax Rates and Bases • Deposit of FICA Taxes and Income Taxes Withheld • Employer's Quarterly Federal Tax Return • Wage and Tax Statements to Employees • Annual Transmittal of Income and Tax Statements • Unemployment Insurance • State Unemployment Tax Returns • Federal Unemployment Tax Returns • Worker's Compensation Insurance

Reporting the Results of Operations

UNIT 17 Depreciation, Bad Debts, and Inventory — 305

Chart of Accounts • New Transactions and Accounts • Depreciation Expense • Bad Debts Expense • The Adjusted Trial Balance • Merchandise on Hand • Completing the Worksheet

UNIT 18 End-of-Period Work for a Merchandising Business — 322

A Service-Merchandising Business • Income Statement • Balance Sheet • Adjusting Entries • Closing Entries • Balancing and Ruling the General Ledger • Postclosing Trial Balance • Beginning Merchandise Inventory • Classified Financial Statements • Classified Balance Sheet • Classified Income Statement

---

PART TWO
financial accounting: basic principles

The Accrual Basis of Accounting

UNIT 19 Accounting Principles and Reporting Standards — 352

The Need for Generally Accepted Accounting Principles • The Sources of Generally Accepted Accounting Principles • The Present Framework of Accounting Principles • The Impact of Accounting Principles, Assumptions, and Modifying Conventions

UNIT 20 Notes Payable and Interest — 368

Negotiable Instruments • Notes Payable • Interest • Partial Payment of a Note Payable • Renewing a Note Payable • Discounting a Note Payable at the Bank • Notes Payable Register • Notes Payable and Interest Expense on the Statements

UNIT 21 Notes Receivable and Drafts — 381

Notes Receivable • Noninterest-Bearing Note Received • Interest-Bearing Note Received • Partial Collection of a Note • Note Not Collected at Maturity • Notes Received at the Time of Sale • Discounting a Note Receivable • Noninterest-Bearing Note Discounted • Notes Receivable Discounted—A Contingent Liability • Discounted Noninterest-Bearing Note Paid at Maturity • Discounted Noninterest-Bearing Note Dishonored at Maturity • Interest-Bearing Note Discounted • Discounted Interest-Bearing Note Paid at Maturity • Discounted Interest-Bearing Note Dishonored at Maturity • Notes Receivable Register • Notes Receivable and Interest Income on the Statements • Drafts • Trade Acceptances

UNIT 22 Accounts Receivable and Bad Debts — 397

Recording Losses When They Occur—The Direct Charge-Off Method • Providing for Losses Before They Occur—The Allowance Method • Recording Actual Uncollectible Accounts • Collecting an Account That Was Written Off • Other Receivables and Bad Debt Losses • Bad Debts Expense on the Income Statement • Allowance for Bad Debts on the Balance Sheet • Recognizing the Effect of Potential Cash Discounts • Installment Sales Procedures • Recording Defaults on Installment Sales

UNIT 23 Valuation of Inventory — 415

Importance of Inventory Valuation • Inventory Costing Methods • Cost or Market, Whichever Is Lower • Inventory Estimation Procedures

UNIT 24 Property, Plant, and Equipment — 430

Classification of Property, Plant, and Equipment • Acquisition of Property, Plant, and Equipment • Costs of Using Property, Plant, and Equipment • Recording Depreciation, Depletion, and Amortization • Methods of Accounting for Depreciation • Depletion Methods • Amortization of Intangible Assets • Disposition of an Asset • Trade-In of an Asset

UNIT 25 Business Taxes — 447

Types of Business Taxes • Property Taxes • Retail Licenses • The Style Clothing Store's Tax Situation • Sales and Excise Taxes • Income Tax Returns for Partnerships • Income Tax Returns for Corporations • Tax Calendar

UNIT 26 Accruals and Deferrals — 465

The Accrual Basis • Preparation of the Worksheet • Recording Bad Debts on the Worksheet • Recording Depreciation on the Worksheet • Recording Accrued and Prepaid Items on the Worksheet • Recording the Ending Inventory on the Worksheet

UNIT 27 The Worksheet and the Financial Statements   486

Entering Adjustments on the Worksheet • Completing the Adjusted Trial Balance Section • Preparing the Balance Sheet Section • Preparing the Income Statement Section • Completing the Worksheet • Preparing the Financial Statements

UNIT 28 Adjusting and Closing Procedures   504

Journalizing the Adjusting Entries • Posting the Adjusting Entries • Journalizing the Closing Entries • Posting the Closing Entries • Taking a Postclosing Trial Balance • Ruling the Accounts • The Need for Reversals • Items Requiring Reversals • Locating Reversals • Posting the Reversing Entries • Posting Reversing Entries to Standard Ledger Accounts

BUSINESS PROJECT 2 The Accrual Basis of Accounting   524

The Trial Balance • Entering Adjustments • Completing the Worksheet • Preparing the Financial Statements • Completing the Cycle

Partnership Accounting

UNIT 29 Partnership Organization   527

Formation of a Partnership • Determining the Value of Net Assets • Adjustments on Proprietorship Books • The Partnership Agreement • Dissolving the Sole Proprietorship • Opening the Partnership Books

UNIT 30 Partnerships: Profit Division and Equity Accounting   540

Partner's Capital Account • Partner's Drawing Account • Division of Partnership Profits • Profit Sharing Agreement • Putting the Plan Into Operation • Partnership Equity on the Statements • Admitting a New Partner

Corporate Accounting

UNIT 31 Characteristics and Formation of a Corporation   557

Legal Aspects of a Corporation • Structure of a Corporation • Characteristics of a Corporation • Forming the Corporation • Types of Stock • Dividends to Stockholders • Values of Capital Stock • Capital Stock on the Balance Sheet • Comparison of Dividend Provisions • Financing With Bonds • Incorporating a Sole Proprietorship • Revaluation of Assets • Revaluation Account • Transfer of Assets and Liabilities to the Corporation • Receipt of Stock From the Corporation • Distribution of Stock to the Proprietor • Acquisition of Assets and Liabilities by the Corporation • Issuance of Stock • Organization Costs • Balance Sheet Immediately After Organization

UNIT 32 Capital Stock Transactions; Corporate Records   584

Corporate Records • Articles of Incorporation • Issuing Stock to the Incorporators • Issuing Additional Stock • Meeting of the Stockholders • Meeting of the Board of Directors • Minute Book • Stock Certificate Books • Capital Stock Ledger and Procedures • Transfer Agent and Registrar • Issuing Stock at a Premium • Issuing Stock at a Discount • Stated Value for No-Par Value Stock • Issuing No-Par Value Stock Above Stated Value • Subscriptions for Capital Stock • Treatment of Defaults on Stock Subscriptions • Records of Stock Subscriptions • Treasury Stock • Redemption of Preferred Stock

UNIT 33 Corporation Earnings and Capital Transactions   612

Determining Corporate Net Income • Net Income and Income Taxes • Estimating the Income Tax • Statement Presentation • Entering Income Taxes and Transferring Net Income • Formal Tax Return • Charge-Off of Intangible Assets • Prior Period Adjustments • Appropriations of Retained Earnings • Dividends • Declaration of a Cash Dividend • Payment of a Cash Dividend • Stock Dividends • Other Stockholders' Equity Accounts • Equity Increase From Appraisal • Additional Paid-In Capital

UNIT 34 Bonds and Other Long-Term Liabilities   639

The Need to Borrow Money • Short-Term and Long-Term Credit • Types of Bonds • Entries for Bond Issue and Interest • Bonds Issued at a Premium • Bonds Issued at a Discount • Balance Sheet Presentation of Premium and Discount • Bonds Issued Between Interest Dates • Bond Sinking Fund and Appropriation of Retained Earnings • Retirement of Bonds • Mortgage Liabilities • Issuance of Noninterest-Bearing Notes for Noncash Assets

UNIT 35 Temporary and Long-Term Investments   **660**

Investments by Business Firms • Temporary Investments • Long-Term Investments

Index   **685**

PREFACE

Accounting plays a vital and constantly expanding role in modern business. A knowledge of accounting is therefore highly important for students who are preparing for a wide range of business occupations as well as for students who are preparing for accounting careers. The fourth edition of *Accounting: Principles and Applications, Parts One and Two* has been specially designed to serve the needs of all students who require a brief but well-rounded introduction to accounting. For students whose career objectives call for only one course in accounting, this book provides the necessary understanding of basic accounting principles and procedures. For students who need a broader knowledge of accounting, this book lays a strong foundation for additional study.

Organization and Content of the Text

The text has been carefully planned to help students master accounting in a logical and efficient manner. The content is divided into two parts. Part One provides thorough coverage of the fundamentals of accounting. Part Two introduces the students to major areas of financial accounting: generally accepted accounting principles and financial reporting standards, the accrual basis of accounting, partnership accounting, and corporation accounting.

Throughout the text material, the teaching of accounting procedures is accompanied by the teaching of sound business practices. For example, Units 6, 7, and 8 emphasize internal control over cash receipts and cash payments. Managerial uses of financial data are also stressed throughout so that the students can understand the importance of accounting within the total framework of business operations. For example, a Managerial Implications section appears at the end of each unit.

Effective application activities are essential to the learning process in accounting. This text provides abundant opportunities for the students to put their knowledge into practice. Every unit is followed by a series of problems, alternate problems, and managerial discussion questions. There are also two business projects, which are intended to help the students integrate the material they have studied.

Learning and Teaching Aids

A number of learning and teaching aids are available for use with Parts One and Two of *Accounting: Principles and Applications*, Fourth Edition. These materials are designed to enhance the effectiveness of the course for both the student and the instructor.

Individualized Performance Guides. There is a separate *Individualized Performance Guide* for each part of the text. This learning aid combines the functions of both a study guide and a workbook. It is correlated with the text on a unit-by-unit basis and contains performance objectives for each unit, directions for studying the unit, self-checking questions and exercises that the students can use to evaluate their understanding of the text material, and working papers for the problems or alternate problems and the business projects. The *Individualized Performance Guide* permits a high degree of self-pacing if the instructor wishes. (The amount of self-pacing can be further increased by duplicating and distributing student check answers for the problem material that are given in the *Course Management and Solutions Manuals*.)

Practice Sets. Three practice sets are available for use with this program. The *Sole Proprietorship Service Business Practice Set* involves a one-month accounting cycle for a real estate agency. Working from source documents, the students record transactions in a combined journal, post to the general ledger and the accounts payable ledger, and prepare banking, payroll, and petty cash records. Because the end-of-cycle procedures in the set do not include adjustments, it can be used after completion of Unit 16 of Part One. This practice set is ideal for situations where the instructor wants to provide intensive experience in handling the daily financial activities of a small office.

The *Sole Proprietorship Merchandising Business Practice Set* is designed for use after Unit 18 of Part One. Working from a narrative of transactions, the students perform one month's accounting activities for a retail furniture store. The accounting system of this firm includes special journals and subsidiary ledgers as well as the general journal and the general ledger. There is a full range of end-of-cycle activities including adjustments. A special series of management questions is also provided so that the students have an opportunity to analyze the accounting records they have prepared.

The *Corporation Accounting Application* is designed for use after Unit 35 of Part Two. This practice set allows the students to complete the accounting cycle of a partnership, add a partner, convert the partnership into a corporation, and perform a variety of activities for the corporation.

Tests. Two sets of tests—one for each part—have been developed for use with the text. These tests measure student progress at important points in the course. Instructors who adopt the text can obtain individual test booklets for each student free of charge.

Course Management and Solutions Manuals. There is a separate *Course Management and Solutions Manual* for each part of the text. In addition to providing a complete key for the problems, alternate problems, and business projects, these manuals contain numerous instructional aids such as transparency masters for major types of accounting forms. For ease in checking student assignments, the solutions for the problem material are given on facsimile pages from the corresponding *Individualized Performance Guide*. Transparencies can be made from the solutions if the instructor wishes to project them.

Material for Further Study of Accounting

Part Three of *Accounting: Principles and Applications,* Fourth Edition, is available in a separate textbook and provides an ideal follow-up to Parts One and Two for students who want to continue their study of accounting. Part Three covers major areas of managerial accounting: responsibility accounting, cost accounting, budgeting, reporting and analyzing operations, and automated accounting procedures.

dedication

The authors dedicate this book to the memory of a distinguished business educator—their friend and colleague—Fred C. Archer.

acknowledgments

A number of accounting instructors have provided valuable assistance with this edition by reviewing manuscript, offering suggestions, checking problems and solutions, and performing other important tasks. The authors are extremely grateful for this assistance. Special recognition must go to Vivian Pacsy of Monroe Business Institute, Bronx, New York, to Nellie Derrick of Kelley Business Institute, Niagara Falls, New York, and to Mary Pretti of the State Technical Institute, Memphis, Tennessee.

Horace R. Brock
Charles E. Palmer

PART ONE

ACCOUNTING:
basic principles

UNIT 1

ANALYZING BUSINESS TRANSACTIONS

Accounting is often called "the language of business." Some people describe accounting as a communication system, and others view it as an information system. Accounting is also defined as an art whose primary purpose is to gather and communicate financial information about an economic or social entity. (A business is an example of an economic entity. A hospital that is not operated for profit is an example of a social entity.) In business accounting, the accountant may be considered the interpreter and communicator of financial information about an economic entity.

Accountants occupy a vital position in business today because they help managers make decisions. Making the right decisions at the right time is the key to successful business operations.

In order for managers to make the right decisions, they need full and accurate financial information about the business. This information must be readily available, and it must be up to date. When an efficient accounting system is in operation and an experienced accountant keeps track of the firm's finances, managers can get quick answers to such questions as the following.

- How much cash does the business have?
- How much money do customers owe the business?
- What is the cost of the merchandise sold this month?
- How much did the volume of sales increase?
- What is the amount owed to suppliers?
- How much profit has the business made?

The facts that accountants provide give managers the information they need to answer thousands of other equally important questions.

Managers are not the only people who need the information contained in accounting records. The owners of a business want to know whether they have made profitable investments. Department heads and supervisors need various records and reports to operate their units efficiently. The government wants data for tax and licensing purposes. Banks and suppliers want figures to help them decide whether to give credit. Accountants provide this information by systematically recording financial facts about the business and using these facts to prepare reports.

However, recording and reporting financial information are only two aspects of accounting. In addition, accountants interpret, or explain, the meaning of the information; give advice about financial problems; and assist in the financial planning of future operations. Accountants are able to perform these functions because of the nature of the recording procedure. This procedure is explained in the present unit and later units.

The recording procedure includes provisions for classifying and summarizing financial information to facilitate the later reporting and interpreting of this information. Classification allows the accountant to sort out similar data and group like items together for clarity and more efficient use. The classified information is then summarized into financial statements. These statements are reports showing the results of operations for the accounting period and the financial position of the business as of the end of the period.

Accounting Begins With Analysis

Long before there can be any recording, reporting, or interpreting of financial information, accountants have to analyze every business transaction. A business transaction may consist of a purchase, a sale, a receipt or payment of cash, or any other financial happening. The effects of each transaction have to be studied in order to know what information to record and where to record it.

Since the accounting process actually begins with an analysis of the transactions of a business, this phase is the natural starting point for a study of accounting. Let us see how the accountant would analyze the transactions of the Modern Cleaning Shop, a dry-cleaning store owned by Paul Reed and operated by Mary Gomez, the manager.

Starting a New Business

Reed obtains the funds to start the business by withdrawing $6,000 from his personal bank account. He deposits the money in a new bank account in the name of the firm, the Modern Cleaning Shop. The new bank account will help Reed keep his financial interest in his business separate from his personal funds. The establishment of this bank account on November 26, 19X1, is the first transaction of the new firm.

George Stein, the accountant who is helping Reed prepare a set of books for the business, explains that there are two important financial facts to be recorded at this time.

a. The business has $6,000 of property in the form of cash, which is on deposit in the bank.
b. Reed has a $6,000 financial interest in the business, called his *equity*, or *capital*.

The firm's position at this time may be expressed in the form of the following simple equation.

MODERN CLEANING SHOP

Property	=	*Financial Interest*
(a) Cash $6,000	=	(b) Paul Reed, Capital $6,000

The equation *property equals financial interest* reflects the basic fact that in a free enterprise system all property is owned by someone. In this case, Reed owns the business because he supplied the property (cash).

Purchasing Business Property for Cash

The manager, Gomez, sees that her first task is to get the shop ready for business operations, which are to begin on December 1, 19X1. She buys cleaning equipment that costs $2,000 and pays for it with money in the form of a check drawn against the firm's bank account. Again, the accountant analyzes the transaction to see what has to be recorded and quickly identifies the following essential elements.

c. The firm has purchased new property (equipment) for $2,000.
d. The firm has paid out $2,000 in cash.

Here is the transaction as the accountant sees it.

MODERN CLEANING SHOP

	Property		=	Financial Interest
	Cash	+ Equipment	=	Paul Reed, Capital
Beginning investment	(a) $6,000		=	(b) $6,000
(c) New property purchased		+$2,000		
(d) Cash paid out	−2,000			
New balances	$4,000 +	$2,000	=	$6,000

Although there is a change in the form of some of the firm's property (cash to equipment), the equation that expresses the change shows that the total value of the property remains the same. Reed's financial interest, or equity, also remains unchanged. Again, *property* (Cash and Equipment) *equals financial interest* (Paul Reed, Capital).

Note carefully that the accountant is recording the financial affairs of the *business entity,* the cleaning shop. Reed's personal assets, such as his personal bank account, home, furniture, and automobile, are kept separate from business assets and are not included in the property of the cleaning shop. Nonbusiness assets are not recorded in the accounting records of the business entity.

Purchasing Property on Credit

Gomez also buys a counter, garment racks, a desk, and several chairs for the shop from Knight, Inc., at a cost of $1,000. Knight agrees to allow the Modern Cleaning Shop 30 days to pay the bill. This arrangement is sometimes called a *charge account,* or *open-account credit.* Amounts that the business must pay in the future are known as *accounts payable.* The companies or individuals to whom the amounts are owed are called *creditors.* This time Stein's analysis reveals the following basic elements.

e. The firm has purchased new property in the form of equipment that cost $1,000.
f. The firm owes $1,000 to Knight, Inc.

This increase in equipment is made without an immediate cash payment because Knight, Inc., is willing to accept a claim against the Modern Cleaning Shop's property until the bill is paid. There are now two different financial interests or claims against the firm's property—the creditor's claim (Accounts Payable) and the owner's claim (Paul Reed, Capital).

Here is how the transaction is expressed in equation form.

	MODERN CLEANING SHOP					
	Property			=	*Financial Interests*	
	Cash	+	Equipment	=	Accounts Payable	+ Paul Reed, Capital
Previous balances	$4,000	+	$2,000	=		$6,000
(e) New property purchased			+1,000			+
(f) Owed to Knight, Inc.					+$1,000	
New balances	$4,000	+	$3,000	=	$1,000	+ $6,000

Notice that when property values and financial interests increase or decrease, the total of the items on one side of the equation still equals the total on the other side. This happens because there are financial interests, or claims against business property, as soon as the property is purchased. The creditor's claim lasts until the debt is paid. The owner's claim lasts as long as he or she continues to own the business. After the creditors are paid, the owner has sole claim or legal right to all property owned by the business.

Paying a Creditor

If the Modern Cleaning Shop's manager decides to pay $700 to Knight, Inc., to reduce the firm's $1,000 debt, the effect of the payment may be analyzed as follows.

g. The firm has paid out $700 in cash.
h. The claim of Knight, Inc., against the firm is reduced by $700.

The effect of this transaction on the firm's property and on the financial interests can be expressed in equation form as shown below.

MODERN CLEANING SHOP

	Property	=	Financial Interests	
	Cash + Equipment	=	Accounts Payable	+ Paul Reed, Capital
Previous balances	$4,000 + $3,000	=	$1,000	+ $6,000
(g) Cash paid out	−700			
(h) Knight's claim reduced			−700	
New balances	$3,300 + $3,000	=	$ 300	+ $6,000

Preparing the Balance Sheet

Accountants use a formal pattern and special accounting terms when they prepare their reports. For instance, they refer to property that a business owns as the business's *assets* and to the debts or obligations of the business as its *liabilities*. The owner's financial interest is called *owner's equity, proprietorship,* or *net worth*. *Owner's equity* is the preferred term and is the term used throughout this book. At regular intervals the Modern Cleaning Shop's accountant will show the status of the firm's assets, liabilities, and owner's equity in a formal report called a *balance sheet*. Here is how the Modern Cleaning Shop's balance sheet looks on November 30, 19X1—the day before operations actually begin.

Modern Cleaning Shop
Balance Sheet
November 30, 19X1

Assets		Liabilities and Owner's Equity	
Cash	3300.00	Liabilities	
Equipment	3000.00	Accounts Payable	300.00
		Owner's Equity	
		Paul Reed, Capital	6000.00
		Total Liabilities and	
Total Assets	6300.00	Owner's Equity	6300.00

Stein lists the assets on the left side of the balance sheet. This arrangement is similar to the equation *property equals financial interests*, which was illustrated earlier. Property was shown on the left side of the equation. Liabilities and owner's equity appear on the right side of the balance sheet—the same side as in the previous equations. Here are several other important details about the form of the balance sheet.

1. The three-line heading of the balance sheet gives the firm's name (who), the title of the report (what), and the date of the report (when). Every balance sheet heading must contain these three lines.
2. On this form of balance sheet, the total of the assets always appears on the same horizontal line as the total of the liabilities and owner's equity.
3. When financial statements are handwritten on ruled accounting paper, dollar signs are usually omitted. However, in typewritten financial statements that are not prepared on ruled forms, dollar signs are generally used at the head of each column and with each total. The dollar signs are placed to the left of the numbers and on the same line.
4. A single line is used to show that the figures above it are being added or subtracted. Double lines are used under the final figure in a column or section of a report. If the report is prepared by hand rather than typewritten, lines should always be drawn with a ruler.

The balance sheet shown on page 6 tells how much and what kind of property the business owns. This statement also shows the amount of accounts payable and the amount of the owner's interest in the firm before the Modern Cleaning Shop opens for business. Paul Reed now has a complete picture of the financial position of the Modern Cleaning Shop as it is ready to start operations.

The Fundamental Accounting Equation

The word *balance* in the title Balance Sheet has a very special meaning. It serves to emphasize that the total of the figures on the left side of the report equals the total of the figures on the right side. In accounting terms, the firm's assets ($6,300) are equal to the total of the liabilities ($300) plus the owner's equity ($6,000). This equality can be expressed in equation form, as illustrated here.

$$\text{Assets} = \text{Liabilities} + \text{Owner's Equity}$$
$$\$6,300 = \$300 + \$6,000$$

This relationship between assets and liabilities plus owner's equity is called the *fundamental accounting equation*. There are many uses for this equation in accounting work. As a matter of fact, the entire process of analyzing, recording, and reporting business transactions is based on the fundamental equation.

Effects of Revenue and Expenses

Shortly after the Modern Cleaning Shop opens for business on December 1, 19X1, the first customer comes in with clothes to be dry-cleaned. Soon more customers follow. This begins a stream of revenue for the business. The result of the revenue is an increase in assets. *Revenue,* or *income,* is the inward flow of money or other assets (including claims to money, such as charge accounts) that results from sales of goods or services or from the use of money or property. An *expense,* on the other hand, involves the outward flow of money. Expenses include the costs of materials, labor, supplies, and services used in an effort to produce revenue. Any excess of revenue over expenses will represent profits for Reed. The chance to make profits is the reason he invested in the Modern Cleaning Shop. The firm's accounting records will show the detailed results of all transactions involving revenue and expenses.

Selling Services for Cash

The cash receipts for dry-cleaning services performed by the Modern Cleaning Shop during the month of December amount to $2,200. The accountant analyzes this fact in the following manner.

i. The business has received $2,200 in cash for services provided to customers.
j. The owner's equity is increased by $2,200 because of this inflow of assets. (Revenue always increases the owner's equity.)

Accountants prefer to keep the revenue figures separate from the owner's equity figure until the financial statements are prepared. Therefore, the revenue appears in equation form as follows.

MODERN CLEANING SHOP

	Assets		= Liabilities +	Owner's Equity	
	Cash +	Equipment =	Accounts Payable +	Paul Reed, Capital	+ Revenue
Previous balances	$3,300 +	$3,000	= $300 +	$6,000	
(i) Cash received	+2,200				
(j) Owner's equity increased					+ $2,200
New balances	$5,500 +	$3,000	= $300 +	$6,000	+ $2,200

Keeping this record of revenue separate from the owner's equity will help Stein compute total revenues much more easily at the end of the month, when the financial reports are prepared.

Selling Services on Credit

The Modern Cleaning Shop has also performed cleaning services for $800 for charge account customers. These customers are allowed 30 days to pay.

Amounts owed by such customers are known as *accounts receivable*. These accounts represent a new form of asset for the firm—claims for future collection from customers. The accountant's analysis breaks the transaction down into the following elements.

k. The firm has a new asset, Accounts Receivable, of $800.
l. The owner's equity is increased by the revenue of $800.

The firm's position now looks like this in equation form.

	Assets					=	Liabilities	+	Owner's Equity		
	Cash	+	Accounts Receivable	+	Equipment	=	Accounts Payable	+	Paul Reed, Capital	+	Revenue
Previous balances	$5,500			+	$3,000	=	$300	+	$6,000	+	$2,200
(k) New asset received			+$800								
(l) Owner's equity increased by revenue											+800
New balances	$5,500	+	$800	+	$3,000	=	$300	+	$6,000	+	$3,000

Collecting Receivables

Near the end of the month, when customers have paid a total of $600 to apply to their accounts, Stein recognizes the following changes.

m. The business has received $600 in cash.
n. Accounts Receivable is reduced by $600.

These changes affect the equation as follows.

	Assets					=	Liabilities	+	Owner's Equity		
	Cash	+	Accounts Receivable	+	Equipment	=	Accounts Payable	+	Paul Reed, Capital	+	Revenue
Previous balances	$5,500	+	$800	+	$3,000	=	$300	+	$6,000	+	$3,000
(m) Cash received	+600										
(n) Accounts receivable reduced			−600								
New balances	$6,100	+	$200	+	$3,000	=	$300	+	$6,000	+	$3,000

Notice that revenue is not recorded when cash is collected from charge account customers. In this transaction there is merely a change in the type of asset (from accounts receivable to cash). Revenue was recorded when the sales on credit took place (see Entry 1). Notice also that the fundamental accounting equation, assets equal liabilities plus owner's equity, holds true, regardless of the changes arising from individual transactions.

Paying Expenses

So far, Reed has done very well. His equity has been increased by sizable revenues. However, keeping a business running costs money. When the business has expenses, they will reduce Reed's equity.

Employees' Salaries

During the first month of operations, the Modern Cleaning Shop pays $1,600 for employees' salaries. The accountant analyzes this transaction as follows.

o. Cash is reduced by the payment of $1,600 to cover an expense.
p. Reed's equity is reduced by the $1,600 outflow of assets.

Stein prefers to keep expense figures separate from the figures for the owner's capital and the revenue. The effect of the expense for salaries is shown below.

	Assets			=	Liabilities	+	Owner's Equity		
	Cash +	Accounts Receivable +	Equipment	=	Accounts Payable	+	Paul Reed, Capital	+ Revenue	− Expenses
Previous balances	$6,100 +	$200 +	$3,000	=	$300	+	$6,000	+ $3,000	
(o) Cash reduced	−1,600								
(p) Owner's equity reduced by expense									$1,600
New balances	$4,500 +	$200 +	$3,000	=	$300	+	$6,000	+ $3,000	− $1,600

The separate record of expenses is kept for the same reason as the separate record of revenue is kept—to help analyze operations for the period.

Rent

Another typical business expense is the payment of rent. When the Modern Cleaning Shop pays $700 for a month's rent, the accountant analyzes the expense in the following terms.

q. Cash is reduced by $700.
r. Reed's equity is reduced by $700.

The equation reflects this payment as shown on page 11. Note that the two expense items are added together to show the total reduction in equity that results from incurring these expenses ($1,600 + $700 = $2,300).

	Assets			= Liabilities +	Owner's Equity		
	Cash +	Accounts Receivable +	Equipment =	Accounts Payable +	Paul Reed, Capital	+ Revenue −	Expenses
Previous balances	$4,500 +	$200 +	$3,000 =	$300 +	$6,000	+ $3,000 −	$1,600
(q) Cash reduced	−700						
(r) Owner's equity reduced by expense							700
New balances	$3,800 +	$200 +	$3,000 =	$300 +	$6,000	+ $3,000 −	$2,300

Supplies Used   At the end of the month, the manager, Gomez, pays $600 for supplies that were used in operations. The use of these supplies represents another business expense. The accountant analyzes the effects of the transaction in this way.

s. Cash is reduced by $600.
t. Reed's equity is reduced by $600 because of the additional expense.

These changes are expressed in equation form as follows.

	Assets			= Liabilities +	Owner's Equity		
	Cash +	Accounts Receivable +	Equipment =	Accounts Payable +	Paul Reed, Capital	+ Revenue −	Expenses
Previous balances	$3,800 +	$200 +	$3,000 =	$300 +	$6,000	+ $3,000 −	$2,300
(s) Cash reduced	−600						
(t) Owner's equity reduced by expense							600
New balances	$3,200 +	$200 +	$3,000 =	$300 +	$6,000	+ $3,000 −	$2,900

The Income Statement   The balance sheet shows the financial condition of a business at a given time. It shows what the business owns and owes, as well as the owner's equity. It does not, however, show the results of business operations, that is, what actually happened to bring about the firm's financial condition. This is the job of another formal accounting report called an *income statement, profit and loss statement,* or *statement of income and expenses.* Income statement is now the most popular term with accountants and is used throughout this book. Here is how the accountant for the Modern Cleaning Shop presents the results of the firm's first month of operations on an income statement.

Modern Cleaning Shop Income Statement Month Ended December 31, 19X1		
Revenue		
Cleaning Service Sales		3 000 00
Less Expenses		
Salaries	1 600 00	
Rent	700 00	
Supplies Used	600 00	
Total Expenses		2 900 00
Net Income for the Month		100 00

The net income or net loss is reported at the bottom of the income statement. This figure is the difference between the sales price of services performed or goods sold (revenue) and the cost of services and goods used (expenses) during a specific period of time. When there is more revenue than expenses, the result is a *net income.* When expenses are greater than revenue, the result is a *net loss.* The income statement illustrated above shows a net income because revenue was greater than expenses. Net income is sometimes called net profit. However, accountants prefer to use net income because it is more precise.

Notice that the three-line heading of the income statement shows who, what, and when. The first line is used for the firm's name (who). The second line gives the title of the report (what). The third line tells the exact period of time covered by the report (when). In the illustration, the third line clearly indicates that the income statement reports the results of operations for the single month of December 19X1.

If the income statement covered the three months of January, February, and March, the third line would read, "Three-Month Period Ended March 31, 19X1." The third line of a statement reporting the results of operations for a 12-month period beginning on January 1 and ending on December 31 of the same calendar year would read, "Year Ended December 31, 19X1." In instances where the 12-month reporting period ends on a date other than December 31, the third line of the income statement would read, "Fiscal Year Ended June 30, 19X1," or "Fiscal Year Ended November 30, 19X1."

Also, note the correct use of single and double lines. This handwritten income statement does not have dollar signs because it was prepared on ruled accounting paper. However, dollar signs would be used on a typewritten income statement that is not prepared on a ruled form.

The Balance Sheet

The income statement by itself is meaningful to business owners, managers, and other interested parties. However, it is even more informative when considered in relation to the assets and the equities that were involved in earning the revenue. Therefore, the balance sheet is once again prepared to give the details of these assets and equities. The final totals in the fundamental accounting equation supply the figures that are required for preparing a balance sheet for the Modern Cleaning Shop.

		Assets			=	*Liabilities*	+		*Owner's Equity*			
Cash	+	Accounts Receivable	+	Equipment	=	Accounts Payable	+	Paul Reed, Capital	+	Revenue	−	Expenses
$3,200	+	$200	+	$3,000	=	$300	+	$6,000	+	$3,000	−	$2,900

The balance sheet prepared from the figures in the above equation summarizes the assets, liabilities, and owner's equity.

Modern Cleaning Shop
Balance Sheet
December 31, 19X1

Assets		Liabilities and Owner's Equity	
Cash	3,200.00	Liabilities	
Accounts Receivable	200.00	Accounts Payable	300.00
Equipment	3,000.00	Owner's Equity	
		Paul Reed, Capital 12/1/X1 6,000.00	
		Net Income for December 100.00	
		Paul Reed, Capital 12/31/X1	6,100.00
Total Assets	6,400.00	Total Liabilities and Owner's Equity	6,400.00

The net income of $100 shown on the December income statement appears on the balance sheet as an increase in owner's equity. The owner's equity on December 31 is determined by adding the net income for December to the owner's equity that existed on December 1. A net loss would be subtracted. The net income or net loss figure is a connecting link that explains the change in owner's equity during the period. Note that the income statement is prepared before the balance sheet because the amount of the net income or net loss for the period is needed to compute the owner's equity that appears on the balance sheet at the end of the period. Of course, the balance sheet also shows the types and amounts of property that the business owns (assets) and the amounts owed to creditors (liabilities) on the reporting date.

The Importance of the Statements

Preparing financial statements is one of the accountant's most important jobs. Therefore, all figures must be checked and double-checked to make sure they are accurate. The figures shown on the balance sheet and the income statement are used by business managers and owners to plan current and future operations. Creditors, prospective investors, governmental agencies, and many others are also vitally interested in the profits of the business and in the asset and equity structure. Each day, millions of business decisions are made on the basis of financial reports.

principles and procedures summary

The accounting process begins with the analysis of business transactions. The accountant analyzes each transaction to determine its effect on the fundamental accounting equation, assets equal liabilities plus owner's equity. The balance sheet is a statement that shows the assets, liabilities, and owner's equity on a given date.

Some changes in owner's equity result from revenue and some from expenses. These changes are summarized on the income statement. The difference between revenue and expenses is the net income or net loss of the business for the period. The net income or net loss for the period also appears on the balance sheet prepared at the close of the same period. Net income or net loss is the connecting link between the owner's equity at the beginning of the period and the owner's equity at the end of the period.

managerial implications

Accurate and informative financial records and statements are necessary so that business people can make sound decisions. Accounting information helps to determine whether a profit has been made, the amount of the assets on hand, the amount owed to creditors, and the amount of owner's equity. Any well-run and efficiently managed business will have a good accounting system to provide timely and useful information.

managerial discussion questions

1. How does an accounting system help managers control operations and make sound decisions?
2. Why should managers be concerned with changes in the amount of creditors' claims against the business?
3. Is it reasonable to expect that all new businesses will have profits from the first month's operations? From the first year's operations?

application of principles

PROBLEM 1-1 The Sunshine Laundry has just been established, and the owner makes a cash deposit of $5,000 in the First State Bank for use in the business.

INSTRUCTIONS Analyze the following transactions. Then record in equation form the changes in property, claims of creditors, and owner's equity. (Use plus, minus, and equal signs.)

a. Beginning investment of $5,000 in cash.
b. Paid $2,200 in cash for the purchase of equipment.
c. Purchased $2,000 of additional equipment on credit.
d. Paid $600 in cash to creditors.
e. Additional investment by the owner of $4,000 in cash.

PROBLEM 1-2 Robert Pond is the sole owner of the Pond Jewelry Repair Service.

INSTRUCTIONS Use the following figures to prepare a balance sheet dated December 31, 19X1. (Use four-column analysis paper.)

Cash	$2,000
Equipment	2,000
Office Furniture	500
Accounts Payable	1,000
Robert Pond, Capital	3,500

PROBLEM 1-3 Lois McKay owns the County Advertising Agency. At the beginning of the month, the books show the following assets, liabilities, and owner's equity.

Cash	$1,600	Accounts Payable	$ 500
Accounts Receivable	400	Expenses	100
Office Furniture	500	Lois McKay, Capital	2,000
Office Machines	600	Revenue	700

INSTRUCTIONS Set up an equation form using the balances given above. Then record the effects of the following transactions in the equation. (Use plus, minus, and equal signs.) Record new balances after each transaction has been entered. Prove the equality of the two sides of the final equation on a separate sheet of paper.

a. Performed services for $200 on credit.
b. Paid $125 in cash for office rent.
c. Performed services for $500 in cash.
d. Paid $50 in cash for supplies used.
e. Sent a check for $200 to a creditor.
f. Paid $50 in cash for the telephone bill.
g. Issued checks for $400 to pay salaries.
h. Performed more services for $600 in cash.
i. Had the adding machine repaired; payment of $10 is due in 30 days. (**Hint:** This transaction has no effect on assets. The firm's liabilities increase. The increase in outsider's claims against the same amount of assets reduces the owner's equity.)
j. Received $300 from accounts receivable.

PROBLEM 1-4 The following equations show the transactions of the Ace Tree Service during February 19X1. The business is owned by John Conte.

	Assets						=	Liabilities	+	Owner's Equity			
	Cash	+	Accts. Rec.	+	Auto	+	Equip.	=	Accts. Pay.	+	John Conte, Capital	+	Revenue	−	Expenses
Balances, Feb. 1	2,500	+	400	+	7,500	+	2,000	=	1,200	+	11,200	+	0	−	0
Paid rent	−250														250
New balances	2,250	+	400	+	7,500	+	2,000	=	1,200	+	11,200	+	0	−	250
Sold services for cash	+1,500												+1,500		
New balances	3,750	+	400	+	7,500	+	2,000	=	1,200	+	11,200	+	1,500	−	250
Paid a creditor	−350								−350						
New balances	3,400	+	400	+	7,500	+	2,000	=	850	+	11,200	+	1,500	−	250
Sold services on credit			+500										+500		
New balances	3,400	+	900	+	7,500	+	2,000	=	850	+	11,200	+	2,000	−	250
Paid salaries	−1,000														1,000
New balances	2,400	+	900	+	7,500	+	2,000	=	850	+	11,200	+	2,000	−	1,250
Paid phone bill	−25														25
New balances	2,375	+	900	+	7,500	+	2,000	=	850	+	11,200	+	2,000	−	1,275

INSTRUCTIONS Analyze each transaction carefully. Then prepare an income statement for the month and a balance sheet for February 28, 19X1. List the expenses in detail on the income statement. Use two-column analysis paper for the income statement and four-column analysis paper for the balance sheet.

alternate problems

PROBLEM 1-1A

The Swift Messenger Service has just been established, and the owner makes a cash deposit of $5,000 in the Valley State Bank for use in the business.

INSTRUCTIONS

Analyze the following transactions. Then use the equation form to record the changes in property, claims of creditors, and owner's equity. (Use plus, minus, and equal signs

a. Beginning investment of $5,000 in cash.
b. Purchased equipment for $3,000 in cash.
c. Purchased $1,000 of additional equipment on credit.
d. Paid $500 in cash to creditors.
e. Additional investment of $1,500 in cash by the owner.

PROBLEM 1-2A

Henry Marks is the sole owner of the Metro Appliance Repair Shop.

INSTRUCTIONS

Use the following figures to prepare a balance sheet dated December 31, 19X1. (Use four-column analysis paper.)

Cash	$4,000
Equipment	3,500
Truck	3,000
Accounts Payable	1,500
Henry Marks, Capital	9,000

PROBLEM 1-3A

Jill Simpson owns the Towne Decorating Service, an interior decorating business. At the beginning of the month, the books showed the following assets, liabilities, and owner's equity.

Cash	$3,000	Accounts Payable	$ 1,700
Accounts Receivable	2,000	Jill Simpson, Capital	10,300
Furniture and Fixtures	1,000	Revenue	5,000
Auto	8,000	Expenses	3,000

INSTRUCTIONS

Set up an equation form using the balances given above. Then record the effects of the following transactions in the equation. (Use plus, minus, and equal signs.) Record new balances after each transaction has been entered. Prove the equality of the two sides of the final equation on a separate sheet.

a. Received $1,100 in cash for services.
b. Paid $150 in cash for supplies used.
c. Received $700 in cash from credit customers.

d. Paid $100 in cash for telephone service.
e. Sent a $600 check in partial payment of the amount due creditors.
f. Paid salaries of $2,000 in cash.
g. Sent a check for $40 to pay an electric bill.
h. Performed services for $2,000 on credit.
i. Paid $260 in cash for auto repairs.
j. Received $1,500 in cash for services.

PROBLEM 1-4A The following equations show the transactions of the Sparkle Window Cleaning Service during March 19X2. The business is owned by Mary Hall.

	Assets						=	Liabilities	+	Owner's Equity			
	Cash	+	Accts. Rec.	+	Truck	+	Equip.	=	Accts. Pay.	+	Mary Hall, Capital	+	Revenue	−	Expenses
Balances, Mar. 1	700	+	500	+	2,000	+	300	=	300	+	3,200	+	0	−	0
Paid rent	−70														70
New balances	630	+	500	+	2,000	+	300	=	300	+	3,200	+	0	−	70
Sold services on credit			+700										+700		
New balances	630	+	1,200	+	2,000	+	300	=	300	+	3,200	+	700	−	70
Paid for supplies used	−50														50
New balances	580	+	1,200	+	2,000	+	300	=	300	+	3,200	+	700	−	120
Sold services for cash	+1,000												+1,000		
New balances	1,580	+	1,200	+	2,000	+	300	=	300	+	3,200	+	1,700	−	120
Paid salaries	−1,000														1,000
New balances	580	+	1,200	+	2,000	+	300	=	300	+	3,200	+	1,700	−	1,120
Paid for truck repairs	−75														75
New balances	505	+	1,200	+	2,000	+	300	=	300	+	3,200	+	1,700	−	1,195

INSTRUCTIONS Analyze each transaction carefully. Then prepare an income statement for the month and a balance sheet for March 31, 19X2. List the expenses in detail on the income statement. Use two-column analysis paper for the income statement and four-column analysis paper for the balance sheet.

UNIT 2
SETTING UP ACCOUNTS

The accountant's methods of analyzing transactions and presenting financial information are discussed in Unit 1. In this unit, we discuss the way in which the accountant keeps records of the changes that are caused by business transactions.

Accounts for Assets, Liabilities, and Owner's Equity

Obviously, accountants do not have time to make up a new equation after every transaction. Instead, they keep separate written records called *accounts* for each asset and liability, as well as for the owner's equity in the business.

Another look at the affairs of the Modern Cleaning Shop helps explain the accountant's recording procedure. When Paul Reed invested $6,000 on November 26, 19X1, the accountant analyzed the transaction and identified two important facts to be recorded.

a. The business had $6,000 worth of property in the form of cash deposited in the bank.
b. Reed had a $6,000 financial interest in the business.

The firm's financial position at that time is illustrated by the following equation.

MODERN CLEANING SHOP		
Property	=	*Financial Interest*
(a) Cash $6,000	=	(b) Paul Reed, Capital $6,000

A formal balance sheet for the firm on November 26 would look like this.

MODERN CLEANING SHOP
Balance Sheet
November 26, 19X1

Assets		Owner's Equity	
Cash	6,000	Paul Reed, Capital	6,000

Reed's financial investment of $6,000 is recorded in an account called Paul Reed, Capital, which appears on the balance sheet under the heading Owner's Equity. This heading identifies the financial interest of the owner. A second set of financial interests are included on the balance sheet under the heading Liabilities. This heading identifies amounts the business owes to creditors. (The Modern Cleaning Shop has no liabilities on November 26, 19X1.)

The total of the two sets of financial interest in a business is equal to the total of the properties that the business owns. These properties are recorded in accounts and are classified on the balance sheet under the heading Assets. For example, Paul Reed's investment of $6,000 in cash is recorded in an asset account called Cash.

The relationship between what a business owns and what it owes is best illustrated by the first simple equation that you learned in Unit 1.

Property = Financial Interest

When this basic proposition is expanded and classified, it becomes the fundamental accounting equation.

Assets = Liabilities + Owner's Equity

Accounts are the separate written records of the assets, liabilities, and owner's equity. Accounts are kept so that financial information can be analyzed, recorded, classified, and summarized. As many accounts are set up as are needed to clearly identify the properties a business owns (assets) and the financial interests in those properties (liabilities and owner's equity). The title of each account describes a separate property or financial interest.

Asset Accounts

One type of account that the accountant might use to analyze and record transactions is called a *T account*. This record consists of two lines, one vertical and one horizontal. The two lines resemble the letter *T*. The name of the account is written on the top line. The increases and decreases are separated and entered on different sides of the vertical line. The location of the items in the fundamental accounting equation shows where amounts will be recorded in the T accounts. For instance, a separate account is set up for the asset Cash. The opening balance of $6,000 (a) is entered on the left side of the account because assets always appear on the left side of the balance sheet and on the left side of the accounting equation. (The plus and minus signs shown below do not normally appear in the accounts. However, they are presented here to help you identify increases and decreases in accounts.)

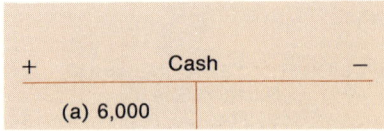

Since increases in assets are recorded on the left side of accounts, decreases are recorded on the right side.

Owner's Equity Accounts

The accountant sets up another account for Reed's equity. Because the owner's equity always appears on the right side of the balance sheet and the accounting equation, Stein enters the opening balance of $6,000 (b) on the right side of the owner's equity account.

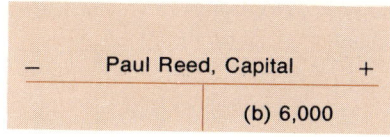

Since the right side of the owner's equity account is used to record increases in the owner's equity, the left side must be used to record decreases.

Making Entries in Asset Accounts

When the Modern Cleaning Shop bought cleaning equipment for $2,000 cash, the accountant made the following analysis.

c. The business purchased new assets in the form of equipment that cost $2,000.
d. The business paid out $2,000 in cash.

To record the purchase of equipment (c), the accountant first opens a new asset account for equipment. The purchase is then recorded on the left, or increase, side.

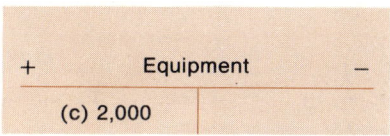

The payment of $2,000 in cash (d) is entered on the right side of the Cash account because decreases in assets are recorded on the right side.

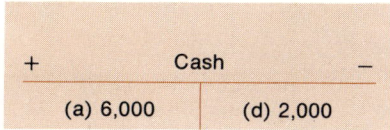

Liability Accounts

Later, when the business bought more equipment for $1,000 on credit from Knight, Inc., the accountant's analysis showed the following effects.

e. The firm had new assets in the form of equipment that cost $1,000.
f. The firm owed $1,000 as an account payable to Knight, Inc.

Again, Stein uses the location on the balance sheet and in the fundamental accounting equation as a recording guide. The increase in equipment (e) is entered on the left side of the Equipment account.

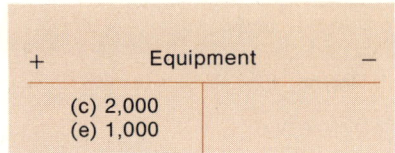

The accountant opens a liability account, Accounts Payable, to record the amount the business owes Knight (f). The $1,000 is entered on the right side of this account because liabilities appear on the right side of the balance sheet and the accounting equation.

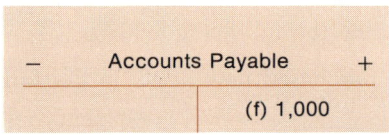

Since the right side of liability accounts is used for increases in liabilities, the left side is used to record decreases.

The firm's position after this transaction appears in equation form below.

	Property	=	*Financial Interest*	
Cash +	Equipment	=	Accounts Payable +	Paul Reed, Capital
$4,000 +	$3,000	=	$1,000 +	$6,000

A formal balance sheet prepared at this time (November 28, 19X1) shows the following situation.

MODERN CLEANING SHOP
Balance Sheet
November 28, 19X1

Assets		Liabilities and Owner's Equity	
Cash	4,000	Liabilities	
Equipment	3,000	Accounts Payable	1,000
		Owner's Equity	
		Paul Reed, Capital	6,000
		Total Liabilities and	
Total Assets	7,000	Owner's Equity	7,000

Recording Payment to a Creditor

On November 30, 19X1, the business paid $700 to Knight, Inc., to apply against the bill of $1,000. Following is the analysis of this transaction.

g. The business paid out $700 in cash.
h. The claim of Knight, Inc., against the firm was reduced by $700.

Stein records the decrease in cash (g) as an entry on the right (decrease) side of the Cash account. The liability (h) is reduced with an entry on the left (decrease) side of the Accounts Payable account.

+	Cash	−	−	Accounts Payable	+
(a) 6,000	(d) 2,000		(h) 700	(f) 1,000	
	(g) 700				

The transactions already discussed took place in November. They were necessary to prepare the Modern Cleaning Shop for business on the morning of December 1, 19X1. After these November transactions have been entered in the accounts, the financial position of the firm is the same as the position shown on the balance sheet of November 30, 19X1 (page 6). Note that this position is represented by the December 1 account balances given below. (The illustration below has been simplified by omitting the individual transactions for November from the accounts. For example, Cash: +$6,000 − $2,000 − $700 = $3,300.)

ASSETS SECTION				LIABILITIES SECTION	
+	Cash	−	−	Accounts Payable	+
3,300				300	
				OWNER'S EQUITY SECTION	
+	Equipment	−	−	Paul Reed, Capital	+
3,000				6,000	

Accounts for Revenue and Expenses

As you learned in Unit 1, many of the transactions of a business involve revenue and expenses. These items are also recorded in accounts. Let's examine the revenue and expense transactions of the Modern Cleaning Shop for December to see how they are recorded in the accounts.

Recording Revenue From Cash Sales

During December, the Modern Cleaning Shop sold cleaning services for $2,200 in cash. The following is the accountant's analysis.

i. The business received $2,200 in cash.
j. The owner's equity was increased by this $2,200 inflow of assets.

The accountant records the receipt of cash (i) as an entry on the left (increase) side of the asset account Cash.

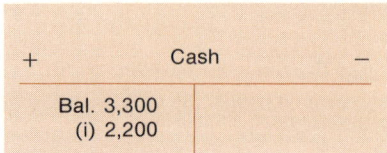

But how is the increase in owner's equity recorded? One way would be to record the $2,200 on the right side of the Paul Reed, Capital account. However, Stein wants to keep the revenue figures separate from the owner's investment until the end of the month (or until the financial reports are prepared). Therefore, he opens a new account called Cleaning Service Sales.

Remember that revenue is a subdivision of owner's equity. The accountant uses this subdivision to classify and summarize the various revenues of the business. The account title Cleaning Service Sales describes the specific type of revenue recorded in that account.

Stein enters the $2,200 on the right side of the Cleaning Service Sales account (j) because revenue increases the owner's equity and an increase in owner's equity is recorded on the right side of the account.

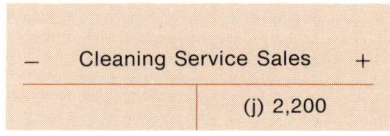

Because the accountant uses the right side of the revenue account to record increases, he uses the left side of the revenue account to record decreases. Decreases in a revenue account may be required by corrections, by transfers to other accounts, or by refunds; however, such entries are not required often.

Other types of revenue would be recorded in separate accounts. For instance, if the Modern Cleaning Shop altered clothing for customers, another account called Alteration Service Sales might be set up. The two accounts would be classified under the heading Revenue on the income statement. The total of the two accounts would be the total revenue of the business for the accounting period.

Recording Revenue From Sales on Credit

During December, the Modern Cleaning Shop also sold cleaning services for $800 to charge account customers. The accountant's analysis showed the following effects.

k. The business obtained a new asset—accounts receivable of $800.
l. The owner's equity was increased by the revenue of $800.

First, the accountant opens a new asset account, Accounts Receivable, and records the $800 (k) on the left (increase) side. Then the increase in owner's equity (l) is recorded as an entry on the right (increase) side of the Cleaning Service Sales account.

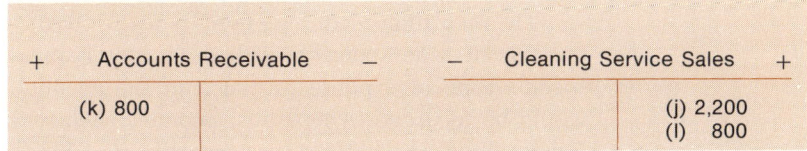

Recording Receipts From Charge Account Customers

When charge account customers paid a total of $600 to apply to their accounts, the accountant made the following analysis.

m. The business received $600 in cash.
n. Accounts Receivable was reduced by $600.

Recording this information involves the use of two asset accounts. The Cash account is increased (left side) by $600 (m), and the Accounts Receivable account is decreased (right side) by $600 (n). Notice that there is no revenue from this transaction. The revenue was recorded when the sales on credit were recorded (Entry 1).

+	Cash	−	+	Accounts Receivable	−
Bal. 3,300			(k) 800		(n) 600
(i) 2,200					
(m) 600					

Recording Expenses

Like other firms, the Modern Cleaning Shop encounters expenses in running its business. The first expense was for employees' salaries of $1,600. The accountant determined that this expense had the following effects.

o. The payment of $1,600 reduced the asset Cash.
p. Reed's equity was reduced by the $1,600 outflow of assets.

The reduction in cash (o) is recorded by an entry on the right (decrease) side of the asset account Cash.

+	Cash	−
Bal. 3,300	(o) 1,600	
(i) 2,200		
(m) 600		

The decrease in Reed's equity that results from the expense could be entered on the left (decrease) side of the Paul Reed, Capital account. However, Stein prefers to keep expenses separate from the owner's equity until the end of the month (or until the financial reports are prepared). Like revenue, expenses are a subdivision of owner's equity. This subdivision is used to classify and summarize the various expenses of the business.

The recording technique used by the Modern Cleaning Shop requires the opening of a new account called Salaries Expense. This title describes the specific type of expense recorded in the account. Other kinds of expenses would be recorded in separate accounts, each with its own descriptive title. For instance, the payment of monthly rent for the store is recorded in an account called Rent Expense. The two expense accounts are classified on the income statement under the heading Expenses. The total of such expense accounts shows the total operating expenses of the business for the accounting period.

The accountant enters the $1,600 (p) on the left side of the Salaries Expense account because expenses decrease owner's equity and an owner's equity account is decreased on the left side. Remember that an increase in an expense is a decrease in the owner's equity. The plus and minus signs shown in the illustration below indicate the effect on the expense account, not the effect on owner's equity.

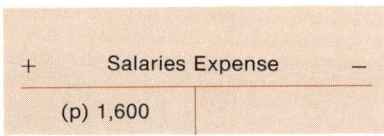

Recording the $700 payment for the December rent follows a similar pattern. The accountant's analysis is as follows.

q. Cash was reduced by $700.
r. Reed's equity was reduced by $700.

The reduction in cash (q) is recorded by another entry on the right side of the Cash account.

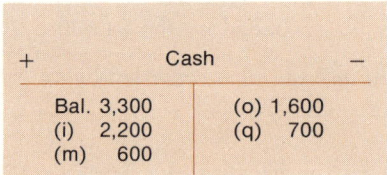

To record the decrease in owner's equity (r), the accountant opens another expense account called Rent Expense. An entry of $700 on the left side of the account shows the increase in this expense as well as the decrease in Reed's equity.

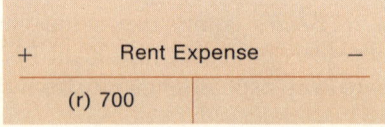

When the Modern Cleaning Shop paid $600 for cleaning supplies that had been used in the month's operations, Stein made the following analysis.

s. The asset Cash was reduced by $600.
t. The additional expense reduced Reed's equity by $600.

Stein records the reduction in the asset Cash (s) on the right side of the Cash account shown below.

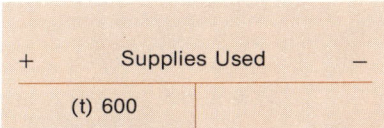

The reduction in Reed's equity (t) is entered on the left side of a new expense account called Supplies Used. An entry is made on the left side because the expense causes a decrease in owner's equity.

```
+           Supplies Used        −
    (t) 600
```

The procedure for recording expenses is logically the opposite of the procedure for recording revenue. Increases in expenses are recorded on the left side of the accounts because expenses reduce owner's equity. Decreases in expenses are recorded on the right side of the expense accounts. These decreases in expenses may result from corrections, transfers to other expense accounts, or refunds. (However, such entries are not required often.)

After the December 19X1 transactions have been recorded, the balances in the various T accounts are the same as those shown in equation form on page 13. This time the accountant can use the T account balances to prepare the income statement and the balance sheet illustrated on the next page. An account balance is computed by first adding the figures on each side of the account. Then the smaller total is subtracted from the larger. The result is the account balance. If the total of the figures on the right side is greater than the total on the left, the balance is recorded on the right. If the total of the figures on the left side is greater, the balance is recorded on the left. For example, the total of the figures on the left side of the T account for Cash is $6,100. The total of the figures on the right side is $2,900. By using the procedure explained above, the balance of the Cash account is computed as $3,200 ($6,100 − $2,900 = $3,200) and is recorded on the left side of the account. Of course, if an account contains only one amount, that figure is the balance.

Notice that items marked "Bal." are balances carried forward from the November transactions.

ASSETS SECTION

Cash

Bal. 3,300	(o) 1,600
(i) 2,200	(q) 700
(m) 600	(s) 600
3,200	

Accounts Receivable

(k) 800	(n) 600
200	

Equipment

Bal. 3,000

LIABILITIES SECTION

Accounts Payable

	Bal. 300

OWNER'S EQUITY SECTION

Paul Reed, Capital

	Bal. 6,000

Salaries Expense

(p) 1,600

Rent Expense

(r) 700

Supplies Used

(t) 600

Cleaning Service Sales

	(j) 2,200
	(l) 800
	3,000

MODERN CLEANING SHOP
Income Statement
Month Ended December 31, 19X1

Revenue		
Cleaning Service Sales		3,000.00
Less Expenses		
Salaries Expense	1,600.00	
Rent Expense	700.00	
Supplies Used	600.00	
Total Expenses		2,900.00
Net Income for the Month		100.00

MODERN CLEANING SHOP
Balance Sheet
December 31, 19X1

Assets		Liabilities and Owner's Equity		
Cash	3,200.00	Liabilities		
Accounts Receivable	200.00	Accounts Payable		300.00
Equipment	3,000.00	Owner's Equity		
		Paul Reed, Capital 12/1/X1	6,000.00	
		Net Income for December	100.00	
		Paul Reed, Capital 12/31/X1		6,100.00
		Total Liabilities and		
Total Assets	6,400.00	Owner's Equity		6,400.00

The Rules of Debit and Credit

Accountants do not say "left side" or "right side" when they talk about making entries in accounts. They use the term *debit*, or *charge*, when they refer to an entry on the left side of an account and the term *credit* when they refer to an entry on the right side of an account. For example, accountants increase assets by debiting asset accounts, and they decrease assets by crediting asset accounts. However, accountants increase liabilities by crediting liability accounts and decrease liabilities by debiting liability accounts. The following illustration summarizes the rules for debiting and crediting accounts.

GUIDE FOR DEBITING AND CREDITING

ASSET ACCOUNTS

DEBIT	CREDIT
Enter the original amount on this side. Enter increases on this side.	Enter decreases on this side.

LIABILITY ACCOUNTS

DEBIT	CREDIT
Enter decreases on this side.	Enter the original amount on this side. Enter increases on this side.

OWNER'S EQUITY ACCOUNT

DEBIT	CREDIT
Enter decreases (withdrawals, and so forth) on this side.	Enter the beginning investment on this side. Enter increases (additional investments, and so forth) on this side.

REVENUE ACCOUNTS

DEBIT	CREDIT
Enter decreases in owner's equity through reduction of revenue (sales returns, allowances, and so forth) on this side.	Enter increases in owner's equity (sales of goods or services) on this side.

EXPENSE ACCOUNTS

DEBIT	CREDIT
Enter decreases in owner's equity through expenses (rent, salaries, utilities, selling expenses, administrative expenses, and so forth) on this side.	Enter increases in owner's equity through reduction of expenses on this side.

The Double-Entry System

The analysis of every transaction produces at least two effects. The effect of an entry on the debit, or left, side of one account is balanced by the effect of an entry on the credit, or right, side of another account. For this reason, the modern system of accounting is sometimes called the *double-entry system*. This system involves recording both effects of a given transaction in order to present a complete picture. The balancing relationship also explains why both sides of the equations shown in Unit 1 were always equal.

Chart of Accounts

Since most businesses have many different accounts, it is necessary to set up a system that allows the accounts to be easily identified and located. A *chart of accounts* represents such a system. Each account is given a number as well as a name. The number is assigned on the basis of the type of account. Similar accounts are grouped and assigned to a certain block of numbers. For example, asset accounts are numbered from 100 to 199. Liability accounts are numbered from 200 to 299. Owner's equity accounts are numbered from 300 to 399, and so on. These numbers help identify the type of account, no matter where it is in a firm's financial records.

Reed's accountant sets up a chart of accounts for the business. Numbers are assigned as shown in the chart of accounts below. Notice that the accounts are not numbered in sequence. For example, the numbering under Assets jumps from 101 to 111. These number gaps are ordinarily left in each block so that additional accounts may be added when needed.

MODERN CLEANING SHOP
Chart of Accounts

Account Number	Account Name
100–199	**ASSETS**
101	Cash
111	Accounts Receivable
141	Equipment
200–299	**LIABILITIES**
202	Accounts Payable
300–399	**OWNER'S EQUITY**
301	Paul Reed, Capital
400–499	**REVENUE**
401	Cleaning Service Sales
500–599	**EXPENSES**
511	Salaries Expense
516	Rent Expense
521	Supplies Used

Permanent and Temporary Accounts

As you have seen, the asset, liability, and owner's equity accounts appear on the balance sheet at the end of an accounting period. The account balances are then carried forward to start the new period. Such accounts are sometimes called *permanent*, or *real, accounts* because they continue from accounting period to accounting period.

In contrast to these permanent accounts are the revenue and expense accounts, which appear on the income statement at the end of an accounting period. Accountants use revenue and expense accounts to classify and summarize changes in owner's equity during the period. Then, as you will see later, the balances of these accounts are transferred to a summary account at the end of the period. In turn, the balance of the summary account is transferred to owner's equity. The revenue and expense accounts are therefore called *temporary*, or *nominal, accounts*.

principles and procedures summary

Each transaction is analyzed to identify its effect on the fundamental accounting equation, assets equal liabilities plus owner's equity. Then the effects of each transaction are recorded in the proper accounts. The location of the entries is based on where the item appears in the fundamental equation and on the balance sheet. An increase in assets is shown on the debit, or left, side of the account because assets appear on the left side of the balance sheet and the equation. The credit, or right, side of the asset account is used to record decreases. In contrast, liability items are on the right side of the equation and the balance sheet. Therefore, increases in liabilities are recorded on the credit, or right, side of the accounts. The opposite side of these accounts is used for recording decreases. Similarly, increases in owner's equity are shown on the credit side of the account. Decreases in owner's equity appear on the debit side.

Revenue is recorded by making entries on the credit side of the separate revenue accounts because revenue increases the owner's equity. Expenses are recorded on the debit side of the separate expense accounts because expenses decrease the owner's equity.

The accounts are usually arranged in a predetermined order for handy reference and speedy identification. The list of the accounts used by a business is called the chart of accounts.

managerial implications

Recording entries in accounts provides an efficient method of gathering data about the financial affairs of a business. From the accounts, the accountant can easily prepare the income statement. This report summarizes the revenue and expenses of the business for a specific period of time. The accountant can also use the accounts to prepare the balance sheet, which summarizes the assets, liabilities, and owner's equity on a given date. Business owners, managers, creditors, banks, and many others use these statements to make decisions concerning the business.

managerial discussion questions

1. How do the income statement and the balance sheet help management make sound decisions?
2. At any time, how can management find out whether a firm can pay its bills as they become due?
3. If a firm's expenses equal or exceed its revenue, what should management do?
4. In discussing a firm's latest financial statements, a manager says that it is the "results on the bottom line" that really count. What does the manager mean?

application of principles

PROBLEM 2-1 The following transactions took place at the Valley Television Repair Service over a period of several months.

INSTRUCTIONS Set up T accounts for the accounts listed in parentheses after the transactions. Analyze each transaction carefully. Then record the amounts in the T accounts affected by that transaction. Use plus and minus signs to show increases and decreases in each account.

a. Al Merritt invested $10,000 cash in the business. (Cash and Al Merritt, Capital.)
b. Purchased testing equipment for $500 in cash. (Shop Equipment and Cash.)
c. Bought store fixtures for $1,200. Payment is due in 30 days. (Store Equipment and Accounts Payable.)
d. Purchased a used truck for $2,500 in cash. (Truck and Cash.)
e. Merritt gave to the firm his personal set of tools that cost $250. (Shop Equipment and Al Merritt, Capital.)
f. Bought a used cash register for $200. Payment is due in 30 days. (Store Equipment and Accounts Payable.)
g. Paid $450 in cash to apply to the amount owed for store fixtures. (Accounts Payable and Cash.)

PROBLEM 2-2

The following transactions occurred at several different businesses and are not related.

INSTRUCTIONS Analyze each of the transactions. Decide what accounts are affected, and enter the proper titles at the top of a pair of T accounts. Then record the effects of the transaction in the T accounts. Use plus and minus signs before the amounts to show the increases and decreases.

a. A firm purchased equipment for $2,000 in cash.
b. The owner, Ann Fields, withdrew $500 of the cash she had invested.
c. A firm sold a piece of surplus equipment for $250 in cash.
d. A firm purchased a used delivery truck for $2,000 in cash.
e. A firm paid $400 in cash to apply against an account owed.
f. A firm purchased office equipment for $450. The amount is to be paid in 60 days.
g. David Black, owner of the Builders Supply Company, made an additional investment of $2,500 in cash.
h. A firm paid $150 by check for office equipment that it had previously purchased on credit.

PROBLEM 2-3

The following revenue and expense transactions took place at the Industrial Cleaning Service.

INSTRUCTIONS Analyze each of the transactions. Decide what accounts are affected, and enter the proper titles at the top of a pair of T accounts. Then record the effects of the transaction in the T accounts. Use plus and minus signs before the amounts to show the increases and decreases.

a. Paid $400 for one month's rent.
b. Sold services for $500 in cash.
c. Paid salaries of $600.
d. Sold additional services for $900 on credit.
e. Paid $75 for the monthly telephone bill.
f. Collected $250 from accounts receivable.
g. Received a $15 refund for an overcharge on the telephone bill.
h. Sold services for $600 on credit.
i. Paid $50 in cash for the monthly electric bill.
j. Received supplies for immediate use. Payment of $75 is due in 30 days.
k. Received $450 from charge account customers.
l. Performed services for $900 in cash.
m. Received credit for $10 as an adjustment for damaged supplies.
n. Issued a check for $65 to pay for supplies previously purchased on credit.

PROBLEM 2-4

The accounts and transactions of the Roper Garage are listed on page 34. (The account numbers have been intentionally omitted.)

INSTRUCTIONS Analyze the transactions. Then record each one in the appropriate T accounts. Use plus and minus signs in front of the amounts to show the increases and decreases. Identify each entry in the T accounts by writing the letter of the transaction next to the entry.

ASSETS
Cash
Accounts Receivable
Office Equipment
Truck

LIABILITIES
Accounts Payable

OWNER'S EQUITY
Dale Roper, Capital

REVENUE
Sales

EXPENSES
Rent Expense
Utilities Expense
Salaries Expense
Repair Parts Expense
Truck Expense

a. Dale Roper invested $5,000 in cash to set up an auto repair shop.
b. Paid $250 for one month's rent.
c. Bought a used tow truck for $800 in cash.
d. Performed services for $800 in cash.
e. Paid $40 for truck repairs.
f. Sold services for $450 on credit.
g. Purchased an office chair for $75 on credit.
h. Received $75 from credit customers.
i. Paid $25 to reduce the amount owed on the office chair.
j. Issued a check for $75 to pay the utility bill.
k. Purchased used office equipment for $400. Half of this amount was paid in cash immediately. The balance is due in 30 days.
l. Issued a check for $1,125 to pay salaries.
m. Performed services for $950 in cash.
n. Performed services for $675 on credit.
o. Paid $375 for parts used in repair work.
p. Collected $450 from accounts receivable.
q. Received a bill for $225, due in 30 days, for repair parts used.
r. Paid $30 in cash for gas and oil for the tow truck.

PROBLEM 2-5 The accountant for the Roper Garage prepares financial statements at the end of each month.

INSTRUCTIONS Use the figures in the T accounts for Problem 2-4 to prepare an income statement and a balance sheet. Use two-column analysis paper for the income statement and four-column analysis paper for the balance sheet. Assume that the transactions took place during the month ended April 30, 19X1. Determine the account balances before you start work on the financial statements.

alternate problems

PROBLEM 2-1A The following transactions took place at the General Accounting Service over a period of several months.

INSTRUCTIONS Set up T accounts for the accounts listed in parentheses after the transactions. Analyze each transaction carefully. Then record the amounts in the T accounts affected by that transaction. Use plus and minus signs to show increases and decreases in each account.

a. Susan Gale invested $7,500 cash in the business. (Cash and Susan Gale, Capital.)
b. Purchased office furniture for $2,000 in cash. (Office Furniture and Cash.)
c. Bought an electronic calculator for $450. Payment is due in 30 days. (Office Equipment and Accounts Payable.)
d. Purchased a used car for the firm for $2,000 in cash. (Automobile and Cash.)
e. Gale gave her personal library of accounting and tax books to the business. The books had a value of $300. (Library Books and Susan Gale, Capital.)
f. Bought a new typewriter for $400. Payment is due in 60 days. (Office Equipment and Accounts Payable.)
g. Paid $450 to settle the amount owed on the calculator. (Accounts Payable and Cash.)

PROBLEM 2-2A The following transactions occurred at several different businesses and are not related.

INSTRUCTIONS Analyze each of the transactions. Decide what accounts are affected, and enter the proper titles at the top of a pair of T accounts. Then record the effects of the transaction in the T accounts. Use plus and minus signs before the amounts to show the increases and decreases.

a. Bill Ramos, an owner, made an additional investment of $5,000 in cash.
b. A firm purchased equipment for $2,500 in cash.
c. A firm sold some surplus office furniture for $200 in cash.
d. A firm purchased a large outdoor sign for $750, to be paid in 60 days.
e. A firm purchased equipment for $1,000 on credit.
f. Alice Scott, owner of the Star Travel Agency, withdrew $1,000 of her original cash investment.
g. A firm bought a delivery truck for $8,000 on credit. Payment is due in 90 days.
h. A firm issued a check for $250 to a supplier in partial payment of an open account balance.

PROBLEM 2-3A

The following revenue and expense transactions took place at the Warren Machine Repair Company.

INSTRUCTIONS

Analyze each of the transactions. Decide what accounts are affected, and enter the proper titles at the top of a pair of T accounts. Then record the effects of the transaction in the T accounts. Use plus and minus signs before the amounts to show the increases and decreases.

a. Sold services for $600 in cash.
b. Paid $200 for the month's rent.
c. Sold additional services for $1,000 on credit.
d. Paid $50 in cash for the monthly electric bill.
e. Bought supplies that cost $100. Payment is due in 30 days.
f. Paid salaries of $1,000.
g. Sold services for $1,500 in cash.
h. Collected $400 from credit customers.
i. Received a $5 cash refund for an overcharge on the electric bill.
j. Paid $25 for the monthly telephone bill.
k. Collected $100 from accounts receivable.
l. Received a $15 credit as an adjustment for damaged supplies.
m. Paid the $85 balance due on supplies previously purchased on credit.
n. Sold additional services for $500 on credit.

PROBLEM 2-4A

Sarah Cohen is an architect who operates her own business. The transactions and account titles for the business are shown below and on the next page. (The account numbers have been intentionally omitted.)

INSTRUCTIONS

Analyze the transactions. Then record each one in the appropriate T accounts. Use plus and minus signs before the amounts to show the increases and decreases. Identify each entry in the T accounts by writing the letter of the transaction next to the entry.

ASSETS	REVENUE
Cash	Fees
Accounts Receivable	
Office Furniture	EXPENSES
Office Equipment	Rent Expense
	Utilities Expense
LIABILITIES	Salaries Expense
Accounts Payable	Telephone Expense
	Miscellaneous Expense
OWNER'S EQUITY	
Sarah Cohen, Capital	

a. Sarah Cohen invested $7,000 in cash to start the business.
b. Paid $300 for one month's rent.
c. Bought office furniture for $1,500 in cash.

d. Performed services for $800 in cash.
e. Paid $135 for the monthly telephone bill.
f. Sold services for $900 on credit.
g. Purchased a typewriter for $350. Paid $100 cash immediately. The balance is due in 30 days.
h. Received a bill for $165 from the office cleaning service. Payment is due in 30 days.
i. Received $400 from accounts receivable.
j. Purchased additional office chairs for $150. Received credit terms of 30 days.
k. Paid $1,000 for salaries.
l. Issued a check for $75 in partial payment of the amount owed for office chairs.
m. Received $700 in cash for services performed.
n. Issued a check for $160 to pay the utility bill.
o. Performed services for $1,200 on credit.
p. Collected $500 from accounts receivable.
q. Paid $65 of the bill from the office cleaning service that was received previously.
r. Paid $90 to Eddy's Duplicating Service for photocopy work performed during the month.

PROBLEM 2-5A

The accountant for Sarah Cohen's business prepares financial statements at the end of each month.

INSTRUCTIONS Use the figures in the T accounts for Problem 2-4A to prepare an income statement and a balance sheet. Use two-column analysis paper for the income statement and four-column analysis paper for the balance sheet. (The first line of the statement headings should read Sarah Cohen, Architect.) Determine the account balances before you start work on the financial statements. Assume that the transactions took place during the month ended June 30, 19X1.

UNIT 3

basic ACCOUNTING RECORDS

In the last unit, you learned that the analysis of each transaction is the basis for recording the effects of the transaction in the accounts. In business, accountants keep written records of each analysis for future reference. These records allow the accountants to recheck their work and trace the details of any transaction long after it has happened.

The General Journal

The analysis of each transaction is kept in a book called the *general journal*. This book is really a diary of business activities that is used to note every event involving financial affairs as it occurs.

When Paul Reed invested $6,000 and started the Modern Cleaning Shop, the accountant analyzed the transaction and identified the following effects.

a. The business had $6,000 of property in the form of cash.
b. Reed had a $6,000 financial investment in the business.

Then, using this analysis as a guide, the accountant decided to record the transaction as follows.

a. Debit the Cash account to record the increase in the asset Cash.
b. Credit the Paul Reed, Capital account to record the new ownership interest.

The accountant's written record of the analysis of the transaction as it appears in the general journal is shown below.

GENERAL JOURNAL		PAGE		
DATE	DESCRIPTION OF ENTRY	POST. REF.	DEBIT	CREDIT
19X1 Nov. 26	Cash		6000 00	
	Paul Reed, Capital			6000 00
	Beginning cash investment of owner.			

Notice that each page in the general journal is given a number and that the year is written at the top of the Date column. The month and day are also written in the Date column on the first line of the first entry. After the first entry, the year and month are written only when a new page is begun or when either the year or the month changes. However, the day of each transaction is written in the Date column on the first line of each entry.

The account to be debited is always entered first in the Description of Entry column. The account title is written close to the left margin, and the debit amount is then entered on the same line in the Debit column.

The account to be credited is always recorded on the line beneath the debit. The account title is indented about half an inch from the left margin. Next, the credit amount is entered on the same line in the Credit column.

A brief explanation follows the credit entry. This explanation begins at the left margin of the Description of Entry column so that as much space as possible is available. Explanations should be complete but concise.

Account titles are written in the general journal exactly as they appear in the chart of accounts and the ledger. Use of the exact wording of each account title minimizes the possibility of errors when the amounts are transferred to the ledger accounts.

Accountants usually leave a blank line between each general journal entry. This separates the transactions and makes them easier to identify and read. Some accountants prefer to use this blank line to number each general journal entry for identification purposes.

Because the accountant writes the transaction analysis in the general journal before making any entry in the accounts, the general journal is known as a *book of original entry*. The process of recording in a journal is called *journalizing*. By journalizing first, the accountant knows that all the data about a transaction is recorded in one place before any details can be forgotten.

General Journal Entries for November

When the Modern Cleaning Shop bought cleaning equipment for $2,000 in cash, the accountant made the following analysis.

c. The business purchased new assets (equipment) that cost $2,000.
d. The business paid out $2,000 in cash.

The accountant made the following entry in the general journal.

GENERAL JOURNAL   Page 1

DATE	DESCRIPTION OF ENTRY	POST. REF.	DEBIT	CREDIT
19 X1 Nov. 27	Equipment		2,000 00	
	Cash			2,000 00
	Purchased cleaning equipment for cash.			

When the Modern Cleaning Shop bought equipment on credit from Knight, Inc., the accountant's analysis was as follows.

e. The business purchased new assets (equipment) that cost $1,000.
f. The business owed $1,000 as an account payable to Knight, Inc.

The entry in the general journal is shown below.

GENERAL JOURNAL				Page 1
DATE	DESCRIPTION OF ENTRY	POST. REF.	DEBIT	CREDIT
19 X1 Nov. 28	Equipment Accounts Payable Purchased equipment on credit from Knight, Inc.		1,000 00	1,000 00

Finally, an analysis of the payment to Knight, Inc., showed the following results.

g. The firm paid out $700 in cash.
h. Knight's claim against the firm was reduced by $700.

The accountant's entry in the journal was as follows.

GENERAL JOURNAL				Page 1
DATE	DESCRIPTION OF ENTRY	POST. REF.	DEBIT	CREDIT
19 X1 Nov. 30	Accounts Payable Cash Paid Knight, Inc., on account.		700 00	700 00

Notice that the debit item is always entered first. This is the case even if the accountant happens to consider the credit first while mentally analyzing the transaction.

General Journal Entries for December

You will recall that the Modern Cleaning Shop officially opened for business on December 1, 19X1, and the following transactions were completed during that month.

1. Sold cleaning services for $2,200 in cash (Entries i and j).
2. Sold cleaning services for $800 on credit to charge customers (Entries k and l).
3. Received $600 in cash from charge account customers to apply to their accounts (Entries m and n).
4. Paid $1,600 for salaries (Entries o and p).
5. Paid $700 for rent (Entries q and r).
6. Paid $600 for supplies used (Entries s and t).

Stein records the December transactions in the general journal. (In actual practice, the transactions would be spread throughout the month and recorded as they occurred. The following general journal entries have been assigned dates to illustrate how these transactions are recorded.)

GENERAL JOURNAL   Page 2

DATE	DESCRIPTION OF ENTRY	POST. REF.	DEBIT	CREDIT
19 X1 Dec. 11	Cash		2,200 00	
	Cleaning Service Sales			2,200 00
	Sold services for cash.			
14	Accounts Receivable		800 00	
	Cleaning Service Sales			800 00
	Sold services on credit.			
16	Cash		600 00	
	Accounts Receivable			600 00
	Received cash from customers on account.			
18	Salaries Expense		1,600 00	
	Cash			1,600 00
	Paid salaries to employees.			
20	Rent Expense		700 00	
	Cash			700 00
	Paid December rent.			
31	Supplies Used		600 00	
	Cash			600 00
	Paid for supplies used.			

Each of the entries illustrated so far consists of a single debit and a single credit. Some transactions may require a record consisting of several debits or several credits. This type of record is called a *compound entry*. In a compound entry, all debits are listed first. All credits are indented and follow the list of debits. Remember, total debits must equal total credits.

For example, a compound entry would be required to record the following transaction. Store fixtures are purchased for $400. The purchaser gives $100 in cash immediately and receives 30 days in which to pay the balance. This transaction would be analyzed as shown below.

1. The asset Store Fixtures is increased by $400.
2. The asset Cash is decreased by $100.
3. The liability Accounts Payable is increased by $300.

The general journal entry for this transaction is illustrated below.

GENERAL JOURNAL				Page 6
DATE	DESCRIPTION OF ENTRY	POST. REF.	DEBIT	CREDIT
19 X2 June 2	Store Fixtures		400 00	
	Cash			100 00
	Accounts Payable			300 00
	Purchased store fixtures, paying $100 cash and receiving 30-day credit terms on balance.			

The General Ledger

The entries in the general journal show what is to be debited and what is to be credited. With this record as a guide, the accountant can enter the information in the individual accounts affected. The accountant actually uses printed forms for the accounts. Each account is kept on a separate form called a *ledger sheet.* All the accounts together make up a *ledger,* or *book of final entry.* (However, some firms keep their ledger accounts on cards and store them in trays.)

The ledger is the master reference file of the accounting system and provides a permanent and classified record of every element involved in the business operation. The following illustrations show how Paul Reed's $6,000 investment would appear in the ledger of the Modern Cleaning Shop. (The use of posting references is explained in the next section.)

GENERAL JOURNAL				PAGE 1
DATE	DESCRIPTION OF ENTRY	POST. REF.	DEBIT	CREDIT
19 X1 Nov. 26	Cash	101	6000 00	
	Paul Reed, Capital	301		6000 00
	Beginning cash investment of owner.			

Cash   NO. 101

DATE	EXPLANATION	POST. REF.	DEBIT	DATE	EXPLANATION	POST. REF.	CREDIT
19 X1 Nov. 26		J1	6000 00				

Paul Reed, Capital   NO. 301

DATE	EXPLANATION	POST. REF.	DEBIT	DATE	EXPLANATION	POST. REF.	CREDIT
				19 X1 Nov. 26	Beginning investment	J1	6000 00

If a question arises later about an item, a look at the proper ledger account will reveal a complete running history of the increases and decreases for the item as well as the source of the original data. The ledger accounts may be kept in a post binder; or, as noted already, if they are in card form, they may be kept in a ledger tray. Ledger accounts are useful records because accountants are able to enter more details in them than in T accounts.

The Explanation column of the ledger account form is used for special notations. Routine entries, however, usually require no explanation.

Posting General Journal Entries to the Ledger

The process of transferring information from the journal to the ledger is called *posting*. Examine the posting of the remainder of the general journal entries for the Modern Cleaning Shop.

The purchase of cleaning equipment for $2,000 was journalized as follows.

GENERAL JOURNAL				Page 1
DATE	DESCRIPTION OF ENTRY	POST. REF.	DEBIT	CREDIT
19 X1 Nov. 27	Equipment		2,000 00	
	Cash			2,000 00
	Purchased cleaning equipment for cash.			

This information was then posted to the proper ledger accounts, as shown below.

Equipment — No. 141

DATE	EXPLANATION	POST. REF.	DEBIT	DATE	EXPLANATION	POST. REF.	CREDIT
19 X1 Nov. 27		J1	2,000 00				

Cash — No. 101

DATE	EXPLANATION	POST. REF.	DEBIT	DATE	EXPLANATION	POST. REF.	CREDIT
19 X1 Nov. 26		J1	6,000 00	19 X1 Nov. 27		J1	2,000 00

In the posting process, the amount in the Debit column of the general journal is transferred to the debit side of the proper account in the ledger. Then, the amount in the Credit column of the journal is entered on the credit side of the proper ledger account.

The procedure usually followed in posting an entry from the general journal is to start with the first account listed in the entry (the account to be debited). The accountant locates this account in the ledger. The date is then entered in the Date column of the account, and the page number of the general journal is entered in the Posting Reference (Post. Ref.) column of the account. (The letter *J* in front of the page number is an abbreviation that identifies the general journal.) The debit amount is then entered in the Debit column of the account. Posting of the debit is complete after the number of the ledger account to which the posting was made is entered in the Posting Reference column of the general journal.

After the debit amount is posted, the same procedure is used to post the credit amount of the transaction. The recording process for the transaction is then complete.

Writing the general journal page number in the ledger account and the account number in the journal shows that the entry has been posted and ensures against posting the same entry twice or not at all. The journal page numbers in the accounts and the account numbers in the journal provide a useful cross-reference when entries must be traced and transactions verified.

The general journal entry is illustrated below as it appears when the posting process has been completed.

GENERAL JOURNAL Page 1

DATE	DESCRIPTION OF ENTRY	POST. REF.	DEBIT	CREDIT
19 X1 Nov. 27	Equipment	141	2,000 00	
	Cash	101		2,000 00
	Purchased cleaning equipment for cash.			

The identical procedure is used in posting the other journal entries for November and December, shown on pages 40 and 41. After those entries are posted, the ledger accounts appear as shown here. Refer to the journal entries, and trace the postings carefully.

Cash No. 101

DATE	EXPLANATION	POST. REF.	DEBIT	DATE	EXPLANATION	POST. REF.	CREDIT
19 X1 Nov. 26		J1	6,000 00	19 X1 Nov. 27		J1	2,000 00
Dec. 11		J2	2,200 00	30		J1	700 00
16		J2	600 00	Dec. 18		J2	1,600 00
				20		J2	700 00
				31		J2	600 00

Accounts Receivable   No. 111

DATE	EXPLANATION	POST. REF.	DEBIT	DATE	EXPLANATION	POST. REF.	CREDIT
19X1 Dec. 14		J2	800 00	19X1 Dec. 16		J2	600 00

Equipment   No. 141

DATE	EXPLANATION	POST. REF.	DEBIT	DATE	EXPLANATION	POST. REF.	CREDIT
19X1 Nov. 27		J1	2,000 00				
28		J1	1,000 00				

Accounts Payable   No. 202

DATE	EXPLANATION	POST. REF.	DEBIT	DATE	EXPLANATION	POST. REF.	CREDIT
19X1 Nov. 30		J1	700 00	19X1 Nov. 28		J1	1,000 00

Paul Reed, Capital   No. 301

DATE	EXPLANATION	POST. REF.	DEBIT	DATE	EXPLANATION	POST. REF.	CREDIT
				19X1 Nov. 26	Beginning investment	J1	6,000 00

Cleaning Service Sales   No. 401

DATE	EXPLANATION	POST. REF.	DEBIT	DATE	EXPLANATION	POST. REF.	CREDIT
				19X1 Dec. 11		J2	2,200 00
				14		J2	800 00

Salaries Expense   No. 511

DATE	EXPLANATION	POST. REF.	DEBIT	DATE	EXPLANATION	POST. REF.	CREDIT
19X1 Dec. 18		J2	1,600 00				

		Rent Expense						No. 516
DATE	EXPLANATION	POST. REF.	DEBIT		DATE	EXPLANATION	POST. REF.	CREDIT
19 X1 Dec. 20		J2	700	00				

		Supplies Used						No. 521
DATE	EXPLANATION	POST. REF.	DEBIT		DATE	EXPLANATION	POST. REF.	CREDIT
19 X1 Dec. 31		J2	600	00				

The pages in the ledger are usually arranged so that the balance sheet accounts—assets, liabilities, and owner's equity—come first. The accounts for the income statement come next, with the revenue accounts first, followed by the expense accounts. The numbering of the accounts in the chart of accounts follows the same order. This arrangement speeds the preparation of the income statement and the balance sheet. All figures are found in the ledger in the order in which they will be presented on the statements.

principles and procedures summary

The accountant's entry in the general journal is a permanent record of the analysis of each transaction. The process of recording in a general journal is called journalizing. The debit item is always entered first. Then the credit item is written on the line below. A brief explanation follows the credit item.

Information is transferred from journal entries to ledger accounts. This process is called posting. The individual accounts together form a ledger. Debits are posted to the left side of the accounts, and credits are posted to the right side. The Posting Reference columns in the general journal and the ledger accounts provide a quick cross-reference if an item needs to be traced or rechecked.

managerial implications

Business managers can always refer to the journal entries and ledger postings if a question comes up about previous transactions. These permanent records allow management to quickly find out what happened in a transaction and how it was recorded. These records also show the effect of a transaction on the assets, liabilities, and owner's equity. By looking at such records, managers can get information they need to make business decisions.

MANAGERIAL DISCUSSION QUESTIONS

1. How do permanent records of transactions help management operate a business effectively and make sound decisions?
2. How does the general ledger make it easier for a newly hired accountant to learn the firm's system of accounts?
3. If the book of original entry contains a complete record of every transaction, why would a manager need to refer to the general ledger at all?
4. How can a manager be sure that the firm's accountant is recording transactions promptly?

APPLICATION OF PRINCIPLES

PROBLEM 3-1 The transactions of City Building Maintenance for October 19X1 are shown below and on page 48.

INSTRUCTIONS Analyze each transaction, and record the effects in general journal form. Use the account titles in the following chart of accounts. Be sure to number the journal page *1* and to put the year at the top of the Date column.

ASSETS
101 Cash
111 Accounts Receivable
141 Truck

LIABILITIES
202 Accounts Payable

OWNER'S EQUITY
301 Margot Conner, Capital

REVENUE
401 Sales

EXPENSES
503 Cleaning Supplies Used
504 Equipment Rental Expense
505 Telephone Expense
506 Truck Expense
511 Salaries Expense
516 Office Rental Expense
522 Utilities Expense

TRANSACTIONS FOR OCTOBER 19X1
Oct. 1 Paid $225 for the October office rent.
     3 Paid a fee of $250 for equipment rental.

5 Sold services for $500 in cash.
6 Paid $55 for the September telephone bill.
9 Sold services for $1,400 on credit.
14 Received a $50 bill for truck repairs. Paid in cash.
15 Paid $1,000 for semimonthly salaries.
18 Collected $300 from credit customers.
21 Paid $100 in cash for supplies used.
24 Sold services for $650 on credit.
25 Received a $45 invoice for cleaning supplies used; terms, 30 days.
26 Received $200 in cash from accounts receivable.
27 Sold services for $600 in cash.
28 Received a $10 cash refund due to an overcharge on the September telephone bill.
29 Paid $150 for the October utilities bill.
30 Paid $1,000 for semimonthly salaries.
31 Sold services for $800 on credit.
31 Received a bill for $100 for additional truck repairs. Payment is due in 30 days.

PROBLEM 3-2 Edith Gardner has opened the Handy Duplicating and Mailing Service. She plans to use the chart of accounts shown below. The financial activities of the business during the first month of operations, July 19X1, are listed below and on the next page.

INSTRUCTIONS
1. Journalize the transactions. Be sure to number the journal page *1* and to write the year at the top of the Date column.
2. Post to the ledger accounts. Before you start the posting process, complete the headings of the account forms by writing the title and the number of each account. (Use the order that the accounts follow in the chart of accounts.)

ASSETS
101 Cash
111 Accounts Receivable
141 Office Equipment

LIABILITIES
202 Accounts Payable

OWNER'S EQUITY
301 Edith Gardner, Capital

REVENUE
401 Sales

EXPENSES
504 Telephone Expense
506 Advertising Expense
507 Salaries Expense
516 Rent Expense
517 Equipment Expense
521 Supplies Used

TRANSACTIONS FOR JULY 19X1
July 1 Edith Gardner invested $3,000 in the business. This amount was deposited in a checking account she opened for the business.

2   Paid $200 office rent by check.
3   Bought duplicating equipment for $3,000, paying $1,000 at once. The balance is payable in 30 days.
4   Paid a $100 advertising bill in cash.
5   Sold services for $350 in cash.
5   Paid $100 for the supplies used.
8   Paid part-time salaries of $200 by check.
11 Sold services for $1,000 on credit.
15 Collected $150 from accounts receivable.
17 Purchased a supply cabinet for $200 in cash.
20 Paid $45 for the monthly telephone bill.
22 Sold services for $500 in cash.
24 Received a bill of $200 for supplies used; terms, 30 days.
25 Paid $100 for equipment repairs.
26 Received a $50 credit to correct an overcharge on the July 24 invoice for supplies used.

PROBLEM 3-3

The accountant for the Rossetti Garage has recommended that the accounts shown below be established in the general ledger of this new firm.

INSTRUCTIONS

Arrange the accounts in the form of a chart of accounts similar to the one shown on page 30 of the text.

ACCOUNTS

301	Gerald Rossetti, Capital	140	Garage Equipment
541	Truck Operating Expense	401	Sales
142	Office Equipment	504	Telephone Expense
202	Accounts Payable	516	Rent Expense
527	Utilities Expense	150	Tow Truck
111	Accounts Receivable	521	Supplies Used
552	Payroll Taxes Expense	101	Cash
512	Salaries Expense		

alternate problems

PROBLEM 3-1A

The transactions listed on page 50 took place at the Kwan Industrial Cleaning Service during July 19X1.

INSTRUCTIONS

Analyze each transaction, and record the effects in general journal form. Choose the account titles from the chart of accounts on page 50. Be sure to number the journal page *1* and to write the year at the top of the Date column.

ASSETS
101 Cash
111 Accounts Receivable
141 Equipment

LIABILITIES
202 Accounts Payable

OWNER'S EQUITY
301 Anna Kwan, Capital

REVENUE
401 Sales

EXPENSES
503 Equipment Repairs Expense
504 Telephone Expense
505 Utilities Expense
511 Salaries Expense
516 Rent Expense
521 Cleaning Supplies Used
522 Office Supplies Used

TRANSACTIONS FOR JULY 19X1

July 1 Paid $160 for the July office rent.
      5 Sold services for $1,000 in cash.
      5 Sold services for $540 on credit.
     10 Paid $60 for the June telephone bill.
     11 Received a bill for $85 for equipment repairs.
     12 Received $400 from credit customers.
     15 Paid $600 for semimonthly salaries.
     18 Issued a $150 check for cleaning supplies used.
     19 Received a $180 invoice for ten cases of detergent used. The payment is due in 30 days.
     20 Paid $1,550 in cash for equipment.
     21 Received $525 from credit customers.
     21 Received a credit of $96 for damaged cleaning supplies previously purchased for the business.
     22 Sold services for $680 in cash.
     22 Sold services for $370 on credit.
     25 Paid $85 for the repair bill received on July 11.
     26 Paid $16 in cash for office stationery.
     28 Issued a $77 check for the monthly electric bill.
     31 Paid $600 for semimonthly salaries.

PROBLEM 3-2A Roberta Brel, a public stenographer, opened an office in the Palace Hotel. She plans to use the chart of accounts shown on page 51. The financial activities of the business during the first month of operations, August 19X1, are also listed on page 51.

INSTRUCTIONS
1. Journalize the transactions. Be sure to number the journal page *1* and to write the year at the top of the Date column.
2. Post to the ledger accounts. Before you start the posting process, complete the headings of the account forms by writing the title and the num-

ber of each account. (Use the order that the accounts follow in the chart of accounts.)

ASSETS
101 Cash
111 Accounts Receivable
141 Office Equipment

LIABILITIES
202 Accounts Payable

OWNER'S EQUITY
301 Roberta Brel, Capital

REVENUE
401 Sales

EXPENSES
504 Telephone Expense
511 Salaries Expense
513 Advertising Expense
516 Rent Expense
517 Equipment Rental Expense
521 Supplies Used

TRANSACTIONS FOR AUGUST 19X1

Aug. 1 Brel invested $2,000 cash in the business. This amount was deposited in the firm's checking account.
    3 Paid $150 in cash for the August office rent.
    5 Bought a desk and other furniture for $600 on credit.
    6 Paid $15 for rental of a typewriter for the month.
    7 Sold stenographic services for $100 in cash.
    10 Paid $21 for an advertisement in the hotel magazine.
    12 Sold services for $240 in cash and $75 on credit. (Use one compound entry.)
    15 Paid $40 for supplies used.
    17 Paid a $300 salary to the assistant.
    18 Bought a file cabinet for $200 on credit.
    20 Paid $200 toward the balance due on a desk and other furniture.
    22 Received a $5 cash refund on supplies due to an overcharge.
    26 Sold services for $275 in cash.
    27 Paid $40 for the monthly telephone bill.
    30 Received $75 in cash from a charge account customer.

PROBLEM 3-3A

The accountant for the Central Air Conditioning Service has recommended that the accounts shown below be established in the firm's general ledger.

INSTRUCTIONS

Arrange the accounts in the form of a chart of accounts similar to the one shown on page 30 of the text.

ACCOUNTS

301	Harold Burkhart, Capital	514	Insurance Expense
140	Office Equipment	401	Sales
111	Accounts Receivable	531	Supplies Used
101	Cash	142	Repair Equipment
145	Truck	202	Accounts Payable
547	Truck Expense	504	Telephone Expense
512	Salaries Expense	552	Payroll Taxes Expense
501	Advertising Expense		

UNIT 4

THE TRIAL BALANCE AND WORKSHEET

As you already know, the purpose of having journals and ledgers is to help gather data that is needed to prepare the financial statements. After an accountant posts all the transactions for the operating period to the ledger accounts, the financial statements are prepared. Because management will use the financial statements to make decisions, the accountant wants to be sure that these reports contain no errors. Before preparing the statements, therefore, the accountant tests the accuracy of the arithmetic used in the recording activities for the period.

The Trial Balance

One testing device accountants use is the *trial balance.* When Reed started the Modern Cleaning Shop with a cash investment, we said that property equaled financial interests. Then, using more technical language, we stated that assets equaled liabilities plus owner's equity. Later, we saw that every entry on the debit, or left, side of one account is matched by an entry of equal amount on the credit, or right, side of another account. The books started with equality of debits and credits and continued that equality in the recording process. Consequently, it follows that the sum of the debit balances in the ledger accounts should equal the sum of the credit balances after all transactions have been posted. If the books do not balance—that is, if the debit balances do not equal the credit balances—accountants know that an error has been made.

To test the equality of the debits and credits in the ledger, accountants use the following procedure.

1. Determine the balance of each account.
2. Add the debit and credit balances separately to see if the totals are equal.

Finding the Balance of an Account

As you saw earlier, two steps are necessary to compute the balance of an account.

1. Add the figures on each side of the account.
2. Subtract the smaller total from the larger to find the balance.

For example, the Cash account of the Modern Cleaning Shop shows total debits of $8,800 and total credits of $5,600. To find the balance, subtract the smaller total ($5,600) from the larger ($8,800). The difference is the account balance of $3,200 ($8,800 − $5,600 = $3,200). This figure is called a *debit balance* because the total of debits is larger than the total of credits.

Cash   No. 101

DATE	EXPLANATION	POST. REF.	DEBIT	DATE	EXPLANATION	POST. REF.	CREDIT
19 X1 Nov. 26		J1	6,000 00	19 X1 Nov. 27		J1	2,000 00
Dec. 11		J2	2,200 00	30		J1	700 00
16		J2	600 00	Dec. 18		J2	1,600 00
	3,200.00		8,800 00	20		J2	700 00
				31		J2	600 00
							5,600 00

Notice that the accountant writes the totals in small figures under the last item on each side of the account. These totals are called *footings* and are written in pencil. The account balance is also written in small pencil figures. Because the Cash account has a debit balance, the balance appears in the Explanation column on the debit side of the account.

Notice that there are no footings in the Debit and Credit columns of the Accounts Receivable account because there are only single amounts in these columns. The difference between the two amounts ($200) is the account balance. This figure appears in the Explanation column on the debit side of the account.

Accounts Receivable   No. 111

DATE	EXPLANATION	POST. REF.	DEBIT	DATE	EXPLANATION	POST. REF.	CREDIT
19 X1 Dec. 14		J2	800 00	19 X1 Dec. 16		J2	600 00
	200.00						

No balance figure is written in the Equipment account because this account has no credit figures. The footing in the Debit column ($3,000) is the account balance.

Equipment   No. 141

DATE	EXPLANATION	POST. REF.	DEBIT	DATE	EXPLANATION	POST. REF.	CREDIT
19 X1 Nov. 27		J1	2,000 00				
28		J1	1,000 00				
			3,000 00				

The balance of the liability account for Accounts Payable appears in the Explanation column on the credit side. This is because the total of credits

53

exceeds the total of debits. When the credits in an account exceed the debits, the account is said to have a *credit balance*.

			Accounts Payable			No. 201
DATE	EXPLANATION	POST. REF.	DEBIT	DATE	EXPLANATION	POST. REF.	CREDIT
19 X1 Nov. 30		J1	700 00	19 X1 Nov. 28	*300.00*	J1	1,000 00

The Paul Reed, Capital account does not have to be balanced because there is only one entry on the credit side. This account has a credit balance of $6,000.

			Paul Reed, Capital			No. 301
DATE	EXPLANATION	POST. REF.	DEBIT	DATE	EXPLANATION	POST. REF.	CREDIT
				19 X1 Nov. 26	Beginning investment	J1	6,000 00

The Cleaning Service Sales account has a credit balance of $3,000. The footing in this case is the sum of the credit entries. Since there are no amounts on the debit side, the footing indicates the account balance.

			Cleaning Service Sales			No. 401
DATE	EXPLANATION	POST. REF.	DEBIT	DATE	EXPLANATION	POST. REF.	CREDIT
				19 X1 Dec. 11 14		J2 J2	2,200 00 800 00 *3,000 00*

The following expense accounts have debit balances. No footings were written in these accounts since each one contains a single entry.

			Salaries Expense			No. 511
DATE	EXPLANATION	POST. REF.	DEBIT	DATE	EXPLANATION	POST. REF.	CREDIT
19 X1 Dec. 18		J2	1,600 00				

		Rent Expense						No. 516
DATE	EXPLANATION	POST. REF.	DEBIT	DATE	EXPLANATION	POST. REF.	CREDIT
19 X1 Dec. 20		J2	700 00				

		Supplies Used						No. 521
DATE	EXPLANATION	POST. REF.	DEBIT	DATE	EXPLANATION	POST. REF.	CREDIT
19 X1 Dec. 31		J2	600 00				

Preparing the Trial Balance

Once Stein finds the balances of the accounts, he lists them on a trial balance form. Preparing a trial balance allows the accountant to see if the total of the debit balances equals the total of the credit balances. The accounts are listed in numeric order. (This is the order followed in the general ledger.) The balance of each account is written in the proper column. Debit balances are shown in the left column, and credit balances are shown in the right column. If an account has no balance, its name and number are still included in the list. However, no figure is entered in the amount columns.

Notice that the trial balance illustrated below has a three-line heading that shows who, what, and when. The date is the closing date for the accounting period. Observe, too, that there are no dollar signs in the amount columns. Accountants usually omit dollar signs when they prepare financial statements, schedules, or working papers on ruled forms.

Modern Cleaning Shop
Trial Balance
December 31, 19X1

Acct. no.	Account Name	Debit	Credit
101	Cash	3200 00	
111	Accounts Receivable	200 00	
141	Equipment	3000 00	
202	Accounts Payable		300 00
301	Paul Reed, Capital		6000 00
401	Cleaning Service Sales		3000 00
511	Salaries Expense	1600 00	
516	Rent Expense	700 00	
521	Supplies Used	600 00	
	Totals	9300 00	9300 00

Purpose of the Trial Balance

When the Debit and Credit columns of the trial balance are equal, the accountant knows that the books are in balance. He is also sure that a debit has been recorded for every credit.

If the Debit and Credit columns are not equal, the accountant knows an error has been made. The error may be in the trial balance, or it may be in the books. The following are some common errors.

1. Making errors in addition.
2. Recording only half an entry. For example, a debit may have been recorded without a credit, or vice versa.
3. Recording both halves of the entry on the same side. (Two debits or two credits may have been recorded in the ledger, rather than one debit and one credit.)
4. Recording one or more amounts incorrectly.
5. Making errors in arithmetic in the journal entry.
6. Making errors in arithmetic when the accounts are balanced.

The trial balance columns can be checked for errors by adding the columns again in the opposite direction. That is, if the columns were first added from top to bottom, they should be verified by adding from bottom to top.

Sometimes the accountant can determine the type of error by the amount of the difference involved. For this reason, when the debit and credit totals on the trial balance are not equal, the accountant computes the difference by subtracting the smaller total from the larger total. If the difference is divisible by 9, there may have been a *transposition* ($357 for $375) or a *slide* ($375 for $37.50). If the difference can be divided by 2, the amount of a debit may have been posted as a credit, or a credit posted as a debit.

Even if the books are in balance, there can be other mistakes. The accountant must also look for errors such as the following.

1. A transaction could be omitted.
2. The same transaction could be recorded more than once.
3. A part of an entry could be recorded in the wrong account.
4. There could be offsetting arithmetic errors in the accounts.
5. There could be offsetting arithmetic errors in totaling the trial balance columns.

Fortunately, these types of errors do not happen often. The trial balance, therefore, is a good test of accuracy.

The Worksheet

When the trial balance shows that the ledger is in balance, the accountant is ready to prepare the financial statements for the period. These statements must be completed as soon as possible if they are to be useful. Therefore, anything that Stein can do to save time is important.

One way that accountants save time is by using a special form called a *worksheet*. Here is how a simple type of worksheet looks.

MODERN CLEANING SHOP
Worksheet
Month Ended December 31, 19X1

ACCT. NO.	ACCOUNT NAME	TRIAL BALANCE		INCOME STATEMENT		BALANCE SHEET	
		DEBIT	CREDIT	DEBIT	CREDIT	DEBIT	CREDIT
101	Cash	3,200 00					
111	Accounts Receivable	200 00					
141	Equipment	3,000 00					
202	Accounts Payable		300 00				
301	Paul Reed, Capital		6,000 00				
401	Cleaning Service Sales		3,000 00				
511	Salaries Expense	1,600 00					
516	Rent Expense	700 00					
521	Supplies Used	600 00					
	Totals	9,300 00	9,300 00				

The Trial Balance Section

The accountant used information from the trial balance to begin to prepare a worksheet. This is why the first two money columns of the worksheet are headed "Trial Balance." The only differences between this form and the one shown on page 55 are the size of the paper used, the inclusion of extra money columns to make it easier to prepare the statements, and the substitution of the period of operation for the closing date on the third line of the heading.

To save time and effort, many accountants combine the trial balance process with the preparation of the worksheet. They list the accounts directly on the worksheet. Then they transfer the account balances from the ledger directly to the Debit and Credit columns of the Trial Balance section of the worksheet. With the account balances on the worksheet, they can then prove the equality of the totals of the debit and credit balances in the usual manner.

The Income Statement and Balance Sheet Sections

The Income Statement and Balance Sheet money columns are used to organize the figures needed for these financial reports. For instance, in order for the accountant to prepare an income statement, all the revenue and expense account balances must be in one place. It is easy for Stein to assemble this information on a worksheet. First, he heads the second pair of money columns "Income Statement." The following pair of columns are for balance sheet figures and are therefore headed "Balance Sheet." The Income Statement and Balance Sheet sections are then subdivided into Debit and Credit columns.

After writing in the headings of the columns, Stein looks at the list of accounts in the Trial Balance section. Starting at the top he examines each item in turn. If an item will appear on the balance sheet, the amount is entered in the Balance Sheet columns. If an item will appear on the income statement, it is entered in the Income Statement columns. Accounts with no balances are ignored. When amounts are *carried over*, or *extended*, from the Trial Balance columns to the statement columns, the accountant must be sure not to enter a debit amount in a credit column or a credit amount in a debit column.

The Balance Sheet Columns. Remember that the accounts are numbered according to type in the following sequence: assets, liabilities, owner's equity, revenue, and expenses. The first three accounts in the Trial Balance section of the worksheet shown below are assets. They are carried over to the Debit column of the Balance Sheet section. As we said before, the debit items continue to appear as debit items after they are carried over.

MODERN CLEANING SHOP
Worksheet
Month Ended December 31, 19X1

ACCT. NO.	ACCOUNT NAME	TRIAL BALANCE DEBIT	TRIAL BALANCE CREDIT	INCOME STATEMENT DEBIT	INCOME STATEMENT CREDIT	BALANCE SHEET DEBIT	BALANCE SHEET CREDIT
101	Cash	3,200 00				3,200 00	
111	Accounts Receivable	200 00				200 00	
141	Equipment	3,000 00				3,000 00	
202	Accounts Payable		300 00				
301	Paul Reed, Capital		6,000 00				
401	Cleaning Service Sales		3,000 00				
511	Salaries Expense	1,600 00					
516	Rent Expense	700 00					
521	Supplies Used	600 00					
	Totals	9,300 00	9,300 00				

The next two items in the Trial Balance section are credit balances for a liability (Accounts Payable) and owner's equity (Paul Reed, Capital). They are carried over to the Credit column of the Balance Sheet section.

MODERN CLEANING SHOP
Worksheet
Month Ended December 31, 19X1

ACCT. NO.	ACCOUNT NAME	TRIAL BALANCE DEBIT	TRIAL BALANCE CREDIT	INCOME STATEMENT DEBIT	INCOME STATEMENT CREDIT	BALANCE SHEET DEBIT	BALANCE SHEET CREDIT
101	Cash	3,200 00				3,200 00	
111	Accounts Receivable	200 00				200 00	
141	Equipment	3,000 00				3,000 00	
202	Accounts Payable		300 00				300 00
301	Paul Reed, Capital		6,000 00				6,000 00
401	Cleaning Service Sales		3,000 00				
511	Salaries Expense	1,600 00					
516	Rent Expense	700 00					
521	Supplies Used	600 00					
	Totals	9,300 00	9,300 00				

The Income Statement Columns. The accountant knows that all revenue and expense items must appear on the income statement. Therefore, he carries over the credit balance in the Cleaning Service Sales account to the Credit column of the Income Statement section of the worksheet. Then he considers the accounts for Salaries Expense, Rent Expense, and Supplies Used. He extends their debit balances across to the Debit column of the Income Statement section of the worksheet, as shown.

MODERN CLEANING SHOP
Worksheet
Month Ended December 31, 19X1

ACCT. NO.	ACCOUNT NAME	TRIAL BALANCE DEBIT	TRIAL BALANCE CREDIT	INCOME STATEMENT DEBIT	INCOME STATEMENT CREDIT	BALANCE SHEET DEBIT	BALANCE SHEET CREDIT
101	Cash	3,200 00				3,200 00	
111	Accounts Receivable	200 00				200 00	
141	Equipment	3,000 00				3,000 00	
202	Accounts Payable		300 00				300 00
301	Paul Reed, Capital		6,000 00				6,000 00
401	Cleaning Service Sales		3,000 00		3,000 00		
511	Salaries Expense	1,600 00		1,600 00			
516	Rent Expense	700 00		700 00			
521	Supplies Used	600 00		600 00			
	Totals	9,300 00	9,300 00				

After Stein has carried each item across the worksheet from the Trial Balance columns to the financial statement columns, he totals the Income Statement columns. In the Income Statement columns of the worksheet we have been discussing, the debits (expenses) total $2,900 and the credits (revenue) total $3,000.

Next, Stein adds the amounts in the Balance Sheet columns. The debits (assets) total $6,400, and the credits (liabilities and owner's equity) total $6,300. These totals are entered as shown on the worksheet below.

MODERN CLEANING SHOP
Worksheet
Month Ended December 31, 19X1

ACCT. NO.	ACCOUNT NAME	TRIAL BALANCE DEBIT	TRIAL BALANCE CREDIT	INCOME STATEMENT DEBIT	INCOME STATEMENT CREDIT	BALANCE SHEET DEBIT	BALANCE SHEET CREDIT
101	Cash	3,200 00				3,200 00	
111	Accounts Receivable	200 00				200 00	
141	Equipment	3,000 00				3,000 00	
202	Accounts Payable		300 00				300 00
301	Paul Reed, Capital		6,000 00				6,000 00
401	Cleaning Service Sales		3,000 00		3,000 00		
511	Salaries Expense	1,600 00		1,600 00			
516	Rent Expense	700 00		700 00			
521	Supplies Used	600 00		600 00			
	Totals	9,300 00	9,300 00	2,900 00	3,000 00	6,400 00	6,300 00

Since the Income Statement columns include all revenue and expenses, these columns are used to determine the net income or net loss. In this instance, the revenue ($3,000) exceeds the expenses ($2,900). Consequently, there is a net income (profit) of $100 ($3,000 − $2,900 = $100).

The net income represents a net increase in owner's equity, resulting from the firm's operations for the month. Therefore, the amount of the net income is carried over to the Balance Sheet section of the worksheet.

A record of the net income is made on the line below the totals.

1. The difference between revenue and expenses is identified on the worksheet as "Net Income for the Month."
2. The amount of $100 is entered in the Debit column of the Income Statement section.
3. The same amount is recorded in the Credit column of the Balance Sheet section.

After the net income is entered on the worksheet, the Income Statement and Balance Sheet columns are totaled again. All pairs of columns should then be in balance.

MODERN CLEANING SHOP
Worksheet
Month Ended December 31, 19X1

ACCT. NO.	ACCOUNT NAME	TRIAL BALANCE DEBIT	TRIAL BALANCE CREDIT	INCOME STATEMENT DEBIT	INCOME STATEMENT CREDIT	BALANCE SHEET DEBIT	BALANCE SHEET CREDIT
101	Cash	3,200 00				3,200 00	
111	Accounts Receivable	200 00				200 00	
141	Equipment	3,000 00				3,000 00	
202	Accounts Payable		300 00				300 00
301	Paul Reed, Capital		6,000 00				6,000 00
401	Cleaning Service Sales		3,000 00		3,000 00		
511	Salaries Expense	1,600 00		1,600 00			
516	Rent Expense	700 00		700 00			
521	Supplies Used	600 00		600 00			
	Totals	9,300 00	9,300 00	2,900 00	3,000 00	6,400 00	6,300 00
	Net Income for the Month			100 00			100 00
				3,000 00	3,000 00	6,400 00	6,400 00

If the business had a loss, the accountant would write "Net Loss for the Month" on the worksheet. The amount of the loss would be entered in the Credit column of the Income Statement section and the Debit column of the Balance Sheet section.

The Income Statement and the Balance Sheet

All the figures Stein needs to prepare the financial statements are now properly organized on the worksheet. The accounts are even arranged in the order in which they appear on the income statement and the balance sheet shown below. The income statement is prepared directly from the Income Statement columns of the worksheet. The balance sheet figures are taken directly from the Balance Sheet columns. Notice that on the balance sheet, the net income of $100 is added to Reed's investment at the beginning of the period. The sum of these two figures is Reed's equity in the business at the end of the month.

MODERN CLEANING SHOP
Income Statement
Month Ended December 31, 19X1

Revenue		
Cleaning Service Sales		3,000 00
Less Expenses		
Salaries Expense	1,600 00	
Rent Expense	700 00	
Supplies Used	600 00	
Total Expenses		2,900 00
Net Income for the Month		100 00

MODERN CLEANING SHOP
Balance Sheet
December 31, 19X1

Assets		Liabilities and Owner's Equity	
Cash	3,200 00	Liabilities	
Accounts Receivable	200 00	Accounts Payable	300 00
Equipment	3,000 00	Owner's Equity	
		Paul Reed, Capital 12/1/X1	6,000 00
		Net Income for December	100 00
		Paul Reed, Capital 12/31/X1	6,100 00
Total Assets	6,400 00	Total Liabilities and Owner's Equity	6,400 00

pRiNciplEs aNd pRocEduREs summaRy

The trial balance is used to prove the equality of the debits and credits in the ledger. Accountants take a trial balance before they prepare the financial reports for the period. Once they know that the books balance, they prepare a worksheet to save time in preparing the statements. First, the trial balance information is recorded on the worksheet. Then the figures needed for the income statement and the balance sheet are organized in the appropriate statement sections. Next, the net income or net loss for the period is determined. Finally, the amounts in the Income Statement and Balance Sheet sections of the worksheet are presented in the formal financial reports.

managerial implications

Taking a trial balance helps to pinpoint errors and identify the kinds of mistakes that may occur. If errors occur repeatedly, managers can take steps to correct careless work habits or to improve the recording procedure. Using the worksheet allows accountants to prepare financial statements more quickly. Consequently, management can get necessary information promptly. The more accounts a business has in its ledger, the more time can be saved by the use of a worksheet.

managerial discussion questions

1. How does the worksheet help management get vital information quickly?
2. Why is it important to make sure that the books balance before preparing the financial statements?

application of principles

PROBLEM 4-1   Ronald West owns and operates an employment service named the West Personnel Agency. The trial balance on February 28, 19X1, and the agency's transactions for March are given on the next page.

INSTRUCTIONS
1. Set up a general ledger for the accounts listed on the trial balance on February 28. Enter the amounts given for the accounts as opening balances. (Record the date, write the word "Balance" in the Explanation column, place a check mark in the Post. Ref. column, and record the amount.)
2. Prepare general journal entries to record the March transactions. (Number the journal page 3.)
3. Post the March general journal entries to the general ledger.
4. Foot each of the accounts. Determine the balance of each account on March 31. Enter the footing and balance figures in proper form.
5. Prepare a trial balance as of March 31.

ACCT. NO.	ACCOUNT NAME	DEBIT	CREDIT
101	Cash	$ 7,810.00	
111	Accounts Receivable	2,590.00	
141	Office Equipment	3,000.00	
143	Office Furniture and Fixtures	3,500.00	
145	Automobile	8,000.00	
202	Accounts Payable		$12,400.00
301	Ronald West, Capital		9,725.00
401	Fees		6,000.00
504	Telephone Expense	375.00	
511	Salaries Expense	1,200.00	
513	Advertising Expense	200.00	
516	Rent Expense	1,000.00	
518	Office Equipment Repairs Expense	15.00	
521	Office Supplies Used	140.00	
522	Utilities Expense	250.00	
523	Auto Repairs Expense	45.00	
	Totals	$28,125.00	$28,125.00

TRANSACTIONS FOR MARCH 19X1

Mar. 1 Paid $500 for the month's rent.
    3 Purchased office furniture that cost $1,000, paying $300 in cash. The balance is due in 30 days.
    5 Collected fees of $1,200 in cash for professional services.
    6 Paid $1,300 in cash for salaries.
    9 Bought a new typewriter for $600 in cash.
   12 Paid $150 in cash for newspaper advertising.
   13 Sold services for $600 in cash. Performed services for $400 on credit. (Use a compound entry.)
   17 Collected $1,500 in cash from accounts receivable.
   18 Paid $125 for the monthly utility bill.
   21 Paid $170 for supplies used.
   24 Paid $160 for the monthly telephone bill.
   26 Sold additional professional services for $500 in cash and $800 on credit.
   27 Paid $6,000 to apply on accounts payable for equipment and furniture previously purchased.
   31 Received a bill for $100 for office supplies used. The bill is payable in 30 days.

PROBLEM 4-2

Pauline Shalsky is an attorney who has her own law practice. Her general ledger accounts and balances on December 31, 19X2, are shown on page 64.

INSTRUCTIONS

1. Complete the worksheet for Pauline Shalsky, Attorney, at the end of six months of operation.

2. Prepare an income statement and a balance sheet. Use two-column analysis paper for the income statement and four-column analysis paper for the balance sheet.

ACCOUNTS

101	Cash ✓	$ 5,000 Dr.	301	Pauline Shalsky, Capital		$28,000 Cr.
111	Accounts Receivable	4,200 Dr.	401	Fees		37,850 Cr.
130	Office Furniture	2,000 Dr.	504	Telephone Expense		2,500 Dr.
132	Professional Library	1,750 Dr.	511	Salaries Expense		14,000 Dr.
134	Building	37,000 Dr.	522	Utilities Expense		1,500 Dr.
202	Accounts Payable	2,500 Cr.	534	Supplies Used		400 Dr.

PROBLEM 4-3

Alan Burke decided to open a house painting and decorating business. The transactions shown below and on page 65 took place during November 19X2, the first month of operations.

INSTRUCTIONS

1. Classify the account titles and numbers given on page 65, and prepare a chart of accounts.
2. Journalize the November transactions.
3. Set up a general ledger.
4. Post all entries to the general ledger.
5. Foot and balance the accounts.
6. Complete a worksheet as of November 30.
7. Prepare the income statement and the balance sheet. Use two-column analysis paper for the income statement and four-column analysis paper for the balance sheet.

TRANSACTIONS FOR NOVEMBER 19X2

Nov. 1 Invested $10,000 in cash.
    3 Paid $400 for the monthly rent.
    7 Purchased equipment for $3,000 in cash.
    9 Purchased a truck for $9,000. Paid $2,500 in cash immediately; the balance is payable in 180 days.
   12 Paid $55 in cash for newspaper advertising.
   14 Sold services for $2,700, $1,200 for cash and $1,500 on credit.
   15 Paid $95 in cash for truck repairs.
   18 Paid $425 for supplies used.
   20 Collected $400 from accounts receivable.
   22 Sold additional services for $2,200, $350 in cash with the balance payable in 30 days.
   24 Paid $1,700 for salaries.
   28 Paid $140 for additional supplies used.

29 Sold surplus equipment for $100 in cash.
30 Paid $75 for the monthly telephone bill.

ACCOUNTS

521	Supplies Used	515	Rent Expense
142	Equipment	202	Accounts Payable
511	Salaries Expense	111	Accounts Receivable
504	Telephone Expense	101	Cash
144	Truck	301	Alan Burke, Capital
401	Sales	512	Advertising Expense
518	Truck Repair Expense		

alternate problems

PROBLEM 4-1A George Modris owns and operates an interior decorating firm called Creative Decorations. The trial balance on March 31, 19X1, and the firm's transactions for April 19X1 are shown below and on page 66.

INSTRUCTIONS
1. Set up a general ledger for the accounts listed on the trial balance on March 31. Enter the amounts as opening balances. (Record the date, write the word "Balance" in the Explanation column, place a check mark in the Post. Ref. column, and record the amount.)
2. Prepare general journal entries to record the April transactions. (Number the journal page 4.)
3. Post the April general journal entries to the general ledger.
4. Foot each of the accounts. Determine the balance of each account on April 30. Enter the footing and balance figures in proper form.
5. Prepare a trial balance as of April 30.

ACCT. NO.	ACCOUNT NAME	DEBIT	CREDIT
101	Cash	$16,089.00	
111	Accounts Receivable	1,375.00	
141	Office Equipment	2,600.00	
143	Display Equipment	5,760.00	
145	Automobile	-0-	
202	Accounts Payable		$ 2,140.00
301	George Modris, Capital		20,495.00
401	Sales		9,700.00
504	Telephone Expense	210.00	
511	Salaries Expense	2,825.00	
513	Advertising Expense	160.00	
516	Rent Expense	550.00	
518	Equipment Repairs Expense	240.00	
521	Office Supplies Used	211.00	
522	Utilities Expense	455.00	
523	Materials Used	1,860.00	
	Totals	$32,335.00	$32,335.00

TRANSACTIONS FOR APRIL 19X1

Apr. 1 Paid $350 for the monthly rent.
 3 Purchased display equipment that cost $900. Paid $300 in cash and agreed to pay the balance in 30 days.
 5 Sold services for $850 in cash.
 5 Paid $775 for the March salaries.
 10 Bought an automobile for the business for $9,000 in cash.
 17 Paid $150 in cash for advertising cards and posters.
 19 Received $950 in cash for professional services. Sold additional services for $625 on credit. (Use a compound entry.)
 22 Paid $68 for the monthly telephone bill.
 23 Collected $450 from credit customers.
 26 Paid $200 to apply on the balance due for display equipment.
 28 Paid $85 for the monthly utility bill.
 30 Paid $25 for office supplies used.
 30 Received an invoice for $620 of materials used on several jobs; the terms are 30 days.
 30 Sold professional services for $500 in cash and $725 on credit.

PROBLEM 4-2A

The general ledger accounts and balances of the Carver Insurance Agency on December 31, 19X1, are shown below.

INSTRUCTIONS
1. Complete the worksheet for the Carver Insurance Agency at the end of six months of operation.
2. Prepare an income statement and a balance sheet. Use two-column analysis paper for the income statement and four-column analysis paper for the balance sheet.

ACCOUNTS

101	Cash	$11,500 Dr.	301	Joanne Carver, Capital	$32,520 Cr.
111	Accounts Receivable	2,200 Dr.	401	Commissions	46,000 Cr.
130	Office Furniture	3,250 Dr.	504	Telephone Expense	2,150 Dr.
132	Automobile	8,900 Dr.	511	Salaries Expense	23,600 Dr.
134	Building	26,000 Dr.	522	Utilities Expense	1,120 Dr.
202	Accounts Payable	1,800 Cr.	534	Maintenance Expense	1,600 Dr.

PROBLEM 4-3A

Steven Adams decided to open a tailoring business. During October 19X1, the first month of operation, the transactions given on page 67 took place.

INSTRUCTIONS
1. Classify the account titles and numbers listed on page 67, and prepare a chart of accounts.
2. Journalize the October transactions.
3. Set up a general ledger.
4. Post all entries to the general ledger.
5. Foot and balance the accounts.

6. Complete a worksheet as of October 31.
7. Prepare the income statement and the balance sheet. Use two-column analysis paper for the income statement and four-column analysis paper for the balance sheet.

TRANSACTIONS FOR OCTOBER 19X1

Oct. 1 Invested $4,000 in cash.
    3 Paid $275 for the monthly rent.
    6 Bought sewing equipment that cost $1,300. Paid $500 in cash; the balance is on credit.
    7 Purchased shop fixtures for $350 in cash.
    10 Sold services for $300, $125 for cash and the balance on credit.
    11 Paid $45 for advertising circulars.
    14 Paid $90 for supplies used.
    17 Sold additional services for $500, $300 for cash and $200 on credit.
    24 Collected $125 from accounts receivable.
    25 Paid $400 for salaries.
    26 Paid $35 for machine repairs.
    28 Sold a surplus sewing machine for $250 in cash.
    29 Paid a $60 telephone bill.
    30 Paid $76 for additional supplies used.
    30 Sold additional services for $900, $700 for cash and $200 on credit.

ACCOUNTS

521	Supplies Used	516	Rent Expense
504	Telephone Expense	202	Accounts Payable
143	Shop Fixtures	111	Accounts Receivable
511	Salaries Expense	101	Cash
141	Sewing Equipment	513	Advertising Expense
401	Sales	301	Steven Adams, Capital
518	Equipment Repairs		

UNIT 5

closing the books for the period

Once the worksheet and financial statements are completed, the accountant enters the results of operations in the ledger as a permanent record for future reference. Since all entries in the ledger are posted from the general journal, the accountant first makes journal entries that summarize the results.

The Revenue and Expense Summary Account

The procedure of journalizing and posting the results of operations is called *closing the books.* The steps in the closing procedure correspond to those used to organize data on the worksheet. (The accountant used the Income Statement columns of the worksheet to assemble the revenue and expense amounts in one place.) In the closing procedure, the accountant also uses a summarizing device for these amounts. Since the summarizing has to take place in the ledger, a special account called Revenue and Expense Summary is used. This special account is sometimes called by other names such as Income Summary or Income and Expense Summary.

In this account, expenses and revenues are arranged as they are on the worksheet. Expenses are entered on the debit side of the Revenue and Expense Summary account, and revenues are entered on the credit side.

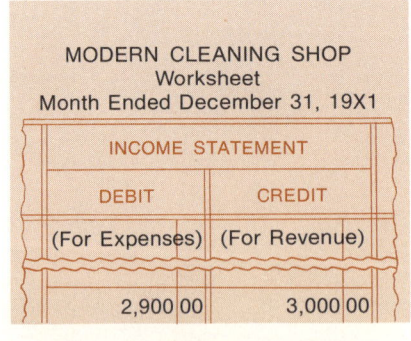

This unit explains the process of journalizing and posting the closing entries to transfer the revenues and expenses to the Revenue and Expense Summary account.

Transferring Revenue Balances

The Cleaning Service Sales account of the Modern Cleaning Shop shows a credit balance of $3,000 on December 31, 19X1, as indicated in the following illustration.

							POST.	
		Cleaning Service Sales					No.	401
DATE	EXPLANATION	POST. REF.	DEBIT	DATE	EXPLANATION	POST. REF.	CREDIT	
				19 X1 Dec. 11		J2	2,200	00
				14		J2	800	00
							3,000	00

Since the Cleaning Service Sales account has a credit balance, it is necessary to debit the account for the same amount in order to close it. The effects of this closing entry are as follows.

1. It transfers the revenue for the period to the credit side of the Revenue and Expense Summary account.
2. It reduces the balance of the revenue account to zero.

The following journal entry shows how the first step of the closing procedure is achieved. The account numbers in the Posting Reference column indicate that the journal entry has been posted to the appropriate ledger accounts.

GENERAL JOURNAL — Page 3

DATE	DESCRIPTION OF ENTRY	POST. REF.	DEBIT	CREDIT

19 X1 Dec. 31	Closing Entries
	Cleaning Service Sales
	   Revenue and Expense Summary
	   To transfer the revenue account balance
	   to the summary account.
		401
		399
			3,000 00	3,000 00

Many accountants prefer to separate the closing entries from the routine journal entries that are recorded throughout the accounting period. Closing entries can be identified in two ways. One method is to write "Closing Entries" in the Description of Entry column of the general journal on the line above the first closing entry. Another method of separation that accountants use is to record the closing entries beginning at the top of a separate general journal page that is used only for this purpose.

Transferring Expense Balances

Expense balances are transferred in a procedure similar to the one just described. On December 31 the Modern Cleaning Shop's expense accounts were as follows.

\	Salaries Expense						No. 511
DATE	EXPLANATION	POST. REF.	DEBIT	DATE	EXPLANATION	POST. REF.	CREDIT
19 X1 Dec. 18		J2	1,600 00				

\	Rent Expense						No. 516
DATE	EXPLANATION	POST. REF.	DEBIT	DATE	EXPLANATION	POST. REF.	CREDIT
19 X1 Dec. 20		J2	700 00				

\	Supplies Used						No. 521
DATE	EXPLANATION	POST. REF.	DEBIT	DATE	EXPLANATION	POST. REF.	CREDIT
19 X1 Dec. 31		J2	600 00				

Since the expense accounts have debit balances, it is necessary to credit each account in order to close it. Usually, the accountant makes a compound journal entry. The expense accounts are closed by crediting each account individually for the amount of its balance. Then, the total amount of the expenses is debited to the Revenue and Expense Summary account. In this way, the summary account will reflect the total expenses for the period, which are shown in the balances of the individual expense accounts. Here is the journal entry that Reed's accountant makes to carry out the second step in the closing procedure. (The account numbers in the Posting Reference column show that the amounts have been posted to the appropriate ledger accounts.)

GENERAL JOURNAL				Page 3
DATE	DESCRIPTION OF ENTRY	POST. REF.	DEBIT	CREDIT
19 X1	Closing Entries			
Dec. 31	Revenue and Expense Summary	399	2,900 00	
	Salaries Expense	511		1,600 00
	Rent Expense	516		700 00
	Supplies Used	521		600 00
	To transfer expense account balances to the summary account.			

After Stein posts the first two closing entries from the general journal to the general ledger, the revenue and expense accounts have no balances. The accountant says that the accounts have been *closed* to the Revenue and Expense Summary account. The ledger sheets look like this.

Revenue and Expense Summary — No. 399

DATE	EXPLANATION	POST. REF.	DEBIT	DATE	EXPLANATION	POST. REF.	CREDIT
19 X1 Dec. 31	Expenses	J3	2,900 00	19 X1 Dec. 31	Revenue	J3	3,000 00

Cleaning Service Sales — No. 401

DATE	EXPLANATION	POST. REF.	DEBIT	DATE	EXPLANATION	POST. REF.	CREDIT
19 X1 Dec. 31	To close	J3	3,000 00	19 X1 Dec. 11		J2	2,200 00
				14		J2	800 00
							3,000 00

Salaries Expense — No. 511

DATE	EXPLANATION	POST. REF.	DEBIT	DATE	EXPLANATION	POST. REF.	CREDIT
19 X1 Dec. 18		J2	1,600 00	19 X1 Dec. 31	To close	J3	1,600 00

Rent Expense — No. 516

DATE	EXPLANATION	POST. REF.	DEBIT	DATE	EXPLANATION	POST. REF.	CREDIT
19 X1 Dec. 20		J2	700 00	19 X1 Dec. 31	To close	J3	700 00

Supplies Used — No. 521

DATE	EXPLANATION	POST. REF.	DEBIT	DATE	EXPLANATION	POST. REF.	CREDIT
19 X1 Dec. 31		J2	600 00	19 X1 Dec. 31	To close	J3	600 00

Notice that Stein has written "To close" in the Explanation column of the individual revenue and expense accounts. This phrase clearly identifies the closing entries in the ledger accounts. Similarly, accountants often write identifying words in the Explanation column of the Revenue and Expense Summary account. The Revenue and Expense Summary account illustrated on page 71 contains notations showing that the expenses have been entered on the debit side and the revenue appears on the credit side.

Note that the Revenue and Expense Summary account now reflects the same information as the first entries in the Income Statement columns of the worksheet on page 59. In other words, the accountant has now formally journalized and posted the information that he had only noted in the Income Statement section of the worksheet before. As a matter of fact, the accountant customarily prepares the closing entries directly from the worksheet. The general journal entry to close the revenue accounts summarizes and transfers the data appearing in the Credit column of the Income Statement section. The general journal entry to close the expense accounts summarizes and transfers the data appearing in the Debit column of the Income Statement section of the worksheet.

Transferring Net Income or Net Loss to Owner's Equity

The next step in the closing procedure is to transfer the balance of the Revenue and Expense Summary account to the owner's equity account. On December 31 the Revenue and Expense Summary account of the Modern Cleaning Shop had a credit balance of $100. This represents the net income for the month (revenue of $3,000 minus expenses of $2,900). Refer to the worksheet on page 60. The transfer of net income was shown on the worksheet by entering a pair of counterbalancing figures in the Income Statement Debit column and the Balance Sheet Credit column. An explanatory notation, "Net Income for the Month," was written in the Account Name column of the worksheet.

The accountant now makes a journal entry to record the transfer of the net income.

GENERAL JOURNAL Page 3

DATE	DESCRIPTION OF ENTRY	POST. REF.	DEBIT	CREDIT
19 X1	Closing Entries			
Dec. 31	Revenue and Expense Summary	399	100 00	
	Paul Reed, Capital	301		100 00
	To transfer net income for the month to the owner's equity account.			

When this entry is posted, the Revenue and Expense Summary account is closed. (This account is not shown on the worksheet.)

		Revenue and Expense Summary					No. 399	
DATE	EXPLANATION	POST. REF.	DEBIT	DATE	EXPLANATION	POST. REF.	CREDIT	
19 X1 Dec. 31	Expenses	J3	2,900 00	19 X1 Dec. 31	Revenue	J3	3,000 00	
31	Net income	J3	100 00					
			3,000 00					

The owner's equity account has been increased by the amount of the net income.

		Paul Reed, Capital					No. 301	
DATE	EXPLANATION	POST. REF.	DEBIT	DATE	EXPLANATION	POST. REF.	CREDIT	
				19 X1 Nov. 26	Beginning investment	J1	6,000 00	
				Dec. 31	Net income	J3	100 00	
							6,100 00	

The new balance of the Paul Reed, Capital account agrees with the final amount shown in the Owner's Equity section of the balance sheet for December 31, 19X1.

MODERN CLEANING SHOP
Balance Sheet
December 31, 19X1

Assets		Liabilities and Owner's Equity	
Cash	3,200 00	Liabilities	
Accounts Receivable	200 00	Accounts Payable	300 00
Equipment	3,000 00	Owner's Equity	
		Paul Reed, Capital 12/1/X1	6,000 00
		Net Income for December	100 00
		Paul Reed, Capital 12/31/X1	6,100 00
Total Assets	6,400 00	Total Liabilities and Owner's Equity	6,400 00

All the changes resulting from operations during the period are now reflected in the ledger accounts. (The example given in this unit shows the closing process at the end of one month for illustrative purposes. Normally, closing takes place only at the end of the fiscal year.)

Ruling the Ledger Accounts

The ledger is not only a complete record of all the accounts, but it is also a continuing record. The same ledger accounts that were used to record the opening transactions and the December transactions are used for the January entries also. If the entries for one fiscal period were combined with those of another, the record would be cluttered and confusing. This is why the accountant separates the entries of one period from those of the next by a process called *ruling* the ledger accounts.

Ruling Closed Accounts

All revenue and expense accounts were closed when their balances were transferred to the Revenue and Expense Summary account. In turn, the Revenue and Expense Summary account was closed when its balance was transferred to the capital account. These accounts are considered closed because they have no balances. A closed account is ruled in the following manner.

1. If only one amount appears on each side of the account, a double line is drawn below the entry, across the Date, Posting Reference, and amount (Debit and Credit) columns on both sides of the account.

Salaries Expense No. 511

DATE	EXPLANATION	POST. REF.	DEBIT	DATE	EXPLANATION	POST. REF.	CREDIT
19 X1 Dec. 18		J2	1,600 00	19 X1 Dec. 31	To close	J3	1,600 00

2. If two or more entries appear on either side of the account, a single line is drawn below the last entry, across the amount (Debit and Credit) columns, on both sides of the account. The total is placed below this line on both sides, and a double line is drawn under all columns except the Explanation columns.

Cleaning Service Sales No. 401

DATE	EXPLANATION	POST. REF.	DEBIT	DATE	EXPLANATION	POST. REF.	CREDIT
19 X1 Dec. 31	To close	J3	3,000 00	19 X1 Dec. 11		J2	2,200 00
				14		J2	800 00
			3,000 00				3,000 00
							3,000 00

Ruling Accounts With Balances

Accounts with balances are ruled so that their balances are *carried forward* to the new period of operations. The accounts whose balances are carried forward are the permanent accounts (assets, liabilities, and owner's equity). The process of ruling and carrying forward works like this.

1. The balance of the account is determined. Often this amount is the same

as the balance computed when the trial balance was prepared. The balance of the Cash account, for example, is $3,200.

Cash No. 101

DATE	EXPLANATION	POST. REF.	DEBIT	DATE	EXPLANATION	POST. REF.	CREDIT
19 X1 Nov. 26 Dec. 11 16	3,200.00	J1 J2 J2	6,000 00 2,200 00 600 00 8,800 00	19 X1 Nov. 27 30 Dec. 18 20 31		J1 J1 J2 J2 J2	2,000 00 700 00 1,600 00 700 00 600 00 5,600 00

2. The balance is entered in the account on the side with the *smaller* total. In the Cash account shown here, the balance of $3,200 is entered on the credit side. The ending date of the old period is written in the Date column, and the notation "Carried Forward" is written in the Explanation column.

Cash No. 101

DATE	EXPLANATION	POST. REF.	DEBIT	DATE	EXPLANATION	POST. REF.	CREDIT
19 X1 Nov. 26 Dec. 11 16	3,200.00	J1 J2 J2	6,000 00 2,200 00 600 00 8,800 00	19 X1 Nov. 27 30 Dec. 18 20 31 31	Carried Forward	J1 J1 J2 J2 J2 ✓	2,000 00 700 00 1,600 00 700 00 600 00 5,600 00 3,200 00

3. The account is totaled and ruled as were the closed accounts discussed on page 74.

Cash No. 101

DATE	EXPLANATION	POST. REF.	DEBIT	DATE	EXPLANATION	POST. REF.	CREDIT
19 X1 Nov. 26 Dec. 11 16	3,200.00	J1 J2 J2	6,000 00 2,200 00 600 00 8,800 00 8,800 00	19 X1 Nov. 27 30 Dec. 18 20 31 31	Carried Forward	J1 J1 J2 J2 J2 ✓	2,000 00 700 00 1,600 00 700 00 600 00 5,600 00 3,200 00 8,800 00

4. The balance is then entered on the opposite side of the account, on the first line below the double ruling. In the Cash account, the balance is entered on the debit side. This entry bears the date of the beginning of the new period (year, month, and day) and is labeled "Brought Forward." The Brought Forward figure becomes the starting point for recording the transactions of the new period. A check mark (✓) is placed in the Posting Reference column beside both the Carried Forward and Brought Forward figures. This indicates that no journal entry was involved. The other two asset accounts in the ledger of the Modern Cleaning Shop—Accounts Receivable and Equipment—are handled in the same manner as the Cash account.

Cash   No. 101

DATE	EXPLANATION	POST. REF.	DEBIT	DATE	EXPLANATION	POST. REF.	CREDIT
19 X1				19 X1			
Nov. 26		J1	6,000 00	Nov. 27		J1	2,000 00
Dec. 11		J2	2,200 00	30		J1	700 00
16	3,200.00	J2	600 00	Dec. 18		J2	1,600 00
			8,800 00	20		J2	700 00
				31		J2	600 00
							5,600 00
				31	Carried Forward	✓	3,200 00
			8,800 00				8,800 00
19 X2							
Jan. 1	Brought Forward	✓	3,200 00				

The liability and owner's equity accounts are balanced, ruled, and carried forward in a similar way. Notice, however, that since each of these accounts has a credit balance, the Brought Forward figure for the new period is entered below the double ruling on the credit side of the account.

Accounts Payable   No. 202

DATE	EXPLANATION	POST. REF.	DEBIT	DATE	EXPLANATION	POST. REF.	CREDIT
19 X1				19 X1			
Nov. 30		J1	700 00	Nov. 28		J1	1,000 00
Dec. 31	Carried Forward	✓	300 00		300.00		
			1,000 00				
			1,000 00				1,000 00
				19 X2			
				Jan. 1	Brought Forward	✓	300 00

			Paul Reed, Capital						No. 301
DATE		EXPLANATION	POST. REF.	DEBIT	DATE		EXPLANATION	POST. REF.	CREDIT
19 X1 Dec. 31		Carried Forward	✓	6,100 00	19 X1 Nov. 26 Dec. 31		Beginning investment Net income	J1 J3	6,000 00 100 00
				6,100 00					*6,100 00* 6,100 00
					19 X2 Jan. 1		Brought Forward	✓	6,100 00

All the asset, liability, and owner's equity accounts shown here required balancing and ruling. However, if a permanent account has only one entry, there is no need to balance and rule it.

The Postclosing Trial Balance

The accountant wants to avoid having mistakes in the ledger at the start of the new period. These mistakes may arise from errors such as carrying forward the wrong amount or putting the Brought Forward balance on the wrong side of an account. If this should happen, the books would not balance at the end of the new period and it might take hours or days to find the error. For this reason, the accountant prepares a *postclosing trial balance*, or *after-closing trial balance*, as the last step in the end-of-period routine. Only the accounts with balances are listed on a postclosing trial balance. This is done to save time. If the postclosing trial balance totals are equal, the accountant can safely proceed with the recording of the entries for the new period. The postclosing trial balance prepared for the Modern Cleaning Shop on December 31 is shown below.

MODERN CLEANING SHOP
Postclosing Trial Balance
December 31, 19X1

ACCT. NO.	ACCOUNT NAME	DEBIT	CREDIT
101	Cash	3,200 00	
111	Accounts Receivable	200 00	
141	Equipment	3,000 00	
202	Accounts Payable		300 00
301	Paul Reed, Capital		6,100 00
	Totals	6,400 00	6,400 00

The completion of the postclosing trial balance is the last of the various steps in the accounting cycle. These same steps are repeated in every fiscal period throughout the life of the business.

Using Dollar Signs

Although the rules involving the use of dollar signs vary among accountants, the basic rules followed in this text are generally accepted by accountants. Fortunately, there are only two rules to remember.

1. No dollar signs are used in the journal or the ledger accounts. Nor are they normally used on handwritten financial forms or statements for internal use by the accountant—such as the worksheet, the postclosing trial balance, and supporting schedules. Dollar signs may also be omitted when financial statements for internal use are typed on ruled accounting forms. (For example, see the balance sheet illustrated on page 73.)
2. Published statements or typed statements prepared for formal use should always have dollar signs. The dollar signs are placed beside the first number in each column and are also placed beside numbers that follow rulings, which are subtotals and totals.

Finding and Correcting Errors

The postclosing trial balance, as well as the trial balance, aids in finding mathematical errors. But even if an error is detected, the accountant still must determine where it was made and take steps to correct it. Refer to page 56 of Unit 4 for a discussion of some of the more common errors in accounting records and how they are found and corrected.

principles and procedures summary

The purpose of the closing procedure is to complete the records of the period before business transactions for the new period are entered in the books. Here are the steps in the closing procedure.

1. Close the revenue accounts by transferring their balances to the Revenue and Expense Summary account.
2. Close the expense accounts by transferring their balances to the Revenue and Expense Summary account.
3. Close the Revenue and Expense Summary account by transferring its balance (net income or net loss) to the owner's equity account.
4. Rule all accounts.
5. Prepare a postclosing trial balance.

This procedure completes the accounting cycle. The entire cycle is listed below.

1. Analyze and record daily transactions in the journal.
2. Post the journal entries to the ledger accounts.
3. Prepare a trial balance at the end of the period.
4. Complete the worksheet.
5. Complete the income statement and the balance sheet.

6. Record the closing entries in the journal.
7. Post the closing entries to the ledger accounts.
8. Balance and rule the ledger accounts.
9. Prepare a postclosing trial balance.

managerial implications

Completion of the closing procedure ends the accounting cycle. For management, this means that the accountant has now completed the analysis of each business transaction and has entered it in both a chronological (day-by-day) record—the journal—and a permanent, classified record—the ledger. The accountant has also summarized the ledger account balances in the form of meaningful financial reports. The data in these reports is useful to people inside and outside the business. The reports allow them to interpret the business's financial condition and measure its profitability without having to review each business transaction individually. These reports also guide managers in making decisions and formulating policies.

managerial discussion questions

1. Why is it important that a firm's books be kept up to date and that management receive the financial statements promptly after the end of each accounting period?
2. What kinds of operating and general policy decisions might be influenced by data on financial statements?

application of principles

PROBLEM 5-1 On December 31, 19X1, the worksheet of the Chambers Secretarial Service includes the accounts shown on page 80.

INSTRUCTIONS
1. Record the closing entries in general journal form. Use 8 as the page number.
2. Compute the balance of the owner's equity account at the end of the period.

ACCOUNTS

301	Doris Chambers, Capital	$17,475 Cr.
401	Sales	29,000 Cr.
501	Rent Expense	3,000 Dr.
505	Salaries Expense	10,000 Dr.
510	Supplies Used	1,400 Dr.
512	Telephone Expense	950 Dr.

PROBLEM 5-2 The Cooley Investment Service opened for business on July 1, 19X4. The accountant who assisted the owner in the organization of the business set up the chart of accounts shown below. The transactions that follow took place during July 19X4.

INSTRUCTIONS
1. Open general ledger accounts, using the chart of accounts as your guide.
2. Journalize the July transactions.
3. Post all entries to the general ledger accounts.
4. Foot and balance the ledger accounts.
5. Complete a worksheet for the month ended July 31.
6. Prepare the income statement and the balance sheet. Use two-column analysis paper for the income statement and four-column analysis paper for the balance sheet.
7. Journalize and post the closing entries.
8. Rule the ledger accounts. Carry forward open account balances.
9. Prepare a postclosing trial balance.

ACCOUNTS

101	Cash		401	Fees
111	Accounts Receivable		503	Telephone Expense
141	Office Equipment		505	Utilities Expense
143	Office Furniture		511	Salaries Expense
202	Accounts Payable		513	Advertising Expense
301	Leon Cooley, Capital		521	Supplies Used
399	Revenue and Expense Summary		525	Miscellaneous Expense

TRANSACTIONS FOR JULY 19X4

July 1 Leon Cooley, the owner, made an initial investment of $7,500 in cash.
 2 Purchased office equipment for $2,000, paying $1,000 cash with the balance due in 30 days.
 3 Paid $750 in cash for used office furniture.
 4 Performed services for $1,500 in cash.
 7 Bought additional office furniture costing $250 on 30-day credit.
 10 Paid $35 in cash for supplies used.
 12 Paid $50 for newspaper advertising.
 15 Performed additional services for $2,500. Collected $1,500 in cash and allowed 30-day credit on the balance.

17 Paid $85 for the monthly telephone bill.
18 Paid $1,500 for salaries of the office staff.
19 Received $500 in cash from accounts receivable.
21 Paid $84 for the monthly utility bill.
22 Paid $500 toward the amount owed on office equipment.
25 Issued a check for $64 to cover miscellaneous expenses.
27 Performed services for $800 in cash.
28 Paid $100 toward the amount owed on office furniture.
31 Paid $25 to have the office cleaned (Miscellaneous Expense).

alternate problems

PROBLEM 5-1A On December 31, 19X2, the worksheet of the McFarland Insurance Agency includes the accounts shown below.

INSTRUCTIONS
1. Record the closing entries in general journal form. Use *12* as the page number.
2. Compute the balance of the owner's equity account at the end of the period.

ACCOUNTS

301	Craig McFarland, Capital	$18,400 Cr.
401	Commissions	34,000 Cr.
501	Rent Expense	7,200 Dr.
505	Salaries Expense	12,000 Dr.
510	Supplies Used	700 Dr.
511	Telephone Expense	1,850 Dr.

PROBLEM 5-2A The E-Z Window Washing Service opened for business on March 1, 19X1. The accountant who assisted the owner in the organization of the business set up the chart of accounts shown on page 82. The transactions that follow took place during March 19X1.

INSTRUCTIONS
1. Open general ledger accounts, using the chart of accounts as your guide.
2. Journalize the March transactions.
3. Post all entries to the general ledger accounts.
4. Foot and balance the ledger accounts.
5. Complete a worksheet for the month ended March 31.
6. Prepare the income statement and the balance sheet. Use two-column analysis paper for the income statement and four-column analysis paper for the balance sheet.
7. Journalize and post the closing entries.
8. Rule the ledger accounts. Carry forward open account balances.
9. Prepare a postclosing trial balance.

ACCOUNTS

101	Cash	401	Sales
111	Accounts Receivable	504	Telephone Expense
141	Cleaning Equipment	505	Utilities Expense
143	Truck	511	Salaries Expense
202	Accounts Payable	513	Advertising Expense
301	Dana Zarin, Capital	519	Truck Repair Expense
399	Revenue and Expense Summary	521	Supplies Used

TRANSACTIONS FOR MARCH 19X1

Mar. 1 Dana Zarin, the owner, made an initial cash investment of $2,000.
     1 Purchased cleaning equipment for $225 in cash.
     2 Bought a used panel truck for $1,500, paying half in cash with the balance due in 30 days.
     3 Sold services for $350 in cash.
     4 Bought cleaning equipment for $285 on credit.
     6 Paid a $35 telephone bill.
     9 Paid $26 for supplies used.
    11 Sold services totaling $450, of which $200 was collected in cash and $250 was to be carried on credit.
    14 Paid $28 in cash for newspaper advertising.
    15 Paid the semimonthly salary of $210 for a part-time helper.
    18 Sold services for $265 in cash and $145 on credit.
    25 Received $85 in cash from credit customers.
    27 Paid $400 in cash to creditors on account.
    29 Paid $74 in cash for truck repairs.
    31 Paid $93 for the monthly utility bill.
    31 Paid the semimonthly salary of $210 for a part-time helper.

business project 1

service business accounting cycle

Now you are given the chance to apply the accounting knowledge you have acquired in the preceding units. You will act as the accountant for the Modern Cleaning Shop for the month of January 19X2. You will analyze and record daily transactions, post to the ledger, and complete the accounting cycle at the end of the month.

Chart of Accounts

The chart of accounts below will be used in the project. These are the same accounts listed in Unit 2, except that two new accounts, Revenue and Expense Summary and Miscellaneous Expense, have been added.

MODERN CLEANING SHOP
Chart of Accounts

Account Number	Account Name
100–199	**ASSETS**
101	Cash
111	Accounts Receivable
141	Equipment
200–299	**LIABILITIES**
202	Accounts Payable
300–399	**OWNER'S EQUITY**
301	Paul Reed, Capital
399	Revenue and Expense Summary
400–499	**REVENUE**
401	Cleaning Service Sales
500–599	**EXPENSES**
511	Salaries Expense
516	Rent Expense
521	Supplies Used
591	Miscellaneous Expense

Preparing the Ledger

Your first task is to prepare the ledger accounts so that the January transactions can be recorded. Enter the amounts from the December 31, 19X1, postclosing trial balance in the proper accounts. The postclosing trial balance is repeated here for your convenience.

MODERN CLEANING SHOP
Postclosing Trial Balance
December 31, 19X1

ACCT. NO.	ACCOUNT NAME	DEBIT	CREDIT
101	Cash	3,200 00	
111	Accounts Receivable	200 00	
141	Equipment	3,000 00	
202	Accounts Payable		300 00
301	Paul Reed, Capital		6,100 00
	Totals	6,400 00	6,400 00

In entering the postclosing trial balance amounts, follow the procedure shown in the Cash account below. Use January 1, 19X2, as the entry date. Write "Brought Forward" in the Explanation column, and place a check mark (✓) in the Posting Reference column.

Cash   No. 101

DATE	EXPLANATION	POST. REF.	DEBIT	DATE	EXPLANATION	POST. REF.	CREDIT
19 X2 Jan. 1	Brought Forward	✓	3,200 00				

Recording the Daily Transactions

Analyze each of the following transactions for January 19X2, and then record it in the general journal. If you have any questions, refer to Unit 3, where similar transactions are journalized. Begin the general journal with page *1*.

To provide a more complete record of each transaction, include the check number when you record a purchase and the sales slip number when you record a sale of services on credit. It is common business practice to prepare an individual sales slip when a credit sale is made. The original is given to the customer, and carbon copies are kept to journalize the transaction and for other purposes. Sales Slip 1 issued by the Modern Cleaning Shop is illustrated on the next page.

MODERN CLEANING SHOP
365 BROAD STREET   DALLAS, TEXAS 75201
Phone: 555-5678

Sold to *Ruth Carr*

Address *14 Oak Lane*

Dallas, Texas 75215

Date *January 7, 19X2*   Terms *30 Days Net*

QUAN.	DESCRIPTION	AMOUNT
6	Slip Covers	
10	Drapes	
	Clean and Dye	60 00

No. 1

TRANSACTIONS FOR JANUARY 19X2

Jan. 2 Purchased cleaning equipment for $770 from the Quality Cleaning Company. Paid with Check 31. (Treat all checks as cash.)

  7 Received $700 for cash sales for cleaning services during the first week.

  7 Performed cleaning services for $60 for Ruth Carr, a charge account customer (Sales Slip 1).

  9 Collected $200 from December sales on credit to charge customers.

  10 Issued Check 32 for $300 to Knight, Inc. to cover balance due.

  11 Bought a used delivery truck for $1,000 from Ace Motors. (Debit Equipment.) Payment is due in one month.

  14 Received $725 for cash sales of cleaning services during the second week.

  14 Performed cleaning services for $25 for John Costa, a charge account customer (Sales Slip 2).

  15 Issued Check 33 for $400 to pay for cleaning supplies used.

  16 Collected $30 from Ruth Carr on account.

  17 Issued Check 34 for $700 for the monthly store rent.

  19 Sold cleaning services for $30 to Roy Hess, a charge account customer (Sales Slip 3).

  21 Received $900 for cash sales of cleaning services during the third week.

23 Collected $45 from charge customers ($30 from Ruth Carr and $15 from John Costa).
24 Issued Check 35 for $500 to Ace Motors to apply on account.
27 Received $800 for cash sales of cleaning services during the fourth week.
28 Paid $600 for a counter and display fixtures for the proposed new accessories department. Issued Check 36 for that amount. (Debit Equipment.) The accessories department will begin operations on February 1, with a complete line of garment bags, hangers, racks, and mothproofing supplies.
28 Sold cleaning services for $60 to charge account customer Janet Bell (Sales Slip 4).
28 Issued Check 37 for $300 for supplies used.
29 Collected $10 on account from charge account customer John Costa.
30 Issued Check 38 for $60 to pay for miscellaneous expenses.
31 Paid $1,700 for monthly salaries. Issued Check 39.

Completing the Cycle

Once you have analyzed and journalized the January transactions, complete the rest of the steps in the accounting cycle. These steps are listed below.

1. Post the daily transactions to the general ledger accounts.
2. Prepare a trial balance to prove the accuracy of the accounts. Follow the procedure of many accountants. Instead of preparing a separate trial balance and transferring the figures to the worksheet, enter the account balances directly in the Trial Balance columns of the worksheet.
3. Complete the worksheet.
4. Prepare an income statement. (Use two-column analysis paper.)
5. Prepare a balance sheet. (Use four-column analysis paper.)
6. Journalize the closing entries.
7. Post the closing entries to the general ledger accounts.
8. Balance and rule the accounts.
9. Prepare a postclosing trial balance.

(**Note:** After your instructor has checked your work, keep all papers relating to the January transactions for future reference.) Key figures are shown below. Use these figures to verify the records you prepared.

Net income for the month	$ 140
Total assets	6,740
Paul Reed, Capital	6,240
Increase in total assets during two months	740
Increase in owner's equity during two months	240

UNIT 6

ACCOUNTING FOR CASH RECEIPTS

A journal provides a chronological record of business transactions. In previous units, you saw how transactions are entered in the general journal. Some firms also have other types of journals called special journals, which improve the efficiency of the journalizing process. In this unit, you will learn about the use of a special journal for transactions involving cash receipts. You will also see how businesses control their cash receipts.

General Journal Entries for Cash Receipts

When the January transactions of the Modern Cleaning Shop were journalized, certain types of entries were repeated many times. For example, eight of the entries were for cash receipts. These transactions resulted in eight different debits to the Cash account. Some of the journal entries for cash receipts are shown below.

Each of these three journal entries, plus the other five not shown, then required posting to the Cash account, as illustrated on page 88.

GENERAL JOURNAL				Page 1
DATE	DESCRIPTION OF ENTRY	POST. REF.	DEBIT	CREDIT
19 X2 Jan. 7	Cash	101	700 00	
	Cleaning Service Sales	401		700 00
	Sold services for cash.			
9	Cash	101	200 00	
	Accounts Receivable	111		200 00
	Collected from December charge customers on account.			
14	Cash	101	725 00	
	Cleaning Service Sales	401		725 00
	Sold services for cash.			

			Cash					No. 101
DATE	EXPLANATION	POST. REF.	DEBIT	DATE	EXPLANATION	POST. REF.	CREDIT	
19 X2 Jan. 1	Brought Forward	✓	3,200 00					
7		J1	700 00					
9		J1	200 00					
14		J1	725 00					
16		J2	30 00					
21		J2	900 00					
23		J2	45 00					
27		J2	800 00					
29		J2	10 00					

You can see the great amount of repetition involved in these journal entries and postings. In the general journal, eight separate entries were required. A look at these entries shows eight debits to Cash, four credits to Cleaning Service Sales, and four credits to Accounts Receivable. For each of the eight journal entries, it was necessary to write two account titles and two amounts as well as an explanation. The posting of 16 items to the ledger accounts represents still further duplication of effort.

The accountant realizes that a more efficient system of recording cash receipts must be developed to save time. Obviously, if only eight transactions for cash receipts required so much space, time, and work, Stein will find it difficult to cope with a larger business volume if he continues using the present recording methods.

The Single-Column Cash Receipts Journal

One way for the accountant to avoid repetition in recording numerous cash transactions is to record receipts in a separate cash receipts journal instead of in the general journal. One type of cash receipts journal is shown below. In this journal, a simple one-line entry can be made for each of the January transactions involving cash receipts.

		CASH RECEIPTS JOURNAL FOR MONTH OF January 19X2		PAGE 1
DATE		ACCOUNT CREDITED	POST. REF.	AMOUNT
Jan. 7		Cleaning Service Sales		700 00
9		Accounts Receivable / December customers		200 00
14		Cleaning Service Sales		725 00
16		Accounts Receivable / Ruth Carr		30 00
21		Cleaning Service Sales		900 00
23		Accounts Receivable / Ruth Carr, $30; John Costa, $15		45 00
27		Cleaning Service Sales		800 00
29		Accounts Receivable / John Costa		10 00

The eight debits to Cash that were necessary in the general journal are eliminated by use of the cash receipts journal. The repetitive explanations needed in the general journal are also eliminated because the title of the journal explains the nature of the transactions entered in it. In other words, the cash receipts journal simplifies the recording process for each receipt. Only the essential elements—the date, the title of the account to be credited, and the amount must be recorded. (The customer's name is recorded for memorandum purposes only, at this time.)

Posting From the Single-Column Cash Receipts Journal

The single-column cash receipts journal offers an important advantage to the accountant when he posts to the Cash account. All he has to do is add the figures in the Amount column and post one summary total ($3,410) as a single debit to the Cash account instead of posting the eight separate debits. When this summary posting is made, the account number is entered in parentheses in the Amount column of the cash receipts journal below the total, as shown.

CASH RECEIPTS JOURNAL FOR MONTH OF January 19 X2   PAGE 1

DATE	ACCOUNT CREDITED	POST. REF.	AMOUNT
Jan. 7	Cleaning Service Sales	401	700 00
9	Accounts Receivable / December customers	111	200 00
14	Cleaning Service Sales	401	725 00
16	Accounts Receivable / Ruth Carr	111	30 00
21	Cleaning Service Sales	401	900 00
23	Accounts Receivable / Ruth Carr, $30; John Costa, $15	111	45 00
27	Cleaning Service Sales	401	800 00
29	Accounts Receivable / John Costa	111	10 00
31	Total Cash Debit		3,410 00
			(101)

Cash   NO. 101

DATE	EXPLANATION	POST. REF.	DEBIT	DATE	EXPLANATION	POST. REF.	CREDIT
19 X2 Jan. 1	Brought Forward	✓	3,200 00				
31		CR1	3,410 00				

By comparing the above Cash account with the Cash account shown on page 88, you can see that eight individual debit postings have been replaced by a single summary posting. (The posting reference *CR1* indicates that the amount was posted from page 1 of the cash receipts journal.) Similarly, if there were 300 cash receipts transactions, use of the single-column cash receipts journal would permit one debit posting to the Cash account instead of the 300 individual cash postings that would be required if the general journal were used to record each transaction.

When the single-column cash receipts journal is used, the credits to Cleaning Service Sales and Accounts Receivable are posted individually as if the posting were being done from the general journal. However, the posting reference *CR1* in these accounts shows that the special journal for cash receipts is the source of the entries. (The four items in the Cleaning Service Sales account with the posting reference *J1* are entries for sales on credit that have been posted from the general journal.)

Cleaning Service Sales NO. 401

DATE	EXPLANATION	POST. REF.	DEBIT	DATE	EXPLANATION	POST. REF.	CREDIT
				19X2 Jan. 7		CR1	700 00
				7		J1	60 00
				14		CR1	725 00
				14		J1	25 00
				19		J1	30 00
				21		CR1	900 00
				27		CR1	800 00
				28		J1	60 00

Accounts Receivable NO. 111

DATE	EXPLANATION	POST. REF.	DEBIT	DATE	EXPLANATION	POST. REF.	CREDIT
19X2 Jan. 1	Brought Forward	✓	200 00	19X2 Jan. 9		CR1	200 00
				16		CR1	30 00
				23		CR1	45 00
				29		CR1	10 00

The general ledger account number is entered in the Posting Reference column of the cash receipts journal as the posting of each item is completed. (Refer to the cash receipts journal shown on page 89.)

The Multicolumn Cash Receipts Journal

Although the single-column cash receipts journal eliminates much of the duplication associated with recording cash receipts, it is apparent that not all the repetition has been avoided. For instance, the repetitive posting of credits to Cleaning Service Sales and to Accounts Receivable still requires much unnecessary work that can be avoided by use of a multicolumn cash receipts journal.

The accountant easily eliminates the repeated posting of credits to Cleaning Service Sales and to Accounts Receivable by adding more columns to the cash receipts journal. In this journal, he now provides three money columns. The first column is used to record credits to the Accounts Receivable account. The credits to the Cleaning Service Sales account are recorded in the second column. The third column is used to record debits to the Cash account (as before). The cash receipts of the Modern Cleaning Shop for January 19X2 are recorded in this new journal as shown on the next page.

CASH RECEIPTS JOURNAL for Month of January 19X2					Page 1
DATE	EXPLANATION	✓	ACCOUNTS RECEIVABLE CR. 111	CLEANING SERVICE SALES CR. 401	CASH DR. 101
Jan. 7	Cash sales			700 00	700 00
9	Collections on account/ December customers		200 00		200 00
14	Cash sales			725 00	725 00
16	Collections on account/ Ruth Carr		30 00		30 00
21	Cash sales			900 00	900 00
23	Collections on account/Ruth Carr, $30; John Costa, $15		45 00		45 00
27	Cash sales			800 00	800 00
29	Collections on account/ John Costa		10 00		10 00

Posting From the Multicolumn Cash Receipts Journal

At the end of the month, the accountant uses the following procedures to complete the recording process for cash receipts.

1. The accountant totals the three money columns of the cash receipts journal and checks to see if the total debits ($3,410) equal the total credits ($285 + $3,125 = $3,410). This verification procedure is known as *crossfooting*.
2. The accountant posts each column total to the ledger account whose number appears in the column heading.
3. The accountant writes the account number below each column total as each summary posting is made.

After these procedures are completed, the multicolumn cash receipts journal and the general ledger accounts appear as shown below and on page 92.

CASH RECEIPTS JOURNAL for Month of January 19X2					Page 1
DATE	EXPLANATION	✓	ACCOUNTS RECEIVABLE CR. 111	CLEANING SERVICE SALES CR. 401	CASH DR. 101
Jan. 7	Cash sales			700 00	700 00
9	Collections on account/ December customers		200 00		200 00
14	Cash sales			725 00	725 00
16	Collections on account/ Ruth Carr		30 00		30 00
21	Cash sales			900 00	900 00
23	Collections on account/ Ruth Carr, $30; John Costa, $15		45 00		45 00
27	Cash sales			800 00	800 00
29	Collections on account/ John Costa		10 00		10 00
31	Totals		285 00	3,125 00	3,410 00
			(111)	(401)	(101)

Cash   No. 101

DATE	EXPLANATION	POST. REF.	DEBIT	DATE	EXPLANATION	POST. REF.	CREDIT
19 X2 Jan. 1	Brought Forward	✓	3,200 00				
31		CR1	3,410 00				

Accounts Receivable   No. 111

DATE	EXPLANATION	POST. REF.	DEBIT	DATE	EXPLANATION	POST. REF.	CREDIT
19 X2 Jan. 1	Brought Forward	✓	200 00	19 X2 Jan. 31		CR1	285 00

Cleaning Service Sales   No. 401

DATE	EXPLANATION	POST. REF.	DEBIT	DATE	EXPLANATION	POST. REF.	CREDIT
				19 X2 Jan. 7		J1	60 00
				14		J1	25 00
				19		J1	30 00
				28		J1	60 00
				31		CR1	3,125 00

Advantages of the Cash Receipts Journal

The multicolumn cash receipts journal permits the accountant to accomplish in three summary postings what would take 16 individual postings if the general journal were used to record cash receipts. Besides saving time, effort, and space, the special journal for cash receipts also permits the accountant to divide the work. While he is using the general journal to record other transactions, another member of the staff can be recording entries in the cash receipts journal.

Balance Ledger Form for the General Ledger Accounts

The accountant for the Modern Cleaning Shop has decided to make another change in the firm's financial records. He will now use the following *balance ledger form* for the general ledger accounts. With this form, the balance of an account is recorded after each entry is posted. Thus there is no need to foot accounts in order to determine their balances. The change to the balance ledger form will speed up the preparation of the trial balance at the end of each month.

	Cash				NO. 101	
DATE	EXPLANATION	POST. REF.	DEBIT	CREDIT	BALANCE	DR. CR.
19X2 Jan 1	Balance	✓			3,200 00	Dr.
31		CR1	3,410 00		6,610 00	Dr.

Examine the balance ledger form shown above. Notice that there are three money columns. The last money column is used for recording the account balance. On January 1, the Cash account had a beginning balance of $3,200. The notation "Dr." shows that this is a debit balance. On January 31, a debit amount of $3,410 was posted from the cash receipts journal, which increased the account balance to $6,610 ($3,200 + $3,410 = $6,610). The posting of a credit amount would, of course, decrease the balance of the Cash account.

Recording Sales Taxes

Some states require merchants to collect a tax on the amount of certain retail sales. Thus, each such sale involves at least three elements. These are the retail price, the tax, and the total amount charged to the customer. For example, a $10 sale subject to a 4 percent sales tax consists of the following elements.

Retail price	$10.00
4% sales tax	0.40
Total charge to customer	$10.40

When sales taxes must be recorded as part of the cash sales transaction, the accountant makes provision for a special Sales Tax Payable column in the cash receipts journal. The illustration below shows how a cash receipts journal looks for a cleaning shop operating in a state that has a tax on such sales.

The total of the Sales Tax Payable column is posted as a credit to a

CASH RECEIPTS JOURNAL for Month of June 19X2 Page 6

DATE	EXPLANATION	✓	ACCOUNTS RECEIVABLE CR. 111	SALES TAX PAYABLE CR. 231	CLEANING SERVICE SALES CR. 401	CASH DR. 101
June 5	Cash sales			40	10 00	10 40
30	Totals		1,200 00	14 56	364 00	1,578 56
			(111)	(231)	(401)	(101)

liability account called Sales Tax Payable. This total represents a liability owed to a unit of government.

	Sales Tax Payable					No. 231
DATE	EXPLANATION	POST. REF.	DEBIT	CREDIT	BALANCE	DR. CR.
19 X2 June 30		CR6		14 56	14 56	Cr.

The merchant is obligated to charge the tax to the customers and to send the tax at regular intervals to the state, city, or other authority imposing the tax. The handling of sales taxes for both cash and credit sales is more fully explained in a later unit.

Recording Cash Discounts on Sales

Like most retail firms doing business on credit, the Modern Cleaning Shop allows its customers 30 days in which to pay (also expressed as *net 30 days*, or *n/30*). However, many manufacturing and wholesaling firms and some retailers allow their credit customers to deduct 1 or 2 percent (or some other percent) of the bill if it is paid within a specified time, often 10 days from the date of sale. That is, customers have 30 days to pay the full amount. But if they pay within 10 days, the amount of the bill is reduced by a certain percentage. These terms might be shown on the bill, for example, as *2%, 10 days, net 30 days*; or simply as *2/10, n/30*. The purpose of this *cash discount* is to encourage prompt payment. Of course, if there is a sales tax involved, no discount is allowed on the tax.

A cash receipt involving a sales discount requires the recording of three elements.

1. The amount of the original sale (as a credit to Accounts Receivable).
2. The amount of discount (as a debit to Sales Discount).
3. The amount of cash received (as a debit to Cash).

In a firm that allows a cash discount, the cash receipts journal would be expanded to provide a new column entitled Sales Discount, as shown below. The entry below was made to record the collection of a $150 receivable from the Hill Company less a 1 percent cash discount for payment within the discount period.

CASH RECEIPTS JOURNAL for Month of December 19X2   Page 12

DATE	EXPLANATION	✓	ACCOUNTS RECEIVABLE CR. 111	SALES TAX PAYABLE CR. 231	CLEANING SERVICE SALES CR. 401	SALES DISCOUNT DR. 453	CASH DR. 101
Dec. 10	Hill Company		150 00			1 50	148 50

The total of the Sales Discount column is posted as a debit to the Sales Discount account at the end of the period. The Sales Discount account balance is deducted from the Sales account balance on the income statement. (Another method for showing sales discounts on the income statement is discussed in a later unit.)

Recording Other Cash Receipts

Every receipt of cash must be recorded in the cash receipts journal. You have already seen how the accountant makes special provisions for transactions that occur frequently, such as cash sales and collections on account. He also designs the cash receipts journal so that transactions that do not occur often enough to warrant special columns in the journal may still be recorded easily. This is accomplished by setting up a new section called Other Accounts Credit. This section provides columns to enter the title of the account to be credited and the amount. There is also a Posting Reference column that is used when the entries in this section are posted.

No end-of-month posting is required for the total of the Other Accounts Credit section; the individual items are posted throughout the month. An "X" is placed below the total of the money column in this section to show that it is not posted.

The following two transactions illustrate the use of the Other Accounts Credit section of the cash receipts journal.

Investment by the Owner

As you learned in Unit 3, an investment of cash by Reed resulted in a debit to Cash and a credit to the Paul Reed, Capital account. Assuming that Reed invested an additional $1,000 in the business on August 1, 19X2, the investment would be recorded in the cash receipts journal as shown below.

CASH RECEIPTS JOURNAL for Month of August 19X2   **Page** 8

DATE	EXPLANATION	✓	ACCOUNTS RECEIVABLE CR. 111	CLEANING SERVICE SALES CR. 401	OTHER ACCOUNTS CREDIT			CASH DR. 101
					ACCOUNT TITLE	POST. REF.	AMOUNT	
Aug. 1	Cash investment				Paul Reed, Capital	301	1,000 00	1,000 00

The $1,000 credit to the Paul Reed, Capital account is entered in the Other Accounts Credit section and then posted individually to the capital account. After the item has been posted, the account number is entered in the cash receipts journal to indicate that the posting has been made. The debit to Cash will, of course, be posted as a part of the total of the Cash column at the end of the month.

Notes Receivable Collection

A *promissory note* may serve as the basis for granting credit in certain sales transactions. The buyer's written promise gives the seller greater assurance of payment than a regular charge account. The note applies moral pressure on the buyer and gives legal protection to the seller. The seller may also earn interest in return for granting credit. When the note is paid, a record must be made of the cash received, including the interest. The recording procedure involved can best be understood through a step-by-step study of a typical example.

Suppose that a charge account customer, David Shaw, owes $200 to the Modern Cleaning Shop. He comes to Mary Gomez and tells her that he is having financial difficulties at the present time. Shaw offers to give a promissory note payable in six months with interest at 9 percent a year to cover his account. Because of the additional security provided by the note, Gomez suggests that Reed accept the offer. Reed agrees, thereby extending the payment date of the debt until October 1. The note, dated April 1, 19X2, is shown below.

```
$ 200.00                                               April 1, 19 X2

Six months          AFTER DATE   I   PROMISE TO PAY

TO THE ORDER OF   Modern Cleaning Shop

Two hundred and no/100 ------------------------------- DOLLARS

PAYABLE AT   City National Bank

VALUE RECEIVED   with interest at 9%

NO.   28    DUE  October 1, 19X2          David Shaw
```

On April 1, an entry for $200 must be made in the firm's books to record the receipt of a new asset, a note receivable. A new account called Notes Receivable is set up in the ledger. This account must be debited for $200. The asset account Accounts Receivable must be credited by the same amount to decrease it. The general journal entry reflecting these changes is illustrated below as it would appear after it was posted.

```
19 X2
Apr.  1   Notes Receivable                         110   200 00
              Accounts Receivable                  111           200 00
          Received a 6-month, 9% note from
          David Shaw to replace open account.
```

On October 1, Shaw pays $209 in cash, representing the amount of the note ($200) plus the interest earned during the period ($9). The accountant uses the Other Accounts Credit section in the cash receipts journal to enter the credit to Notes Receivable and the credit to Interest Earned, as shown on the next page.

CASH RECEIPTS JOURNAL for Month of October 19X2								Page 10
DATE		EXPLANATION	ACCOUNTS RECEIVABLE	CLEANING SERVICE SALES	OTHER ACCOUNTS CREDIT			CASH DR. 101
			✓ CR. 111	CR. 401	ACCOUNT TITLE	POST. REF.	AMOUNT	
Oct.	1	Collection of note from David Shaw			Notes Receivable Interest Earned	110 491	200 00 9 00	209 00

Again, the individual items in the Other Accounts Credit section are posted to the proper accounts. The account numbers are then entered in the cash receipts journal to show that the items have been posted. The use of the Interest Earned account and its presentation on the income statement is discussed in a later unit.

Safeguarding Receipts

One of the advantages of having an efficient and speedy procedure for recording cash receipts is that the funds reach the bank sooner. Many firms have a policy of making daily bank deposits so that cash receipts are not kept on the premises for more than a short period of time. Cash receipts are not only safer in the bank, but as deposits they become funds available for paying bills owed by the depositor.

Need for Internal Control Over Business Operations

The firm studied so far, the Modern Cleaning Shop, has a single owner. Such firms represent a form of business organization called a *sole proprietorship.* When businesses become larger, it is more difficult for one owner to personally supervise all the operations of the business. That is why several owners might pool their activities and form a partnership or a corporation. However, regardless of the form of business organization, great reliance must be placed on the accounting system to help control operations.

Losses to American business from employee carelessness, inaccuracy, and dishonesty are estimated to total billions of dollars a year. No business is immune from this hazard, and to ignore it may mean the difference between a profitable operation and complete failure. That is why the public accountant serving a firm such as the Modern Cleaning Shop would recommend a strong system of internal control.

General Principles of Internal Control

Internal control is a system designed to safeguard the assets of a business and to help ensure the accuracy and reliability of the accounting records. The system should be organized and operated so that the work of one person provides a check on the work of another, with minimum duplication of effort. If the business has enough employees to permit the necessary separation of duties, a strong system of internal control can be established. If the number of employees is small, internal control will be weaker and will have to be supplemented by more careful supervision from the owner or manager of the firm.

Stein recommends that Reed give careful consideration to the following points when planning the operating routines for the Modern Cleaning Shop.

1. No one person should be in complete charge of any important business transaction. Two or more employees should be assigned to every important operation, and the work of one should be planned so that it will be checked against the work of the other at some point in the routine.
2. The person or persons who handle cash should not be the same as those who have responsibility for recording the cash.
3. Every employee should be trained to do his or her job and should also understand why the job or procedure is to be performed in the specified manner.
4. Only capable and experienced personnel of demonstrated reliability should be assigned to key positions in the internal control system. Unannounced changes in these assignments are also desirable. Annual vacations should be required for each employee, and his or her regular work should be performed by other employees during vacations.
5. Management must review and evaluate the established system of internal control periodically to make sure that it is operating as planned and continues to provide adequate safeguards.
6. The control system should include mechanical devices as well as forms, records, and routines to provide maximum protection. For example, cash registers, cashier cages, and locked storerooms make theft or mishandling of assets more difficult.

Internal Control Over Cash Receipts

Cash is the most precious and most easily stolen or lost asset of the average business. Every penny received in payment for goods or services must be protected so that the funds will be available to pay bills, salaries, and the many other obligations that a business has. The principles of internal control already discussed should be applied to the handling of cash receipts. The following precautionary routines are especially important for cash receipts.

1. One person should receive the cash, whether it is delivered by mail or in person (over the counter). After making a record of the receipts, this person should turn the cash over to another person for deposit in the bank.
2. All cash receipts should be deposited in the bank promptly, preferably every day. They should not be used for making cash payments.
3. The entries for cash receipts in the firm's accounting records should be made by a person other than the one who receives the cash or the one who deposits it in the bank.
4. At the end of each month, a person other than the three discussed above should obtain the bank statement directly from the bank and should prepare a bank reconciliation.

Obviously, in a business as small as the Modern Cleaning Shop, there are not enough employees to have each procedure handled by a separate person. However, every effort must be made to have as great a division of duties as possible.

Control of Cash Receipts in a Small Business

One of the first things Reed did when he started his business was open a bank account for the cleaning shop. This was the first step in the development of a complete system of control over cash. Reed decided that all cash receipts would be deposited daily. He also decided that all payments would be made by check and that only he would be authorized to sign checks drawn against the firm's funds.

Stein, the accountant hired by Reed to help him set up the books and establish operating procedures, recommended that cash items coming in by mail (checks and money orders) be handled by two persons—one to receive and list the cash items and another to deposit them. Gomez, the manager, is assigned to receive and list cash receipts that come in by mail. At the end of each day, she turns the receipts over to Reed for deposit and gives the list of cash items to the accountant for entry in the firm's accounting records.

Cash and checks received from customers in person are recorded on a cash register in the shop by Ann Schmidt, the salesclerk. Since she needs to make change for customers, a special *change fund* was established by drawing a check payable to her. (Schmidt is in charge of and responsible for the change fund.) After this check was cashed, Schmidt had a variety of coins and bills to meet her needs for change.

At the end of each day, Schmidt separates the change fund from the cash receipts. The change fund is put in a secure place for storage overnight. (Stein recommended a fireproof safe.) Schmidt checks the day's cash receipts against the figures shown on an audit tape printed by the cash register. (This tape is locked inside the machine during the day.) Schmidt prepares a cash register proof form and gives this form along with the audit tape to the accountant. The accountant uses the information to make the necessary entries in the accounting records.

The day's receipts from the cash register go to Reed for deposit. At this time, Reed has the receipts from both Gomez and Schmidt. He now sorts and counts all cash and cash items for listing on a deposit slip, and proceeds to make the deposit at the bank.

The banking procedures to be used by the Modern Cleaning Shop are discussed more thoroughly in Unit 8.

The Cash Receipts Journal

The accountant in charge of a firm's books plays a vital role in the internal control system.

Recording

Each day the accountant for the Modern Cleaning Shop enters the cash receipts in the cash receipts journal. He uses the list of cash items received by mail that Gomez prepared and the cash register proof form that Schmidt prepared as the basis for the entries. Then he compares the amount shown on the day's receipted deposit slip with his records to make sure that all money received has been deposited on the same day, in accordance with company policy.

Cash Short or Over

In making change, some errors are almost certain to occur. If such errors are made, the cash available for deposit from cash sales will be either more or less than the amount listed on the cash register tape. If the amount of cash available for deposit is greater than the amount shown on the tape, cash is said to be *over*. If there is less cash than the tape shows, cash is *short*. In practice, cash tends to be short more often than over, perhaps because customers are more likely to notice and complain if they receive too little change than if they receive too much.

For proper control over cash receipts, amounts short or over should be recorded. Since a net shortage is expected, they are recorded in an expense account. Reed's accountant set up the Cash Short or Over account for this purpose. As already noted, when the cash register is cleared at the end of each day, the cash is compared with the total of the register tape. The amount short or over is then determined. This information appears on the cash register proof form that is given to the accountant.

Stein has expanded the cash receipts journal for the Modern Cleaning Shop by adding a column headed Cash Short or Over. The debits for cash short are entered in the usual manner. If cash is over, the amount is entered in red or circled or placed in parentheses to show that it is a credit. At the end of the month, the net amount short is posted as a debit to the Cash Short or Over account.

Although errors in handling cash receipts can be expected, large shortages or overages should be investigated. Similarly, if shortages or overages occur too often, it is wise to investigate the situation.

Posting   At the end of the month of February, the cash receipts journal used by the Modern Cleaning Shop looks, in part, like this.

CASH RECEIPTS JOURNAL for Month of February 19X2 — Page 2

DATE	EXPLANATION	✓	ACCOUNTS RECEIVABLE CR. 111	CLEANING SERVICE SALES CR. 401	OTHER ACCOUNTS CREDIT			CASH SHORT OR OVER DR. 529	CASH DR. 101
					ACCOUNT TITLE	POST. REF.	AMOUNT		
Feb. 1	Joan Casey		29 20						29 20
1	Robert Dahl		73 50						73 50
28	Cash sales			140 00				(25)	140 25
28	Totals		395 00	4,107 75			240 00	2 75	4,740 00
			(111)	(401)			(X)	(529)	(101)

From this journal, the total cash received during the month, $4,740, is posted as a debit to Cash. The net cash shortage for the month, $2.75, is posted as a debit to Cash Short or Over. A credit of $395 is posted to Accounts Receivable, and a credit of $4,107.75 is posted to Cleaning Service Sales. (The total of the Other Accounts Credit column, $240, is of course not posted because the individual amounts in this column were posted during the month.)

principles and procedures summary

A special journal is used for cash receipts in order to save time, effort, and recording space. In a small business, the accountant may use a single-column cash receipts journal that provides for one summary debit to the Cash account and for individual postings of credit amounts.

However, it is even more efficient for the accountant to use a multicolumn cash receipts journal. This journal requires as few as three postings to the general ledger to record the cash receipts for a whole month. Special columns may be provided in the cash receipts journal to record transactions involving sales tax, cash discounts, and other items.

All businesses, whether they are large or small, should have a system of internal control. This system is intended to protect assets and ensure the accuracy and reliability of the accounting records.

managerial implications

By deciding to use a cash receipts journal, a manager ensures that recording work is reduced. Also, the work can be divided, with one person using the general journal and another recording transactions in the cash receipts journal.

Because cash can easily be lost or stolen, management must use special care in safeguarding receipts. A system for the internal control of cash receipts must be set up by management and the accountant. One important control procedure is to deposit each day's cash receipts intact in the bank so that they can be easily traced from the journal to the bank statement. Another important control procedure is to divide the duties of receiving, recording, and depositing cash among different persons.

managerial discussion questions

1. What procedures can management devise to ensure full internal control of cash receipts?
2. From the viewpoint of efficiency, what are the advantages of a cash receipts journal?
3. Why might the management of a firm offer cash discounts to customers?
4. How can the management of a small business divide duties in order to achieve internal control over cash receipts?

application of principles

PROBLEM 6-1 The Jones Hardware Store sells building hardware and paints. Some customers pay for their purchases with cash; others are given 30-day credit terms. The firm uses a single-column cash receipts journal. The general ledger accounts involved in the cash receipts transactions for January 19X2 and the balances of those accounts at the first of the month are as follows.

ACCOUNTS

101	Cash	$3,455.85
111	Accounts Receivable	4,528.55
401	Sales	-0-

The January transactions relating to the receipt of cash are shown below.

INSTRUCTIONS
1. Open the ledger accounts, and enter the balances.
2. Record all transactions in the cash receipts journal. Use *1* for the journal page number.
3. Total the cash receipts journal.
4. Make the individual and summary postings to the proper ledger accounts. Since this firm uses the balance ledger form, be sure to enter the new account balance after each posting.

TRANSACTIONS FOR JANUARY 19X2

Jan. 2 Received $120 for cash sales.
    7 A customer, Helen Wall, paid $200 on account.
    9 Received $2,400 in cash sales for the week.
  11 Collected $200 from Sid Levy to apply toward his account.
  12 Checks totaling $425 were received from Ted Long and Linda Browne to balance their accounts.
  15 Collected $3,150 in cash sales for the week.
  18 Received an additional $300 in cash from Kate Morely to apply toward her account.
  22 Received $2,600 in cash, $2,350 of which represents cash sales. The balance is to be applied to the account of Bert Olson.
  28 Received a check for $150 from David Zorn to balance his account.
  31 Receipts from cash sales amounted to $1,975.

PROBLEM 6-2 This problem covers the cash receipts procedures for Bob's Sporting Goods Store for the month of February 19X1. Because of the volume of transactions, the business uses a multicolumn cash receipts journal with special columns for Accounts Receivable Cr. 111, Sales Cr. 401, and Cash Dr. 101. The ledger accounts involved in the cash receipts transactions for February and their balances at the first of the month are as follows.

ACCOUNTS

101	Cash	$3,509
111	Accounts Receivable	3,120
401	Sales	-0-

The February 19X1 transactions involving the receipt of cash are shown below.

INSTRUCTIONS
1. Open the ledger accounts, and enter the balances.
2. Record each transaction in the cash receipts journal. Use 2 for the journal page number.
3. Foot and prove the money columns of the journal. Then enter the totals, and rule the journal.
4. Make the summary postings to the ledger accounts.

TRANSACTIONS FOR FEBRUARY 19X1

Feb. 1 Received a check for $125 from Tom Cameron, a charge customer, to pay his account.
    2 Received $275 for cash sales.
    3 Received $750 from various customers to apply toward their accounts.
    4 Collected $300 for goods sold today.
    5 Received checks totaling $850 from various charge customers.
    9 Gail Hall, a charge customer, sent a check for $150 to balance her account.
  13 Today's receipts from cash sales total $182.
  17 Collected $300 on accounts receivable from the Maple School.
  24 Received $1,000 in cash, of which $450 represents cash sales. The balance is from various accounts receivable.
  27 Received a $100 check from Harry Segal, a charge customer.
  28 Received $610 from cash sales today.

PROBLEM 6-3 The Deroy Company sells radio, television, and stereo equipment for cash and on various credit terms. The firm's cash receipts journal has columns for Accounts Receivable Cr. 111, Sales Tax Payable Cr. 231, Sales Cr. 401, Other Accounts Credit, Sales Discount Dr. 453, and Cash Dr. 101. Selected transactions that took place during July 19X2 are shown below and on page 104.

INSTRUCTIONS
1. Record all the transactions in the cash receipts journal. Use 7 for the journal page number.
2. Foot, total, and rule the money columns. Prove the accuracy of your work by adding the credit column totals and the debit column totals and comparing them for equality.

TRANSACTIONS FOR JULY 19X2

July 1 Received $546 in cash, which resulted from cash sales of $525 plus 4% sales tax of $21.

103

5		Paul Wagner, a charge customer, sent a check for $441 in payment of a June 25 invoice for $450, less 2% discount.
11		Received $137.20 from Susan Wong, a charge customer, to pay for a July 2 invoice of $140, less 2% discount.
14		Collected $606 from Frank Burdi to cover his $600 note due plus the interest of $6.
17		Collected a total of $832 for cash sales, of which $800 represents the total selling price of goods and $32 represents a 4% sales tax.
21		Received an additional investment of $2,000 from the owner, Bill Deroy.
24		Received a $160 check from Mary Miller to apply toward her account.
27		Collected $392 from a charge customer, John Leister, to cover an invoice of July 21 for $400 less 2% discount.
31		Doris Van Horn sent a check for $505 to pay her June 1 note for $500 plus interest of $5.

alternate problems

PROBLEM 6-1A The ABC Venetian Blind Company sells and installs venetian blinds. Some customers pay cash on installation; others are given credit terms. A single-column cash receipts journal is used. The ledger accounts involved in the cash receipts transactions for February 19X1, and their balances at the first of the month are as follows.

ACCOUNTS

101	Cash	$4,452.60
111	Accounts Receivable	2,142.70
401	Sales	-0-

The February 19X1 transactions relating to the receipt of cash are shown below and on the next page.

INSTRUCTIONS
1. Open the ledger accounts, and enter the balances.
2. Record all transactions in the cash receipts journal. Use 2 for the journal page number.
3. Total the cash receipts journal.
4. Make the individual and summary postings to the proper ledger accounts. Since this firm uses the balance ledger form, be sure to enter the new account balance after each posting.

TRANSACTIONS FOR FEBRUARY 19X1

Feb. 3 Sam Pappas paid $78.50 in cash for blinds.
      5 Clark Sampson paid $226.70 by check for blinds installed.
      7 Received a check for $50 from Rita Blackwell to apply toward her account.

11 Carol O'Brien sent in a check for $126.35 to pay her January account in full.
13 Receipts consisted of $229.15 in cash for blinds installed today for Edward Teague and $87.60 in cash for blinds installed today for Cliff Jones.
17 Installed blinds for three customers and received $337.55 in cash.
21 Received $157.25 from Brenda Parker in payment of her January account and $217.30 for blinds installed today.
22 Received $415.25 in cash for blinds installed today.
23 Mary Kohl sent in a check for $100 to apply toward her account.
25 Collected $302.50 for blinds installed today.

PROBLEM 6-2A

This problem covers the cash receipts procedures for the Suburban Drapery Company for the month of March 19X1. Because of the volume of transactions, the business uses a multicolumn cash receipts journal with special columns for Account Receivable Cr. 111, Sales Cr. 401, and Cash Dr. 101. The ledger accounts involved in the cash receipts transactions for March and their balances at the first of the month are as follows.

ACCOUNTS

101	Cash	$3,416.85
111	Accounts Receivable	2,889.68
401	Sales	-0-

The March 19X1 transactions involving the receipt of cash are shown below and on page 106.

INSTRUCTIONS
1. Open the ledger accounts, and enter the balances.
2. Record each transaction in the cash receipts journal. Use 3 for the journal page number.
3. Foot and prove the money columns of the journal. Then enter the totals, and rule the journal.
4. Make the summary postings to the proper ledger accounts.

TRANSACTIONS FOR MARCH 19X1

Mar. 1 Received a check for $167.50 from John Caruso to pay his January account.
2 Collected $199.75 in cash for draperies installed today.
5 Collected $232.60 for draperies installed today, and also received $20 from Calvin Johnson to apply toward his account.
9 Cash sales of $347.50 for draperies installed.
10 Cash sales of $117.75 for draperies installed.
13 Brenda Farber sent a check for $75 in partial payment of her February account. Collected $98.80 from one customer for draperies installed today.
20 A check for $336.90 was received from Carter Eken to pay his February account.

23 Collected $132.75 in cash for draperies installed today.
24 Received a check for $97.65 from Margaret Lucas to pay her February account.
27 Received a check from the County Library for $1,017.35 to pay its January account for draperies installed in the reference rooms.
30 Received cash totaling $180 for draperies installed today and checks from Wilma Owens, $110.50, and Rita Galvez, $19.50, to pay their February accounts.

PROBLEM 6-3A The Parton Company sells musical instruments for cash and on various credit terms. The firm's cash receipts journal has columns for Accounts Receivable Cr. 111, Sales Tax Payable Cr. 231, Sales Cr. 401, Other Accounts Credit, Sales Discount Dr. 453, and Cash Dr. 101. Selected transactions that took place during May 19X1 are shown below.

INSTRUCTIONS
1. Record all the transactions in the cash receipts journal. Use 5 for the journal page number.
2. Foot, total, and rule the money columns. Prove the accuracy of your work by adding the credit column totals and the debit column totals and comparing them for equality.

TRANSACTIONS FOR MAY 19X1

May 4 Total cash of $444.96 received from cash sales of $432 plus sales tax of $12.96.
   7 Received a check for $220.50 from Roy Miller, a charge customer, in payment of a May 1 invoice for $225, less a 2% discount.
  12 Received a check for $812 from Frank Bronsky to pay for his February 12 note for $800 with interest at 6%.
  14 Check for $122.50 received from Sonia Davis to pay for a May 7 invoice for $125, less a 2% discount.
  15 Rita Case, owner of the Parton Company, made an additional investment of $2,000 in cash.
  25 Fay Cades delivered a check for $404 to pay her March 25 note for $400, plus interest of $4.
  26 Received $100 in cash from Donald Bunch to apply toward his account.
  28 Received total cash of $789.39 from cash sales of $766.40, plus sales tax of $22.99.
  31 Received a check for $970.20 from Frances Baker, a charge customer, to pay for a May 1 invoice for $980, less a 1% discount.

UNIT 7

ACCOUNTING FOR CASH PAYMENTS

In Unit 6 you learned how the accountant reduces the amount of effort and time necessary to record repetitive entries for cash receipts by using a special cash receipts journal. There are also many repetitive entries involving cash payments. In this unit, you will see how the efficiency of the accounting system is further increased by the use of a special journal for cash payments.

General Journal Entries for Cash Payments

Nine of the January transactions for the Modern Cleaning Shop involved credits to the Cash account because cash was paid out. Some of the general journal entries made to record these payments are shown below.

19 X2					
Jan.	2	Equipment	141	770 00	
		Cash	101		770 00
		Purchased cleaning equipment, Check 31.			
	10	Accounts Payable	202	300 00	
		Cash	101		300 00
		Paid Knight, Inc., in full, Check 32.			
	15	Supplies Used	521	400 00	
		Cash	101		400 00
		Paid for cleaning supplies, Check 33.			
	17	Rent Expense	516	700 00	
		Cash	101		700 00
		Paid January rent, Check 34.			

Each of these four entries in the general journal, plus the other five entries not shown, required a credit posting to the Cash account in the general ledger as illustrated on the next page.

107

		Cash						No. 101
DATE	EXPLANATION	POST. REF.	DEBIT	DATE	EXPLANATION	POST. REF.	CREDIT	
19 X2 Jan. 1	Brought Forward	✓	3,200 00	19 X2 Jan. 2		J1	770 00	
				10		J1	300 00	
				15		J2	400 00	
				17		J2	700 00	
				24		J2	500 00	
				28		J2	600 00	
				28		J2	300 00	
				30		J2	60 00	
				31		J3	1,700 00	

It is apparent that this procedure for recording cash payments is too time-consuming. The accountant must develop a method to eliminate some of the duplication.

The Single-Column Cash Payments Journal

To avoid so much repetition in recording cash payments, the accountant can set up a separate journal for these transactions. One possibility is a single-column cash payments journal. The journal illustrated here might be used to record the January 19X2 transactions of the Modern Cleaning Shop. The accountant needs only one line in this journal to record the facts about each payment—the date of the check, the check number, the title of the account debited, and the amount.

CASH PAYMENTS JOURNAL FOR MONTH OF January 19X2				PAGE 1
DATE	CHECK NO.	ACCOUNT DEBITED	POST. REF.	AMOUNT
Jan. 2	31	Equipment		770 00
10	32	Accounts Payable / Knight Inc		300 00
15	33	Supplies Used		400 00
17	34	Rent Expense		700 00
24	35	Accounts Payable / Ace Motors		500 00
28	36	Equipment		600 00
28	37	Supplies Used		300 00
30	38	Miscellaneous Expense		60 00
31	39	Salaries Expense		1,700 00

The nine credits to Cash that are required in the general journal are no longer necessary. The explanations are also left out because the title of this special journal is self-explanatory. The purpose of entering the check number in the cash payments journal is to permit ready reference to the record of payment on the checkbook stub.

Posting From the Single-Column Cash Payments Journal

The time-saving advantage in posting from the single-column cash payments journal occurs when the Cash account is to be credited. The accountant does not need to post individual credits. Instead, he adds the figures in the Amount column of the cash payments journal at the end of the month and posts the total as a single credit to the Cash account. He then writes the abbreviation *CP1* in the Posting Reference column of the Cash account. This abbreviation represents the journal (cash payments journal) and page (1) from which the posting was made.

After the accountant posts the total to the Cash account, he enters the account number in the cash payments journal. This number is written in parentheses in the Amount column below the total.

CASH PAYMENTS JOURNAL FOR MONTH OF January 19X2   PAGE 1

DATE	CHECK NO.	ACCOUNT DEBITED	POST. REF.	AMOUNT
Jan. 2	31	Equipment	141	770 00
10	32	Accounts Payable / Knight Inc.	202	300 00
15	33	Supplies Used	521	40 00
17	34	Rent Expense	516	70 00
24	35	Accounts Payable / Ace Motors	202	500 00
28	36	Equipment	141	600 00
28	37	Supplies Used	521	300 00
30	38	Miscellaneous Expense	591	60 00
31	39	Salaries Expense	511	1700 00
31		Total Cash Credit		5330 00
				(101)

Cash NO. 101

DATE	EXPLANATION	POST. REF.	DEBIT	CREDIT	BALANCE	DR. CR.
19X2 Jan. 1	Balance	✓			3200 00	Dr.
31		CR1	3410 00		6610 00	Dr.
31		CP1		5330 00	1280 00	Dr.

As you can see, the single credit entry for $5,330 to the Cash account covers all the January cash payments. This entry takes the place of the nine postings that would be necessary if the payments had been recorded in the general journal.

The single-column cash payments journal requires the posting of individual debits to the asset, expense, or liability accounts involved. As each entry is posted, the accountant writes the number of the account being debited in the Posting Reference column of the cash payments journal. (See the journal illustrated above.) The accountant enters the abbreviation *CP1* in

109

the Posting Reference column of the ledger accounts involved to show the journal and page from which the posting was made.

Equipment   No. 141

DATE	EXPLANATION	POST. REF.	DEBIT	CREDIT	BALANCE	DR./CR.
19X2 Jan. 1	Balance	✓			3000 00	Dr
2		CP1	770 00		3770 00	Dr
11		J1	1000 00		4770 00	Dr
28		CP1	600 00		5370 00	Dr

Accounts Payable   No. 202

DATE	EXPLANATION	POST. REF.	DEBIT	CREDIT	BALANCE	DR./CR.
19X2 Jan. 1	Balance	✓			300 00	Cr
10		CP1	300 00		-0-	
11		J1		1000 00	1000 00	Cr
24		CP1	500 00		500 00	Cr

Salaries Expense   No. 511

DATE	EXPLANATION	POST. REF.	DEBIT	CREDIT	BALANCE	DR./CR.
19X2 Jan. 31		CP1	1700 00		1700 00	Dr

Rent Expense   No. 516

DATE	EXPLANATION	POST. REF.	DEBIT	CREDIT	BALANCE	DR./CR.
19X2 Jan. 17		CP1	700 00		700 00	Dr

Supplies Used   No. 521

DATE	EXPLANATION	POST. REF.	DEBIT	CREDIT	BALANCE	DR./CR.
19X2 Jan. 15		CP1	400 00		400 00	Dr
28		CP1	300 00		700 00	Dr

		Miscellaneous Expense				NO. 591	
DATE		EXPLANATION	POST. REF.	DEBIT	CREDIT	BALANCE	DR. CR.
19X2 Jan. 30			CP1	60 00		60 00	Dr.

The Multicolumn Cash Payments Journal

In most businesses there are many repetitive transactions involving cash payments. For example, there are usually many cash payments on accounts payable and many payments for expenses such as salaries, rent, and utilities. When the single-column cash payments journal is used, each payment results in an individual debit being posted to the appropriate account. For example, if there were 200 payments on accounts payable during the month, there would be 200 debit postings to the Accounts Payable account.

By increasing the number of columns in the cash payments journal, the accountant can avoid posting numerous individual debits. The three-column journal illustrated below is one that Stein might develop for the Modern Cleaning Shop. In the first money column, the accountant records all debits to the Accounts Payable account. The next section of the cash payments journal is used to record debits for items that do not occur often enough to warrant special columns. This section is called Other Accounts Debit. Notice that it has space for entering account titles as well as amounts. The third money column is used to accumulate the amounts to be included in the total credit to the Cash account. The January 19X2 transactions of the Modern Cleaning Shop involving cash payments are recorded in the multicolumn cash payments journal as illustrated below.

CASH PAYMENTS JOURNAL for Month of January 19X2   Page 1

DATE	CHECK NO.	EXPLANATION	ACCOUNTS PAYABLE √	ACCOUNTS PAYABLE DR. 202	OTHER ACCOUNTS DEBIT ACCOUNT TITLE	OTHER ACCOUNTS DEBIT POST. REF.	OTHER ACCOUNTS DEBIT AMOUNT	CASH CR. 101
Jan. 2	31	Cleaning equipment			Equipment		770 00	770 00
10	32	Knight, Inc.		300 00				300 00
15	33	Cleaning supplies			Supplies Used		400 00	400 00
17	34	January rent			Rent Expense		700 00	700 00
24	35	Ace Motors		500 00				500 00
28	36	Store fixtures			Equipment		600 00	600 00
28	37	Cleaning supplies			Supplies Used		300 00	300 00
30	38	Miscellaneous items			Miscellaneous Expense		60 00	60 00
31	39	January payroll			Salaries Expense		1,700 00	1,700 00

Posting From the Multicolumn Cash Payments Journal

Each amount in the Other Accounts Debit column of the cash payments journal is posted individually. As each item is posted, the account number is entered in the Posting Reference column of the journal. These postings are made throughout the month. For example, the payment on January 2 is posted to the Equipment account as shown below.

CASH PAYMENTS JOURNAL for Month of January 19X2 — Page 1

DATE	CHECK NO.	EXPLANATION	√	ACCOUNTS PAYABLE DR. 202	OTHER ACCOUNTS DEBIT ACCOUNT TITLE	POST. REF.	AMOUNT	CASH CR. 101
Jan. 2	31	Cleaning equipment			Equipment	141	770 00	770 00

Equipment — No. 141

DATE	EXPLANATION	POST. REF.	DEBIT	CREDIT	BALANCE	DR. CR.
19X2 Jan. 1	Balance	√			3,000 00	Dr.
2		CP1	770 00		3,770 00	Dr.

At the end of the month, the accountant uses the following procedures to complete the recording process for cash payments.

1. The accountant totals the three money columns of the cash payments journal and checks to see that the total debits ($800 + $4,530 = $5,330) equal the total credits ($5,330).
2. The accountant posts the total in the Accounts Payable column ($800) as a debit to the Accounts Payable account in the general ledger.
3. The accountant posts the total of the Cash column ($5,330) as a credit to the Cash account in the general ledger.
4. The accountant writes the account number below the total of each column as each posting is completed. (The Other Accounts Debit total is not posted because it is composed of items that have already been posted individually. An "X" is written below the Other Accounts Debit total to indicate that it is not posted.)

The cash payments journal and the related general ledger accounts to which column totals are posted are shown on the next page.

Advantages of the Cash Payments Journal

The multicolumn cash payments journal saves a great deal of time, effort, and recording space. The posting of the January cash payments at the Modern Cleaning Shop was completed with only 9 entries instead of the 18 entries that would be needed if the general journal were used for these transactions. More-

CASH PAYMENTS JOURNAL for Month of January 19X2 — Page 1

DATE	CHECK NO.	EXPLANATION	ACCOUNTS PAYABLE ✓	ACCOUNTS PAYABLE DR. 202	OTHER ACCOUNTS DEBIT — ACCOUNT TITLE	POST. REF.	AMOUNT	CASH CR. 101
Jan. 2	31	Cleaning equipment			Equipment	141	770 00	770 00
10	32	Knight, Inc.		300 00				300 00
15	33	Cleaning supplies			Supplies Used	521	400 00	400 00
17	34	January rent			Rent Expense	516	700 00	700 00
24	35	Ace Motors		500 00				500 00
28	36	Store fixtures			Equipment	141	600 00	600 00
28	37	Cleaning supplies			Supplies Used	521	300 00	300 00
30	38	Miscellaneous items			Miscellaneous Expense	591	60 00	60 00
31	39	January payroll			Salaries Expense	511	1,700 00	1,700 00
31		Totals		800 00			4,530 00	5,330 00
				(202)			(X)	(101)

Accounts Payable — No. 202

DATE	EXPLANATION	POST. REF.	DEBIT	CREDIT	BALANCE	DR. CR.
19 X2 Jan. 1	Balance	✓			300 00	Cr.
11		J1		1,000 00	1,300 00	Cr.
31		CP1	800 00		500 00	Cr.

Cash — No. 101

DATE	EXPLANATION	POST. REF.	DEBIT	CREDIT	BALANCE	DR. CR.
19 X2 Jan. 1	Balance	✓			3,200 00	Dr.
31		CR1	3,410 00		6,610 00	Dr.
31		CP1		5,330 00	1,280 00	Dr.

over, the savings in posting effort would increase with additional activity involving payments to suppliers. Most businesses actually have many more accounts payable transactions than are included in the example given here. Another advantage of using a cash payments journal is that it allows further division of the accounting work. If the volume of transactions is heavy, three people can record journal entries at the same time. One person can enter transactions in the general journal, a second can work with the cash receipts journal, and a third can be assigned to make entries in the cash payments journal. This division of journalizing activities increases the efficiency of the accounting system.

Recording Other Cash Payments

While most of a firm's payments relate to routine transactions, the accounting system must be versatile enough to handle special types of payments as well. This section shows how a variety of special cash payments are recorded.

Withdrawals by the Owner

In Unit 2 you learned that decreases in owner's equity are recorded as debits. One type of decrease in owner's equity arises from cash withdrawals by the owner. Since the owner does not receive a salary with which to pay his personal living expenses, he draws cash against previously earned profits that have become a part of his capital or in anticipation of profits to be earned. No withdrawals have yet been recorded for Paul Reed because his capital is so limited and his business is so new. However, when Reed does make a cash withdrawal, it will be done by check and will be recorded in the cash payments journal. The account to be debited and the amount will be entered in the Other Accounts Debit section. The accountant usually prefers to debit a special owner's equity account, such as Paul Reed, Drawing, instead of making a direct debit to the capital account. He does this so that all withdrawals can be recorded in one place for ready reference and identification. A typical entry for a cash withdrawal by the owner appears as shown below.

CASH PAYMENTS JOURNAL for Month of February 19X2   Page 2

DATE	CHECK NO.	EXPLANATION	ACCOUNTS PAYABLE ✓	DR. 202	OTHER ACCOUNTS DEBIT ACCOUNT TITLE	POST. REF.	AMOUNT	CASH CR. 101
Feb. 28	55	Cash withdrawal			Paul Reed, Drawing	302	50 00	50 00

At the end of the period, the separate drawing account makes it easy to provide complete information about the changes in owner's equity that took place during the period. This information is presented in the Owner's Equity section of the balance sheet, as shown.

Owner's Equity

Paul Reed, Capital, February 1, 19X2		$6,240.00
Net Income for February	$94.70	
Less Withdrawals	50.00	44.70
Paul Reed, Capital, February 28, 19X2		$6,284.70

Payment of Sales Taxes

Only one payment of all the sales tax collected is ordinarily made to the taxing authority in any given month. Thus, there is no need for a special column in the cash payments journal for this item. Payment of the tax collected is made by check and is entered in the cash payments journal, with the account title and amount shown in the Other Accounts Debit section.

CASH PAYMENTS JOURNAL for Month of July 19X2   Page 7

DATE	CHECK NO.	EXPLANATION	ACCOUNTS PAYABLE ✓	DR. 202	OTHER ACCOUNTS DEBIT ACCOUNT TITLE	POST. REF.	AMOUNT	CASH CR. 101
July 2	549	Remittance of June taxes			Sales Tax Payable	231	14 56	14 56

If a firm buys supplies, materials, or other items for its own use at retail and pays a sales tax on each transaction, ordinarily no distinction is made between the cost of the material and the tax on it. For example, if the firm buys office supplies for $20 plus a 4 percent sales tax ($0.80), the entire amount of $20.80 is ordinarily debited to an expense account such as Supplies Used.

Payment of Notes and Interest

The previous unit described how a seller might accept a note receivable in settlement of a bill owed by a customer. The seller later collects the amount of the note plus interest. Look at a similar transaction from the opposite side. Suppose that on June 10, 19X2, the Modern Cleaning Shop buys a piece of cleaning equipment for $300 and gives the seller a 6-month, 10 percent note to settle the bill. At the time of the purchase, the transaction is recorded in the general journal by a debit of $300 to the asset account Equipment and a credit of $300 to the liability account Notes Payable.

19X2				
June 10	Equipment	141	300 00	
	Notes Payable	201		300 00
	Issued a 6-month, 10% note for new cleaning equipment.			

On December 10 Reed pays the $300 note plus $15 interest by issuing a check for $315. This transaction is recorded in the cash payments journal. The entry involves a credit of $315 to Cash and offsetting debits to Notes Payable for $300 and to Interest Expense for $15.

CASH PAYMENTS JOURNAL for Month of December 19X2   Page 12

DATE	CHECK NO.	EXPLANATION	ACCOUNTS PAYABLE ✓	DR. 202	OTHER ACCOUNTS DEBIT ACCOUNT TITLE	POST. REF.	AMOUNT	CASH CR. 101
Dec. 10	968	Note paid to Warren Company			Notes Payable	201	300 00	
					Interest Expense	593	15 00	315 00

115

The Interest Expense account will, of course, be shown on the income statement.

Cash Discount on Purchases

You learned in Unit 6 that some suppliers permit their customers to deduct 1 or 2 percent for paying a bill within a specified period, usually 10 days. You also learned that the seller recorded this discount in the Sales Discount account. The purchaser must also record the discount taken on such payments. When a payment involves a discount, the accountant must record three items in the cash payments journal.

1. The total amount of the purchase (as a debit to Accounts Payable).
2. The amount of the discount (as a credit to Purchases Discount).
3. The amount of cash paid out (as a credit to Cash).

In a firm that takes advantage of cash discounts on purchases, the accountant will design the cash payments journal to facilitate the recording of discounts. The following illustration shows how special columns are provided for recording the three elements listed above.

CASH PAYMENTS JOURNAL for Month of November 19X2 — Page 11

DATE	CHECK NO.	EXPLANATION	✓	ACCOUNTS PAYABLE DR. 202	OTHER ACCOUNTS DEBIT			PURCH. DISCOUNT CR. 504	CASH CR. 101
					ACCOUNT TITLE	POST. REF.	AMOUNT		
Nov. 1	884	Lane Company		1,000 00				10 00	990 00

At the end of the month, the amounts in the Purchases Discount column are added and the total is credited to the Purchases Discount account in the general ledger. The account number is written under the total in the cash payments journal to indicate that the posting has been made. Other procedures for recording purchase discounts are discussed in a later unit.

Internal Control Over Cash Payments

The importance of internal control over cash receipts was emphasized in Unit 6. The control procedures for cash receipts are only one part of a well-designed system of internal control. There must also be control over payments so that none of the firm's cash is spent without proper authorization or supervision. Obviously, a company's cash is safe only if there is complete control over both incoming and outgoing funds.

Internal control over cash payments may be achieved by adopting certain policies and by planning work assignments. For example, here are the recommendations that public accountants make to people who are starting businesses.

1. All payments should be made by check, except for minor payments from petty cash. (The use of a petty cash fund is discussed later in this unit.)
2. No check should be written without a properly approved payment voucher to authorize the payment.

3. Bills should be approved only by experienced and responsible personnel.
4. The records covering bills and payments should be kept by someone other than the person who authorizes payments.
5. Still another person should sign and mail the checks to creditors.

In a small business like the Modern Cleaning Shop, it may not be possible to achieve as much division of responsibilities as is desirable. However, no matter what the size of a business, efforts should be made to set up effective control over cash payments.

The Voucher System for Control of Liabilities and Payments of Cash

The five recommendations made by public accountants to achieve internal control over cash payments require divided responsibilities, separate approvals, and documentation for all payments. A chain of suitable procedures should be set up. These procedures must include control of the liabilities a business incurs. Only certain staff members should be allowed to place orders and incur liabilities. Others should maintain records of liabilities and payments. Still other employees should be responsible for approving payments. After one employee approves a payment, another employee issues a check. Still another person should sign and mail the check. As a further precaution, many businesses require that bank accounts be reconciled periodically by officers or employees who are not involved in other cash control procedures.

The *voucher system* is a widely used method for establishing internal control over the incurring of liabilities and the payment of cash. In this system, all liabilities are recorded as soon as they occur. This system also requires that expenditures be made only by check and that checks be issued only in payment of debts approved independently in advance.

Because of its importance and widespread usage, the voucher system is discussed in greater depth in Unit 14.

The Petty Cash Fund

Although bills should be paid only by check and only after proper authorization has been given for the payment, it is not practical to make every payment by check. There are times when small expenditures must be made in cash. For example, if 12 cents' postage is due on the morning's mail, the letter carrier cannot be expected to sit down and wait until the proper approval has been secured and a check written. Most businesses find it convenient to pay such small expense items from a *petty cash fund*.

Establishing the Fund

To set up a petty cash fund, a check is written to the order of the person in charge of the fund—usually the office manager, the cashier, or a secretary. The check is cashed, and the money is placed in a safe or a locked cash box to be used for payments as needed. The original entry to record the check establishing the petty cash fund involves a debit to a new asset account called Petty Cash. The cash payments journal entry made by the Modern Cleaning Shop's accountant to set up a petty cash fund of $25 on May 1, 19X2, is illustrated.

CASH PAYMENTS JOURNAL for Month of May 19X2   Page 5

DATE	CHECK NO.	EXPLANATION	✓	ACCOUNTS PAYABLE DR. 202	OTHER ACCOUNTS DEBIT ACCOUNT TITLE	POST. REF.	AMOUNT	CASH CR. 101
May 1	302	Establish petty cash fund			Petty Cash	105	25 00	25 00

Making Payments From the Fund

Each payment from the petty cash fund is usually limited to some relatively small amount, such as $5. When a payment is made from the fund, a receipt, called a *petty cash voucher,* is prepared. The petty cash vouchers are numbered in sequence and are dated as they are used. When a payment is made, the amount is entered on the voucher, the purpose of the expenditure is noted, and the account to be charged is identified. The person receiving payment is asked to sign the voucher as a receipt, and the person in charge of the petty cash fund initials the voucher to indicate that it has been checked for completeness.

A petty cash voucher to record the payment of $4.75 for office supplies is shown below.

PETTY CASH VOUCHER 1

NOTE: this form must be filled out in ink or typewritten.

DESCRIPTION OF EXPENDITURE	CHARGE TO ACCOUNT	AMOUNT
Office Supplies	Supplies Used 521	4 75
	TOTAL	4 75

RECEIVED
THE SUM OF Four ———————————— DOLLARS AND 75/100 CENTS
SIGNED a. C. Abbott   DATE 5/5/X2   APPROVED BY M.D.   DATE 5/5/X2
Delta Office Supply Co.

The Petty Cash Analysis Sheet

A memorandum record of petty cash transactions is made on an *analysis sheet.* (Sometimes analysis sheets are kept in a *petty cash book.*) Cash put in the fund is listed in the Receipts column, and cash paid out is listed in the Payments column. Special columns are provided for expenses that occur frequently, such as Supplies Used and Miscellaneous Expense. An Other Accounts Debit column is provided for accounts that are not involved in petty cash transactions often. The petty cash analysis sheet for the Modern Cleaning Shop after the payments for May 19X2 have been entered is shown below.

PETTY CASH ANALYSIS SHEET FOR MONTH OF May 19X2									PAGE 1	
DATE	VOU. NO.	EXPLANATION	RECEIPTS	PAYMENTS	SUP. USED DR. 521	DEL. EXPENSE DR. 532	MISC. EXPENSE DR. 591	OTHER ACCOUNTS DEBIT ACCOUNT TITLE	ACCT. NO.	AMOUNT
May 1	—	Establish fund	25 00							
5	1	Delta Office Supply Company		4 75	4 75					
12	2	Ace Express Company		3 00		3 00				
17	3	Swift Delivery Service		3 20		3 20				
26	4	Postage stamps		1 10			1 10			
27	5	Cash withdrawal		5 00				Paul Reed, Drawing	302	5 00

Replenishing the Fund

At the end of each month (or sooner if the fund runs low), the petty cash fund is replenished so that there will be an adequate amount of money on hand to meet anticipated needs. The total of the vouchers for payments from the fund plus the cash on hand should always equal the fixed amount of the fund—$25 in this case.

The first step in replenishing the fund is to total each column on the petty cash analysis sheet. A check is then written for an amount sufficient to restore the petty cash fund to its original balance. The amount of this check is recorded in the cash payments journal. The analysis sheet indicates the accounts to be debited when the check is entered in the cash payments journal. The column totals for May showed the following information.

ACCOUNTS

521	Supplies Used	$ 4.75	
532	Delivery Expense	6.20	
591	Miscellaneous Expense	1.10	
302	Paul Reed, Drawing	5.00	
	Total	$17.05	

The reimbursement check for $17.05 is issued to the person in charge of the petty cash fund and is recorded in the cash payments journal as shown below.

CASH PAYMENTS JOURNAL for Month of May 19X2								Page 5
DATE	CHECK NO.	EXPLANATION	✓	ACCOUNTS PAYABLE DR. 202	OTHER ACCOUNTS DEBIT ACCOUNT TITLE	POST. REF.	AMOUNT	CASH CR. 101
May 31	330	Replenish petty cash fund			Supplies Used	521	4 75	
					Delivery Expense	532	6 20	
					Miscellaneous Expense	591	1 10	
					Paul Reed, Drawing	302	5 00	17 05

It is important to note that the petty cash analysis sheet is not a record of original entry and the figures are *not posted* from it to the general ledger accounts. The expenditures from the petty cash fund are recorded in the cash payments journal only when the fund is replenished. The expenses are posted to the general ledger from the cash payments journal.

The reimbursement check is entered on the petty cash analysis sheet, and the sheet is balanced and ruled as shown.

DATE	VOU. NO.	EXPLANATION	RECEIPTS	PAYMENTS	SUP. USED DR. 521	DEL. EXPENSE DR. 532	MISC. EXPENSE DR. 591	OTHER ACCOUNTS DEBIT ACCOUNT TITLE	ACCT. NO.	AMOUNT
May 1	—	Establish fund	25 00							
5	1	Delta Office Supply Company		4 75	4 75					
12	2	Ace Express Company		3 00		3 00				
17	3	Swift Delivery Service		3 20		3 20				
26	4	Postage stamps		1 10			1 10			
27	5	Cash withdrawal		5 00				Paul Reed, Drawing	302	5 00
31	—	Totals	25 00	17 05	4 75	6 20	1 10			5 00
31	—	Balance on hand		7 95						
			25 00	25 00						
31	—	Balance on hand	7 95							
31	—	Replenish fund	17 05							
31	—	Carried forward	25 00							

Petty Cash Analysis Sheet for month of May 19X2 — Page 1

The balance of $25 will be brought forward on the first line of the petty cash analysis sheet for June. The amount will be entered in the Receipts column. A dash will be placed in the Voucher Number column, and "Brought Forward" will be used as the explanation.

Internal Control of Petty Cash

Whenever there is valuable property or cash to protect, the accountant must establish safeguards. Petty cash is no exception. This is how the principles of internal control have been applied to petty cash by the Modern Cleaning Shop.

1. The petty cash fund is used only for payments of a minor nature that cannot conveniently be made by check.
2. The amount of money set aside for the fund does not exceed an approximate amount needed to cover one month's payments from the fund.
3. The check to establish the fund is made out to the person in charge of the fund—never to the order of Cash.
4. The person in charge of the fund has sole control of the money and is the only one authorized to make payments from the fund.
5. The money for the petty cash fund is kept in a safe. (A locked box or a locked drawer could also be used.)
6. All payments made from the fund are covered by petty cash vouchers signed by the persons who received the money. The vouchers show the details of the payments and thus are valuable for future reference.

principles and procedures summary

The use of a special cash payments journal saves time, effort, and recording space in journalizing and posting transactions involving cash payments. The single-column cash payments journal requires individual posting of debits to the accounts affected but only one credit posting to the Cash account in the general ledger.

The multicolumn cash payments journal saves a great deal more time in posting. The amounts in the Accounts Payable column are totaled and posted as a single debit. Since the Cash account is also credited in a total figure from the journal, only the items in the Other Accounts Debit section must be posted individually.

Minor payments may be made in cash through a petty cash fund. A petty cash voucher is prepared for each payment and signed by the person receiving the money. A petty cash analysis sheet is kept, with special columns for accounts that are used often. The fund is replenished periodically, with a check drawn for the amount spent. At that time an entry is made in the cash payments journal to record the debits to the accounts involved.

managerial implications

Management ensures greater efficiency in the firm's accounting work through the use of a special journal for cash payments. In addition, management and the accountant must set up internal control procedures for the recording and handling of cash payments. These procedures provide added safeguards over cash. Proper authorization must be given before liabilities are incurred and before payments are made to settle bills. The payments, except for small expenditures, are made only by check. Management achieves control over small expenditures through the use of a petty cash fund, which requires that written vouchers be obtained for all payments. The responsibility for the petty cash fund is delegated to one person.

managerial discussion questions

1. Explain how procedures for recording and handling cash payments can ensure management of effective internal control.
2. Why is it important for management to control the liabilities that the firm incurs?

application of principles

PROBLEM 7-1 The Stevens Company uses a single-column cash payments journal. The general ledger accounts involved in the cash payments for March 19X1 and their balances at the first of the month are as follows.

ACCOUNTS

101	Cash	$5,050	511	Salaries Expense	-0-
141	Store Equipment	9,000	513	Advertising Expense	-0-
202	Accounts Payable	2,600	516	Rent Expense	-0-
504	Telephone Expense	-0-	521	Supplies Used	-0-
505	Utilities Expense	-0-			

The March transactions relating to the payment of cash are shown below.

INSTRUCTIONS
1. Open the ledger accounts, and enter the balances.
2. Record each transaction in the cash payments journal. Use 3 for the journal page number.
3. Total the journal.
4. Complete the individual and summary postings to the proper ledger accounts.

TRANSACTIONS FOR MARCH 19X1
Mar. 1 Paid $200 for the monthly rent, Check 750.
    3 Paid $50 for the monthly telephone bill, Check 751.
    6 Paid William Kraus $100 to apply on account, Check 752.
    7 Issued Check 753 for $50 to pay for supplies used.
  10 Issued Check 754 for $1,000 to purchase additional store equipment.
  12 Paid $1,100 for semimonthly salaries, Check 755.
  14 Issued Check 756 for $200 to pay an advertising bill due today.
  17 Sent Check 757 for $200 to Kenneth Oyler in payment of account.
  18 Sent Check 758 for $100 to Jill Carmody to cover balance due.
  23 Made a $60 payment for additional supplies used, Check 759.
  24 Issued Check 760 for $125 to cover account payable to Michael Remp due today.
  25 Paid $100 for newspaper advertisement, Check 761.
  27 Sent Check 762 for $200 to Saul Stanburg to settle an account payable.
  31 Paid semimonthly salaries of $1,100, Check 763.
  31 Paid $90 for the monthly utility services, Check 764.

PROBLEM 7-2 This problem covers the cash payments procedures for the Chan Laboratory for the month of April 19X1. The firm uses a multicolumn cash payments journal with special columns for Accounts Payable Dr. 202, Other Accounts

Debit, and Cash Cr. 101. The general ledger accounts involved in the cash payments for April and their balances at the first of the month are as follows.

ACCOUNTS

101	Cash	$6,100	513	Advertising Expense	-0-
141	Laboratory Equipment	8,000	516	Rent Expense	-0-
			518	Equipment Repairs Expense	-0-
202	Accounts Payable	2,500			
504	Telephone Expense	-0-	521	Supplies Used	-0-
505	Utilities Expense	-0-	591	Miscellaneous Expense	-0-
511	Salaries Expense	-0-			

The April transactions involving the payment of cash are shown below.

INSTRUCTIONS
1. Open the ledger accounts, and enter the balances.
2. Record each transaction in the cash payments journal. Use 3 for the journal page number.
3. Foot and prove the money columns of the journal. Then enter the totals, and rule the journal.
4. Complete the individual and summary postings to the proper general ledger accounts.

TRANSACTIONS FOR APRIL 19X1

Apr. 1 Paid $300 for the monthly rent, Check 171.
    2 Issued Check 172 for $500 to pay for the equipment that was purchased from the Olson Brothers last month on credit.
    3 Made a $100 payment to Ellen Goodhart to cover the balance due on account, Check 173.
    4 Paid $135 for the monthly utility bill, Check 174.
    7 Issued Check 175 for $200 to the Gunder Equipment Company in payment of their invoice for equipment. The terms were net cash.
   10 Sent Check 176 for $100 to Sarah Weigle for legal advice. (Debit Miscellaneous Expense.)
   12 Paid $125 for the telephone bill, Check 177.
   15 Issued Check 178 for $1,200 to pay salaries for the first half of the month.
   18 Issued Check 179 for $100 to pay an advertising bill.
   20 Sent Check 180 for $200 to the Harbor Supply Company for supplies used.
   22 Issued Check 181 for $40 to Cleary Repairs, Inc., for equipment repairs performed today.
   23 Paid $400 for new laboratory equipment. Issued Check 182 to the Laboratory Machinery Company.
   25 Issued Check 183 for $25 for supplies used.
   27 Paid $750 on account to Rosenberg Brothers, Check 184.
   28 Issued Check 185 for $35 to cover miscellaneous expenses.
   30 Issued Check 186 for $1,200 to pay salaries for the second half of the month.

PROBLEM 7-3 The Ludwig Company is a retail jewelry store owned and operated by William Ludwig. The firm uses a cash payments journal with columns for Accounts Payable Dr. 202, Other Accounts Debit, Purchases Discount Cr. 504, and Cash Cr. 101. The petty cash analysis sheet has special columns for Advertising Expense Dr. 513, Office Supplies Expense Dr. 521, Postage Expense Dr. 522, and Miscellaneous Expense Dr. 591. During July 19X1, the following accounts were used in the cash payments transactions.

ACCOUNTS

101	Cash	505	Utilities Expense
105	Petty Cash Fund	513	Advertising Expense
201	Notes Payable	516	Rent Expense
202	Accounts Payable	521	Office Supplies Expense
231	Sales Tax Payable	522	Postage Expense
302	William Ludwig, Drawing	591	Miscellaneous Expense
504	Purchases Discount	593	Interest Expense

The cash payments for the month are shown below and on the next page.

INSTRUCTIONS
1. Record all payments by check in the cash payments journal. Use 7 as the journal page number.
2. Record all payments from the petty cash fund on the petty cash analysis sheet. Use 7 as the sheet number.
3. Foot and prove the petty cash analysis sheet. (Add the totals of the columns in the Distribution of Payments section. The sum of these amounts should equal the total of the Payments column.) Enter the totals, and rule the petty cash analysis sheet. Then enter the receipt of Check 113, which was issued to replenish the fund.
4. Foot the money columns of the cash payments journal, and prove their accuracy. Then enter the totals, and rule the journal.

TRANSACTIONS FOR JULY 19X1
July 1 Issued Check 101 for $250 to Colonial Realtors for July rent.
   2 Set up a petty cash fund of $100, issuing Check 102 for the required amount. (Enter the transaction in the cash payments journal in the usual manner, debiting the Petty Cash Fund account. Also record the transaction on the first line of the petty cash analysis sheet.)
   3 Issued Check 103 for $147.50 to the Shamoto Watch Company to pay the invoice of June 10, which had terms of net 30 days.
   4 Sent Check 104 for $147 to the Jewelers' Exchange to cover the invoice of June 27 for $150 less a 2% cash discount.
   7 Paid $2.50 from the petty cash fund for postage, Petty Cash Voucher 1. (Remember to record such payments on the petty cash analysis sheet.)
   8 Made a payment of $202 to the Peoples National Bank to cover a $200 note due today plus $2 interest, Check 105.
   10 Issued Check 106 for $250 to William Ludwig, the owner, as a cash withdrawal for personal use.

	12	Issued Check 107 for $643.50 to pay the July 7 invoice of $650 from Gem Imports Inc. (terms 1% in 10 days, net 30 days).
	14	Paid $4 from the petty cash fund for office supplies, Petty Cash Voucher 2.
	15	Issued Check 108 for $245 to Mino Supply Company to cover the July 7 invoice for $250 less a 2% discount.
	18	William Ludwig issued Check 109 for $250, payable to himself, as a cash withdrawal for personal use.
	20	Paid $7 from the petty cash fund for delivery service, Petty Cash Voucher 3. (Debit Miscellaneous Expense.)
	21	Issued Check 110 for $40 to Rapid Printing Company for advertising leaflets.
	25	Paid $60 for the monthly utility bill, Check 111.
	27	Paid $10 from the petty cash fund for an advertising poster, Petty Cash Voucher 4.
	30	Sent Check 112 for $160.40 to the State Tax Commission to pay the sales taxes due today.
	31	Replenished the petty cash fund for $23.50 by issuing Check 113. (Get the analysis of the payments from the solution of Instruction 3 on page 124.)
	31	Issued Check 114 for $505 to Jewel Creations Corporation to pay a $500 note and interest of $5.
	31	Issued Check 115 to Parker Tools for their $200 invoice dated July 22, taking the 1% cash discount allowed.

alternate problems

PROBLEM 7-1A The Precision Tile Company uses a single-column cash payments journal. The general ledger accounts involved in the cash payments for February 19X1 and their balances at the first of the month are as follows.

ACCOUNTS

101	Cash	$9,452.60	511	Salaries Expense	-0-
141	Equipment	7,227.50	513	Advertising Expense	-0-
202	Accounts Payable	3,476.25	516	Rent Expense	-0-
504	Telephone Expense	-0-	521	Supplies Used	-0-
505	Utilities Expense	-0-			

The February transactions relating to cash payments are shown on page 126.

INSTRUCTIONS
1. Open the ledger accounts, and enter the balances.
2. Record each transaction in the cash payments journal. Use 2 as the journal page number.
3. Total the journal.
4. Complete the individual and summary postings to the proper ledger accounts.

TRANSACTIONS FOR FEBRUARY 19X1

Feb. 2 Paid $612.20 for new equipment, Check 54.
3 Sent Check 55 for $235 to the Bauer Company to apply toward the account owed.
6 Paid $350 for the monthly rent, Check 56.
10 Issued Check 57 for $133.85 to pay the January utility bill.
12 Paid the Manero Brothers $888.20 on account, Check 58.
14 Paid $126.50 for the January telephone bill, Check 59.
15 Issued Check 60 for $1,600 to pay salaries for the first half of the month.
16 Issued Check 61 for $56.35 in payment for supplies used.
18 Paid $75.60 for an advertising bill that was due today. Issued Check 62.
22 Paid $112.70 to the Palm Supply Company for an invoice of February 12 that was due today. Check 63 was issued for that amount.
25 Paid $218.15 for supplies used, Check 64.
27 Sent $1,179.50 for full payment to Romanoff Mills, Check 65.
28 Paid $736.75 for a piece of new equipment by issuing Check 66.
28 Issued Check 67 for $1,625 to pay salaries for the last half of the month.

PROBLEM 7-2A This problem covers the cash payments procedures for the Gable Manufacturing Company for the month of March 19X1. The firm uses a multicolumn cash payments journal with special columns for Accounts Payable Dr. 202, Other Accounts Debit, and Cash Cr. 101. The general ledger accounts involved in the cash payments for March and their balances at the first of the month are as follows.

ACCOUNTS

101	Cash	$7,519.84	513	Advertising Expense	-0-
141	Equipment	6,876.35	516	Rent Expense	-0-
202	Accounts Payable	2,425.39	518	Equipment Repairs Expense	-0-
504	Telephone Expense	-0-			
505	Utilities Expense	-0-	521	Supplies Used	-0-
511	Salaries Expense	-0-	591	Miscellaneous Expense	-0-

The March 19X1 transactions involving the payment of cash are shown on the next page.

INSTRUCTIONS
1. Open the ledger accounts, and enter the balances.
2. Record each transaction in the cash payments journal. Use 3 as the journal page number.
3. Foot and prove the money columns of the journal. Then enter the totals and rule the journal.
4. Complete the individual and summary postings to the proper general ledger accounts.

TRANSACTIONS FOR MARCH 19X1

Mar. 1 Paid $122.70 on account to Madison Paint Company, Check 68.
2 Paid $465 for new equipment obtained today, Check 69.
4 Paid $325 to the Bauer Company for the balance of their account, Check 70.
5 Paid $297.75 to the General Supply Company for the invoice due today. Payment was made by Check 71.
8 Issued Check 72 for $350 to pay the March rent.
9 Issued Check 73 for $43.35 for supplies used.
10 Paid $130.60 for the monthly utilities bill, Check 74.
13 Paid $126.50 for the monthly telephone bill, Check 75.
15 Paid $950 by Check 76 for salaries for the first half of the month.
18 Paid $210 to Lee Brothers for payment of account in full, Check 77.
19 Paid $73.65 to Electrical Repairs Inc. for repairing equipment, Check 78.
23 Paid $98.25 for supplies used, Check 79.
24 Issued Check 80 for $155.80 to pay the February advertising bill.
25 Sent Check 81 for $500 to the Capital Manufacturing Company on account.
29 Paid $22.55 by Check 82 for miscellaneous expenses.
30 Issued Check 83 for $925 for salaries for the last half of the month.

PROBLEM 7-3A The Diaz Company is a retail clothing store owned and operated by Juan Diaz. The firm uses a cash payments journal with columns for Accounts Payable Dr. 202, Other Accounts Debit, Purchases Discount Cr. 504, and Cash Cr. 101. The petty cash analysis sheet has special columns for Advertising Expense Dr. 513, Office Supplies Expense Dr. 521, Postage Expense Dr. 522, and Miscellaneous Expense Dr. 591. During June 19X1, the following accounts were used in the cash payments transactions.

ACCOUNTS

101	Cash	505	Utilities Expense
105	Petty Cash Fund	513	Advertising Expense
201	Notes Payable	516	Rent Expense
202	Accounts Payable	521	Office Supplies Expense
231	Sales Tax Payable	522	Postage Expense
302	Juan Diaz, Drawing	591	Miscellaneous Expense
504	Purchases Discount	593	Interest Expense

The cash payments for the month are shown on page 128.

INSTRUCTIONS
1. Record all payments by check in the cash payments journal. Use 6 as the journal page number.
2. Record all payments from the petty cash fund on the petty cash analysis sheet. Use 6 as the sheet number.
3. Foot and prove the petty cash analysis sheet. (Add the totals of the col-

umns in the Distribution of Payments section. The sum of these amounts should equal the total of the Payments column.) Enter the totals, and rule the petty cash analysis sheet. Then enter the receipt of Check 465, which was issued to replenish the fund.
4. Foot the money columns of the cash payments journal, and prove their accuracy. Then enter the totals, and rule the journal.

TRANSACTIONS FOR JUNE 19X1

June 1 Issued Check 452 for $300 to Sarno Real Estate for the June rent.
4 Issued Check 453 for $50 to set up a petty cash fund. (Enter the transaction in the cash payments journal in the usual manner, debiting the Petty Cash Fund account. Also record the transaction on the first line of the petty cash analysis sheet.)
5 Issued Check 454 for $237.60 to Miller Brothers for a $240 invoice of May 27, less a 1% discount.
6 Paid $1.50 from the petty cash fund for office supplies, Petty Cash Voucher 1. (Remember to record such payments on the petty cash analysis sheet.)
7 Diaz issued Check 455 for $100 to himself as a cash withdrawal for personal use.
8 Paid $644.84 to Fashion Fabrics by Check 456 for an invoice dated June 1 in the amount of $658 (credit terms 2/10, n/30).
9 Paid $4 from petty cash for postage stamps, Petty Cash Voucher 2.
12 Issued Check 457 for $1,015 to the Westgate Bank to cover a note for $1,000 plus interest at 6% for 90 days.
13 Issued Check 458 for $355 to the Warren Wholesale Company to pay the invoice of May 15. The terms are net cash 30 days.
14 Diaz issued Check 459 for $150 to himself as a cash withdrawal for personal use.
15 Paid $5 from the petty cash fund to the high school newspaper for advertising, Petty Cash Voucher 3.
18 Paid $744.80 to Teen Creations for the June 8 invoice of $760 that was due today. A 2% discount was deducted, and Check 460 was issued.
20 Paid $34.65 for the May utilities bill, Check 461.
21 Took $10 from the petty cash fund to have store windows washed, Petty Cash Voucher 4. (Debit Miscellaneous Expense.)
22 Issued Check 462 to pay an invoice of May 25 for $390 from the Alabama Woolen Mills. A $3.90 discount was deducted, and the check was made payable for $386.10.
25 Issued Check 463 for $277.80 to the State Tax Commission for the May sales tax collected.
26 Took $3.75 from the petty cash fund for office supplies, Petty Cash Voucher 5.
28 Issued Check 464 for $606 to Clinton Distributors to pay a $600 note plus interest.
29 Paid $24.25 to replenish the petty cash fund by issuing Check 465. (Get the analysis of the payments from the solution of Instruction 3.)

UNIT 8

banking procedures and reconciliations

Rapid developments in computers in recent years have permitted the introduction of electronic banking devices and techniques that are dramatically different from the manual procedures so long in use. However, the basic banking transactions remain the same and, whatever means are used to do the work, the requirements for analyzing and recording, classifying and summarizing, reporting and interpreting must still be met. In this unit you will learn how businesses use checking accounts to control cash and make payments efficiently.

Cash Controls

When Paul Reed was organizing his business in November 19X1, he consulted his accountant about the records that would be required to keep track of his financial affairs. The accountant realized at once that there would be a considerable amount of cash received over the counter and that additional amounts would be received by mail from charge customers. In order to protect and control this cash, the accountant knew that more would be needed than a set of detailed records. He therefore recommended procedures to ensure safety in the physical handling of the funds.

As you saw in Unit 6, the cash items (checks and money orders) arriving at the Modern Cleaning Shop by mail are handled by two persons. One person, Mary Gomez, receives and lists the cash items that come in by mail. At the end of the day, she gives the list to the accountant for entry in the cash receipts journal and delivers the cash to Reed for deposit. The accountant also suggested that the cash and checks received from customers in person be recorded on a cash register by Ann Schmidt, the store's salesclerk. At the end of each day, she gives the accountant a cash register proof form showing the receipts from cash sales. The accountant enters this information in the cash receipts journal. The day's over-the-counter receipts are given to Reed for deposit in the firm's bank account. At this time, Reed has both the mail receipts and the over-the-counter receipts. The next step for him is to sort and count all the cash items for listing on a deposit slip.

The Deposit Slip

A form called a *deposit slip*, or a *deposit ticket*, must be prepared for each bank deposit. These forms are usually provided to the depositor by the bank in which the account is maintained and are usually preprinted with the assigned account number. Reed has completed the deposit slip on page 130 for the deposit of January 9, 19X2.

129

CHECKING ACCOUNT DEPOSIT		DOLLARS	CENTS
CURRENCY		45	00
COIN		4	75
CHECKS List each separately			
1	32-1182	20	00
2	32-1182	15	00
3	32-1216	35	00
4	32-1216	40	00
5	32-1450	30	25
6	32-1450	10	00
7			
8			
9			
10			
11			
12			
13			
TOTAL FROM OTHER SIDE OR ATTACHED LIST			
TOTAL		200.00	

DATE January 9, 19X2

MODERN CLEANING SHOP
365 BROAD STREET
DALLAS, TEXAS 75201

CITY NATIONAL BANK
DALLAS, TEXAS 75201

Checks and other items are received for deposit subject to the terms and conditions of this bank's collection agreement.

⑈1110⑆3604⑈ ⑉80⑉00 42269⑈

Note the series of numbers preprinted along the edge of the deposit slip. The same series of numbers is also preprinted on the bottom of the checks that Reed uses (see the illustration on page 134). A special kind of type (MICR type) that can be "read" by machine is used for the preprinted numbers.

Numbers of this nature contain codes that are used in sorting and routing checks and deposit slips. The first half of the series shown above, 1110 3604, identifies the Federal Reserve District and the bank. In this system, set up by the American Bankers Association, the first pair of numbers (11) shows that Reed's bank is located in the eleventh Federal Reserve District, and the second pair (10) is a routing number used in the processing of the document. The numbers 3604 identify the City National Bank. The second half of the series, 80 00 42269, is the number the bank gave to the Modern Cleaning Shop's account.

Banks prefer to use deposit slips and checks encoded with these special numbers so that such documents can be processed rapidly and efficiently by computers and other electronic devices. Documents that are not encoded must be handled manually outside the regular processing. This is a slow and costly procedure with much greater possibility of error.

Preparing the Deposit

Deposit slips for checking accounts are usually prepared on multicopy sets of forms. The name of the depositor is either preprinted or handwritten on the deposit slip. (Note that the deposit slip used by the Modern Cleaning Shop has the firm's name preprinted.)

The current date is written on the deposit slip (January 9, 19X2, in this case). The total value of the paper money is entered opposite the word *cur-*

rency on the deposit slip. Currency to be deposited should be sorted by denomination, with the smallest denomination on top of the pile. If there is a large amount of currency, the bank may require that the bills be placed in currency bands. The total value of the coins is entered opposite the word *coin*. If there is a large number of coins of any one denomination, they should be packaged in coin wrappers provided by the bank. The name of the depositor is written or stamped on each currency band and each coin wrapper to identify the source, in case of possible error.

Checks and other items presented for deposit should be listed individually on the deposit slip. Some banks require that an identification number be entered for each item as well as the amount. The identification number is taken from the top part of the fraction that appears in the upper right corner of each check. For example, the number 32-3604 would be taken from the check shown on page 134. This identification number is known as the *ABA* (American Bankers Association) *transit number*.

Endorsements

Checks to be deposited must be *endorsed*. This is the legal process by which the Modern Cleaning Shop, as the *payee* (firm to which the checks are payable), transfers ownership of the checks to the bank. The reason for transferring ownership is to give the bank the legal right to collect payment from the *drawers*, or *payors* (the persons or firms that issued the checks). In the event that a check cannot be collected, the endorser guarantees payment to all subsequent holders.

There are several forms of endorsement that are in common use. Individuals often use a *blank endorsement*. This endorsement consists of the signature of the payee written on the back of the check, preferably at the left end (the perforated end that was torn away from the stub). A check that has a blank endorsement can be further endorsed by the bearer (anyone into whose hands it should fall by intentional transfer or through loss).

A *full endorsement* is much safer. The payee indicates, as part of the endorsement, the name of the person, firm, or bank to whom the check is to be payable. Only the person, firm, or bank named in the full endorsement can transfer it to someone else.

The most appropriate form of endorsement for business purposes is the *restrictive endorsement*, which limits further use of the check to a stated purpose. Usually, the purpose is deposit in the firm's bank account. For maximum safety and speedy handling, the Modern Cleaning Shop uses a rubber stamp to make a restrictive endorsement.

All three types of endorsement are illustrated below.

Blank Endorsement	Full Endorsement	Restrictive Endorsement
Paul Reed 80-00-42269	PAY TO THE ORDER OF CITY NATIONAL BANK MODERN CLEANING SHOP 80-00-42269	PAY TO THE ORDER OF CITY NATIONAL BANK FOR DEPOSIT ONLY MODERN CLEANING SHOP 80-00-42269

Delivering the Deposit   Once the deposit has been prepared, it should be delivered promptly to the bank. In most businesses, the owner or an employee takes the deposit to the bank during regular banking hours. This person gets a stamped duplicate copy of the deposit slip from the teller as a receipt for the funds.

Some businesses make deposits by mail because of the distance to the bank, the inconvenience and loss of time caused by the travel involved, or other reasons. For such depositors, the bank may provide special deposit slips and envelopes preaddressed to the mail teller of the bank. These businesses usually receive by mail a receipt for the deposit. (The depositors may be given special forms or envelopes that they can address to themselves. The bank uses these forms or envelopes to mail receipts.)

Because the Modern Cleaning Shop is a retail business that receives cash throughout the day, its bank deposit is prepared at the end of the day. Reed carries the deposit to the bank in a locked bag. Since the bank is not open, he places the bag in the night depository at the door of the bank. The bag slides down a chute into the bank vault for safekeeping overnight. Then, at his convenience during banking hours the next day, Reed visits the bank, unlocks the bag, makes the deposit in the usual manner, and takes the bag back to the shop for reuse.

The Deposit Receipt   The bank may acknowledge receipt of a deposit in a variety of ways. One method widely used for many years was to provide a *passbook* to the depositor and record the date and amount of each deposit in it, along with the teller's validating initials. This required that the passbook be brought or sent to the bank so that the information could be entered personally by the teller. Many banks issue a machine-printed receipt form indicating the date and amount of money received. This method is widely used for deposits by mail and when deposits are made in automatic teller machines. However, the most common method is for the bank teller to stamp and return one copy of the multicopy deposit slip form. In this way, the depositor obtains a receipt copy with all the details of the deposit. This copy can be retained indefinitely among the depositor's financial records as proof of the deposit, in case it is needed.

Dishonored Checks   Sometimes a check that has been deposited is returned and charged back to the depositor's account. This occurs when the bank on which the check was drawn has refused to honor it, usually because there are not sufficient funds in the drawer's account to cover it. (The bank usually stamps the letters NSF for "Not Sufficient Funds" on the check.) Such a check is said to be *dishonored*. The depositor's records must be adjusted (by means of a journal entry) to reflect the dishonored check. It is also necessary to correct the balance of the bank account shown on the check stubs.

If a firm is notified of a dishonored check by its bank, it must contact the drawer in order to arrange for collection. The drawer may instruct the firm to redeposit the check on a certain date after it places the necessary funds in its account. The firm's records are again adjusted when the check is redeposited.

Postdated Checks   Occasionally, a business will receive a *postdated check*, which is a check dated some time in the future. The drawer of such a check may not have sufficient funds in the bank to cover the check but expects to make a deposit to cover the amount before the check is presented for payment. Such a check should not be deposited before its date. If it is deposited and payment of the check is then refused by the drawer's bank, the check becomes a dishonored check. The issuing or accepting of postdated checks is not considered proper business practice.

Making Payments by Check

Remember that Reed's accountant recommended that all payments be made by check. Stein also advised that Reed be the only person authorized to sign checks for the firm. Reed's signature was supplied to the bank when the account for the Modern Cleaning Shop was opened in November. The *signature card* illustrated below serves as a contract between the depositor and the bank. It authorizes the bank to make payments from funds in the depositor's account on checks that have the authorized signature.

CITY NATIONAL BANK

CHECKING ACCOUNT AGREEMENT WITH: Modern Cleaning Shop

ADDRESS: 365 Broad Street, Dallas, Texas 75201   PHONE: 555-5678

The undersigned certifies that he or she, as sole proprietor, is doing business under the name of Modern Cleaning Shop, an unincorporated trade name, that no person other than the undersigned has any interest in said business except as employee and that the following employees, whose signatures appear below, are hereby authorized to sign checks and endorse negotiable instruments in my name and/or in said trade name. Such authority is to continue until written notice to the contrary from the undersigned shall have been received by you.

Witness my hand and seal this the 26th day of November, 19 X1.

Proprietor: *Paul Reed* (L.S.)
(Signature)

Paul Reed (Employee) will sign *Paul Reed*

_____ (Employee) will sign _____

DATE OPENED: Nov. 26, 19X1   INITIAL DEPOSIT: $ 6,000

OFFICER ACCEPTING: *R. Sadowski*   ACCOUNT NO.: 80-00-42269

Larger business firms may provide for two signatures on checks. This is an excellent internal control procedure and is particularly appropriate when the owners are not actively involved in the management. Provisions are sometimes made authorizing any two of several responsible officers or employees to sign checks for the firm. This assures that checks may be issued in the absence of one or more of the authorized signers.

Checkwriting Procedures

A *check* is a written order signed by the depositor or other authorized person (the drawer) instructing the bank (the *drawee*) to pay a specific sum of money to the person designated (the payee). Such a check is negotiable, which means

133

that ownership of the check can be transferred to another person or firm. As you have already seen, the payee can endorse the check and transfer (negotiate) it to a third party for presentation to the bank.

The Checkbook Most individuals and many small businesses use checkbooks provided by the bank. Ordinarily, the checks are written by hand. However, many businesses have their own checks printed on forms that can easily be typed. Each check form has a carbon copy that is kept as a record of the payment and serves as the basis for the necessary accounting entry. Reed has obtained the bank's standard checkbook. It contains checks with stubs attached, like those illustrated below.

Preparing the Check Notice in the illustration below that the check number appears on both the check and the check stub along with other data that is important from an accounting standpoint. Check numbers are usually preprinted.

There are a number of procedures that should be followed in writing a check. For instance, in a standard checkbook, the check stub should always be filled out first. Otherwise, the stub might be forgotten. The stub contains information that is important for future reference. Notice that on the check stub illustrated above, the opening balance of $3,200 is at the top, next to the words *Balance Brought Forward*. The amount of the first check, $770, is written next to the words *Amount This Check*. It is then subtracted from the total to obtain the balance of $2,430. The rest of the details recorded on the stub are the date (January 2, 19X2), the name of the payee (Quality Cleaning Company), and the purpose of the payment (equipment).

134

Once the stub is completed, the check portion is filled out. The date, the name of the payee, and the amount in figures and words are written very carefully. A line is drawn to fill any empty space after the payee's name and after the amount in words. Some firms use a checkwriting machine that imprints the amount in distinctive type and perforates the check paper under the writing to prevent fraudulent alteration. When all the data is entered on the check, it should be examined for accuracy before it is signed and sent out.

On the second stub shown on page 134, two deposits have been entered and the dates noted. On January 7 a deposit of $700 was made, and on January 9 a deposit of $200 was made. Before the second check is written, the balance of $2,430 (which was brought forward from the first stub) is added to the two deposits. The total of $3,330 is then entered. The amount of the second check, $300, is written in the proper space and is immediately deducted from the total to obtain a new balance of $3,030. The rest of the check stub and check are filled out as was previously explained.

Look again at the checks illustrated and notice how the amounts are expressed. The amount of each check is written in figures in the space to the right of the dollar sign following the name of the payee. Special care must be taken to write the figures clearly so that they can be read easily. The dollar amount of the check is restated in words on the line below the name of the payee. The writing should begin at the extreme left of the space provided in order to prevent the insertion of additional words. The cents amount is usually shown as a fraction of a dollar. Thus, 15 cents is written as $\frac{15}{100}$. If the check is for an even dollar amount, $\frac{00}{100}$ or $\frac{no}{100}$ is written. (On a typewritten check, the form used is 22/100 or no/100.) The cents amount is usually separated from the dollar amount by the word *and*. It is customary to draw a line from the fraction to the word *Dollars* in order to fill the empty space.

If through error, the amount expressed in figures is not the same as the amount in words, the bank will pay the amount written in words or will return the check unpaid.

Note the numbers printed in machine-readable type on the bottom of each check. This is the same MICR technique discussed earlier in this unit. The first bank to receive the check after it has been issued will encode the amount of the check in the same type in the lower right corner. The check (and similar deposit slips) may then be handled automatically by electronic devices (called *magnetic character readers*) through regular banking procedures. Checks that are not encoded with the bank number, the account number, and the check amount must be processed manually outside regular procedures.

Using Specially Printed Check Forms

Later, Reed purchases specially prepared checks; and the standard bank checks previously described are no longer used. The new check form is in two parts. At the top, there is the check itself. At the bottom, there is a detachable part (called the *remittance advice*) that is used for writing explanatory information, such as the amount, number, and date of the invoice being paid. The first of the new checks, numbered 301, was issued by the Modern Cleaning

Shop on May 1, 19X2, to the Star-Herald Papers for $300 in payment for advertising. This voucher check is illustrated below.

```
Modern Cleaning Shop                              No. 301      32-3604
365 Broad Street                                               1110
Dallas, Texas 75201

                                          May 1       , 19 X2

Pay to the
order of     Star-Herald Papers                    $ 300.00

Three hundred and no/100---------------------------------DOLLARS
                                          Modern Cleaning Shop
         CITY NATIONAL BANK               Paul Reed
         DALLAS, TEXAS 75201              AUTHORIZED SIGNATURE

⑈1110⑈3604⑈ ⑈80⑈00 42269⑈
- - - - - - - - - - - - - - - - - - - - - - - - - - - - - - - - -
Modern Cleaning Shop, Dallas, Texas 75201    DETACH BEFORE DEPOSITING

April advertising, Invoice 27641              $300
```

The Bank Statement

Once a month the bank sends each depositor a statement of the deposits received and the checks paid. A typical bank statement is illustrated below. At this time, the bank also returns the checks that were paid during the month. The depositor may also receive deposit slips, debit memorandums for special bank charges, credit memorandums for special amounts paid into the account (such as the amount of a note that the bank has collected for the depositor), or other papers that have a bearing on the account balance.

CITY NATIONAL BANK

MODERN CLEANING SHOP   ACCOUNT NO. 80-00-42269
365 BROAD STREET
DALLAS, TX 75201   PERIOD ENDING JAN 31, 19X2

CHECKS	DEPOSITS	DATE	BALANCE
AMOUNT BROUGHT FORWARD		19X2 JAN 1	3,200.00
770.00-		JAN 3	2,430.00
	700.00+	JAN 8	3,130.00
	200.00+	JAN 10	3,330.00
300.00-		JAN 11	3,030.00
	725.00+	JAN 15	3,755.00
400.00-		JAN 16	3,355.00
	30.00+	JAN 17	3,385.00
700.00-		JAN 18	2,685.00
	900.00+	JAN 22	3,585.00
	45.00+	JAN 24	3,630.00
500.00-		JAN 26	3,130.00
600.00-		JAN 29	2,530.00
300.00-		JAN 30	2,230.00

Bank Reconciliation—Modern Cleaning Shop

Immediately after receiving the bank statement (and after posting all amounts involving cash to the general ledger) the accountant should reconcile the bank statement with the firm's records. The bank statement received by the Modern Cleaning Shop at the close of January 19X2 shows a balance in the firm's bank account of $2,230. But the balance reflected in the Cash account in the general ledger (see page 113) and also on the last stub of the checkbook is only $1,280. The accountant must determine why this difference exists and bring the records into balance. This process of determining the reasons for the difference is known as *reconciling the bank statement*.

An analysis by the accountant of the bank statement and the firm's records on January 31 reveals two types of differences between the bank statement and the Cash account. These two types of differences, which are very common, are discussed below.

1. Two checks, one written on January 30 and one on January 31, were recorded in the cash payments journal and the checkbook. However, the January 31 bank statement does not show that these two checks have cleared the bank, that is, been paid by the bank. The two checks, known as *outstanding checks*, are as follows.
   Check 38 for $60, dated January 30, payable to S.S. Baker for miscellaneous expenses.
   Check 39 for $1,700, dated January 31, payable to Reed for salaries of the firm's employees.
2. A deposit of $810 was made during evening hours on January 31. This deposit arrived too late to be entered on the bank statement issued that day. The amount of the deposit represented the receipts of January 27 and January 29 that were entered in the cash receipts journal. An amount that has been recorded on the books but was not deposited in sufficient time to be included on the current bank statement is known as a *deposit in transit*.

The accountant proceeds to reconcile the bank balance to the cash balance in the firm's books as shown in the *reconciliation statement* illustrated below.

MODERN CLEANING SHOP
Bank Reconciliation Statement
January 31, 19X2

Balance on bank statement		$2,230
Add deposit of Jan. 31, in transit		810
		$3,040
Deduct outstanding checks		
No. 38, January 30	$ 60	
No. 39, January 31	1,700	1,760
Balance in books		$1,280

Many banks have adopted the practice of printing a *reconciliation form* on the back of the monthly bank statement to assist depositors in reconciling their accounts. The following reconciliation form shows how Reed's accountant would have completed such a form.

THIS FORM IS PROVIDED TO HELP YOU BALANCE YOUR BANK STATEMENT

Date **January 31**, 19 **X2**

Balance Shown on Bank Statement	$ 2,230.00	Balance Shown in Your Checkbook	$ 1,280.00
Add Deposits Not on Statement:	$ 810.00	Add Any Deposits Not Already Entered in Checkbook:	$
Total...	$ 3,040.00	Total....	$ 1,280.00

Subtract Checks Issued But Not on Statement:

No. 38 $ 60.00
　 39 1,700.00

Subtract Service Charges and Other Bank Charges Not in Checkbook:

$ _____

| Total......... $ 1,760.00 | Total........ $ |
| Adjusted Balance........ $ 1,280.00 | Adjusted Balance..... $ 1,280.00 |

No entries are made in Reed's books for the outstanding checks and the deposit in transit. Stein will examine the next month's bank statement to verify that the deposit is credited and that the checks were charged to the firm's account.

Bank Reconciliation— Extended Illustration

The accountant for the Modern Cleaning Shop found it a simple task to reconcile the January bank statement because there were very few transactions with the bank during the month. However, as a business grows and transactions become more numerous, the task of reconciling the bank statement becomes more difficult. To illustrate the steps used in a larger business, the bank reconciliation procedure for the Varsity Sporting Goods Store for February, 19X1 is explained in this section. February is the first month of operations for the business.

The Bank Statement On March 1, the Varsity Sporting Goods Store receives the bank statement shown below. This statement covers the firm's checking account transactions for the month of February. The accountant's first step is to see if the balance of $28,501.72 shown by the bank agrees with the balance in the firm's Cash account and in its checkbook.

CITY NATIONAL BANK

VARSITY SPORTING GOODS STORE ACCOUNT NO. 34-10-60821
180 PARK AVENUE
DALLAS, TX 75201 PERIOD ENDING FEB 28, 19X1

CHECKS		DEPOSITS	DATE	BALANCE
AMOUNT BROUGHT FORWARD				0.00
			19X1	
50.00-	25.00-	27,000.00+	FEB 1	26,925.00
		425.00+	FEB 2	27,350.00
250.00-		575.00+	FEB 3	27,675.00
		500.00+	FEB 4	28,175.00
		1,030.00+	FEB 7	
		1,395.00+	FEB 7	30,600.00
		775.00+	FEB 8	31,375.00
		1,240.00+	FEB 9	32,615.00
1,960.00-		1,080.00+	FEB 10	31,735.00
300.00-		975.00+	FEB 11	32,410.00
200.00-	490.00-	2,050.00+	FEB 14	
719.81-	56.35-	805.00+	FEB 14	33,798.84
82.50-	102.77-	275.00+	FEB 15	33,888.57
101.01-	127.56-	525.00+	FEB 16	34,185.00
		490.00+	FEB 17	34,675.00
		550.00+	FEB 18	35,225.00
		710.00+	FEB 21	35,935.00
		625.00+	FEB 21	36,560.00
		210.00+	FEB 22	36,770.00
5,135.20-		265.00+	FEB 23	31,899.80
4,838.26-		305.00+	FEB 24	27,366.54
25.00-DM		330.00+	FEB 25	27,671.54
102.77-	17.05-	720.00+	FEB 28	28,271.72
400.00-	0.00-SC	730.00+	FEB 28	28,601.72
100.00-			FEB 28	28,501.72

LAST AMOUNT IN THIS COLUMN IS YOUR BALANCE

Codes: CC Certified Check EC Error Correction Please examine this
CM Credit Memorandum OD Overdrawn statement upon receipt
DM Debit Memorandum RI Returned Item and report any errors
DC Deposit Correction SC Service Charge within ten days.

Book Balance of Cash At the end of the month, the Cash account in the general ledger has had entries posted to it from two sources—the cash receipts journal and the cash payments journal. From the cash receipts journal, a debit posting of $43,805 was made to the Cash account. From the cash payments journal, a credit posting of $15,561.85 was made. With the total cash receipts and payments posted for the month, the Cash account shows a debit balance of $28,243.15. This is called the *book balance*. The latest stub in the firm's checkbook also shows this balance.

\multicolumn{7}{c}{Cash}						No. 101
DATE	EXPLANATION	POST. REF.	DEBIT	CREDIT	BALANCE	DR. CR.
19 X1 Feb. 28		CR1	43,805 00		43,805 00	Dr.
28		CP1		15,561 85	28,243 15	Dr.

Difference Between Book Balance and Bank Balance

Since the difference between the book balance and the bank balance may be due to errors made by either the depositor or the bank, the reconciliation process must be undertaken at once. Errors in the firm's records should be corrected immediately. Errors made by the bank should be called to its attention at the earliest possible time.

Even if no errors have been made in the calculation of the book balance or the bank balance, there are four basic reasons why the balances may not agree. You learned about the first two reasons when the reconciliation procedure for the Modern Cleaning Shop was discussed.

1. Outstanding checks may have been written and entered in the firm's cash payments journal, but they may not have been paid by the bank and charged to the depositor's account before the end of the month.
2. There may be a deposit in transit. A deposit recorded in the firm's cash receipts journal may have reached the bank too late to be included in the bank statement for the current month.
3. The bank may have deducted service charges or other items that have not yet been entered in the firm's records.
4. The bank may have credited the firm's account for collections made or for other items that have not yet been entered in the firm's records.

Differences stemming from the first two causes require no entries in the firm's records. However, they must be considered in the preparation of the reconciliation statement. Then, the next bank statement must be checked to make sure that the outstanding checks and deposits in transit have been picked up in the bank records. Differences arising from the last two of the causes listed above must be corrected by making entries in the firm's records so that these records will reflect the increases or decreases of cash.

In addition to the differences already discussed, there are other differences that occur less often. The bank may have made an arithmetic error, may have given credit to the wrong depositor, or may have charged a check against the wrong depositor's account. Similarly, a check may have been recorded in the books at an amount different than the amount for which it was actually written, or it may not have been entered at all.

Steps in the Bank Reconciliation

There are several steps that should be followed in reconciling a bank statement.

Step 1. The canceled checks and debit memorandums sent by the bank are compared with the deductions listed on the bank statement. Charges other than checks are explained in the debit memorandums.

Two debit memorandums are included with the bank statement received by the Varsity Sporting Goods Store. The first debit memorandum covers a check from Thomas Hunt for $25 that the bank could not collect because there were not sufficient funds in Hunt's account. This *NSF check*, as it is called, is charged back against Varsity's bank account because the firm had endorsed it, deposited it, and received credit for it. The debit memorandum is shown below.

DEBIT	Varsity Sporting Goods Store 180 Park Avenue Dallas, TX 75201	CITY NATIONAL BANK	
	34-10-60821	DATE Feb. 25, 19X1	
	NSF Check-Thomas Hunt	25	00
		APPROVED *W.E.H.*	

The second debit memorandum covers monthly bank service charges. These charges vary among banks. They may include a flat maintenance charge plus charges for checks paid on the account, for checks deposited or cashed, and for use of the night depository. Some banks give the depositor a credit against the service charges to reflect the earning power of the minimum balance kept in the account. Varsity's bank allows such a credit. Because of the very large balance in the account during February, the credit exceeds the charges. Thus no service charges were deducted from the account. The amount of the service charges (in this case 0.00) is indicated by the letters *SC* on Varsity's bank statement shown on page 139.

Step 2. The canceled checks are arranged in numeric order so that they can be compared with the entries made in the cash payments journal. In making this comparison, the accountant verifies the amount of each check and the check number. (Any differences must be corrected in the general journal.) The endorsement on each canceled check should be examined to make sure that it agrees with the payee.

In verifying the canceled checks, the accountant finds that a $100 check was charged by mistake to the account of the Varsity Sporting Goods Store on February 28, 19X1, and is included in the canceled checks. The check was issued by the Varsity Clothing Company and should have been charged to its account. The accountant will, of course, immediately notify the bank of the error and return the check to the bank. The Varsity Sporting Goods Store will be given credit for $100.

The numbers and amounts of checks that have been written but have not yet been returned by the bank (outstanding checks) should be listed for later use. This list for Varsity includes Check 117, $127.56; Check 118, $101.01; and Check 120, $375.

Step 3. The deposits shown on the bank statement are compared with the daily receipts listed in the cash receipts journal. In the case of the Varsity Sporting Goods Store, the bank statement agrees with the firm's records except for an amount of $220 for the receipts of February 28. The money was placed in the night depository on February 28 but was not deposited in the bank until the following day, March 1. A note is made of $220 as a deposit in transit. When the next bank statement arrives, the accountant will check to see that the bank has included this deposit in its records.

Step 4. The final step is to prove that all differences between the book balance and the bank balance are accounted for. This is done by preparing a formal bank reconciliation statement, such as the one shown below.

VARSITY SPORTING GOODS STORE
Bank Reconciliation Statement
February 28, 19X1

Balance on bank statement		$28,501.72
Add: Deposit of February 28, in transit	$220.00	
Check incorrectly charged		
by bank to firm's account	100.00	320.00
		$28,821.72
Deduct outstanding checks		
No. 117, February 27	$127.56	
No. 118, February 28	101.01	
No. 120, February 28	375.00	
Total outstanding checks		603.57
Adjusted bank balance		$28,218.15
Balance in books		$28,243.15
Deduct NSF check		25.00
Adjusted book balance		$28,218.15

Note that there are two main sections in the reconciliation statement. The upper section starts with the balance on the bank statement ($28,501.72). To this amount are added any items that increase the bank balance, such as receipts that were entered on the firm's books but have not yet been recorded by the bank. The deposit in transit of $220 and the $100 check of the Varsity Clothing Company that was incorrectly charged to the store's account are the only two items in this category. The accountant adds these two amounts to the bank balance, which results in a new total of $28,821.72. Then, from this total he subtracts items that decrease the bank balance, such as the three outstanding checks that were entered on the firm's books but have not yet been deducted by the bank. After the subtraction, there is an adjusted bank balance of $28,218.15.

The second section of the reconciliation statement starts with the balance in the books ($28,243.15 from the Cash account). To this balance, any increases are added, such as special collection items recorded by the bank but not yet entered in the firm's books. Varsity did not have any such items during February. Next, items that were deducted by the bank but are not yet shown in the firm's records must be subtracted from the previous book balance. There is one item of this type—the NSF check issued by Thomas Hunt for $25. Subtracting this check from the original book balance results in an adjusted book balance of $28,218.15. The adjusted bank balance and the adjusted book balance agree, as they always should at the end of reconciliation.

Adjusting the Records

Items in the second section of the reconciliation statement require entries in the firm's books to correct the Cash account balance. In the case of the Varsity Sporting Goods Store, an entry must be made for Thomas Hunt's NSF check. The entry is recorded in the general journal by debiting Accounts Receivable (to charge Hunt's dishonored check back to him) and by crediting Cash.

After this entry is posted, the Cash account balance will be $28,218.15, the same figure as the adjusted book balance on the reconciliation statement. If checks with stubs are being used, the balance shown on the last stub should be corrected at this point to agree with the adjusted balance shown in the Cash account.

19 X1				
Mar. 1	Accounts Receivable	111	25 00	
	Cash	101		25 00
	NSF check from Thomas Hunt returned by bank.			

Cash   No. 101

DATE	EXPLANATION	POST. REF.	DEBIT	CREDIT	BALANCE	DR. CR.
19 X1						
Feb. 28		CR1	43,805 00		43,805 00	Dr.
28		CP1		15,561 85	28,243 15	Dr.
Mar. 1		J3		25 00	28,218 15	Dr.

pRiNciplEs ANd pRocEduREs summARy

A checking account is essential to a business firm if the firm is to achieve adequate cash control and efficiency in making payments. Once the account is opened, receipts should be deposited daily. Payments can be made conveniently by check.

Checkwriting requires careful attention to details. If a standard checkbook is used, the stub should be completed before the check itself. The stub will provide the information needed to journalize the payment.

As soon as the bank statement is received, it should be promptly reconciled with the Cash account. Frequently, differences arise because of deposits in transit, outstanding checks, and other factors. Some differences may require that the firm's records be adjusted after the bank statement is reconciled.

managerial implications

The use of banking services by a business firm is an important method for safeguarding cash. The formal procedure for receiving, recording, and depositing cash and for making and recording cash payments must provide for authorization, verification, and proof all along the line. In order for management to maintain an adequate amount of cash to meet obligations, it must know the true cash position of the company at all times. Management should therefore insist that reconciliations be made promptly so that errors can be quickly corrected and other differences can be accounted for.

managerial discussion questions

1. How can the accounting system keep management informed of the firm's true cash position at all times?
2. Why should a manager insist that the endorsement on each canceled check be examined by the person reconciling the bank statement?
3. Would closer supervision of procedures for recording cash receipts and payments save time by eliminating the need for a monthly bank statement reconciliation? Why or why not?
4. Many banks now offer a variety of computer services to clients. Why is it not advisable for a firm to pay its bank to complete the reconciliation procedure at the end of each month?

application of principles

PROBLEM 8-1 At the end of February 19X1, George Nakos received his monthly bank statement for the Nakos Towing Service from the Peoples National Bank. The opening balance shown on the bank statement shown on page 145 agrees with the balance of the business's Cash account on January 31. Since the two figures agree, the Cash account on January 31 has been automatically verified. A list of deposits that were made and checks that were issued during February is supplied below. The balance of the Cash account and the checkbook on February 28 was $8,311.

INSTRUCTIONS
1. Verify the Cash account on February 28 by preparing a bank reconciliation statement.
2. Record in general journal form the entry to correct the Cash account balance. Charge the amount to Miscellaneous Expense. Use 2 as the journal page number.

TRANSACTIONS FOR FEBRUARY 19X1

Feb.	1	Balance	$6,500
	1	Check 421	100
	3	Check 422	10
	3	Deposit	500
	6	Check 423	225
	10	Deposit	410
	11	Check 424	200
	15	Check 425	75
	21	Check 426	60
	22	Deposit	730
	25	Check 427	4
	25	Check 428	20
	27	Check 429	35
	28	Deposit	900

PEOPLES NATIONAL BANK

NAKOS TOWING SERVICE
401 BELL STREET
CLEVELAND, OH 44106

ACCOUNT NO. 110-624-0

PERIOD ENDING FEB 28, 19X1

CHECKS		DEPOSITS	DATE	BALANCE
AMOUNT BROUGHT FORWARD			19X1 JAN 31	6,500.00
		500.00+	FEB 4	7,000.00
100.00-			FEB 6	6,900.00
200.00-	10.00-	410.00+	FEB 11	7,100.00
225.00-			FEB 15	6,875.00
60.00-			FEB 19	6,815.00
		730.00+	FEB 23	7,545.00
20.00-	4.00-		FEB 25	7,521.00
3.75-SC			FEB 28	7,517.25

145

PROBLEM 8-2 On June 30, 19X1, the balance in the Haig Company's checkbook and Cash account was $6,418.59. The balance shown on the bank statement on the same date was $7,542.03.

- The records indicate that a deposit of $944.07 made on the night of June 30 does not appear on the bank statement.
- A service charge of $14.34 and a debit memorandum of $120 covering an NSF check have not yet been entered in the firm's books.
- The following checks were issued but have not yet been paid by the bank.
  Check 533 for $148.95.
  Check 535 for $97.50.
  Check 536 for $425.40.
- On the last day of the month the bank collected a $1,500 note receivable plus $30 interest for the firm.

INSTRUCTIONS
1. Reconcile the book balance and the bank balance as of June 30, 19X1.
2. Record entries in general journal form to correct the Cash account. Use 6 as the journal page number.

alternate problems

PROBLEM 8-1A At the end of April 19X1, Linda Monet received her monthly bank statement for Monet Florists from the Century National Bank. The opening balance shown on the bank statement shown on the next page agrees with the balance of the Cash account on March 31. Since the two figures agree, the Cash account on March 31 has been automatically verified. A list of deposits made and checks issued during April is supplied below. The balance of the Cash account and the checkbook on April 30 was $3,972.

TRANSACTIONS FOR APRIL 19X1

Apr.	1	Balance	$6,089
	1	Check 244	100
	3	Check 245	300
	5	Deposit	350
	5	Check 246	275
	10	Check 247	2,000
	17	Check 248	50
	19	Deposit	150
	22	Check 249	9
	23	Deposit	150
	26	Check 250	200
	28	Check 251	18
	30	Check 252	15
	30	Deposit	200

INSTRUCTIONS 1. Verify the Cash account by preparing a reconciliation statement.

2. Record in general journal form the entry to correct the Cash account balance. Charge the amount to Miscellaneous Expense. Use 4 as the journal page number.

```
                    CENTURY NATIONAL BANK

MONET FLORISTS                          ACCOUNT NO. 454-623016
376 KING AVENUE
ATLANTA, GA 30305                       PERIOD ENDING APR 30, 19X1

        CHECKS              DEPOSITS       DATE        BALANCE
AMOUNT BROUGHT FORWARD                     19X1
                                           MAR 31      6,089.00
                             350.00+       APR  6      6,439.00
     100.00-                               APR  6      6,339.00
     275.00-   300.00-                     APR 10      5,764.00
   2,000.00-                               APR 13      3,764.00
       1.65-SC                             APR 14      3,762.35
                             150.00+       APR 20      3,912.35
      50.00-                               APR 22      3,862.35
                             150.00+       APR 25      4,012.35
       9.00-                               APR 26      4,003.35
     200.00-                               APR 29      3,803.35


                                            LAST AMOUNT IN THIS
                                            COLUMN IS YOUR BALANCE

Codes:  CC   Certified Check        EC   Error Correction    Please examine this
        CM   Credit Memorandum      OD   Overdrawn           statement upon receipt
        DM   Debit Memorandum       RI   Returned Item       and report any errors
        DC   Deposit Correction     SC   Service Charge      within ten days.
```

PROBLEM 8-2A On July 31, 19X1, the balance in the checkbook and the Cash account of Maria's Dress Shop was $11,549. The balance shown on the bank statement on the same date was $11,267.05.

- The records indicate that an $879.60 deposit dated July 30, 19X1, and a $476.80 deposit dated July 31, 19X1, do not appear on the bank statement.

147

- A service charge of $4.50 and a debit memorandum of $80 covering an NSF check have not yet been entered in the firm's books.
- The checks listed below were issued but have not yet been paid by the bank.
  Check 864 for $110.50.
  Check 865 for $11.60.
  Check 868 for $238.20.
  Check 870 for $576.30.
  Check 871 for $77.35.
  Check 873 for $145.

INSTRUCTIONS
1. Reconcile the book balance with the bank balance for the month ended July 31, 19X1.
2. Record entries in general journal form to correct the Cash account. Use 7 as the journal page number.

UNIT 9

THE SALES JOURNAL

You have already learned that much of the repetitive work involved in recording cash receipts and cash payments can be reduced by the use of special journals. Naturally, the accountant also devises special journals to handle other types of transactions that occur often. In this unit, you will see how a special journal is used for recording credit sales. You will also learn about the procedures that businesses use to manage their credit sales efficiently.

General Journal Entries for Credit Sales

Another look at the January 19X2 transactions in the general journal of the Modern Cleaning Shop reveals repetitive entries for sales of cleaning services on credit.

19X2					
Jan.	7	Accounts Receivable	111	60 00	
		Cleaning Service Sales	401		60 00
		Sold services on credit to Ruth Carr, Sales Slip 1.			
	14	Accounts Receivable	111	25 00	
		Cleaning Service Sales	401		25 00
		Sold services on credit to John Costa, Sales Slip 2.			
	19	Accounts Receivable	111	30 00	
		Cleaning Service Sales	401		30 00
		Sold services on credit to Roy Hess, Sales Slip 3.			
	28	Accounts Receivable	111	60 00	
		Cleaning Service Sales	401		60 00
		Sold services on credit to Janet Bell, Sales Slip 4.			

As you can see, there is a great amount of repetition involved in both journalizing and posting the credit sales. In the general journal, the four credit sales made during January required four separate entries. These entries involved four debits to Accounts Receivable, four credits to Cleaning Service Sales, and four explanations. The posting of eight items to the two general ledger accounts shown on page 150 represents still further duplication of effort. The accountant realizes that a more efficient system of recording credit sales must be developed to save time and effort.

Accounts Receivable No. 111

DATE	EXPLANATION	POST. REF.	DEBIT	DATE	EXPLANATION	POST. REF.	CREDIT
19 X2 Jan. 1	Brought Forward	✓	200 00				
7		J1	60 00				
14		J1	25 00				
19		J1	30 00				
28		J1	60 00				

Cleaning Service Sales No. 401

DATE	EXPLANATION	POST. REF.	DEBIT	DATE	EXPLANATION	POST. REF.	CREDIT
				19 X2 Jan. 7		J1	700 00
				7		J1	60 00
				14		J1	725 00
				14		J1	25 00
				19		J1	30 00
				21		J1	900 00
				27		J1	800 00
				28		J1	60 00

Recording Entries in the Sales Journal

A third special journal, one used only for credit sales, provides an efficient system for recording these sales. The January credit sales of the Modern Cleaning Shop are shown below in a *sales journal* to illustrate how entries are made in this special journal.

SALES JOURNAL FOR MONTH OF January 19 X2 PAGE ___

DATE	SALES SLIP NO.	CUSTOMER'S NAME	✓	AMOUNT
Jan. 7	1	Ruth Carr		60 00
14	2	John Costa		25 00
19	3	Roy Hess		30 00
28	4	Janet Bell		60 00

The columns and headings in the sales journal speed up the recording process. The accountant needs only one line to record the date, the sales slip number, the customer's name, and the amount for each entry. In addition, since the sales journal is used only to record credit sales, the accountant does not have to record an explanation for each entry. All needless repetition is avoided, and all entries for credit sales can now be found grouped together in one place.

The Sales Slip Number column in the sales journal is useful for future reference. For instance, suppose the accountant needs to check some details about the sale to Ruth Carr. He would look for the sales slip number in the proper column of the journal, find a carbon copy of Sales Slip 1 (illustrated on page 85) in the firm's file of sales slips, and have the information he is seeking in a short time.

Posting From the Sales Journal

The sales journal also eliminates repetition in posting to the Accounts Receivable account and the Cleaning Service Sales account. The accountant does not have to post each entry to the individual general ledger accounts. Instead, no posting is made to these accounts until the end of the month, when Stein adds the figures in the Amount column of the sales journal. This total, representing all the credit sales for the month, is posted as a debit to the Accounts Receivable account and as a credit to the Cleaning Service Sales account. The account numbers of the two general ledger accounts are entered in parentheses in the Amount column of the sales journal immediately below the total. When the posting is finished, the sales journal and the related general ledger accounts appear as illustrated below. The *S1* abbreviation in the Posting Reference column of the accounts shows that the amount was posted from page 1 of the sales journal.

SALES JOURNAL FOR MONTH OF *January* 19 X2   PAGE ___

DATE	SALES SLIP NO.	CUSTOMER'S NAME	✓	AMOUNT
Jan. 7	1	Ruth Carr		60 00
14	2	John Costa		25 00
19	3	Roy Hess		30 00
28	4	Janet Bell		60 00
31		Total Credit Sales		175 00
				(111)(401)

Accounts Receivable   NO. 111

DATE	EXPLANATION	POST. REF.	DEBIT	CREDIT	BALANCE	DR. CR.
19X2 Jan. 1	Balance	✓			200 00	Dr.
31		S1	175 00		375 00	Dr.

Cleaning Service Sales   NO. 401

DATE	EXPLANATION	POST. REF.	DEBIT	CREDIT	BALANCE	DR. CR.
19X2 Jan. 31		S1		175 00	175 00	Cr.

Advantages of the Sales Journal

The previous examples show that time, effort, and recording space can be saved by the use of the special sales journal for entries involving credit sales. If you compare the Accounts Receivable and Cleaning Service Sales accounts with those shown on page 150, you can see that even more time is saved in the posting process. When the sales journal is used, the four individual postings to each of these accounts are replaced by a single summary posting to each. If there had been 300 credit sales during the month, 300 postings to each account would have been necessary if the transactions had been recorded in the general journal. However, when a special sales journal is used, only one summary posting to each account at the end of the month is needed. The use of a special sales journal also permits more division of work. For example, in a large business, the recording of the credit sales may be a full-time job for one accounting clerk.

Recording Sales Tax

You have already learned that in some states certain retail sales of goods and services are subject to a sales tax, which retailers must collect from their customers. The retailers are then required to send the sales tax at specific intervals to the state or other taxing authority.

When a sales tax applies to goods sold on credit, the tax must, of course, be charged to the customer and recorded at the time of the sale. A business that collects sales tax could use the sales journal shown below. This journal provides a separate column for recording sales tax.

SALES JOURNAL for Month of June 19X2						Page 6
DATE	SALES SLIP NO.	CUSTOMER'S NAME	✓	ACCOUNTS RECEIVABLE DR. 111	SALES TAX PAYABLE CR. 231	CLEANING SERVICE SALES CR. 401
June 1	241	Alice Ryan		22 66	66	22 00
30		Totals		480 00	13 98	466 02
				(111)	(231)	(401)

At the end of the month, each column is added and the total is posted to the appropriate general ledger account. The account number in parentheses below each total in the sales journal shows that the amount has been posted to the proper general ledger account. The total of the Sales Tax Payable column is posted as a credit to the Sales Tax Payable account because it represents a liability. (Cash and credit sales and the related sales taxes are discussed more fully in a later unit.)

Accounts Receivable					No. 111	
DATE	EXPLANATION	POST. REF.	DEBIT	CREDIT	BALANCE	DR. CR.
19 X2 June 1	Balance	✓			3,600 00	Dr.
30		S6	480 00		4,080 00	Dr.

	Sales Tax Payable				No.	231
DATE	EXPLANATION	POST. REF.	DEBIT	CREDIT	BALANCE	DR. CR.
19 X2 June 30		S6		13 98	13 98	Cr.

	Cleaning Service Sales				No.	401
DATE	EXPLANATION	POST. REF.	DEBIT	CREDIT	BALANCE	DR. CR.
19 X2 June 30		S6		466 02	466 02	Cr.

Recording Sales Returns and Allowances

A sale is recorded on the books of a business firm at the time goods are sold or a service is provided. However, not every sale produces satisfaction. If something is wrong with the goods or the service, the firm may take back the goods (resulting in a *sales return*) or give the customer an allowance on the price of the goods or the service (resulting in a *sales allowance*). For example, suppose that Frank Sanchez, one of Reed's customers, complains that a rug was not cleaned properly. After examining the rug, Reed agrees to allow a $6 credit, reducing the bill from $24 to $18. How would the allowance be handled?

This allowance is recorded in the general journal because it does not belong in any of the special journals that the firm has set up so far. The Accounts Receivable account is credited to record the reduction in the amount owed by Sanchez. A new account called Sales Returns and Allowances is debited.

19 X2 June 2	Sales Returns and Allowances	451	6 00	
	Accounts Receivable	111		6 00
	Allowance given to Frank Sanchez because of improper rug cleaning.			

The accountant prefers to use the Sales Returns and Allowances account rather than make a direct debit to the Cleaning Service Sales account. This procedure gives the firm a complete record of its sales returns and allowances for the period. Merchants consider this record one of several measures of operating efficiency. The total of the sales returns and allowances is later deducted from the revenue for the period in the Revenue section of the income statement as shown below.

<u>Revenue</u>
    Cleaning Service Sales $4,725.60
    Less Sales Returns and Allowances   39.75
    Net Sales $4,685.85

Returns and Allowances Involving Sales Tax

Sales taxes are imposed only on the net amount of the sale to a customer. This means that a customer who returns goods or is given an allowance on goods or services for which sales tax was charged is entitled to a credit not only for the amount of the sales price involved but also for the amount of sales tax. Similarly, the business is not obligated to pay to the taxing authority the sales tax on returns and allowances. In these cases, the reduction in sales tax liability must be entered with the return or allowance in the business's records. For example, assume that on June 4, 19X2, Alice Ryan is given an allowance of $3 on the sale of June 1, recorded in the sales journal on page 152. The allowance and the reduction in tax liability are recorded in the general journal as shown below.

19X2					
June	4	Sales Returns and Allowances	451	3 00	
		Sales Tax Payable	231	09	
		Accounts Receivable	111		3 09
		Allowance given to Alice Ryan for improper cleaning on sale of June 1.			

If there are numerous sales returns and allowances, a firm may set up a special journal for such transactions. The sales returns and allowances journal is discussed in Unit 10.

List Price and Trade Discounts

The operations of the Modern Cleaning Shop are typical of the activities of thousands of firms called *retailers* that sell their goods and services at retail prices to consumers. In turn, retailers purchase goods from wholesalers, manufacturers, and other distributors. The basic accounting procedures for sales used by wholesalers, manufacturers, and other distributors are the same as for retailers. However, such firms have two sales procedures that are not commonly found in retail businesses. These are cash discounts and trade discounts.

In Unit 6, you saw how cash discounts on sales are handled. These cash discounts are examined again in a later unit. Trade discounts are discussed in this section.

A wholesale business must offer its goods to trade customers at less than retail prices so that trade customers can resell the goods at a profit. This price adjustment by wholesale businesses often takes the form of *trade discounts,* which are reductions from the established retail price. There may be a single trade discount or a series of discounts. The *net price* (list price less all trade discounts) is the amount that the wholesaler records in its sales journal as the sales price of the goods.

Computation of a Single Trade Discount

Suppose that the list price of some goods is $500 and the trade discount is 40 percent. The amount of the discount is $200, and the net price to be shown on the invoice and recorded in the sales journal is $300.

List price	$500
Less 40% discount	200
Invoice price	$300

Computation of a Series of Trade Discounts

If the list price of some goods is $500 and the trade discount is quoted in a series such as 25 percent and 15 percent, a different net price will result.

List price	$500.00
Less first discount	
(25% of $500)	125.00
Difference	$375.00
Less second discount	
(15% of $375)	56.25
Invoice price	$318.75

The same goods or services may be offered to different customers at different trade discounts, depending on the size of the order and the costs of selling to the various types of customers.

Use of Credit

The use of credit is considered to be one of the most important factors in the rapid growth of the American economic system. It is common practice to buy and sell goods and services on credit, rather than for cash. Sales on credit are made by producers, manufacturers, wholesalers, and retailers, as well as by professionals and service businesses of all kinds. The assumption is that both sales and profit volumes will increase if buyers are permitted to pay for purchases over a period of a month or more following the sale.

However, the increases in sales and profits that a business expects when it grants credit will only be realized if each customer completes the transaction by paying for the goods purchased or the services received. If payment is not received, the expected profits become actual losses and the purpose for granting the credit is defeated. Business firms protect against the possibility of such losses by investigating a customer's credit record and ability to pay for purchases before allowing any credit to the customer.

Professionals, such as doctors, lawyers, architects, and owners of small businesses like the Modern Cleaning Shop, usually make their own decisions about granting credit. Such decisions may be based on personal judgment or on reports available from local credit bureaus, information supplied by other creditors, and credit ratings supplied by national firms such as Dun & Bradstreet Companies, Inc. The owner decides whether to extend credit to a customer or require immediate cash payment.

Larger business firms maintain a credit department to determine the amounts and types of credit that should be granted to customers. In addition to using credit data supplied by institutions, the credit department may obtain financial statements and related reports from customers who have applied for credit. This information is analyzed to help determine the maximum amount of credit that may safely be granted to each customer and suitable credit terms for the customer. Financial statements that have been audited by certified public accountants are used extensively by credit departments.

Credit Policies

Sometimes, even though the credit investigation is thorough, some accounts receivable become uncollectible. Unexpected business developments, errors of judgment, incorrect financial data, and many other causes may lead to defaults in payments by customers. Many managers believe that some uncollectible accounts are to be expected in normal business operations and that limited losses indicate that a firm's credit policies are sound. Provisions for such limited bad debt losses are usually made in budgets and other financial projections.

Each business must reach its own decisions as to the most desirable credit policies for it to use to achieve maximum sales with minimum bad debt losses. A credit policy that is too tight results in low bad debt losses at the expense of increases in the sales volume that might otherwise be achieved. A credit policy that is too lenient may result in increased sales volume accompanied by high bad debt losses. Good judgment based on knowledge and experience must be used to achieve a well-balanced credit policy. This policy must be realistic and yet liberal enough to contribute to increases in profitable sales. However, it must also be conservative and strict enough to hold losses from uncollectible accounts to acceptable levels.

Open-Account Credit

The form of credit most commonly used by professionals and small businesses permits the sale of services and goods to the customer with the understanding that the amount is to be paid at a later date. This type of arrangement is called *open-account credit*. It is usually granted on the basis of personal acquaintance or knowledge of the customer by the professional or the owner of the business. However, formal credit checks may also be used. The amount involved in each transaction is usually small, and payment is expected within 30 days or on receipt of a monthly statement.

You are already familiar with the open-account credit arrangement used by the Modern Cleaning Shop. Sales transactions are recorded by debits to the Accounts Receivable account and credits to the Cleaning Service Sales account. Collections on account are recorded by debits to the Cash account and credits to the Accounts Receivable account.

Business Credit Cards

Many retail businesses, especially large ones such as department store chains, gasoline companies, and car rental companies, provide a form of credit card (often called a *charge plate*) that they issue to customers who have established credit. The charge plate serves as a means of identification and as an indicator that the customer has an account with the issuing firm. Such firms usually have a credit department, which makes a thorough check of each customer before an account is opened and the customer is given the charge plate.

The name of the customer and the account number assigned are printed on the charge plate in raised letters and numbers. Whenever a sale is made, a sales slip is prepared in the usual manner. Then the sales slip and the charge plate are placed in a mechanical device that prints the customer's name, account number, and other data on all copies of the sales slip. In addition to the use of the charge plate, many retail businesses require the salesclerk to telephone the credit department to verify the customer's credit status before delivering the merchandise or performing the service.

The credit card sales discussed in this section are similar to the open-account credit sales explained previously. Sales of this type are also referred to as *charge account sales*. The sales transactions are recorded by debits to the Accounts Receivable account and credits to a revenue account. Collections on account are recorded by debits to Cash and credits to Accounts Receivable.

Bank Credit Cards

An increasingly popular method for making credit sales while minimizing or avoiding the risk of bad debt losses is by allowing customers to use *bank credit cards*. The most widely accepted bank credit cards are Mastercard and VISA. Many banks participate in one or both of these credit card arrangements, and other banks have their own credit cards.

These credit cards are issued to consumers by banks rather than by the businesses that accept the cards in sales transactions. Bank credit cards are given to applicants who satisfy credit requirements. Individuals who want such credit cards must fill out an application form. If an applicant meets the necessary requirements, a plastic card is issued with the name and identifying account number printed in raised characters.

Almost any type of business may participate in these credit card programs by meeting the conditions set by the bank. When a sale is made to a cardholder, the business completes a special sales slip (sometimes referred to as a sales invoice). This form must be imprinted with data from the customer's bank credit card and then signed by the customer. Many businesses continue to complete their regular sales slips for internal control and other purposes in addition to preparing the special sales slip required by the bank.

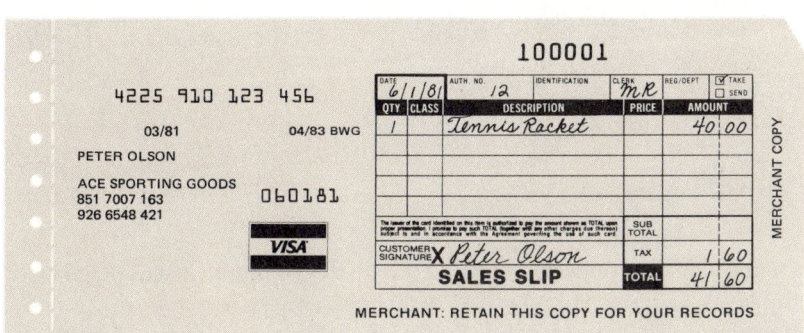

When a business makes a sale on the basis of a bank credit card, it acquires an asset that can be converted into cash immediately without responsibility for later collection from the customer. Periodically (preferably each day), the completed sales slips from the bank credit card sales are totaled. The number of sales slips and the total amount of the sales are recorded on a special deposit form. (See the illustration on page 158.) This form along with the completed sales slips is presented to the bank in much the same manner as a cash deposit. Depending upon the arrangements that have been made, the bank will either deduct a fee, called a *discount* (usually in the $2\frac{1}{2}$ to 6 percent range) and credit the depositor's account immediately with the net amount of the sales, or it may credit the depositor's account for the full amount of the sales and then deduct the discount at the end of the month. (If the second procedure is used, the total discount for the month will appear on the bank statement.)

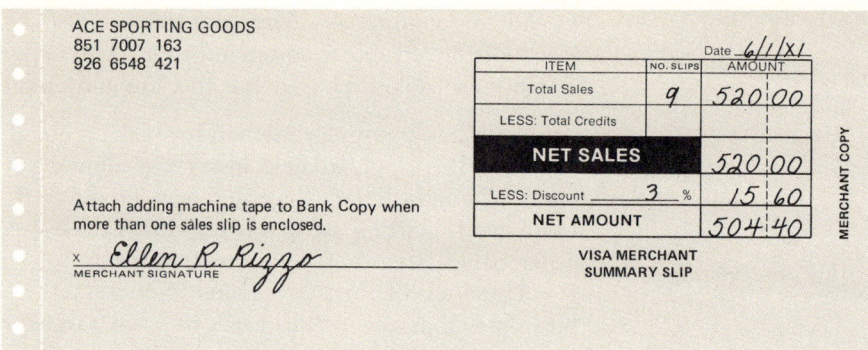

The bank has responsibility for collecting from the cardholders. If any amounts are uncollectible, the bank sustains the loss. For the retailer, bank credit card sales are like cash sales. The accounting procedures for such sales are therefore quite similar to the accounting procedures for cash sales, with which you are familiar. If the business is billed once each month for the bank's discount, the total amount involved in the daily deposit of the credit card sales slips is debited to Cash and credited to Sales. This entry is made in the cash receipts journal as shown below.

CASH RECEIPTS JOURNAL for Month of August 19X1   Page 8

DATE	EXPLANATION	✓	ACCOUNTS RECEIVABLE CR. 111	SALES CR. 401	CASH DR. 101
Aug. 1	Cash sales			638 00	638 00
1	Credit card sales			290 00	290 00

When the bank statement is received and the monthly discount charge against the bank account is known, a "noncheck" entry is made in the cash payments journal. The accountant debits the Discount Expense on Bank Credit Card Sales account and credits the Cash account. An example of this type of entry is illustrated below.

CASH PAYMENTS JOURNAL for Month of September 19X2   Page 9

DATE	CHECK NO.	EXPLANATION	✓	ACCOUNTS PAYABLE DR. 202	OTHER ACCOUNTS DEBIT ACCOUNT TITLE	POST. REF.	AMOUNT	CASH CR. 101
Sept. 2	—	Discount on August sales (3% of $12,000)			Disc. Exp. on Bank Credit Card Sales	592	360 00	360 00

If the bank deducts the discount at the time each deposit of credit card sales is made, the entry in the cash receipts journal is made as shown on the next page. In this situation the daily entry includes the expense for the discount. To facilitate the recording of credit card sales, a special column has been set up for the Discount Expense on Bank Credit Card Sales account. (Notice that these sales were subject to a 4 percent sales tax.)

		ACCOUNTS RECEIVABLE		SALES TAX PAYABLE CR. 231	SALES CR. 401	OTHER ACCOUNTS CREDIT			DISC. EXP./ BANK CR. CARD SALES DR. 592	CASH DR. 101
DATE	EXPLANATION		CR. 111			ACCOUNT TITLE	POST. REF.	AMOUNT		
June 1	Cash sales			44 00	1,100 00					1,144 00
1	Credit card sales			20 00	500 00				15 60	504 40

CASH RECEIPTS JOURNAL for Month of June 19X2 — Page 6

Credit Card Companies

Many well-known credit cards, such as American Express, Diners Club, and Carte Blanche, are issued by business firms established for that specific purpose. The individual seeking to become a cardholder must submit an application containing the required information and must pay an annual fee to the credit card company. If the individual's credit references are satisfactory, the credit card is issued. It is normally reissued at one-year intervals so long as the company's credit experience with the cardholder remains satisfactory.

Hotels, restaurants, airline companies, many types of retail stores, and a wide variety of other businesses may make arrangements to accept these credit cards. When making sales to cardholders, sellers usually make out their own sales slip or bill and then complete a special sales slip required by the credit card company. As with the sales slips for bank credit cards, the forms must be imprinted with the identifying data on the customer's card and signed by the customer. (Such sales slips are sometimes referred to as *sales invoices, sales drafts,* or *sales vouchers.* The term used varies from one credit card company to another.)

The effect of such a sale is that the seller acquires an account receivable from the credit card company rather than from the customer. Periodically, the seller summarizes the completed sales slips and submits them to the credit card company, which pays the seller promptly. At approximately one-month intervals, the credit card company bills the cardholders for all sales slips it has acquired during the period. It is the responsibility of the company to collect from the cardholders.

The accounting procedures for such sales are much like those for sales on open account. The difference is that the account receivable is with the credit card company. If the number of transactions is small and the dollar volume is low, these sales may be recorded in the sales journal as shown below.

SALES JOURNAL for Month of April 19X1 — Page 4

DATE	SALES SLIP NO.	CUSTOMER'S NAME	ACCOUNTS RECEIVABLE		SALES TAX PAYABLE CR. 231	SALES CR. 401
			✓	DR. 111		
Apr. 2	714	American Express (Ann Walsh)		36 40	1 40	35 00
9	751	Diners Club (Robert Treat)		43 68	1 68	42 00

159

The receipt of payment from the credit card company is recorded in the cash receipts journal as shown below.

CASH RECEIPTS JOURNAL for Month of April 19X2									Page 4
			ACCOUNTS RECEIVABLE CR. 111	SALES TAX PAYABLE CR. 231	SALES CR. 401	OTHER ACCOUNTS CREDIT		DISC. EXP. ON CREDIT CARD SALES DR. 592	CASH DR. 101
DATE	EXPLANATION	✓				ACCOUNT TITLE	POST. REF.	AMOUNT		
Apr. 28	American Express (Ann Walsh)		36 40						2 55	33 85
30	Diners Club (Robert Treat)		43 68						3 06	40 62

If the transactions are numerous or the dollar volume is large, the transactions may be recorded in the general journal. When a summary statement and the completed sales slips are submitted to the credit card company, the accountant makes the following entry. He uses a separate Accounts Receivable account as shown below.

GENERAL JOURNAL				Page 5
DATE	DESCRIPTION OF ENTRY	POST. REF.	DEBIT	CREDIT

19 X1 May 31	Accounts Receivable—Credit Card Companies
	    Sales Tax Payable
	    Sales
	Sent summary statement to American Express for credit card sales made during the week.
		114
		231
		401
			1,872 00	72 00
				1,800 00

Later, when payment less the discount is received from the credit card company, the receipt of the cash is recorded as shown below.

CASH RECEIPTS JOURNAL for Month of June 19X1									Page 6
			ACCOUNTS RECEIVABLE CR. 111	SALES TAX PAYABLE CR. 231	SALES CR. 401	OTHER ACCOUNTS CREDIT		DISC. EXP. ON CREDIT CARD SALES DR. 592	CASH DR. 101
DATE	EXPLANATION	✓				ACCOUNT TITLE	POST. REF.	AMOUNT		
June 14	American Express (5/31 summary)					Accounts Receivable—Credit Card Companies	114	1,872 00	131 04	1,740 96

Layaway or Will-Call Sales   In a *layaway sale*, or *will-call sale*, the customer makes a deposit on a certain item and the store puts it aside. The customer must pay the rest of the price (usually within a specified time) before taking possession of the goods. A customer who does not complete the payments within the time allowed may legally forfeit the amount that has already been paid. However, in many cases, the store refunds the payments made or credits them against other purchases in an effort to retain customer goodwill. Experience with sales of this type indicates that most customers complete their payments and receive the goods.

The accounting procedure for layaway sales is as follows. The sale is recorded when the customer makes the deposit and the merchandise is put aside. Cash is debited for the amount of the deposit, and Accounts Receivable is debited for the balance. The Sales account is credited for the entire price of the item. In effect, the transaction is recorded as a credit sale, on which a part payment has been made. Later payments are recorded as collections on account. When the price of the goods has been paid in full (there is no longer an accounts receivable balance for the sale), the goods are given to the customer.

COD Sales Procedures

COD (cash on delivery) sales are made to customers without established credit who want goods delivered or shipped to them. The cash is collected from the customer at the time of delivery. If the customer cannot pay, the goods are returned to the seller. The simplest accounting procedure for such sales is to prepare a sales slip marked "COD" to accompany the goods. The deliveryperson is instructed to collect the amount shown on the sales slip. No entry is made in the Accounts Receivable account. If the customer pays, the transaction is then processed as a cash sale. If the customer does not pay, the sales slip is voided and the merchandise is returned to stock.

principles and procedures summary

The sales journal is a special journal used for recording sales on credit. These sales are recorded in the sales journal as they take place during the period. At the end of the period, the total amount sold on credit is posted as a debit to the Accounts Receivable account and a credit to a revenue account.

Sales tax collection may be recorded in a special column in the sales journal. Sales returns and allowances may be entered in the general journal if they occur infrequently. However, a special journal is used when the returns and allowances are numerous. The sales tax liability on sales returns and allowances is adjusted so the customer pays tax only on the net amount. In turn, the seller remits only the sales tax collected on the net sales for the period.

Credit sales are very common, and many different credit arrangements are used. Each firm must choose the credit policy that suits its needs.

managerial implications

Management must be certain that all sales are promptly, efficiently, and accurately recorded because sales represent the source of revenue for the business. The use of the sales journal saves time and effort, reduces office costs, and permits the division of labor.

The sales journal also provides a convenient record of sales tax collections. An accurate record is necessary, since the seller is required to send the tax collections to the taxing authority. The complete and systematic tax record in the sales journal speeds the completion of the periodic tax report form and provides proof that would be needed in the event of a tax audit.

Management must select a well-balanced credit policy. This policy should help to increase sales volume but should also keep bad debt losses at an acceptable level.

MANAGERIAL DISCUSSION QUESTIONS

1. Why should management insist that sales are recorded promptly and efficiently?
2. How does management use the Sales Returns and Allowances account as a measure of operating efficiency? Whose efficiency is involved?
3. How often should special journals, such as the sales journal, be redesigned?
4. Under what circumstances would an accountant recommend the use of a sales returns and allowances journal to the management of a business?
5. How can a firm's credit policy affect its profitability?

APPLICATION OF PRINCIPLES

PROBLEM 9-1 The AA Refrigeration Company has a single-column sales journal. The general ledger accounts used in recording the firm's credit sales are as follows.

ACCOUNTS

111	Accounts Receivable	$18,500
401	Refrigeration Sales	-0-

The June 19X1 transactions involving credit sales are shown below.

INSTRUCTIONS
1. Open the general ledger accounts, and enter the balance of the Accounts Receivable account.
2. Record each transaction in the sales journal. Use 6 as the journal page number.
3. Total and rule the journal.
4. Make the required postings to the proper general ledger accounts.

TRANSACTIONS FOR JUNE 19X1

June 1 Sold an air conditioner for $450 to Robert Cleary on 30-day credit, Sales Slip 59.

2 Sold a refrigerator for $375 on 30-day credit to Susan Moy, Sales Slip 60.

5 Delivered and installed a $3,000 cooling system at The Shopping Mart on credit, Sales Slip 61.

7   Sold a dehumidifier for $400 to Alex Weller on credit, Sales Slip 62.
9   Installed an $800 refrigerator for Carl Shamoto, Sales Slip 63. Half the amount is payable in 15 days, and the balance is due in 30 days.
12 Delivered and installed a $500 air conditioner for Mary Callas on credit, Sales Slip 64.
14 Sold portable fans to Carol VanStaden for $75 on credit, Sales Slip 65, and to Philip Aster for $95 on credit, Sales Slip 66.
16 Sold an exhaust fan for $225 to Corner Sweet Shop on credit, Sales Slip 67. Also sold another $75 fan to Carol VanStaden on credit, Sales Slip 68.
19 Sold an air filter for $60 to Rolf Broner on credit, Sales Slip 69.
20 Mario Ramos purchased a $600 refrigerator on credit, Sales Slip 70.
22 Delivered and installed a $500 air conditioner for Mary Jalenos on credit, Sales Slip 71.
23 Made the following sales on credit: $100 to Joseph Pulaski, Sales Slip 72; $140 to Hope Gillies, Sales Slip 73; $175 to Edward Mahoney, Sales Slip 74.
24 Recorded a $210 sale on credit to George Goetz, Sales Slip 75.
26 Installed an attic fan for $345 in the home of Anthony Caruso, Sales Slip 76. The amount is payable in 30 days.
28 Sold a $400 automobile air conditioner to Larry Bates on credit, Sales Slip 77.
30 Made the following sales on credit: Frank Jensen, $200, Sales Slip 78; and Donna Helm, $315, Sales Slip 79.

PROBLEM 9-2

This problem covers the procedures for recording cash and credit sales at the City Supply Company. The firm's books include a single-column sales journal and a cash receipts journal with columns for Accounts Receivable Cr. 111, Sales Cr. 401, and Cash Dr. 101. The general ledger shows the following accounts and balances at the opening of business on March 1, 19X1.

ACCOUNTS

101	Cash	$1,880
111	Accounts Receivable	3,600
401	Sales	-0-

The March 19X1 transactions involving sales are shown on page 164.

INSTRUCTIONS
1. Open the general ledger accounts, and enter the balances.
2. Record each transaction in the appropriate journal. Use 3 as the page number for each journal.
3. Foot and prove the cash receipts journal. Then total and rule both journals.
4. Make the necessary postings to the general ledger accounts.

TRANSACTIONS FOR MARCH 19X1

Mar. 1 Received $150 in cash for the sale of merchandise.
3 Received $258.50 from accounts receivable.
5 Sold merchandise for $175 on account to Pablo Garcia, Sales Slip 601.
6 Received $250 in cash from credit customers.
8 Sold merchandise for $240 on credit to Theresa Ulrich, Sales Slip 602.
10 Received $100 to cover cash sales.
12 Made the following sales on credit: George Fong, $55, Sales Slip 603; and Patrick McSweeney, $35, Sales Slip 604.
13 Sold merchandise totaling $1,500 to the following: on credit to Gale Petersen, $300, Sales Slip 605; on credit to Sam Goldberg, $900, Sales Slip 606; for cash, $300.
15 Sold merchandise for $215 on credit to Paul Wujek, Sales Slip 607.
17 Made credit sales to Carla Fuentes, $25, Sales Slip 608; Frank Conti, $10, Sales Slip 609; and Sarah Freeman, $22, Sales Slip 610.
20 Issued Sales Slip 611 for $25 to cover a credit sale to Roberta Werth.
21 Sold merchandise for $15 on credit to Ellen Dallow, Sales Slip 612.
22 Sold merchandise for $85 on credit to Mark Bassin, Sales Slip 613.
23 Sold merchandise on credit to Joan Brendel, $15, Sales Slip 614; Franklin Jones, $40, Sales Slip 615; and Erin Mahoney, $17, Sales Slip 616.
24 Issued Sales Slip 617 for $85 for a credit sale to Thomas Valentine.
25 Collected $2,500 in cash from accounts receivable.
26 Sold merchandise for $16 on credit to Janet Holmgaard, Sales Slip 618.
27 Sold merchandise on credit to Elio Marchi, $75, Sales Slip 619, and John Becker, $45, Sales Slip 620.
29 Sold $110 of merchandise on account to Franz Hofmann, Sales Slip 621.
31 Issued Sales Slip 622 for $90 for a credit sale to Peter Lomax.

PROBLEM 9-3 The Imperial Gift Shop sells china, glassware, and other gift items that are subject to a 6 percent state sales tax. The shop uses a general journal and a sales journal with special columns for Accounts Receivable Dr. 111, Sales Tax Payable Cr. 231, and Sales Cr. 401. The credit transactions shown on the next page took place during a week in November 19X1.

INSTRUCTIONS
1. Record the proper transactions in the sales journal and the general journal. Use *11* as the page number for each journal.
2. Foot the sales journal, and prove the accuracy of your work.

TRANSACTIONS FOR NOVEMBER 1–5, 19X1

Nov. 1 Sold china for $106 to Michele King; the price was $100 plus $6 sales tax, Sales Slip 141.
1 Sold a brass serving tray for $50 plus $3 sales tax to Robin Cooley, Sales Slip 142.
2 Sold a vase for $40 plus $2.40 tax to Werner Knerr, Sales Slip 143.
3 Sold a punch bowl and glasses for $80 plus tax to Lisa Mariani on Sales Slip 144.
3 Sold a set of serving bowls for $20 plus tax to Margot Durand, Sales Slip 145.
3 Allowed a $5 credit, plus sales tax, to Michele King because of a broken cup she discovered when unpacking the china sold on Nov. 1, Sales Slip 141. (Use the Sales Returns and Allowances account.)
4 Sold a coffee table for $60 plus sales tax to Hans Rheinhold, Sales Slip 146.
4 Sold sterling silver teaspoons for $110 plus tax to Emily Gunther, Sales Slip 147.
5 Accepted the return of the serving tray bought by Robin Cooley on Nov. 1. It was a duplicate of one already owned by the person for whom it was intended. Item is in perfect condition. Full credit allowed.
5 Sold table linen to David Smith for $175 plus sales tax, Sales Slip 148.
5 Sold a clock to Victor Costello for $100 plus $6 tax, Sales Slip 149.

alternate problems

PROBLEM 9-1A

The Royal Venetian Blind Company has a single-column sales journal. The general ledger accounts used in recording the firm's credit sales are as follows.

ACCOUNTS

111 Accounts Receivable $3,242.70
414 Venetian Blind Sales   -0-

The April 19X1 transactions involving credit sales are shown below and on page 166.

INSTRUCTIONS
1. Open the general ledger accounts, and enter the balance of the Accounts Receivable account.
2. Record each transaction in the sales journal. Use 4 as the journal page number.
3. Total and rule the journal.
4. Make the required postings to the proper general ledger accounts.

TRANSACTIONS FOR APRIL 19X1

Apr. 2 Sold a venetian blind for $22.50 to Lester Berg, Sales Slip 32.
3 Installed venetian blinds for Marie Taylor, $132.15, Sales Slip 33, and for Jacob Levai, $56, Sales Slip 34.

5   Sold venetian blinds for $563.70 to Lakeview School, Sales Slip 35.
6   Sold venetian blinds for $28.70 to Lillian Shaw, Sales Slip 36.
9   Sold venetian blinds for $1,215.65 to Seaside Apartments on Sales Slip 37.
10 Installed venetian blinds costing $388.40 for Mark DuPree, Sales Slip 38. Half the amount is payable in 30 days and the other half in 60 days.
11 Made the following sales: Sales Slip 39, $43.20, to Jean Cartwright; Sales Slip 40, $22, to Michael Wu; Sales Slip 41, $67.35, to Francine Minott.
13 Installed extra-long blinds costing $166.80 for Jack O'Reilly, Sales Slip 42.
14 Sold blinds for $47.95 to Floyd Schmidt, Sales Slip 43.
16 Sold venetian blinds for $832.50 to County College, Sales Slip 44.
17 Sold $96.60 of venetian blinds to Sam Solomon, Sales Slip 45.
20 Made the following sales: Sales Slip 46, $31.95, to Jack Holden; Sales Slip 47, $24.75, to Stan Goldberg; Sales Slip 48, $95, to Tom Saxon.
23 Installed venetian blinds sold to Kathy Lauren for $92.30, Sales Slip 49.
25 Made the following sales: Sales Slip 50 for $118.85 to James Buckman, Sales Slip 51 for $33.55 to Ann Norris.
27 Sold venetian blinds for $337.75 to Fred Ehmer, Sales Slip 52.

PROBLEM 9-2A

This problem covers procedures for recording the cash and credit sales at Sloan Floor Coverings. The firm's books include a single-column sales journal and a cash receipts journal with special columns for Accounts Receivable Cr. 111, Sales Cr. 401, and Cash Dr. 101. The following accounts and balances on May 1, 19X1, are taken from the firm's general ledger.

ACCOUNTS

101	Cash	$2,238.45
111	Accounts Receivable	783.20
401	Sales	-0-

The May 19X1 transactions involving sales are shown below and on page 167.

INSTRUCTIONS

1. Open the general ledger accounts, and enter the balances.
2. Record each transaction in the appropriate journal. Use 5 as the page number for each journal.
3. Foot and prove the cash receipts journal. Total and rule both journals.
4. Make the necessary postings to the general ledger accounts.

TRANSACTIONS FOR MAY 19X1

May 2 Sold $102.25 of floor tiles on credit to Taylor's Clothing Shop, Sales Slip 53.
    3 Sold a $42.75 area rug for cash.

4	Sold floor tiles for $44.60 on credit to Vito Parelli, Sales Slip 54.
5	Sold a $89.50 rug on credit to Anna Sweetman, Sales Slip 55.
6	Installed wall-to-wall carpeting for $1,335.75 on credit in United Can Company office, Sales Slip 56.
9	Made the following sales on credit: Sales Slip 57 for $111.25 to Leroy Johnson, Sales Slip 58 for $55 to Susan McNeill, and Sales Slip 59 for $87.65 to Felder's Drug Store.
10	Sold a rug for $352.50 on 60 days' credit to Gloria Mendez, Sales Slip 60.
11	Gave special credit terms on a $195 sale to Joe Medov, Sales Slip 61. One-third is payable in 30 days, one-third in 60 days, and one-third in 90 days.
12	Collected $84.50 in cash from the sale of floor tiles.
13	Installed linoleum for $136 on credit for Douglas Kinmore, Sales Slip 62.
17	Made a $71.35 credit sale to Marcia Tollman, Sales Slip 63. Made a $60.35 credit sale to Bridget Connolly, Sales Slip 64.
18	Sold $427.55 worth of floor tiles to George Saffos on credit, Sales Slip 65.
19	Sold an area rug for $99 to Collette duPres, Sales Slip 66, 30 days' credit.
20	Sold Brenda Harris floor mats for $53.75 on credit, Sales Slip 67.
23	Installed floor tiles on credit for Kenneth Chin, Sales Slip 68, $146.35, and for Elsa Luchow, $33.95, Sales Slip 69.
25	Installed floor tiles on credit for $989.95 in Liberty School, Sales Slip 70.
26	Made cash sales of $31.25.
27	Made a credit sale of $64.25 to John Roberts, Sales Slip 71.
30	Sold Ray Silverton a $219.50 rug on credit, Sales Slip 72.
31	Made the following sales on credit: Sales Slip 73 for $91 to Juanita Lopez, Sales Slip 74 for $37.50 to Mary Whitman, and Sales Slip 75 for $13.65 to Helen Pierce.

PROBLEM 9-3A The Greenery is a shop that sells flowers, plants, and plant supplies. All sales are subject to a 3 percent sales tax. The shop uses a general journal and a sales journal with special columns for Accounts Receivable Dr. 111, Sales Tax Payable Cr. 231, and Sales Cr. 401. The credit transactions shown below and on page 168 took place during a week in January 19X1.

INSTRUCTIONS
1. Record the proper transactions in the sales journal and the general journal. Use *1* for the page number of each journal.
2. Foot the sales journal, and prove the accuracy of your work.

TRANSACTIONS FOR JANUARY 8–13, 19X1

Jan. 8 Sold $41.20 of floral arrangements to Lynn Jonas, Sales Slip 19, at the cost of $40 plus a sales tax of $1.20.

8   Sold a potted plant for $24.72 to Lena Sorrento, Sales Slip 20—$24 plus a sales tax of $0.72.
9   Sold a floral arrangement for $50 plus sales tax to The Heinberg Restaurant, Sales Slip 21.
10 Sold a corsage for $8.50 plus $0.26 sales tax, to Jonathan Wright, Sales Slip 22.
11 Allowed Lynn Jonas a credit of $5 plus sales tax because of withered blossoms discovered in one of the floral arrangements. The transaction was covered by Sales Slip 19, January 8. (Use the Sales Returns and Allowances account.)
11 Sold plants to Anna Popov for $22 plus sales tax, Sales Slip 23.
11 Sold one dozen roses for $30 plus sales tax to Walter Craven, Sales Slip 24.
12 Sold clay pots for $22 plus sales tax to Karen McLean, Sales Slip 25.
12 Sold two sprays to Conlon Hotel for $60 plus sales tax, Sales Slip 26.
13 Sold table arrangements for $80 plus sales tax to City College for Parents' Day, Sales Slip 27.
13 Accepted a return of roses sold to Walter Craven on January 11, Sales Slip 24, and allowed him full credit because of late delivery.

UNIT 10

THE ACCOUNTS RECEIVABLE LEDGER

In previous units, you saw how special journals for cash receipts, cash payments, and sales are used to increase the efficiency of an accounting system. Another way to improve efficiency is to set up individual accounts for credit customers. Such accounts are kept in a subsidiary ledger called the accounts receivable ledger. *This ledger provides detailed information that does not appear in the general ledger.*

Recording Credit Sales

The sales journal and the cash receipts journal simplify the handling of sales on credit. As the January credit sales were made at the Modern Cleaning Shop, the accountant recorded them in the sales journal. Then, at the end of the month, the Accounts Receivable account in the general ledger was debited for the total of the credit sales and the Cleaning Service Sales account was credited for the same amount.

SALES JOURNAL for Month of January 19X2 Page 1

DATE	SALES SLIP NO.	CUSTOMER'S NAME	✓	AMOUNT
Jan. 7	1	Ruth Carr		60 00
14	2	John Costa		25 00
19	3	Roy Hess		30 00
28	4	Janet Bell		60 00
31		Total Credit Sales		175 00
				(111)
				(401)

Accounts Receivable No. 111

DATE	EXPLANATION	POST. REF.	DEBIT	CREDIT	BALANCE	DR. CR.
19X2 Jan. 1	Balance	✓			200 00	Dr.
31		S1	175 00		375 00	Dr.

Cleaning Service Sales No. 401

DATE	EXPLANATION	POST. REF.	DEBIT	CREDIT	BALANCE	DR. CR.
19X2 Jan. 31		S1		175 00	175 00	Cr.

As customers paid their bills, the accountant entered each receipt in the multicolumn cash receipts journal. Then the total of the Accounts Receivable column in the cash receipts journal was posted at the end of the month as a credit to the Accounts Receivable account.

CASH RECEIPTS JOURNAL for Month of January 19X2   Page 1

DATE		EXPLANATION	✓	ACCOUNTS RECEIVABLE CR. 111	CLEANING SERVICE SALES CR. 401	CASH DR. 101
Jan.	7	Cash sales			700 00	700 00
	9	December customers		200 00		200 00
	14	Cash sales			725 00	725 00
	16	Ruth Carr		30 00		30 00
	21	Cash sales			900 00	900 00
	23	Ruth Carr		30 00		30 00
	23	John Costa		15 00		15 00
	27	Cash sales			800 00	800 00
	29	John Costa		10 00		10 00
	31	Totals		285 00	3,125 00	3,410 00
				(111)	(401)	(101)

Accounts Receivable   **No. 111**

DATE		EXPLANATION	POST. REF.	DEBIT	CREDIT	BALANCE	DR. CR.
19 X2							
Jan.	1	Balance	✓			200 00	Dr.
	31		S1	175 00		375 00	Dr.
	31		CR1		285 00	90 00	Dr.

The end-of-month posting to the Cleaning Service Sales account and the Cash account is not shown at this time to save space.

The Need for More Information

After the sales and cash receipts figures have been posted to the Accounts Receivable account, the accountant knows that the balance of $90 represents the amount owed by credit customers at the end of January. Although this balance is useful, it does not give the accountant all the information he needs. For instance, it does not tell him who owes the money or how long each debt has remained unpaid.

To understand the accountant's problem more clearly, suppose that Ruth Carr, a credit customer, telephones and asks how much she owes to the Modern Cleaning Shop. Under the present system, Stein would have to check through all the entries in the sales journal to find the amounts sold to Carr. Next, he would have to look through all the entries in the cash receipts journal to find out how much Carr had paid on her debt. Then he would have to check the general journal for possible sales returns and allowances. Finally, after adding all sales and deducting all amounts paid and credits allowed, Stein would be able to determine the amount still owed by the customer.

The accountant is too busy to spend this much time answering a routine question. Also, the customer cannot be expected to wait so long for an answer. If a few requests like this one were made every day, the accountant would have to neglect his other work. It is obvious that a better system must be devised.

Accounts for Individual Credit Customers

In order to give customers the information they ask for, the firm needs an individual account for each credit customer. This account shows all transactions with the customer and the balance owed at any given time. Requests for information may also come from managers and salespeople in the company and from banks and credit bureaus. This makes individual customer accounts even more necessary.

Although the customer's account may be recorded on the standard ledger form, which has debits on the left side and credits on the right side, this form is not the most efficient. An account form is needed that will show the balance the customer owes at all times. To meet this need, it is customary to use a three-column balance ledger form for the accounts of credit customers. This form is similar to the balance ledger form that the Modern Cleaning Shop has adopted for its general ledger accounts.

The balance owed on January 31, 19X2, by each customer of the Modern Cleaning Shop has been entered in the balance-form ledger sheets shown below and on page 172. The date used for the balances is February 1, 19X2, the first day of the next accounting period.

Balances in these accounts are presumed to be debit balances because asset accounts usually have debit balances. Occasionally, there are credit bal-

NAME: Janet Bell
ADDRESS: 1069 Warren Street
Dallas, TX 75215
TERMS: n/30

DATE	DESCRIPTION	POST. REF.	DEBIT	CREDIT	BALANCE
19 X2 Feb. 1	Balance	✓			60 00

NAME: Ruth Carr
ADDRESS: 14 Oak Lane
Dallas, TX 75226
TERMS: n/30

DATE	DESCRIPTION	POST. REF.	DEBIT	CREDIT	BALANCE
19 X2 Feb. 1	Balance	✓			–0–

NAME:	John Costa				TERMS: n/30
ADDRESS:	49 Vista Road Dallas, TX 75217				

DATE	DESCRIPTION	POST. REF.	DEBIT	CREDIT	BALANCE
19 X2 Feb. 1	Balance	✓			—0—

NAME:	Roy Hess				TERMS: n/30
ADDRESS:	611 Tenth Avenue Dallas, TX 75203				

DATE	DESCRIPTION	POST. REF.	DEBIT	CREDIT	BALANCE
19 X2 Feb. 1	Balance	✓			30 00

ances because a customer has overpaid the account or has returned goods that have already been paid for and has received credit. In these cases, the credit balances are indicated by a "Cr." notation, parentheses, or a circle around the balance amount.

The accounts for credit customers are kept alphabetically or by account number in the accounts receivable ledger. This ledger is known as a subsidiary ledger because it is separate from and subordinate to the general ledger. The establishment of the accounts receivable ledger is another example of the way in which the accountant designs the accounting system so that similar items are grouped together for convenient reference. Beginning in February, all transactions that the Modern Cleaning Shop has with credit customers will be posted to the accounts receivable ledger.

Revising the Sales Journal

You may recall that the Modern Cleaning Shop plans to open an accessories department on February 1, 19X2. Obviously, the owner will want to keep a close watch on the progress made by the new department. To help Reed do this more easily, the accountant arranges to gather separate revenue figures for sales of cleaning services and sales of accessories. A new revenue account, Accessories Sales 402, is therefore opened in the general ledger.

Then, separate columns are set up in the sales journal for assembling the information that will be posted to the separate revenue accounts at the end of the period. Since sales of cleaning services and accessories may be made to a single customer and listed on a single sales slip, the sales journal should also provide a column for entering the charge to the customer's account, as was done before.

Recording the Sale

The procedure for recording a credit sale remains very much the same. The total of each sale is entered in the Accounts Receivable Debit column and in the appropriate Sales column (or columns) as a credit (or credits). The revenue columns permit classification of the sales according to type. When the Modern Cleaning Shop sells cleaning services for $20 on credit to a new customer, James Allen, on February 1, the following entry is made in the sales journal.

SALES JOURNAL for Month of February 19X2   Page 2

DATE	SALES SLIP NO.	CUSTOMER'S NAME	✓	ACCOUNTS RECEIVABLE DR. 111	CLEANING SERVICE SALES CR. 401	ACCES- SORIES SALES CR. 402
Feb. 1	5	James Allen		20 00	20 00	

Posting the Sale to the Customer's Account

Because the Modern Cleaning Shop is now using an accounts receivable ledger, a new procedure is added when a credit sale is recorded. The amount of the sale is posted immediately to the customer's account in the accounts receivable ledger. The posting of the sale to the account for James Allen is shown below.

NAME: James Allen
ADDRESS: 216 Lawson Street
Dallas, TX 75227   **TERMS:** n/30

DATE	DESCRIPTION	POST. REF.	DEBIT	CREDIT	BALANCE
19 X2 Feb. 1	Sales Slip 5	S2	20 00		20 00

After the entry is posted to Allen's account, the accountant puts a check mark (✓) in the Accounts Receivable section of the sales journal, as shown.

SALES JOURNAL for Month of February 19X2   Page 2

DATE	SALES SLIP NO.	CUSTOMER'S NAME	✓	ACCOUNTS RECEIVABLE DR. 111	CLEANING SERVICE SALES CR. 401	ACCES- SORIES SALES CR. 402
Feb. 1	5	James Allen	✓	20 00	20 00	

Revising the Cash Receipts Journal

The establishment of the accessories department also requires that the cash receipts journal be expanded to include separate columns for the revenue that each department earns from cash sales. Therefore, the accountant adds a new column headed Accessories Sales Cr. 402.

Recording Collections

The procedure for journalizing a collection from a credit customer remains the same as before. If Allen pays $5 on his account on February 4, the entry in

173

a multicolumn cash receipts journal would be made as shown in the following illustration. Note that only the customer's name is recorded in the Explanation column, since the debit to Cash and the credit to Accounts Receivable indicate a collection on account.

CASH RECEIPTS JOURNAL for Month of February 19X2   Page 2

DATE	EXPLANATION	✓	ACCOUNTS RECEIVABLE CR. 111	CLEANING SERVICE SALES CR. 401	ACCESSORIES SALES CR. 402	CASH DR. 101
Feb. 4	James Allen		5 00			5 00

Posting the Receipt to the Customer's Account

After the cash received from the customer is journalized, it is posted immediately to the customer's account in the accounts receivable ledger as shown below. Again, this is a new procedure.

NAME: James Allen
ADDRESS: 216 Lawson Street
Dallas, TX 75227   **TERMS:** n/30

DATE	DESCRIPTION	POST. REF.	DEBIT	CREDIT	BALANCE
19 X2 Feb. 1	Sales Slip 5	S2	20 00		20 00
4		CR2		5 00	15 00

A check mark is placed in the Accounts Receivable section of the cash receipts journal to show that the entry has been posted to the subsidiary ledger.

CASH RECEIPTS JOURNAL for Month of February 19X2   Page 2

DATE	EXPLANATION	✓	ACCOUNTS RECEIVABLE CR. 111	CLEANING SERVICE SALES CR. 401	ACCESSORIES SALES CR. 402	CASH DR. 101
Feb. 4	James Allen	✓	5 00			5 00

Recording Sales Returns and Allowances

As you learned in Unit 9, a customer may find that goods are not satisfactory for some reason. In some cases, the seller permits the customer to return the merchandise for credit. This is a sales return. In other cases, the customer may keep the goods and accept a reduction in the amount paid or owed. This reduction is called a sales allowance.

In the accounting system used by the Modern Cleaning Shop, the entry for a sales return or allowance is recorded in the general journal. With the addition of the accessories department, separate accounts must be kept for the returns and allowances on service transactions and those on merchandise transactions. Thus, from now on, the entry for a return or allowance will consist of a debit to either Sales Returns and Allowances—Cleaning Service 451 or Sales Returns and Allowances—Accessories 452. The Accounts Receivable account is credited as before. However, since an accounts receivable ledger is now being used, it is also necessary to credit the individual customer's account.

For example, suppose that Anthony Bruno, a credit customer, returns defective goods to the Modern Cleaning Shop on February 5. The entry in the general journal for this return is shown below.

19X2				
Feb. 5	Sales Ret. and Allow.—Accessories	452	10 00	
	Accounts Receivable/Anthony Bruno	111/✓		10 00
	Return of accessories sold on February 4, Sales Slip 7.			

Notice that the accountant indicates by means of a diagonal line in the Posting Reference column that two credit postings have been made. The 111 refers to the Accounts Receivable account in the general ledger. The check mark refers to Bruno's account in the accounts receivable ledger.

Posting Sales Returns and Allowances

General journal entries are always posted immediately to the proper accounts in the general ledger and in the accounts receivable ledger. The accounts affected by the general journal entry illustrated above are shown below and on page 176.

Sales Returns and Allowances—Accessories   No. 452

DATE	EXPLANATION	POST. REF.	DEBIT	CREDIT	BALANCE	DR. CR.
19X2 Feb. 5		J2	10 00		10 00	Dr.

Accounts Receivable   No. 111

DATE	EXPLANATION	POST. REF.	DEBIT	CREDIT	BALANCE	DR. CR.
19X2 Jan. 1	Balance	✓			200 00	Dr.
31		S1	175 00		375 00	Dr.
31		CR1		285 00	90 00	Dr.
Feb. 5		J2		10 00	80 00	Dr.

NAME:	Anthony Bruno				
ADDRESS:	9 Glen Road				
	Dallas, TX 75216			**TERMS:**	n/30

DATE	DESCRIPTION	POST. REF.	DEBIT	CREDIT	BALANCE
19 X2					
Feb. 4	Sales Slip 7	S2	25 00		25 00
5		J2		10 00	15 00

Sales Returns and Allowances Journal

At the Modern Cleaning Shop, sales returns and allowances are recorded in the general journal because the firm has few such transactions. However, in a larger business, these transactions may occur often enough to justify the use of another special journal, the sales returns and allowances journal. Here is how a sales returns and allowances journal might look in a company whose sales are subject to a sales tax.

SALES RETURNS AND ALLOWANCES JOURNAL for Month of July 19X1   Page 1

DATE	SALES SLIP NO.	CUSTOMER'S NAME		ACCOUNTS RECEIVABLE CR. 111	SALES TAX PAYABLE DR. 231	SALES RET. & ALLOW.— CLEAN. SERV. DR. 451	SALES RET. & ALLOW.— ACCES. DR. 452
July 2	2346	James Doyle	✓	20 60	60	20 00	
2	2347	Sally Hanson	✓	15 45	45	15 00	
30	2861	Tom Wilenski	✓	6 18	18		6 00
31		Totals		540 00	15 72	518 28	6 00
				(111)	(231)	(451)	(452)

The credits are posted daily from this special journal to the individual customers' accounts in the accounts receivable ledger. A check mark is entered in the Accounts Receivable section after each posting has been made. At the end of the month, the column totals are posted to the proper general ledger accounts (Accounts Receivable, Sales Tax Payable, Sales Returns and Allowances—Cleaning Service, and Sales Returns and Allowances—Accessories).

Daily Routine

Each credit sale made during the month at the Modern Cleaning Shop is recorded in the sales journal and is then posted at once to the account of the customer involved. The February transactions of this type are illustrated below as they appear in the sales journal.

SALES JOURNAL for Month of February 19X2 Page 2

DATE	SALES SLIP NO.	CUSTOMER'S NAME	ACCOUNTS RECEIVABLE ✓	DR. 111	CLEANING SERVICE SALES CR. 401	ACCESSORIES SALES CR. 402
Feb. 1	5	James Allen	✓	20 00	20 00	
2	6	Helen Pace	✓	10 00	10 00	
4	7	Anthony Bruno	✓	25 00		25 00
10	8	Marilyn Diaz	✓	25 00		25 00
12	9	James Allen	✓	7 00	7 00	
15	10	Ruth Carr	✓	10 00		10 00
19	11	John Costa	✓	15 00		15 00
23	12	David Fisher	✓	20 00	20 00	
26	13	Karen Drake	✓	12 00		12 00

Each cash receipt from a credit customer making a payment on account is entered in the cash receipts journal and then posted at once to the customer's account. The February transactions of this type are shown below.

CASH RECEIPTS JOURNAL for Month of February 19X2 Page 2

DATE	EXPLANATION	ACCOUNTS RECEIVABLE ✓	CR. 111	CLEANING SERVICE SALES CR. 401	ACCESSORIES SALES CR. 402	CASH DR. 101
Feb. 4	James Allen	✓	5 00			5 00
10	Helen Pace	✓	10 00			10 00
11	Anthony Bruno	✓	15 00			15 00
20	Marilyn Diaz	✓	20 00			20 00
21	James Allen	✓	15 00			15 00
26	John Costa	✓	15 00			15 00

Each return or allowance is entered in the general journal and posted at once to the general ledger and subsidiary ledger accounts involved. The only other credit customer besides Anthony Bruno to return defective accessories during February was Karen Drake. The general journal entry gives all the details.

19X2				
Feb. 28	Sales Ret. and Allow.—Accessories	452	2 00	
	Accounts Receivable/Karen Drake	111/✓		2 00
	Return of accessories sold on February 26, Sales Slip 13.			

177

Subsidiary Ledger Account Balances

After the February transactions have been posted, the customers' accounts in the accounts receivable ledger reflect a variety of entries, as shown below and on pages 179 and 180.

NAME: James Allen
ADDRESS: 216 Lawson Street
Dallas, TX 75227
TERMS: n/30

DATE	DESCRIPTION	POST. REF.	DEBIT	CREDIT	BALANCE
19 X2					
Feb. 1	Sales Slip 5	S2	20 00		20 00
4		CR2		5 00	15 00
12	Sales Slip 9	S2	7 00		22 00
21		CR2		15 00	7 00

NAME: Janet Bell
ADDRESS: 1069 Warren Street
Dallas, TX 75215
TERMS: n/30

DATE	DESCRIPTION	POST. REF.	DEBIT	CREDIT	BALANCE
19 X2					
Feb. 1	Balance	✓			60 00

NAME: Anthony Bruno
ADDRESS: 9 Glen Road
Dallas, TX 75216
TERMS: n/30

DATE	DESCRIPTION	POST. REF.	DEBIT	CREDIT	BALANCE
19 X2					
Feb. 4	Sales Slip 7	S2	25 00		25 00
5		J2		10 00	15 00
11		CR2		15 00	-0-

NAME: Ruth Carr
ADDRESS: 14 Oak Lane
Dallas, TX 75226
TERMS: n/30

DATE	DESCRIPTION	POST. REF.	DEBIT	CREDIT	BALANCE
19 X2					
Feb. 1	Balance	✓			-0-
15	Sales Slip 10	S2	10 00		10 00

NAME: John Costa
ADDRESS: 49 Vista Road
Dallas, TX 75217
TERMS: n/30

DATE		DESCRIPTION	POST. REF.	DEBIT	CREDIT	BALANCE
19X2						
Feb.	1	Balance	✓			-0-
	19	Sales Slip 11	S2	15 00		15 00
	26		CR2		15 00	-0-

NAME: Marilyn Diaz
ADDRESS: 2147 Lake Drive
Dallas, TX 75219
TERMS: n/30

DATE		DESCRIPTION	POST. REF.	DEBIT	CREDIT	BALANCE
19X2						
Feb.	10	Sales Slip 8	S2	25 00		25 00
	20		CR2		20 00	5 00

NAME: Karen Drake
ADDRESS: 1026 Barr Street
Dallas, TX 75217
TERMS: n/30

DATE		DESCRIPTION	POST. REF.	DEBIT	CREDIT	BALANCE
19X2						
Feb.	26	Sales Slip 13	S2	12 00		12 00
	28		J2		2 00	10 00

NAME: David Fisher
ADDRESS: 147 First Street
Dallas, TX 75226
TERMS: n/30

DATE		DESCRIPTION	POST. REF.	DEBIT	CREDIT	BALANCE
19X2						
Feb.	23	Sales Slip 12	S2	20 00		20 00

NAME: Roy Hess
ADDRESS: 611 Tenth Avenue
Dallas, TX 75203
TERMS: n/30

DATE		DESCRIPTION	POST. REF.	DEBIT	CREDIT	BALANCE
19X2						
Feb.	1	Balance	✓			30 00

NAME:	Helen Pace				
ADDRESS:	10 Station Plaza				
	Dallas, TX 75219			**TERMS:**	n/30

DATE	DESCRIPTION	POST. REF.	DEBIT	CREDIT	BALANCE
19 X2					
Feb. 2	Sales Slip 6	S2	10 00		10 00
10		CR2		10 00	-0-

End-of-Month Routine

At the end of the month, the accountant totals the columns in the sales journal. He then posts the totals to the general ledger accounts indicated: $144 to Accounts Receivable, $57 to Cleaning Service Sales, and $87 to Accessories Sales.

SALES JOURNAL for Month of February 19X2 Page 2

DATE	SALES SLIP NO.	CUSTOMER'S NAME	✓	ACCOUNTS RECEIVABLE DR. 111	CLEANING SERVICE SALES CR. 401	ACCESSORIES SALES CR. 402
Feb. 1	5	James Allen	✓	20 00	20 00	
2	6	Helen Pace	✓	10 00	10 00	
4	7	Anthony Bruno	✓	25 00		25 00
10	8	Marilyn Diaz	✓	25 00		25 00
12	9	James Allen	✓	7 00	7 00	
15	10	Ruth Carr	✓	10 00		10 00
19	11	John Costa	✓	15 00		15 00
23	12	David Fisher	✓	20 00	20 00	
26	13	Karen Drake	✓	12 00		12 00
28		Totals		144 00	57 00	87 00
				(111)	(401)	(402)

The procedure for posting totals from the cash receipts journal is similar. All columns are totaled, and then the totals are posted to the accounts named in the column headings. The total of the Accounts Receivable Credit column is shown here to illustrate the procedure.

CASH RECEIPTS JOURNAL for Month of Feburary 19X2 Page 2

DATE	EXPLANATION	✓	ACCOUNTS RECEIVABLE CR. 111	CLEANING SERVICE SALES CR. 401	ACCESSORIES SALES CR. 402	CASH DR. 101
Feb. 4	James Allen	✓	5 00			5 00
28	Totals		80 00			
			(111)			

After the totals from the sales journal and the cash receipts journal are posted to the general ledger, the Accounts Receivable account looks like this.

DATE		EXPLANATION	POST. REF.	DEBIT	CREDIT	BALANCE	DR. CR.
19 X2							
Jan.	1	Balance	✓			200 00	Dr.
	31		S1	175 00		375 00	Dr.
	31		CR1		285 00	90 00	Dr.
Feb.	5		J2		10 00	80 00	Dr.
	28		J2		2 00	78 00	Dr.
	28		S2	144 00		222 00	Dr.
	28		CR2		80 00	142 00	Dr.

Accounts Receivable No. 111

Proving the Subsidiary Ledger

After all the postings are made from the sales journal, cash receipts journal, and general journal to the subsidiary and general ledger accounts, the accountant checks the accuracy of his work. This is a two-step process.

1. The accountant prepares a list of the credit customers and the balances they owe. This list is called a *schedule of accounts receivable*. The accountant then adds all balances to determine the total owed by the customers. Here are the balances taken from the accounts illustrated on pages 178-180.

Modern Cleaning Shop
Schedule of Accounts Receivable
February 28, 19X2

Customer	Balance
James Allen	7 00
Janet Bell	60 00
Ruth Carr	10 00
Marilyn Diaz	5 00
Karen Drake	10 00
David Fisher	20 00
Roy Hess	30 00
Total Due From Customers	142 00

Notice that when a schedule of accounts receivable is prepared only the accounts that have balances are listed in order to save time and space. The accounts of Anthony Bruno, John Costa, and Helen Pace are omitted because they have no balances on February 28.

2. The accountant compares the total due from the credit customers with the balance of the Accounts Receivable account in the general ledger. In this case, the total of $142 obtained in Step 1 agrees with the balance of the Accounts Receivable account shown above.

The procedure described in Step 2 is called proving the subsidiary ledger accounts against the control account. The Accounts Receivable account in the general ledger is known as a *control account* because it summarizes many amounts and thereby provides an independent proof of accuracy. At the end of each month, the Accounts Receivable account contains several important totals. For example, on February 28 the Accounts Receivable account for the Modern Cleaning Shop showed the following figures for February.

1. What customers owed at the beginning of the month, $90. (This amount is indicated by the balance on January 31.)
2. What customers bought on credit, increasing their debts, $144.
3. What customers received as credits on returns and allowances, $10 and $2.
4. What customers paid to reduce their debts, $80.

The balance of the Accounts Receivable account is the amount that credit customers still owe. This account provides a proof of the subsidiary ledger for accounts receivable because its final balance should be the same as the total of all the balances in the customers' accounts. From now on, the Accounts Receivable account in the general ledger of the Modern Cleaning Shop will be called the Accounts Receivable Control account.

Accounts Receivable From Credit Card Company Sales

In previous units, you learned that open-account credit arrangements such as those adopted by the Modern Cleaning Shop are widely used by small businesses and by many professionals. The amounts of these credit sales are debited to the Accounts Receivable Control account and credited to a revenue account in the general ledger. Individual accounts for the credit customers are maintained in an accounts receivable subsidiary ledger.

Credit sales made on the basis of credit cards that a firm has issued to its own customers are accounted for in the same way as open-account sales. This is understandable because the firm itself is providing the credit. Bank credit card sales, on the other hand, are accounted for in much the same manner as cash sales. For these sales, no accounts receivable records are needed by the seller.

The procedure used to account for sales made on the basis of credit cards issued by credit card companies is similar to the procedure for recording open-account sales. However, an important difference is that the account receivable is with the credit card company, not with the cardholders who buy the goods or services. Such sales are usually credited to the same revenue account that is used for other types of credit sales. The debit part of the entry can be handled in two ways.

Businesses that have few transactions with credit card companies may debit the amounts of such sales to the usual Accounts Receivable Control account in the general ledger and provide an individual account for each credit card company in the accounts receivable subsidiary ledger.

On the other hand, firms that do a large volume of business with credit card companies may debit all such sales to a special Accounts Receivable From Credit Card Companies account in the general ledger, thus separating this type of receivable from the accounts receivable resulting from open-account sales. Subsidiary ledger accounts may not be needed. Instead, a file is maintained of copies of the periodic summaries submitted to the credit card companies for payment. The total amount of the unpaid summaries in the file at any time should equal the balance of the Accounts Receivable From Credit Card Companies account in the general ledger at the same time. Selected transactions of this nature are illustrated below and on page 184. (For purposes of this illustration, opening and closing account balances and the effects of other transactions have been ignored.)

SALES JOURNAL for Month of July 19X1 — Page 7

DATE	SALES SLIP NO.	CUSTOMER'S NAME	ACCOUNTS RECEIVABLE DR. 111	ACCTS. REC.— CREDIT CARD COMPANIES DR. 114	SALES TAX PAYABLE CR. 231	SALES CR. 401	SALES— CREDIT CARD COMPANIES CR. 404
July 6		Summary of credit card sales/American Express		3,090 00	90 00		3,000 00
10		Summary of credit card sales/Diners Club		2,008 50	58 50		1,950 00
31		Totals		18,952 00	552 00		18,400 00
				(114)	(231)		(404)

CASH RECEIPTS JOURNAL for Month of July 19X1 — Page 7

DATE	EXPLANATION	ACCOUNTS RECEIVABLE CR. 111	ACCTS. REC.— CREDIT CARD COMPANIES CR. 114	SALES TAX PAYABLE CR. 231	SALES CR. 401	DISC. EXP. ON CREDIT CARD SALES DR. 592	CASH DR. 101
July 20	Summary of 7/6/American Express		3,090 00			216 30	2,873 70
25	Summary of 7/10/Diners Club		2,008 50			140 60	1,867 90
31	Totals		16,391 00			1,147 37	15,243 63
			(114)			(592)	(101)

Cash — No. 101

DATE	EXPLANATION	POST. REF.	DEBIT	CREDIT	BALANCE	DR. CR.
19X1 July 31		CR7	15,243 63		15,243 63	Dr.

Accounts Receivable From Credit Card Companies — No. 114

DATE	EXPLANATION	POST. REF.	DEBIT	CREDIT	BALANCE	DR. CR.
19X1 July 31		S7	18,952 00		18,952 00	Dr.
31		CR7		16,391 00	2,561 00	Dr.

Sales Tax Payable					No. 231	
DATE	EXPLANATION	POST. REF.	DEBIT	CREDIT	BALANCE	DR. CR.
19X1 July 31		S7		552 00	552 00	Cr.

Sales—Credit Card Companies					No. 404	
DATE	EXPLANATION	POST. REF.	DEBIT	CREDIT	BALANCE	DR. CR.
19X1 July 31		S7		18,400 00	18,400 00	Cr.

Discount Expense on Credit Card Sales					No. 592	
DATE	EXPLANATION	POST. REF.	DEBIT	CREDIT	BALANCE	DR. CR.
19X1 July 31		CR7	1,147 37		1,147 37	Dr.

principles and procedures summary

Accounts with individual credit customers are usually kept in a subsidiary ledger called the accounts receivable ledger. Daily postings are made to this ledger from the sales journal, the cash receipts journal, and the general journal. The current balance of a customer's account is computed after each posting so that the amount owed is known at all times.

When all entries have been posted for the month, the balances in the customers' accounts are added together to compute the total amount owed. This total is then compared with the balance of the Accounts Receivable Control account in the general ledger. The two amounts should be the same.

When a firm has more than one type of sales revenue, separate revenue accounts may be used. If this is done, provision must be made in the sales journal and the cash receipts journal for recording each type of revenue.

managerial implications

The use of an accounts receivable subsidiary ledger provides the manager and the credit department with up-to-date information about the balance owed by each customer. This is of special value in setting, reappraising, or carrying out credit and collection policies. The control feature of the accounts receivable subsidiary ledger system provides an additional proof of the accuracy of the accounting records. When customers' accounts are maintained efficiently and proved periodically, there will be better customer relations and less chance of misunderstanding.

managerial discussion questions

1. How can accounting records help management develop and maintain sound credit and collection policies?
2. What are some of the advantages of keeping an accounts receivable subsidiary ledger?
3. How does a control account aid management?

application of principles

PROBLEM 10-1   On October 1, 19X1, the Sun Electronic Service opened a new department for the sale of radios, television sets, and cassette players. Its repair service operations will continue as before. The revenue received from the sale of merchandise is to be recorded separately from the revenue arising from services provided. The general ledger accounts used in recording the firm's credit sales are as follows.

ACCOUNTS

101	Cash	$4,021.00
111	Accounts Receivable Control	1,439.24
401	Repair Service Sales	-0-
402	Merchandise Sales	-0-
403	Sales Returns and Allowances	-0-

The company uses a sales journal with special columns for Accounts Receivable Dr. 111, Repair Service Sales Cr. 401, and Merchandise Sales Cr. 402. The cash receipts journal has special columns for Accounts Receivable Cr. 111, Repair Service Sales Cr. 401, Merchandise Sales Cr. 402, and Cash Dr. 101.

Beginning October 1, 19X1, an accounts receivable subsidiary ledger is to be kept using balance-form ledger sheets. A list of the individual account balances as of September 30 follows. (Addresses are intentionally omitted here and in future problems containing subsidiary ledgers.)

ACCOUNTS

Armstrong Hospital	$ 55.40
Cannon College	225.60
Linda Glenn	9.26
Susan Harvey	40.00
Henry Heller	5.25
Lee's Garden Apartments	110.50
Mesa Motel	210.69
Newville Community Center	167.29
Charles Searle and Co.	245.15
Star Nursing Home	370.10
Total Due From Customers	$1,439.24

The October 19X1 transactions involving the sale of merchandise and services as well as the receipt of cash are shown below and on the next page.

INSTRUCTIONS
1. Open the general ledger accounts, and enter the balances.
2. Open the accounts receivable subsidiary ledger. (A separate ledger account should be used for each customer listed here.) Enter the customer's name, the year, the date of October 1, the word "Balance" in the Description column, a check mark in the Posting Reference column, and the amount in the Balance column. Open accounts for new customers as required. The customary terms are 30 days net.
3. Prove the accuracy of your work by doing the following. List the balances owed by credit customers as shown in the accounts receivable subsidiary ledger. Add the balances, and compare the resulting total with the balance of the Accounts Receivable Control account in the general ledger and with the total of the schedule of accounts receivable shown above. Use a separate sheet of paper for this step.
4. Record each transaction in the appropriate journal. Use *10* as the journal page number.
5. Complete the required daily and summary postings to the general ledger and to the accounts receivable ledger.
6. Prepare a schedule of accounts receivable as of October 31, 19X1, and prove the total by comparing it with the balance of the control account.

TRANSACTIONS FOR OCTOBER 19X1

Oct. 1 Received $210.69 from the Mesa Motel in payment of Sept. 5 sale. Sold repair services on credit for $48.50 to James Carpenter, Sales Slip 101.

3 Sold a $249.75 portable television set for cash. Sold repair services for $25 to Arthur Salsky, Sales Slip 102, payable in 30 days.

3 Received a check for $35.40 from Armstrong Hospital to apply on account. Sold a cassette player for $46.85 to Susan Harvey on credit, Sales Slip 103. A check for $135.10 was received from the Star Nursing Home to apply toward its account.

5   Received $5.25 from Henry Heller to balance his account. Sold a portable AM-FM radio for $179.50 to Linda Glenn, Sales Slip 104, due in 30 days.

6   Sold and delivered two television sets for a total of $685 to Cannon College, Sales Slip 105, terms net 30 days. Cash sales for the day were services, $150.50, and merchandise, $265.90.

9   Made the following credit sales of merchandise: Sales Slip 106 to Eastern College, $218.75, and Sales Slip 107 to Robert Miller, $55. Also received $20 in cash for a small repair job.

10 Received a check for $225.60 from Cannon College in payment of its September balance. Received $32.50 cash for repair services provided today.

11 Made a $75.95 credit sale of merchandise to Ronald Nelson, Sales Slip 108. Sales Slip 109 covers a $49.10 credit sale of a portable radio to Harold Geiger.

12 Sold $130.50 worth of merchandise for cash.

13 Received a check for $40 from Susan Harvey, in payment of her September account. Sold merchandise for $110 on credit to The Bus Depot Shop, Sales Slip 110.

16 Sold merchandise for $117.50 in cash. Sold merchandise for $45.56 on credit to the Star Nursing Home, Sales Slip 111.

17 Received a $50 check from Newville Community Center to apply on its September account. Provided $30 of repair services on credit for the Mesa Motel, Sales Slip 112.

18 Made cash sales of $85.60 for merchandise sold today. Also sold $275 of merchandise to Eastern College on credit, Sales Slip 113.

19 Sold merchandise for $85 to James Carpenter on Sales Slip 114. Received a $25 check from Arthur Salsky in payment of Sales Slip 102.

22 Gave credit of $342.50 to Cannon College for the return of one of the television sets originally charged on Sales Slip 105, dated October 6.

23 Sold $57.95 of merchandise for cash.

24 Sold a $61.55 cassette player to Ronald Nelson, Sales Slip 115.

25 Henry Heller, a charge customer, bought a $45.95 portable radio on Sales Slip 116; Robert Christianson purchased a $30.50 clock radio on Sales Slip 117, also on credit.

27 Sold merchandise for $150.25 in cash today. Received a $110.50 check from Lee's Garden Apartments in payment of the September account.

29 Gave an allowance of $15 to James Carpenter due to a scratch on a radio purchased on October 19, Sales Slip 114.

30 Sold merchandise amounting to $65.15 in cash. Issued Sales Slip 118 to cover the credit sale of $40 of repair services to Charles Searle and Co.

31 Sold merchandise for $129.49 to The Bus Depot Shop on credit, Sales Slip 119.

alternate problem

PROBLEM 10-1A On July 1, 19X1, a new department of the Royal Venetian Blind Company was established for repairing and cleaning venetian blinds. The revenue received from services provided and merchandise sold is to be recorded separately. The general ledger accounts to be used in recording the firm's sales are as follows.

ACCOUNTS

101	Cash	$4,760.25
111	Accounts Receivable Control	2,409.05
401	Venetian Blind Sales	-0-
402	Repair and Cleaning Service Sales	-0-
403	Sales Returns and Allowances	-0-

The company uses a sales journal with special columns for Accounts Receivable Dr. 111, Venetian Blind Sales Cr. 401, and Repair and Cleaning Service Sales Cr. 402. The cash receipts journal has special columns for Accounts Receivable Cr. 111, Venetian Blind Sales Cr. 401, Repair and Cleaning Service Sales Cr. 402, and Cash Dr. 101.

Beginning July 1, 19X1, an accounts receivable subsidiary ledger is to be kept, using balance-form ledger sheets. A list of the individual account balances as of June 30 follows. (Addresses are intentionally omitted here and in future problems containing subsidiary ledgers.)

ACCOUNTS

George Aiken	$ 15.65
Allied Can Company	1,335.75
Alpine School	-0-
Broadway School	289.95
Rufus Collins	88.50
Raymond Gano	115.75
Hatton Clothing	-0-
Milton Apartments	315.05
Judy Paine	23.40
Perkins Drug Store	-0-
Leon Rowland	225.00
Total Due From Customers	$2,409.05

The July 19X1 transactions involving the sale of merchandise and services as well as the receipt of cash are shown on pages 189 and 190.

INSTRUCTIONS
1. Open the general ledger accounts, and enter the balances.
2. Open the accounts receivable subsidiary ledger. (A separate ledger account should be used for each customer listed here.) Enter the customer's name, the year, the date of July 1, the word "Balance" in the Description column, a check mark in the Posting Reference column, and the amount

in the Balance column. Open accounts for new customers as required. The customary terms are 30 days net.
3. Prove the accuracy of your work by doing the following. List the balances owed by credit customers as shown in the accounts receivable subsidiary ledger. Add the balances, and compare the resulting total with the balance of the Accounts Receivable Control account in the general ledger and with the total of the schedule of accounts receivable shown on page 188. Use a separate sheet of paper for this step.
4. Record each transaction in the appropriate journal. Use 7 for the journal page number.
5. Complete the required daily and summary postings to the general ledger and to the accounts receivable subsidiary ledger.
6. Prepare a schedule of accounts receivable as of July 31, 19X1, and prove the total by comparing it with the balance of the control account.

TRANSACTIONS FOR JULY 19X1

July 1 Sold venetian blinds for $63.35 on credit to Jenny Spangler, Sales Slip 102. Received $1,335.75 from the Allied Can Company in payment of a May 6 sale.

2 Received cash totaling $163.80 for installing blinds on two jobs. Charged $43 to repair blinds on credit for Olga Patterson, Sales Slip 103.

3 Received a $100 check from Milton Apartments to apply on account. Sold venetian blinds for $136.95 on credit to Hatton Clothing, Sales Slip 104. Sold Judy Paine one $12.50 venetian blind on credit, Sales Slip 105. Received $23.40 from Judy Paine in payment of her account as of June 30.

5 Sold venetian blinds costing $956.65 on credit to the Alpine School, Sales Slip 106. Received $88.50 on account from Rufus Collins.

6 Installed blinds at $422.80 for Perkins Drug Store on credit, Sales Slip 107. Cash sales today totaled $134 ($114 on the sale of blinds and $20 for cleaning service).

9 Made the following sales of blinds on credit today: Sales Slip 108, $55.95, to Larry Davis on special 60-day net terms; Sales Slip 109, $17.50, to George Aiken. Made a $27.35 repair for cash.

10 Received a check for $289.95 from the Broadway School in payment of the June 30 balance. Also received $39.25 in cash for blinds repaired today.

11 Made a credit sale of $38.45 for blinds to Noreen Langley, Sales Slip 110. Sales Slip 111 covers a credit sale of $76.75 for blinds to Edward Comary.

12 Received $235.70 in cash for blinds installed today.

13 Received a $15.65 check from George Aiken in payment of his account as of June 30. Sold $348 worth of venetian blinds on credit to Zeigler Radio Company, Sales Slip 112.

16 Received $97.50 in cash for venetian blinds. Sold venetian blinds on credit for $122.40, Sales Slip 113, to Milton Apartments.

17 Cleaned blinds for $24 on credit for Rufus Collins, Sales Slip 114. Leon Rowland delivered a check for $112.50 to apply to his account and promised to pay the balance on August 15.

18 Received a total of $164.30 from three different customers for cash sales of venetian blinds. Sales Slip 115 for $180 covers a special installation for the Broadway School.

19 Repaired venetian blinds for $24.65 on credit for Jenny Spangler, Sales Slip 116. Received a $43 check from Olga Patterson in payment of Sales Slip 103, dated July 2.

22 Gave a credit of $26.65 to the Alpine School for a venetian blind returned. It was originally charged on Sales Slip 106, dated July 5.

23 Installed blinds for $112 cash in one home today.

24 Made a credit sale of $21.55 for blinds today to Noreen Langley, Sales Slip 117.

25 Made credit sales of blinds for $46.80 to Leon Rowland, Sales Slip 118, and for $39.50 to Judy Paine, Sales Slip 119.

27 Collected $102.90 for venetian blinds installed today on a cash basis. Received a $215.05 check from Milton Apartments to complete payment of the June 30 balance of that account.

UNIT 11

THE PURCHASES JOURNAL

In the past few units, you have seen how an accountant can adjust a firm's accounting procedures to get the work done faster and more efficiently. The accountant must constantly be alert to make sure that the procedures being used are adequate to meet changes in the operations of the business.

Studying New Plans

When the accountant for the Modern Cleaning Shop hears about the owner's plans to open an accessories department on February 1, 19X2, he gives careful thought to the new accounting problems that may arise. He knows that a stock of merchandise must be bought and replenished from time to time. He can reasonably expect that most of the stock will be bought on credit. He can also expect the new department to increase both cash sales and credit sales. With these things in mind, the accountant then considers whether or not the firm's present recording methods are adequate to meet the new conditions.

The new demands from increased sales activities offer no problem. The added volume of credit sales can easily be handled through the sales journal. The revenue from sales in the new department can be identified and accumulated in a multicolumn sales journal with separate columns for Cleaning Service Sales and Accessories Sales. Collections from credit customers can be efficiently recorded in a multicolumn cash receipts journal. Provision can even be made for the possibility of returns and allowances arising from sales of both cleaning services and accessories by the use of new accounts called Sales Returns and Allowances–Cleaning Service and Sales Returns and Allowances–Accessories.

However, the firm's buying activities for the new department must be studied carefully. The cash payments made to cover purchases of merchandise on credit can be recorded in a multicolumn cash payments journal. But the accountant realizes that the only existing place to record the credit purchases themselves is in the general journal. Stein knows what will happen if the new transactions are recorded by using the present methods. For instance, suppose that the Modern Cleaning Shop makes the following credit purchases during February 19X2.

TRANSACTIONS OF FEBRUARY 19X2

Feb. 1 Purchased an initial stock of merchandise for $1,200 on credit from the Warren Wholesale Company. This amount is payable in 30 days. The supplier issues Invoice 649, dated February 1, 19X2, which is shown below.

WARREN WHOLESALE COMPANY
671 Valley Street
Topeka, Kansas 66614

SOLD TO: Modern Cleaning Shop
365 Broad Street
Dallas, TX 75201

INV. NO.: **649**

INV. DATE: 2/1/X2

TERMS: 30 days net

SHIP VIA: Truck prepaid

QUANTITY	ITEM	UNIT PRICE	AMOUNT
800	Sets, assorted hangers, 8 in set	$1.25	$1,000.00
100	Hat racks	2.50	250.00
50	Shoe racks	3.75	187.50
20	Tie racks	3.125	62.50
			$1,500.00
	Less 20%		300.00
			$1,200.00

13 Purchased additional merchandise for the accessories department for $300 on credit from the Best Products Company, payable in 30 days. The supplier issues Invoice A4973, dated February 12. (This invoice covers merchandise with a list price of $416.66, but Reed is given trade discounts of 20% and 10%.)

17 Purchased more merchandise for the accessories department on 20-day credit terms from Prestige Plastics, Inc. The supplier issues Invoice 43691 for $100 (net of discounts), dated February 15.

24 Purchased merchandise for $210 (net invoice price) from the Warren Wholesale Company to replace items sold. The same 30-day terms apply. The supplier issues Invoice 855, dated February 22.

Recording Merchandise Purchases in the General Journal

If the accountant records the February credit purchases of merchandise in the general journal, it would be necessary to make a separate entry for each purchase. When goods are bought, a new account, Merchandise Purchases 501, is debited so that a record of the stock acquired for the accessories department can be kept. The purchases of goods by a firm are considered a cost of doing business. The Merchandise Purchases account is therefore in the same group as the expense accounts. (This group is now called Costs and Expenses on the chart of accounts.) The liability, Accounts Payable, is credited for the goods bought on credit. Note that each purchase is recorded at the net invoice price (after trade discounts have been deducted). The four entries for February credit purchases would appear in the general journal as shown below.

19X2					
Feb. 1	Merchandise Purchases	501	1,200 00		
	Accounts Payable	202		1,200 00	
	Purchased merchandise from Warren Wholesale Company, terms 30 days; Invoice 649, dated 2/1/X2.				
13	Merchandise Purchases	501	300 00		
	Accounts Payable	202		300 00	
	Purchased merchandise from Best Products Company, terms 30 days; Invoice A4973, dated 2/12/X2.				
17	Merchandise Purchases	501	100 00		
	Accounts Payable	202		100 00	
	Purchased merchandise from Prestige Plastics, Inc., terms 20 days; Invoice 43691, dated 2/15/X2.				
24	Merchandise Purchases	501	210 00		
	Accounts Payable	202		210 00	
	Purchased merchandise from Warren Wholesale Company, terms 30 days; Invoice 855, dated 2/22/X2.				

These general journal entries would require four debit postings to the Merchandise Purchases account in the general ledger and four credit postings to the Accounts Payable account as shown below.

Merchandise Purchases   No. 501

DATE	EXPLANATION	POST. REF.	DEBIT	CREDIT	BALANCE	DR. CR.
19X2						
Feb. 1		J2	1,200 00		1,200 00	Dr.
13		J2	300 00		1,500 00	Dr.
17		J2	100 00		1,600 00	Dr.
24		J2	210 00		1,810 00	Dr.

Accounts Payable   No. 202

DATE	EXPLANATION	POST. REF.	DEBIT	CREDIT	BALANCE	DR. CR.
19X2						
Feb. 1	Balance	✓			500 00	Cr.
1		J2		1,200 00	1,700 00	Cr.
13		J2		300 00	2,000 00	Cr.
17		J2		100 00	2,100 00	Cr.
24		J2		210 00	2,310 00	Cr.

It is clear that it will be too time-consuming to make these repetitive entries in the general journal and repetitive postings to the general ledger accounts. The accountant avoids this wasted effort by designing a *purchases journal* to be used for recording purchases of merchandise made on credit.

Recording Entries in the Purchases Journal

The single-column purchases journal illustrated below reflects the same credit purchases that are shown on page 193 in general journal form.

The columns organize the vital information about each credit purchase. The record of the supplier's invoice number, invoice date, and terms helps the accountant relate the purchase to a specific invoice. It is especially important that the invoice date and terms be clearly shown so that the bills are paid at the proper time and any cash discounts are taken. The information necessary for each entry comes from the supplier's invoice, such as the one illustrated on page 192.

PURCHASES JOURNAL	FOR MONTH OF February 19 X2					PAGE 1
DATE	PURCHASED FROM	INV. NO.	INVOICE DATE	TERMS	✓	AMOUNT
Feb. 1	Warren Wholesale Company	649	2/1	n/30		1200 00
13	Best Products Company	A4973	2/12	n/30		300 00
17	Prestige Plastics, Inc.	43691	2/15	n/20		100 00
24	Warren Wholesale Company	855	2/22	n/30		210 00

Posting From the Purchases Journal

The posting process for the purchases journal is as simple as that used for the sales journal. The accountant waits until he has recorded the last credit purchase for the month. Then he adds the figures in the Amount column and enters the total of the purchases. Next, he posts the total as a debit to the Merchandise Purchases account and as a credit to the Accounts Payable account in the general ledger. The account numbers are entered beneath the total in the Amount column of the purchases journal to show that the figure has been posted. The following illustrations show how the purchases journal and the related general ledger accounts look when the posting is completed. Note that the abbreviation *P1* is used to identify the first page of the purchases journal as the source of the entry.

PURCHASES JOURNAL	FOR MONTH OF February 19 X2					PAGE 1
DATE	PURCHASED FROM	INV. NO.	INVOICE DATE	TERMS	✓	AMOUNT
Feb. 1	Warren Wholesale Company	649	2/1	n/30		1200 00
13	Best Products Company	A4973	2/12	n/30		300 00
17	Prestige Plastics, Inc.	43691	2/15	n/20		100 00
24	Warren Wholesale Company	855	2/22	n/30		210 00
28	Total Credit Purchases					1810 00
						(501)(202)

		Merchandise Purchases				NO. 501	
DATE	EXPLANATION		POST. REF.	DEBIT	CREDIT	BALANCE	DR. CR.
19 X2 Feb. 28			P1	1810 00		1810 00	Dr.

		Accounts Payable				NO. 202	
DATE	EXPLANATION		POST. REF.	DEBIT	CREDIT	BALANCE	DR. CR.
19 X2 Feb. 1	Balance		✓			500 00	Cr.
28			P1		1810 00	2310 00	Cr.

Advantages of the Purchases Journal

By using the purchases journal, the accountant simplifies the process of journalizing and posting purchases of merchandise on credit. Other credit purchases, such as equipment, must still be recorded in the general journal. In contrast to the many lines needed to record the four purchases in the general journal, only four lines are needed to record the same facts in the purchases journal. The posting process is also simplified because the accountant makes only two postings to the general ledger from the purchases journal at the end of the month. Even if more than four purchases were recorded in the purchases journal, at the end of the month the accountant would only have to make two postings. In addition to the saving in time and effort, there is still another advantage in using this special journal. There is now additional opportunity to divide the accounting work among different employees.

Recording Freight In

Some purchases are made with the understanding that the buyer will pay the cost of shipping the goods from the seller's warehouse. If the buyer pays the transportation company directly for the freight, a check is written and the transaction is entered in the cash payments journal. An account called Freight In 506 is used to record the cost of shipping goods from the seller. The amount paid is entered as a debit to Freight In and a credit to Cash. If freight payments are made often, a special column for recording them may be set up in the cash payments journal.

Sometimes the shipping cost is paid by the seller and then included in the bill for the goods sent to the purchaser. In this case, the entire entry is made in the purchases journal. Three elements are recorded, as in this example.

Cost of goods (to be debited to Merchandise Purchases)	$126.00
Shipping cost (to be debited to Freight In)	6.00
Amount of invoice (to be credited to Accounts Payable)	$132.00

The accountant can make up a multicolumn purchases journal that will permit recording of invoices that involve freight charges. Such a journal is shown below. As in the case of other multicolumn special journals, the columns are totaled and posted only at the end of the month in order to eliminate duplication of work.

PURCHASES JOURNAL for Month of June 19X2   **Page** 6

DATE	PURCHASED FROM	INVOICE NO.	INVOICE DATE	TERMS	✓	ACCOUNTS PAYABLE CR. 202	MERCH. PURCH. DR. 501	FREIGHT IN DR. 506
June 3	Dantz Company	2596	6/1	30 days		132 00	126 00	6 00

The balance of the Freight In account is shown on the income statement where it is added to the balance of the Merchandise Purchases account.

Purchases Returns and Allowances

After the information from the purchase invoice has been recorded in the purchases journal, the buyer may find that the goods are damaged or defective or different from the items ordered. If this is so, the seller is informed so that an allowance can be obtained or the goods can be returned for credit. Suppose that on February 27, Mary Gomez inspects the goods purchased from the Warren Wholesale Company on February 24. She finds that items with a price of $10 were not the ones ordered. She arranges with Warren to return these items and to give the Modern Cleaning Shop a $10 credit on the bill. The accountant records this return in the following way. Accounts Payable is reduced by $10, and a new account called Purchases Returns and Allowances 509 is credited. The entry is made in the general journal as shown below.

19 X2				
Feb. 27	Accounts Payable	202	10 00	
	Purchases Returns and Allowances	509		10 00
	Returned accessories purchased from Warren Wholesale Company on February 24, Invoice 855; found not as ordered.			

If there are numerous purchases returns and allowances, a special journal may be set up to record them.

Although it would be possible to credit Merchandise Purchases for the amounts of the purchases returns and allowances, the accountant prefers to keep a separate record of all such items. This separate record is useful for studies of purchasing efficiency and suppliers' performance and for preparing the income statement. (As you will learn later, the balance of the Purchases Returns and Allowances account is deducted from the balance of the Merchandise Purchases account in the Cost of Goods Sold section of the income statement.)

Internal Control of Purchases

Because of the large amounts of money spent for purchases, most businesses develop careful procedures for the control of purchases and their payment. In Unit 13 you will learn many of the detailed procedures that are used by businesses to achieve this internal control. Essentially, however, the control process involves the following safeguards.

1. All purchases are made only after proper authorization has been given in writing.
2. Goods are carefully checked when they are received. Then they are compared with the purchase order and with the invoice received from the supplier.
3. The computations on the invoice are checked for accuracy.
4. Authorization for payment is made by someone other than the person who ordered the goods. This authorization is given only after all the verifications have been made.
5. Still another person writes the check for payment.

The main objective of these procedures is to ensure that several different people are involved in the process of buying and receiving goods and making the necessary payments. This division of responsibility provides a system of checks and balances.

Purchases by Use of Credit Cards

In many firms, owners and employees use credit cards to purchase services. These services are usually connected with business travel or entertainment. Generally, individuals have separate credit cards for personal (nonbusiness) purchases. Credit cards that bear the firm's name are used for business-related expenses such as airline, hotel, restaurant, and car rental charges. Businesses almost never use credit cards for purchases of assets or merchandise for resale.

Purchases made with business credit cards are accounted for in the same manner as purchases on open account. The firm assumes an obligation that is recorded by debiting an appropriate account (usually an expense account) and crediting the Accounts Payable account. Later, when the firm pays the bill, the Accounts Payable account is debited and the Cash account is credited.

Many professional firms and small businesses prefer not to record business credit card purchases until they receive the periodic statement. In such cases, the usual procedure is to pay the amount of the bill promptly by check. The appropriate expense or other account is debited, and the Cash account is credited. This procedure avoids journalizing and posting numerous small accounts payable transactions, thus saving time and effort.

The accounts payable liability that arises from a bank credit card purchase may be recorded at the time of purchase in the same manner as a purchase on open account or by business credit card is recorded. However, the use of a bank credit card to make a purchase creates a liability to the participating bank, not to the seller. The most commonly used procedure is to record the transaction at the time of payment. The buyer usually receives a periodic bill from the bank. When the check is issued to pay the bill, an entry is made in the cash payments journal. The appropriate expense or other account is debited and the Cash account is credited.

Generally, purchases made by use of cards issued by credit card companies are not recorded by the buyer until the buyer receives a statement. The transaction is journalized at the time of payment. The appropriate expense or other account is debited, and the Cash account is credited. Large firms with many employees may use many individual credit cards issued on one credit card account. Periodic billings received on such accounts may be recorded at the time of receipt, crediting the Accounts Payable account and debiting the appropriate expense accounts or other accounts. Some companies will debit such charges to a special *clearing account* until the amounts are verified by the individual employees who incurred the liabilities. Following verification by the individual employees, the appropriate expense accounts are debited and the special clearing account is credited. Here again, it is important to remember that the liability is owed by the business firm that holds the credit cards. The credit card company issued the cards on the basis of an agreement with the firm. When verification of the statements is completed and payment is made, the Accounts Payable account (or the clearing account) is debited and the Cash account is credited.

principles and procedures summary

Each credit purchase is recorded in the purchases journal at the time it is made. Because of the design of the journal, only one line is required for recording a purchase. At the end of the month, the total amount purchased on credit is posted to the general ledger as a debit to Merchandise Purchases and a credit to Accounts Payable.

Freight costs on purchases can be handled in several ways. For example, if the buyer pays a freight bill directly, a simple cash payment is involved. This is recorded by debiting Freight In and crediting Cash. On the other hand, if the seller pays the freight in advance for the buyer, the freight cost is added to the seller's invoice. In this case, the invoice total must be analyzed so that the appropriate charges can be made to Merchandise Purchases and Freight In when the invoice is recorded in the purchases journal.

The amounts received for returns or allowances on purchases are credited to the Purchases Returns and Allowances account. The offsetting debit reduces the liability account Accounts Payable.

managerial implications

The use of the special journal for credit purchases helps provide accurate, up-to-date information to management efficiently and quickly. The special purchases journal also permits division of accounting work, which saves time. The use of a Freight In account permits the later study of costs of this nature. The use of a Purchases Returns and Allowances account also provides information that is valuable to management.

Internal control of purchasing operations is attained by a carefully designed system of checks and balances. Such a system helps to protect a business firm from excessive investment in merchandise and from fraud.

managerial discussion questions

1. How can proper accounting procedures protect a firm from excessive investment in merchandise and from fraud?
2. Why would management insist on absolute completeness and accuracy in recording suppliers' invoice dates and terms in the purchases journal?
3. How would management benefit from an accounting system that includes separate revenue accounts for each operating department?
4. Why is the use of special journals for cash receipts, cash payments, sales, and purchases likely to be more efficient than the use of a general journal for all these transactions?

application of principles

PROBLEM 11-1 The Santos Glass Company uses a single-column purchases journal. On January 1, 19X2, the general ledger accounts used in recording the firm's credit purchases were as follows.

ACCOUNTS

202	Accounts Payable	$5,964.20
501	Merchandise Purchases	-0-

The January 19X2 transactions involving the purchase of merchandise on credit are shown on page 200.

INSTRUCTIONS
1. Open the general ledger accounts, and enter the balances.
2. Record each transaction in the purchases journal. Use *1* for the journal page number.
3. Total and rule the purchases journal.
4. Make the required postings to the proper ledger accounts.

TRANSACTIONS FOR JANUARY 19X2

Jan. 3 Purchased window glass for $995.69 from the I-O-F Glass Works, Invoice 1694, dated January 2; terms are 30 days net.
    4 Bought mirror glass for $290 from the Allied Products Company, Invoice A491-64, dated January 2; terms are 2% 10 days, net 30 days.
    8 Purchased plate glass for $150 from Lake Manufacturing Company on Invoice 6920, dated January 5, payable in 30 days.
   11 Bought safety glass for $175.50 from the Plastic Specialties Corporation. Invoice 44-98-A-1 is dated January 9 and is due in 30 days.
   18 Purchased tinted glass for $60 from Charles and Company, covered by Invoice 648, dated January 17; terms are 2% 10 days, net 30 days.
   24 Purchased $250.14 of special window glass from Bell Glass Distributors. Invoice 301-296 is dated January 20, with net payment due in 30 days.
   28 Purchased frame mouldings for $200 from Boyle's Mill Products. The supplier issued Invoice 4596, dated January 25; terms are 1% 10 days, net 30 days.

PROBLEM 11-2

The Russell Stores Corporation purchases its merchandise from various suppliers for cash and on credit. The firm uses a single-column purchases journal and a cash payments journal with special columns for Accounts Payable Dr. 202, Other Accounts Debit, and Cash Cr. 101. The general ledger accounts used in recording the firm's purchases are as follows at the beginning of June 19X1.

ACCOUNTS

101	Cash	$7,421.60
202	Accounts Payable	4,709.40
501	Merchandise Purchases	-0-

The June 19X1 transactions involving the purchase of merchandise are shown below and on the next page.

INSTRUCTIONS
1. Open the general ledger accounts, and enter the balances.
2. Record each transaction in the appropriate journal. Use 6 for the page number of each journal.
3. Foot and prove the cash payments journal. Then total and rule both journals.
4. Make the required individual and summary postings to the proper general ledger accounts.

TRANSACTIONS FOR JUNE 19X1

June 4 Purchased womens' wear for $449.80 in cash from Sarto Products, Check 116.
    6 Bought swimsuits for $785.15 from the Central Wholesale Company; Invoice 11098, dated June 3, is due in 30 days.

11 Purchased a new stock of curtains and draperies for $740.10 on credit from the County Distributors Company. Invoice 2941 is dated June 8; terms are 2/10, net 30.

14 Paid $362.20 in cash for hardware and house furnishings from East Fixtures Company, Check 136.

22 Bought boys' clothing for $279.20 in cash from Waynesboro Mills, Check 152.

23 Purchased rugs for $1,187.15 from the McCormick Fabric Company; terms are 30 days net. Invoice 869 is dated June 21.

27 Bought a stock of new appliances for $690.40 from Acme Electric Supply. The invoice is dated June 25 and numbered 45269. Terms are 1% 10 days, net 60 days.

30 Bought women's shoes for $586 from the Hanover Shoe Manufacturing Company; terms are net 30 days. Invoice 60-4091 is dated June 29.

PROBLEM 11-3 The Office Supplies Company purchases its merchandise from various suppliers. Its accounting records include a purchases journal with special columns for Accounts Payable Cr. 202, Merchandise Purchases Dr. 501, and Freight In Dr. 506. The firm also has a general journal and a cash payments journal with columns for Accounts Payable Dr. 202, Other Accounts Debit, and Cash Cr. 101. During a typical week in July 19X1, the selected transactions shown below and on page 202 took place.

INSTRUCTIONS
1. Record each transaction in the appropriate journal. Use 7 for each journal page number.
2. Foot all money columns in the purchases journal and the cash payments journal, and prove the accuracy of your work.

TRANSACTIONS FOR JULY 2–7 19X1

July 2 Bought stationery for $450 on credit from the Fulton Paper Company. Invoice A431, dated July 1, is due in 30 days, with no freight charge.

3 Purchased $1,469.40 of filing equipment from the Smead Manufacturing Company, terms 2% 10 days, 30 days net. Invoice J2-41-7 is dated July 2.

3 Paid freight charges of $46.10 on the shipment of filing equipment received from the Smead Manufacturing Company. Issued Check 981.

5 Purchased office desks and other furniture for $1,980 from the Superior Products Company. Invoice A4290 is dated July 3 and shows terms of 30 days net.

5 Purchased $860.15 of duplicator supplies from Sharpe Visual Products. Invoice 80681, dated July 2, allows terms of 2% 10 days, net 60 days, with no freight charge.

5 Issued Check 1012 for $80.50 to pay freight charges on the shipment received from the Superior Products Company.
6 Purchased an additional stock of electric typewriters for $2,469.60. The supplier, Modern Equipment Wholesalers, allows 60-day terms. Invoice T91-648 is dated July 3 and includes freight charges of $69.60.
7 Returned a chair bought for $37.50 from the Superior Products Company on Invoice A4290 of July 3. When this item was unpacked, it was found to be badly damaged.
7 Bought a stock of time clocks for $1,200 from the Nigon Corporation, covered by Invoice 9816, dated July 5; terms are net 60 days, with no freight charges.

alternate problems

PROBLEM 11-1A The Decorative Blind Company uses a single-column purchases journal. On April 1, 19X1, the general ledger accounts used in recording the firm's credit purchases were as follows.

ACCOUNTS

| 202 | Accounts Payable | $3,476.25 |
| 501 | Merchandise Purchases | -0- |

The April 19X1 transactions involving the purchase of merchandise on credit are shown below and on the next page.

INSTRUCTIONS
1. Open the general ledger accounts, and enter the balances.
2. Record each transaction in the purchases journal. Use 4 as the journal page number.
3. Total and rule the purchases journal.
4. Make the required postings to the proper general ledger accounts.

TRANSACTIONS FOR APRIL 19X1
Apr. 2 Purchased slats for $995 from the Western Aluminum Company, Invoice 3445, dated April 1; terms are 30 days net.
8 Bought tapes for $247.50 from the Bronson Milling Company, Invoice A11021, dated April 6, net payable in 60 days.
12 Purchased cords for $126.30 from the LeMay Cordage Company, Invoice 2783, dated April 11, net due in 30 days.
20 Purchased additional slats for $1,064.85 from the Western Aluminum Company, Invoice 3558, dated April 19; terms are 30 days net.
23 Purchased gears for raising and lowering blinds for $469.20 from the Universal Gear Company, Invoice G1090, dated April 20, net due and payable in 30 days.

26 Purchased slats of special lengths for $115 from the Extruded Aluminum Company on 60-day credit terms, Invoice 309B, dated April 25.

28 Purchased 100 gallons of paint for $595 from the Farber Paint Company; terms are net May 10; Invoice 301-388 is dated April 27.

PROBLEM 11-2A

This problem covers the purchases of the Stein Venetian Blind Company for the month of May 19X1. The manager has determined that certain items of merchandise can be purchased for cash more economically than on credit. The company uses a single-column purchases journal and a cash payments journal with special columns for Accounts Payable Dr. 202, Other Accounts Debit, and Cash Cr. 101. The general ledger accounts used in recording the firm's purchases were as follows at the beginning of the month.

ACCOUNTS

101	Cash	$3,612.20
202	Accounts Payable	2,895.25
501	Merchandise Purchases	-0-

The May 19X1 transactions involving the purchase of merchandise are shown below.

INSTRUCTIONS
1. Open the general ledger accounts, and enter the balances.
2. Record each transaction in the appropriate journal. Use 5 for the page number of each journal.
3. Foot and prove the cash payments journal. Then total and rule both journals.
4. Make the required individual and summary postings to the proper general ledger accounts.

TRANSACTIONS FOR MAY 19X1

May 4 Purchased slats for $1,450 from the Western Aluminum Company, Invoice 6698, dated May 2; terms are 30 days net.

5 Paid $42.50 in cash for special green tapes, Check 773.

10 Bought cords for $212.35 from the LeMay Cordage Company, Invoice 3642, dated May 9, net due in 30 days.

15 Paid $15.30 in cash for a set of special ratchet gears for extra wide blinds from Wayne Products Inc., Check 782.

18 Purchased 10 gallons of paint for $69.50 from the Gandolf Paint Company, net due in 30 days, Invoice 2412C, dated May 16.

21 Bought tapes for $522.50 from the Bronson Milling Company, Invoice B23368, dated May 18, net payable in 60 days.

25 Purchased a supply of wood bottom slats for $249.25 from the Asheville Lumber Company, Invoice 788, dated May 23, net payable on June 10.

PROBLEM 11-3A The College Bookstore purchases textbooks from various publishers and sells them to students. For recording purposes, the bookstore uses a general journal, a purchases journal with special columns for Accounts Payable Cr. 202, Merchandise Purchases Dr. 501, and Freight In Dr. 506, and a cash payments journal with columns for Accounts Payable Dr. 202, Other Accounts Debit, and Cash Cr. 101. During a typical week in October 19X1, the transactions shown below took place.

INSTRUCTIONS
1. Record each transaction in the appropriate journal. Use *10* for the page number of each journal.
2. Foot all money columns in the purchases journal and the cash payments journal, and prove the accuracy of your work.

TRANSACTIONS FOR OCTOBER 16–20, 19X1

Oct. 16 Bought books for $280 from United Publishers, Invoice 835, dated October 12; terms, net cash 30 days.

16 Paid $14.50 in freight charges on a shipment received from United Publishers, by Check 1214.

17 Purchased books for $376 plus prepaid freight of $18.75 from the Scientific Book Company, Invoice 10-213, dated October 13; terms are 2/10, net/30; the total invoice is $394.75.

18 Bought books for $763 from the Tri-State Depository, Invoice 1875, dated October 16; terms are net cash 30 days.

18 Paid freight charges of $36.15 on a shipment received from the Tri-State Depository, by Check 1221.

19 Discovered that books costing $155 received from the Tri-State Depository were the wrong edition and returned them for credit. (Use the Purchases Returns and Allowances account.)

19 Bought books for $188 plus prepaid freight of $11.70 from Technical Printers, Inc., Invoice 364, dated October 17; terms are net cash 60 days.

20 Purchased a set of reference books at the delivered price of $440 from the Almanac Publishing Company, Invoice A534, dated October 16; terms are net 30 days.

20 Bought books for $615 plus freight of $43.40 from the Brooks Printing Company, Invoice B832, dated October 17; terms are 2/30, net 60 days.

UNIT 12
THE ACCOUNTS PAYABLE LEDGER

In Unit 11 you saw how the accountant designed a purchases journal for recording the expected credit purchases of merchandise. The efficient handling of these purchases also requires the use of a subsidiary ledger called the accounts payable ledger.

Recording Procedures for Purchases

The February 19X2 purchases of merchandise on credit for the new accessories department of the Modern Cleaning Shop were entered in the purchases journal as follows.

PURCHASES JOURNAL for Month of February 19X2 — Page 1

DATE	PURCHASED FROM	INVOICE NO.	INVOICE DATE	TERMS	✓	AMOUNT
Feb. 1	Warren Wholesale Company	649	2/1	n/30		1,200 00
13	Best Products Company	A4973	2/12	n/30		300 00
17	Prestige Plastics, Inc.	43691	2/15	n/20		100 00
24	Warren Wholesale Company	855	2/22	n/30		210 00
28	Total Credit Purchases					1,810 00
						(501)
						(202)

The total of the Amount column in the purchases journal was posted at the end of the month. The Merchandise Purchases account was debited to record the cost of the goods purchased, and the Accounts Payable account was credited to show the firm's liability to its suppliers.

Merchandise Purchases — No. 501

DATE	EXPLANATION	POST. REF.	DEBIT	CREDIT	BALANCE	DR. CR.
19X2 Feb. 28		P1	1,810 00		1,810 00	Dr.

	Accounts Payable					No. 202
DATE	EXPLANATION	POST. REF.	DEBIT	CREDIT	BALANCE	DR. CR.
19 X2 Feb. 1	Balance	✓			500 00	Cr.
28		P1		1,810 00	2,310 00	Cr.

During the same month, there was only one return on a purchase of merchandise. It was recorded in the general journal as follows.

19 X2 Feb. 27	Accounts Payable/Warren Wholesale Co.	202	10 00	
	Purchases Returns and Allowances	509		10 00
	Returned accessories purchased on February 24, Invoice 855; found not as ordered.			

After the entry was posted, the general ledger accounts appeared as shown below.

	Accounts Payable					No. 202
DATE	EXPLANATION	POST. REF.	DEBIT	CREDIT	BALANCE	DR. CR.
19 X2 Feb. 1	Balance	✓			500 00	Cr.
27		J2	10 00		490 00	Cr.
28		P1		1,810 00	2,300 00	Cr.

	Purchases Returns and Allowances					No. 509
DATE	EXPLANATION	POST. REF.	DEBIT	CREDIT	BALANCE	DR. CR.
19 X2 Feb. 27		J2		10 00	10 00	Cr.

As payments are sent to creditors, the accountant enters the details in the cash payments journal. The illustration on the next page shows how a multi-column cash payments journal would be used for recording such transactions. To simplify the presentation, only payments made on accounts payable are shown in this journal.

CASH PAYMENTS JOURNAL for Month of February 19X2   Page 2

DATE	CHECK NO.	EXPLANATION	✓	ACCOUNTS PAYABLE DR. 202	OTHER ACCOUNTS DEBIT ACCOUNT TITLE	POST. REF.	AMOUNT	CASH CR. 101
Feb. 3	41	Warren Wholesale Co.		600 00				600 00
10	44	Ace Motors		500 00				500 00
15	47	Best Products Company		150 00				150 00
24	51	Prestige Plastics, Inc.		100 00				100 00
28		Totals		1,350 00				
				(202)				

At the end of the month, the total of the Accounts Payable Debit column is posted to the Accounts Payable account in the general ledger.

Accounts Payable   No. 202

DATE	EXPLANATION	POST. REF.	DEBIT	CREDIT	BALANCE	DR. CR.
19 X2 Feb. 1	Balance	✓			500 00	Cr.
27		J2	10 00		490 00	Cr.
28		P1		1,810 00	2,300 00	Cr.
28		CP2	1,350 00		950 00	Cr.

The Need for More Information

The final balance of the Accounts Payable account shows how much the firm owes to all its creditors. This figure is reported on the balance sheet that the accountant prepares at the end of the month. However, when the time comes for the accountant to pay the firm's bills, he quickly realizes that the balance of the Accounts Payable account does not give him all the information he needs. For example, the accountant must find out the exact amount that is owed to each creditor and the date that each bill is to be paid. It is difficult to obtain such information from the firm's present financial records.

Stein would have to check through all the entries in the purchases journal to find out what purchases were made from a particular creditor. Then he would have to check through all the entries in the cash payments journal to find out how much had already been paid to the same creditor. Next, he would have to check the general journal for purchases returns and allowances. Finally, by deducting the total payments and the returns and allowances from the total purchases, he could compute the amount still due.

Obviously, this procedure is impractical. It is much simpler to set up an accounts payable ledger. This subsidiary ledger will contain individual accounts for the firm's creditors, just as the accounts receivable ledger contains individual accounts for the firm's customers. By having an accounts payable ledger, the accountant can quickly find out the amount owed to each creditor.

Accounts With Individual Creditors

Each creditor's account can be kept on a standard ledger form. However, most accountants prefer the three-column balance ledger form for such accounts. The advantage of this form is that the account balance is always available. For example, the balance that the Modern Cleaning Shop owes to Ace Motors on January 31, 19X2, is shown in the following account set up on February 1.

NAME:	Ace Motors				
ADDRESS:	204 Drake Avenue				
	Dallas, TX 75228				TERMS: n/30

DATE	DESCRIPTION	POST. REF.	DEBIT	CREDIT	BALANCE
19 X2 Feb. 1	Balance	✓			500 00

All accounts with creditors are kept alphabetically or according to the creditor's account number in the accounts payable subsidiary ledger. Since liability accounts usually have credit balances, the balances in this ledger are presumed to be credit balances. Occasionally, debit balances result from such transactions as purchases returns and allowances on goods already paid for. These debit balances are indicated by the use of a "Dr." notation, parentheses, or a circle around the amount.

Recording a Purchase

The procedure for journalizing each credit purchase remains the same as before. The necessary entry is made in the purchases journal. For example, the purchase from the Warren Wholesale Company on February 1 is recorded exactly as it appears on page 205.

PURCHASES JOURNAL for Month of February 19X2   Page 1

DATE	PURCHASED FROM	INVOICE NO.	INVOICE DATE	TERMS	✓	AMOUNT
Feb. 1	Warren Wholesale Company	649	2/1	n/30		1,200 00

Posting a Purchase to the Creditor's Account

A new procedure is involved, however, in posting purchases. Each entry in the purchases journal must be posted immediately as a credit to the proper supplier's account in the accounts payable ledger. The balance of the account is computed as each posting is made.

NAME:	Warren Wholesale Company				
ADDRESS:	671 Valley Street				
	Topeka, KA 66614			TERMS:	n/30

DATE	DESCRIPTION	POST. REF.	DEBIT	CREDIT	BALANCE
19X2					
Feb. 1	Invoice 649, 2/1/X2	P1		1,200 00	1,200 00

After an entry is posted to the accounts payable ledger, a check mark is placed in the purchases journal.

PURCHASES JOURNAL for Month of February 19X2   Page 1

DATE	PURCHASED FROM	INVOICE NO.	INVOICE DATE	TERMS	✓	AMOUNT
Feb. 1	Warren Wholesale Company	649	2/1	n/30	✓	1,200 00

Recording a Cash Payment to a Creditor

The procedure for journalizing a payment to a creditor remains basically the same as before. When a check is issued, an entry is made in the cash payments journal. For example, the payment of $600 to the Warren Wholesale Company is recorded in the cash payments journal as shown below.

CASH PAYMENTS JOURNAL for Month of February 19X2   Page 2

DATE	CHECK NO.	EXPLANATION	✓	ACCOUNTS PAYABLE DR. 202	OTHER ACCOUNTS DEBIT ACCOUNT TITLE	POST. REF.	AMOUNT	CASH CR. 101
Feb. 3	41	Warren Wholesale Co.		600 00				600 00

Posting a Payment to the Creditor's Account

The procedure for posting payments to the creditor's account is new. After the amount paid has been entered in the cash payments journal, it is posted immediately as a debit to the creditor's account in the accounts payable ledger as shown below.

NAME:	Warren Wholesale Company				
ADDRESS:	671 Valley Street				
	Topeka, KA 66614			TERMS:	n/30

DATE	DESCRIPTION	POST. REF.	DEBIT	CREDIT	BALANCE
19X2					
Feb. 1	Invoice 649, 2/1/X2	P1		1,200 00	1,200 00
3		CP2	600 00		600 00

A check mark is then placed in the Accounts Payable section of the cash payments journal to indicate that the posting to the creditor's account has been completed.

CASH PAYMENTS JOURNAL for Month of February 19X2				ACCOUNTS PAYABLE		OTHER ACCOUNTS DEBIT			Page 2
DATE		CHECK NO.	EXPLANATION	√	DR. 202	ACCOUNT TITLE	POST. REF.	AMOUNT	CASH CR. 101
Feb.	3	41	Warren Wholesale Co.	√	600 00				600 00

Remember that the Posting Reference column in the Other Accounts Debit section of the cash payments journal is used only for amounts posted to the general ledger accounts.

Recording a Purchase Return or Allowance

The use of an accounts payable ledger does not change the recording of a purchase return or allowance in the general journal. For example, on February 27 the Modern Cleaning Shop returned accessories that cost $10 to the Warren Wholesale Company. The accountant entered the return in the general journal as shown on page 206.

Posting a Purchase Return or Allowance

When a business has an accounts payable ledger, a new procedure is used to post purchases returns and allowances. After the purchase return or allowance is entered in the general journal, the accountant posts the debit part of the entry to the Accounts Payable account in the general ledger and to the creditor's account in the accounts payable ledger. He indicates the double posting by means of a diagonal line in the Posting Reference column of the general journal. The number of the general ledger account debited (202) is shown to the left of the diagonal line. The check mark on the right of the diagonal line indicates the debit posting to the subsidiary ledger account. The credit to the Purchases Returns and Allowances account is posted as before. The general journal entry below is shown as it appears after these postings have been completed.

19 X2					
Feb. 27	Accounts Payable/Warren Wholesale Co.	202/√	10 00		
	Purchases Returns and Allowances	509		10 00	
	Returned accessories purchased on				
	February 24, Invoice 855; found				
	not as ordered.				

Daily Routine

Each credit purchase is recorded in the purchases journal and is then posted to the proper creditor's account in the accounts payable ledger. The Modern

Cleaning Shop's credit purchases for February are shown in the purchases journal illustrated below.

PURCHASES JOURNAL for Month of February 19X2 — Page 1

DATE	PURCHASED FROM	INVOICE NO.	INVOICE DATE	TERMS	✓	AMOUNT
Feb. 1	Warren Wholesale Company	649	2/1	n/30	✓	1,200 00
13	Best Products Company	A4973	2/12	n/30	✓	300 00
17	Prestige Plastics, Inc.	43691	2/15	n/20	✓	100 00
24	Warren Wholesale Company	855	2/22	n/30	✓	210 00

Each payment to a creditor is recorded in the cash payments journal and is then posted immediately to the creditor's account. The new balance of the account is computed after each posting so that the amount owed will always be available for quick reference. The following cash payments journal shows the payments that the Modern Cleaning Shop made to creditors during February.

CASH PAYMENTS JOURNAL for Month of February 19X2 — Page 2

DATE	CHECK NO.	EXPLANATION	✓	ACCOUNTS PAYABLE DR. 202	OTHER ACCOUNTS DEBIT ACCOUNT TITLE	POST. REF.	AMOUNT	CASH CR. 101
Feb. 3	41	Warren Wholesale Co.	✓	600 00				600 00
10	44	Ace Motors	✓	500 00				500 00
15	47	Best Products Company	✓	150 00				150 00
24	51	Prestige Plastics, Inc.	✓	100 00				100 00

Each purchase return or allowance is recorded in the general journal and is then posted immediately. The debit is posted to the Accounts Payable account in the general ledger and to the creditor's account in the accounts payable ledger. The credit is posted to the Purchases Returns and Allowances account in the general ledger.

Subsidiary Ledger Account Balances

The creditors' accounts in the accounts payable subsidiary ledger of the Modern Cleaning Shop at the end of February 19X2 are illustrated on the next page.

NAME:	Ace Motors				TERMS: n/30
ADDRESS:	204 Drake Avenue Dallas, TX 75228				

DATE	DESCRIPTION	POST. REF.	DEBIT	CREDIT	BALANCE
19 X2 Feb. 1	Balance	✓			500 00
10		CP2	500 00		-0-

NAME:	Best Products Company				TERMS: n/30
ADDRESS:	1210 Penn Plaza Pittsburgh, PA 15222				

DATE	DESCRIPTION	POST. REF.	DEBIT	CREDIT	BALANCE
19 X2 Feb. 13	Invoice A4973, 2/12/X2	P1		300 00	300 00
15		CP2	150 00		150 00

NAME:	Prestige Plastics, Inc.				TERMS: n/20
ADDRESS:	267 Spring Street St. Louis, MO 63119				

DATE	DESCRIPTION	POST. REF.	DEBIT	CREDIT	BALANCE
19 X2 Feb. 17	Invoice 43691, 2/15/X2	P1		100 00	100 00
24		CP2	100 00		-0-

NAME:	Warren Wholesale Company				TERMS: n/30
ADDRESS:	671 Valley Street Topeka, KA 66614				

DATE	DESCRIPTION	POST. REF.	DEBIT	CREDIT	BALANCE
19 X2 Feb. 1	Invoice 649, 2/1/X2	P1		1,200 00	1,200 00
3		CP2	600 00		600 00
24	Invoice 855, 2/22/X2	P1		210 00	810 00
27		J2	10 00		800 00

End-of-Month Routine

The procedure for posting totals from the purchases journal at the end of the month is the same as before. The Amount column is totaled as shown on the next page. Then the total of the credit purchases is posted as a debit to the Merchandise Purchases account and as a credit to the Accounts Payable account in the general ledger. The account numbers are entered in the journal as posting is completed.

PURCHASES JOURNAL for Month of February 19X2 — Page 1

DATE	PURCHASED FROM	INVOICE NO.	INVOICE DATE	TERMS	✓	AMOUNT
Feb. 1	Warren Wholesale Company	649	2/1	n/30	✓	1,200 00
13	Best Products Company	A4973	2/12	n/30	✓	300 00
17	Prestige Plastics, Inc.	43691	2/15	n/20	✓	100 00
24	Warren Wholesale Company	855	2/22	n/30	✓	210 00
28	Total Credit Purchases					1,810 00
						(501)
						(202)

The procedure for posting totals from the cash payments journal also remains the same. All columns are totaled, and the totals of the Cash and Accounts Payable columns are posted to the general ledger. As each posting is completed, the account number is placed below the column total. The following illustration shows only the Accounts Payable column after posting in order to simplify the presentation.

CASH PAYMENTS JOURNAL for Month of February 19X2 — Page 2

DATE	CHECK NO.	EXPLANATION	✓	ACCOUNTS PAYABLE DR. 202	OTHER ACCOUNTS DEBIT ACCOUNT TITLE	POST. REF.	AMOUNT	CASH CR. 101
Feb. 3	41	Warren Wholesale Co.	✓	600 00				600 00
10	44	Ace Motors	✓	500 00				500 00
15	47	Best Products Company	✓	150 00				150 00
24	51	Prestige Plastics, Inc.	✓	100 00				100 00
28		Totals		1,350 00				
				(202)				

When the postings have been made from the purchases journal, the cash payments journal, and the general journal, the Accounts Payable account in the general ledger appears as shown below.

Accounts Payable — No. 202

DATE	EXPLANATION	POST. REF.	DEBIT	CREDIT	BALANCE	DR. CR.
19X2 Feb. 1	Balance	✓			500 00	Cr.
27		J2	10 00		490 00	Cr.
28		P1		1,810 00	2,300 00	Cr.
28		CP2	1,350 00		950 00	Cr.

Proving the Subsidiary Ledger

After all postings are made from the purchases journal, cash payments journal, and general journal to the subsidiary and general ledger accounts, the accountant checks the work for accuracy. As in the previous unit, the checking process involves two steps.

1. The accountant prepares a list of the creditors and the balances owed to them. This list is called a *schedule of accounts payable.* The accountant adds all the balances to obtain the total that the firm owes to its creditors. The information shown on the following schedule of accounts payable was taken from the accounts illustrated on page 212.

```
              Modern Cleaning Shop
           Schedule of Accounts Payable
                February 28, 19X2
        Creditor                           Balance
  Best Products Company                     150 00
  Warren Wholesale Company                  800 00
       Total Owed to Creditors              950 00
```

Notice that when the schedule of accounts payable is prepared only accounts that have balances are listed. This is done to save time and space. Ace Motors and Prestige Plastics, Inc., are omitted because these accounts have no balances on February 28.

2. The accountant compares the total of the schedule of accounts payable with the balance of the Accounts Payable account in the general ledger. In this case, the total of $950 obtained in Step 1 agrees with the balance of the Accounts Payable account shown on page 213.

The Accounts Payable account is called a control account for reasons similar to those pointed out in connection with the Accounts Receivable Control account. When an accounts payable subsidiary ledger is used, the Accounts Payable account in the general ledger summarizes many different activities and thereby provides an independent proof of accuracy. From now on, this account is called the Accounts Payable Control account at the Modern Cleaning Shop.

Accounts Payable Resulting From Credit Card Purchases

As you learned in the discussion of credit card purchases in Unit 11 (page 197), there is seldom any need for separate general ledger or subsidiary ledger accounts for accounts payable resulting from credit card purchases. These transactions are normally handled within the usual accounting procedures covering purchases on credit. If necessary, adaptations are possible similar to those illustrated for the sales journal and the accounts receivable ledger.

principles and procedures summary

The accounts payable ledger contains an account for each supplier. As soon as a purchase is made and journalized, the amount must be credited to the individual supplier's account in the accounts payable ledger. When a payment is made, the amount is posted at once as a debit to the proper subsidiary ledger account from the cash payments journal. Each purchase return or allowance is immediately posted as a debit to the proper subsidiary ledger account from the general journal. End-of-month postings to the general ledger are made in the usual way. When all entries are posted, a schedule of accounts payable is prepared. The balances in the accounts payable subsidiary ledger are added to determine the total amount owed to creditors. This total is then compared with the balance of the Accounts Payable Control account in the general ledger. The two amounts should be equal.

managerial implications

It is important for a firm to have detailed information about the amounts owed to creditors. This information helps to ensure that bills are paid promptly, that good relations are kept with suppliers, and that cash can be made available as needed. The process of proving the total of the balances in the accounts payable ledger to the control account balance is a valuable check on the accuracy of a firm's records.

The more elaborate accounting system used by the Modern Cleaning Shop in February resembles that used in many medium-sized businesses. Firms of this size have a steady volume of transactions that must be handled quickly and efficiently. In a business with a greater volume of transactions, an accounting clerk might be assigned to each journal and ledger to speed the recording process. However, no matter how many or how few employees are involved, each journal and ledger in the system should be interlocked so that resulting records will be accurate and complete.

managerial discussion questions

1. What purpose does the accounts payable ledger serve?
2. Why is it important for management to know how much is owed to each of the firm's creditors?
3. How does a control account serve as a check on accuracy?

application of principles

PROBLEM 12-1 The Barker Electronic Service uses a cash payments journal with special columns for Accounts Payable Dr. 202, Other Accounts Debit, and Cash Cr. 101; a single-column purchases journal; and a general journal. The general ledger accounts used in recording the firm's purchases are as follows on December 1, 19X1.

ACCOUNTS

101	Cash	$4,506.21
202	Accounts Payable Control	2,736.84
501	Merchandise Purchases	-0-
503	Purchases Returns and Allowances	-0-

The individual accounts on December 1, 19X1, in the accounts payable subsidiary ledger show the following data. (Addresses are omitted intentionally.)

BARKER ELECTRONIC SERVICE
Schedule of Accounts Payable
December 1, 19X1

Creditor	Balance
ATC Communications System	$ 275.10
Apollo Sound Systems	371.74
Bryan Laboratories	75.00
Central Radio/TV Distributors	1,005.00
Colonial Radio Corporation	150.00
General Electronics, Inc.	735.00
Lincoln Television Sales Corporation	-0-
Repair Parts and Supply Company	125.00
Total Owed to Creditors	$2,736.84

The transactions of the Barker Electronic Service involving purchases of merchandise on credit and payments of cash for December 19X1 are shown on pages 217 and 218.

INSTRUCTIONS
1. Open the general ledger accounts, and enter the balances.
2. Open the accounts in the accounts payable ledger. Write each creditor's name, the year, and the date "Dec. 1." Write "Balance" in the Explanation column, place a check mark in the Posting Reference column, and enter the amount owed to the creditor in the Balance column. Open an

account for each creditor listed on the schedule of accounts payable, even though there may be no balance as of this date. Open accounts for new creditors as needed.

3. Prove the accuracy of your work in Instruction 2 by doing the following. List the balances owed to creditors as shown in the accounts payable ledger. Then add the balances, and compare the resulting total with the balance of the Accounts Payable Control account in the general ledger and with the total of the schedule of accounts payable illustrated on page 216. Use a separate sheet of paper for this step.

4. Record each transaction in the appropriate journal. Use 12 for the page number of each journal.

5. Complete the required daily and summary postings to the general ledger and to the accounts payable ledger.

6. Prepare a schedule of accounts payable as of December 31, 19X1, and prove the total against the balance of the control account.

TRANSACTIONS FOR DECEMBER 19X1

Dec. 2 Purchased merchandise for $1,205.60 from the Colonial Radio Corporation, Invoice 4964, December 1; terms are 30 days.

3 Issued Check 741 for $125 to the Repair Parts and Supply Company for Invoice 10469 dated November 4.

4 Issued Check 742 for $510 to General Electronics, Inc., to pay for Invoice 694J6, dated October 6.

6 Paid $150 to the Colonial Radio Corporation for Invoice 4721 dated November 8, Check 743.

8 Purchased merchandise for $34.10 in cash. Issued Check 744. (Charge to Merchandise Purchases.)

11 Bought a stock of clock-radios costing $208.40 from Emery Radio Corporation, Invoice 941, dated December 9; terms are 30 days net.

12 Purchased color TV sets for $1,180 from Central Radio/TV Distributors, Invoice B10-941, dated December 10; terms are net 30 days.

14 Bought merchandise for $125 from the Repair Parts and Supply Company, Invoice 12631, dated December 12; terms are 30 days net.

14 Paid $371.74 by Check 745 for the balance of the account owed to Apollo Sound Systems.

15 Issued Check 746 for $275.10 to pay ATC Communications Systems.

18 Bought $100 of merchandise for cash, Check 747.

19 Purchased additional merchandise for $40 from Bryan Laboratories, Invoice 207-B, dated December 15; terms are 60 days.

20 Received an $85 allowance from Central Radio/TV Distributors for damaged merchandise purchased on their invoice dated November 25.

22 Purchased new merchandise for $415 from Apollo Sound Systems, Invoice 509731, December 20, net 30 days.

24 Paid $920 to Central Radio/TV Distributors for the net balance due on the purchase of November 25, Invoice A14-680, Check 748.

26 Bought cassette players for $605 from General Electronics, Inc., Invoice 97849, dated December 23; terms are net 60 days.

27 Received an allowance of $18.40 from Emery Radio Corporation to cover a shortage in the shipment of December 9, Invoice 941.

31 Purchased radios for $65.20 from ATC Communications Systems, Invoice 41276, December 29, net 30 days.

alternate problem

PROBLEM 12-1A The Decorative Blind Company uses a cash payments journal with special columns for Accounts Payable Dr. 202, Other Accounts Debit, and Cash Cr. 101; a single-column purchases journal; and a general journal. The general ledger accounts used in recording the firm's purchases are as follows on April 1, 19X1.

ACCOUNTS

101	Cash	$4,550.25
202	Accounts Payable Control	3,122.95
501	Merchandise Purchases	3,916.65
503	Purchases Returns and Allowances	-0-

The individual accounts on April 1, 19X1, in the accounts payable subsidiary ledger show the following information. (Addresses are omitted intentionally.)

DECORATIVE BLIND COMPANY
Schedule of Accounts Payable
April 1, 19X1

Creditor	Balance
Asheville Lumber Company	$ 249.25
Bronson Milling Company	770.00
Extruded Aluminum Corporation	115.00
Farber Paint Company	-0-
Gandolf Paint Company	69.50
LeMay Cordage Company	-0-
Universal Gear Company	469.20
Western Aluminum Company	1,450.00
Total Owed to Creditors	$3,122.95

The transactions involving purchases of merchandise on credit and payments of cash for April 19X1 are shown on pages 219 and 220.

INSTRUCTIONS
1. Open the general ledger accounts, and enter the balances.
2. Open the accounts in the accounts payable ledger. Write each creditor's name, the year, and the date "April 1." Write "Balance" in the Explanation column, place a check mark in the Posting Reference column, and enter the amount owed to the creditor in the Balance column. Open an account for each creditor listed on the schedule of accounts payable, even though there may be no balance as of this date. Open accounts for new creditors as needed.
3. Prove the accuracy of your work in Instruction 2 by doing the following. List the balances owed to creditors as shown in the accounts payable ledger. Then add the balances, and compare the resulting total with the balance of the Accounts Payable Control account in the general ledger and with the total of the schedule of accounts payable illustrated on page 218. Use a separate sheet of paper for this step.
4. Record each transaction in the appropriate journal. Use 4 for the page number of each journal.
5. Complete the required daily and summary postings to the general ledger and to the accounts payable ledger.
6. Prepare a schedule of accounts payable as of April 30, 19X1, and prove the total against the control account.

TRANSACTIONS FOR APRIL 19X1

Apr. 1 Purchased slats for $1,023.65 from the Western Aluminum Company, Invoice 7211, April 1; the terms are net 30 days.
1 Issued Check 537 for $1,450 to the Western Aluminum Company in payment for Invoice 6698, dated March 2.
4 Issued Check 538 for $469.20 to the Universal Gear Company for Invoice G1090, dated March 5.
5 Issued Check 539 for $15.50 to purchase purple paint for special job. (Charge to Merchandise Purchases.)
6 Issued Check 540 for $247.50 to the Bronson Milling Company in payment for Invoice A11021, dated February 6.
8 Bought special trim material from the Lexington Supply Company, Invoice 434, April 6, $33.75, net due in 30 days.
11 Paid $249.25 owed to the Asheville Lumber Company, Check 541.
12 Bought cords for $255.15 from the LeMay Cordage Company, Invoice 4718, April 10, due in 30 days net.
14 Purchased special gears for wide blinds costing $198.50 from Wayne Products Inc., Invoice 976, dated April 12, net due in 30 days.
15 Paid $69.50 to the Gandolf Paint Company for Invoice 2412C, dated March 16, Check 542.
18 Paid $5.50 for special tassels, Check 543.
19 Received a $100 allowance from the Western Aluminum Company. Slats purchased on Invoice 7211, April 1, were of inferior quality.

20 Purchased paint for $433.90 from Gandolf Paint Company, Invoice 2567D, April 15, net due in 30 days.

21 Wood bottom slats costing $125 were bought from the Asheville Lumber Company, net payable on May 10, Invoice 813, April 20.

25 Issued Check 544 for $115 to the Extruded Aluminum Corporation to cover Invoice 309B, dated February 25.

28 Purchased tapes costing $342.80 from the Bronson Milling Company, net payable in 60 days, Invoice C24413, dated April 27.

29 Bought two drums of paint for $565.75 from the Farber Paint Company; terms are net May 10; Invoice 301-493 is dated April 25.

30 Received $24.50 credit for gears returned to Wayne Products Inc. The original purchase was on Invoice 976, dated April 12.

UNIT 13

THE COMBINED JOURNAL

In earlier units, it was shown how a business might record all its transactions in a two-column general journal. Then, as the transactions became more numerous, time and effort were saved through the use of special journals. In this unit, we will discuss the way in which a small business may obtain many of the advantages of special journals while using only a single book of original entry. The cornerstone of this simple, yet effective, system is a combined journal, sometimes called a combined cash journal.

Designing a Combined Journal

For a small business, journalizing transactions in a combined journal is faster and easier than it is in a general journal. As in the special journals, a single line is usually all that is required to record a particular transaction. Special columns are used to record the transactions that occur most often. Other Accounts columns are provided for handling less frequent types of entries that would normally be made in the general journal.

Special Columns

The combined journal of a business should be designed with the firm's specific needs in mind. First, the accountant studies the firm's proposed operations in order to develop an appropriate chart of accounts. Then, each account should be considered individually in planning the journal. Accounts that are likely to be used often in recording routine business operations are the ones for which special columns are justified in the new journal. Suppose that the Modern Cleaning Shop had decided to use a combined journal. Study its chart of accounts on page 83, and follow this step-by-step explanation of how the accountant would set up a combined journal for the firm.

The first account in the chart of accounts, Cash, is certainly used often enough to require special columns. Both debit and credit entries are frequently made in the Cash account. Thus, the accountant provides both a Debit column and a Credit column in the Cash section of the journal. Generally, the first two money columns of a combined journal are used for cash transactions.

Another asset account, Accounts Receivable, also requires frequent recording of both debits and credits. Therefore, the accountant sets up two amount columns in the combined journal for Accounts Receivable and provides a check column to show that individual debits and credits have been posted to the accounts receivable subsidiary ledger.

On the other hand, the next asset account in the chart of accounts, Equipment, will probably be used in relatively few transactions. Therefore, it does not justify a special column. The few transactions that do occur can be recorded in the Other Accounts columns of the combined journal.

The liability Accounts Payable will usually be debited and credited a number of times each month. For this reason, the accountant provides two amount columns in the new combined journal for Accounts Payable plus a check column to show when amounts have been posted to the accounts payable subsidiary ledger. There should be very few transactions affecting the owner's capital account. Therefore, a special column is not needed for it.

Numerous sales transactions will require that many credits be recorded in the revenue account during the month. Therefore, the accountant places a column called Cleaning Service Sales in the combined journal.

Turning to the expense items, the accountant finds that Salaries Expense might have several debit entries each month and should therefore be given a special debit column in the combined journal. The Rent Expense account is normally debited for only one payment each month—not enough to warrant a special column. However, the Supplies Used account might be debited in a number of transactions and should have a special column in the combined journal. In addition to these accounts, the new account, Miscellaneous Expense, first used in the January transactions, may have frequent debit entries during the month. The accountant sets up a special column in which to record such entries.

Other Accounts Columns

The combined journal also contains Other Accounts columns for recording both debit and credit entries in accounts for which no special columns are provided. An Account Title column is included for noting the titles of the accounts involved. There is also a Posting Reference column, which is used to record the account numbers as each entry in the Other Accounts columns is posted to the general ledger.

When all designing is done, the combined journal for the Modern Cleaning Shop would appear in the form shown on pages 224 and 225.

Recording Transactions in the Combined Journal

As usual, the accountant analyzes each transaction before recording it in the combined journal. Once he has a mental picture of the entry to be made, he records the date, explanation, and debit and credit figures in their proper columns. If special columns are available, the amounts are entered in them. Otherwise it is necessary to record the amounts in the Other Accounts columns and enter the account titles. Ordinarily, each transaction can be recorded on a single line. Of course, the debits recorded in the entry must equal the credits recorded for the same transaction. The procedures for using the combined journal can be seen by retracing the January 19X2 transactions of the Modern Cleaning Shop that were first presented in Business Project 1 (pages 83–86).

For example, consider the recording procedure for the January 2 transaction: *Purchased cleaning equipment for $770 from the Quality Cleaning Company. Paid with Check 31.*

As this transaction is analyzed, the accountant realizes that he must debit the Equipment account and credit the Cash account. Since there is no special column in the combined journal for Equipment, the $770 debit must be entered in the Other Accounts Debit column and the account title must be written in the Account Title column. The credit to Cash is entered in the special Cash Credit column. The first entry in the combined journal is shown in the illustration provided on pages 224 and 225.

Other January transactions would be recorded in the combined journal as follows.

January 7—Received $700 for cash sales of cleaning services during the first week. The entry in the combined journal involves a debit to Cash and a credit to Cleaning Service Sales. Both amounts are recorded in the special columns provided. (See the second entry in the illustration.) Similar transactions occurred in successive weeks, on January 14, 21, and 27.

January 7—Performed cleaning services for $60 for Ruth Carr, a charge account customer (Sales Slip 1). This transaction is recorded by a debit to Accounts Receivable and a credit to Cleaning Service Sales. Again, special columns are available in the combined journal. Similar credit sales took place on January 14, 19, and 28.

January 9—Collected $200 from December sales on credit to charge customers. For this entry, special columns are used to record a debit to Cash and a credit to Accounts Receivable. Other collections on account occurred on January 16, 23, and 29.

January 10—Issued Check 32 for $300 to Knight, Inc., to cover balance due. This payment is recorded as a debit to Accounts Payable and a credit to Cash. Both parts of the entry are made in special columns. There was another payment to a creditor on January 24.

January 11—Bought a used delivery truck for $1,000 from Ace Motors. Payment is due in one month. The debit to the Equipment account is entered in the Other Accounts Debit column, and the credit to Accounts Payable is recorded in the appropriate special column.

January 15—Issued Check 33 for $400 to pay for cleaning supplies used. The debit is entered in the special column for Supplies Used, and the credit is recorded in the Cash Credit column. More supplies were bought and paid for in a similar way on January 28.

January 17—Issued Check 34 for $700 for the monthly store rent. A debit to the Rent Expense account is recorded in the Other Accounts Debit column, and a credit to Cash is recorded in the appropriate special column.

January 28—Paid $600 for a counter and display fixtures for the proposed new accessories department. Issued Check 36 for that amount. This transaction is recorded by a debit to Equipment in the Other Accounts Debit column and a credit to Cash.

January 30—Issued Check 38 for $60 to pay miscellaneous expenses. Since a special column has been provided for Miscellaneous Expense, the necessary debit can be quickly recorded there. The offsetting credit to Cash is entered in the Cash Credit column.

January 31—Paid $1,700 for monthly salaries. Issued Check 39. The expense account is debited by using the special column for Salaries Expense, and Cash is credited.

The completed combined journal for January is shown below.

COMBINED JOURNAL for Month of January 19X2

DATE	CHECK NO.	EXPLANATION	CASH DR. 101	CASH CR. 101	✓	ACCOUNTS RECEIVABLE DR. 111	✓	ACCOUNTS RECEIVABLE CR. 111
Jan. 2	31	Equipment purchased		770 00				
7		Cash sales	700 00					
7		Ruth Carr			✓	60 00		
9		December accounts	200 00		✓			200 00
10	32	Knight, Inc.		300 00				
11		Ace Motors						
14		Cash sales	725 00					
14		John Costa			✓	25 00		
15	33	Cleaning supplies		400 00				
16		Ruth Carr	30 00		✓			30 00
17	34	Rent for month		700 00				
19		Roy Hess			✓	30 00		
21		Cash sales	900 00					
23		Ruth Carr	30 00		✓			30 00
23		John Costa	15 00		✓			15 00
24	35	Ace Motors		500 00				
27		Cash sales	800 00					
28	36	Fixtures for accessories dept.		600 00				
28		Janet Bell			✓	60 00		
28	37	Cleaning supplies		300 00				
29		John Costa	10 00		✓			10 00
30	38	Miscellaneous items		60 00				
31	39	Payroll for month		1,700 00				
31		Totals	3,410 00	5,330 00		175 00		285 00
			(101)	(101)		(111)		(111)

Daily Postings From the Combined Journal

The individual items in the Other Accounts columns must be posted as promptly as possible to the accounts shown in the Account Title column. In the combined journal illustrated above, these items include three debits to Equipment for $770, $1,000, and $600 and a debit to Rent Expense for $700. The account numbers are written in the Posting Reference column to note the posting of these entries to the general ledger accounts.

Daily postings are made to the accounts receivable and accounts payable ledgers. After each debit or credit posting is made, a check mark is placed in the Accounts Receivable section or the Accounts Payable section of the combined journal.

Proving the Combined Journal

When the month's transactions have been entered, the next step is to total each column and prove the equality of the debits and credits before posting the column totals. The proof can be shown in a simple schedule like the one on page 225.

Page 1

ACCOUNTS PAYABLE		CLEANING SERVICE SALES CR. 401	SALARIES EXPENSE DR. 511	SUPPLIES USED DR. 521	MISC. EXPENSE DR. 591	OTHER ACCOUNTS				
✓	DR. 202	CR. 202					ACCOUNT TITLE	POST. REF.	DEBIT	CREDIT
							Equipment	141	770 00	
			700 00							
			60 00							
✓	300 00									
✓		1,000 00					Equipment	141	1,000 00	
			725 00							
			25 00							
					400 00					
							Rent Expense	516	700 00	
			30 00							
			900 00							
✓	500 00									
			800 00				Equipment	141	600 00	
			60 00							
					300 00					
						60 00				
				1,700 00						
	800 00	1,000 00	3,300 00	1,700 00	700 00	60 00			3,070 00	
	(202)	(202)	(401)	(511)	(521)	(591)			(X)	(X)

MODERN CLEANING SHOP
Proof of Combined Journal
January 31, 19X2

Acct. No.	Account Name	Debit	Credit
101	Cash	$3,410	$5,330
111	Accounts Receivable	175	285
202	Accounts Payable	800	1,000
401	Cleaning Service Sales		3,300
511	Salaries Expense	1,700	
521	Supplies Used	700	
591	Miscellaneous Expense	60	
	Other Accounts	3,070	
	Totals	$9,915	$9,915

End-of-Month Postings From the Combined Journal

When the proof of the combined journal is completed, all column totals, except those in the Other Accounts section, are posted. The account number is recorded beneath each column total as the posting is made to the account involved. An "X" is written beneath the amount columns in the Other Accounts section to show that the totals are not posted. Thus, for the operations of the Modern Cleaning Shop in January 19X2, the bulk of the posting is completed in ten summary figures.

Typical Uses

The combined journal is sometimes used in small professional offices, service businesses, and merchandising businesses.

Professional Offices

The combined journal may be ideal to record the transactions that occur in a professional office, such as the office of a doctor, lawyer, accountant, or architect. However, special journals are more efficient if the transactions become very numerous or are too varied.

Service Businesses

The use of the combined journal to record the January transactions of the Modern Cleaning Shop has already been discussed. The combined journal may be advantageous for small service businesses, provided that the volume of transactions does not become excessive and provided that the nature of the transactions does not become too involved.

Merchandising Businesses

The combined journal may be used by a merchandising business, but only if the firm is relatively small and has a limited variety of transactions involving a very small number of accounts. In fact, even for a small merchandising business (such as the Modern Cleaning Shop after the accessories department is opened), the use of special journals may prove more advantageous.

If the variety of transactions is so great that many different accounts are required, the combined journal will not work well. The accountant will either have to use so many columns that the journal will become unwieldy, or he will have to record so many transactions in the Other Accounts columns that little efficiency will result. As a general rule, if the transactions of a business are numerous enough to merit the use of special journals, any attempt to substitute the combined journal is a mistake. Remember that each special journal can be designed for maximum efficiency in recording transactions.

principles and procedures summary

The combined journal unites the functions of the various special journals and the general journal into one book of original entry. In designing a combined journal, the accountant should review the chart of accounts so that he can set up special columns for accounts that are expected to have numerous entries. Other Accounts columns are provided to take care of any transactions for which no special column has been established. Items recorded in the Other Accounts columns are posted daily. At the end of the month, the journal is totaled and the equality of the debits and credits is proved. Then, the totals of all the special columns are posted.

managerial implications

The combined journal is of special benefit in a small business or a small professional office. It enables the business owner or professional person to easily keep track of the firm's financial affairs. For an operation of limited size, the combined journal is a time-saving and efficient recording device. However, if the volume of the firm's transactions is large and varied, the combined journal becomes unwieldy and does not allow for a division of labor.

managerial discussion questions

1. Why is the combined journal of special benefit only to the small business owner or professional person?
2. How would an accountant design a combined journal?

application of principles

PROBLEM 13-1 Rose Cavalier opened an office for a management consulting service on May 1, 19X1. Her accountant designed a simple accounting system consisting of a general ledger and a combined journal with the following money columns: Cash Dr. 101 and Cr. 101; Accounts Receivable Dr. 111 and Cr. 111; Professional Fees Cr. 401; Salaries Expense Dr. 511; Office Supplies Used Dr. 521; Traveling Expense Dr. 522; Duplicating Expense Dr. 533; and Other Accounts Debit and Credit. A chart of accounts and the transactions for Cavalier's first month of consulting work are given below and on pages 228–229.

ACCOUNTS

ASSETS

101	Cash
111	Accounts Receivable
141	Office Furniture
143	Automobile

LIABILITIES

202	Accounts Payable

OWNER'S EQUITY

301	Rose Cavalier, Capital
399	Revenue and Expense Summary

REVENUE

401	Professional Fees

EXPENSES

504	Telephone Expense
505	Utilities Expense
511	Salaries Expense
516	Rent Expense
521	Office Supplies Used
522	Traveling Expense
533	Duplicating Expense
591	Miscellaneous Expense

227

INSTRUCTIONS
1. Record each transaction in the combined journal.
2. Foot the combined journal at the end of the month, and prepare a schedule to prove the journal.
3. Enter the totals, and rule the combined journal.

TRANSACTIONS FOR MAY 19X1

May 1 Rose Cavalier deposited $12,500 of her personal savings in the City National Bank to open a checking account for the Cavalier Consulting Service.
1 Paid $500 for office rent for May, Check 1.
3 Issued Check 2 for $200 to pay for duplicating service.
4 Purchased office furniture for $550 by Check 3.
5 Paid $50 for office supplies by Check 4.
5 Bought an $8,000 automobile for use in the business; the terms are $2,000 cash down, with the balance payable in 60 days. Check 5 was issued for the down payment.
7 Check 6 for $150 was issued to pay the weekly salary of the office assistant.
7 Received $400 cash in fees for professional services to clients. Also earned $550 for professional services on credit.
9 Paid $20 by Check 7 for gasoline, oil, and routine servicing of the automobile. (Debit Traveling Expense.)
10 Paid the $34 telephone bill by Check 8.
10 Bought bookcases costing $200 for the office. Paid $50 by Check 9. The balance is due in 30 days.
12 Purchased $60 worth of additional office supplies; the terms are 30 days net.
14 Issued Check 10 for $150 to pay the weekly salary of the office assistant.
14 Sold professional services during the week for $500 in cash and $600 on credit.
16 Paid $260 for airline tickets and hotel accommodations in connection with a convention, Check 11.
17 Paid $75 for the utility bill by Check 12.
18 Paid $20 for trash removal service, Check 13. (Debit Miscellaneous Expense.)
19 Issued Check 14 for $50 to pay for additional duplicating service.
21 Paid $150 for the salary of the office assistant by Check 15.
21 Sold professional services during the week for $400 in cash and $625 on credit.
21 Received $550 cash from clients on account.
23 Paid $20 for gasoline and minor servicing of the automobile, Check 16.
25 Issued Check 17 for $85 to buy airline tickets for a business trip to a client's plant.
25 Received checks amounting to $800 from clients to apply toward their accounts.

28 Issued Check 18 for $150 to pay the weekly salary of the office assistant.

28 Performed professional services during the week for $250 in cash and $750 on credit.

29 Issued Check 19 for $75 for additional office supplies.

alternate problem

PROBLEM 13-1A Dr. William Henderson reestablished his medical practice when he returned from military service. Based upon his previous experience, he decided to use a simple accounting system consisting of a general ledger and a combined journal with the following money columns: Cash Dr. 101 and Cr. 101; Accounts Receivable Dr. 111 and Cr. 111; Medical Fees Cr. 401; Salaries Expense Dr. 511; Office Supplies Used Dr. 521; Medical Supplies Used Dr. 522; Automobile Expense Dr. 533; and Other Accounts Debit and Credit. A chart of accounts and the transactions for Henderson's first month of practice are given below and on page 230.

ACCOUNTS

ASSETS		REVENUE	
101	Cash	401	Medical Fees
111	Accounts Receivable		
141	Equipment		**EXPENSES**
143	Automobile	504	Telephone Expense
		505	Utilities Expense
LIABILITIES		511	Salaries Expense
202	Accounts Payable	516	Rent Expense
		521	Office Supplies Used
OWNER'S EQUITY		522	Medical Supplies Used
		533	Automobile Expense
301	William Henderson, Capital	591	Miscellaneous Expense
399	Revenue and Expense Summary		

INSTRUCTIONS
1. Record each transaction in the combined journal.
2. Foot the combined journal at the end of the month, and prepare a schedule to prove the journal.
3. Enter the totals, and rule the combined journal.

TRANSACTIONS FOR APRIL 19X1

Apr. 3 William Henderson deposited $6,000 of his savings to open an account for his medical practice in the First National Bank.

3 Signed a lease and paid $400 in advance for one month's rent for a suite of offices in the Medical Arts Building, Check 1.

3 Paid $575 for office and examining equipment by Check 2.

4 Paid $76.75 for office supplies by Check 3.

5 Paid $273.50 for medical supplies by Check 4.

7	Bought a used automobile for the practice. Paid $2,000 by Check 5 and agreed to pay the balance of $3,100 in ten monthly installments of $310 each.
8	Issued Check 6 for $160 for the weekly salary of the receptionist.
8	Revenue from medical services during the first week amounted to $136 in cash and $244 in accounts receivable.
10	Paid $16.50 for gasoline and oil for the automobile, Check 7.
10	Bought a new typewriter for $650, paying $150 by Check 8 and promising to make five monthly payments of $100 each. (Use only one line for this entry.)
11	Paid $71.65 for medical supplies by Check 9.
14	Paid $37.75 for office supplies by Check 10.
15	Paid $160 for the weekly salary of the receptionist by Check 11.
15	Received revenue from medical services of $192 in cash and $563 in accounts receivable during the week.
17	Paid $9.35 for an item of miscellaneous expense by Check 12.
19	Paid $44.95 for office supplies by Check 13.
21	Paid $19.80 for gasoline and oil for the automobile by Check 14.
22	Paid the $160 weekly salary of the receptionist by Check 15.
22	Received $145 in cash from patients to apply on accounts receivable.
22	Received $288 in cash and $852 in accounts receivable for medical services performed this week.
25	Paid $81.75 for the utilities bill, Check 16.
26	Paid $98.50 for the telephone bill by Check 17.
27	Paid $84.25 for medical supplies, Check 18.
28	Received a total of $166 in checks to apply toward accounts receivable.
29	Paid $160 for the receptionist's weekly salary, Check 19.
29	Received $235 in cash and $490 in accounts receivable for medical services performed during the week.

UNIT 14

THE VOUCHER SYSTEM

Earlier we discussed the need for internal control over business operations. In this unit, you will learn about the voucher system, a widely used method of controlling liabilities and payments. This system and two accounting records used with it, the voucher register and the check register, will be examined in detail.

Internal Control in a Medium-Sized Business

The firm you have studied so far, the Modern Cleaning Shop, is small, has relatively simple operations, and has a limited number of transactions. For example, the business makes only a few credit purchases each month and deals with only a small group of creditors. A simple system of control over liabilities and payments therefore works effectively in this firm. However, a business with more complex operations requires a more elaborate set of control procedures. The firm that we discuss in this unit, the Style Clothing Store, is an example of such a business.

The Modern Cleaning Shop has a single owner and is known as a *sole proprietorship*. As you study the operations of the Style Clothing Store, you will become familiar with another type of business organization, the *partnership*, in which there are two or more owners. When a firm grows and engages in a wide range of activities, it often becomes difficult for a single owner to personally handle all operational and financial details of the business. This is one major reason why two or more individuals might form a partnership.

The Style Clothing Store is owned by three partners: Linda Hanson, Steven Casey, and Janet Miller. The partnership was formed on February 1, 19X1. At that time Hanson, formerly sole owner of the Style Clothing Store, transferred the assets and liabilities of the store as her investment in the new business. Casey and Miller contributed additional capital in the form of cash.

Actually, there are very few differences in the routine accounting procedures followed by sole proprietorships and partnerships. At this point, it is sufficient that you know that a separate capital account and a separate drawing account are opened for each partner. Thus, the chart of accounts for the Style Clothing Store contains the following owners' equity accounts.

ACCOUNTS

301 Linda Hanson, Capital
302 Linda Hanson, Drawing
311 Steven Casey, Capital
312 Steven Casey, Drawing
321 Janet Miller, Capital
322 Janet Miller, Drawing

The public accountant hired by the Style Clothing Store makes the following recommendations for effective internal control over liabilities and cash payments.

Internal Control Over Liabilities and Cash Payments

1. No liabilities should be incurred without prior authorization. For example, a properly approved purchase order should be required for each credit purchase of merchandise.
2. All payments should be made by check, except for minor payments from petty cash.
3. No check should be written without a properly approved voucher to authorize payment.
4. Bills should be approved for payment only by experienced and responsible personnel.
5. The records covering bills and payments should be kept by someone other than the person approving the bills for payment.
6. Still another person should sign the checks and mail them to creditors.

The Payment Voucher

As indicated in Recommendation 3, control over payments at the Style Clothing Store is achieved through the use of a *voucher system*. A form called a *voucher* is prepared to authorize the payment of obligations, to establish cash funds, and to make cash transfers.

For example, the first obligation that the Style Clothing Store had to meet was the rent on the building it occupies, which is due on the first of the month. The accountant in charge of the books of the firm prepared Voucher 2-01 on February 1, 19X1, in favor of the Fisher Realty Company for $250, the monthly rental. Since Casey is the partner in charge of purchasing goods and services, the next step was to obtain his signature on the voucher to authorize payment. Then Susan Bates, the office clerk, was instructed to write out the check and have Hanson sign and mail it.

Note how the principles of internal control have been applied. One person (the accountant) prepared the voucher, and a second person (Casey) approved it. Then, a third person (Bates) wrote the check, and a fourth person (Hanson) signed the check and mailed it. (Casey should not sign the check because he approved the voucher in the first place.)

The same procedure is followed in the issuance of two other vouchers that are required almost at once to facilitate business operations. Voucher 2-02 for $50 provides for the establishment of a change fund for use by Robert Gallo, the salesclerk for the Style Clothing Store. This fund was mentioned in an earlier unit in connection with the receipt of cash over the counter. Another voucher, 2-03, is drawn in favor of Susan Bates to set up a petty cash fund of $25, which Bates will maintain.

Payment vouchers are often prenumbered consecutively. However, the accountant for the Style Clothing Store has suggested that the firm use a two-part number—the number to the left of the dash representing the month and the number to the right showing the sequence within the month. Thus, Voucher 2-01 identifies the first voucher prepared in February.

When an invoice for merchandise or supplies is received, the voucher procedure is more elaborate than that required for the rent payment. The first step is to verify the invoice. For example, on February 1 the Style Clothing Store received an invoice for merchandise from Valley Wholesale Clothiers. Bates, who opened the mail, passed the invoice along to Casey, who is responsible for store operations. He inspected the incoming shipment and made sure that it contained everything that was listed on the invoice. Then he passed the invoice to Hanson, who referred to the purchase order files to see that the prices charged on the invoice did not exceed those specified when the order was placed. (A small check mark is often made on the invoice beside each item verified.)

At this point the office clerk, Bates, checked the arithmetic on the invoice. In technical terms, she verified the extensions and the total. Checking the extensions involves multiplying the quantity of each item by its unit price. Checking the total involves re-adding the extensions and refiguring the discounts. After these verifications were made, the invoice appeared as shown below.

```
        VALLEY WHOLESALE CLOTHIERS
           123 PONCE DE LEON AVENUE
             ATLANTA, GEORGIA 30308
                                            Invoice No.  R-47651

    SOLD  Style Clothing Store            Date  February 1, 19X1
     TO   246 Main Street
          Greenville, SC 29610
                                            Customer's
                                            Order No.  1-34

                                            Terms  2/10, n/30

    ┌──────────┬──────────────────────┬──────────┬──────────────┐
    │ QUANTITY │ DESCRIPTION OF ITEMS │ PER UNIT │    AMOUNT    │
    ├──────────┼──────────────────────┼──────────┼──────────────┤
    │ ✓  20    │ Corduroy Suits D-4786│ ✓ $45.00 │ ✓$    900.00 │
    │ ✓  8 pr. │ Denim Jeans P-537    │ ✓  12.50 │ ✓     100.00 │
    │ ✓  1     │ Denim Jacket R-258   │ ✓  20.14 │ ✓      20.14 │
    │          │                      │          │ ✓$  1,020.14 │
    │          │        Less 20%      │          │ ✓     204.03 │
    │          │                      │          │ ✓     816.11 │
    │          │        Less 10%      │          │ ✓      81.61 │
    │          │                      │          │ ✓$    734.50 │
    └──────────┴──────────────────────┴──────────┴──────────────┘

              VERIFICATIONS
         QUANTITIES  │  J.C.
         RECEIVED    │
         PRICES      │  L.H.
         CHARGED     │
         EXTENSIONS  │  S.B.
         & TOTAL     │
```

Notice the use of a *verification stamp* on this invoice. As the Style Clothing Store receives each invoice, the office clerk applies a rubber stamp to imprint the block of control information shown. Each person who verifies part of the invoice puts his or her initials in the proper space to indicate that the invoice is correct in that respect. Bates entered her initials to show that she had verified the extensions and total, Casey initialed the invoice to show that he had verified the quantity received, and Hanson initialed it to show that she had checked the prices billed.

Preparing and Approving the Voucher

The verified invoice now becomes the basis for the preparation of a voucher (2-04) to authorize the payment when due. When completed, this voucher indicates the amount ($734.50) and the number (501) of the account to be debited (Merchandise Purchases). Then the verified invoice of Valley Wholesale Clothiers is attached to the voucher and given to Casey, who is in charge of purchasing operations. After Casey records his approval on the voucher, it is ready for recording in the voucher register. The completed payment voucher is shown below.

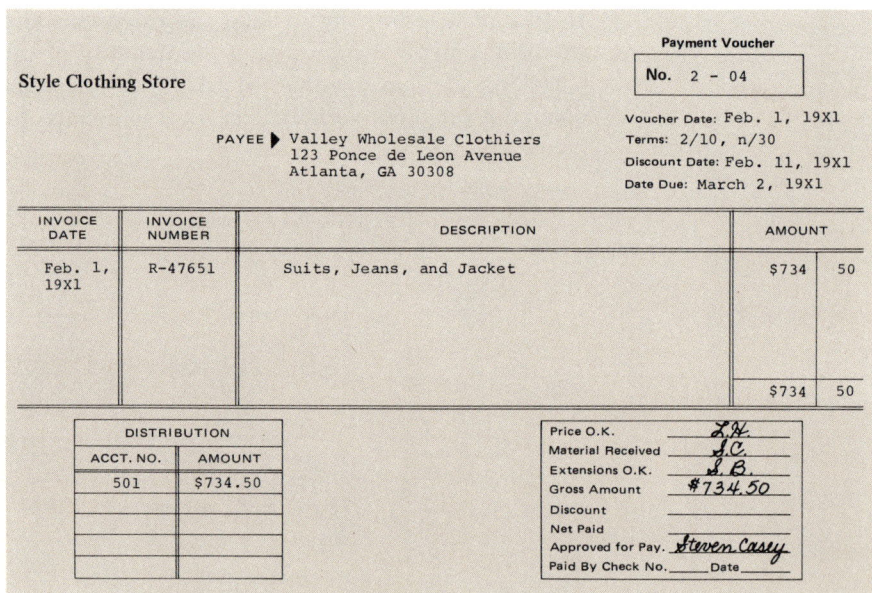

Note that the Distribution section of the voucher illustrated above shows only the number of the account to be debited (501). No account to be credited is specified because vouchers are normally credited to the Accounts Payable account. (Since an accounts payable subsidiary ledger is not used with the voucher system, the Accounts Payable account in the general ledger is not called a control account.)

Sometimes it may be necessary to credit accounts other than the Accounts Payable account. In this case, it is customary to enter *all debits and credits* in the Distribution section of the voucher. For example, Voucher 2-14 payable to Susan Bates is for $182.55. This represents her gross earnings of $225 for the pay period, less $13.50 FICA deducted (at an assumed 6 percent rate) and less $28.95 income tax withheld. Recording her salary involves the following entries to the firm's accounts. Office Salaries Expense (551) is debited for $225.00, Accounts Payable (205) is credited for $182.55, Employee Deductions—FICA Tax (221) is credited for $13.50, and Employee Deductions—Income Tax Withheld (222) is credited for $28.95. The Distribution section of the voucher would look like this.

DISTRIBUTION

Acct. No.	Amount
Dr. 551	$225.00
Cr. 205	182.55
Cr. 221	13.50
Cr. 222	28.95

The Voucher Register

Vouchers are listed in numerical order in an accounting record called a *voucher register*. The voucher register provides space for recording the date and number of each voucher, the payee, the amount to be paid (which is usually to be credited to Accounts Payable), and the account to be debited. Special columns are set up for accounts having frequent transactions, and Other Accounts Debit and Credit columns are provided for accounts that are used less often. Columns are also provided for recording the date paid and the number of the check issued to make the payment. The voucher register used by the Style Clothing Store is shown on the next page.

Unpaid vouchers are filed according to the date on which they should be paid. The file of unpaid vouchers thus represents the accounts payable of the firm, and no formal accounts payable subsidiary ledger is required.

Vouchers that have been paid are stamped "Paid" and then filed in the paid vouchers file in numeric order. In some cases, paid vouchers may be filed according to the name of the payee to permit more ready reference and avoid the possibility of duplication of payment.

Posting From the Voucher Register

The completed voucher register covering the operations of the Style Clothing Store for the month of February is shown on pages 236 and 237. At the end of January, when the firm was still solely owned by Linda Hanson, it owed the following vouchers: 1-22, $2,000; 1-26, $300; 1-27, $200; 1-28, $500. As you saw previously, Hanson transferred the assets and liabilities of her store to the partnership she formed with Casey and Miller on February 1, 19X1. The vouchers remaining unpaid at the end of January were assumed as accounts payable by the partnership.

Each item in the Other Accounts Debit or Credit column is posted shortly after entry to the account indicated. At the end of the month, all the columns

VOUCHER REGISTER for Month of February 19X1

	DATE	VOU. NO.	PAYABLE TO	PAID DATE	PAID CHECK NO.	ACCTS. PAYABLE CR. 205	EMPLOYEE DEDUC. FICA CR. 221	EMPLOYEE DEDUC. INC. TAX CR. 222
1	Feb. 1	2-01	Fisher Realty Co.	2/1	101	250 00		
2	1	2-02	Robert Gallo	2/1	102	50 00		
3	1	2-03	Susan Bates	2/1	103	25 00		
4	1	2-04	Valley Wholesale Clothiers	2/10	108	734 50		
5	3	2-05	Graham Paper Co.			189 50		
6	5	2-06	Office Suppliers			57 75		
7	9	2-07	Kelly & Smith, Attys.			200 00		
8	10	2-08	G. Thompson, CPA			75 00		
9	10	2-09	Burke Clothing Co.	2/19	114	5,240 00		
10	10	2-10	Southern Express Co.	2/11	109	56 35		
11	10	2-11	Fashions, Inc.	2/19	115	4,937 00		
12	10	2-12	Fast Truckers	2/11	110	82 50		
13	12	2-13	Moore Insurance			240 00		
14	15	2-14	Susan Bates	2/15	111	182 55	13 50	28 95
15	15	2-15	Robert Gallo	2/15	112	209 40	15 00	25 60
16	15	2-16	Alfred White	2/15	113	182 00	12 60	15 40
17	18	2-17	Better Box Co.			95 00		
18	25	2-18	Greenville Water Co.			12 50		
19	25	2-19	State Utilities Co.			157 25		
20	27	2-20	Valley Wholesale Clothiers			3,465 00		
21	27	2-21	Central Telephone Co.			26 75		
22	28	2-22	Star-Herald Papers			329 75		
23	28	2-23	Jiffy Delivery Co.			245 00		
24	28	2-24	Susan Bates	2/28	116	182 55	13 50	28 95
25	28	2-25	Robert Gallo	2/28	117	209 40	15 00	25 60
26	28	2-26	Alfred White	2/28	118	182 00	12 60	15 40
27	28	2-27	Linda Hanson	2/28	119	400 00		
28	28	2-28	Steven Casey	2/28	120	375 00		
29	28	2-29	Susan Bates	2/28	121	17 05		
	28		Totals			18,408 80	82 20	139 90
						(205)	(221)	(222)

in the voucher register are totaled and the equality of the debits and credits is proved by cross-footing.

When the proof is completed, the totals of all columns except the Other Accounts columns are posted to the accounts shown in the column headings. An "X" is placed under the totals of the Other Accounts columns to indicate that the amounts are not posted.

The Check Register

In the accounting system of the Modern Cleaning Shop, the cash payments journal contained columns for the accounts to be debited as cash was paid out. In the voucher system used by the Style Clothing Store, the function of classifying expenditures is performed by use of the voucher register. The actual payment of cash is always made to settle a specific voucher that was previously recorded in the voucher register as an account payable. Therefore, each check written under the voucher system results in a debit to Accounts Payable and a credit to Cash. Checks are recorded in numeric order in a *check register*

MERCH. PURCH. DR. 501	FREIGHT IN DR. 506	STORE SUP. AND EXP. DR. 523	OTHER ACCOUNTS			
			ACCOUNT TITLE	POST. REF.	DEBIT	CREDIT
			Rent Expense	542	250 00	
			Change Fund	106	50 00	
734 50			Petty Cash	105	25 00	
		189 50				
			Office Supplies and Expense	553	57 75	
			Professional Fees Expense	554	200 00	
5,240 00			Professional Fees Expense	554	75 00	
	56 35					
4,937 00						
		82 50				
			Insurance Expense	536	240 00	
			Office Salaries Expense	551	225 00	
			Sales Salaries Expense	521	250 00	
			Sales Salaries Expense	521	210 00	
		95 00				
			Utilities Expense	543	12 50	
3,465 00			Utilities Expense	543	157 25	
			Office Supplies and Expense	553	26 75	
			Advertising Expense	522	329 75	
			Delivery Expense	532	245 00	
			Office Salaries Expense	551	225 00	
			Sales Salaries Expense	521	250 00	
			Sales Salaries Expense	521	210 00	
			Linda Hanson, Drawing	301	400 00	
			Steven Casey, Drawing	311	375 00	
	2 55	3 45	Advertising Expense	522	2 00	
			Office Supplies and Expense	553	9 05	
14,376 50	141 40	287 95			3,825 05	
(501)	(506)	(523)			(X)	

that provides space for entering the date, check number, payee's name, voucher number, and amount of the payment. The following illustration shows how Checks 101 to 103 issued by the Style Clothing Store up to this point are entered in the check register.

CHECK REGISTER for Month of February 19X1   Page 1

DATE		CHECK NO.	PAYABLE TO	VOU. NO.	ACCTS. PAYABLE DR. 205	PURCH. DISCOUNT CR. 512	CASH CR. 101
Feb.	1	101	Fisher Realty Co.	2-01	250 00		250 00
	1	102	Robert Gallo	2-02	50 00		50 00
	1	103	Susan Bates	2-03	25 00		25 00

The Style Clothing Store uses a specially printed check form that is similar to the one illustrated on page 134 in Unit 8.

Paying an Invoice Less Discount

The Style Clothing Store uses the procedure in accounting for cash discounts on purchases that you learned in Unit 7. Invoices are recorded at total price. When discounts are taken, they are credited to the Purchases Discount account and are shown on the income statement as a reduction in the cost of goods sold.

The invoice of Valley Wholesale Clothiers (Voucher 2-04) was recorded in the voucher register for its full amount, $734.50. The terms are stated on the invoice as 2/10, n/30. This means that a discount of 2 percent may be taken if payment is made within 10 days; otherwise, the full amount is due within 30 days. The discount amounts to $14.69 ($734.50 × 0.02).

While 2 percent may not seem like a significant amount, remember that it is offered for paying the invoice only 20 days earlier. On a yearly basis, this saving amounts to slightly more than 36 percent (365 ÷ 20 days × 0.02). A business cannot afford to lose such a generous return on its money by not paying within the discount period.

As previously explained, unpaid vouchers are usually filed according to their due dates. If a cash discount is offered, the filing date is the last date on which payment can be made to take the discount. The invoice from Valley Wholesale Clothiers must be paid on February 10 in order to obtain the discount. Since the amount of the discount is $14.69, the amount of the actual payment should be $719.81 ($734.50 − $14.69). However, if $719.81 is debited to Accounts Payable, the balance of $734.50 payable to Valley Wholesale Clothiers would not be closed.

This recording problem is easily solved by providing a special column in the check register for purchases discounts. The full amount of the invoice is entered as a debit in the Accounts Payable column; the amount of the discount is entered as a credit in the Purchases Discount column; and the amount of the check is entered as a credit in the Cash column. Here is how the check issued to Valley Wholesale Clothiers is recorded in the check register.

CHECK REGISTER for Month of February 19X1   Page 1

DATE	CHECK NO.	PAYABLE TO	VOU. NO.	ACCTS. PAYABLE DR. 205	PURCH. DISCOUNT CR. 512	CASH CR. 101
Feb. 10	108	Valley Wh. Clothiers	2-04	734 50	14 69	719 81

Posting From the Check Register

The partial check register for the Style Clothing Store for the month of February is shown on the next page. Vouchers 1-26, 1-22, 1-27, and 1-28 represent liabilities of the original firm owned solely by Linda Hanson. These liabilities were assumed by the partnership when it was formed on February 1.

At the end of the month, all the money columns in the check register are totaled and the equality of the debits and credits is proved. Then the totals are posted to the general ledger accounts indicated in each of the column head-

CHECK REGISTER for Month of February 19X1						Page 1	
DATE	CHECK NO.	PAYABLE TO	VOU. NO.	ACCTS. PAYABLE DR. 205		PURCH. DISCOUNT CR. 512	CASH CR. 101
Feb. 1	101	Fisher Realty Co.	2-01	250	00		250 00
1	102	Robert Gallo	2-02	50	00		50 00
1	103	Susan Bates	2-03	25	00		25 00
8	104	Star-Herald Papers*	1-26	300	00		300 00
8	105	Madison Wholesalers*	1-22	2,000	00	40 00	1,960 00
8	106	Jiffy Delivery Co.*	1-27	200	00		200 00
8	107	Burke Cothing Co.*	1-28	500	00	10 00	490 00
10	108	Valley Wh. Clothiers	2-04	734	50	14 69	719 81
28	119	Linda Hanson	2-27	400	00		400 00
28	120	Steven Casey	2-28	375	00		375 00
28	121	Susan Bates	2-29	17	05		17 05
28		Totals		16,315	30	268 23	16,047 07
				(205)		(512)	(101)

*Liabilities of Style Clothing Store assumed by the partnership of Hanson, Casey, and Miller.

ings. The postings arising from the February totals of the check register can be summarized as follows.

    Dr. 205 Accounts Payable $16,315.30

        Cr. 512 Purchases Discount $ 268.23
        Cr. 101 Cash   16,047.07
        $16,315.30

Proving the Accounts Payable Balance

After the postings from the voucher register and the check register have been made, the balance of the Accounts Payable account in the general ledger is $5,093.50. The following illustration of this account shows the amount carried over from the original firm ($3,000) as well as the February transactions of the partnership. The abbreviation *CR* in the Posting Reference column indicates the amount that was posted from the check register. The abbreviation *VR* indicates the amount that was posted from the voucher register.

Accounts Payable						No. 205
DATE	EXPLANATION	POST. REF.	DEBIT	CREDIT	BALANCE	DR. CR.
19X1 Feb. 1		J1		3,000 00	3,000 00	Cr.
28		VR1		18,408 80	21,408 80	Cr.
28		CR1	16,315 30		5,093 50	Cr.

As already noted, under the voucher system, no subsidiary ledger of accounts payable is maintained. The unpaid vouchers identify the persons or firms to whom amounts are owed. These unpaid vouchers are listed on a schedule at the end of the month, and their total is checked against the balance of the Accounts Payable account in the general ledger. This schedule should also be checked against the voucher register to be sure that it includes all items that have not been marked "Paid." The schedule of unpaid vouchers for February 19X1 prepared at the Style Clothing Store is shown below.

STYLE CLOTHING STORE
Schedule of Vouchers Payable
February 28, 19X1

Voucher Number	Payable to	Amount
2–05	Graham Paper Company	$ 189.50
2–06	Office Suppliers	57.75
2–07	Kelly & Smith, Attorneys	200.00
2–08	G. E. Thompson, CPA	75.00
2–13	Moore Insurance Agency	240.00
2–17	Better Box Company	95.00
2–18	Greenville Water Company	12.50
2–19	State Utilities Company	157.25
2–20	Valley Wholesale Clothiers	3,465.00
2–21	Central Telephone Company	26.75
2–22	Star-Herald Papers	329.75
2–23	Jiffy Delivery Company	245.00
	Total	$5,093.50

Transactions Requiring Special Treatment

As long as invoices are received, verified, vouchered, and paid in the normal manner, businesses using the voucher system can efficiently handle a great volume of transactions. However, the procedures are rather rigid, and certain infrequent transactions may be awkward to record. Here are some typical examples.

Partial Payments

After a voucher has been prepared for the full amount of an invoice, a firm may decide to pay in two or more installments. For instance, suppose that the Style Clothing Store bought furniture and fixtures costing $4,000 on April 4, and Voucher 4-08 was prepared to cover the purchase. Being short of cash at the end of April, the firm arranged to pay only half the amount at that time and to pay the other half at the end of May.

In this case, the original voucher (4-08) is canceled by issuing two new vouchers (4-33 and 4-34). The new vouchers are recorded in the voucher register separately, each entry involving a credit of $2,000 to the Accounts Payable account in the usual manner. However, each entry also involves a debit of $2,000 to Accounts Payable, which is recorded in the Other Accounts Debit column to cancel the original voucher. (The original debit of $4,000 to the Furniture and Fixtures account is not affected.) A notation of the cancellation is made in the Paid Date column of the voucher register on the line where Voucher 4-08 (the original voucher) was recorded, and the new voucher numbers are entered in the Paid Check Number column, as illustrated below.

The first new voucher (4-33) is paid at the end of April (right away), and the second new voucher (4-34) is filed for payment at the end of May.

VOUCHER REGISTER for Month of April 19X1 — Page 3

DATE	VOU. NO.	PAYABLE TO	PAID DATE	PAID CHECK NO.	ACCTS. PAYABLE CR. 205	OTHER ACCOUNTS — ACCOUNT TITLE	POST. REF.	DEBIT	CREDIT
Apr. 4	4-08	Office Suppliers	Canc.	V4-33 V4-34	4,000 00	Furniture and Fixtures	131	4,000 00	
30	4-33	Office Suppliers	4/30	208	2,000 00	Accounts Payable	205	2,000 00	
30	4-34	Office Suppliers			2,000 00	Accounts Payable	205	2,000 00	

Notes Payable The Style Clothing Store owes $10,000 to the First National Bank on a 9 percent 60-day note, dated February 1. This transaction was recorded in the cash receipts journal on February 1 by debiting Cash and crediting Notes Payable—Bank for $10,000. On April 2, when the note falls due, a voucher must be prepared to authorize payment of $10,150 ($10,000 face value of the note plus $150 interest). By means of an entry in the voucher register, Notes Payable—Bank is debited for $10,000, Interest Expense is debited for $150, and Accounts Payable is credited for $10,150. Then a check for $10,150 is issued and entered in the check register to settle the obligation. The entry in the voucher register is shown below.

VOUCHER REGISTER for Month of April 19X1 — Page 3

DATE	VOU. NO.	PAYABLE TO	PAID DATE	PAID CHECK NO.	ACCTS. PAYABLE CR. 205	OTHER ACCOUNTS — ACCOUNT TITLE	POST. REF.	DEBIT	CREDIT
Apr. 2	4-04	First Nat'l Bank	4/2	204	10,150 00	Notes Payable— Bank	201	10,000 00	
						Interest Expense	591	150 00	

Another recording problem involving notes payable might arise after a voucher has been prepared for an invoice in the normal manner. Suppose that the debtor decides, instead of writing a check, to issue a note payable to the supplier as a means of postponing payment. The amount owed is no longer an account payable. Therefore, a general journal entry is made debiting Accounts Payable (thus canceling the original voucher) and crediting Notes Payable— Trade. When the time comes for paying the note, the entries are the same as those previously described for paying the note owed to the bank. A new voucher is prepared for the note (plus interest, if any), and it is paid.

Purchases Returns and Allowances

If the Style Clothing Store receives goods that are unsatisfactory for some reason, the items may be returned to the supplier. At other times, such goods may be kept and an allowance will be made by the supplier to reduce the purchase price. In either case, the amount finally owed to the supplier is less than the amount of the original invoice. If the original invoice has already been vouchered, the accounting records must be adjusted.

For example, suppose that on March 2 the Style Clothing Store receives an invoice for $750 for merchandise purchased from Madison Wholesalers. Voucher 3-05 is prepared for the invoice. Then, on March 8, an allowance of $50 is made by the supplier to cover damage in transit. The revised amount is to be paid on March 11, less a 2 percent cash discount, as computed here.

Voucher 3-05	$750
Allowance granted on March 8	50
Amount still owed	$700
Less 2% cash discount	14
Amount to be paid on March 11	$686

Method 1. On March 8, when the allowance is made, a new voucher for the revised amount owed, $700, can be issued crediting Accounts Payable. Accounts Payable is also debited for $750 to cancel the original voucher (3-05), and Purchases Returns and Allowances is credited for $50. Using the Other Accounts Debit and Credit columns in the voucher register, this entry would appear as shown in the first illustration on the next page.

On the line for Voucher 3-05, a notation is made in the Paid section, "Canceled by Voucher 3-12." This paves the way for the issuance on March 11 of a check for $686 ($700 less the discount). This check is entered in the check register by debiting Accounts Payable for $700 and crediting Purchases Discount for $14 and Cash for $686.

Method 2. Some accountants use a simpler method for handling this type of adjustment. Since the voucher register for March was not closed and posted before the allowance was agreed upon, the original entry can be corrected by making a notation for the $50 allowance on the same line as the original voucher entry. The notation is circled. This method is shown in the second illustration on the next page.

The adjustment is recorded on the original voucher, and when approved by Casey, payment is made for the net amount. At the end of the month, the figures that are circled are totaled separately from the original figures in each column of the voucher register. The $50 item illustrated is posted as a debit to Accounts Payable and a credit to Purchases Returns and Allowances, thereby accomplishing the same result as the first method. Note, however, that the second method can be used only if the revision is made before the voucher register has been summarized for the period.

VOUCHER REGISTER for Month of March 19X1											Page 2	
			PAID		ACCTS. PAYABLE CR. 205	MERCH. PURCH. DR. 501	OTHER ACCOUNTS					
DATE	VOU. NO.	PAYABLE TO	DATE	CHECK NO.			ACCOUNT TITLE		POST. REF.	DEBIT		CREDIT
Mar. 2	3-05	Madison Wholesalers	Canc.	V3-12	750 00	750 00						
8	3-12	Madison Wholesalers			700 00		Accounts Payable Purchases Ret. and Allow.		205 509	750 00		50 00

VOUCHER REGISTER for Month of March 19X1											Page 2	
			PAID		ACCTS. PAYABLE CR. 205	MERCH. PURCH. DR. 501	OTHER ACCOUNTS					
DATE	VOU. NO.	PAYABLE TO	DATE	CHECK NO.			ACCOUNT TITLE		POST. REF.	DEBIT		CREDIT
Mar. 2	3-05	Madison Wholesalers			(50 00) 750 00	(50 00) 750 00						
31		Totals			(50 00) 19,980 00	(50 00) 15,960 00				5,000 00		2,000 00
					(205)	(501)				(X)		(X)

Recording Purchase Discounts Lost

The procedures that you have learned for recording purchases and cash discounts are very commonly used. However, there is a disadvantage that may make them undesirable if a good system of internal control is to be developed. If, due to inefficiency, a discount is not taken because an invoice is not paid promptly, the accounting records will not reveal the loss of the discount. To overcome this shortcoming, many accountants prefer to record vouchers for purchases in such a way that discounts not taken will stand out for investigation, while discounts taken are not separately stated in the records.

Under this procedure, purchase invoices are recorded in the voucher register *net of discount*; that is, the amount used for the entry is the invoice price minus the cash discount that may be taken. If the invoice is paid within the discount period, the check is drawn for the exact amount of the original voucher. On the other hand, if the invoice is paid too late to take the discount, the total amount of the invoice must be paid. This will be larger than the amount of the original voucher. The difference is recorded in the check register by debiting an account called Discount Lost 507. The balance of this account is added to the balance of the Merchandise Purchases account for presentation on the income statement under Cost of Goods Sold. To illustrate how this procedure works, assume that the Style Clothing Store uses the system. On February 1, when the firm receives the invoice for a purchase of $734.50 from Valley Wholesale Clothiers with terms of 2/10, n/30, the invoice is recorded in the voucher register at the net amount ($734.50 − $14.69 = $719.81), as shown below.

VOUCHER REGISTER for Month of February 19X1   Page 1

DATE	VOU. NO.	PAYABLE TO	PAID DATE	CHECK NO.	ACCTS. PAYABLE CR. 205	MERCH. PURCH. DR. 501
Feb. 1	2-04	Valley Wh. Clothiers	2/10	108	719 81	719 81

When payment is made within the discount period, it is recorded as follows.

CHECK REGISTER for Month of February 19X1   Page 1

DATE	CHECK NO.	PAYABLE TO	VOU. NO.	ACCTS. PAYABLE DR. 205	DISCOUNT LOST DR. 507	CASH CR. 101
Feb. 10	108	Valley Wh. Clothiers	2-04	719 81		719 81

If the payment is made too late to take the discount, the amount of discount lost is recorded in the check register and management's attention will immediately be directed to this failure. The check register entry shown below reflects the lost discount.

CHECK REGISTER for Month of February 19X1   Page 1

DATE	CHECK NO.	PAYABLE TO	VOU. NO.	ACCTS. PAYABLE DR. 205	DISCOUNT LOST DR. 507	CASH CR. 101
Feb. 20	116	Valley Wh. Clothiers	2-04	719 81	14 69	734 50

Other Cash Control Procedures

As you learned in Unit 7, a business should maintain a petty cash fund because it is not practical to make each small payment by check. The procedures necessary to properly control a petty cash fund were discussed and illustrated in that unit. Another important aspect of cash control is the prompt and accurate preparation of the bank reconciliation statement each month. Bank reconciliations were explained in Unit 8.

principles and procedures summary

Internal control is an important factor in the protection of a business firm. Each step in the accounting routine should be planned to involve more than one person and to provide a basis for double-checking the work performed.

The voucher system provides a control over cash payments. A voucher is prepared for every expenditure and then approved. The voucher is entered in the voucher register and then filed with other approved vouchers. This file serves in place of an accounts payable subsidiary ledger. When a check is issued to pay the voucher, an entry is made in the check register and the voucher register. The voucher is then transferred to a paid vouchers file.

Certain transactions such as purchases returns and allowances, partial payments, and notes payable may require special treatment when they are being recorded under the voucher system.

Purchases may be recorded net of discount. Then, if discounts are not taken, the discounts lost will stand out for investigation.

managerial implications

Because of its nature, cash is easily lost or stolen. Management must make sure that the system of internal control is adequate to prevent misuse of cash funds and other valuable assets. Good control procedures not only guard against loss, but they also help improve employee relations. Each employee is able to clearly show the amount of cash or property for which he or she is responsible and how it was handled.

The protection given by the voucher system is invaluable to management in safeguarding the outward flow of funds. Every step is recorded, checked, and documented. Responsibility all along the line is clear and definite. The answers to "What?," "Why?," "Who?," "When?," and so on, are available at all times for reference or auditing purposes.

managerial discussion questions

1. How does the voucher system protect management from the misuse of cash?

2. How can management avoid unnecessary red tape as a by-product of its search for adequate internal controls?
3. In a small business there may be only one or two experienced and reliable employees capable of assuming key positions in an internal control system. Is it impractical to introduce internal controls in this type of situation? Why or why not?
4. How can the management of a firm establish internal control over the liabilities that are incurred?

application of principles

PROBLEM 14-1 The Lincoln Hardware Store was established on August 1, 19X1 by James and Sandra Rose to carry on a retail business. The chart of accounts that the firm's accountant set up is given below.

ACCOUNTS

101	Cash
111	Accounts Receivable
121	Merchandise Inventory
131	Store Equipment
141	Office Equipment
201	Notes Payable
202	Accounts Payable
221	Employee Deductions—FICA
222	Employee Deductions—Income Tax Withheld
301	James Rose, Capital
311	Sandra Rose, Capital
401	Sales
501	Merchandise Purchases
502	Freight In
503	Purchases Returns and Allowances
504	Purchases Discount
521	Sales Salaries Expense
522	Advertising Expense
523	Store Supplies and Expense
529	Cash Short or Over
542	Rent Expense
551	Office Salaries Expense
553	Office Supplies and Expense

The business transactions that the Lincoln Hardware Store completed during August 19X1 are shown on pages 247 and 248.

INSTRUCTIONS

1. Set up a general journal and three special journals: a cash receipts journal, a voucher register, and a check register. (Use the same column headings as are in the forms illustrated on pages 236–237 of the text.) Use *1* as the page number for each journal.
2. Set up general ledger accounts for Cash and Accounts Payable.
3. Record the transactions shown below and on page 248. Then, foot and prove the special journals.
4. Post from the special journals to the Cash account and the Accounts Payable account.
5. Prepare a schedule of vouchers payable, and prove its total with the balance of the Accounts Payable account.

TRANSACTIONS FOR AUGUST 19X1

Aug. 1 James Rose invests $6,000 cash in the new business, and Sandra Rose invests $5,000.

    1 Purchased office equipment for $800 from the Zip Office Supply Company, giving a noninterest-bearing, 30-day note. (In the general journal, debit the Office Equipment account and credit the Notes Payable account.)

    2 Prepared Voucher 8-01 for $700 in rent owed to the Apex Realty Company. Paid the voucher by Check 101.

    3 Prepared Voucher 8-02 for $125 owed to the Zip Office Supply Company for office supplies used.

    4 Prepared Voucher 8-03 for $500 owed to Town Builders for building fixtures in the store. (Debit the Store Equipment account.)

    5 Prepared Voucher 8-04 for $136.65 owed to the Madison Railroad for freight on merchandise purchased.

    6 Paid Voucher 8-04 by Check 102.

    8 Prepared Voucher 8-05 for $2,500 of merchandise purchased from the American Hardware Company; the terms are 2/10, n/30.

    9 Purchased a used cash register for $500 from the Machine Supply Company; the terms are $250 cash with the balance due in 30 days. Vouchers 8-06 and 8-07 were prepared for the two installments. Issued Check 103 for $250 to pay Voucher 8-06.

    10 Prepared Voucher 8-08 for $3,000 owed to the Tester Hardware Company for merchandise; the terms are 2/10, n/30.

    12 Prepared Voucher 8-09 for $100 owed to the Kell Supply Company for store supplies used.

    13 Received $400 in cash for merchandise sold.

    15 Returned merchandise costing $100 for credit to the Tester Hardware Company. (Make a circled entry in the voucher register over the entry for Voucher 8-08.)

    16 Issued Check 104 to pay Voucher 8-05, net of 2% discount.

    17 Sold merchandise for $525 in cash; cash short is $1.50.

    18 Prepared Voucher 8-10 for $45 owed to the *Daily Herald* for advertising. Paid by Check 105.

247

19 Prepared Voucher 8-11 for $231.40 owed to the Madison Railroad for freight on merchandise purchased.
20 Issued Check 106 to pay Voucher 8-11.
20 Issued Check 107 to pay Voucher 8-08, net of return and 2% discount.
23 Sold merchandise for $470 in cash; cash over is $0.50.
25 Prepared Voucher 8-12 for merchandise costing $2,150 purchased from the American Hardware Company; the terms are 2/10, n/30.
26 Sold merchandise for $460 in cash; cash short is $1.
27 Prepared Voucher 8-13 for $133 owed to City Utilities for electricity used in the store during the month. Issued Check 108 to pay the voucher.
28 Prepared Voucher 8-14 for $91.60 owed to the Central Telephone Company for office service during the month. The voucher was paid by Check 109.
30 Prepared Voucher 8-15 for an $800 note payable of August 1 owed to the Zip Office Supply Company. Isssued Check 110 to pay the voucher.
31 Sold merchandise for $475 in cash; cash short is $0.80.
31 Prepared Voucher 8-16 for Frank Sims, the salesclerk, for his salary of $800, less $48 deducted for FICA tax and $80 deducted for income tax. Paid the voucher by Check 111. Prepared Voucher 8-17 for Mary Kee, the office clerk, for her salary of $600 less $36 deducted for FICA tax and $54 deducted for income tax. Paid the voucher by Check 112.

PROBLEM 14-2

On April 10, 19X1, the Ames Department Store purchased merchandise from the Gross Manufacturing Company. The total invoice price was $1,600, and the terms were 3/20, n/60.

INSTRUCTIONS

1. Record the purchase made by Ames in general journal form, assuming:
   a. Ames records purchases at the total invoice price.
   b. Ames records purchases at the net invoice price.
2. Suppose that Ames paid the invoice on April 28. Record the payment in general journal form, assuming:
   a. Ames recorded the purchase at the total invoice price.
   b. Ames recorded the purchase at the net invoice price.
3. Suppose that the Ames Department Store paid the invoice on June 7 (after the discount period). Record the payment in general journal form, assuming:
   a. Ames recorded the purchase at the total invoice price.
   b. Ames recorded the purchase at the net invoice price.

alternate problems

PROBLEM 14-1A Steven Meyers and Laura Regan established the Quality Toy Store on August 1, 19X1, to carry on a retail business. The chart of accounts for the store is given below.

ACCOUNTS

101	Cash
111	Accounts Receivable
121	Merchandise Inventory
131	Store Equipment
141	Office Equipment
201	Notes Payable
202	Accounts Payable
221	Employee Deductions—FICA
222	Employee Deductions—Income Tax Withheld
301	Steven Meyers, Capital
311	Laura Regan, Capital
401	Sales
501	Merchandise Purchases
502	Freight In
503	Purchases Returns and Allowances
504	Purchases Discount
521	Sales Salaries Expense
522	Advertising Expense
523	Store Supplies and Expense
529	Cash Short or Over
542	Rent Expense
551	Office Salaries Expense
553	Office Supplies and Expense

The business transactions for August 19X1 are shown on pages 250 and 251.

INSTRUCTIONS
1. Set up a general journal and three special journals: a cash receipts journal, a voucher register, and a check register. (Use the same column headings as are in the forms illustrated on pages 236–237 of the text.) Use *1* as the page number for each journal.
2. Set up general ledger accounts for Cash and Accounts Payable.
3. Record the transactions shown on pages 250 and 251. Then, foot and prove the special journals.
4. Post from the special journals to the Cash account and the Acounts Payable account.
5. Prepare a schedule of vouchers payable, and prove its total with the balance of the Accounts Payable account.

TRANSACTIONS FOR AUGUST 19X1

Aug. 1 Steven Meyers invests $10,000 cash in the new business, and Laura Regan invests $12,000.
1 Purchased office equipment for $900 from the Central Supply Company, giving a noninterest-bearing, 30-day note. (In the general journal, debit the Office Equipment account and credit the Notes Payable account.)
2 Prepared Voucher 8-01 for $900 owed to the Jordan Realty Company for the monthly rent. Paid by Check 101.
3 Prepared Voucher 8-02 for $55 owed to the ABC Supply Company for office supplies used.
4 Prepared Voucher 8-03 for $500 owed to the York Company for building fixtures in the store. (Debit the Store Equipment account.)
5 Prepared Voucher 8-04 for $188 owed to the Mountain Railroad for freight on merchandise purchased.
6 Paid Voucher 8-04 by Check 102.
8 Prepared Voucher 8-05 for $1,000 owed to the Chan Toy Company for merchandise previously purchased. The terms are 2/10, n/30.
9 Purchased a used cash register for $500 from the Town Supply Company; the terms are $200 cash with the balance due in 30 days. Vouchers 8-06 and 8-07 were prepared for the two installments. Issued Check 103 for $200 to pay Voucher 8-06.
10 Prepared Voucher 8-08 for $3,000 owed to the Chan Toy Company for merchandise previously purchased. The terms are 2/10, n/30.
12 Prepared Voucher 8-09 for $100 owed to the TY Supply Company for store supplies used.
13 Received $400 in cash for merchandise sold.
15 Returned merchandise costing $100 for credit to the Chan Toy Company. (Make a circled entry in the voucher register over the entry for Voucher 8-08.)
16 Issued Check 104 to pay Voucher 8-05, net of 2% discount.
17 Sold merchandise for $600 in cash; cash short is $1.50.
18 Prepared Voucher 8-10 for $80 owed to the *Weekend News* for advertising. Paid by Check 105.
19 Prepared Voucher 8-11 for $156.40 owed to the Mountain Railroad for freight on merchandise purchased.
20 Issued Check 106 to pay Voucher 8-11.
20 Issued Check 107 to pay Voucher 8-08, net of return and 2% discount.
23 Sold merchandise for $470 in cash; cash over is $0.50.
25 Prepared Voucher 8-12 for $2,150 owed to the Chan Toy Company for merchandise; the terms are 2/10, n/30.
26 Sold merchandise for $510 in cash; cash short is $1.90.
27 Prepared Voucher 8-13 for $86 owed to City Utilities for electricity used in the store during the month. The amount was paid by Check 108.
28 Prepared Voucher 8-14 for $54 owed to the Central Telephone

Company for office telephone service. Payment was made by Check 109.

30 Prepared Voucher 8-15 for a $900 note payable of August 1 owed to the Central Supply Company. This amount was paid by Check 110.

31 Sold merchandise for $610 in cash; cash short is $0.90.

31 Prepared Voucher 8-16 for Tom Perry, the salesclerk, for his salary of $900 less $54 deducted for FICA tax and $82 deducted for income tax. Paid the voucher by Check 111. Prepared Voucher 8-17 for Mary Hernandez, the office clerk, for her salary of $600 less $36 deducted for FICA tax and $43.20 deducted for income tax. Paid the voucher by Check 112.

PROBLEM 14-2A On March 1, 19X1, the State Supply Company sold merchandise to City Retailers. The total invoice price was $2,000, and the terms were 2/10, n/30.

INSTRUCTIONS
1. Record the purchase made by City Retailers in general journal form assuming:
   a. City Retailers records purchases at the total invoice price.
   b. City Retailers records purchases at the net invoice price.
2. Suppose that City Retailers paid the invoice on March 9. Record the payment in general journal form, assuming:
   a. City Retailers recorded the purchase at the total invoice price.
   b. City Retailers recorded the purchase at the net invoice price.
3. Suppose that City Retailers paid the invoice on March 30 (after the discount period). Record the payment in general journal form, assuming:
   a. City Retailers recorded the purchase at the total invoice price.
   b. City Retailers recorded the purchase at the net invoice price.

UNIT 15
PAYROLL COMPUTATIONS, RECORDS, AND PAYMENT

In the discussion of accounting records up to this point, there has been no detailed treatment of salary and wage payments to employees. A consideration of payroll accounting would have interrupted the sequence of the general accounting procedures being described. Also, payroll accounting, including the related payroll taxes and tax returns, is so important that it requires concentrated attention and extended treatment. Such coverage is provided in this unit and the next.

Objectives of Payroll Work

The primary objective of payroll work is to compute the amount of wages or salary due employees and to pay these amounts promptly. Another objective is to classify payments to employees properly and to charge these amounts to the appropriate expense accounts. Until the mid-1930s, payroll accounting involved few other considerations.

In 1935 the federal Social Security Act was passed. Under the terms of this legislation, it became necessary for businesses to keep detailed payroll and employee earnings records. The withholding of federal income tax started in 1943, and several states also enacted plans for income tax withholding that added to payroll recordkeeping work. The wage and hour provisions of the federal Fair Labor Standards Act of 1938 (as amended) affected the computation of earnings. The various state worker's compensation insurance laws are a further concern in payroll accounting because they require careful classification of payrolls according to the type of work done by employees. The provisions of each law are discussed in greater detail in the paragraphs that follow.

The Social Security System

The federal Social Security Act has been amended several times and is likely to be further amended. The present social security system has two principal parts. The first, discussed in this unit, consists of the old-age, survivors, and disability insurance program and the hospital insurance program (Medicare). This part of the system is financed entirely by the federal government through taxes levied under the Federal Insurance Contributions Act (FICA). The second part, discussed in Unit 16, is the federal unemployment insurance program. This part is financed jointly by the federal government and the states through taxes levied under the Federal Unemployment Tax Act (FUTA) and the corresponding state unemployment tax laws. Changes occur in the rates and base figures more often than in the methods of computation. Learn the methods, and then always be sure to use the latest rates and bases.

Coverage. Most employers and employees are covered by the social security system. Agricultural workers, domestic workers, and most self-employed persons are covered under special provisions. Railroad workers have a separate program of their own and are therefore exempt. Employees of state and local governments and of certain religious and nonprofit organizations are also exempt but may choose to be covered. Only ordinary business employers and employees that are covered by the system are considered here.

Benefits. Insured workers may claim retirement benefits after they retire at age 62 or later. Disability benefits for insured workers over 50 and under 65 are based on average monthly earnings. They are the same as old-age insurance benefits would be if the disabled worker were already 65 and retired. In each case, the amount of benefits depends upon the average monthly earnings of the insured person. In addition to the cash benefits mentioned here, hospital insurance benefits are available for people who are 65 or over and are covered by social security. Further details about benefits, including survivors' benefits, may be obtained from the government publication *Your Social Security* or from district offices of the Social Security Administration (which are listed in telephone directories under United States Government: Department of Health and Human Services).

Identification Numbers. Each employer and each employee must obtain an identification number because millions of employers and employees are covered by the social security system. These numbers help ensure that proper credits for taxes paid are given in cases in which there may be more than one person or company with the same name. Social security records are stored in computers, and the use of identification numbers makes it easier to handle the tremendous volume of entries that must be recorded each year.

The Fair Labor Standards Act

The Fair Labor Standards Act of 1938 (as amended) applies only to firms engaged directly or indirectly in interstate commerce. This federal statute, which is often referred to as the Wage and Hour Law, fixes a minimum hourly rate of pay and maximum hours of work per week to be performed at the regular rate. The minimum hourly rate of pay proposed for 1981 is $3.35. At present, the maximum number of hours is 40. Hours worked in excess of 40 in any week must be paid for at an overtime premium rate of at least one and a half times the regular hourly rate of pay. (This overtime rate is called *time and a half*.) Many employers who are not covered by the federal law pay time and a half for overtime because of union contracts or simply as a good business practice.

The Fair Labor Standards Act requires covered employers to maintain records for each employee to show that the provisions of the law have been followed. No particular form is specified for these records, but they should indicate the name and address of the employee, date of birth, hours worked each day and week, wages paid at the regular rate, and overtime premium wages. Similar information is required for employees subject to the FICA taxes previously discussed. One record for each employee ordinarily serves both purposes.

Worker's Compensation Insurance

State laws covering worker's compensation insurance require employers to pay for insurance that will reimburse employees for losses suffered from injuries or will compensate their families if death occurs in the course of their employment. Benefits are paid directly to the injured workers or to their survivors.

Illustrative Case—The Kent Novelty Company

The first step in payroll work is to determine the gross amount of wages or salary earned by each employee. There are a number of common ways of paying employees. Some workers are paid at a stated rate per hour, and their gross pay depends on the number of hours they work. This method is called the *hourly-rate basis*. Other workers are paid an agreed amount for each week or month or other period. This arrangement is called the *salary basis*.

The Kent Novelty Company is used in this unit and the next to illustrate typical payroll procedures and records. This firm, which is owned by Howard Scott, produces a variety of novelty items and sells them by mail. It is staffed by three production workers and a helper, who are paid weekly on the hourly-rate basis, and by one office clerk, who is paid a monthly salary. The employees are subject to FICA tax and federal income tax withholding. Scott manages the company himself and withdraws a portion of the profits from time to time, but he receives no regular salary.

The Kent Novelty Company is subject to FICA tax and to federal and state unemployment insurance taxes. Since the mail-order business involves interstate commerce, the firm is also subject to the Fair Labor Standards Act. In addition, the business is required by state law to carry worker's compensation insurance.

Determining Gross Pay for Hourly Workers

To determine the gross pay earned by an employee on an hourly-rate basis, it is necessary to know the rate of pay and the number of hours the employee has worked.

Hours Worked

There are various methods of keeping track of the hours worked by each employee. At the Kent Novelty Company, the shop supervisor keeps a time book in which she enters the number of hours worked each day by each employee who is paid on an hourly basis. At the end of the week, the office clerk uses this record to prepare the payroll.

If the time book system is used in a larger firm, each supervisor keeps a record of the time worked by the employees under his or her supervision. More often, however, a larger business uses a time clock. Each employee has a time card and inserts it in the time clock to record the time of arrival and the time of departure. The payroll clerk collects each card at the end of the week, determines the hours worked, multiplies the number of hours by the proper rate, and computes the gross pay.

Gross Pay

Suppose that the time book kept at the Kent Novelty Company during the week ended January 7, 19X1, shows that the first employee, Peter Brown, worked 40 hours. His rate of pay is $6 an hour. His gross pay of $240 is found by multiplying 40 hours by $6.

The second employee, George Dunn, has worked 44 hours. Four of these hours are overtime. Thus, they must be paid for at Dunn's regular rate ($4) plus a premium rate of one-half of his regular rate ($4 × 0.50 = $2 premium rate). Dunn's gross pay is calculated as follows.

Total time × regular rate:	44 hours × $4	$176
Overtime premium:	4 hours × $2	8
Gross pay		$184

This method is the one specified under the Wage and Hour Law and is therefore the one used in the illustrations. Another method, which gives the same gross pay, uses the steps shown below.

Regular time earnings:	40 hours × $4	$160
Overtime earnings:	4 hours × $6	24
Gross pay		$184

The second method quickly answers the employee's question, "How much more did I earn by working overtime than I would have earned for only 40 hours of work?" The employer, however, is more concerned with the amount of premium the firm could have saved if all the hours had been paid for at the regular rate. The first method gives this information.

The third employee, Joan King, worked 40 hours. Her hourly rate is $5. Her gross pay is therefore 40 hours times $5, or $200. The fourth employee, Rita Lopez, is the supervisor. She worked 40 hours, and her rate of pay is $8 per hour. Thus, her gross pay is 40 hours times $8, or $320.

Deductions From Gross Pay Required by Law

There are two principal deductions from employees' gross pay that are required by federal law—social security (FICA) tax and income tax withholding. These deductions are explained below and on succeeding pages.

FICA Tax

The taxes required by the Federal Insurance Contributions Act are levied in an equal amount on both the employer and the employee. Since, as was previously mentioned, rates and bases change often, a hypothetical rate and base are used in this discussion. We will assume that a tax rate of 6.13 percent is applied to a base consisting of the first $22,900 of wages paid to an employee during the calendar year. Wages paid in excess of the base amount (called *tax-exempt wages*) are not taxed. If an employee works for more than one employer during the year, the FICA tax is deducted on the current base, such as the first $22,900 paid by each employer. The excess tax is later refunded to the employee by the government or applied to payment of his or her income taxes for the year.

Although, technically, there are two separate rates for (1) old age, survivors, and disability insurance and (2) hospital insurance, they are generally combined into one rate and referred to simply as *social security tax,* or *FICA tax.* The latter term is used in this textbook.

In the following examples, the FICA tax is deducted from the earnings of each employee of the Kent Novelty Company at the assumed rate of 6.13 percent on the first $22,900 earned. The amount to be deducted can be computed either by multiplying the taxable wages by the FICA rate or by referring to tax tables available from the government and from commercial sources, such as office supply stores.

Tax Computed by the Percentage Method. When the employee's FICA tax is computed by the percentage method, the employer multiplies the taxable wages by the tax rate and rounds the answer to the nearest penny. The FICA taxes to be deducted by the Kent Novelty Company, based on the gross pay previously calculated and a tax rate of 6.13 percent, are shown below.

Employee	*Gross Pay*	*Tax Rate*	*FICA Tax*
Peter Brown	$240	6.13%	$14.71
George Dunn	184	6.13%	11.28
Joan King	200	6.13%	12.26
Rita Lopez	320	6.13%	19.62
Total			$57.87

Tax Determined From Tax Table. FICA taxes on wages can be determined from the Social Security Employee Tax Table in *Circular E,* the *Employer's Tax Guide,* which is published by the Internal Revenue Service. At the assumed 6.13 percent rate, the FICA tax due on the $240 of wages earned by Peter Brown would amount to $14.71. This is the same amount that was calculated by using the percentage method. The table shows FICA tax of $12.26 on wages of $200 and $2.45 on wages of $40. These two tax amounts are added as shown below to find the FICA tax to be withheld.

WAGES	FICA TAX
On $200	$12.26
On 40	2.45
On $240	$14.71

Federal Income Tax Withholding

A substantial portion of the federal government's revenue comes from the income tax on individuals. Many rules and regulations are used in determining the amount of federal income tax that each person must pay. Also keep in mind that rates, rules, and regulations change often. The rates used in this text are for illustrative purposes only. In actual practice, a current edition of the Internal Revenue Service's *Circular E* would be consulted for up-to-date rates and other information.

Most taxpayers are on a pay-as-you-go basis. This means that the income tax due from a person earning a salary or wages must be withheld by the employer and paid to the government periodically—at the same time the FICA taxes are paid. At the end of each year, the individual employee files a tax return. If the amount withheld does not cover the taxes due, the employee pays the balance. If too much has been withheld, the employee will receive a refund.

Claiming Withholding Exemptions and Allowances. The amount of income tax a person must pay depends on the amount of income, the number of personal exemptions and withholding allowances, and marital status. The matter of exemptions and allowances is a technical subject that cannot be fully explored here. In brief, a person is ordinarily entitled to one exemption for himself or herself, one for a spouse (unless the spouse also works and claims an exemption), and one for each dependent for whom the person provides more than half the support during the year. A person may also be entitled to a special withholding allowance; to withholding allowances based on various tax credits, if eligible; and to other withholding allowances based on itemized deductions and alimony, if any.

Employees claim the number of exemptions and withholding allowances to which they are entitled by completing an *Employee's Withholding Allowance Certificate, Form W-4.* This form is filed with the employer. Peter Brown's Form W-4 is illustrated on pages 258–259. Due to the highly individual and complex nature of the withholding allowances based on tax credits, itemized deductions, and alimony, they are not considered here.

If an employee fails to file a Form W-4, the employer must withhold tax from the wages as though there were no exemptions or allowances. If the number of exemptions or allowances decreases, the employee must file a new Form W-4 within ten days. If the number of exemptions or allowances increases, the employee may file an amended certificate.

If the employee desires, he or she may use Form W-4 to instruct the employer to withhold a specified amount of income tax each pay period above the amount required by law. This reduces the possibility that a balance may be due when the individual files the yearly income tax return.

Computing Income Tax Withholding. There are several methods that can be used to compute the amount of income tax to be withheld from an employee's earnings. However, all except one require cumbersome computations. The exception is the *wage-bracket table method,* which involves the use of tables to determine the amount of tax. The simplicity of this method explains why it is used almost universally. *Circular E,* the *Employer's Tax Guide,* contains withholding tables for weekly, biweekly, semimonthly, monthly and daily or miscellaneous payroll periods for single and married persons. Sections of the tables for single and married persons paid weekly are illustrated on pages 261 and 262.

After the proper table has been chosen, the first step in using the table is to find the line that covers the amount of wages the employee earned. Follow

Form W-4 — Employee's Withholding Allowance Certificate
(Use for Wages Paid After December 31, 19X1)

Rev. December 19X1
Department of the Treasury — Internal Revenue Service

This certificate is for income tax withholding purposes only. It will remain in effect until you change it. If you claim exemption from withholding, you will have to file a new certificate on or before April 30 of next year.

Type or print your full name: **Peter Brown**
Your social security number: **324-76-1245**

Home address (number and street or rural route): **24 Oak Street**
City or town, State, and ZIP code: **Manchester, NH 03104**

Marital Status:
- [ ] Single [X] Married
- [ ] Married, but withhold at higher Single rate

Note: *If married, but legally separated, or spouse is a nonresident alien, check the single block.*

1. Total number of allowances you are claiming **3**
2. Additional amount, if any, you want deducted from each pay (if your employer agrees) . . . . . . $
3. I claim exemption from withholding (see instructions). Enter "Exempt" . . . .

Under the penalties of perjury, I certify that the number of withholding allowances claimed on this certificate does not exceed the number to which I am entitled. If claiming exemption from withholding, I certify that I incurred no liability for Federal income tax for last year and I anticipate that I will incur no liability for Federal income tax for this year.

Signature ▶ **Peter Brown**   Date ▶ **January 1**, 19 **X1**

---------- Detach along this line ----------

▲ Give the top part of this form to your employer; keep the lower part for your records and information ▲

Instructions
The explanatory material below will help you determine your correct number of withholding allowances, and will assist you in completing the Form W-4 at the top of this page.

See **Publication 505** for more information on withholding.

Avoid Overwithholding or Underwithholding
By claiming the number of withholding allowances you are entitled to, you can fit the amount of tax withheld from your wages to your tax liability. In addition to the allowances for personal exemptions to be claimed in item (a), be sure to claim any additional allowances you are entitled to in item (b), "Special withholding allowance," and item (c), "Allowance(s) for credit(s) and/or deduction(s)." While you may claim these allowances on Form W-4 for withholding purposes, you may not claim them under "Exemptions" on your tax return Form 1040 or Form 1040A.

You may claim the special withholding allowance if you are single with only one employer, or married with only one employer and your spouse is not employed. If you have unusually large itemized deductions, make alimony payments, or credit(s) for child care expenses, earned income, credit for the elderly, or residential energy credits, you may claim additional allowances to avoid having too much income tax withheld from your wages.

If you and your spouse are both employed or you have more than one employer, you should make sure that enough has been withheld. If you find that you need more withholding, claim fewer allowances or ask for additional withholding or request to be withheld at the higher "Single" status. If you are currently claiming additional withholding allowances based on itemized deductions, check the worksheet on the back to see that you are claiming the proper number of allowances.

How Many Withholding Allowances May You Claim?
Use the schedule below to determine the number of allowances you may claim for tax withholding purposes. In determining the number, keep in mind these points: if you are single and hold more than one job, you may not claim the same allowances with more than one employer at the same time; or, if you are married and both you and your spouse are employed, you may not both claim the same allowances with your employers at the same time. A nonresident alien, other than a resident of Canada, Mexico, or Puerto Rico, may claim only one personal allowance.

Completing Form W-4
If you find you are entitled to one or more allowances in addition to those you are now claiming, increase your number of allowances by completing the form above and filing it with your employer. If the number of allowances you previously claimed decreases, you must file a new Form W-4 within 10 days. (If you expect to owe more tax than will be withheld, you may increase your withholding by claiming fewer or "0" allowances on line 1, or by asking for additional withholding on line 2, or both.)

You may claim exemption from withholding of Federal income tax if you had no liability for income tax for last year, and you anticipate that you will incur no liability for income tax for this year. You may not claim exemption if your joint or separate return shows tax liability before the allowance of any credit for income tax withheld. If you are exempt, your employer will not withhold Federal income tax from your wages. However, social security tax will be withheld if you are covered by the Federal Insurance Contributions Act.

You must revoke this exemption (1) within 10 days from the time you anticipate you will incur income tax liability for the year or (2) on or before December 1 if you anticipate you will incur Federal income tax liability for the next year. If you want to stop or are required to revoke this exemption, you must file a new Form W-4 with your employer showing the number of withholding allowances you are entitled to claim. This certificate for exemption from withholding will expire on April 30 of next year unless a new Form W-4 is filed on or before that date.

The Following Information is Provided in Accordance with the Privacy Act of 1974
The Internal Revenue Code requires every employee to furnish his or her employer with a signed withholding allowance certificate showing the number of withholding allowances that the employee claims (section 3402(f)(2)(A) and the Regulations thereto). Individuals are required to provide their Social Security Number for proper identification and processing (section 6109 and the Regulations thereto).

The principal purpose for soliciting withholding allowance certificate information is to administer the Internal Revenue laws of the United States.

If an employee does not furnish a signed withholding allowance certificate, the employee is considered as claiming no withholding allowances (section 3401(e)) and shall be treated as a single person (section 3402(l)).

The routine uses of the withholding allowance certificate information include disclosure to the Department of Justice for actual or potential criminal prosecution or civil litigation.

Figure Your Total Withholding Allowances Below
(a) Allowance(s) for exemption(s)—Enter 1 for each personal exemption you can claim on your Federal income tax return* . . . **2**
(b) Special withholding allowance—Enter 1 if single with 1 employer, or married with 1 employer and spouse not employed** . . . **1**
(c) Allowance(s) for credit(s) and/or deduction(s)—Enter number from tables on page 2 . . . .
(d) Total (add lines (a) through (c) above)—Enter here and on line 1, Form W-4, above **3**

*If you are in doubt as to whom you may claim as a dependent, see the instructions that came with your last Federal income tax return or call your local Internal Revenue Service office.
**This allowance is used solely for purposes of figuring your withholding tax, and cannot be claimed when you file your tax return.

Form W-4 (Rev. 12-X1)

TABLE A.—Table for Determining Number of Withholding Allowances Based on Tax Credits

Figure the number of additional withholding allowances for the amount of tax credits for child care expenses, earned income credit, credit for the elderly, or residential energy credits, from the appropriate column (see line (c) on other side). For an explanation of these credits, see the Instructions for Form 1040.
Note: Watch for announcements that could affect the number of withholding allowances you may claim.

Allowances ▶	0	1		2		3		4		5		6	
Estimated salaries and wages from all sources:		If the amount of estimated tax credits is:											
	Under	At least	But less than	At least	But less than	At least	But less than	At least	But less than	At least	But less than	At least	But less than
Part I — Single Employees													
Under $5,000	No additional allowances												
5,000–15,000	250	250	500	500	700	700	900	900 or more					
15,001–25,000	350	350	700	700	1,000	1,000 or more							
25,001–35,000	550	550	950	950 or more									
Part II — Head of Household Employees													
Under $5,000	No additional allowances												
5,000–20,000	150	150	400	400	650	650	900	900 or more					
20,001–35,000	1	1	300	300	650	650	1,000	1,000 or more					
35,001–45,000	450	450	850	850 or more									
Part III — Married Employees (When Spouse is Not Employed)													
Under $8,000	No additional allowances												
8,000–15,000	200	200	350	350	500	500	700	700	800	800	950	950 or more	
15,001–25,000	250	250	500	500	700	700	950	950 or more					
25,001–35,000	300	300	650	650	950	950 or more							
35,001–45,000	650	650	1,050	1,050 or more									
Part IV — Married Employees (When Both Spouses are Employed)													
Under $8,000	No additional allowances												
8,000–15,000	250	250	400	400	450	450 or more							
15,001–25,000	550	550	800	800	950	950 or more							

How to Use Table A

1 Find your filing status under Part I, II, III, or IV.
2 Using your filing status, find your estimated salaries and wages in the left column.
3 Read the shaded amounts to the right until you get to the amount of your estimated tax credits.
4 Look to the top of the column to find the number of allowances you may take for your estimated tax credits.
5 Enter this number on page 1, line (c), together with the number of allowances from Table B for itemized deductions, and alimony payments.

Example: A taxpayer who expects to file a Federal income tax return as a **single** person estimates annual wages of $12,000 and tax credits of $650. The taxpayer uses Part I for single employees. The $12,000 falls in the wage bracket of $5,000 to 15,000 in the left column. Reading in the shaded area to the right, $650 falls within the estimated tax credits bracket of At least 500 But less than 700. Looking to the top of the column, the taxpayer finds that 2 allowances are permitted. The taxpayer adds "2" to the number of any allowances from Table B below and enters the total on page 1, line (c).

TABLE B.—Table for Determining Number of Withholding Allowances Based on Itemized Deductions and Alimony Payments, if Any*

Estimated salaries and wages from all sources:	Column (A) Single Employees (only one job)	Column (B) Married Employees (one spouse working and one job only)	Column (C) Married Employees (both spouses working or employees with more than one job)
Under $10,000	$2,800	$3,900	$4,000
10,000–30,000	2,800	3,900	5,800
30,001–40,000	3,500	3,900	8,000
Over $40,000	15% of estimated salaries and wages	13% of estimated salaries and wages	23% of estimated salaries and wages

*If you are paying alimony but will not itemize deductions, figure the number of withholding allowances by dividing the estimated alimony payments by $1,000 (round off fractions to the nearest whole number) and enter on page 1, line (c).

How to Use Table B

1 Enter the amount of your estimated itemized deductions, including alimony payments, for the year . . . . . .
2 Find your total estimated salary and wage amount in the left column. Read to the right and enter the amount from column (A), (B), or (C) for your filing status . . . .
3 Subtract line 2 from line 1 . . . . .
4 Divide the amount on line 3 by $1,000. Enter here and on page 1, line (c) together with the number of any allowances for tax credits from Table A, above. (Round off fractions to the nearest whole number.) . . . . .

☆U.S. GOVERNMENT PRINTING OFFICE: 19X1—0-263-299 58-040-1110 across this line until you reach the column corresponding to the number of withholding allowances claimed. The amount shown at this point in the table is the income tax to be withheld. For example, Peter Brown has three withholding allowances and earned $240 for the week. In the section of the table for married persons paid weekly that appears on page 262, the appropriate line is the one covering wages between $240 and $250. On this line, under the column headed "3," the amount of tax is given as $23. The amount to be withheld from each of the other hourly employees of the Kent Novelty Company can be obtained in a similar manner from the sections of the weekly wage-bracket withholding tables illustrated on pages 261 and 262.

The income tax to be withheld from the pay of the four hourly workers is summarized below.

Employee	Gross Pay	Marital Status	Withholding Allowances	Income Tax to Be Withheld
Peter Brown	$240	Married	3	$23.00
George Dunn	184	Married, wife works	1	19.10
Joan King	200	Single with dependents	3	21.00
Rita Lopez	320	Married	4	35.10
Total				$98.20

Other Deductions Required by Law

Some states require that state income tax be withheld from employees. The principles and procedures are similar to those already explained for federal income tax withholding. Of course, the appropriate state withholding tables or tax rates must be used.

In certain states, unemployment tax or disability and sickness tax must also be deducted from employees' wages. The amounts to be deducted are determined by applying the specified rates to taxable wages as defined in the law. The procedures involved in such deductions are similar to those that have already been illustrated.

At this time, we will assume that no other deductions are required by law from the wages of the employees of the Kent Novelty Company.

Deductions From Gross Pay Not Required by Law

Many kinds of deductions not required by law may be made from the pay of an employee by agreement or contract between the employee and the employer. For example, a specified deduction from the pay of the employee may be made each month or each payroll period for group life insurance or group hospital insurance. The employer often pays a share of the cost of such programs.

Company retirement plans may be financed entirely by the employer or by the employee and employer jointly. In the latter case, the contributions are

SINGLE Persons — WEEKLY Payroll Period

And the wages are—		And the number of withholding allowances claimed is—										
At least	But less than	0	1	2	3	4	5	6	7	8	9	10 or more
		The amount of income tax to be withheld shall be—										
$0	$28	$0	$0	$0	$0	$0	$0	$0	$0	$0	$0	$0
28	29	.20	0	0	0	0	0	0	0	0	0	0
29	30	.30	0	0	0	0	0	0	0	0	0	0
30	31	.50	0	0	0	0	0	0	0	0	0	0
31	32	.60	0	0	0	0	0	0	0	0	0	0
32	33	.80	0	0	0	0	0	0	0	0	0	0
33	34	.90	0	0	0	0	0	0	0	0	0	0
34	35	1.10	0	0	0	0	0	0	0	0	0	0
35	36	1.20	0	0	0	0	0	0	0	0	0	0
36	37	1.40	0	0	0	0	0	0	0	0	0	0
37	38	1.50	0	0	0	0	0	0	0	0	0	0
38	39	1.70	0	0	0	0	0	0	0	0	0	0
39	40	1.80	0	0	0	0	0	0	0	0	0	0
40	41	2.00	0	0	0	0	0	0	0	0	0	0
41	42	2.10	0	0	0	0	0	0	0	0	0	0
42	43	2.30	0	0	0	0	0	0	0	0	0	0
43	44	2.40	0	0	0	0	0	0	0	0	0	0
44	45	2.60	0	0	0	0	0	0	0	0	0	0
45	46	2.70	0	0	0	0	0	0	0	0	0	0
46	47	2.90	0	0	0	0	0	0	0	0	0	0
47	48	3.00	.10	0	0	0	0	0	0	0	0	0
48	49	3.20	.30	0	0	0	0	0	0	0	0	0
49	50	3.30	.40	0	0	0	0	0	0	0	0	0
50	51	3.50	.60	0	0	0	0	0	0	0	0	0
51	52	3.60	.70	0	0	0	0	0	0	0	0	0
52	53	3.80	.90	0	0	0	0	0	0	0	0	0
53	54	3.90	1.00	0	0	0	0	0	0	0	0	0
54	55	4.10	1.20	0	0	0	0	0	0	0	0	0
55	56	4.20	1.30	0	0	0	0	0	0	0	0	0
56	57	4.40	1.50	0	0	0	0	0	0	0	0	0
57	58	4.50	1.60	0	0	0	0	0	0	0	0	0
58	59	4.70	1.80	0	0	0	0	0	0	0	0	0
59	60	4.80	1.90	0	0	0	0	0	0	0	0	0
60	62	5.10	2.20	0	0	0	0	0	0	0	0	0
62	64	5.40	2.50	0	0	0	0	0	0	0	0	0
64	66	5.70	2.80	0	0	0	0	0	0	0	0	0
66	68	6.10	3.10	.20	0	0	0	0	0	0	0	0
68	70	6.40	3.40	.50	0	0	0	0	0	0	0	0
70	72	6.80	3.70	.80	0	0	0	0	0	0	0	0
72	74	7.10	4.00	1.10	0	0	0	0	0	0	0	0
74	76	7.50	4.30	1.40	0	0	0	0	0	0	0	0
76	78	7.90	4.60	1.70	0	0	0	0	0	0	0	0
78	80	8.20	4.90	2.00	0	0	0	0	0	0	0	0
80	82	8.60	5.20	2.30	0	0	0	0	0	0	0	0
82	84	8.90	5.50	2.60	0	0	0	0	0	0	0	0
84	86	9.30	5.80	2.90	0	0	0	0	0	0	0	0
86	88	9.70	6.20	3.20	.30	0	0	0	0	0	0	0
88	90	10.00	6.60	3.50	.60	0	0	0	0	0	0	0
90	92	10.40	6.90	3.80	.90	0	0	0	0	0	0	0
92	94	10.70	7.30	4.10	1.20	0	0	0	0	0	0	0
94	96	11.10	7.60	4.40	1.50	0	0	0	0	0	0	0
96	98	11.50	8.00	4.70	1.80	0	0	0	0	0	0	0
98	100	11.80	8.40	5.00	2.10	0	0	0	0	0	0	0
100	105	12.50	9.00	5.50	2.60	0	0	0	0	0	0	0
105	110	13.40	9.90	6.40	3.40	.50	0	0	0	0	0	0
110	115	14.30	10.80	7.30	4.10	1.20	0	0	0	0	0	0
115	120	15.20	11.70	8.20	4.90	2.00	0	0	0	0	0	0
120	125	16.10	12.60	9.10	5.70	2.70	0	0	0	0	0	0
125	130	17.00	13.50	10.00	6.60	3.50	.60	0	0	0	0	0
130	135	17.90	14.40	10.90	7.50	4.20	1.40	0	0	0	0	0
135	140	19.00	15.30	11.80	8.40	5.00	2.10	0	0	0	0	0
140	145	20.00	16.20	12.70	9.30	5.80	2.90	0	0	0	0	0
145	150	21.10	17.10	13.60	10.20	6.70	3.60	.70	0	0	0	0
150	160	22.60	18.60	15.00	11.50	8.10	4.70	1.80	0	0	0	0
160	170	24.70	20.70	16.80	13.30	9.90	6.40	3.30	.50	0	0	0
170	180	26.80	22.80	18.80	15.10	11.70	8.20	4.80	2.00	0	0	0
180	190	28.90	24.90	20.90	16.90	13.50	10.00	6.50	3.50	.60	0	0
190	200	31.00	27.00	23.00	18.90	15.30	11.80	8.30	5.00	2.10	0	0
200	**210**	33.60	29.10	25.10	**21.00**	17.10	13.60	10.10	6.70	3.60	.70	0
210	220	36.20	31.20	27.20	23.10	19.10	15.40	11.90	8.50	5.10	2.20	0
220	230	38.80	33.80	29.30	25.20	21.20	17.20	13.70	10.30	6.80	3.70	.80
230	240	41.40	36.40	31.40	27.30	23.30	19.20	15.50	12.10	8.60	5.20	2.30
240	250	44.00	39.00	34.00	29.40	25.40	21.30	17.30	13.90	10.40	6.90	3.80
250	260	46.60	41.60	36.60	31.60	27.50	23.40	19.40	15.70	12.20	8.70	5.30
260	270	49.20	44.20	39.20	34.20	29.60	25.50	21.50	17.50	14.00	10.50	7.10

261

MARRIED Persons — WEEKLY Payroll Period

And the wages are—		And the number of withholding allowances claimed is—										
At least	But less than	0	1	2	3	4	5	6	7	8	9	10 or more
		The amount of income tax to be withheld shall be—										
$0	$46	$0	$0	$0	$0	$0	$0	$0	$0	$0	$0	$0
46	47	.10	0	0	0	0	0	0	0	0	0	0
47	48	.20	0	0	0	0	0	0	0	0	0	0
48	49	.40	0	0	0	0	0	0	0	0	0	0
49	50	.50	0	0	0	0	0	0	0	0	0	0
50	51	.70	0	0	0	0	0	0	0	0	0	0
51	52	.80	0	0	0	0	0	0	0	0	0	0
52	53	1.00	0	0	0	0	0	0	0	0	0	0
53	54	1.10	0	0	0	0	0	0	0	0	0	0
54	55	1.30	0	0	0	0	0	0	0	0	0	0
55	56	1.40	0	0	0	0	0	0	0	0	0	0
56	57	1.60	0	0	0	0	0	0	0	0	0	0
57	58	1.70	0	0	0	0	0	0	0	0	0	0
58	59	1.90	0	0	0	0	0	0	0	0	0	0
59	60	2.00	0	0	0	0	0	0	0	0	0	0
60	62	2.20	0	0	0	0	0	0	0	0	0	0
62	64	2.50	0	0	0	0	0	0	0	0	0	0
64	66	2.80	0	0	0	0	0	0	0	0	0	0
66	68	3.10	.20	0	0	0	0	0	0	0	0	0
68	70	3.40	.50	0	0	0	0	0	0	0	0	0
70	72	3.70	.80	0	0	0	0	0	0	0	0	0
72	74	4.00	1.10	0	0	0	0	0	0	0	0	0
74	76	4.30	1.40	0	0	0	0	0	0	0	0	0
76	78	4.60	1.70	0	0	0	0	0	0	0	0	0
78	80	4.90	2.00	0	0	0	0	0	0	0	0	0
80	82	5.20	2.30	0	0	0	0	0	0	0	0	0
82	84	5.50	2.60	0	0	0	0	0	0	0	0	0
84	86	5.80	2.90	.10	0	0	0	0	0	0	0	0
86	88	6.10	3.20	.40	0	0	0	0	0	0	0	0
88	90	6.40	3.50	.70	0	0	0	0	0	0	0	0
90	92	6.70	3.80	1.00	0	0	0	0	0	0	0	0
92	94	7.00	4.10	1.30	0	0	0	0	0	0	0	0
94	96	7.30	4.40	1.60	0	0	0	0	0	0	0	0
96	98	7.60	4.70	1.90	0	0	0	0	0	0	0	0
98	100	7.90	5.00	2.20	0	0	0	0	0	0	0	0
100	105	8.50	5.60	2.70	0	0	0	0	0	0	0	0
105	110	9.20	6.30	3.40	.50	0	0	0	0	0	0	0
110	115	10.00	7.10	4.20	1.30	0	0	0	0	0	0	0
115	120	10.70	7.80	4.90	2.00	0	0	0	0	0	0	0
120	125	11.50	8.60	5.70	2.80	0	0	0	0	0	0	0
125	130	12.20	9.30	6.40	3.50	.70	0	0	0	0	0	0
130	135	13.10	10.10	7.20	4.30	1.40	0	0	0	0	0	0
135	140	14.00	10.80	7.90	5.00	2.20	0	0	0	0	0	0
140	145	14.90	11.60	8.70	5.80	2.90	0	0	0	0	0	0
145	150	15.80	12.40	9.40	6.50	3.70	.80	0	0	0	0	0
150	160	17.20	13.70	10.60	7.70	4.80	1.90	0	0	0	0	.0
160	170	19.00	15.50	12.10	9.20	6.30	3.40	.50	0	0	0	0
170	180	20.80	17.30	13.80	10.70	7.80	4.90	2.00	0	0	0	0
180	190	22.60	19.10	15.60	12.20	9.30	6.40	3.50	.60	0	0	0
190	200	24.40	20.90	17.40	14.00	10.80	7.90	5.00	2.10	0	0	0
200	210	26.20	22.70	19.20	15.80	12.30	9.40	6.50	3.60	.80	0	0
210	220	28.10	24.50	21.00	17.60	14.10	10.90	8.00	5.10	2.30	0	0
220	230	30.20	26.30	22.80	19.40	15.90	12.50	9.50	6.60	3.80	.90	0
230	240	32.30	28.30	24.60	21.20	17.70	14.30	11.00	8.10	5.30	2.40	0
240	250	34.40	30.40	26.40	23.00	19.50	16.10	12.60	9.60	6.80	3.90	1.00
250	260	36.50	32.50	28.50	24.80	21.30	17.90	14.40	11.10	8.30	5.40	2.50
260	270	38.60	34.60	30.60	26.60	23.10	19.70	16.20	12.70	9.80	6.90	4.00
270	280	40.70	36.70	32.70	28.60	24.90	21.50	18.00	14.50	11.30	8.40	5.50
280	290	42.80	38.80	34.80	30.70	26.70	23.30	19.80	16.30	12.90	9.90	7.00
290	300	45.10	40.90	36.90	32.80	28.80	25.10	21.60	18.10	14.70	11.40	8.50
300	310	47.50	43.00	39.00	34.90	30.90	26.90	23.40	19.90	16.50	13.00	10.00
310	320	49.90	45.30	41.10	37.00	33.00	28.90	25.20	21.70	18.30	14.80	11.50
320	330	52.30	47.70	43.20	39.10	35.10	31.00	27.00	23.50	20.10	16.60	13.20
330	340	54.70	50.10	45.50	41.20	37.20	33.10	29.10	25.30	21.90	18.40	15.00
340	350	57.10	52.50	47.90	43.30	39.30	35.20	31.20	27.20	23.70	20.20	16.80
350	360	59.50	54.90	50.30	45.70	41.40	37.30	33.30	29.30	25.50	22.00	18.60
360	370	61.90	57.30	52.70	48.10	43.50	39.40	35.40	31.40	27.30	23.80	20.40
370	380	64.60	59.70	55.10	50.50	45.90	41.50	37.50	33.50	29.40	25.60	22.20
380	390	67.40	62.10	57.50	52.90	48.30	43.70	39.60	35.60	31.50	27.50	24.00
390	400	70.20	64.80	59.90	55.30	50.70	46.10	41.70	37.70	33.60	29.60	25.80
400	410	73.00	67.60	62.30	57.70	53.10	48.50	43.80	39.80	35.70	31.70	27.60
410	420	75.80	70.40	65.00	60.10	55.50	50.90	46.20	41.90	37.80	33.80	29.70
420	430	78.60	73.20	67.80	62.50	57.90	53.30	48.60	44.00	39.90	35.90	31.80
430	440	81.40	76.00	70.60	65.20	60.30	55.70	51.00	46.40	42.00	38.00	33.90
440	450	84.20	78.80	73.40	68.00	62.70	58.10	53.40	48.80	44.20	40.10	36.00

usually based on the wages or salary earned and may be deducted each pay period.

In some cases, employees may ask to have amounts deducted from their earnings and deposited in a company credit union or a bank, or accumulated and used to buy United States savings bonds, shares of stock, or other investments. The employee signs an authorization for such deductions and may change this authorization or withdraw it at any time. Employees who have received advances from their employers or who have bought merchandise from the firm often repay such debts through payroll deductions.

These and other possible payroll deductions increase the payroll record-keeping work but do not involve any new principles or procedures. They are handled in the same way as the required deductions for FICA and income taxes, which have been discussed in detail.

Determining Gross Pay for Salaried Workers

A salaried employee earns an agreed sum of money each payroll period. Salaried workers may be paid by the week but more often are paid semimonthly or monthly. For example, the office clerk at the Kent Novelty Company is paid monthly.

Hours Worked

Unless they are not eligible because of the level of their position or the amount of their salary, salaried workers are covered under the maximum hours and overtime premium pay provisions of the Wage and Hour Law. The employer should keep a time record for each salaried worker to make sure that hourly earnings meet legal requirements.

Gross Pay

During January, Ellen Gold, the office clerk at the Kent Novelty Company, worked her regular schedule of 38 hours a week. Therefore, no overtime premium is involved. Her agreed salary of $750 is her gross pay for the month of January.

Deductions From Gross Pay

Regardless of the method of paying an employee, FICA tax is deducted on the base amount earned during the calendar year. For Ellen Gold this tax is 6.13 percent of $750 for January, or $45.98.

Ellen Gold is not married and claims only one personal exemption for federal income tax withholding purposes. The amount of income tax to be withheld for her is determined by referring to the monthly wage-bracket withholding table illustrated on the next page. Her gross pay of $750 for the month is included in the line that reads "At least $720, but less than $760." Under the column for one withholding allowance, $94.90 is shown as the amount of income tax to be withheld from her January earnings.

Recording Gross Pay and Deductions for Hourly Workers

Payroll personnel must compute the payroll accurately and promptly so that the net amount can be paid to the workers at the scheduled times. The payroll information for the workers is entered in a record called a *payroll register* or *payroll journal*.

SINGLE Persons — MONTHLY Payroll Period

And the wages are—		And the number of withholding allowances claimed is—										
At least	But less than	0	1	2	3	4	5	6	7	8	9	10 or more
		The amount of income tax to be withheld shall be—										
$0	$120	$0	$0	$0	$0	$0	$0	$0	$0	$0	$0	$0
120	124	.60	0	0	0	0	0	0	0	0	0	0
124	128	1.20	0	0	0	0	0	0	0	0	0	0
128	132	1.80	0	0	0	0	0	0	0	0	0	0
132	136	2.40	0	0	0	0	0	0	0	0	0	0
136	140	3.00	0	0	0	0	0	0	0	0	0	0
140	144	3.60	0	0	0	0	0	0	0	0	0	0
144	148	4.20	0	0	0	0	0	0	0	0	0	0
148	152	4.80	0	0	0	0	0	0	0	0	0	0
152	156	5.40	0	0	0	0	0	0	0	0	0	0
156	160	6.00	0	0	0	0	0	0	0	0	0	0
160	164	6.60	0	0	0	0	0	0	0	0	0	0
164	168	7.20	0	0	0	0	0	0	0	0	0	0
168	172	7.80	0	0	0	0	0	0	0	0	0	0
172	176	8.40	0	0	0	0	0	0	0	0	0	0
176	180	9.00	0	0	0	0	0	0	0	0	0	0
180	184	9.60	0	0	0	0	0	0	0	0	0	0
184	188	10.20	0	0	0	0	0	0	0	0	0	0
188	192	10.80	0	0	0	0	0	0	0	0	0	0
192	196	11.40	0	0	0	0	0	0	0	0	0	0
196	200	12.00	0	0	0	0	0	0	0	0	0	0
200	204	12.60	.10	0	0	0	0	0	0	0	0	0
204	208	13.20	.70	0	0	0	0	0	0	0	0	0
208	212	13.80	1.30	0	0	0	0	0	0	0	0	0
212	216	14.40	1.90	0	0	0	0	0	0	0	0	0
216	220	15.00	2.50	0	0	0	0	0	0	0	0	0
220	224	15.60	3.10	0	0	0	0	0	0	0	0	0
224	228	16.20	3.70	0	0	0	0	0	0	0	0	0
228	232	16.80	4.30	0	0	0	0	0	0	0	0	0
232	236	17.40	4.90	0	0	0	0	0	0	0	0	0
236	240	18.00	5.50	0	0	0	0	0	0	0	0	0
240	248	18.90	6.40	0	0	0	0	0	0	0	0	0
248	256	20.10	7.60	0	0	0	0	0	0	0	0	0
256	264	21.30	8.80	0	0	0	0	0	0	0	0	0
264	272	22.50	10.00	0	0	0	0	0	0	0	0	0
272	280	23.70	11.20	0	0	0	0	0	0	0	0	0
280	288	25.10	12.40	0	0	0	0	0	0	0	0	0
288	296	26.60	13.60	1.10	0	0	0	0	0	0	0	0
296	304	28.00	14.80	2.30	0	0	0	0	0	0	0	0
304	312	29.40	16.00	3.50	0	0	0	0	0	0	0	0
312	320	30.90	17.20	4.70	0	0	0	0	0	0	0	0
320	328	32.30	18.40	5.90	0	0	0	0	0	0	0	0
328	336	33.80	19.60	7.10	0	0	0	0	0	0	0	0
336	344	35.20	20.80	8.30	0	0	0	0	0	0	0	0
344	352	36.60	22.00	9.50	0	0	0	0	0	0	0	0
352	360	38.10	23.20	10.70	0	0	0	0	0	0	0	0
360	368	39.50	24.50	11.90	0	0	0	0	0	0	0	0
368	376	41.00	26.00	13.10	.60	0	0	0	0	0	0	0
376	384	42.40	27.40	14.30	1.80	0	0	0	0	0	0	0
384	392	43.80	28.80	15.50	3.00	0	0	0	0	0	0	0
392	400	45.30	30.30	16.70	4.20	0	0	0	0	0	0	0
400	420	47.80	32.80	18.80	6.30	0	0	0	0	0	0	0
420	440	51.40	36.40	21.80	9.30	0	0	0	0	0	0	0
440	460	55.00	40.00	25.00	12.30	0	0	0	0	0	0	0
460	480	58.60	43.60	28.60	15.30	2.80	0	0	0	0	0	0
480	500	62.20	47.20	32.20	18.30	5.80	0	0	0	0	0	0
500	520	65.80	50.80	35.80	21.30	8.80	0	0	0	0	0	0
520	540	69.40	54.40	39.40	24.40	11.80	0	0	0	0	0	0
540	560	73.00	58.00	43.00	28.00	14.80	2.30	0	0	0	0	0
560	580	76.70	61.60	46.60	31.60	17.80	5.30	0	0	0	0	0
580	600	80.90	65.20	50.20	35.20	20.80	8.30	0	0	0	0	0
600	640	87.20	70.60	55.60	40.60	25.60	12.80	.30	0	0	0	0
640	680	95.60	78.10	62.80	47.80	32.80	18.80	6.30	0	0	0	0
680	720	104.00	86.50	70.00	55.00	40.00	25.00	12.30	0	0	0	0
720	760	112.40	94.90	77.40	62.20	47.20	32.20	18.30	5.80	0	0	0
760	800	120.80	103.30	85.80	69.40	54.40	39.40	24.40	11.80	0	0	0
800	840	129.20	111.70	94.20	76.70	61.60	46.60	31.60	17.80	5.30	0	0
840	880	138.10	120.10	102.60	85.10	68.80	53.80	38.80	23.80	11.30	0	0
880	920	148.50	128.50	111.00	93.50	76.00	61.00	46.00	31.00	17.30	4.80	0
920	960	158.90	137.20	119.40	101.90	84.40	68.20	53.20	38.20	23.30	10.80	0
960	1,000	169.30	147.60	127.80	110.30	92.80	75.40	60.40	45.40	30.40	16.80	4.30
1,000	1,040	179.70	158.00	136.40	118.70	101.20	83.70	67.60	52.60	37.60	22.80	10.30
1,040	1,080	190.10	168.40	146.80	127.10	109.60	92.10	74.80	59.80	44.80	29.80	16.30
1,080	1,120	200.50	178.80	157.20	135.50	118.00	100.50	83.00	67.00	52.00	37.00	22.30
1,120	1,160	210.90	189.20	167.60	145.90	126.40	108.90	91.40	74.20	59.20	44.20	29.20

Payroll Register

The payroll register illustrated on pages 266 and 267 shows payroll information for Kent's four hourly workers.

Each employee's name, withholding allowances, and regular hourly rate can be entered in the register in advance to save time in payroll preparation. From the completed time records, the hours worked each day are entered in the register, along with the total and overtime hours for the week. Gross pay computations are made in the manner previously described and are entered in the Earnings section. These amounts are classified according to regular and overtime premium earnings. The sum of the earnings is entered in the Total column.

The next two columns of the payroll register are used only when an employee has earned wages that are tax exempt (above $6,000 for FUTA and above the assumed base of $22,900 for FICA). This information comes from the Cumulative Total column of the employee's individual earnings record. (See the illustration on page 268. This record is explained in a later section.)

The computation of FICA tax and the determination of the amount of income tax to be withheld are made as previously described. The figures are entered in the appropriate columns of the Deductions section of the payroll register. Any other deductions are entered with a proper explanation in the Other column. Then the deductions for each employee are subtracted from the gross pay to find the net amount to be paid. This figure is recorded in the Net Amount column.

When the payroll information for all employees in the group has been recorded in the payroll register, the columns are totaled as shown. The accuracy of the register should be proved at this point, before the payroll is paid. This proof is accomplished by cross-footing—adding and subtracting the column totals across the register. The total of the Regular Earnings column plus the total of the Overtime Premium column should equal the total of the Total Earnings column. The total of the Total Earnings column minus the totals of the Deductions columns should equal the total of the Net Amount column. For the payroll register shown on pages 266 and 267, this proof would be expressed in the following way: $936.00 + $8.00 = $944.00; $944.00 − $57.87 − $98.20 = $787.93.

Once the payroll register has been checked for accuracy, the payroll information is recorded in the firm's accounting records. The column totals from the payroll register supply all the necessary figures. Each item in the entry may be traced back to the payroll register.

The Accounting Entry for Payroll

The gross pay should be charged to the appropriate expense account. For the production workers at the Kent Novelty Company, this account might be entitled Shop Labor Expense 601. Separate liability accounts should be set up for each type of deduction made from the employees. A liability account should also be used to record the amount of net pay due, since the accounting entry for the payroll is made before the employees are actually paid.

HOURLY PAYROLL No. 1												Week Beginning January 1, 19X1 and Ending	
			HOURS BY DAYS							HOURS WORKED			
NAME	INC. TAX ALLOW.	MARITAL STATUS	S	M	T	W	T	F	S	TOTAL	OVER-TIME	REG. HRLY. RATE	
Brown, Peter	3	M		8	4	8	8	8	4	40		6	00
Dunn, George	1	M		8	8	8	8	8	4	44	4	4	00
King, Joan	3	S		8	8	8	4	8	4	40		5	00
Lopez, Rita	4	M		8	8	4	8	8	4	40		8	00

The entry for Kent's January 7 payroll in the general journal is shown below after posting is completed.

19	X1						
Jan.	7	Shop Labor Expense	601	944	00		
		Employee Ded.—FICA Tax	221			57	87
		Employee Ded.—Inc. Tax Withheld	222			98	20
		Wages Payable	203			787	93
		Gross earnings, deductions, and net wages payable to shop employees for week ended Jan. 7, 19X1.					

Paying the Payroll

Some firms, particularly smaller firms, pay their employees in cash. However, most firms prefer to make such payments by check. The canceled check provides a record of the payment and the employee's endorsement serves as a receipt. The use of checks avoids the inconvenience of obtaining the cash and putting it in pay envelopes. Using checks also eliminates the risk involved in handling large amounts of currency.

Paying in Cash

When the payroll is to be paid in cash, one check is written for the total amount of net pay earned by all the employees. Then this check is cashed, and the firm obtains bills and coins of suitable denominations so that the correct net pay amount can be inserted in the pay envelope of each worker. The pay envelope usually has an information block printed on it. This area is used to enter the amount of gross pay, the deductions, and the net pay. The employees may be asked to sign a receipt or to sign on their lines in the payroll register as evidence that the pay was received.

January 7, 19X1   Paid January 9, 19X1

EARNINGS			TAX-EXEMPT WAGES		DEDUCTIONS			PAID	
REGULAR	OVERTIME PREMIUM	TOTAL	FICA	FUTA	FICA TAX	INC. TAX WITHHELD	OTHER	NET AMOUNT	CHECK NO.
240 00		240 00			14 71	23 00		202 29	4725
176 00	8 00	184 00			11 28	19 10		153 62	4726
200 00		200 00			12 26	21 00		166 74	4727
320 00		320 00			19 62	35 10		265 28	4728
936 00	8 00	944 00			57 87	98 20		787 93	

Paying by Check   When employees are paid by check, an individual check is written for each employee. The check number is entered in the Check Number column of the payroll register on the same line as the employee's other information. (See the payroll register illustrated above.) Information about the employee's gross pay, deductions, and net pay are usually shown on a stub of the payroll check. The employee detaches the stub and keeps it as a record of his or her payroll data for the period.

Of course, the payroll check is written to the employee for the net pay amount. The effect of the payments is to decrease the Wages Payable account and to decrease the Cash account. Thus, when the checks are issued, the amounts are recorded in the cash payments journal by debiting Wages Payable and crediting Cash.

Payroll checks may be drawn on the firm's regular bank account or on a separate payroll bank account. If a separate payroll bank account is used, one check is usually drawn on the regular bank account for the net amount of wages payable and deposited in the payroll bank account. This check is entered in the cash payments journal as a debit to Wages Payable and a credit to Cash. Since individual checks totaling this amount are immediately written on the payroll bank account, this account never has a balance. Thus it does not appear on the financial statements.

Recording Gross Pay and Deductions for Salaried Workers   If there were several salaried workers, a payroll register similar to the one illustrated for the hourly workers might be used. Since the Kent Novelty Company has only one salaried employee, her earnings and deductions are recorded by a separate general journal entry, as illustrated on page 268.

Note that the Office Salaries Expense account is debited for the gross pay of Ellen Gold. Her deductions are recorded in the same liability accounts as those of the hourly-rate workers, and the net amount due her is recorded in the same Wages Payable account. Salaried workers are ordinarily paid by

	19	X1								
	Jan.	31	Office Salaries Expense		501	750	00			
			Employee Ded.—FICA Tax		221			45	98	
			Employee Ded.—Inc. Tax Withheld		222			94	90	
			Wages Payable		203			609	12	
			Gross earnings, deductions, and net salary payable to Ellen Gold for the month of January 19X1.							

check. The payment is recorded in the cash payments journal by debiting Wages Payable and crediting Cash.

Individual Earnings Records

At the beginning of each year, or when a new employee is hired during the year, an *individual earnings record* (sometimes called a *compensation record*) is set up for each worker. This record contains the employee's name, address, social security number, date of birth, number of withholding allowances claimed, and any other information that may be needed. The details for each pay period are posted to the employee's individual earnings record from the payroll register. The record for Peter Brown illustrated below shows the data for the first payroll in January.

NAME: Peter Brown   **EMPL. NO.:** 1   **SOC. SEC. NO.:** 324-76-1245
ADDRESS: 24 Oak Street, Manchester, NH 03104   **DATE OF BIRTH:** Jan. 23, 1948
WITHHOLDING ALLOWANCES: 3   **MARITAL STATUS:** Married

PAYROLL NO.	DATE		HOURS WORKED		RATE PER HOUR	EARNINGS			CUMU-LATIVE TOTAL	DEDUCTIONS		
	WK. END.	PAID	TOT. HRS.	O.T. HRS.		REGULAR AMOUNT	OVERTIME PREMIUM AMOUNT	TOTAL AMOUNT		FICA TAX	INCOME TAX WITHHELD	OTHER
1	1/7	1/9	40	0	6 00	240 00		240 00	240 00	14 71	23 00	

Note that the details shown on this record include the payroll date (entered in the Week Ended column), the date paid, the hours worked, the hourly rate, the earnings (broken down into regular earnings and overtime premium earnings as indicated in the payroll register), and each deduction. One item is not posted from the payroll register—the cumulative total. This amount is the employee's year-to-date gross pay. It is computed whenever a payroll entry is made in an employee's earnings record.

The earnings records may be totaled monthly and at the end of every calendar quarter. In this way, they provide information needed in making tax payments and filing tax returns, as described in the next unit.

An individual earnings record is also kept for each salaried employee. The employer may use either the same form of record as the one used for hourly workers or a slightly modified form designed especially for salaried workers. Whatever the form of the record, the details of the earnings and deductions are entered in it for each pay period, just as is done for the hourly workers.

Completing January Payrolls

In order to complete the January payrolls for the Kent Novelty Company, assume that all employees worked the same number of hours a week during the month as they did in the first week. Thus, they also earned the same gross pay, had the same deductions, and had the same net pay each week.

Journal Entries

As explained already, a general journal entry is made to record the payroll for the hourly employees of the Kent Novelty Company. Since we are assuming an identical payroll for each week of the month, the four weekly payrolls require entries similar to the one shown on page 266. The office clerk is paid monthly. Her earnings and deductions for January are recorded in a separate general journal entry, as shown on page 268.

Ledger Accounts Posted

The entries for the weekly payrolls involving hourly workers and for the monthly salaried worker are posted to the proper accounts in the general ledger. At the end of January, these accounts appear as shown below and on page 270. (The debits to the Wages Payable account for the payments to employees have not yet been posted.)

Wages Payable   No. 203

DATE	EXPLANATION	POST. REF.	DEBIT	CREDIT	BALANCE	DR. CR.
19 X1 Jan. 7		J1		787 93	787 93	Cr.
14		J1		787 93	1,575 86	Cr.
21		J2		787 93	2,363 79	Cr.
28		J2		787 93	3,151 72	Cr.
31		J2		609 12	3,760 84	Cr.

Employee Deductions—FICA Tax   No. 221

DATE	EXPLANATION	POST. REF.	DEBIT	CREDIT	BALANCE	DR. CR.
19 X1 Jan. 7		J1		57 87	57 87	Cr.
14		J1		57 87	115 74	Cr.
21		J2		57 87	173 61	Cr.
28		J2		57 87	231 48	Cr.
31		J2		45 98	277 46	Cr.

Employee Deductions—Income Tax Withheld   No. 222

DATE	EXPLANATION	POST. REF.	DEBIT	CREDIT	BALANCE	DR. CR.
19 X1 Jan. 7		J1		98 20	98 20	Cr.
14		J1		98 20	196 40	Cr.
21		J2		98 20	294 60	Cr.
28		J2		98 20	392 80	Cr.
31		J2		94 90	487 70	Cr.

Office Salaries Expense   No. 501

DATE	EXPLANATION	POST. REF.	DEBIT	CREDIT	BALANCE	DR. CR.
19 X1 Jan. 31		J2	750 00		750 00	Dr.

Shop Labor Expense   No. 601

DATE	EXPLANATION	POST. REF.	DEBIT	CREDIT	BALANCE	DR. CR.
19 X1 Jan. 7		J1	944 00		944 00	Dr.
14		J1	944 00		1,888 00	Dr.
21		J2	944 00		2,832 00	Dr.
28		J2	944 00		3,776 00	Dr.

Proving the Individual Earnings Records

As previously mentioned, the earnings and deductions of each employee are posted to an individual earnings record. At the end of each month, the postings to these records for the period can be checked against the amounts posted to the general ledger accounts. Each earnings record is totaled for the month. Then a list is made of the column totals for gross pay and for each deduction, usually on an adding machine. The totals from the earnings records shown on the adding machine tape are compared with the current month's postings to the corresponding general ledger accounts. Any differences are found and corrected.

    The individual earnings record for Peter Brown at the end of January is shown on the next page. The record for each of the other employees is similar.

    The adding machine tapes illustrated on the next page show the total earnings and deductions entered in the individual earnings records kept by the Kent Novelty Company.

NAME: Peter Brown **EMPL. NO.:** 1 **SOC. SEC. NO.:** 324-76-1245
ADDRESS: 24 Oak Street, Manchester, NH 03104 **DATE OF BIRTH:** Jan. 23, 1948
WITHHOLDING ALLOWANCES: 3 **MARITAL STATUS:** Married

PAYROLL NO.	DATE WK. END.	DATE PAID	HOURS WORKED TOT. HRS.	HOURS WORKED O.T. HRS.	RATE PER HOUR	EARNINGS REGULAR AMOUNT	EARNINGS OVERTIME PREMIUM AMOUNT	EARNINGS TOTAL AMOUNT	CUMULATIVE TOTAL	DEDUCTIONS FICA TAX	DEDUCTIONS INCOME TAX WITHHELD	DEDUCTIONS OTHER
1	1/7	1/9	40	0	6 00	240 00		240 00	240 00	14 71	23 00	
2	1/14	1/16	40	0	6 00	240 00		240 00	480 00	14 71	23 00	
3	1/21	1/23	40	0	6 00	240 00		240 00	720 00	14 71	23 00	
4	1/28	1/30	40	0	6 00	240 00		240 00	960 00	14 71	23 00	
January						960 00		960 00		58 84	92 00	

```
Gross Earnings       FICA Tax Withheld    Income Tax Withheld
        .00*                 .00*                 .00*
     960.00              58.84                92.00
     736.00              45.12                76.40
     800.00              49.04                84.00
   1,280.00              78.48               140.40
     750.00              45.98                94.90
   4,526.00*            277.46*              487.70*
```

Note that the totals for FICA tax deducted and income tax withheld on the adding machine tape (which represent the amounts from the individual earnings records) agree with the general ledger account balances for these items. (The accounts are illustrated on pages 269 and 270.) The gross earnings total equals the sum of the debits to the Office Salaries Expense account and the Shop Labor Expense account shown on page 270. With this proof completed as shown, the records are ready for the transactions of the next month.

PROOF OF BALANCES IN PAYROLL ACCOUNTS					
Earnings:	Office Salaries Expense	501	$ 750.00		
	Shop Labor Expense	601	3,776.00	$4,526.00 (Dr.)	
Deductions:	FICA Tax	221		$ 277.46 (Cr.)	
	Income Tax Withheld	222		487.70 (Cr.)	
Net Pay:	Wages Payable	203		3,760.84 (Cr.)	
				$4,526.00 (Cr.)	

Recording the Liability for Unpaid Wages

In many cases, it is not possible for the employer to pay all wages in the month in which they are earned. As a result, there are wages owed to employees at the end of the month. These are called *accrued wages payable*. When the amount is large enough to be important, the accountant should make an adjusting entry at the end of the month to record the fact that the expense has been incurred and that a liability exists. The adjusting entry on the worksheet consists of a debit to the appropriate expense account and a credit to Wages Payable.

The accountant of the Kent Novelty Company did not choose to record the accrued shop wages on January 31 because the amount was small. However, many accountants would feel that in order to report the expenses of January properly, the earnings of the employees for Monday, January 30, and Tuesday, January 31, should be recorded on January 31. The wages expense for those two days would then appear on the income statement for January, and the amount owed would appear as a liability on the balance sheet. The total wages earned by the four shop workers in the last two days of January was $378. If an adjusting entry had been made, it would have been recorded on the worksheet and later in the general journal as follows.

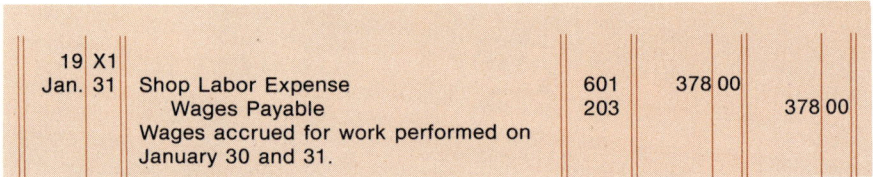

Note that only the gross pay is recorded as an expense and as a liability. No recognition is given to the withholding amounts because the withholdings are not technically made until the employees are paid. The accountant is merely interested in recording the total expense and the total liability so that the financial statements will accurately report the net income for the period and the total liabilities as of the end of the period.

principles and procedures summary

The main objective of payroll work is to compute the amounts due employees and to pay these amounts promptly. The employer is required to withhold at least two taxes from the employees' pay: the employees' FICA tax and federal income tax. Instructions for computing the amount of each of these taxes are provided by the government to the employer. Other required deductions may be made for state and city income taxes. Many employees also have voluntary deductions that are made by agreement between the employees and the employer. The employer keeps a record of the employees' gross pay and deductions in a payroll register. Information from this record is used to prepare a payroll entry in the general journal.

Details of earnings and deductions for each employee are kept on an individual earnings record. All of these records may be proved monthly against the entries in the general ledger accounts for payroll.

managerial implications

Employers must be very careful that their payroll procedures and their wage rates comply with governmental requirements, including the provisions of the federal Wage and Hour Law, which requires additional pay for overtime hours. Similarly, care must be taken to be sure that proper withholdings are made.

Payrolls make up a large part of the operating costs in most business firms. Thus, proper and adequate payroll records are also essential to management as an aid in controlling expenses. These records show how much has been spent for labor and the use made of the labor so that the proper expense accounts can be charged. Payroll records must be kept accurately and must be carefully audited to prevent errors in payment or fraud.

managerial discussion questions

1. Why is it important for a firm to have detailed payroll records?
2. How do proper and adequate payroll records aid management in controlling expenses?

application of principles

PROBLEM 15-1 The Wilton Electronic Service pays its employees on an hourly basis, and the employees receive one and a half times the regular rate for hours worked in excess of 40 in one week. Data for the week ended January 22, 19X1, is shown on the next page.

INSTRUCTIONS
1. Set up a payroll register containing columns with the following headings: Name, Number of Allowances, Marital Status, Total Hours Worked, Overtime Hours, Regular Hourly Rate, Regular Earnings, Overtime Premium, Total Earnings, FICA Tax Withheld, Income Tax Withheld, and Net Amount. Enter each employee's name, allowances, marital status, hours worked, and rate.

2. Compute the total earnings for each employee, including regular earnings and overtime premium earnings. Enter this information in the payroll register.
3. Compute the FICA tax to be withheld from each employee's earnings. Use the assumed rate of 6.13 percent of total earnings. Enter the amounts in the payroll register.
4. Determine the income tax to be withheld from each employee's earnings. Use the withholding tax tables given on pages 261 and 262. Enter the amounts in the payroll register.
5. Compute the net pay for each employee, and enter the amount in the payroll register.
6. Total and rule the money columns of the payroll register. Prove the totals by cross-footing.

Employee	Total Hours Worked	Hourly Rate	Withholding Allowances	Marital Status
Carole Burke	43	$6.00	3	Married
Harry Kohn	36	4.00	5	Married
Neil Larson	39	4.50	5	Single
Tom Wyler	45	6.50	3	Married

PROBLEM 15-2 Janet Thomas operates a woodworking shop. She pays employees an hourly wage, with time and a half for hours over 40 worked in one week.

Data for the week ended December 31, 19X1 is shown on the next page. All four employees are married.

INSTRUCTIONS
1. Set up a payroll register with the following headings: Name, Number of Allowances, Marital Status, Total Hours Worked, Overtime Hours, Regular Hourly Rate, Regular Earnings, Overtime Premium, Total Earnings, FICA Tax Withheld, Income Tax Withheld, and Net Amount. Enter each employee's name, allowances, marital status, hours worked, and rate.
2. Compute the total earnings for each employee, including regular earnings and overtime premium. Enter this information in the payroll register.
3. Compute the FICA tax to be withheld from each employee's earnings. Use the assumed rate of 6.13 percent. Enter the amounts in the payroll register.
4. Determine the income tax to be withheld from each employee's earnings. Use the withholding tax tables on pages 261 and 262. Enter the amounts in the payroll register.
5. Compute the net pay for each employee, and enter the amount in the payroll register.
6. Total and rule the money columns of the payroll register. Prove the totals.
7. Make the general journal entry to record the payroll. Debit Wages Expense. For the other accounts involved, use the account titles given in the text illustrations.

Employee	Total Hours Worked	Hourly Rate	Withholding Allowances	Cumulative Earnings Through Dec. 24
Kevin Connor	40	$5.20	2	$ 5,640
Lauren Mirs	48	6.00	3	6,400
Toby Reese	26	9.50	3	11,910
Wendy Lee	40	4.50	4	7,000

PROBLEM 15-3 A portion of the individual earnings record of John Coker is shown in the *Individualized Performance Guide*. Coker is married and claims three withholding allowances. He earned $3.50 an hour through the month of March. During the week ended March 31, he worked 38 hours, for which he was paid on that day. Beginning April 1, Coker's wages were increased to $4 an hour; and during the week ended April 7, he worked 42 hours, for which he was paid on that date.

INSTRUCTIONS
1. Compute Coker's total earnings, cumulative total, FICA deduction (assuming a rate of 6.13 percent), and federal income tax withholding (using the table on page 262) for the week ended March 31. Enter the data for that week in Coker's earnings record.
2. Total all money columns for the month of March, and place a single rule under the totals.
3. Bring down the totals in all money columns for the quarter, and place a double rule under these amounts.
4. Compute Coker's total earnings, cumulative total, FICA deduction, and federal income tax withholding for the week ended April 7. (Don't forget Coker's pay increase.) Enter the payroll data in Coker's earnings record.

PROBLEM 15-4 The Russo Milling Company pays its three production employees on Friday of each week. On Wednesday, April 30, 19X1, the accountant wishes to record accrued wages for the last three days of April. These amounts will be paid on Friday, May 2. Data concerning wage rates, hours worked, and so on, for the three employees is shown below and on the next page.

INSTRUCTIONS Make the general journal entry on April 30 to record the accrued wages so that an income statement can be properly prepared for the period ended on that date. This firm uses an account called Mill Labor Expense for recording the wages of production employees.

EMPLOYEE INFORMATION

- Marian Adams, single, one withholding allowance, hourly wage rate, $6. Worked 8 hours on each of the three days.

- Howard Benson, married, three withholding allowances, hourly wage rate, $4. Worked 8 hours on Monday, did not work on Tuesday, and worked 8 hours on Wednesday.
- Carla Rinaldo, single, one withholding allowance, hourly wage rate, $5.50. Worked 10 hours on Monday, 8 hours on Tuesday, and 9 hours on Wednesday.

alternate problems

PROBLEM 15-1A   Braun's Repair Shop pays its employees on an hourly basis, and the employees receive one and a half times the regular rate for hours worked in excess of 40 in one week. The data for the week ended January 8, 19X1, is shown below.

INSTRUCTIONS
1. Set up a payroll register containing columns with the following headings: Name, Number of Allowances, Marital Status, Total Hours Worked, Overtime Hours, Regular Hourly Rate, Regular Earnings, Overtime Premium, Total Earnings, FICA Tax Withheld, Income Tax Withheld, and Net Amount. Enter each employee's name, allowances, marital status, hours worked, and rate.
2. Compute the total earnings for each employee, including regular earnings and overtime premium earnings. Enter the amounts in the payroll register.
3. Compute the FICA tax to be withheld from each employee's earnings. Use the assumed rate of 6.13 percent of total earnings. Enter the amounts in the payroll register.
4. Determine the income tax to be withheld from each employee's earnings. Use the withholding tax tables given on pages 261 and 262. Enter the amounts in the payroll register.
5. Compute the net pay for each employee, and enter the amount in the payroll register.
6. Total and rule the money columns of the payroll register. Prove the totals by cross-footing.

Employee	Total Hours Worked	Hourly Rate	Withholding Allowances	Marital Status
Bonnie Willis	44	$5.40	4	Married
Glen Lanski	42	6.10	3	Married
Diane Taylor	36	4.50	2	Single
Tom Levine	45	6.00	3	Married

PROBLEM 15-2A   Robert Mendez operates the Morris Appliance Shop. He pays the workers on an hourly basis, with time and a half for hours over 40 worked in one week. Data for the week ended December 24, 19X1, is shown on the next page. All three workers are married.

INSTRUCTIONS
1. Set up a payroll register with the following columns: Name, Number of Allowances, Marital Status, Total Hours Worked, Overtime Hours, Regu-

lar Hourly Rate, Regular Earnings, Overtime Premium, Total Earnings, FICA Tax Withheld, Income Tax Withheld, and Net Amount. Enter each employee's name, allowances, marital status, hours worked, and rate.
2. Compute the total earnings for each employee, including regular earnings and overtime premium. Enter these amounts in the payroll register.
3. Compute the FICA tax to be withheld from each employee's earnings. Use the assumed rate of 6.13 percent. Enter the amounts in the payroll register.
4. Determine the income tax to be withheld from each employee's earnings. Use the withholding tax tables on pages 261 and 262. Enter the amounts in the payroll register.
5. Compute the net pay for each employee, and enter the amount in the payroll register.
6. Total and rule the money columns of the payroll register. Prove the totals.
7. Make the general journal entry to record the payroll. Debit Wages Expense. For the other accounts involved, use the account titles given in the text illustrations.

Employee	Total Hours Worked	Hourly Rate	Withholding Allowances	Cumulative Earnings Through Dec. 17
Joanne Mazzeo	41	$4.10	3	$ 7,800
Tom Ness	48	3.50	4	5,400
John Ortiz	24	6.50	2	11,940

PROBLEM 15-3A A portion of the individual earnings record of John Coker is shown in the *Individualized Performance Guide.* Coker is married and claims three withholding allowances. He earns $3.50 an hour. During the week ended March 31, he worked 43 hours, for which he was paid on that day. During the week ended April 7, he worked 45 hours, for which he was paid on that day.

INSTRUCTIONS
1. Compute Coker's total earnings, cumulative total, FICA deduction (assuming a rate of 6.13 percent), and federal income tax withholding (using the table on page 262) for the week ended March 31. Enter the data for that week in Coker's earnings record.
2. Total all money columns for the month of March, and place a single rule under the totals.
3. Bring down the totals in all money columns for the quarter, and place a double rule under these amounts.
4. Compute the total earnings, cumulative total, FICA deduction, and federal income tax withholding for the week ended April 7. Enter the data for that week in Coker's earnings record.

PROBLEM 15-4A The two truck drivers who work for the City Delivery Service are paid on Friday of each week. Rhonda Smith is single, claims one withholding allowance, and earns $5.10 an hour. She worked 8 hours on Monday, February 27, and 8 hours on Tuesday, February 28. James Monroe is married, claims two withholding allowances, and earns $6.00 an hour. He worked 6 hours on February 27 and 8 hours on February 28.

INSTRUCTIONS   Make the general journal entry on February 28, 19X1, to record the accrued wages so that an income statement can be properly prepared for the period ended on that date. This firm uses an account called Delivery Wages Expense for recording the wages of the truck drivers.

UNIT 16

PAYROLL TAXES

Businesses are required by law to act as collection agents for the FICA tax and the income tax due from employees. Firms must deduct, account for, and transmit these taxes to the government. They are also responsible for paying unemployment taxes and reporting employee earnings to the government. This unit explains how the accountant makes tax payments and files the required tax returns and reports.

Changes in Tax Rates and Bases

In recent years, frequent and substantial changes have been made in the social security (FICA) and federal unemployment (FUTA) taxes. The tax rates for employees and employers have increased greatly, and the maximum amount of wages subject to FICA taxes has risen significantly. The maximum amount of wages subject to FUTA taxes has also increased. In actual practice, always be sure to use the latest rates and bases and follow the latest instructions. *Circular E,* the *Employer's Tax Guide,* and other publications of the Internal Revenue Service are very helpful in keeping informed about current developments and requirements.

Deposit of FICA Taxes and Income Taxes Withheld

Generally, income taxes withheld and FICA taxes are deposited in a Federal Reserve Bank or other authorized financial institution. Most commercial banks are authorized to receive such deposits. The employer enters the amount of the deposit on a preprinted government form, which must be included with a check for the taxes owed. This form is the Federal Tax Deposit, Form 501.

The frequency of deposits is determined by the amount of taxes. The taxes are owed when the wages and salaries are paid, not when the payroll periods end. The requirements for depositing FICA taxes and income taxes withheld vary according to the total amount of such taxes. The total amount of federal income taxes, the total amount of FICA taxes withheld from employee earnings, and the total amount of FICA taxes owed by the employer will determine how often the employer must make deposits.

If at the end of the quarter the total undeposited taxes are less than $200, no deposit is required. The taxes may be paid to the Internal Revenue Service when Form 941 is filed (see page 285), or they may be deposited by the end of the following month. If at the end of the quarter the total undeposited taxes are $200 or more but less than $2,000, they must be deposited by the end of the following month.

If at the end of the first or second month of the quarter, the total undeposited taxes for the quarter are $200 or more but less than $2,000, the taxes must be deposited within 15 days after the end of the month. If the taxes are less than $200, they may be carried over to the next month.

If at the end of any quarter-monthly period (approximately one-fourth of a month) the total undeposited taxes for the quarter amount to $2,000 or more, they must be deposited within three banking days after the end of the quarter-monthly period. A quarter-monthly period ends on the 7th, 15th, 22d, and last day of any month. (Local holidays observed by authorized financial institutions, Saturdays, Sundays, and legal holidays are not counted as banking days.)

Employer's FICA Tax

Since a business firm pays the FICA tax at the same rate and on the same taxable wages as its employees, the amount of tax the firm owes is usually the same as that deducted from the employees. However, when the Kent Novelty Company applies the assumed 6.13 percent rate to the total wages paid for January ($4,526), the resulting tax is $277.44 rather than the $277.46 deducted from employee earnings. Small differences of this type occur due to rounding off individual tax deductions. Some firms handle such a situation by matching the amount deducted from the employees when making the tax deposit. Any final difference is settled on the quarterly tax return. However, Kent will deposit the exact employer's FICA tax that it owes ($277.44).

Because the Kent Novelty Company is keeping its records on the cash basis, the employer's FICA tax is not recorded until the cash is actually paid out.

Deposit of January Taxes

The January tax deductions from the employees of the Kent Novelty Company and the employer's FICA tax are as follows.

Employees' FICA Tax Deducted	$ 277.46
Employees' Income Tax Withheld	487.70
Employer's FICA Tax	277.44
Total	$1,042.60

The total at the end of the first month of the quarter exceeds $200, and therefore it must be deposited in an authorized bank by February 15, 19X1. The employer makes this payment by writing a check to the depository bank, which in this case is the Security National Bank. This payment is recorded in the cash payments journal. The debit amounts are entered in the Other Accounts section. (An account called Employer's FICA Tax Expense 551 is used to record the firm's FICA contribution.) The amount of the check, $1,042.60, is entered in the Cash Credit column. This entry in the cash payments journal is illustrated on the next page.

			ACCOUNTS PAYABLE		OTHER ACCOUNTS DEBIT			
DATE	CHECK NO.	EXPLANATION	✓	DR. 202	ACCOUNT TITLE	POST. REF.	AMOUNT	CASH CR. 101
Feb. 1	248	Deposit of Jan. taxes			Employee Deduc.— FICA Tax	221	277 46	
					Employee Deduc.— Income Tax With.	222	487 70	
					Employer's FICA Tax Expense	551	277 44	1,042 60

CASH PAYMENTS JOURNAL for Month of February 19X1 — Page 2

As noted already, the deposit must be accompanied by a properly filled out Federal Tax Deposit, Form 501. When this punched card form is processed, the amount paid is credited to the employer by the Internal Revenue Service. Both sides of the Form 501 filed in February by the Kent Novelty Company are shown below. This form covers the payment of the firm's January FICA taxes and income tax withholdings.

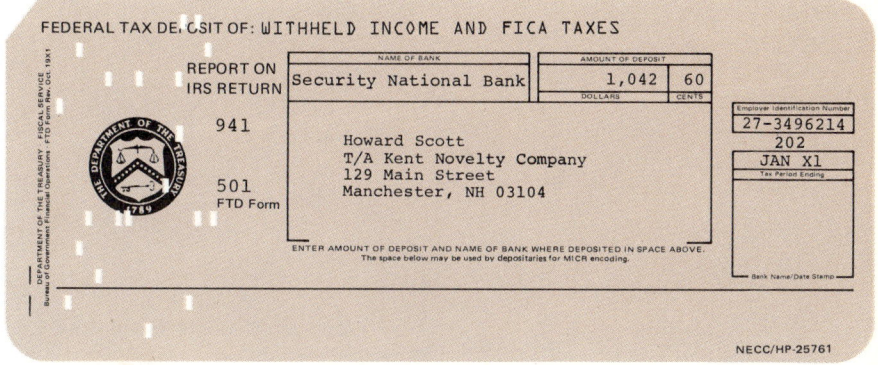

FRONT OF FORM 501

REVERSE SIDE OF FORM 501

281

February Payroll Records

There are four payroll weeks in February for the Kent Novelty Company. To simplify the example, assume that each hourly employee worked the same number of hours each week as in January and had the same gross pay and deductions. Assume also that the office clerk, Ellen Gold, earned her regular salary and had the same deductions as in January. The individual earnings records for the employees would be posted and proved in the manner previously described. Then a tax deposit form would be prepared and the taxes deposited in the bank. Finally, an entry would be made in the cash payments journal, as illustrated on page 281.

March Payroll Records

In March, the Kent Novelty Company had five payroll weeks, making a total of 13 weekly payrolls for the quarter. Assume again that the earnings and deductions of each hourly employee were the same for each week as in January and February and that the office clerk's monthly salary and deductions were the same as before.

The ledger accounts for the taxes withheld from employees' earnings are shown below as they would appear after the payroll transactions for March are posted.

Employee Deductions—FICA Tax					No. 221
DATE	EXPLANATION	POST. REF.	DEBIT	CREDIT	BALANCE	DR. CR.
19 X1 Mar. 3		J3		57 87	57 87	Cr.
10		J3		57 87	115 74	Cr.
17		J3		57 87	173 61	Cr.
24		J3		57 87	231 48	Cr.
31		J3		57 87	289 35	Cr.
31		J3		45 98	335 33	Cr.

Employee Deductions—Income Tax Withheld					No. 222
DATE	EXPLANATION	POST. REF.	DEBIT	CREDIT	BALANCE	DR. CR.
19 X1 Mar. 3		J3		98 20	98 20	Cr.
10		J3		98 20	196 40	Cr.
17		J3		98 20	294 60	Cr.
24		J3		98 20	392 80	Cr.
31		J3		98 20	491 00	Cr.
31		J3		94 90	585 90	Cr.

Quarterly Summary of Earnings Records

At the end of each calendar quarter, the earnings record of each employee is totaled for the quarter. This involves adding the three monthly totals in the Total Earnings, FICA Tax, and Income Tax Withheld columns. The sums are placed on the line for the appropriate quarter. The cumulative total of the employee's earnings is also entered on this line. The record for Peter Brown, completely posted and summarized for the first quarter, is illustrated on the next page. Those for the other employees are completed in the same way.

NAME: Peter Brown EMPL. NO.: 1 SOC. SEC. NO.: 324-76-1245
ADDRESS: 24 Oak Street, Manchester, NH 03104 DATE OF BIRTH: Jan. 23, 1948
WITHHOLDING ALLOWANCES: 3 MARITAL STATUS: Married

PAYROLL NO.	DATE WK. END.	DATE PAID	HOURS WORKED TOT. HRS.	HOURS WORKED O.T. HRS.	RATE PER HOUR	EARNINGS REGULAR AMOUNT	EARNINGS OVERTIME PREMIUM AMOUNT	EARNINGS TOTAL AMOUNT	CUMULATIVE TOTAL	DEDUCTIONS FICA TAX	DEDUCTIONS INCOME TAX WITHHELD	OTHER
1	1/7	1/9	40	0	6 00	240 00		240 00	240 00	14 71	23 00	
2	1/14	1/16	40	0	6 00	240 00		240 00	480 00	14 71	23 00	
3	1/21	1/23	40	0	6 00	240 00		240 00	720 00	14 71	23 00	
4	1/28	1/30	40	0	6 00	240 00		240 00	960 00	14 71	23 00	
	January					960 00		960 00		58 84	92 00	
1	2/4	2/6	40	0	6 00	240 00		240 00	1,200 00	14 71	23 00	
2	2/11	2/13	40	0	6 00	240 00		240 00	1,440 00	14 71	23 00	
3	2/18	2/20	40	0	6 00	240 00		240 00	1,680 00	14 71	23 00	
4	2/25	2/27	40	0	6 00	240 00		240 00	1,920 00	14 71	23 00	
	February					960 00		960 00		58 84	92 00	
1	3/3	3/5	40	0	6 00	240 00		240 00	2,160 00	14 71	23 00	
2	3/10	3/12	40	0	6 00	240 00		240 00	2,400 00	14 71	23 00	
3	3/17	3/19	40	0	6 00	240 00		240 00	2,640 00	14 71	23 00	
4	3/24	3/26	40	0	6 00	240 00		240 00	2,880 00	14 71	23 00	
5	3/31	3/31	40	0	6 00	240 00		240 00	3,120 00	14 71	23 00	
	March					1,200 00		1,200 00		73 55	115 00	
	First Quarter							3,120 00	3,120 00	191 23	299 00	

The quarterly totals for each employee, taken from the individual earnings records, are shown below.

Employee	Total Earnings	FICA Tax	Income Tax
Peter Brown	$ 3,120.00	$191.23	$ 299.00
George Dunn	2,392.00	146.64	248.30
Joan King	2,600.00	159.38	273.00
Rita Lopez	4,160.00	255.06	456.30
Ellen Gold	2,250.00	137.94	284.70
Totals	$14,522.00	$890.25	$1,561.30

Employer's Quarterly Federal Tax Return

During the month following the end of each calendar quarter (April, July, October, and January), the employer must file a tax return and pay any balance of tax due for the quarter. This return is called the Employer's Quarterly Federal Tax Return, Form 941.

Purpose of Form 941

Form 941 was recently revised. Much of the social security information concerning individual employees previously reported on Form 941 is now shown on each employee's Form W-2, as is explained on pages 286–287. Form 941 now requires only the reporting of total wages and other income subject to income tax withholding, total wages and tips subject to FICA taxes, the totals of the taxes for each of the deposit periods in the quarter, and the amounts and dates of the various deposits made by the employer. In effect, Form 941 provides a verification of the employer's compliance with the applicable laws.

Filing Form 941

Form 941 must be filed quarterly by all employers subject to income tax withholding, FICA taxes, or both, with certain exceptions as specified in *Circular E*. The due dates for the returns and tax payments are the last day of the month following the end of each calendar quarter. If all taxes were deposited when due during the calendar quarter, the employer may file the return by the 10th day of the second month following the end of the quarter. Howard Scott, the owner of the Kent Novelty Company, prepared his Form 941 for the first quarter of 19X1 as shown opposite.

Completing Form 941

Much of the data needed to complete Form 941 is obtained from the quarterly summary of earnings records illustrated on page 283. The top of Form 941 shows the employer's name and identification number. The wages and other income subject to withholding are entered on Line 2, and the total income tax withheld of $1,561.30 is entered on Line 3. Since there is no adjustment of income tax to be reported on this return, the amount of $1,561.30 is also entered on Line 5. Note that this amount is the same as the total of income tax withheld for the quarter from all employees, as shown in the summary on page 283.

The $14,522 of total wages subject to income tax withholding and FICA taxes reported on Lines 2 and 6 is the Total Earnings amount shown in the quarterly summary. This amount is multiplied by 12.26 percent, which represents the combined rate (6.13 percent × 2) of FICA taxes for both the employer and the employees. The result is $1,780.40, the amount of FICA taxes due. (When taxable tips are reported, they are entered on Line 7. The tips are subject to the employee's FICA tax, but the employer is not required to pay any FICA tax on tips.) Reference to the quarterly summary shows that the total amount of FICA taxes deducted from employee earnings during the quarter was $890.25. To this sum is added the amount of the employer's FICA tax ($890.19), resulting in the total of $1,780.44, which was deposited during the quarter as required. The "fractions only" difference of $0.04 is entered on Line 9 as an adjustment. This brings the total of FICA taxes due into agreement with the total FICA tax deposits made each month and also reported on Form 941.

The sum of the adjusted total of income tax withheld (Line 5) and the adjusted total of FICA taxes (Line 10) is the total tax due (Line 11). From this total, the sum of the amounts remitted with the Federal Tax Deposits, Form

Form **941** (Rev. July 19X1) Department of the Treasury Internal Revenue Service		Employer's Quarterly Federal Tax Return			
Your name, address, employer identification number, and calendar quarter of return. (If not correct, please change) ▶	Name (as distinguished from trade name) HOWARD SCOTT		Date quarter ended MAR 31, 19X1 D27 C	T FF	
	Trade name, if any KENT NOVELTY COMPANY		Employer identification number TD 27-3496214	FD FP	
	Address and ZIP code 129 MAIN STREET, MANCHESTER, NH 03104			I T	
				If address is different from prior return, check here ▶	

1	Number of employees (except household) employed in the pay period that includes March 12th (complete for first quarter only)		5
2	Total wages and tips subject to withholding, plus other compensation . . . . ▶		14,522 00
3	Total income tax withheld from wages, tips, annuities, gambling, etc. (see instructions)		1,561 30
4	Adjustment of withheld income tax for preceding quarters of calendar year		-0-
5	Adjusted total of income tax withheld		1,561 30
6	Taxable FICA wages paid . . . . $ 14,522.00 multiplied by 12.26% = TAX . .		1,780 40
7	Taxable tips reported . . . . $_____ multiplied by 6.13% = TAX . .		-0-
8	Total FICA taxes (add lines 6 and 7)		1,780 40
9	Adjustment of FICA taxes (see instructions) . . . . Fractions only . .		04.
10	Adjusted total of FICA taxes . . . . ▶		1,780 44
11	Total taxes (add lines 5 and 10)		3,341 74
12	Advance earned income credit (EIC) payments, if any (see instructions)		-0-
13	Net taxes (subtract line 12 from line 11)		3,341 74

Deposit period ending:		I. Tax liability for period	II. Date of deposit	III. Amount deposited
Overpayment from previous quarter				
First month of quarter	1st through 7th day	213.94		
	8th through 15th day	213.94		
	16th through 22d day	213.94		
	23d through last day	400.78		
A First month total . . . . . . ▶ A		1,042.60	Feb.1,19X1	1,042.60
Second month of quarter	1st through 7th day	213.94		
	8th through 15th day	213.94		
	16th through 22d day	213.94		
	23d through last day	400.78		
B Second month total . . . . . . ▶ B		1,042.60	Mar.2,19X1	1,042.60
Third month of quarter	1st through 7th day	213.94		
	8th through 15th day	213.94		
	16th through 22d day	213.94		
	23d through last day	614.72		
C Third month total . . . . . . ▶ C		1,256.54	Apr.5,19X1	1,256.54
D Total for quarter (add items A, B, and C) . .		3,341.74		3,341.74
E Final deposit made for quarter. (Enter zero if the final deposit made for the quarter is included in item D)				-0-

14	Total deposits for quarter (including final deposit made for quarter) and overpayment from previous quarter. (See instructions for deposit requirements on page 4) . . . . Note: If undeposited taxes at the end of the quarter are $200 or more, deposit the full amount with an authorized financial institution or a Federal Reserve bank according to the instructions on the back of the Federal Tax Deposit Form 501. Enter this deposit in the Record of Federal Tax Deposits and include it on line 14.	3,341 74
15	Undeposited taxes due (subtract line 14 from line 13—this should be less than $200). Pay to Internal Revenue Service and enter here . . . . ▶	
16	If line 14 is more than line 13, enter overpayment here ▶ $_____ and check if to be: ☐ Applied to next return, or ☐ Refunded.	
17	If you are not liable for returns in the future, write "FINAL" (See instructions) ▶ Date final wages paid ▶	

Under penalties of perjury, I declare that I have examined this return, including accompanying schedules and statements, and to the best of my knowledge and belief it is true, correct, and complete.

Date ▶ April 15, 19X1   Signature ▶ *Howard Scott*   Title ▶ Owner

Please file this form with your Internal Revenue Service Center (see instructions on "Where to File").   Form **941** (Rev. 7-X1)

501, is deducted to determine any undeposited taxes. If a balance is due, it must be sent with the return to the Internal Revenue Service Center serving the region where the principal place of business of the employer is located.

Since the total undeposited taxes at the end of the first and second months were more than $200 but less than $2,000, Kent deposited the taxes within 15 days after the end of each month as required. At the end of the quarter, Kent could have waited until the end of the next month (April) to deposit the taxes due and then could have filed the return by the 10th of the second month following (May 10). However, the owner decided to follow established procedures and deposit the taxes on April 5, immediately after the close of the payroll period at the end of the month. Form 941 was then filed on April 15, 19X1, well in advance of the required due date.

Recording the Payment

If there are any undeposited taxes due when Form 941 is completed, a check is written to the Internal Revenue Service for the amount owed. The Kent Novelty Company made its deposits each month when they were due. Thus, there are no taxes owed. The entry to record the March taxes of $1,256.54, deposited on April 5, is shown below as it appears in the cash payments journal.

CASH PAYMENTS JOURNAL for Month of April 19X1   Page 4

DATE	CHECK NO.	EXPLANATION	ACCOUNTS PAYABLE √	ACCOUNTS PAYABLE DR. 202	OTHER ACCOUNTS DEBIT ACCOUNT TITLE	POST. REF.	AMOUNT	CASH CR. 101
Apr. 5	419	Deposit of March taxes			Employee Deduc.—FICA Tax	221	335 33	
					Employee Deduc.—Income Tax With.	222	585 90	
					Employer's FICA Tax Expense	551	335 31	1,256 54

If the employer has not deducted enough taxes from the employees, the firm must make up any difference. This increases the charge to the firm's tax expense account. Although the employer is supposed to remit excess collections, small overages resulting from rounding off are often absorbed in the tax expense account.

Using Form 941c to Correct Errors

If an employer incorrectly reports FICA information, Form 941c can be used to correct the error.

Wage and Tax Statements to Employees

Employers must give each employee a Wage and Tax Statement, Form W-2, by January 31. If an employee leaves the firm before this date, the firm must provide a Form W-2 within 30 days after the end of the person's employment. Form W-2 shows the employer's name, address, and identification number, as well as the employee's name, address, and social security number. In addition, this form contains information about the employee's earnings and deductions, both federal and state (if applicable). There are two kinds of Forms W-2. One is used in states where only federal tax is withheld, and the other is used where both federal and state taxes are withheld.

The information for Form W-2 is obtained from the individual earnings records, after they have been posted and summarized for the year. The form of earnings record used by the Kent Novelty Company shows earnings and withholding information for the first six months on the front of the record. (Information for the second quarter is identical to that for the first quarter, which is illustrated on page 283.) The reverse side of the earnings record contains information for the third and fourth quarters and also provides a line for entering yearly totals for each item. Most large employers use computers to gather this information. The Internal Revenue Service encourages employers who have computers to use magnetic tape to file the data for the Forms W-2.

Assume that the individual earnings records for the employees of the Kent Novelty Company show the following totals for the year. (Notice that none of the employees earned more than $22,900 during the year. Therefore, all wages paid were subject to FICA tax.)

Employee	Total Earnings	FICA Tax	Income Tax
Peter Brown	$12,480.00	$ 764.92	$1,196.00
George Dunn	9,568.00	586.56	993.20
Joan King	10,400.00	637.52	1,092.00
Rita Lopez	16,640.00	1,020.24	1,825.20
Ellen Gold	9,000.00	551.76	1,138.80
Totals	$58,088.00	$3,561.00	$6,245.20

Wage and Tax Statements are sometimes referred to as withholding statements. The one for Peter Brown is illustrated below. (For purposes of this discussion, state and local tax considerations have been omitted.)

1 Control number	222	2 Employer's State number		For Official Use Only
3 Employer's name, address, and ZIP code Howard Scott T/A Kent Novelty Company 129 Main Street Manchester, NH 03104		4 Sub-total / Cor-rection / Void		Make No Entry Here See Note on the Back of Copy D
		7 Employer's identification number 27-3496214		
10 Employee's social security number 324-76-1245	11 Federal income tax withheld $1,196.00	12 Wages, tips, other compensation $12,480.00	13 FICA tax withheld $764.92	14 Total FICA wages $12,480.00
15 Employee's name (first, middle, last) Peter Brown		16 Pension plan coverage? Yes/No No	17*	18 FICA tips
24 Oak Street Manchester, NH 03104		20 State income tax withheld	21 State wages, tips, etc.	22 Name of State
		23 Local income tax withheld	24 Local wages, tips, etc.	25 Name of locality
19 Employee's address and ZIP code				
Wage and Tax Statement		19X1	COPY A For Social Security Administration *See instructions for Forms W-2 and W-2P and back of Copy D	
Form W-2				Department of the Treasury—Internal Revenue Service

If there is a state income tax in addition to the federal income tax, six copies of Form W-2 are prepared. Three are given to the employee, who must attach one to his federal income tax return, attach one to his state income tax return, and keep the other for his records. The employer keeps one copy for the firm's records, sends one to the state tax department, and sends one to the Social Security Administration with the annual Transmittal of Income and Tax Statements, Form W-3, which is described next. If there is a city or local income tax as well as the state tax, the firm must prepare more copies of Form W-2.

Annual Transmittal of Income and Tax Statements

After filing the last quarterly return for the year on Form 941, the employer must also prepare a Transmittal of Income and Tax Statements, Form W-3. This form must be submitted with all Forms W-2 for the employees to the Social Security Administration. Form W-3, discussed below, is due by February 28 following the end of the calendar year. The Social Security Administration processes these forms, records the employees' FICA wages, and sends the employees' FICA and income tax information to the Internal Revenue Service.

Form W-3 reports the total of FICA wages; total FICA tax withheld; total wages, tips, and other compensation; total federal income tax withheld; and other information. Each of these totals must be the same as those reported on the Forms W-2 submitted. In turn, the totals of the Forms W-2 must agree with the totals reported on the quarterly Forms 941 for the year. Thus, the government requires the employer at this time to identify the employees from whom federal income tax and FICA tax were withheld during the year, as reported on their Forms W-2, and to show that the totals withheld agree with the amounts sent to the government. The following illustration shows a completed Form W-3 for the Kent Novelty Company.

1 Control number	333	2 Employer's State number		For Official Use Only		
Kind of Tax Statements Transmitted	3 Official use	4 Military	5 Agriculture	6 W-2 ☒	7 Original ☒	8 With TIN ☒
	9 Railroad	10 Household	11 State or Local Gov.	12 W-2P	13 Corrected	14 Without TIN
15 State SSA number		16 Number of statements attached 5			17 Date of report 01/31/X2	
18 Total FICA tax withheld 3,561.00		19 Total Federal income tax withheld 6,245.20			20 Total FICA tips	
21 Total FICA wages 58,088.00		22 Total wages, tips, and other compensation 58,088.00			23 Gross annuities, pensions, retired pay, etc.	
24 Employer's identification number 27-3496214			25 Establishment number	26 Taxable annuities, pensions, retired pay, etc.		
27 Howard Scott T/A Kent Novelty Company 129 Main Street Manchester, NH 03104				Internal Revenue Service—Department of the Treasury Form W-3 Transmittal of Income and Tax Statements 19X1		

Under penalties of perjury, I declare that I have examined this return, including accompanying documents, and to the best of my knowledge and belief, it is true, correct, and complete. In the case of documents without recipients' identifying numbers, I have complied with the requirements of the law by requesting such numbers from the recipients, but did not receive them.

Signature *Howard Scott*   Title Owner   Date 01/31/X2

The filing of Form W-3 marks the end of the routine procedures needed to account for payrolls and for FICA taxes and income tax withholdings. As you learned in Unit 15, protection of workers against the risks of unemployment is the second major part of the social security program. Federal and state provisions for unemployment insurance require additional taxes, records, and reports by the employer. This area of payroll work is discussed below.

Unemployment Insurance

You will be able to better understand the purpose of the procedures used to account for unemployment insurance if you first know about unemployment legislation.

Coverage The basic unemployment legislation of 1935 imposed a direct payroll tax on certain employers to provide funds for an unemployment insurance program. Under the Federal Unemployment Tax Act (FUTA), an "employer" usually includes any person or organization that (1) pays wages of $1,500 or more during any calendar quarter in the current or preceding calendar year, or (2) employs 1 or more persons, on at least some portion of 1 day, in each of 20 or more calendar weeks during the current or preceding taxable year. Employers who qualify as exempt organizations under Section 501(c)(3) of the Internal Revenue Code (such as nonprofit schools and institutions) are not subject to the FUTA tax. Beginning in 1978, coverage was extended to agricultural and domestic service employees in certain situations.

Benefits Before receiving unemployment benefits, a worker who loses his or her job must register with the state employment office and must accept any satisfactory position in his or her field of work that is offered. If, after a waiting period (one week in most cases), work cannot be found, the state pays the unemployed person a specified weekly amount designed to help relieve the financial problems resulting from a period of temporary unemployment. The length of time that state unemployment benefits are paid varies from state to state but is normally about 26 weeks. However, the unemployed person must actively look for work during this period and accept a suitable job, if one becomes available.

In 1972, because of high rates of unemployment, an extended federal-state unemployment compensation benefits program was instituted to help those unemployed persons whose regular state unemployment benefits were used up. Under certain conditions, the regular state benefits can be extended for a period of about 13 weeks. Other measures of an emergency nature have been taken occasionally to provide additional extensions of unemployment benefits in states having unusually severe conditions of unemployment.

Taxes Under the original act, a gross tax amounting to 3 percent of the first $3,000 paid each covered worker during the calendar year was levied on the employer by the federal government. The act was further designed to encourage the states to provide their own unemployment insurance programs. Special provisions permitted employers to deduct a credit of as much as 90 percent of the 3 percent federal tax for payments made to states with approved plans. Employers can take advantage of these provisions because each state has set up an approved unemployment insurance program.

The gross FUTA tax has been changed a number of times. At this writing, it is 3.4 percent. Similarly, the base wages subject to the tax have been increased in several stages to the current $6,000.

Since the maximum credit deductible by employers from their FUTA tax for payments made to state unemployment compensation plans is still 2.7 percent (90 percent of 3 percent), only the remaining 0.7 percent of the FUTA tax is actually paid to the federal government.

In addition to the tax on the employer, a few states also levy an unemployment tax on the employee. This tax is determined by the employer at the rates and on the bases required by the state law. The amount is sent to the appropriate state agency at the specified time and in the specified manner. The handling of this tax is similar in principle to the handling of the employee's FICA tax, which you learned about previously.

Experience Ratings

One of the purposes of the unemployment insurance program is to stabilize employment and reduce unemployment. Firms that provide steady employment are granted a lower state tax rate under an *experience-rating,* or *merit-rating, system.* With this system, the employer may take a credit against the FUTA tax as though he paid at the normal state rate (to a maximum of 2.7 percent). Hence, the employer may pay as little as a fraction of 1 percent to the state instead of the usual 3.5 to 4 percent without experience rating. Penalty rates as high as 6 to 7.5 percent may be levied in some states if a firm has a poor record of providing steady employment.

State Unemployment Tax Returns

Employers subject to state unemployment tax (SUTA) laws must file returns and pay the tax on a quarterly basis. The individual state forms differ in detail, but they generally include information similar to the information required under FUTA. The state limits for taxable wages are usually the same as those of FUTA.

Taxable Wages

The employer obtains the information concerning the taxable wages paid from the individual employee earnings records in the same way that the data for Form 941 was compiled at the Kent Novelty Company. In some quarters, the data for unemployment tax and FICA tax may be identical. For example, in the first calendar quarter, the amount of wages subject to state unemployment tax at the Kent Novelty Company is the same as the taxable wages reported on Form 941. However, in later quarters, the amounts will differ. Keep in mind that the base of taxable wages used for computing each employee's FICA tax is much higher than that used for unemployment tax. In this text, we are assuming a base of $22,900 for FICA tax, while the base for unemployment tax is $6,000.

Payment of Taxes

The SUTA tax is usually due by the last day of the month following the end of the calendar quarter, and the amount owed must be deposited at that time. For example, in April, the Kent Novelty Company must pay its tax for the first quarter of the year and file the proper return with the required information concerning employees and their taxable wages.

During the first calendar quarter of 19X1, the Kent Novelty Company paid wages totaling $14,522 to its five employees (see the summary on page 283). No employee had cumulative earnings in excess of $6,000. Therefore, all wages paid were subject to the state unemployment tax. Assume that the Kent Novelty Company has earned an experience rating and that its SUTA rate is 1.3 percent. At this rate, on the taxable wages of $14,522 paid during the first quarter, the total unemployment tax due to the state is $188.79.

The accountant draws a check payable to the proper tax collection authority, such as the State Division of Employment Security, for the amount of the tax due ($188.79) and sends the check with the tax return. The entry to record the tax expense and the payment is made in the cash payments journal. An account called Payroll Tax Expense 552 is debited for the amount paid.

The same procedure is followed in later quarters. The taxable wages are determined from the data in the individual earnings records. Note that in the earnings record for Peter Brown, illustrated on page 283, there is a Cumulative Total column showing the year-to-date wages. This column is used to find out when the tax exemption point is reached. Thus, the record would show that Peter Brown reached the $6,000 maximum for unemployment insurance with his wages for the week ended June 23. The amount of tax-exempt wages for each employee for each tax would be entered in the columns of the payroll register provided for that purpose (see page 267).

When preparing state unemployment returns at the end of each quarter, the accountant examines the individual earnings records to determine the amounts of taxable wages. Then the accountant computes the state unemployment tax to be paid. The necessary data for the Kent Novelty Company for each quarter during the year is shown below.

Quarter Ended	Taxable Wages	SUTA Tax Paid
March 31	$14,522.00	$188.79
June 30	11,962.00	155.51
September 30	3,516.00	45.71
December 31	-0-	-0-
Totals	$30,000.00	$390.01°

°$0.01 overage due to rounding off.

Federal Unemployment Tax Returns

The tax levied under the Federal Unemployment Tax Act (FUTA) is paid only by the employer in a manner similar to the unemployment taxes levied by the various states. The relationship between the federal and state programs was discussed earlier in this unit.

Deposit of FUTA Taxes

As already noted, at this writing, the FUTA tax rate is 3.4 percent of the first $6,000 of annual wages paid to each employee who is covered by the law. FUTA taxes must be deposited in a Federal Reserve Bank or other authorized financial institution, and must be accompanied by a preprinted tax form—the Federal Tax Deposit, Form 508. The employer must compute the amount of the FUTA tax liability on a quarterly basis and deposit any amount due by the last day of the first month following the end of the calendar quarter.

To determine if a deposit must be made for any of the first three quarters, the employer multiplies that part of the first $6,000 of each employee's wages paid during the quarter by 0.7 percent. If the total tax owed for the quarter and any undeposited tax from a prior quarter amount to more than $100, the sum must be deposited by the last day of the first month following the quarter.

If the amount is $100 or less, it need not be deposited but must be added to the amount subject to deposit for the next quarter.

The net federal unemployment tax for the year is reported on the Employer's Annual Federal Unemployment Tax Return, Form 940. After computing the net tax, the employer subtracts all the amounts deposited during the year. If the remainder is more than $100, the entire sum must be deposited by January 31. If the net tax for the year minus any deposits is $100 or less, it may be deposited or it may be paid with Form 940 by January 31.

From the schedule on page 283, you will note that the total earnings of the Kent Novelty Company's five employees for the first calendar quarter amounted to $14,522. No employee had earnings of as much as $6,000. Therefore, the entire $14,522 was subject to FUTA tax computed at the rate of 0.7 percent. The resulting tax was $101.65. Since this amount exceeded $100, it was deposited on April 21, 19X1. The Federal Tax Deposit, Form 508, properly completed, is illustrated below.

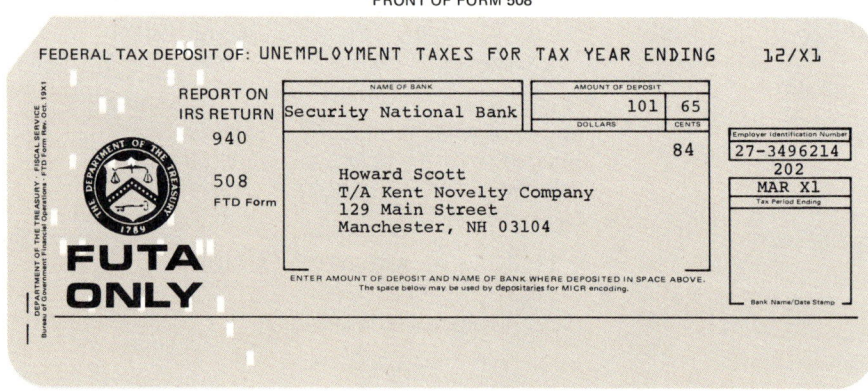

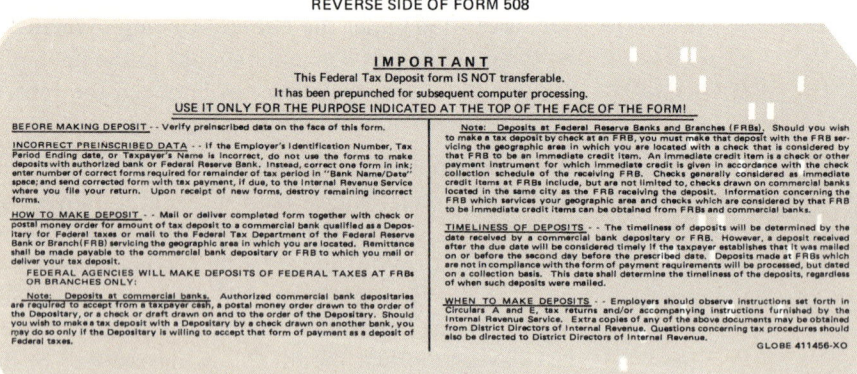

Filing Form 940

Each employer covered by FUTA must file a Form 940 and pay any tax due for the year by the following January 31. The information for this return comes partly from the individual earnings records and partly from copies of the state unemployment tax returns that the employer has filed during the year. Form 940 prepared at the Kent Novelty Company for the calendar year 19X1 is shown below.

Form 940
Department of the Treasury
Internal Revenue Service

Employer's Annual Federal Unemployment Tax Return

19X1

If incorrect, make any necessary change

Name (as distinguished from trade name): HOWARD SCOTT
Trade name, if any: KENT NOVELTY COMPANY
Address and ZIP code: 129 MAIN STREET, MANCHESTER, NH 03104
Calendar Year: 19X1
Employer Identification number: 27-3496214

T / FF / FD / FP / I / T

A Have you paid all required contributions to your State unemployment fund by the due date of Form 940? ... ☒ Yes ☐ No
If you check the "Yes" box, enter amount of contributions timely paid to your State unemployment fund ... ▶ 390.01
B Are you required to pay contributions to only one State? ... ☒ Yes ☐ No
If you check the "Yes" box: (1) Enter the name of the State that you are required to pay contributions to ... ▶ NH
(2) Enter your State experience rate(s) for 19X1 (see instructions for Part V, columns 4 and 5) ... ▶ 1.3 %. ... %. ... %

Part I Computation of Taxable Wages (To Be Completed by All Taxpayers)

1 Total payments (including exempt payments) during the calendar year for services of employees ... 58,088|00
  Exempt Payments ... Amount paid
2 Exempt payments. (Explain each exemption shown, attaching additional sheets if necessary) ▶ ... -0-
3 Payments for services in excess of $6,000. Enter only the excess over the first $6,000 paid to individual employees exclusive of exempt amounts entered on line 2. Do not use State wage limitation ▶ ... 28,088|00
4 Total exempt payments (add lines 2 and 3) ... 28,088|00
5 Total taxable wages (subtract line 4 from line 1). (If any portion is exempt from State contributions, see instructions) ▶ 30,000|00

Part II Tax Due or Refund (Complete if You Checked the "Yes" boxes in Both Items A and B Above)

1 FUTA tax. Multiply the wages on line 5, Part I, by .007 and enter here ... 210|00
2 (a) Delaware wages included on line 5, Part I ▶ $............... multiplied by .003 ... -0-
  (b) Pennsylvania wages included on line 5, Part I ▶ $............... multiplied by .003 ... -0-
3 Total FUTA tax (add lines 1, 2a, and 2b) ... 210|00
4 Less: Total FUTA tax deposited from line 5, Part IV ... 210|00
5 Balance due (subtract line 4 from line 3—this should not be over $100). Pay to Internal Revenue Service ▶ -0-
6 Overpayment (subtract line 3 from line 4) ▶ -0-

Part III Tax Due or Refund (Complete if You Checked the "No" Box in Either Item A or Item B Above)

1 Gross FUTA tax. Multiply the wages on line 5, Part I, by .034 ...
2 Maximum credit. Multiply the wages on line 5, Part I, by .027 ...
3 Enter the smaller of the amount on line 11, Part V, or line 2, above ...
4 (a) Delaware wages included on line 5, Part I ▶ $............... multiplied by .003
  (b) Pennsylvania wages included on line 5, Part I ▶ $............... multiplied by .003
5 Credit allowable (subtract lines 4a and 4b from line 3) ...
6 Net FUTA tax (subtract line 5 from line 1) ...
7 Less: Total FUTA tax deposited from line 5, Part IV ...
8 Balance due (subtract line 7 from line 6—this should not be over $100). Pay to Internal Revenue Service ▶
9 Overpayment (subtract line 6 from line 7) ▶

Part IV Record of Federal Tax Deposits for Unemployment Tax (Form 508)

	a. Quarter	b. Liability by period	c. Date of deposit	d. Amount of deposit
1	First	101.65	April 21, 19X1	101|65
2	Second	83.73		
3	Third	24.62	Oct. 21, 19x1	108|35
4	Fourth	-0-		

5 Total FUTA tax deposited (add column d, lines 1 through 4) (do not include contributions paid to State) ▶ 210|00
If you will not have to file returns in the future, write "Final" here (see general instruction "Who Must File") ▶

Under penalties of perjury, I declare that I have examined this return, including accompanying schedules and statements, and to the best of my knowledge and belief, it is true, correct, and complete, and that no part of any payment made to a State unemployment fund claimed as a credit was or is to be deducted from the payments to employees.

Date ▶ January 10, 19X2 Signature ▶ *Howard Scott* Title (Owner, etc.) ▶ Owner

Form **940** (19X1)

Computing Credit

Note in the illustration of Form 940 that the Kent Novelty Company's contributions for state unemployment tax payable at its 1.3 percent experience rate amounted to $390.01 (including an overage of $0.01 due to rounding off) and that the required sum was actually paid. The data about the state tax appears on lines A and B at the top of Form 940.

Computing Taxable Wages

The first part of Form 940 requires a listing of total remuneration paid during the calendar year less remuneration exempt from taxation. The difference between these two amounts equals the total taxable FUTA wages. As shown in the form illustrated, total remuneration for the year paid by the Kent Novelty Company was $58,088 (see also page 288). Tax-exempt wages for the year amounted to $28,088, leaving $30,000 taxable. (This is easily proved, since the Kent Novelty Company had five employees, all of whom earned more than $6,000 during the calendar year.)

The gross federal tax based on $30,000 of taxable wages at the required 3.4 percent rate is $1,020. However, Kent earned a maximum credit of $810 (1.3 percent actually paid to the state + 1.4 percent credit = 2.7 percent maximum credit $\times$ $30,000 = $810). Thus, the balance due the federal government is $210 ($30,000 $\times$ .007). The computation of the FUTA tax owed by Kent is shown in the second part of Form 940.

Reporting FUTA Tax Deposits

In the fourth part of Form 940, the employer records the deposits of federal unemployment tax made during the year. The deposit of $101.65 for the first quarter's tax is shown. At the end of the second quarter, computation of the tax showed that only $83.73 was due ($11,962 of taxable wages $\times$ 0.7 percent = $83.73). Since that amount was less than $100, no deposit was made and the amount was carried over to the following quarter. At the end of the third quarter, computation of the tax showed that only $24.62 was due. By itself, the $24.62 did not need to be deposited. However, when this amount was added to the $83.73 brought forward from the second quarter, the resulting total was $108.35, which had to be deposited. The deposit was made on October 21, 19X1.

Payment of FUTA Taxes

On April 21, 19X1, a check for the amount of FUTA tax due for the first quarter, $101.65, was written to the order of the Internal Revenue Service and deposited with Form 508 in the Security National Bank. This payment was recorded in the cash payments journal as a debit to Payroll Tax Expense. On Oct. 21, another check was drawn in the amount of $108.35 to cover the FUTA tax for the second and third quarters. The required deposit was then made, and the payment was recorded in the cash payments journal. As shown on the Form 940 illustrated on page 293, there was no balance of FUTA tax due at the end of the calendar year. Therefore, no check was written, no deposit was made, and no entry was recorded.

Worker's Compensation Insurance

Employers required by state law to carry worker's compensation insurance generally pay an estimated premium in advance. Then, after the end of the year, they pay an additional premium (or receive credit for overpayment) based on an audit of the payroll for the year. The rate of the insurance premium varies with the risk involved in the work performed. Therefore, it is important to have employees classified properly according to the kind of work they do and to summarize labor costs according to the insurance premium classifications.

For the purpose of this insurance rating, there are only two different work classifications at the Kent Novelty Company: office work and shop work. The premium rates are $0.20 per $100 for office work and $3.20 per $100 for shop work. Based on the payroll for the previous year, the Kent Novelty Company paid an estimated premium of $1,500 on January 15, 19X1. This premium was paid in advance to cover the year of 19X1. A check was written to the insurance company for this amount. The accountant then made an entry in the cash payments journal debiting Worker's Compensation Insurance Expense 555 and crediting Cash.

At the end of 19X1, the accountant analyzed the payroll data for that year and applied the proper rates to determine the year's premium. As a result of this analysis, the accountant found that a balance was owed for the worker's compensation insurance.

Classification	Payroll	Rate	Premium
Office Work	$ 9,000.00	$0.20/$100	$ 18.00
Shop Work	49,088.00	$3.20/$100	1,570.82
Totals	$58,088.00		$1,588.82
Less Estimated Premium Paid			1,500.00
Balance of Premium Due			$ 88.82

The final balance due the insurance company, $88.82, is paid by check and entered in the cash payments journal as a debit to Worker's Compensation Insurance Expense and a credit to Cash.

principles and procedures summary

Employers serve as collection agents for FICA taxes and income tax withheld from employees and must remit these amounts, together with the employer's FICA tax, to the government as required by law. These taxes must be deposited in an authorized bank if they amount to a certain sum. The schedule for deposits varies according to the sums involved. A Federal Tax Deposit, Form 501, is prepared and submitted with each deposit.

At the end of each calendar quarter, the employer must file a quarterly tax return on Form 941 reporting taxable wages paid to employees during the quarter, the income tax withheld, and FICA taxes. Any balance of taxes due must by paid with this return.

By the end of January, each employee must be given a Wage and Tax Statement, Form W-2, showing his or her earnings for the year and deductions for FICA tax and income tax. The employer prepares an annual Transmittal of Income and Tax Statements, Form W-3, and files it together with copies of the Forms W-2 issued to the employees.

Unemployment insurance protects workers against the financial problems of temporary unemployment. It is administered by the various state governments. The tax for this insurance is paid by the employer, although some states levy a tax on employees also. Unemployment taxes must be paid to both the state and federal governments.

State unemployment tax returns differ in detail but usually require a list of employees, their social security numbers, and the taxable wages paid. An Employer's Annual Federal Unemployment Tax Return, Form 940, must be filed each January for the preceding calendar year. It shows the total wages paid, the amount of taxable wages, and the gross federal tax. As of this writing, the gross tax is 3.4 percent of the first $6,000 paid each employee each year. Credit of up to 2.7 percent against the gross tax is allowed for unemployment tax paid under state plans or waived because of state experience ratings.

Employers may be required under state law to carry worker's compensation insurance. Ordinarily, an estimated premium is paid at the beginning of each year. A final settlement is made with the insurance company on the basis of an audit of the payroll after the end of the year. Premiums vary according to the type of work performed by each employee.

managerial implications

Management must make sure that payroll taxes are computed properly and paid on time. It is also essential that payroll tax returns and forms be prepared accurately and filed promptly in order to avoid penalties imposed by law. The accounting records must facilitate the preparation of these reports in an efficient manner. Today's manager must thoroughly understand the various payroll tax laws in order to control both direct and indirect labor in the firm's operations.

managerial discussion questions

1. Why is it important for a manager to thoroughly understand the various payroll tax laws and procedures?
2. What is the significance to management of the experience-rating, or merit-rating, system used to determine the employer's tax under the state unemployment insurance laws?

application of principles

PROBLEM 16-1 During the month following the end of each calendar quarter, an employer is required to file Form 941, the Employer's Quarterly Federal Tax Return. Assume that the McLean Company, owned by Keith McLean, received the required form from the Internal Revenue Service for the third quarter of 19X1. A summary of the employee earnings, FICA tax deductions, and income tax withheld during the quarter appears below.

PAYROLL SUMMARY

Payroll Period Ended		Total Earnings	FICA Tax Deducted	Income Tax Withheld
July	7	$ 940	$ 57.62	$ 95.62
	14	980	60.07	99.69
	21	940	57.62	95.62
	28	960	58.85	97.65
		$ 3,820	$234.16	$ 388.58
Aug.	4	$ 920	$ 56.40	$ 93.58
	11	940	57.62	95.62
	18	940	57.62	95.62
	25	960	58.85	97.65
		$ 3,760	$230.49	$ 382.47
Sept.	1	$ 980	$ 60.07	$ 99.69
	8	940	57.62	95.62
	15	960	58.85	97.65
	22	940	57.62	95.62
	29	920	56.40	93.58
		$ 4,740	$290.56	$ 482.16
Totals		$12,320	$755.21	$1,253.21

McLean prepared the required tax deposit forms and issued checks as follows.

a. Federal Tax Deposit, Form 501, $856.90, was paid on August 15, 19X1.
b. Federal Tax Deposit, Form 501, $843.45, was paid on September 15, 19X1.

INSTRUCTIONS

1. Complete Form 941 in accordance with the discussions in this unit and the instructions on the form itself. Use the assumed 12.26 percent total FICA rate in computations. Use the following address for the company: 1111 Glen Drive, Green Bay, Wisconsin 54303. Use 57-0202222 as the employer identification number. Sign the form with your name, and use the title "accountant." Date the return October 30, 19X1. (Hint to student: A "fractions only" $0.01 adjustment of FICA taxes will be needed as a reduction on Line 9 of Form 941.)
2. On October 30 the owner issued a check to deposit the taxes for the third month (September) as computed and entered during completion of Form 941. In general journal form, make the entry needed to record issuance of the check.

PROBLEM 16-2 Certain transactions and procedures relating to unemployment taxes and to worker's compensation insurance are given below for the Wayne Construction Company owned by Claude Krantz. The company's address is 128 University Drive, Kansas City, Missouri 64120. The employer's identification number is 57-6161611. Carry out the procedures as instructed in each of the following steps.

INSTRUCTIONS

1. Account for the yearly settlement of the worker's compensation insurance premium. The insurance company auditor examined the firm's accounting records and made the following analysis of payrolls for the previous year (19X0).

COMPUTATION OF ACTUAL PREMIUM			
Classification	Amount of Wages Paid	Insurance Rates	Premium Earned
Construction Work	$61,000	$3.10/$100	$1,891
Office Work	8,000	$0.15/$100	12
Totals	$69,000		$1,903
Less Estimated Premium Paid			1,800
Balance of Premium Due			$ 103

On January 25, 19X1, the owner issued a check for $103. In general journal form, make the entry needed to record payment of the premium due the insurance company.

2. Account for the payment of the current year's estimated premium for worker's compensation insurance. The estimated wages and the premium are as follows.

COMPUTATION OF ESTIMATED PREMIUM			
Classification	Amount of Estimated Wages	Insurance Rates	Estimated Premium
Construction Work	$65,000	$3.10/$100	$2,015
Office Work	8,000	$0.15/$100	12
Totals	$73,000		$2,027

On January 28, 19X1, the owner issued a check for $2,027. In general journal form, record the payment of the estimated premium to the insurance company.

3. Compute the state unemployment insurance tax owed on the employees' wages for the quarter ended March 31, 19X1. This information will be shown on the employer's quarterly report to the state agency that collects the SUTA tax. The Wayne Construction Company has received an experience rating and therefore pays only 1.5 percent on a state unemployment tax rate of 2.7 percent. The wages paid to the employees during the first quarter are given on the next page.

EARNINGS SUMMARY

Social Security Number	Name of Employee	Total Earnings
444–00–1234	Curtis Johnson	$ 1,625
444–09–4325	Geraldine Franklin	2,400
333–01–3456	Glenn Mahoney	1,800
333–09–5431	William Harrison	2,800
222–02–4567	Michael Romano	2,130
222–09–7531	Barbara Hundley	2,800
111–03–5678	Irene DuPres	2,050
		$15,605

4. On April 28, 19X1, the owner issued a check for the amount you computed in Instruction 3. Make an entry in general journal form to record the issuance of the check.
5. Complete Form 940, the Employer's Annual Federal Unemployment Tax Return. Assume that all weekly and monthly payrolls have been paid and that all quarterly reports have been submitted as required. The payroll information for 19X1 is as follows.

PAYROLL SUMMARY

Quarter Ended	Total Wages Paid	Wages Paid in Excess of $6,000	State Unemployment Tax Paid
Mar. 31	$15,605.00	-0-	$234.08
June 30	17,200.00	$ 3,400.00	207.00
Sept. 30	17,500.00	13,300.00	63.00
Dec. 31	19,100.00	15,100.00	60.00
Totals	$69,405.00	$31,800.00	$564.08

The required federal tax deposit forms and checks were submitted as follows.
   a. Federal Tax Deposit, Form 508, and a check for $109.24, were submitted on April 21, 19X1.
   b. Federal Tax Deposit, Form 508, and a check for $126, were submitted on October 21, 19X1.

Sign Form 940 with your name, and use the title "accountant." Date the return January 28, 19X1.

6. On January 28, 19X2, the owner issued a check for the amount shown on Line 5 of Part II of Form 940. In general journal form, record issuance of the check.

PROBLEM 16-3 The table illustrated on page 300 shows cumulative earnings of the four employees of the Noles Company at the end of June, September, and December, 19X1.

	Cumulative Earnings		
Employee	Through June	Through September	Through December
Peter Estes	$4,800	$7,200	$ 9,600
Francis Fagan	5,480	8,720	11,960
Jean Goodman	3,900	5,850	7,800
Manuel Carillo	-0-	1,800	4,500

INSTRUCTIONS

1. Compute the amount of state unemployment tax that would be due on the wages paid by the Noles Company for the third quarter of the year. Use 2.7 percent as the tax rate.
2. In general journal form, make the entry on October 12 to record payment of the state unemployment tax when the third quarterly return is filed. (Refer to the text illustrations for the account titles to be used throughout this problem.)
3. Compute the federal unemployment tax due through June. (The total for the first two quarters amounts to less than $100 and is carried over to the third quarter.)
4. Compute the federal unemployment tax due through September. Then, make an entry in general journal form to record payment of the tax deposit on October 15. (The gross federal tax is 3.4 percent, less a credit for the state tax of 2.7 percent, which gives a net federal tax of 0.7 percent on the first $6,000 paid each employee.)
5. On January 5, 19X1, the Noles Company paid the estimated worker's compensation insurance premium for 19X1. The estimated premium was based on an expected payroll of $33,000 and a premium rate of $2.75 per $100 of wages.
    a. In general journal form, make the entry to record payment of the estimated premium on January 5.
    b. Compute the balance due for the worker's compensation insurance premium based on the actual payroll for the year. Then make a general journal entry to record the payment of the amount due on January 20, 19X2.

alternate problems

PROBLEM 16-1A During the month following the end of each calendar quarter, an employer is required by law to file Form 941, the Employer's Quarterly Federal Tax Return. Assume that the Shelton Company, owned by Robert Shelton, received the required form from the Internal Revenue Service for the second quarter of 19X1. A summary of the payrolls that the firm paid during the quarter appears on the next page.

Shelton prepared the required tax deposit forms and issued checks as follows.

   a. Federal Tax Deposit, Form 501, $1,023.74, paid on May 15, 19X1.
   b. Federal Tax Deposit, Form 501, $1,080.37, paid on June 15, 19X1.

PAYROLL SUMMARY

Payroll Period Ended		Total Earnings	FICA Tax Deducted	Income Tax Withheld
Apr.	7	$ 1,080	$ 66.20	$ 119.88
	14	1,120	68.66	124.32
	21	1,150	70.50	127.65
	28	990	60.69	119.79
		$ 4,340	$266.05	$ 491.64
May	5	$ 1,050	$ 64.37	$ 116.55
	12	1,230	75.40	138.99
	19	1,190	72.95	124.95
	26	1,160	71.10	132.24
		$ 4,630	$283.82	$ 512.73
June	2	$ 980	$ 60.07	$ 116.62
	9	1,060	64.98	117.66
	16	1,140	69.88	140.22
	23	1,090	66.82	122.08
	30	1,210	74.17	143.10
		$ 5,480	$335.92	$ 639.68
Totals		$14,450	$885.79	$1,644.05

INSTRUCTIONS

1. Complete Form 941 in accordance with the discussions in the textbook and the instructions on the form itself. Use the assumed 12.26 percent total FICA rate in computations. Use 3415 Broad Street, Denver, Colorado 80215 as the business's address and 57-0202745 as the employer's identification number. (Hint to student: A "fractions only" $0.01 adjustment of FICA taxes will be needed as an increase on Line 9 of Form 941.)
2. On July 30 the owner issued a check to deposit the taxes for the third month (June) as computed and entered during completion of Form 941. In general journal form, record issuance of the check.

PROBLEM 16-2A Certain transactions and procedures relating to unemployment taxes and to worker's compensation insurance are given below for the Wilson Toy Company, owned by Rita Wilson. The firm's address is 1616 Main Street, Cleveland, Ohio 44115. The employer's identification number is 57-0202746. Carry out the procedures as instructed in each of the following steps.

INSTRUCTIONS

1. Account for the yearly settlement of the worker's compensation insurance premium. The auditor for the insurance company that issues the policy to the Wilson Toy Company made the following analysis of payrolls for the previous year (19X0).

COMPUTATION OF ACTUAL PREMIUM

Classification	Amount of Wages Paid	Insurance Rates	Premium Earned
Shop Labor	$27,342.00	$3.90/$100	$1,066.34
Office Work	6,300.00	$0.16/$100	10.08
Totals	$33,642.00		$1,076.42
Less Estimated Premium Paid			960.00
Balance of Premium Due			$ 116.42

On January 20, 19X1, the owner issued a check for $116.42. In general journal form, make an entry to record the payment of the premium due the insurance company.

2. Account for the payment of the current year's estimated premium for worker's compensation insurance. A bill has been received from the insurance company for the estimated premium for the current year. This premium is based upon the actual premium for the previous year, as adjusted for the owner's estimate of wages to be paid this year and higher rates to be charged by the insurance company. The data from the bill that the insurance company issued to the Wilson Toy Company is shown in the following table.

COMPUTATION OF ESTIMATED PREMIUM

Classification	Amount of Estimated Wages	Insurance Rates	Estimated Premium
Shop Labor	$34,000.00	$4.29/$100	$1,458.60
Office Work	6,600.00	$0.18/$100	11.88
Totals	$40,600.00		$1,470.48

On January 31, 19X1, the owner issued a check for $1,470.48. In general journal form, make an entry to record payment of the estimated premium to the insurance company.

3. Compute the state unemployment insurance tax owed on the employees' wages for the quarter ended March 31, 19X1. This information will be shown on the employer's quarterly report to the state agency that collects SUTA tax. The Wilson Toy Company has received an experience rating and therefore pays only a 2 percent state unemployment tax rate. (The maximum rate of tax in the state is normally 2.7 percent.) The wages that the business paid to its employees during the first quarter are illustrated in the table on page 303.

EARNINGS SUMMARY

Social Security Number	Name of Employee	Total Earnings
251-07-4400	Sarah Abbott	$ 1,840.00
586-22-1401	Kenneth Hoffman	1,841.00
247-15-3302	Greta Mann	1,840.00
322-08-9903	Carla Todd	2,196.00
333-11-8504	Ben Thomas	2,007.50
538-13-4905	Mark Petersen	900.00
Totals		$10,624.50

4. On April 29, 19X1, the owner issued a check for the amount you computed in Instruction 3. Record the check in general journal form.
5. Complete Form 940, the Employer's Annual Federal Unemployment Tax Return. Assume that all weekly and monthly payrolls have been paid and that all quarterly reports have been submitted as required. The payroll information for 19X1 is as follows.

PAYROLL SUMMARY

Quarter Ended	Total Wages Paid	Wages Paid in Excess of $6,000	State Unemployment Tax Paid
Mar. 31	$10,624.50	-0-	$212.49
June 30	10,916.50	$ 66.50	217.00
Sept. 30	10,400.00	8,400.00	40.00
Dec. 31	10,500.00	10,200.00	6.00
Totals	$42,441.00	$18,666.50	$475.49

The required federal tax deposit in the amount of $150.32 was made on July 14, 19X1, using Form 508.

Sign Form 940 with your name, and use the title "accountant." Date the return January 22, 19X2.

6. On January 22, 19X2, the owner issued a check for the amount shown on Line 5 of Part II of Form 940. In general journal form, record issuance of the check.

PROBLEM 16-3A The Samuels Company has four employees. The following table shows their cumulative earnings through June 19X1 and their July wages.

Employee	Cumulative Earnings Through June	July Wages
Herbert Strauss	$5,520	$920
Brenda Warren	4,725	825
Alice Taylor	4,500	750
Donald McIntyre	3,600	600

INSTRUCTIONS
1. Assuming that the four employees had earnings in August and September equal to their July wages, compute the amount of state unemployment tax that the Samuels Company would owe on the wages for the third quarter of the year. Use 2.7 percent as the tax rate.
2. In general journal form, make the entry on October 10 to record the payment of the state tax when the third quarterly return is filed. (Refer to text illustrations for the account titles to be used throughout this problem.)
3. Compute the federal unemployment tax due through June. (The gross federal tax is 3.4 percent, less a credit for the state tax of 2.7 percent, which gives a net federal tax of 0.7 percent on the first $6,000 paid each employee.) Assume that if the total taxes amount to less than $100, they are carried over to the third quarter. However, if they amount to $100 or more, they are deposited as required by law.
4. Compute the federal unemployment tax due for the third quarter. Indicate by a general journal entry or a statement how the amount due is properly handled according to law.
5. On January 4, 19X1, the Samuels Company paid the estimated worker's compensation insurance premium for 19X1. The estimated premium was based on an expected payroll of $34,000 and a premium rate of $3 per $100 of wages.
   a. In general journal form, make the entry to record payment of the estimated premium on January 4.
   b. Compute the balance due based on the actual payroll for the year, $35,040. Then make a general journal entry to record the payment on January 18, 19X2.

[Handwritten notes at top: Accelerated Depreciation: 1. Sum of years digit 2. Double Declining Balance — 10/55 120,000/55 × 10 55 = Adding 1 through 10 together]

UNIT 17

depreciation, bad debts, and inventory

In Units 6 through 12, you saw how the accounting system of the Modern Cleaning Shop was expanded to include four special journals as well as the general journal. You also saw how two subsidiary ledgers for accounts receivable and accounts payable were established to support the general ledger. In addition to these changes, the continuing growth of the Modern Cleaning Shop has made it necessary to set up more accounts in the general ledger. These accounts are needed to properly record several new types of transactions and make end-of-period adjustments.

Chart of Accounts

The Modern Cleaning Shop's entry into the merchandising of accessories made it necessary to revise the firm's chart of accounts as shown below. Accounts described in recent units have been added. The five accounts to be explained in this unit are also included at this time to avoid the need for a further revision of the chart of accounts within the next few pages. These expanded records will make it possible to efficiently produce information about the expected larger volume of operations at the Modern Cleaning Shop. Again, notice that number gaps are left within each grouping so that more accounts may be added when required.

MODERN CLEANING SHOP
Chart of Accounts

Account Number	Account Name
100–199	**ASSETS**
101	Cash
111	Accounts Receivable Control
111A	Allowance for Bad Debts
121	Merchandise Inventory
141	Equipment
141A	Accumulated Depreciation
200–299	**LIABILITIES**
202	Accounts Payable Control
300–399	**OWNER'S EQUITY**
301	Paul Reed, Capital
302	Paul Reed, Drawing
399	Revenue and Expense Summary

305

Account Number	Account Name
400-499	**REVENUE**
401	Cleaning Service Sales
402	Accessories Sales
451	Sales Returns and Allowances—Cleaning Service
452	Sales Returns and Allowances—Accessories
500-599	**COSTS AND EXPENSES**
501	Merchandise Purchases
509	Purchases Returns and Allowances
511	Salaries Expense
516	Rent Expense
521	Supplies Used
561	Bad Debts Expense
564	Depreciation Expense
591	Miscellaneous Expense

New Transactions and Accounts

After the February 19X2 transactions for the Modern Cleaning Shop were journalized and posted, the trial balance shown below was completed as a proof of accuracy.

MODERN CLEANING SHOP
Trial Balance
February 28, 19X2

ACCT. NO.	ACCOUNT NAME	DEBIT	CREDIT
101	Cash	1,586 00	
111	Accounts Receivable Control	142 00	
111A	Allowance for Bad Debts		
121	Merchandise Inventory		
141	Equipment	5,400 00	
141A	Accumulated Depreciation		
202	Accounts Payable Control		950 00
301	Paul Reed, Capital		6,240 00
302	Paul Reed, Drawing	50 00	
401	Cleaning Service Sales		4,282 00
402	Accessories Sales		1,287 00
451	Sales Returns and Allowances—Cleaning Service		
452	Sales Returns and Allowances—Accessories	22 00	
501	Merchandise Purchases	1,810 00	
509	Purchases Returns and Allowances		10 00
511	Salaries Expense	1,950 00	
516	Rent Expense	700 00	
521	Supplies Used	934 00	
561	Bad Debts Expense		
564	Depreciation Expense		
591	Miscellaneous Expense	175 00	
	Totals	12,769 00	12,769 00

The word *Control* was added to the titles of the Accounts Receivable account and the Accounts Payable account because subsidiary ledgers are now being used. Certain new accounts warrant special attention. A new revenue account, Accessories Sales, reflects the revenue from the first month's activities of the new accessories department, and the Sales Returns and Allowances—Accessories account reflects the returns and allowances for the new department. The Merchandise Purchases account also appears for the first time. The $1,810 balance in this account represents the cost of the stock of merchandise bought for the new department. Similarly, the $10 balance in the Purchases Returns and Allowances account represents the cost of goods returned.

There are also several other less obvious elements that require the accountant's careful consideration after the trial balance is entered on the worksheet. For example, the accountant notices the following problems.

1. There is no recognition of any merchandise that remains unsold at the end of the period.
2. The asset Equipment is being shown at the original cost, without regard for the decrease in its useful life during the month.
3. The balance of $142 in the Accounts Receivable Control account may include amounts that will not be collected.

Unless such missing elements are recognized and recorded at this time, the financial statements that are prepared will not present a complete and true picture of the financial condition of the business and the net income or net loss for the period. The simplest solution is to give these matters special treatment on the worksheet.

Depreciation Expense

The Equipment account on the trial balance has a balance of $5,400, representing the original cost of the equipment purchased for use in the business. However, the accounting system must reflect the fact that equipment has a limited useful life. It gradually wears out or must be discarded because it no longer serves the purpose intended. The accountant seeks to apportion the cost of the asset over its useful life by recording an expense, called *depreciation expense*, at the end of each period. This process is called *matching*, because the proportionate expense recognized during the period is matched, or charged, against the revenue of that period.

The apportionment of depreciation expense is accomplished by an *adjusting entry* at the end of each period. For example, if an asset costs $5,000 and is expected to be completely worthless at the end of five years, it seems logical that $1,000 of its cost should be charged off as an expense each year. There are several ways of determining how much expense should be charged to each period. But in this unit, only one simple and widely used procedure, known as *straight-line depreciation*, will be presented. With this procedure, an equal amount of depreciation expense is charged off in each period of an asset's useful life.

Schedule of Equipment

The first step in determining the amount of depreciation expense is to prepare a list of the equipment items. The cost, expected useful life, and estimated salvage value of each item must be determined. Estimates of the useful life are based on the experience of the individual business or of other businesses with similar items of equipment. The accountant for the Modern Cleaning Shop has prepared the following schedule of equipment.

MODERN CLEANING SHOP
Schedule of Equipment
February 28, 19X2

Date Purchased	Description	Cost	Estimated Useful Life	Estimated Salvage Value
19X1				
Nov. 27	Cleaning Equipment	$2,000	5 years	–0–
28	Counter, Garment Racks, Desk, and Chairs	1,000	5 years	–0–
19X2				
Jan. 2	Cleaning Equipment	770	5 years	–0–
11	Delivery Truck	1,000	5 years	–0–
28	Counter and Display Fixtures	600 }	5 years	–0–
Feb. 3	Freight on Counter and Display Fixtures	30 }		
	Total in Ledger Account	$5,400		

Note that the useful life of each item is estimated as five years and that it is assumed that there will be no salvage value. In practice, the different items would probably have different estimated lives, but the assumption of a uniform five-year life simplifies the discussion at this point. It is also assumed that the five-year life starts on February 1 for each item. (Depreciation has been deliberately ignored in previous periods to permit concentration on other matters.) Keeping these assumptions in mind, let us figure out how much depreciation expense should be recorded for the month of February.

Determining the Depreciation Expense

With the aid of the information shown in the schedule of equipment—the cost, the estimated useful life, and the expected salvage value—the depreciation expense for February can be determined by following this formula.

$$\frac{\text{Cost} - \text{Salvage Value}}{\text{Useful Life}} = \text{Depreciation Expense}$$

In this formula, the useful life must be expressed in months. Since five years = 60 months, the depreciation expense for February is computed as shown below.

$$\frac{\$5,400 - 0}{60} = \$90$$

Recording Depreciation Expense

When Stein revised the Modern Cleaning Shop's chart of accounts as of February 1, 19X2, he also anticipated the need to record depreciation on the books. The amount of depreciation is debited to a new general ledger account called Depreciation Expense. The offsetting credit is recorded in another new account called Accumulated Depreciation. (An older title, Reserve for Depreciation, is still in occasional use. However, in modern practice, Accumulated Depreciation is generally preferred, although some accountants use the title Allowance for Depreciation.) Depreciation expense is first recorded on the worksheet.

Worksheet Adjustment for Depreciation Expense

Having determined the amount of depreciation expense to be recorded, the accountant immediately enters the amount as a debit to the Depreciation Expense account and a credit to the Accumulated Depreciation account on the worksheet. Notice that a new pair of columns entitled Adjustments is used for this entry, as shown in the illustration below. Notice also that both figures are labeled "(a)" to help identify them for future reference, particularly when journalizing the adjustment later.

MODERN CLEANING SHOP
Worksheet (Partial)
Month Ended February 28, 19X2

ACCT. NO.	ACCOUNT NAME	TRIAL BALANCE DEBIT	TRIAL BALANCE CREDIT	ADJUSTMENTS DEBIT	ADJUSTMENTS CREDIT
101	Cash	1,586 00			
111	Accounts Receivable Control	142 00			
111A	Allowance for Bad Debts				
121	Merchandise Inventory				
141	Equipment	5,400 00			
141A	Accumulated Depreciation				(a)90 00
202	Accounts Payable Control		950 00		
301	Paul Reed, Capital		6,240 00		
302	Paul Reed, Drawing	50 00			
401	Cleaning Service Sales		4,282 00		
402	Accessories Sales		1,287 00		
451	Sales Ret. and Allow.—Cleaning Service				
452	Sales Ret. and Allow.—Accessories	22 00			
501	Merchandise Purchases	1,810 00			
509	Purchases Returns and Allowances		10 00		
511	Salaries Expense	1,950 00			
516	Rent Expense	700 00			
521	Supplies Used	934 00			
561	Bad Debts Expense				
564	Depreciation Expense			(a)90 00	
591	Miscellaneous Expense	175 00			
	Totals	12,769 00	12,769 00		

Recording the credit in the separate Accumulated Depreciation account permits the accountant to maintain a record of the original cost of the asset items in the Equipment account. The Accumulated Depreciation account then provides a record of the total amount of depreciation taken on the items.

Accumulated Depreciation and similar accounts are called *contra asset accounts* because their balances are offset against the balances of the related asset accounts. The credit balance of a contra asset account is deducted from the debit balance of the related asset account. The resulting difference is the balance sheet valuation of the asset and is referred to as the *book value,* or the *carrying value,* of the asset.

Bad Debts Expense

A second element requiring attention at this time is the probability that the Modern Cleaning Shop will be unable to collect some of the amounts owed by credit customers. Most business people who sell goods and services on credit find that there is some *bad debts expense.* There are two procedures that the accountant might use for recognizing losses from bad debts.

Recording a Loss When It Occurs

One procedure used by most small businesses is to wait until they are sure the account of a specific customer is definitely uncollectible and then record the expense. The amount to be charged off as a loss is debited to an expense account, usually called Bad Debts Expense, and credited to the asset account Accounts Receivable Control in the general ledger and the customer's account in the accounts receivable ledger.

Providing for a Loss Before It Occurs

Instead of waiting to record a loss when a particular account proves uncollectible, it is possible to anticipate bad debt losses and provide for them ahead of time. This method permits the seller to match the estimated bad debts expense against the sales revenue from which the accounts receivable resulted. It also allows the accountant to show the accounts receivable on the balance sheet at the amount that is probably collectible, rather than at the gross amount, even though it is not known which specific customers will not pay their accounts.

There are numerous methods for determining the amount of estimated bad debt losses for each period. The accountant for the Modern Cleaning Shop decides to base the estimate on a percentage of credit sales. This is a widely used method.

Determining the Amount of Bad Debts Expense. The accountant realizes that after the Modern Cleaning Shop has been in business for several years and has had more experience with credit losses, it will be possible to estimate fairly accurately what percent of credit sales will be uncollectible. In the meantime, the accountant decides to rely upon data compiled by a trade association in estimating the bad debt losses. These figures show that for similar businesses, bad debt losses average about 2.5 percent of *net credit sales* (sales on credit less returns and allowances on such sales). The estimated bad debts expense for February is thus $3.30, as computed below. (Again, for the sake of simplicity and clarity, estimated bad debt losses from sales made prior to February are being ignored.)

Credit Sales for Month (from sales journal)	$144.00
Less Sales Returns and Allowances on Credit Sales	12.00
Net Credit Sales	$132.00
Estimated Percentage of Loss (2.5%)	× 0.025
Estimated Bad Debts on February Sales	$ 3.30

Recording Bad Debts Expense. The revised chart of accounts for the Modern Cleaning Shop provides the new general ledger accounts required to record the expense arising from bad debts. The amount for the month is debited to Bad Debts Expense. The offsetting credit is to Allowance for Bad Debts. This adjustment is first recorded on the worksheet as shown below.

MODERN CLEANING SHOP
Worksheet (Partial)
Month Ended February 28, 19X2

ACCT. NO.	ACCOUNT NAME	TRIAL BALANCE DEBIT	TRIAL BALANCE CREDIT	ADJUSTMENTS DEBIT	ADJUSTMENTS CREDIT
101	Cash	1,586 00			
111	Accounts Receivable Control	142 00			
111A	Allowance for Bad Debts				(b) 3 30
121	Merchandise Inventory				
141	Equipment	5,400 00			
141A	Accumulated Depreciation				(a) 90 00
202	Accounts Payable Control		950 00		
301	Paul Reed, Capital		6,240 00		
302	Paul Reed, Drawing	50 00			
401	Cleaning Service Sales		4,282 00		
402	Accessories Sales		1,287 00		
451	Sales Ret. and Allow.—Cleaning Service				
452	Sales Ret. and Allow.—Accessories	22 00			
501	Merchandise Purchases	1,810 00			
509	Purchases Returns and Allowances		10 00		
511	Salaries Expense	1,950 00			
516	Rent Expense	700 00			
521	Supplies Used	934 00			
561	Bad Debts Expense			(b) 3 30	
564	Depreciation Expense			(a) 90 00	
591	Miscellaneous Expense	175 00			
	Totals	12,769 00	12,769 00		

Worksheet Adjustment for Bad Debts Expense. The amount of the adjustment for bad debts, $3.30, is entered in the Adjustments section of the worksheet as a debit to Bad Debts Expense and a credit to Allowance for Bad Debts. Note that both figures are identified by the letter *b* in parentheses in the illustration above to help in the later preparation of a journal entry for this adjustment.

The Allowance for Bad Debts account is called a *valuation account.* The amount of the adjustment for bad debts is recorded as a credit in this account so that the accountant can keep a separate record of the estimated total of uncollectible debts. The Accounts Receivable Control account shows the gross amount owed by customers. It therefore remains in balance with the subsidiary ledger. On the balance sheet, the accountant subtracts the balance of the Allowance for Bad Debts account from the balance of the Accounts Receivable Control account to show the estimated value (collectible amount) of the accounts receivable. The effect of the debit entry in the Bad Debts Expense account is to charge the estimated loss against operations of the period. This information is presented on the income statement.

Charging Off Uncollectible Accounts. Under the system of providing for bad debt losses before they occur, an entry must also be made whenever a particular account becomes uncollectible. This entry consists of a debit to the Allowance for Bad Debts account and a credit to Accounts Receivable Control and the customer's account in the accounts receivable ledger. Note that the Bad Debts Expense account is not involved in this entry. It is used only in the adjusting entry. Writing off a particular uncollectible account does not affect the bad debts expense for the period. This expense was recorded when the bad debt losses were estimated in the period of sale.

The Adjusted Trial Balance

The adjustments for depreciation and for bad debts are the only adjustments required for the Modern Cleaning Shop. Therefore, the figures in the Adjustments columns of the worksheet may now be added to verify the equality of debits and credits, as shown in the illustration below.

Next, another pair of columns, entitled Adjusted Trial Balance, is set up immediately to the right of the Adjustments section. The items in the original Trial Balance section are combined with the items in the Adjustments section, and the results are entered in the Adjusted Trial Balance section. Each column of the Adjusted Trial Balance section is then added to prove the equality of the debits and credits. Thus, the Adjusted Trial Balance section permits the accountant to verify that the debits and credits remain equal after the adjustments have been made. Study the partial worksheet given below.

MODERN CLEANING SHOP
Worksheet (Partial)
Month Ended February 28, 19X2

ACCT. NO.	ACCOUNT NAME	TRIAL BALANCE DEBIT	TRIAL BALANCE CREDIT	ADJUSTMENTS DEBIT	ADJUSTMENTS CREDIT	ADJUSTED TRIAL BALANCE DEBIT	ADJUSTED TRIAL BALANCE CREDIT
101	Cash	1,586 00				1,586 00	
111	Accounts Receivable Control	142 00				142 00	
111A	Allowance for Bad Debts				(b) 3 30		3 30
121	Merchandise Inventory						
141	Equipment	5,400 00				5,400 00	
141A	Accumulated Depreciation				(a) 90 00		90 00
202	Accounts Payable Control		950 00				950 00
301	Paul Reed, Capital		6,240 00				6,240 00
302	Paul Reed, Drawing	50 00				50 00	
401	Cleaning Service Sales		4,282 00				4,282 00
402	Accessories Sales		1,287 00				1,287 00
451	Sales Ret. and Allow.—Cl. Serv.						
452	Sales Ret. and Allow.—Access.	22 00				22 00	
501	Merchandise Purchases	1,810 00				1,810 00	
509	Purchases Returns and Allow.		10 00				10 00
511	Salaries Expense	1,950 00				1,950 00	
516	Rent Expense	700 00				700 00	
521	Supplies Used	934 00				934 00	
561	Bad Debts Expense			(b) 3 30		3 30	
564	Depreciation Expense			(a) 90 00		90 00	
591	Miscellaneous Expense	175 00				175 00	
	Totals	12,769 00	12,769 00	93 30	93 30	12,862 30	12,862 30

Merchandise on Hand

Before completing the worksheet, the accountant must recognize one other element. Some of the merchandise purchased during the period has not been sold and is still on hand. With this in mind, the accountant reasons as follows.

1. The cost of the merchandise that has not been sold should be recorded in an asset account called Merchandise Inventory.
2. The operations of the period should be charged only with the cost of goods actually sold—not with the total cost of all merchandise purchased.

Taking an Inventory

The first step for the accountant is to find out how much merchandise remains unsold at this time. The process of checking and counting stock is called *taking an inventory*. A list, called an *inventory sheet,* is prepared. It shows the quantity and description of all items on hand. Later, the quantity is multiplied by the unit cost of each item. Then the extensions are added together to determine the total cost of the stock remaining unsold.

Suppose a count made in the stockroom of the accessories department of the Modern Cleaning Shop reveals the following inventory data at the end of February.

MODERN CLEANING SHOP
Inventory Sheet
Accessories Department

DATE February 28, 19X2

QUANTITY	DESCRIPTION	UNIT COST	TOTAL
600 sets	Assorted hangers, 8 in set	$1.00	$ 600.00
35	Hat racks	2.00	70.00
38	Tie racks	2.50	95.00
20	Shoe racks	3.00	60.00
62	Shoeshine kits	2.25	139.50
18	3-suit garment bags, plastic	.75	13.50
40	2-suit garment bags, plastic	.40	16.00
10	Mothproofing spray cans	.60	6.00
	Total inventory		$1,000.00

Counted by *a. s.*   Priced by *m. g.*   Checked by *P. R.*

Having determined the amount of the inventory, the accountant can quickly compute the *cost of goods sold.*

Total Merchandise Purchases	$1,810
Less Purchases Returns and Allowances	10
Net Purchases	$1,800
Less Cost of Goods Remaining (Inventory)	1,000
Cost of Goods Sold	$ 800

Entering Ending Inventory on the Worksheet

The accountant records the inventory figure directly on the worksheet to avoid any delay in the preparation of the financial statements. The entries are made in the Income Statement and Balance Sheet columns of the worksheet as shown on page 315.

Merchandise Asset. The amount of the ending inventory is recorded as an asset on the Merchandise Inventory line in the Debit column of the Balance Sheet section. The $1,000 entry is identified by the letter *c* in parentheses.

Cost of Goods Sold. The other half of the inventory entry is made on the same line, as a credit in the Income Statement section. The letter *c* is again used for identification. The effect of this entry is more easily understood by extending the balances of Merchandise Purchases and Purchases Returns and Allowances to the Income Statement section at once, as shown on page 315.

Observe that the resulting combination of purchases and inventory figures in the Income Statement section now reflects the cost of goods sold. Specifically, the debit for Merchandise Purchases of $1,810 is offset by credits for Purchases Returns and Allowances of $10 and for Merchandise Inventory of $1,000. Thus, we get the calculation: $1,810 − $10 − $1,000 = $800. This $800 figure is the same as the cost of goods sold shown on page 313.

Completing the Worksheet

From this point on, the steps for completing the worksheet are as before. Refer to the worksheet shown on page 316 in order to trace the steps.

1. Extend the remaining asset, liability, owner's capital, and owner's drawing account balances (Accounts 101–302) to the appropriate columns in the Balance Sheet section. Then extend the remaining revenue and expense account balances to the columns in the Income Statement section. Total the columns in the Income Statement and Balance Sheet sections.
2. Notice that the total of the Income Statement Credit column exceeds the total of the Debit column by $894.70. Also notice that the total of the Balance Sheet Debit column exceeds the total of the Credit column by the same amount of $894.70, which is the net income for the month. Enter the net income of $894.70 for February in the Debit column of the Income Statement section and in the Credit column of the Balance Sheet section, thus transferring the net income for the month from the Income Statement section to the Balance Sheet section.
3. Compute the final totals of the columns in the Income Statement and Balance Sheet sections. The debits and credits should then be equal for each pair of columns in the entire worksheet.

pRiNciples aNd pRoceduRes suMMaRy

Before the financial statements can be prepared, the accountant must (1) determine the depreciation expense, (2) estimate the bad debts expense, and (3) determine the inventory of the merchandise on hand.

A new section on the worksheet, entitled Adjustments, is used to record the end-of-period data about depreciation and bad debts. For example, depreciation is recorded by a debit to Depreciation Expense and a credit to Accumulated Depreciation. The same columns are used to record the bad debts by

MODERN CLEANING SHOP
Worksheet
Month Ended February 28, 19X2

ACCT. NO.	ACCOUNT NAME	TRIAL BALANCE DEBIT	TRIAL BALANCE CREDIT	ADJUSTMENTS DEBIT	ADJUSTMENTS CREDIT	ADJUSTED TRIAL BALANCE DEBIT	ADJUSTED TRIAL BALANCE CREDIT	INCOME STATEMENT DEBIT	INCOME STATEMENT CREDIT	BALANCE SHEET DEBIT	BALANCE SHEET CREDIT
101	Cash	1,586 00				1,586 00					
111	Accounts Receivable Control	142 00				142 00					
111A	Allowance for Bad Debts				(b) 3 30		3 30				
121	Merchandise Inventory									(c)1,000 00	(c)1,000 00
141	Equipment	5,400 00				5,400 00					
141A	Accumulated Depreciation				(a)90 00		90 00				
202	Accounts Payable Control		950 00				950 00				
301	Paul Reed, Capital		6,240 00				6,240 00				
302	Paul Reed, Drawing	50 00				50 00					
401	Cleaning Service Sales		4,282 00				4,282 00				
402	Accessories Sales		1,287 00				1,287 00				
451	Sales Ret. and Allow.—Cleaning Serv.										
452	Sales Ret. and Allow.—Accessories	22 00				22 00					
501	Merchandise Purchases	1,810 00				1,810 00		1,810 00			
509	Purchases Returns and Allowances		10 00				10 00		10 00		
511	Salaries Expense	1,950 00				1,950 00					
516	Rent Expense	700 00				700 00					
521	Supplies Used	934 00				934 00					
561	Bad Debts Expense			(b) 3 30		3 30					
564	Depreciation Expense			(a)90 00		90 00					
591	Miscellaneous Expense	175 00				175 00					
	Totals	12,769 00	12,769 00	93 30	93 30	12,862 30	12,862 30				

MODERN CLEANING SHOP
Worksheet
Month Ended February 28, 19X2

ACCT. NO.	ACCOUNT NAME	TRIAL BALANCE DEBIT	TRIAL BALANCE CREDIT	ADJUSTMENTS DEBIT	ADJUSTMENTS CREDIT	ADJUSTED TRIAL BALANCE DEBIT	ADJUSTED TRIAL BALANCE CREDIT	INCOME STATEMENT DEBIT	INCOME STATEMENT CREDIT	BALANCE SHEET DEBIT	BALANCE SHEET CREDIT
101	Cash	1,586 00				1,586 00				1,586 00	
111	Accounts Receivable Control	142 00				142 00				142 00	
111A	Allowance for Bad Debts				(b) 3 30		3 30				3 30
121	Merchandise Inventory								(c)1,000 00	(c)1,000 00	
141	Equipment	5,400 00				5,400 00				5,400 00	
141A	Accumulated Depreciation				(a)90 00		90 00				90 00
202	Accounts Payable Control		950 00				950 00				950 00
301	Paul Reed, Capital		6,240 00				6,240 00				6,240 00
302	Paul Reed, Drawing	50 00				50 00				50 00	
401	Cleaning Service Sales		4,282 00				4,282 00		4,282 00		
402	Accessories Sales		1,287 00				1,287 00		1,287 00		
451	Sales Ret. and Allow.—Cleaning Serv.										
452	Sales Ret. and Allow.—Accessories	22 00				22 00		22 00			
501	Merchandise Purchases	1,810 00				1,810 00		1,810 00			
509	Purchases Returns and Allowances		10 00				10 00		10 00		
511	Salaries Expense	1,950 00				1,950 00		1,950 00			
516	Rent Expense	700 00				700 00		700 00			
521	Supplies Used	934 00				934 00		934 00			
561	Bad Debts Expense			(b) 3 30		3 30		3 30			
564	Depreciation Expense			(a)90 00		90 00		90 00			
591	Miscellaneous Expense	175 00				175 00		175 00			
	Totals	12,769 00	12,769 00	93 30	93 30	12,862 30	12,862 30	5,684 30	6,579 00	8,178 00	7,283 30
	Net Income for the Month							894 70			894 70
								6,579 00	6,579 00	8,178 00	8,178 00

a debit to Bad Debts Expense and a credit to Allowance for Bad Debts. The items in the Trial Balance section of the worksheet are combined with those in the Adjustments section and extended to the Adjusted Trial Balance section.

The ending inventory is determined by counting and pricing the merchandise on hand. The total amount is entered in the Credit column of the Income Statement section of the worksheet and in the Debit column of the Balance Sheet section. The balance of Merchandise Purchases is then extended to the Debit column of the Income Statement section. The balance of Purchases Returns and Allowances is extended to the Credit column of the same section. The remainder of the worksheet procedure is the same as before.

managerial implications

In determining the net income or net loss for the period, management must consider the effects of the depreciation of equipment, possible uncollectible accounts, and the ending merchandise inventory. Matching expenses against the revenues of the period is a sound accounting practice. The adjustments are also reflected on the balance sheet where they help to present the most accurate picture of the business's current financial position. Recording this information on the worksheet helps the accountant to prepare complete and accurate financial statements as quickly as possible. The sooner reliable results are known, the quicker management can make decisions and develop new plans.

managerial discussion questions

1. How is the measurement of the results of operations for the period affected by the application of the matching principle of accounting?
2. Which of the two procedures for recognizing bad debt losses discussed in this unit would a conservative management be most likely to choose?
3. If the useful life of a valuable asset is considerably overestimated, what is the effect of the mistake on the firm's financial statements?

application of principles

PROBLEM 17-1 The Ondrias Wholesale Supply Company purchased $64,246.18 of merchandise for resale during the fiscal year ended December 31, 19X1. Purchases returns and allowances for the period were $1,106.41. The actual inventory of merchandise on hand as of December 31, 19X1, amounted to $21,269.12.

INSTRUCTIONS   Compute the cost of goods sold for the fiscal year ended December 31, 19X1.

PROBLEM 17-2   During the month of January 19X2, the Ondrias Wholesale Supply Company sold merchandise for $60,618.21. Of this sum, cash sales amounted to $5,460.08. The rest of the sales were on credit. Sales returns and allowances of $746.88 are related to credit transactions. The company's experience indicates that 3 percent of net credit sales will not be collected.

INSTRUCTIONS   Compute the estimated bad debt loss on January sales.

PROBLEM 17-3   The Durant Products Company uses a 10-column worksheet. The data from the Account Number, Account Name, and Trial Balance columns of the worksheet for the year ended December 31, 19X1 is shown below. The firm started its operations at the beginning of 19X1. All equipment was purchased on January 2 19X1, and is estimated to have a useful life of 10 years. Included in the balance of the Sales account is $748.17 of cash sales. All sales returns and allowances relate to credit transactions. The firm estimates that 2 percent of net credit sales will not be collected.

INSTRUCTIONS   1. Enter the trial balance as of December 31, 19X1, on a 10-column worksheet.

Acct. No.	Account Name	Trial Balance Debit	Trial Balance Credit
101	Cash	$ 2,396.04	
111	Accounts Receivable Control	3,519.08	
111A	Allowance for Bad Debts		
121	Merchandise Inventory		
141	Equipment	7,526.50	
141A	Accumulated Depreciation		
202	Accounts Payable Control		$ 3,210.81
301	Barbara Durant, Capital		8,000.00
302	Barbara Durant, Drawing	200.00	
401	Sales		27,531.41
402	Sales Returns and Allowances	300.00	
501	Merchandise Purchases	5,007.46	
503	Purchases Returns and Allowances		375.00
511	Salaries Expense	10,000.00	
519	Rent Expense	9,000.00	
522	Supplies Used	1,000.00	
562	Bad Debts Expense		
565	Depreciation Expense		
591	Miscellaneous Expense	168.14	
	Totals	$39,117.22	$39,117.22

2. If you are not using preprinted forms, insert all other column headings in the worksheet. (Use the illustration on page 316 as a guide.)
3. Compute the bad debt loss for the year, and enter it on the worksheet. Use the letter *a* to identify both parts of the entry. Show your computations.
4. Compute the depreciation for the year, and enter it on the worksheet. Use the letter *b* to identify both parts of the entry. Show your computations.
5. Foot and prove the Adjustments columns. Then enter the totals.
6. Extend the proper figures into the Adjusted Trial Balance columns. Foot and prove these columns. Then enter the totals.
7. Enter the merchandise inventory of $1,941.86 as of December 31, 19X1. Use the letter *c* to identify both parts of the entry.
8. Extend the amounts in the Adjusted Trial Balance columns to the proper columns of the Income Statement and Balance Sheet sections. Then total these sections.
9. Compute and enter the net income for the period.
10. Foot and prove the columns in the Income Statement and Balance Sheet sections. Then enter the final totals, and rule all columns.

Alternate problems

PROBLEM 17-1A The Northland Trading Company purchased $39,462.50 of merchandise for resale during the fiscal year ended March 31, 19X1. Purchases returns and allowances for the period were $787.50. The actual inventory of merchandise on hand as of March 31, 19X1, amounted to $6,975.

INSTRUCTIONS Compute the cost of goods sold for the fiscal year ended March 31, 19X1.

PROBLEM 17-2A During the month of April 19X1, the Northland Trading Company sold $3,850 of merchandise. Of this sum, cash sales amounted to $1,142.60. The rest of the sales were on credit. Sales returns and allowances of $157.40 are related to credit transactions. The company's experience indicates that 2 percent of net credit sales will not be collected.

INSTRUCTIONS Compute the estimated bad debt loss on April sales.

PROBLEM 17-3A The Bowen Furniture Company uses a 10-column worksheet. The data from the Account Number, Account Name, and Trial Balance columns of the worksheet for the month ended June 30, 19X8, is shown on page 320. The company began operations on June 1, 19X8. All of the equipment represented in the Equipment account was purchased on June 1 and is estimated to have a useful life of ten years. Included in the balance of the Sales account is $459.55 of cash sales. All sales returns and allowances relate to credit transactions. Richard Bowen estimates that 3 percent of the company's net credit sales will not be collected.

BOWEN FURNITURE COMPANY
Worksheet (Partial)
Month Ended June 30, 19X8

Acct. No.	Account Name	Trial Balance Debit	Trial Balance Credit
101	Cash	$ 1,977.50	
111	Accounts Receivable Control	2,944.25	
111A	Allowance for Bad Debts		
121	Merchandise Inventory		
141	Equipment	6,672.25	
141A	Accumulated Depreciation		
202	Accounts Payable Control		$ 3,115.60
301	Richard Bowen, Capital		11,960.35
302	Richard Bowen, Drawing	100.00	
401	Sales		4,909.55
402	Sales Returns and Allowances	200.00	
501	Merchandise Purchases	6,779.98	
503	Purchases Returns and Allowances		389.53
511	Salaries Expense	725.00	
516	Rent Expense	600.00	
521	Supplies Used	256.70	
561	Bad Debts Expense		
564	Depreciation Expense		
591	Miscellaneous Expense	119.35	
	Totals	$20,375.03	$20,375.03

INSTRUCTIONS

1. Enter the company's trial balance data as of June 30, 19X8, on a 10-column worksheet.
2. If you are not using preprinted forms, insert all other column headings in the worksheet. (Use the worksheet illustrated on page 316 of the text as a guide.)
3. Compute the depreciation for the month of June, and enter it on the worksheet. Use the letter *a* to identify both parts of the entry. Show your computations.
4. Compute the bad debt loss for the month of June, and enter it on the worksheet. Use the letter *b* to identify both parts of the entry. Show your computations.
5. Foot and prove the Adjustments columns of the worksheet. Then enter the totals.
6. Extend the proper figures from the Trial Balance and Adjustments columns into the Adjusted Trial Balance columns. Foot and prove these columns. Then enter the totals.

7. Enter the merchandise inventory of $4,864.30 as of June 30, 19X8. Use the letter *c* to identify both parts of the entry for the ending merchandise inventory.
8. Extend the amounts in the Adjusted Trial Balance columns to the proper columns of the Income Statement and Balance Sheet sections. Then total these sections.
9. Compute the net income for the period and enter it on the worksheet.
10. Foot and prove the columns in the Income Statement and Balance Sheet sections. Then enter the final totals, and rule all columns of the worksheet.

UNIT 18

END-OF-PERIOD WORK FOR A MERCHANDISING BUSINESS

In earlier units, you saw how the accountant prepares financial statements for a small service business that has relatively simple operations. In this unit, you will learn about the financial statements prepared in a firm that sells merchandise and has more complex operations. You will also see how closing entries are made in such a business.

A Service-Merchandising Business

When the Modern Cleaning Shop opened its accessories department, it changed from a purely service business to a service-merchandising enterprise. A merchandising firm is one that buys and sells goods in the regular course of operations. Thus, the Modern Cleaning Shop now sells both services and goods. The new merchandising aspect of the business requires certain changes in the form of the financial statements.

Income Statement

At the end of January 19X2, the Modern Cleaning Shop's income statement looked like this.

MODERN CLEANING SHOP
Income Statement
Month Ended January 31, 19X2

Revenue		
Cleaning Service Sales		$3,300
Less Operating Expenses		
Salaries Expense	$1,700	
Rent Expense	700	
Supplies Used	700	
Miscellaneous Expense	60	
Total Operating Expenses		3,160
Net Income for the Month		$ 140

Of course, Paul Reed, the owner, wishes to know how much revenue is being received from each type of operation. Thus, beginning in February the income statement will show revenue from two sources—Cleaning Service Sales and Accessories Sales. See the Revenue section of the income statement illustrated below.

Note that the revenue from Cleaning Service Sales of $4,282 is handled as before. However, the revenue from Accessories Sales of $1,287 is reduced by the Sales Returns and Allowances—Accessories of $22 to arrive at the Net Accessories Sales of $1,265. The Cost of Goods Sold ($800) is deducted from this figure to determine the Gross Profit on Accessories Sales of $465. This $465 amount is added to the Cleaning Service Sales to arrive at the Total Gross Profit on Sales of $4,747. Next, the various operating expenses of the business are subtracted from the Total Gross Profit on Sales in order to arrive at the Net Income for the Month of $894.70.

MODERN CLEANING SHOP
Income Statement
Month Ended February 28, 19X2

Revenue
  Cleaning Service Sales $4,282.00
  Gross Profit on Accessories Sales
    Accessories Sales $1,287.00
    Less Sales Returns and Allowances   22.00
    Net Accessories Sales $1,265.00
  Less Cost of Goods Sold
    Inventory, February 1, 19X2 $ –0–
    Purchases During Period $1,810.00
    Less Purchases Returns and Allowances   10.00
    Net Purchases   1,800.00
    Total Merchandise Available for Sale $1,800.00
    Less Inventory, February 28, 19X2   1,000.00
    Cost of Goods Sold   800.00
  Gross Profit on Accessories Sales   465.00
Total Gross Profit on Sales $4,747.00
Less Operating Expenses
  Salaries Expense $1,950.00
  Rent Expense   700.00
  Supplies Used   934.00
  Bad Debts Expense   3.30
  Depreciation Expense   90.00
  Miscellaneous Expense   175.00
  Total Operating Expenses   3,852.30
Net Income for the Month $ 894.70

Balance Sheet   There are four new elements on the balance sheet for February 28, 19X2. The first new element is the Allowance for Bad Debts, which is subtracted from Accounts Receivable Control to arrive at the estimated collectible accounts receivable of $138.70. The second new element is an asset, Merchandise Inventory. The amount shown for this asset is the result of the inventory taken at the close of business on the last day of the period. The third new element is the Accumulated Depreciation, which is subtracted from the related asset, Equipment, to determine the book value of $5,310 for this asset. These items are shown on the asset side of the balance sheet illustrated below.

In the Owner's Equity section of the balance sheet, the fourth new element, the owner's drawing account, is subtracted from the net income for February to arrive at the net increase in owner's capital, or investment, during the period, which is $844.70.

MODERN CLEANING SHOP
Balance Sheet
February 28, 19X2

Assets				Liabilities and Owner's Equity			
Cash			$1,586.00	Liabilities			
Accounts Receivable Control		$142.00		Accounts Payable Control			$950.00
Less Allowance for Bad Debts		3.30	138.70	Owner's Equity			
Merchandise Inventory			1,000.00	Paul Reed, Capital, Feb. 1, 19X2		$6,240.00	
Equipment	$5,400.00			Net Income for February	$894.70		
Less Accumulated Depreciation		90.00	5,310.00	Less Withdrawals	50.00	844.70	
				Paul Reed, Capital, Feb. 28, 19X2			7,084.70
				Total Liabilities and Owner's Equity			
Total Assets			$8,034.70				$8,034.70

Adjusting Entries

After the financial statements have been prepared from the worksheet, the accountant turns to the task of making a permanent record of the end-of-period adjustments so that the general ledger accounts will agree with the worksheet and the financial statements. The account titles and amounts needed to journalize the adjustments are taken directly from the Adjustments section of the worksheet. For example, the completed worksheet shown on page 316 is the source of the adjusting entries made at the Modern Cleaning Shop on February 28, 19X2. The first adjusting entry is to record the estimated depreciation of $90 for the month. This entry is made in the general journal as illustrated below. (The account numbers are shown as they would appear after the posting procedure is completed.)

19 X2	Adjusting Entries			
Feb. 28	Depreciation Expense	564	90 00	
	Accumulated Depreciation	141A		90 00
	Adjustment a for depreciation of equipment in February.			

The second adjusting entry records the estimated bad debts loss of $3.30 from February credit sales.

	19 X2						
	Feb. 28	Bad Debts Expense		561	3 30		
		Allowance for Bad Debts		111A			3 30
		Adjustment b for estimated bad debt loss on February credit sales.					

The adjusting entries are then posted to the general ledger accounts affected. Refer to the accounts illustrated below.

Depreciation Expense   No. 564

DATE	EXPLANATION	POST. REF.	DEBIT	CREDIT	BALANCE	DR. CR.
19 X2 Feb. 28	Adjustment a	J2	90 00		90 00	Dr.

Accumulated Depreciation   No. 141A

DATE	EXPLANATION	POST. REF.	DEBIT	CREDIT	BALANCE	DR. CR.
19 X2 Feb. 28	Adjustment a	J2		90 00	90 00	Cr.

Bad Debts Expense   No. 561

DATE	EXPLANATION	POST. REF.	DEBIT	CREDIT	BALANCE	DR. CR.
19 X2 Feb. 28	Adjustment b	J2	3 30		3 30	Dr.

Allowance for Bad Debts   No. 111A

DATE	EXPLANATION	POST. REF.	DEBIT	CREDIT	BALANCE	DR. CR.
19 X2 Feb. 28	Adjustment b	J2		3 30	3 30	Cr.

After the adjusting entries have been posted to the general ledger accounts, the accounts reflect the same balances as are shown in the Adjusted Trial Balance columns of the worksheet on page 316.

Closing Entries

With the adjustments now journalized and posted, the accountant for the Modern Cleaning Shop is ready to begin the closing process. The procedure for February is very similar to that used in December and January.

1. The accountant transfers the balances that appear in the Credit column of the Income Statement section of the worksheet shown below, including the ending merchandise inventory, to the Revenue and Expense Summary account. This is accomplished by making the following entry in the general journal. After the entry is recorded, the amounts are posted to the proper ledger accounts.

MODERN CLEANING SHOP
Worksheet (Partial)
Month Ended February 28, 19X2

ACCT. NO.	ACCOUNT NAME	INCOME STATEMENT DEBIT	INCOME STATEMENT CREDIT	BALANCE SHEET DEBIT	BALANCE SHEET CREDIT
101	Cash			1,586 00	
111	Accounts Receivable Control			142 00	
111A	Allowance for Bad Debts				3 30
121	Merchandise Inventory		(c)1,000 00	(c)1,000 00	
141	Equipment			5,400 00	
141A	Accumulated Depreciation				90 00
202	Accounts Payable Control				950 00
301	Paul Reed, Capital				6,240 00
302	Paul Reed, Drawing			50 00	
401	Cleaning Service Sales		4,282 00		
402	Accessories Sales		1,287 00		
451	Sales Ret. and Allow.—Cleaning Service				
452	Sales Ret. and Allow.—Accessories	22 00			
501	Merchandise Purchases	1,810 00			
509	Purchases Returns and Allowances		10 00		
511	Salaries Expense	1,950 00			
516	Rent Expense	700 00			
521	Supplies Used	934 00			
561	Bad Debts Expense	3 30			
564	Depreciation Expense	90 00			
591	Miscellaneous Expense	175 00			
	Totals	5,684 30	6,579 00	8,178 00	7,283 30
	Net Income for the Month	894 70			894 70
		6,579 00	6,579 00	8,178 00	8,178 00

		Closing Entries			
19 X2 Feb. 28		Merchandise Inventory	121	1,000 00	
		Cleaning Service Sales	401	4,282 00	
		Accessories Sales	402	1,287 00	
		Purchases Returns and Allowances	509	10 00	
		Revenue and Expense Summary	399		6,579 00
		To record ending inventory and transfer revenue and other credit items to the summary account.			

2. Then the accountant transfers the balances that appear in the Debit column of the Income Statement section of the worksheet to the Revenue and Expense Summary account by recording and posting the following general journal entry.

19 X2 Feb. 28	Revenue and Expense Summary	399	5,684 30	
	Sales Ret. and Allow.—Accessories	452		22 00
	Merchandise Purchases	501		1,810 00
	Salaries Expense	511		1,950 00
	Rent Expense	516		700 00
	Supplies Used	521		934 00
	Bad Debts Expense	561		3 30
	Depreciation Expense	564		90 00
	Miscellaneous Expense	591		175 00
	To transfer expense account balances and other debit items to the summary account.			

3. After the closing entries are posted to the general ledger, the accounts affected appear as follows.

Merchandise Inventory — No. 121

DATE	EXPLANATION	POST. REF.	DEBIT	CREDIT	BALANCE	DR. CR.
19 X2 Feb. 28	Ending inventory	J2	1,000 00		1,000 00	Dr.

Revenue and Expense Summary — No. 399

DATE	EXPLANATION	POST. REF.	DEBIT	CREDIT	BALANCE	DR. CR.
19 X2 Feb. 28	Revenue	J2		6,579 00	6,579 00	Cr.
28	Expenses	J2	5,684 30		894 70	Cr.

Cleaning Service Sales — No. 401

DATE	EXPLANATION	POST. REF.	DEBIT	CREDIT	BALANCE	DR. CR.
19 X2 Feb. 28		CR2		4,225 00	4,225 00	Cr.
28		S2		57 00	4,282 00	Cr.
28	Closing	J2	4,282 00		–0–	

Accessories Sales — No. 402

DATE	EXPLANATION	POST. REF.	DEBIT	CREDIT	BALANCE	DR. CR.
19 X2 Feb. 28		CR2		1,200 00	1,200 00	Cr.
28		S2		87 00	1,287 00	Cr.
28	Closing	J2	1,287 00		–0–	

Sales Returns and Allowances—Accessories   No. 452

DATE	EXPLANATION	POST. REF.	DEBIT	CREDIT	BALANCE	DR. CR.
19X2 Feb. 5		J1	10 00		10 00	Dr.
28		J2	2 00		12 00	Dr.
28		CP2	10 00		22 00	Dr.
28	Closing	J2		22 00	–0–	

Merchandise Purchases   No. 501

DATE	EXPLANATION	POST. REF.	DEBIT	CREDIT	BALANCE	DR. CR.
19X2 Feb. 28		P1	1,810 00		1,810 00	Dr.
28	Closing	J2		1,810 00	–0–	

Purchases Returns and Allowances   No. 509

DATE	EXPLANATION	POST. REF.	DEBIT	CREDIT	BALANCE	DR. CR.
19X2 Feb. 27		J2		10 00	10 00	Cr.
28	Closing	J2	10 00		–0–	

Salaries Expense   No. 511

DATE	EXPLANATION	POST. REF.	DEBIT	CREDIT	BALANCE	DR. CR.
19X2 Feb. 28		CP2	1,950 00		1,950 00	Dr.
28	Closing	J2		1,950 00	–0–	

Rent Expense   No. 516

DATE	EXPLANATION	POST. REF.	DEBIT	CREDIT	BALANCE	DR. CR.
19X2 Feb. 16		CP2	700 00		700 00	Dr.
28	Closing	J2		700 00	–0–	

Supplies Used   No. 521

DATE	EXPLANATION	POST. REF.	DEBIT	CREDIT	BALANCE	DR. CR.
19 X2						
Feb. 8		CP2	250 00		250 00	Dr.
13		CP2	124 00		374 00	Dr.
21		CP2	160 00		534 00	Dr.
27		CP2	400 00		934 00	Dr.
28	Closing	J2		934 00	-0-	

Bad Debts Expense   No. 561

DATE	EXPLANATION	POST. REF.	DEBIT	CREDIT	BALANCE	DR. CR.
19 X2						
Feb. 28	Adjustment b	J2	3 30		3 30	Dr.
28	Closing	J2		3 30	-0-	

Depreciation Expense   No. 564

DATE	EXPLANATION	POST. REF.	DEBIT	CREDIT	BALANCE	DR. CR.
19 X2						
Feb. 28	Adjustment a	J2	90 00		90 00	Dr.
28	Closing	J2		90 00	-0-	

Miscellaneous Expense   No. 591

DATE	EXPLANATION	POST. REF.	DEBIT	CREDIT	BALANCE	DR. CR.
19 X2						
Feb. 2		CP2	60 00		60 00	Dr.
14		CP2	75 00		135 00	Dr.
22		CP2	40 00		175 00	Dr.
28	Closing	J2		175 00	-0-	

4. The next step is to transfer the net income (or net loss) to the owner's capital account. The journal entry necessary to transfer the net income for February to the Paul Reed, Capital account is shown below.

19 X2				
Feb. 28	Revenue and Expense Summary	399	894 70	
	Paul Reed, Capital	301		894 70
	To close the summary account by transferring net income for period to the capital account.			

After this entry has been posted, the Revenue and Expense Summary account and the Paul Reed, Capital account appear as follows.

Revenue and Expense Summary					No. 399	
DATE	EXPLANATION	POST. REF.	DEBIT	CREDIT	BALANCE	DR. CR.
19 X2 Feb. 28	Revenue	J2		6,579 00	6,579 00	Cr.
28	Expenses	J2	5,684 30		894 70	Cr.
28	Net income	J2	894 70		–0–	

Paul Reed, Capital					No. 301	
DATE	EXPLANATION	POST. REF.	DEBIT	CREDIT	BALANCE	DR. CR.
19 X2 Feb. 1	Balance	✓			6,240 00	Cr.
28	Net income	J2		894 70	7,134 70	Cr.

5. The final step is to transfer the balance of the Paul Reed, Drawing account to the Paul Reed, Capital account. The journal entry to accomplish this is shown below.

19 X2 Feb. 28	Paul Reed, Capital	301	50 00	
	Paul Reed, Drawing	302		50 00
	To close the drawing account to the capital account.			

After this entry is posted, the Paul Reed, Drawing account and the Paul Reed, Capital account appear as follows.

Paul Reed, Capital					No. 301	
DATE	EXPLANATION	POST. REF.	DEBIT	CREDIT	BALANCE	DR. CR.
19 X2 Feb. 1	Balance	✓			6,240 00	Cr.
28	Net income	J2		894 70	7,134 70	Cr.
28	Withdrawals	J2	50 00		7,084 70	Cr.

Paul Reed, Drawing					No. 302	
DATE	EXPLANATION	POST. REF.	DEBIT	CREDIT	BALANCE	DR. CR.
19 X2 Feb. 28		CP2	50 00		50 00	Dr.
28	Closing	J2		50 00	–0–	

Balancing and Ruling the General Ledger

When a balance ledger form is used for the general ledger accounts, the end-of-period work is simplified because the balancing and ruling procedures are eliminated. This is one of the advantages of using the balance ledger form.

Postclosing Trial Balance

Finally, the accountant prepares the postclosing trial balance at the end of February. Remember that the purpose of this procedure is to check the equality of the debits and credits in the general ledger accounts that remain open after the closing process has been completed.

MODERN CLEANING SHOP
Postclosing Trial Balance
February 28, 19X2

ACCT. NO.	ACCOUNT NAME	DEBIT	CREDIT
101	Cash	1,586 00	
111	Accounts Receivable Control	142 00	
111A	Allowance for Bad Debts		3 30
121	Merchandise Inventory	1,000 00	
141	Equipment	5,400 00	
141A	Accumulated Depreciation		90 00
202	Accounts Payable Control		950 00
301	Paul Reed, Capital		7,084 70
	Totals	8,128 00	8,128 00

Beginning Merchandise Inventory

The ending inventory of $1,000 on February 28, 19X2, becomes the beginning inventory for the new period that starts on March 1. This beginning inventory will also become part of the cost of goods sold during March because it is assumed that the stock carried over from the previous period will be the first sold in the new period. The treatment of beginning inventory on the worksheet is simple. As a part of the cost of goods sold and similar to an expense, the inventory figure is extended to the Debit columns of the Adjusted Trial Balance and Income Statement sections of the worksheet just as is done with the expense items. This procedure is illustrated in a partial worksheet dated March 31, 19X2, which is shown on page 333. To complete the inventory data, the March 31 inventory of $1,100, the Merchandise Purchases of $1,305, and the Purchases Returns and Allowances of $22 are also extended, as you learned in Unit 17.

The figures for purchases, returns and allowances, and inventory that are assembled in the Income Statement section reflect the cost of goods sold for March. The effect becomes clear when this data is arranged in the format used in the Cost of Goods Sold section of the Modern Cleaning Shop's income statement for the month ended March 31, 19X2.

Less Cost of Goods Sold		
Inventory, March 1, 19X2		$1,000
Purchases During Period	$1,305	
Less Purch. Returns and Allowances	22	
Net Purchases		1,283
Total Merchandise Available for Sale		$2,283
Less Inventory, March 31, 19X2		1,100
Cost of Goods Sold		$1,183

The ending inventory on March 31 is deducted from the Total Merchandise Available for Sale to arrive at the Cost of Goods Sold. Hence, the ending inventory is entered in the Credit column of the Income Statement section as a reduction of the costs for the period. The ending inventory also represents an asset on hand on March 31 and must appear on the March 31 balance sheet. Therefore, it is entered in the Debit column of the Balance Sheet section of the worksheet.

When the closing entries for March are prepared from the worksheet, the ending inventory is recorded in the usual way along with the other items in the Credit column of the Income Statement section. Next, the total of the Debit column of the Income Statement section is journalized in the usual way as a debit to Revenue and Expense Summary. This time, however, the total will include the $1,000 beginning inventory figure that has been extended to the Debit column. The Merchandise Inventory account must be credited for $1,000 to show that this amount has been used as part of the cost of goods sold during March. Study the following closing entries for March and the postings to the Merchandise Inventory account.

19X2		Closing Entries			
Mar.	31	Merchandise Inventory	121	1,100 00	
		Cleaning Service Sales	401	5,455 00	
		Accessories Sales	402	1,620 00	
		Purchases Returns and Allowances	509	22 00	
		Revenue and Expense Summary	399		8,197 00
		To record the ending inventory and to transfer the revenue account balances and other credit items to the summary account.			
	31	Revenue and Expense Summary	399	7,976 50	
		Merchandise Inventory	121		1,000 00
		Sales Ret. and Allow.—Accessories	452		25 00
		Merchandise Purchases	501		1,305 00
		Salaries Expense	511		3,000 00
		Rent Expense	516		700 00
		Supplies Used	521		1,495 00
		Bad Debts Expense	561		11 50
		Depreciation Expense	564		90 00
		Miscellaneous Expense	591		350 00
		To transfer the expense account balances, other debit items, and the beginning inventory to the summary account.			

MODERN CLEANING SHOP
Worksheet
Month Ended March 31, 19X2

ACCT. NO.	ACCOUNT NAME	TRIAL BALANCE DEBIT	TRIAL BALANCE CREDIT	ADJUSTMENTS DEBIT	ADJUSTMENTS CREDIT	ADJUSTED TRIAL BALANCE DEBIT	ADJUSTED TRIAL BALANCE CREDIT	INCOME STATEMENT DEBIT	INCOME STATEMENT CREDIT	BALANCE SHEET DEBIT	BALANCE SHEET CREDIT
101	Cash	1,839 00									
111	Accounts Receivable Control	492 00									
111A	Allowance for Bad Debts		11 50								
121	Merchandise Inventory	1,000 00				1,000 00		1,000 00	(c)1,100 00	(c)1,100 00	
501	Merchandise Purchases	1,305 00				1,305 00		1,305 00			
509	Purchases Ret. and Allow.		22 00				22 00		22 00		

333

	Merchandise Inventory				No. 121	
DATE	EXPLANATION	POST. REF.	DEBIT	CREDIT	BALANCE	DR. CR.
19 X2 Feb. 28	Ending inventory	J2	1,000 00		1,000 00	Dr.
Mar. 31	Ending inventory	J3	1,100 00		2,100 00	Dr.
31	Closing	J3		1,000 00	1,100 00	Dr.

There are various methods for handling inventory on the worksheet and in the adjusting and closing entries. However, the method illustrated above is preferred by many accountants because it permits them to prepare the adjusting and closing entries directly from the worksheet, using the figures exactly as they are. Most other methods require that alterations be made to the amounts shown on the worksheet before the adjusting or closing entries can be prepared.

Classified Financial Statements

The operations of the Modern Cleaning Shop are typical of those of thousands of small businesses that open every year. When these businesses begin, their accounting records are usually quite simple. Then, as they expand operations, the records are changed to meet new demands. To see how this process affects the financial statements, look at the Modern Cleaning Shop's balance sheet dated December 31, 19X5, four years after the business started. This balance sheet is illustrated on page 335.

Notice that the form of the statement is more elaborate and that many account titles have been added. These differences are explained below.

Classified Balance Sheet

The accountant adds new accounts from time to time to meet special recording problems, as has been explained in Units 6–17. In turn, as the accounts become more numerous, a more elaborate statement, called a *classified balance sheet*, is commonly used to group and classify the various assets and liabilities for more effective presentation. This type of balance sheet, which is shown on page 335, is prepared in *report form*. A report-form balance sheet lists assets, liabilities, and owner's equity in vertical order on the page. The report form is usually preferred when there are a great many accounts and when the statement is prepared on the typewriter. Let us examine each section of the classified balance sheet illustrated here.

Current Assets

The first section of the classified balance sheet lists current assets. *Current assets* consist of cash, items that will normally be converted into cash within one year, and items that will be used up within one year. These items are usually listed in order of liquidity—ease of conversion into cash. Current assets are vital to a firm's survival because they provide the funds needed to pay bills and meet expenses.

A number of current assets, such as cash, accounts receivable, and merchandise inventory, have been presented many times before in this book.

MODERN CLEANING SHOP
Balance Sheet
December 31, 19X5

Assets

Current Assets			
Cash in Bank		$ 4,015	
Petty Cash Fund		100	
Change Fund		150	
Investment in U.S. Treasury Securities		5,500	
Notes Receivable		2,750	
Accounts Receivable Control	$ 6,600		
Less Allowance for Bad Debts	350	6,250	
Prepaid Insurance		840	
Merchandise Inventory		3,625	
Total Current Assets			$23,230
Plant and Equipment			
Buildings and Cleaning Equipment	$60,000		
Less Accumulated Depreciation	11,500	$48,500	
Store Equipment	$ 4,800		
Less Accumulated Depreciation	2,100	2,700	
Delivery Equipment	$ 8,450		
Less Accumulated Depreciation	2,640	5,810	
Office Equipment	$ 3,170		
Less Accumulated Depreciation	1,430	1,740	
Land		15,000	
Total Plant and Equipment			73,750
Total Assets			$96,980

Liabilities and Owner's Equity

Current Liabilities			
Notes Payable		$ 8,000	
Accounts Payable Control		3,100	
Sales Tax Payable		635	
Employee Deductions:			
FICA Tax	$ 920		
Income Tax Withheld	2,440	3,360	
Total Current Liabilities			$15,095
Long-Term Liabilities			
9% Mortgage Payable on Plant, 19Y4			38,000
Total Liabilities			$53,095
Owner's Equity			
Paul Reed, Capital, January 1, 19X5		$38,015	
Net Income for Year 19X5	$13,070		
Less Withdrawals	7,200		
Net Increase in Investment in 19X5		5,870	
Paul Reed, Capital, December 31, 19X5			43,885
Total Liabilities and Owner's Equity			$96,980

However, some new account titles appear in the Current Assets section of the December 31, 19X5, balance sheet. For example, Cash is listed as Cash in Bank, and there are two additional cash accounts and three other new accounts for current assets.

- Petty Cash Fund is a small, fixed sum set aside to pay for minor cash outlays, such as postage due, carfare, and special supplies, as explained in Unit 7.
- Change Fund is a fixed sum of cash kept in the cash registers for making change.
- Investments usually represent securities bought as a means of earning interest on funds that are temporarily not required in the firm's operations. Government bonds and treasury notes are common investments for this purpose.
- Notes Receivable might be obtained as a result of sales transactions, as described in Unit 6. Notes are sometimes accepted from credit customers in settlement of their overdue accounts. They are usually listed before Accounts Receivable on the balance sheet to reflect the stronger legal claim that notes represent against the debtors.
- Prepaid Insurance represents insurance premiums paid in advance for protection that will cover future periods. In its first few years, the Modern Cleaning Shop purchased insurance policies that covered only short periods and charged the premiums to an expense account when the policies were bought. However, the owner later realized that it was more economical to purchase insurance policies covering more than a one-year period. When a long-term policy is purchased, it is more appropriate to record the premium in an asset account. Thus, as of January 1, 19X5, the accountant set up an asset account called Prepaid Insurance to record the premiums paid when long-term insurance policies are purchased. At the end of each month, the portion of the insurance premium that applies to the period will be transferred to the Insurance Expense account. On January 2, 19X5, the firm paid a premium of $1,680 for a two-year insurance policy. The entry to record this payment is shown below in general journal form.

19X5					
Jan. 2	Prepaid Insurance	126	1,680 00	
	Cash in Bank	101		1,680 00
	Paid premium on two-year fire insurance policy.			

Since the policy covers two years, each month 1/24th of the prepaid insurance is used up. The monthly expense is computed by dividing the total cost of the policy by the number of months ($1,680 ÷ 24 = $70). At the end of each month, an adjusting entry is made to transfer $70 of the prepaid insurance to the Insurance Expense account, as shown below.

19X5					
Jan. 31	Insurance Expense	536	70 00	
	Prepaid Insurance	126		70 00
	Expired insurance for month of January.			

Thus, during 19X5 a total of $840 ($70 × 12), which represented the cost of one year's premium, was charged off as an expense for the period. The $840 balance in the Prepaid Insurance account is the unused premium applicable to the remaining life of the policy (one-half of the original premium of $1,680).

Similar adjustments may be made for other prepaid expense items, such as office supplies purchased in large quantities and prepaid rent.

Plant and Equipment

The section on the classified balance sheet that follows Current Assets is Plant and Equipment. Plant and equipment consists of property that will be used for a long time in the conduct of business operations. Accountants keep a close watch on these assets because they usually represent a very sizable investment; and, because of their special nature, it is often difficult and costly to replace them. All the accounts listed under Plant and Equipment on the Modern Cleaning Shop's balance sheet are new.

- The all-inclusive Equipment account used earlier has been replaced by several more specialized accounts: Buildings and Cleaning Equipment, Store Equipment, Delivery Equipment, and Office Equipment. In each of these accounts, the value of the asset is carried at cost.
- A separate Accumulated Depreciation account is set up for each asset to accumulate the total depreciation charges recorded over the life of the asset.
- The firm has also acquired a new asset, Land. The owner bought land on which to build a new dry-cleaning plant. Land is not subject to charges for depreciation.

Current Liabilities

The Current Liabilities section appears in the Liabilities and Owner's Equity portion of the classified balance sheet. Current liabilities are debts that must be paid within one year. They are usually listed in order of priority of payment. Since the firm's credit reputation depends upon prompt settlement of its debts, the accountant must make sure that funds are available when these obligations become due. The Modern Cleaning Shop's current liabilities include several new items.

- Notes Payable are debts based on short-term written promises to pay, usually given to suppliers and banks. They are normally listed before Accounts Payable on the balance sheet to reflect the preferred nature of these claims against the firm.
- The Sales Taxes Payable account was set up to record the obligation for paying taxes collected on retail sales, as described in Unit 6.
- Employee Deductions—FICA Tax represents the firm's liability for payment of the taxes deducted from workers' earnings to support the federal social security program.
- Employee Deductions—Income Tax Withheld is a liability account that shows the firm's obligation for amounts deducted from workers' earnings under federal and other income tax regulations.

Long-Term Liabilities

Following current liabilities on the classified balance sheet are long-term liabilities—debts of the business due more than a year in the future. Although repayment of these obligations may not be due for several years, the accountant must plan ahead so that the money for settlement can be obtained when needed. In the meantime, the accountant must make sure that periodic interest is paid promptly when due.

There is only one long-term liability shown for the Modern Cleaning Shop. A long-term loan on the plant buildings is secured by a mortgage. Thus, the account is entitled Mortgage Payable on Plant and identified by the year due, 19Y4.

Owner's Equity The Owner's Equity section of the balance sheet is very much the same as it was in earlier periods. The owner's additional investments (when there are any) and withdrawals of profits during the period are clearly presented in this section.

Classified Income Statement The Modern Cleaning Shop's income statement for the year ended December 31, 19X5, which is shown on page 339, also reveals a more elaborate grouping of items and a number of new accounts. Notice that the information on operating revenue and cost of goods sold is broken down by department. The totals for the entire business are presented in the right column. Starting at the top of this income statement, consider the changes within each major section.

Operating Revenues A more descriptive title is now used in the first section of the income statement to emphasize the source of the revenue. Only revenue from operations belongs here. Other income is presented near the bottom of the form and is discussed on page 341.

- There are now three accounts for recording revenue from sales: Accessories Sales, Cleaning Supplies Sales, and Cleaning Service Sales. (The cleaning supplies department was set up in 19X5.)
- For each department, the total of Sales Returns and Allowances and Sales Discounts is deducted from Sales to determine Net Sales. (Accountants agree that Sales Returns and Allowances should be deducted from Sales. However, some accountants suggest that Sales Discounts should not be offset against Sales but should be shown as Other Expense because Sales Discount is, in effect, interest paid to customers to encourage them to pay quickly.)

Cost of Goods Sold There are several new items in the Cost of Goods Sold section.

- Merchandise Inventory, January 1, shows no figure for Cleaning Supplies Sales because the department started operations during the current year.
- Freight In is added to Merchandise Purchases to find the total cost of the goods purchased during the period.
- Purchases Returns and Allowances, along with Purchases Discounts, are shown as a reduction in the cost of purchases during the period. The treatment of Purchases Returns and Allowances was discussed in Unit 11. (Some accountants prefer to show Purchases Discounts as Other Income on the basis that these discounts represent interest earned for prompt payment of bills.)

Gross Profit on Sales The Gross Profit on Sales remains as before.

Operating Expenses The Operating Expenses section is now subdivided to permit grouping of these expenses into three categories: plant operating expenses, selling expenses, and administrative expenses.

MODERN CLEANING SHOP
Income Statement
Year Ended December 31, 19X5

	Accessories Sales		Cleaning Supplies Sales		Cleaning Service Sales		Total	
Operating Revenue								
Sales		$20,364		$12,161		$89,189		$121,714
Less: Sales Ret. and Allow.	$ 286		$ 108		$ 427			
Sales Discounts	230	516	257	365		427		1,308
Net Sales		$19,848		$11,796		$88,762		$120,406
Cost of Goods Sold								
Merchandise Inventory, Jan. 1		$ 1,510		$ -0-				
Merchandise Purchases	$15,960		$12,010					
Freight In	260		190					
Total Cost of Purchases		16,220		12,200				
Less: Purchases Ret. and Allow.	$ 155		$ 45					
Purchases Discounts	285	440	175	220				
Total Merchandise Available for Sale		$17,290		$11,980				
Less Merchandise Inventory, Dec. 31		1,625		2,000				
Cost of Goods Sold		$15,665		$ 9,980		-0-		$ 25,645
Gross Profit on Sales		$ 4,183		$ 1,816		$88,762		$ 94,761
Operating Expenses								
Plant Operating Expenses								
Plant Salaries and Wages Expense					$25,600			
Plant Supplies and Expense					4,780			
Utilities Expense					1,910			
Depreciation Expense on Buildings and Cleaning Equipment					1,500			
Total Plant Operating Expenses						$33,790		
Selling Expenses								
Sales Salaries and Commissions Expense					$15,520			
Store Supplies and Expense					1,160			
Advertising Expense					1,620			
Store Taxes and Licenses					760			
Depreciation Expense on Store Equipment					480			
Delivery Expense					7,450			
Depreciation Expense on Delivery Equipment					690			
Total Selling Expenses						27,680		
Administrative Expenses								
Office Salaries Expense					$ 8,200			
Office Supplies and Expense					1,920			
Depreciation Expense on Office Equipment					400			
Insurance Expense					1,400			
Bad Debts Expense					250			
Donations and Contributions					575			
Payroll Tax Expense					3,024			
Property Tax Expense					780			
Miscellaneous Expense					2,675			
Total Administrative Expenses						19,224		
Total Operating Expenses								80,694
Net Income From Operations								$ 14,067
Other Income								
Interest Earned								368
Other Expense								$ 14,435
Interest Expense								1,365
Net Income for the Year								$ 13,070

Plant Operating Expenses. These are the expenses involved in running the new plant that opened on January 1 of the current year, 19X5.

- Plant Salaries and Wages Expense includes the pay of all plant officials and workers.
- Plant Supplies and Expense includes all the supplies and services, except utilities, required in plant operations.
- Utilities Expense is recorded separately because it represents a significant amount.
- Depreciation Expense on Buildings and Cleaning Equipment shows the expense for 19X5 of the depreciation taken on these assets based on their various estimated useful lives.

Selling Expenses. This category includes all expenses directly related to the sale and delivery of cleaning services, cleaning supplies, and accessories. Several new account titles are used to identify specific expenses.

- The Sales Salaries and Commissions Expense account and the Store Supplies and Expense account are adaptations of the familiar Salaries Expense account and Supplies Used account.
- Other accounts that have been added to meet the needs of expanded operations are: Advertising Expense, Store Taxes and Licenses, Delivery Expense, Depreciation Expense on Store Equipment, and Depreciation Expense on Delivery Equipment.

Administrative Expenses. This section includes expenses relating to all other activities of the more complex business besides plant operations and selling operations. There are a number of new accounts.

- The accounts for Office Salaries Expense, Office Supplies and Expense, Depreciation Expense on Office Equipment, Bad Debts Expense, and Miscellaneous Expense have all been used before.
- Insurance Expense is a natural outgrowth of the purchase of plant, equipment, and inventory. The business now needs protection against the risk of various types of losses. Included in the total yearly expense of $1,400 is the expired insurance premium of $840 discussed on page 336.
- Donations and Contributions are another cost of modern business operations. A firm often makes contributions to charitable and civic organizations to build goodwill and improve the welfare of the community.
- Payroll Tax Expense, explained in Unit 16, represents the employer's costs under various payroll tax laws.
- Property Tax Expense is a result of the ownership of plant, equipment, inventory, and other property. A business may be subject to a variety of property taxes levied by different taxing authorities.

Net Income From Operations

Like the heading Operating Revenue, Net Income From Operations emphasizes the source of the net income. Many businesses have a small income from nonoperating sources, but the two amounts must be kept separate to allow appraisal of true operating efficiency.

Other Income   The Other Income section provides a place to show the sources of nonoperating income, such as Interest Earned. This interest might arise from interest-bearing notes receivable (Unit 6) or from investments the firm has made.

Other Expenses   Typically, nonoperating expenses relate to the costs of financial dealings. In the case of the Modern Cleaning Shop, Interest Expense represents interest that the firm has to pay on interest-bearing notes payable and on the plant mortgage.

Net Income for the Period   The final total on the income statement shows the combined results of all types of revenue and expenses. (If the firm had a net loss for the period, the amount would be shown in parentheses or italics.)

principles and procedures summary

The income statement for a merchandising business shows the sources and amounts of revenue, the cost of goods sold, the gross profit on sales, operating expenses, and the net income or net loss. The balance sheet normally includes the Merchandise Inventory account among the assets, the Allowance for Bad Debts account as a deduction from the Accounts Receivable Control account, and the Accumulated Depreciation account as a deduction from the Equipment account. In the Owner's Equity section, the owner's withdrawals are deducted from the net income, or added to the net loss.

The merchandising aspect of a business has little effect on the rest of the firm's end-of-period routine. Immediately after the financial statements are completed, the adjusting entries are journalized and posted. Next, the closing entries are journalized and posted in almost the same manner as for a service business. Then a postclosing trial balance is taken, as before. (If a balance ledger form is used for the general ledger, there is no need to balance and rule the accounts.)

As businesses become larger, their financial statements become more elaborate. However, new accounts quickly fall into familiar patterns and groupings once the basic principles of statement preparation are learned.

A classified balance sheet is commonly used to group a firm's assets and liabilities for effective presentation. Assets are usually arranged in two groups—current assets and plant and equipment. Liabilities are also divided into two groups—current liabilities and long-term liabilities.

Current assets consist of cash, items that will normally be converted into cash within one year, and items that will be used up within one year. Plant and equipment consists of property that will be used for a long time in business operations. Current liabilities are debts that must be paid within one year, whereas long-term liabilities are obligations that are due more than a year in the future.

A classified income statement for a large merchandising business would probably include the following sections: operating revenue, cost of goods sold, gross profit on sales, operating expenses, net income from operations, other income, and other expense. To make the statement even more meaningful, the operating expenses might be broken down into several categories such as plant operating expenses, selling expenses, and administrative expenses.

Regardless of the size or type of business, the basic accounting principles and procedures discussed so far can be applied to the needs of the firm. An accountant must often adapt records and procedures to devise an accounting system that is workable for a particular business.

MANAGERIAL implications

Financial statements can be easily adapted to meet the reporting needs of service, merchandising, or service-merchandising businesses. Management must understand the significance of the accounts used to record depreciation and bad debts in order to interpret the balance sheet figures correctly. A knowledge of the methods for determining the value of the ending inventory and for computing the cost of goods sold also helps management to understand how net income and loss figures are derived. Knowing where these figures came from and where to find more details is extremely important for auditing, comparison, and control purposes.

Classified financial statements are prepared so that management and others can more easily draw meaningful conclusions from the statements. The classification of items helps management to analyze both the financial condition of the business and the results of operations for the period. However, management must understand the nature and significance of the groupings. When classified statements are prepared, management has an extremely useful means of comparing the current year with prior years to see trends and patterns. Also, classified statements make it possible for management to compare its business with similar firms in the same industry.

MANAGERIAL discussion questions

1. Why does management need to know how the value of the ending inventory and the cost of goods sold were computed?
2. Refer to the partial income statement on page 332. Is it a good idea for management to allow its investment in inventory to grow by as much as 10 percent in a month? Explain.
3. Why might an owner refrain from making sizable and frequent drawings from a business?

4. Why does management compare the business's current financial statements with those of prior years and with those of other firms?
5. On the 19X5 income statement for the Modern Cleaning Shop (page 339), the information about operating revenue and cost of goods sold is broken down by departments. Why is this helpful to management?
6. Why would management consider it important to compare the amount of the firm's current assets and the amount of its current liabilities?
7. Should management be concerned if the balance sheet shows that the business's cash is less than the total of its current liabilities? Why or why not?
8. Suppose that the net income of a firm has dropped during the last three years. When comparing the income statement figures for each year, what items should management pay particular attention to in order to find the reason behind the decrease?

application of principles

PROBLEM 18-1 The Reliable Auto Parts Company is a wholesale business owned and operated by Ted Porter. A completed worksheet for the firm is shown on page 344. This worksheet is for the year ended December 31, 19X4.

INSTRUCTIONS
1. From the completed worksheet, prepare an income statement for the year ended December 31, 19X4.
2. From the completed worksheet, prepare a balance sheet dated December 31, 19X4.
3. Journalize the necessary adjusting entries for the accounting period.
4. Journalize the entries to close all the revenue, cost, and expense balances and to account for the balances of the beginning and ending merchandise inventory.
5. Journalize the entry to transfer the net income or net loss for the period from the Revenue and Expense Summary account to the owner's capital account.

PROBLEM 18-2 The Jordan Company is a retail business owned and operated by Alice Jordan. The firm sells household appliances such as refrigerators, laundry equipment, and dishwashers. Adjusted trial balance data for the company is given on page 345. This data was prepared at the end of the year's operations on December 31, 19X2. A count of the merchandise on hand in the business on that day showed an ending inventory of $62,500.

RELIABLE AUTO PARTS COMPANY
Worksheet
Year Ended December 31, 19X4

ACCT. NO.	ACCOUNT NAME	TRIAL BALANCE DEBIT	TRIAL BALANCE CREDIT	ADJUSTMENTS DEBIT	ADJUSTMENTS CREDIT	ADJUSTED TRIAL BALANCE DEBIT	ADJUSTED TRIAL BALANCE CREDIT	INCOME STATEMENT DEBIT	INCOME STATEMENT CREDIT	BALANCE SHEET DEBIT	BALANCE SHEET CREDIT
101	Cash in Bank	7,602 63				7,602 63				7,602 63	
111	Accounts Receivable Control	5,194 45				5,194 45				5,194 45	
121	Merchandise Inventory	15,000 00				15,000 00		15,000 00	(c)16,500 00	(c)16,500 00	
131	Furniture and Equipment	3,000 00				3,000 00				3,000 00	
131A	Acc. Depr.—Furn. and Equipment		900 00		(a)300 00		1,200 00				1,200 00
141	Delivery Truck	2,775 00				2,775 00				2,775 00	
141A	Acc. Depr.—Delivery Truck		1,200 00		(b)600 00		1,800 00				1,800 00
202	Accounts Payable Control		3,511 20				3,511 20				3,511 20
301	Ted Porter, Capital		14,372 50				14,372 50				14,372 50
401	Sales		183,101 45				183,101 45		183,101 45		
451	Sales Discount	2,266 73				2,266 73		2,266 73			
501	Merchandise Purchases	83,237 70				83,237 70		83,237 70			
509	Purchases Discount		822 26				822 26		822 26		
511	Rent Expense	1,800 00				1,800 00		1,800 00			
521	Sales Salaries Expense	26,960 00				26,960 00		26,960 00			
523	Store Supplies and Expense	3,546 25				3,546 25		3,546 25			
525	Depreciation Expense—Furn. and Equip.			(a)300 00		300 00		300 00			
531	Advertising Expense	1,738 90				1,738 90		1,738 90			
541	Delivery Salaries Expense	23,295 00				23,295 00		23,295 00			
543	Delivery Truck Expense	1,081 40				1,081 40		1,081 40			
545	Depreciation Expense—Delivery Truck			(b)600 00		600 00		600 00			
551	Office Salaries Expense	23,360 00				23,360 00		23,360 00			
553	Office Supplies and Expense	3,049 35				3,049 35		3,049 35			
	Totals	203,907 41	203,907 41	900 00	900 00	204,807 41	204,807 41	186,235 33	200,423 71	35,072 08	20,883 70
	Net Income for Year							14,188 38			14,188 38
								200,423 71	200,423 71	35,072 08	35,072 08

JORDAN COMPANY
Worksheet (Partial)
Year Ended December 31, 19X2

Account Name	Adjusted Trial Balance Debit	Credit
Cash in Bank	$ 43,060.20	
Petty Cash	200.00	
Change Fund	800.00	
Investment in U.S. Treasury Bonds	5,390.00	
Notes Receivable	5,000.00	
Accounts Receivable Control	50,375.15	
Allowance for Bad Debts		$ 982.71
Interest Receivable	50.00	
Merchandise Inventory, Jan. 1	65,200.00	
Prepaid Insurance	1,820.00	
Supplies on Hand	800.00	
Building	30,500.00	
Accum. Depr.—Building		2,750.00
Furniture and Equipment	38,500.00	
Accum. Depr.—Furniture and Equipment		7,700.00
Land	7,500.00	
Deposits With Utility Companies	100.00	
Notes Payable		9,200.00
Accounts Payable Control		29,505.45
Sales Taxes Payable		1,235.20
Wages Payable		990.00
Employee Deductions—FICA Tax		115.35
Employee Deductions—Income Taxes Withheld		673.20
Alice Jordan, Capital		161,072.70
Sales		495,138.35
Sales Returns and Allowances	3,782.15	
Interest Earned		240.00
Merchandise Purchases	269,795.10	
Depreciation Expense—Building	750.00	
Depreciation Expense—Furniture and Equipment	2,400.00	
Insurance Expense	4,530.20	
Property Taxes Expense	6,217.30	
Sales Salaries Expense	26,225.00	
Payroll Tax Expense—Sales Salaries	2,210.30	
Delivery Expense	18,240.60	
Sales Supplies and Expense	31,248.75	
Advertising Expense	11,710.20	
Officers' Salaries Expense	55,000.00	
Office Salaries Expense	17,325.00	
Payroll Tax Expense—Officers' and Office Salaries	3,615.10	
Office Supplies and Expense	6,310.20	
Miscellaneous Expense	100.00	
Bad Debts Expense	847.71	
Totals	$709,602.96	$709,602.96

INSTRUCTIONS
1. From the adjusted trial balance data, prepare a classified income statement for the year ended December 31, 19X2. (No departmental columns are required on this income statement.)
2. From the adjusted trial balance data, prepare a classified balance sheet dated December 31, 19X2.

alternate problems

PROBLEM 18-1A The Pelham Hardware Store is a retail business owned and operated by Barbara Katz. A completed worksheet for the firm is shown on page 347. This worksheet is for the year ended December 31, 19X3.

INSTRUCTIONS
1. From the completed worksheet, prepare an income statement for the year ended December 31, 19X3.
2. From the completed worksheet, prepare a balance sheet dated December 31, 19X3.
3. Journalize the necessary adjusting entries for the accounting period.
4. Journalize the entries to close all the revenue, cost, and expense balances and to account for the balances of the beginning and ending merchandise inventory.
5. Journalize the entry to transfer the net income or net loss for the period from the Revenue and Expense Summary account to the owner's capital account.
6. Journalize the entry to transfer the balance of the owner's drawing account to the owner's capital account.

PROBLEM 18-2A The Jackson Distributing Company is a wholesale business owned and operated by George Jackson. The firm sells canned food products to retail stores, schools, hospitals, and restaurants. The last three sections of its completed worksheet for the year ended December 31, 19X4 are shown on pages 348 and 349.

Note the manner in which numbers have been assigned to the accounts. This will give you a clue to the classification of the accounts. For instance, the Jackson Distributing Company classifies expenses into three groups: warehouse expenses, 600 series; selling expenses, 700 series; and administrative expenses, 800 series.

INSTRUCTIONS
1. From the worksheet, prepare a classified income statement for the year ended December 31, 19X4. (No departmental columns are required on this income statement.)
2. From the worksheet, prepare a classified balance sheet dated December 31, 19X4.

PELHAM HARDWARE STORE
Worksheet
Year Ended December 31, 19X3

ACCT. NO.	ACCOUNT NAME	TRIAL BALANCE DEBIT	TRIAL BALANCE CREDIT	ADJUSTMENTS DEBIT	ADJUSTMENTS CREDIT	ADJUSTED TRIAL BALANCE DEBIT	ADJUSTED TRIAL BALANCE CREDIT	INCOME STATEMENT DEBIT	INCOME STATEMENT CREDIT	BALANCE SHEET DEBIT	BALANCE SHEET CREDIT
101	Cash in Bank	4,156 00				4,156 00				4,156 00	
111	Accounts Receivable Control	14,860 00				14,860 00				14,860 00	
111A	Allowance for Bad Debts		40 50		(d)300 00		340 50				340 50
121	Merchandise Inventory	35,000 00				35,000 00		35,000 00	(e)36,000 00	(e)36,000 00	
131	Store Equipment	950 00				950 00				950 00	
131A	Acc. Depr.—Store Equipment		180 00		(a) 90 00		270 00				270 00
135	Delivery Truck	2,250 00				2,250 00				2,250 00	
135A	Acc Depr.—Delivery Truck		750 00		(b)375 00		1,125 00				1,125 00
141	Office Equipment	720 00				720 00				720 00	
141A	Acc. Depr.—Office Equipment		130 00		(c) 65 00		195 00				195 00
202	Accounts Payable Control		4,235 00				4,235 00				4,235 00
301	Barbara Katz, Capital		38,378 50				38,378 50				38,378 50
302	Barbara Katz, Drawing	600 00				600 00				600 00	
401	Sales		212,700 00				212,700 00		212,700 00		
501	Merchandise Purchases	108,375 00				108,375 00		108,375 00			
521	Rent Expense	3,600 00				3,600 00		3,600 00			
523	Sales Salaries Expense	36,500 00				36,500 00		36,500 00			
525	Store Supplies and Expense	583 00				583 00		583 00			
527	Depreciation Expense—Store Equip.			(a) 90 00		90 00		90 00			
531	Advertising Expense	2,275 00				2,275 00		2,275 00			
541	Delivery Wages Expense	22,400 00				22,400 00		22,400 00			
543	Delivery Truck Expense	760 00				760 00		760 00			
545	Depreciation Expense—Delivery Truck			(b)375 00		375 00		375 00			
551	Office Salaries Expense	23,000 00				23,000 00		23,000 00			
553	Office Supplies and Expense	385 00				385 00		385 00			
555	Depreciation Expense—Office Equip.			(c) 65 00		65 00		65 00			
561	Bad Debts Expense			(d)300 00		300 00		300 00			
	Totals	256,414 00	256,414 00	830 00	830 00	257,244 00	257,244 00	233,708 00	248,700 00	59,536 00	44,544 00
	Net Income for Year							14,992 00			14,992 00
								248,700 00	248,700 00	59,536 00	59,536 00

347

JACKSON DISTRIBUTING COMPANY
Worksheet (Partial)
Year Ended December 31, 19X4

Acct. No.	Account Name	Adjusted Trial Balance Dr.	Adjusted Trial Balance Cr.	Income Statement Dr.	Income Statement Cr.	Balance Sheet Dr.	Balance Sheet Cr.
101	Cash in Bank	6,775				6,775	
105	Petty Cash Fund	100				100	
111	Notes Receivable	2,700				2,700	
112	Accounts Receivable Control	13,625				13,625	
112A	Allowance for Bad Debts		275				275
113	Investments—Stocks and Bonds	10,000				10,000	
121	Merchandise Inventory	18,500		18,500	(f)16,000	(f)16,000	
126	Prepaid Insurance	1,800				1,800	
141	Office Equipment	4,400				4,400	
141A	Acc. Depr.—Office Equipment		1,550				1,550
143	Warehouse Buildings	32,000				32,000	
143A	Acc. Depr.—Warehouse Buildings		12,000				12,000
144	Warehouse Equipment	8,000				8,000	
144A	Acc. Depr.—Warehouse Equipment		3,000				3,000
145	Delivery Equipment	11,500				11,500	
145A	Acc. Depr.—Delivery Equipment		4,300				4,300
151	Land	9,000				9,000	
201	Notes Payable		4,800				4,800
202	Accounts Payable Control		10,500				10,500
203	Salaries and Wages Payable		2,350				2,350
221	Employee Ded.—FICA Tax		95				95
222	Employee Ded.—Inc. Tax Withheld		235				235
231	Sales Tax Payable		440				440
251	Mortgage Payable on Buildings		14,000				14,000
301	George Jackson, Capital		52,865				52,865
302	George Jackson, Drawing	7,200				7,200	
405	Sales		198,400		198,400		
451	Sales Ret. and Allow.	1,125		1,125			
453	Sales Discounts	325		325			
501	Merchandise Purchases	92,600		92,600			
506	Freight In	3,200		3,200			
509	Purchases Ret. and Allow.		830		830		

348

		Adjusted Trial Balance		Income Statement		Balance Sheet	
Acct. No.	Account Name	Dr.	Cr.	Dr.	Cr.	Dr.	Cr.
510	Purchases Discounts		350		350		
601	Warehouse Salaries and Wages Expense	7,400		7,400			
602	Warehouse Supplies and Expense	525		525			
603	Utilities Expense	1,400		1,400			
604	Building Repairs Expense	250		250			
605	Depr. Exp.—Warehouse Buildings and Equip.	2,000		2,000			
701	Sales Salaries Expense	34,800		34,800			
702	Sales Supplies and Expense	975		975			
703	Advertising Expense	4,150		4,150			
704	Travel and Entertainment Expense	760		760			
705	Sales Licenses Expense	300		300			
706	Delivery Expense	1,800		1,800			
707	Depr. Exp.—Delivery Equipment	3,000		3,000			
801	Office Salaries Expense	16,200		16,200			
802	Office Supplies and Expense	850		850			
803	Insurance Expense	1,200		1,200			
804	Contributions Expense	350		350			
805	Payroll Tax Expense	2,900		2,900			
806	Property Tax Expense	1,175		1,175			
807	Telephone Expense	1,200		1,200			
808	Depr. Exp.—Office Equipment	225		225			
809	Bad Debts Expense	1,075		1,075			
901	Interest Income		375		375		
951	Interest Expense	980		980			
	Totals	306,365	306,365	199,265	215,955	123,100	106,410
	Net Income for Year			16,690			16,690
				215,955	215,955	123,100	123,100

349

PART TWO
financial accounting: basic principles

UNIT 19
ACCOUNTING PRINCIPLES AND REPORTING STANDARDS

In Part One you learned how accounting procedures are used to properly record business transactions in a sole proprietorship. You also learned how to prepare an income statement and a balance sheet to reflect the net income or net loss of a business and to show its financial condition. In Part Two you will learn to apply generally accepted accounting principles so that information about a firm's operations and its financial position will be even more clearly reported and will meet the needs of owners, managers, creditors, investors, governmental units, and other interested parties.

The Need for Generally Accepted Accounting Principles

The use of proper accounting principles is especially important when the business entity is not a sole proprietorship but is instead a partnership or a corporation. Accounting principles and procedures for both types of entity are examined in Part Two. In this unit you will learn the basic assumptions, concepts, and modifying conventions underlying accounting principles. In addition, you will get an insight into how accounting principles are developed and put into use.

The various needs for reliable financial information can be satisfied only if there are rules, procedures, and principles of accounting that are generally accepted and used. If each company made up its own rules, there could be no basis for comparing the earnings and financial position of different firms. Even the records and reports of a particular company could not be compared for different periods unless accounting principles were applied consistently. In addition, users of the statements would probably be misinformed and misled.

The Sources of Generally Accepted Accounting Principles

Today's accounting principles were developed over a period of years in response to the changing needs for business reports. The process has worked very much like this. A particular procedure is devised by an accountant as a solution to a specific problem. Then other accountants find the procedure suitable for their problems and start to use it. Eventually, the procedure may become widely used and may be recognized by the professional accountants, accounting writers, and organizations that are responsible for developing generally accepted accounting principles.

Accounting principles, or standards, that have "authoritative support" in this country are developed through a cooperative effort between the private (business) sector and the public (governmental) sector of the economy. Currently, the main bodies involved are the Securities and Exchange Commission

(SEC) in the public sector and the Financial Accounting Standards Board (FASB) in the private sector.

The SEC In 1934 the Securities and Exchange Commission was set up to administer the Securities Act of 1933 and the Securities Exchange Act of 1934. Among other powers, the SEC has authority to define accounting terms and to prescribe accounting principles. The SEC also determines the form and content of accounting reports filed by companies under its jurisdiction. Since all publicly held companies (those whose stocks are traded in the organized securities markets) and all companies with 500 or more shareholders (owners) are subject to SEC regulations, the SEC is a dominant force in accounting. However, historically, the SEC has used these powers rather sparingly, preferring to let the accounting profession develop acceptable accounting principles and financial reporting standards.

Since 1937 the SEC has issued over 200 *Accounting Series Releases* (ASRs) giving its preferences or requirements on various accounting matters. Some, but not all, of these releases prescribe accounting principles to be followed. In one of the releases (ASR 150, issued in 1973), the SEC stated that it would view the pronouncements of the Financial Accounting Standards Board as having "authoritative support." In addition, the release said that generally the SEC would rely on the FASB's pronouncements as the proper accounting principles to be followed by companies under the SEC's jurisdiction. Even though the SEC does rely on the private sector to take the lead in developing accounting principles, the SEC is still responsible for setting the rules for the financial statements filed with it.

The FASB and Its Predecessors The Financial Accounting Standards Board is the result of efforts by the private sector, especially the American Institute of Certified Public Accountants (AICPA), to develop an organization responsible for formulating financial accounting standards. A brief review of the predecessors of the FASB will help you understand its structure and functions.

From 1939 through 1959, the American Institute of Certified Public Accountants issued a series of *Accounting Research Bulletins* through its Committee on Accounting Procedure. In these bulletins, the committee tried to give practical solutions to a number of current problems. While the opinions were not mandatory, most members of the AICPA followed them.

In 1959 the Committee on Accounting Procedure was disbanded. A new body, called the Accounting Principles Board (APB), was formed to issue authoritative statements on accounting principles. The APB existed until 1973 and issued 31 *Opinions*. If members of the AICPA did not follow these opinions, they were required to justify the principles they chose. If the principles could not be justified, members were subject to sanctions by the AICPA. These sanctions had the effect of discrediting members and included, at the extreme, expulsion. Obviously, the APB opinions had a major impact on accounting practices.

In addition to the opinions, the APB issued four *Statements,* which did not have the same binding effect as the opinions. Statement No. 4, issued in 1970, was entitled *Basic Concepts and Accounting Principles Underlying Financial*

Statements of Business Enterprises. This statement was a comprehensive listing of basic assumptions, postulates, and principles of accounting that were generally accepted at the time. One other publication of the AICPA should be mentioned. Since 1947 its research department has conducted annual surveys to determine the accounting and reporting practices of some 600 representative corporations. The results of each survey are provided in a publication called *Accounting Trends and Techniques in Published Corporate Annual Reports.*

In 1972 the AICPA, the American Accounting Association, the National Association of Accountants, the Financial Executives' Institute, and the Financial Analysts Federation jointly established the Financial Accounting Standards Board (FASB). The FASB is responsible for developing financial accounting standards and principles. By having groups other than the AICPA involved, the organizations that formed the FASB hoped that its rulings would have wide support in the economy.

The FASB receives its funding from the Financial Accounting Foundation. The organizations that set up the FASB choose the trustees of the Financial Accounting Foundation. These trustees are responsible for general oversight of the foundation and for securing financial support through contributions from the private sector. (No governmental funds are used.) More important, the trustees select the seven members of the Financial Accounting Standards Board. The board members, who develop and issue accounting pronouncements, are full-time employees with distinguished accounting backgrounds.

The authoritative pronouncements of the FASB are known as *Statements of Financial Accounting Standards.* Through 1979 the FASB had issued approximately 30 statements. As previously pointed out, the Securities and Exchange Commission recognizes these pronouncements as authoritative. The AICPA gives these statements additional support by requiring that its members make sure that the companies whose statements they audit follow the accounting and reporting standards specified in the FASB statements. Any departures from these standards must be justified. Thus, the pronouncements of the FASB automatically become generally accepted accounting principles.

One of the FASB's most important projects is called the "conceptual framework project." This project is expected to last for many years. Its aim is to develop a series of documents that will provide a theoretical framework for financial accounting and reporting. These documents will, among other things:

1. Define the objectives of accounting.
2. Identify users of financial reports and the uses made of these reports.
3. Develop the best possible definition of financial elements such as assets, liabilities, revenues, and expenses.
4. Establish the form and content of financial statements.
5. Develop measurement standards for income and other items.

The documents produced by the conceptual framework project should lead to more logical and concise accounting principles and reporting standards.

To some extent, the conceptual framework project reflects the suggestion by a number of accountants that accounting principles should be arrived at deductively. This means that rules should be based on observations of the general needs and uses of financial accounting. The following steps might be involved in the deductive process.

Step 1: Identify the users of financial reports.
Step 2: Define what uses are made of financial reports.
Step 3: Determine what kinds of accounting information best serve these uses.
Step 4: Define basic assumptions about the society in which business exists and about the nature of business activities and functions.
Step 5: Develop broad principles, standards, or guides for providing the information needed, based on the assumptions that have been made.
Step 6: Develop detailed rules and procedures for implementing the broad principles.

The first publication issued by the FASB in the conceptual framework project was *Objectives of Financial Statements,* which attempts to identify the users of general-purpose financial reports and to examine the uses of those statements.

Other Organizations

Other organizations have also played an important role in developing accounting principles. The Executive Committee of the American Accounting Association published "A Tentative Statement of Accounting Principles Underlying Corporate Financial Statements" in *The Accounting Review* for June 1936. The association has issued revised statements in 1941, 1948, and 1957, with several supplements between the last two revisions. In 1966 a special research committee of the association published a study entitled *A Statement of Basic Accounting Theory.* About half the members of the association are teachers of accounting, and a number of them have written textbooks and articles dealing with accounting principles. Thus, in a variety of ways, the association has been able to stimulate the acceptance of the principles it has developed and perfected throughout the years.

As early as 1900, the New York Stock Exchange began requiring corporations whose stock and bonds it listed to publish annual reports. Later, quarterly reports were required, and in 1933 the Exchange insisted upon independent audits for all corporations that applied to have their securities listed.

Government regulatory agencies have prescribed detailed systems of accounting for various public utilities, including the railroad industry and the electric power industry. Such agencies are more concerned with regulation, however, than with the development of accounting principles. Similarly, federal income tax requirements have had an impact on financial accounting even though it is not usually necessary that financial accounting practices and tax accounting practices be the same.

The Present Framework of Accounting Principles

The rules of accounting that you have already learned and that you will study in the remaining units of this textbook are embodied in what is known today as the *historical cost framework* of accounting. There are a number of ideas underlying this framework. Some accountants refer to all of these ideas as accounting *principles*; other accountants refer to them as accounting *concepts*. The exact term one uses for them is immaterial; the ideas involved are the important elements. For the convenience of discussion, we shall separate the ideas into three groups: (1) general principles or concepts, (2) underlying assumptions, and (3) modifying conventions.

General Principles or Concepts

In deciding how a transaction should be recorded and how its effects should be reported on the financial statements, accountants must keep in mind several basic accounting principles or concepts that serve as guides.

Cost Basis. Business transactions are, almost without exception, recorded on the basis of cost; that is, for an amount of money determined through dealings in the market between the business and outsiders. Assets are carried at cost until they are used. At that time, the cost (or an appropriate part of it) is charged against revenue. Cost is preferred to some possible alternatives, such as appraisal value, because cost, when determined in an "arm's length" transaction (a transaction with outsiders), is an objective, verifiable measure of economic value. In recent years, the cost principle has come under severe criticism. Many people have pointed out that the high rate of inflation throughout the world makes original costs meaningless. The FASB and the SEC have both recognized this problem by requiring certain large companies to disclose the impact of inflation on their financial statements.

Realization. Since accounting reports today focus on the measurement of income for the fiscal period, one critical problem is the determination of the period in which to record revenue and to report it on the income statement. Revenue represents the inflow of new assets resulting from the sale of goods or services. Thus, as a general rule, revenue is recognized when a sale is made or a service is provided to an outsider. It is at this time that revenue is *realized*—new assets are created in the form of money or in the form of claims against others. Thus accountants usually say that revenue should not be recognized until it has been realized.

The realization principle has been the subject of much criticism. For example, it is argued by many people, including some accountants, that if a company owns shares of stock in another corporation and those shares are traded on a stock exchange, the quoted market value of the stock should be recorded in the accounts and any increase in value should be recognized as income. However, under the realization principle, no income is recognized until the increase is realized through sale or exchange. (However, a decrease in value might be recognized under our present accounting principles.)

The argument usually given for insistence on the realization principle is that an increase in value might be eliminated by a later decrease in value before the asset is sold. Also, the realization principle ensures that objective, verifiable evidence underlies the accounting records.

There are a number of important exceptions to the general rule that revenue is recognized at the time of sale. One exception involves accounting for installment sales, which is discussed in Unit 22. In an installment sale, the difference between the selling price and the cost of the merchandise may be credited to a deferred income account at the time of sale. Part of the deferred income is recognized as revenue whenever a collection is made on the installment account receivable. This method should be used only when it is not possible to estimate losses from defaults on installments.

Another exception to the realization principle that is interesting, but seldom encountered, involves commodities for which there is an assured price and few costs to be incurred in getting the items to market. In this case, the revenue may be recognized at the time the commodity is produced. The best example of the recording of revenue when production is completed has historically been in connection with the mining of gold. For many years in this country, gold had a guaranteed market with few after-production costs. Thus the immediate recognition of revenue at the time of production was justified.

Still another, and more complex, exception to the realization principle for reporting revenue is the *percentage-of-completion basis* for measuring income on long-term construction contracts. For example, a contractor may build a bridge that requires three years to complete. It is not logical to wait until the bridge is entirely finished and report all income in the year of completion. Instead, each year a portion of the estimated profit may be recorded as earned. The profit recorded is based on the portion of estimated total costs incurred during that year.

Still other businesses, especially service firms such as those operated by physicians, attorneys, and accountants, record revenues only when cash is received. This procedure is followed for federal income tax purposes and because of high losses on the outstanding bills owed by patients or clients.

By far the greatest number of businesses follow the general rule that revenue is recognized at the time of sale.

Matching Costs With Revenue. If income is to be properly measured, revenues must be matched against the expired costs incurred in earning those revenues. This is sometimes referred to as matching effort and accomplishment. To achieve matching, the accountant seeks systematic, rational approaches for determining the period in which costs should be charged against revenues.

Some costs, such as manufacturing costs, can easily be identified with specific products. It is customary to treat these costs as inventory costs and charge them to cost of goods sold when the products are sold. Some other costs, such as office salaries, do not clearly benefit future periods and are charged as expenses when they are incurred. Still other costs benefit many future periods. The accountant therefore seeks to estimate the periods benefited and to charge the costs as expenses during the periods involved. For example, the cost of a store building is depreciated over its estimated useful life.

Many of the controversial questions in accounting involve determining the period or periods in which a cost should be charged as an expense.

The Accrual Basis. Inherent in the realization principle and the matching principle is the *accrual* principle. As you have already seen in Part One, sometimes a transaction occurs in one period but the cash involved is not received or paid out until a later period. Under the accrual principle, transactions are recorded in the period in which they occur, rather than in the period when the cash inflow or outflow takes place. For example, suppose that employees work in December but are not paid until January of the following year. Their earnings should be recorded as an expense in December, and the amount owed to them at the end of December should be shown as a liability on the December 31 balance sheet. Similarly, if a firm purchases office supplies in December and uses only a portion of them in that month, the cost should be allocated so that the part used is treated as an expense and the part still on hand is reported as an asset.

Consistency. The need for consistent application of a given accounting procedure from one period to the next in a particular company was mentioned previously. Any lack of consistency would result in financial reports that are not comparable with earlier reports and are therefore misleading.

However, the consistency rule does not mean that no changes in accounting principles or methods can be made. If the application of another accounting method would clearly give a fairer presentation of earnings or financial position, it is proper to change to the new method. Detailed rules have been developed for reporting the effects of the change so that statement users are completely informed.

Full Disclosure. It is necessary to disclose all information that might affect the statement user's interpretation of the profitability and financial position of a business. This must be done either in the actual financial statements or in footnotes to the statements. In recent years, there have been numerous lawsuits by statement users against certified public accountants and against companies issuing financial statements. The lawsuits have charged that the statements of these companies did not disclose facts that would have influenced investor decisions. As a result, accountants are very careful to include enough information so that the informed reader can obtain a complete and accurate picture. The financial reports issued by large companies usually include a thorough explanation of the accounting principles and methods that have been used in preparing the statements. The SEC has long maintained that the key element of financial reporting is full disclosure.

Underlying Assumptions

In applying the present body of accounting theory, accountants have used several assumptions about the economy, business enterprises, and business activities that make accounting principles meaningful. We will refer to these assumptions as: (1) the separate entity assumption, (2) the going concern assumption, (3) the stable monetary unit assumption, (4) the objectivity assumption, and (5) the periodicity of income assumption.

Separate Entity. Accounting records are kept for a particular business organization. It is assumed that the firm is an entity separate from other businesses and even separate from its owners and creditors. Transactions are recorded in relation to their effects on the business entity. Statements summarize these effects for owners, managers, and others. The fundamental accounting equation (assets equal liabilities plus owner's equity) expresses the concept concisely.

It is easy to understand the difference between the business entity and its owners in the case of a corporation such as General Motors because the accounting concept of separation agrees with the legal facts. However, the entity concept in accounting applies equally to a sole proprietorship or a partnership, even though owners of these types of business may be legally liable for all debts of the business and for actions carried out on behalf of the business.

Going Concern (**Continuity of Existence**). When periodic financial reports are prepared for a business, it is generally assumed that the firm is a going concern and will continue to operate indefinitely. This assumption permits carrying forward a portion of the cost of assets that will be used in future periods. If accountants could not assume that the activities of each business entity would continue into the future, they would have to try to estimate the current value of assets in case of immediate liquidation.

Stable Monetary Unit. Accounting records are kept in terms of money. It is convenient for accountants to assume that the value of money is stable or that changes in its value are not great enough to affect the recorded financial data. The costs of assets purchased many years ago are therefore added to the costs of assets recently purchased, and a total dollar amount is reported.

As a matter of fact, the value of money *has* changed substantially in recent years. For this reason, many people have questioned the validity of the assumption that money is a stable measure of value. However, until recently, accounting organizations have been reluctant to give effect to changes in the value of the dollar. In the past few years, research committees of the American Accounting Association and a research study sponsored by the American Institute of Certified Public Accountants have suggested that this problem should be recognized and perhaps be reflected in the financial statements or in supplementary statements. In addition, the FASB and the SEC have recommended that certain larger companies disclose the impact of price-level changes on their financial statements.

Objectivity. Users of financial reports have a right to expect that the statements are objective—that they are unbiased and fair to all parties. In addition, users are entitled to assume that the statements are based on verifiable evidence rather than on opinions. In accounting, this is taken to mean that two competent accountants who look at the same evidence would arrive at the same conclusion. However, the concepts of objectivity and verifiability do not eliminate the factor of judgment from accounting. For example, estimates of the useful lives of plant and equipment, selection of depreciation methods, and estimates of salvage value are all largely subjective decisions. These decisions affect the computation of depreciation expense for each fiscal period. Subjective judgments must also be made in many other cases.

Periodicity of Income. Accountants realize that the final and correct results of a firm's operations cannot actually be determined until the business has ceased to exist. Only when all assets have been sold and all liabilities settled is it known for certain what is left for the owners and whether they have experienced a gain or a loss. However, owners, managers, and others need some idea of operating results at short intervals. Accountants must therefore have techniques for interim determination of values so that financial statements can be prepared at least yearly for all businesses and as often as monthly for many firms. The accrual basis of accounting is widely used because it allows accountants to provide financial information for each year or other fiscal period.

If yearly statements (or statements prepared at other intervals during the life of the business) are to have validity, it must be assumed that the nature of a firm's activities is such that they do, in fact, lend themselves to reasonable periodic income determination.

Modifying Conventions

Although the basic accounting principles and underlying assumptions provide a means for analyzing each business transaction to determine its proper treatment in the accounts, a number of practical considerations have come to be accepted as limiting or modifying the application of the general principles. Among the most important of these "modifying conventions" are materiality, conservatism, and industry practice.

Materiality. *Materiality* concerns the significance of an item in relation to the particular situation of which it is a part. An item of a certain dollar amount might be material in a small company and thus would have to be disclosed. However, the same amount might not be significant in a larger firm and could therefore be combined with other figures or be presented in a different manner on the statements.

Although no hard-and-fast rules for judging materiality have been laid down, an item is usually compared with the firm's net income and with total owner's equity in deciding whether it is material. It is generally accepted that a deviation from normal accounting principles is permissible if the amount is immaterial. For example, a business that has sales of $10,000,000 a year might buy a small tool with a useful life of three years for $5. Practicality dictates that this item be charged as an expense rather than recorded as an asset and then depreciated. The amount of this transaction is immaterial in such a large business. Although this is an extreme example, it indicates the concept involved.

Conservatism. Accountants have long followed a doctrine of conservatism. Assets are understated rather than overstated if any question exists. Recognition of income is deferred until it is realized, and losses and expenses are recognized as soon as they occur.

Although this doctrine is still basically accepted by most accountants, an increasing number concede that undue conservatism in the present may make for a lack of conservatism in the future. For example, if too much of the cost of an asset is charged as depreciation expense in the present period, the firm's net income will be conservatively reported and the book value of the asset will be conservatively stated. But in later years, during which the asset still performs useful services, the depreciation expense will be understated and the net income will be correspondingly overstated, which is not conservative. Increased accuracy of valuation and timing has come to be more important to many accountants than the old-style conservatism.

Industry Practice. Sometimes accounting practices have become acceptable in certain industries although not generally acceptable in other industries. These exceptions are often created because of tax laws, regulatory requirements, or high risk involved. For example, in the public utility industry, it is customary to capitalize, as part of asset costs, all interest expense incurred on money borrowed to build a power plant during the period that the plant is being constructed. This practice is not generally followed in other industries. It has developed in the public utility industry because interest capitalization is permitted by regulatory agencies for rate-making purposes.

Another example of a unique practice is found in accounting for pension funds. There it is common to report investments in the stocks and bonds of corporations at the fair market value of the investments even though that value may be higher than the original cost. This procedure is prohibited for almost all other types of business investments under generally accepted accounting principles, although other businesses do record *declines* in the value of investments in marketable securities.

The Impact of Accounting Principles, Assumptions, and Modifying Conventions

Throughout the remainder of this book, you will find many references to accounting principles, assumptions, and modifying conventions. A thorough knowledge of these concepts will help you to understand how individual transactions are accounted for and why they are handled in a specific way. Often, the accountant is faced with new or unusual transactions that give rise to accounting questions that do not appear to have simple solutions. Almost invariably the accountant will fall back on the concepts discussed in this unit in deciding how to handle the transaction. Thus, an understanding of this unit is essential to an understanding of complex accounting issues.

principles and procedures summary

Some of the most important ideas underlying accounting are the cost principle, the realization principle, the matching principle, the accrual principle, the consistency principle, and the full disclosure principle. There are also certain assumptions that have an important influence on accounting. These are the separate entity assumption, the going concern assumption, the stable monetary unit assumption, the objectivity assumption, and the periodicity of income assumption.

In order to obtain greater uniformity and improve reliability, accounting organizations, especially the American Institute of Certified Public Accountants, have taken an active role in developing accounting principles. The ever-increasing interest of government, stockholders, analysts, creditors, and economists in financial reports ensures that there will be continuing progress in the search for accounting principles that will make the reports more meaningful and reliable. Never in the history of accounting has there been such a large and diverse group interested in accounting principles and financial reporting standards.

MANAGERIAL implications

Financial statements are of great importance in managerial decision making. Thus, management should understand the basic principles that underlie financial statements. Of particular importance in large firms is the need for comparability between statements so that the management of one firm can compare the results of its operations with those of its competitors. Comparisons of this type are made possible only by the existence of a body of basic accounting concepts, assumptions, principles, and standards that are applied by all businesses.

MANAGERIAL discussion questions

1. Why must management understand the principles and assumptions underlying a firm's financial statements?
2. How can the element of personal judgment, which is involved in such matters as selection of depreciation methods and estimates of salvage value and useful life, be minimized to preserve the objectivity of an accounting system?
3. Why might management argue that the historical cost framework should be abandoned?
4. The management of a firm suggests that all financial statements of debtors be stated at "the current value of assets." What objection do you see to this procedure? What benefits do you see in this procedure?
5. Suppose that you are employed as an accountant. An officer of the firm where you work asks why you use generally accepted accounting principles and where these rules come from. Explain the sources of generally accepted accounting principles and the reasons for using them.

application of principles

PROBLEM 19-1 The accounting treatment or statement presentation of various items is discussed below. The items pertain to different businesses and are unrelated.

INSTRUCTIONS Indicate in each case whether or not the item has been handled in accordance with generally accepted accounting principles. If so, indicate which of the basic concepts has been followed. If not, indicate which concept has been violated and tell how the item should have been recorded or presented.

1. The Ace Company manufactured some machinery for its own use at a cost of $45,000. The lowest bid price from an outsider was $52,000. The company records the machinery at $45,000.
2. At the beginning of the year 19X1, the Jordan Company bought a building for $100,000. At the end of 19X1, the building's value is appraised at $105,000. Since there is an increase in value, the company does not record depreciation on the building.
3. The balance sheet of the Marlow Shoe Store reports prepaid insurance at $300, the cash value of the policy on the date when the statement is prepared. The prepaid insurance consists of the last year of a three-year fire insurance policy that originally cost $1,500.
4. The assets listed in the accounting records of the Jiffy Laundry include the residence of Margaret Lee, the owner of the business.
5. On December 31, 19X1, the Accounts Receivable account of the Thompson Company includes $500 owed by Leroy Holt. Holt is in the county jail on charges of passing bad checks. The owner of the Thompson Company writes off the amount because he feels certain that the debt will not be paid, even though Holt insists that he will pay after he gets out of jail and obtains a job.
6. The machinery of the Precision Manufacturing Company has a depreciated cost of $60,000. However, the machinery could not be sold for more than $25,000 today. The owner thinks that the machinery should nevertheless be reported on the balance sheet at $60,000.
7. The Lakeside Hotel owns certain land purchased about 40 years ago for $10,000. Jane Johnson, the owner, thinks that since the price level today is almost three times the price level at the time the land was purchased, the balance of the account for this asset should be increased to reflect the price-level change.

PROBLEM 19-2 The income statement shown on page 364 was prepared by Roy Smith, the owner of Smith's Hardware Store, for the year ended December 31, 19X4. The business is a sole proprietorship. An accountant who looked at the income statement told Smith that it does not conform to generally accepted accounting principles.

INSTRUCTIONS Prepare an income statement in accordance with generally accepted accounting principles.

SMITH'S HARDWARE STORE
Income Statement
Year Ended December 31, 19X4

Cash Receipts From Customers		$265,000
Cost of Goods Sold		
Merchandise Inventory, Jan. 1	$ 24,000	
Payments to Suppliers	200,000	
	$224,000	
Less Merchandise Inventory, Dec. 31	30,000	
Cost of Goods Sold		194,000
Gross Profit on Sales		$ 71,000
Operating Expenses		
Salaries Expense	$ 42,000	
Taxes and Insurance Expense	6,000	
Repairs Expense	1,000	
Other Office Expenses	8,000	
Other Selling Expenses	10,000	
Interest Expense	3,000	
Total Expenses		70,000
Net Income From Operations		$ 1,000
Increase in Market Value of Equipment		3,200
Net Income for Year		$ 4,200

The following additional information is made available by Smith.
1. On December 31, 19X4, accounts receivable from customers total $15,500. On January 1, 19X4, the receivables totaled $20,000.
2. On December 31, 19X4, doubtful accounts receivable are estimated to be $1,700. On January 1, 19X4, accounts receivable amounting to $800 were expected to be uncollectible.
3. On December 31, 19X4, accounts payable owed to suppliers are $21,000. On January 1, 19X4, the outstanding accounts payable were $12,000.
4. Included in Salaries Expense is $6,000 that Smith withdrew for his personal use.
5. Included in Interest Expense is $1,200 that Smith withdrew as interest on his capital investment.
6. Miscellaneous repairs of $500 were charged to the Equipment account during the year. No new equipment was purchased during the year.
7. Smith explains that since the estimated value of his equipment has increased by $3,200 during the year, no depreciation expense was recorded. The equipment has a total cost of $33,000, and a total estimated useful life of 10 years with no salvage value.

alternate problems

PROBLEM 19-1A The accounting treatment or statement presentation of various items is discussed below. The items pertain to different businesses and are unrelated.

INSTRUCTIONS Indicate in each case whether or not the item has been handled in accordance with generally accepted accounting principles. If so, indicate which of the basic concepts has been followed. If not, indicate which concept has been violated and tell how the item should have been recorded or presented.

1. Included on the balance sheet of the Spotless Cleaning Shop is the personal automobile of Harry McKay, the owner.
2. The Lindsey Manufacturing Company makes furniture. The cost of a particular chair is $35. However, when the inventory figures are computed for the balance sheet, the amount used for this chair is $68, the normal selling price.
3. On December 1, 19X2, the Crystal Rock Company purchased some highly specialized, custom-made equipment for $400,000. Since the equipment is of no use to anyone else and has no resale value, it is shown on the December 31, 19X2, balance sheet at $1.
4. On December 31, 19X1, the Pennco Corporation valued its inventory according to an acceptable accounting method. On December 31, 19X2, the inventory was valued by a different but also acceptable method; and on December 31, 19X3, the inventory was valued by the method that was used in 19X1.
5. Each year the Arkansas Company values its investments in land at the current market price.
6. In 19X3 the Latex Corporation had sales of $8 million, all on credit. Statistics of the company for prior years show that bad debt losses are equal to about 1 percent of sales each year. However, the Latex Corporation charges off part of its accounts receivable as a bad debt loss only when a specific account is found to be uncollectible.
7. The Hermanson Company owns office equipment that was purchased seven years ago. It is still carried in the firm's accounting records at the original cost. No depreciation has ever been taken on the equipment.

PROBLEM 19-2A The income statement shown on page 366 was sent by Ann Kenzo, the owner of the Kenzo Clothing Store, to several of her creditors who had asked for financial statements. The business is a sole proprietorship. An accountant for one of the creditors looked over the income statement and found that it did not conform to generally accepted accounting principles.

INSTRUCTIONS Prepare an income statement for the Kenzo Clothing Store in accordance with generally accepted accounting principles.

KENZO CLOTHING STORE
Income Statement
Year Ended December 31, 19X6

Cash Collected From Customers		$460,000
Cost of Goods Sold		
Merchandise Inventory, Jan. 1	$ 50,000	
Payments to Creditors	290,000	
	$340,000	
Less Merchandise Inventory, Dec. 31	55,000	
Cost of Goods Sold		285,000
Gross Profit on Sales		$175,000
Expenses		
Salary to Owner	$ 18,000	
Salaries to Employees	54,000	
Depreciation Expense	17,500	
Income Tax of Owner	12,200	
Other Taxes of Business	8,800	
Advertising and Other Selling Expenses	15,000	
Repairs Expense	6,000	
Office Expenses	18,000	
Insurance Expense	3,000	
Interest Expense	8,000	
Utility and Telephone Expenses	6,000	
Legal and Audit Expenses	2,000	
Miscellaneous Expense	19,000	
Total Expenses		187,500
Net Loss From Operations		($ 12,500)
Increase in Appraised Value of Land During Year		10,000
Net Loss for Year		($ 2,500)

The following additional information was made available by Kenzo.

1. On December 31, 19X6, accounts receivable from customers total $22,000. On January 1, 19X6, the receivables totaled $18,000.
2. No effort has been made to charge off worthless accounts. An analysis shows that probably $1,900 of the accounts receivable on December 31, 19X6, will never be collected and that about $1,000 of the accounts receivable on January 1, 19X6, were worthless.
3. The beginning and ending inventories were valued at their estimated selling price. The actual cost of the ending inventory is estimated to be $33,000, and the actual cost of the beginning inventory was estimated at $30,000.
4. On December 31, 19X6, suppliers of merchandise are owed $29,000, while on January 1, 19X6, they were owed $26,000.

5. The owner paid herself a salary of $1,500 a month from the business's funds and charged this amount to an account called Salary to Owner.
6. The owner also withdrew cash from the firm's bank account in order to pay herself $5,000 interest on her capital investment. This amount was charged to Interest Expense.
7. A check for $12,200 to cover the owner's personal income tax for the previous year was issued from the firm's bank account.
8. Depreciation on assets was computed at 10 percent of the gross profit. An analysis of assets showed that the original cost of the equipment and fixtures totaled $40,000. Their estimated useful life is 10 years with no salvage value. The building had a cost of $75,000. Its useful life is expected to be 25 years with no salvage value.
9. Included in Repairs Expense was a $3,000 payment on December 22 for paving a new parking lot.
10. The increase in land value was based on an appraisal by a qualified appraiser.

UNIT 20

NOTES PAYABLE AND INTEREST

Checks are not the only kind of negotiable instruments used in financing and settling business transactions. Promissory notes, drafts, and trade acceptances are sometimes used, especially for larger transactions and for obligations that extend for a longer time than the typical open-account credit period.

Negotiable Instruments

The law dealing with negotiable instruments is a part of the Uniform Commercial Code, which has been adopted by the legislatures of all the states. This law specifies that in order to be negotiable, instruments must meet the following requirements.

1. They must be in writing and must be signed by the *maker* (or drawer).
2. They must contain an unconditional promise or order to pay a definite amount of money.
3. They must be payable either on demand or at a future time that is fixed or that can be determined.
4. They must be payable to the order of a specific person or to the bearer.
5. If addressed to a drawee, they must clearly name or identify that person.

The checks illustrated in Unit 8 were negotiable instruments because they met all these requirements. The promissory note discussed in this unit and shown below also meets all the requirements of negotiability.

$ 3,000.00   Greenville, S.C. March 18 19X2
Ninety days ———————— AFTER DATE We ———— PROMISE TO PAY
TO THE ORDER OF Columbia Equipment Company
Three Thousand and 00/100 ———————————————— DOLLARS
PAYABLE AT City National Bank
VALUE RECEIVED PLUS INTEREST AT THE RATE OF 10 PERCENT PER ANNUM
                                                    Style Clothing Store
NO. 1   DUE June 16, 19X2   Linda Hanson

Notes Payable

The note illustrated here is actually a promise by the Style Clothing Store to pay $3,000 to the Columbia Equipment Company in 90 days. It is negotiable because:

1. It is in writing and signed by the maker (Linda Hanson for the Style Clothing Store).
2. It is an unconditional promise for payment of a definite sum.
3. It is payable on a date that can be determined.
4. It is payable to a named party.

The note also specifies that interest at the rate of 10 percent a year must be paid at maturity. However, this provision is not needed for negotiability, and some notes may not show any interest.

The amount listed on the note ($3,000) is called the *principal, face value,* or *face amount*. The total that must be paid when the note becomes due (the principal plus the interest) is known as the *maturity value*.

The interest-bearing note illustrated on page 368 was created under the following circumstances.

Interest-Bearing Note Given in Purchase of an Asset

On March 18 the Style Clothing Store purchased furniture and store fixtures for $3,000 from the Columbia Equipment Company. Columbia agreed to allow the store 90 days in which to pay for the goods if the store would issue a promissory note bearing interest at 10 percent a year. Columbia worked out this arrangement so that the Style Clothing Store could pay for the goods later, but it also wanted as much legal protection as possible for itself.

Recording the Issuance of the Note.   The Style Clothing Store records this transaction on its books by making a general journal entry, as shown below. This entry involves a debit to Furniture and Fixtures and a credit to Notes Payable—Trade.

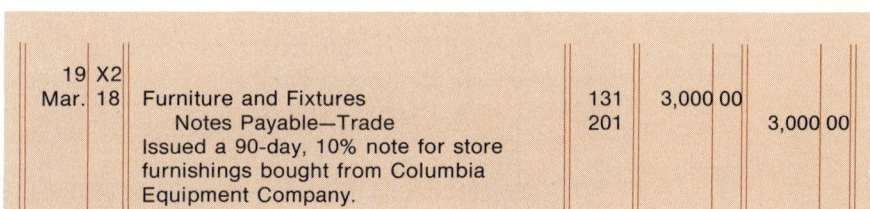

19 X2 Mar. 18	Furniture and Fixtures	131	3,000 00	
	Notes Payable—Trade	201		3,000 00
	Issued a 90-day, 10% note for store furnishings bought from Columbia Equipment Company.			

The Style Clothing Store makes no entry for the interest at the time the note is given. It will record the interest later.

Maturity Date.   When the note payable becomes due, the Columbia Equipment Company will ask its bank to collect the funds. Obviously, the Style Clothing Store needs to know when to expect the demand for payment so that it can have enough money on deposit to cover the amount due. It is therefore important to determine the maturity date of the note immediately. This is done by counting the number of days from the date the note was issued. (The issue date itself is not counted.) For example, a 30-day note issued on January 1 matures 30 days after January 1—on January 31. The following steps are needed to find the maturity date of a 30-day note issued on January 15.

1. Determine the number of days the note will run in the month of issue. In this case, it will run for 16 days in January (31 − 15).   <u>16 days</u>
2. Subtract the number of days the note will run in the month of issue from the total time for which the note was issued. In this case, the remaining time is 14 days (30 − 16). Thus, the note will run for 14 days in February.   <u>14 days</u>
3. Prove the computations. Add the previous figures together to see whether they equal the total period of the note in days: 16 days + 14 days = 30 days.   <u>30 days</u>

Since the note must run 14 days in February, the maturity date is February 14. More than two months may be involved if the time period of the note is longer. For example, the note issued on March 18 to the Columbia Equipment Company was for 90 days. The steps needed to find its maturity date are as follows.

1. Determine the number of days the note will run in the month of issue. In this case, it will run for 13 days in March (31 − 18).   <u>13 days</u>
2. Add to that number the total days in the following months until within one month of the total time period.
Number of days in April   <u>30 days</u>
Number of days in May   <u>31 days</u>

Total number of days from the issue date to the end of May   74 days
3. Determine the number of days the note will run in the month in which it matures. In this case, the note will run for 16 days in June (90 − 74).   <u>16 days</u>
4. Prove the computations. Add the previous figures together to see whether they equal the total period of the note in days: 74 days + 16 days = 90 days.   <u>90 days</u>

Thus the maturity date is June 16.

Sometimes the period of a note is described in months instead of days. For example, the note issued to the Columbia Equipment Company might have been for three months rather than for 90 days. When the period is defined in months, the maturity date is determined by counting ahead to the same date in the following month or months. Three months from March 18 is June 18, regardless of the fact that March and May have 31 days and April has 30. No count of the actual days is required. A three-month note dated March 31 would be due on July 1.

Interest   When a firm grants credit by accepting a promissory note, it must wait for payment and thus forego the use of money during the credit period. The party receiving the credit postpones payment and has the use of the money during the credit period. Since the use of money is a valuable privilege, creditors often charge debtors for it. *Interest* is the name given to the price charged for the use of money or credit.

The interest specified in a credit transaction is accounted for separately. It is recorded as interest expense or interest income, as the case may be. The following section describes how the interest on a note payable is computed and recorded.

Interest Calculations The amount of interest for any time period can be determined by using this formula.

$$\text{Interest} = \text{Principal} \times \text{Interest Rate} \times \text{Time in Years}$$

The time period is indicated by a fraction. The exact number of days the note is to run is generally used as the numerator, and 360 is used as the denominator. (Although most years have 365 days, 360 is used for convenience.) The 90-day term of the Style Clothing Store's note is therefore expressed as $\frac{90}{360}$ of a year.

If we apply the interest formula to the promissory note issued by the Style Clothing Store to the Columbia Equipment Company, we will find that the interest on $3,000 for 90 days at 10 percent is $75.

$$\text{Interest} = \$3{,}000 \times 0.10 \times \frac{90}{360}$$
$$\text{Interest} = \$75$$

Shortcut Interest Calculations If interest is at the rate of 6 percent and the credit period is 60 days, the 6 percent, 60-day method of calculation can be used. This method operates as follows.

$$\text{Interest} = \text{Principal} \times \text{Rate} \times \text{Time}$$
$$\text{Interest} = \text{Principal} \times 0.06 \times \frac{60}{360}$$
$$\text{Interest} = \text{Principal} \times \frac{6}{100} \times \frac{60}{360}$$
$$\text{Interest} = \text{Principal} \times \frac{\cancel{6}}{100} \times \frac{\cancel{60}}{\cancel{360}}$$
$$\text{Interest} = \text{Principal} \times \frac{1}{100} = \text{Principal} \times 0.01$$

A quick way of multiplying any figure by 0.01 is simply to move the decimal point two places to the left. Thus, interest at 6 percent for 60 days is computed by moving the decimal point two places to the left in the principal amount. For example, interest at 6 percent for 60 days on $800 is $8.

$$\$800 \times 0.01 = \$8$$

Since interest is in direct proportion to rate and time, the shortcut method can also be used to determine interest where the rate is more or less than 6 percent or where the time is more or less than 60 days. For example, interest at 6 percent for 75 days on $1,200 can be computed as follows.

$$\text{Interest at 6\% for 60 days } (0.01 \times \$1,200) = \$12$$

$$\text{Interest at 6\% for } \underline{15} \text{ days } \left(\frac{15}{60} = \frac{1}{4} \text{ of } \$12\right) = 3$$

$$\text{Interest at 6\% for } \underline{\underline{75}} \text{ days} = \underline{\underline{\$15}}$$

Similarly, interest at 8 percent for 60 days on $1,500 is determined as shown below.

$$\text{Interest at 6\% for 60 days } (0.01 \times \$1,500) = \$15$$

$$\text{Interest at } \underline{2}\% \text{ for 60 days } \left(\frac{2}{6} = \frac{1}{3} \times 15\right) = \underline{5}$$

$$\text{Interest at } \underline{\underline{8}}\% \text{ for 60 days} = \underline{\underline{\$20}}$$

Such calculations are shortcuts in some cases. However, in other cases, they may become so involved that it is simpler and more accurate to use the regular formula.

Payment of the Note and Interest

On the maturity date, June 16, the Style Clothing Store pays the Columbia Equipment Company the $3,000 principal of the note and the $75 interest. As explained in Unit 14, the Style Clothing Store uses the voucher system to control its payments. Thus, a voucher must be prepared and approved for payment of the note and the interest due. The voucher would then be entered in the voucher register. The effect of this entry is shown in general journal form below.

19 X2				
June 16	Notes Payable—Trade	201	3,000 00	
	Interest Expense	591	75 00	
	Accounts Payable	205		3,075 00

Next, the Style Clothing Store issues a check in settlement of the note and interest and enters it in the check register. The effect of this entry is illustrated in general journal form.

19 X2				
June 16	Accounts Payable	205	3,075 00	
	Cash in Bank	101		3,075 00

Partial Payment of a Note Payable

If only partial payment of a note is made at its maturity, the voucher and check are prepared for the amount that is being paid. This amount is endorsed on the note by the payee, or the old note is canceled and a new one is issued for the balance due.

If there is no agreement to the contrary, a noninterest-bearing note that is not paid at maturity begins at that time to bear interest at a rate established by law in each state. It continues to do so until it is paid.

Renewing a Note Payable

Sometimes the firm that has issued a note asks for an extension of time in which to pay. If the note payable is renewed for another period of time, no additional accounting entries are required. The usual accounting entry is made when the note is paid on the deferred maturity date.

Discounting a Note Payable at the Bank

Business firms often borrow money from banks and sign notes payable as evidence of the debts. Banks invariably charge interest on loans. Like the interest on the note payable to the Columbia Equipment Company, the interest on a bank loan may be paid at maturity. In many cases, however, the bank deducts the interest in advance, and the borrower receives only the difference between the face amount of the note and the interest on it to maturity. This arrangement, which is called *discounting*, works in the following way.

Suppose that the Style Clothing Store arranges to borrow $5,000 at 8 percent from its bank on April 30 by discounting a 30-day note payable. The interest is calculated according to the formula given earlier.

$$\text{Interest} = \$5,000 \times 0.08 \times \frac{30}{360}$$

$$\text{Interest} = \$33.33$$

The bank deducts the $33.33 interest from the $5,000 face amount of the note and the Style Clothing Store receives the difference, which is $4,966.67. The firm will probably have the bank deposit this amount in its checking account.

Recording the Issuance of the Note

The effect of this transaction is shown below in general journal form. Notes Payable—Bank is credited because the accountant wishes to distinguish notes payable to banks from notes payable to businesses. Cash in Bank is debited for the amount of cash actually received, and Interest Expense is debited for the amount of interest that was deducted.

19 X2				
Apr. 30	Cash in Bank	101	4,966 67	
	Interest Expense	591	33 33	
	Notes Payable—Bank	203		5,000 00

Since the transaction involves a cash receipt, it would normally be entered in the cash receipts journal. The entry presents a problem, however, because of the debit to Interest Expense. The typical cash receipts journal is not set up to handle such a debit conveniently. The transaction can nevertheless be recorded in the cash receipts journal if the accountant enters the amount of interest expense in the Other Accounts Credit section as a circled figure to indicate that it is a debit. This entry is shown below.

CASH RECEIPTS JOURNAL for Month of April 19X2   Page 4

DATE	EXPLANATION	ACCOUNTS RECEIVABLE CR. 111	SALES CR. 401	OTHER ACCOUNTS CREDIT			CASH IN BANK DR. 101
		✓		ACCOUNT TITLE	POST. REF.	AMOUNT	
Apr. 30	Discounted note			Notes Payable—Bank	203	5,000 00	
				Interest Expense	591	⟨33 33⟩	4,966 67

Notice that the entry requires two lines in the cash receipts journal, one to credit Notes Payable—Bank and the other to debit Interest Expense and Cash in Bank. Other techniques can also be used for recording this transaction.

Paying the Note The maturity date of the Style Clothing Store's note is May 30. (Since it is dated April 30, there are no days to run in April.) The firm prepares a voucher for $5,000 on May 30 to pay the note. The accountant, Gloria Thompson, debits Notes Payable—Bank and credits Accounts Payable in the voucher register entry. Thompson then issues a check for $5,000 and makes an entry in the check register, debiting Accounts Payable and crediting Cash in Bank. Since the interest was deducted in advance by the bank and was recorded at the time the note was issued, no further entry for it is required. Only the face amount of the note is paid at maturity.

Notes Payable Register If many notes payable are issued, it may be convenient to keep a record of the details by maintaining a *notes payable register.* This record shows the important information about each note payable on a single line. The information includes the date of the note, the payee, where the note is payable, the time it is to run, its maturity date, its face amount, and the interest rate and amounts of interest, if any. At the end of each accounting period, a *schedule of notes payable* can be prepared by listing the unpaid notes that appear in the notes payable register. The total must agree with the total of the Notes Payable account(s) in the general ledger, as though proving to a control account.

The two notes issued in March by the Style Clothing Store are entered in a notes payable register as illustrated below.

NOTES PAYABLE REGISTER

DATE OF ENTRY	PAYEE	WHERE PAYABLE	DATE OF NOTE	TIME TO RUN
19 X2			19 X2	
Mar. 18	Columbia Equipment Co.	City National Bank	Mar. 18	90 days
Apr. 30	City National Bank	City National Bank	Apr. 30	30 days

In the form shown here, the notes payable register is a memorandum record. However, it can also be designed for use as a book of original entry from which postings are made to the ledger accounts. If the notes payable register is used in this way, the entry for the issuance of a note that is recorded in the register takes the place of a journal entry. The posting of the transaction is done directly from the register. The Style Clothing Store does not have enough notes payable to use the register as a book of original entry.

Notes Payable and Interest Expense on the Statements

Notes payable represent obligations of the business. Thus they appear on the balance sheet as liabilities. As explained earlier, the Style Clothing Store has set up separate accounts called Notes Payable—Trade and Notes Payable—Bank. Both of these accounts are shown on the balance sheet. Notes due within one year are usually classified as current liabilities, and notes due in more than one year are classified as long-term liabilities. The notes presented in this unit are current liabilities. Some special aspects of long-term notes are discussed in Unit 34.

Interest expense usually appears on the income statement as a nonoperating expense. It is listed under Other Expense, and it is deducted from the figure for Net Income From Operations, as shown below.

Net Income From Operations	$9,675.25
Other Expense	
Interest Expense	125.30
Net Income	$9,549.95

principles and procedures summary

Notes payable can be noninterest-bearing, but usually they do bear interest. When a note is given for the purchase of an asset, the amount is credited to a notes payable account and debited to an asset account. At the maturity date, a voucher is prepared for payment of the note and entered in the voucher register. Only the principal is debited to the Notes Payable account when the

Page 1

	MATURITY DATE												FACE AMOUNT OF NOTE	INTEREST		DATE PAID	REMARKS
YEAR	J	F	M	A	M	J	J	A	S	O	N	D		RATE	AMOUNT		
19X2						16							3,000 00	10%	75 00		
19X2			30										5,000 00	8%	33 33		Discounted

voucher is issued. The interest is debited to the Interest Expense account, and the entire amount to be paid—principal and interest—is credited to Accounts Payable. When the check is issued, Accounts Payable is debited and Cash in Bank is credited in the check register.

When money is borrowed from a bank and a note is given to the bank, the bank may deduct the interest in advance (discount the note), giving the borrower only the difference between the principal of the note and the interest on it. In this case, Notes Payable—Bank is credited for the principal, Interest Expense is debited for the interest, and Cash in Bank is debited for the difference (the cash actually received from the bank). This entry is made when the note is issued.

If a business issues many notes, it may keep a notes payable register. Notes payable appear as a liability on the balance sheet. Interest expense is usually classified as a nonoperating expense on the income statement.

MANAGERIAL implications

Managers must be aware of opportunities to finance operations through the use of short-term notes payable that temporarily provide cash. Sources of such funds include suppliers (through credit extension) and banks. For funds secured through bank loans, the discounting of notes payable results in a higher interest rate than that shown on the face of each note. Since the interest is deducted in advance, the borrower does not have the use of all the funds indicated on the face of the note.

Managers must also be familiar with the Uniform Commercial Code if they are to understand the rights and obligations involved in notes payable commitments.

MANAGERIAL discussion questions

1. Why might managers use outside sources of funds for their business operations? How do they acquire these funds?
2. Of what benefit to managers is the notes payable register?
3. Suppose that you work for a company that often discounts notes payable at the bank. The bank's current discount rate is 10 percent. A member of your company's board of directors suggests that the effective interest rate is more than 10 percent because the company does not have the use of the amount of money shown on the face of the note that is being discounted. Comment on this argument.

application of principles

PROBLEM 20-1
1. Compute the total interest on each of the following notes, using the interest formula method. Show all computations.
   a. $680 at 7 percent for 90 days.
   b. $1,856.80 at 8 percent for 6 months.
2. Compute the interest on each of the following notes, using the 6 percent, 60-day method. Show all computations.
   a. $800 at 6 percent for 90 days.
   b. $2,908.50 at 6 percent for 60 days.
   c. $7,850 at 5 percent for 120 days.
3. Compute the discount on the following noninterest-bearing notes. Show all computations.
   a. $8,000 discounted at 8 percent for 60 days.
   b. $4,500 discounted at 10 percent for 40 days.

PROBLEM 20-2 Carlos Montez operates a business that makes large purchases of equipment. As a result, there are numerous transactions involving notes payable. Montez maintains a notes payable register to help him keep track of due dates and interest payments. Selected accounts used by the business are given below. Transactions involving notes payable that took place during the month of July 19X1 are given on the next page.

INSTRUCTIONS
1. Enter the following as notes of July 1, 19X1, in a notes payable register with columns as shown on pages 374 and 375 of the text. Compute and enter the maturity date and interest, if any, when recording each note.
   a. Note issued to Sadowski Equipment Company on May 24, 19X1, for $7,000, payable in two months without interest. (This note and all others in this problem are payable at the First State Bank.)
   b. Note issued to Mallard Distributors on May 28, 19X1, for $9,000, due in 60 days with interest at 8 percent.
2. Analyze each of the July transactions, and make the necessary entry or entries. Use the following journals and registers. (Keep in mind that this firm uses the notes payable register as a memorandum record and not as a book of original entry.)
   a. A general journal.
   b. The notes payable register listed above.
   c. A cash receipts journal with columns as illustrated on page 374.
   d. A voucher register with columns as illustrated in Unit 14.

ACCOUNTS

101 Cash in Bank	201 Notes Payable—Trade
131 Factory Equipment	203 Notes Payable—Bank
133 Delivery Equipment	205 Accounts Payable
141 Land	591 Interest Expense

TRANSACTIONS FOR JULY 19X1

July 9   Purchased factory equipment from the Wayne Company and issued a note for $12,000 for three months with interest at 7 percent. (Enter in the general journal and the notes payable register.)

16   Purchased delivery equipment from West Auto Company; Invoice 888, dated July 16, 19X1. The initial payment of $4,000 was authorized by Voucher 7-10 and was made by Check 701. A $4,000 note due in six months with interest at 7 percent was given to cover the balance of the purchase price. (Enter Voucher 7-10 in the voucher register.)

18   Issued a 90-day, 8 percent note for $5,000 to Bay Realty in payment for land to be used by the company.

23   A 50-day note for $1,500, bearing interest at 9 percent, was given to the Able Manufacturing Company for factory equipment that was previously purchased on credit and recorded as Voucher 6-3.

24   Renewed a $7,000 note dated May 24 that is owed to the Sadowski Equipment Company and was due today. Gave a new note for 60 days with interest at 8 percent. (No journal entry is required. Make a notation in the notes payable register.)

26   Discounted an $8,000 note at the First State Bank. The bank deducted an 8 percent discount charge for the 120-day loan.

28   Paid half of the note due Mallard Distributors today and all of the interest owed by Check 745 for $4,620, authorized by Voucher 7-34. Issued a new note for $4,500 payable in 60 days with interest at 8 percent. (Enter Voucher 7-34 in the voucher register. No entry is required in the general journal. Make a notation of the cash payment and the renewal note opposite the original note in the Remarks column of the notes payable register. Then enter the new note.)

AlTERNATE pRObLEMS

PROBLEM 20-1A

1. Compute the total interest on each of the following notes, using the interest formula method. Show all computations.
    a. $800 at 9 percent for 90 days.
    b. $1,400 at 7 percent for 4 months.
2. Compute the interest on each of the following notes, using the 6 percent, 60-day method. Show all computations.
    a. $400 at 6 percent for 90 days.
    b. $812.50 at 7 percent for 60 days.
    c. $1,450.56 at 5 percent for 30 days.
3. Compute the discount on the following noninterest-bearing notes. Show all computations.
    a. $7,200 discounted at 8 percent for 6 months.
    b. $3,456 discounted at 7 percent for 45 days.

PROBLEM 20-2A East and West is a chain of dry-cleaning stores owned and operated by Linda James and Sam Clay. The owners have decided to start a program of modernization and expansion to increase efficiency, reduce operating costs, and increase sales. Since the funds for this program will come partly from their own cash reserves but mostly from notes payable, the partners have decided to set up a notes payable register. This memorandum record will help them maintain control over the due dates and interest payments. Selected accounts used by the business are given below. Transactions involving notes payable that took place during the month of December 19X1 are listed below and on the next page.

INSTRUCTIONS
1. Enter the following notes as of December 1, 19X1, in a notes payable register with columns as shown on pages 374 and 375 of the text. Compute and enter the maturity date and interest, if any, when recording each note.
    a. Note issued to the Jackson Equipment Company on November 1, 19X1, for $5,000, due in 45 days without interest. (This note and all others in this problem are payable at the First National Bank.)
    b. Note issued to the Jackson Equipment Company on November 1, 19X1, for $10,000, due in 60 days with interest at 9 percent.
2. Analyze each of the December transactions, and make the necessary entry or entries. Use the following journals and registers. (Keep in mind that this firm uses the notes payable register as a memorandum record and not as a book of original entry.)
    a. A general journal.
    b. The notes payable register listed above.
    c. A cash receipts journal with columns as illustrated in this unit.
    d. A voucher register with columns as illustrated in Unit 14.

ACCOUNTS

101	Cash in Bank	201	Notes Payable—Trade
131	Cleaning Equipment	203	Notes Payable—Bank
133	Delivery Equipment	205	Accounts Payable
141	Land	591	Interest Expense

TRANSACTIONS FOR DECEMBER 19X1

Dec. 1 Purchased additional cleaning equipment from the Jackson Equipment Company, and issued a note for $8,000 for 90 days with interest at 9 percent. (Enter in the general journal and the notes payable register.)

8 Purchased a small delivery truck from the Auto-Truck Sales Company, Invoice 857, dated December 8, 19X1. The initial payment of $3,000 was authorized by Voucher 12-10 and was made by Check 316 on this date. A $3,000 note due in six months with interest at 8 percent was given to cover the balance of the purchase price. (Enter Voucher 12-10 in the voucher register.)

10 Issued a 60-day, 6 percent note for $4,500 to Builders, Inc., in payment for land to be used as a parking area for one of the dry-cleaning stores.

11 Issued a 30-day note for $1,250 with interest at 8 percent to the Cleaners Supply Company in order to obtain an extension of credit on an overdue account payable. The account payable was previously recorded as Voucher 11-26.

16 Renewed a $5,000 note dated November 1, which was due today. The note was owed to the Jackson Equipment Company. Gave a new note for 30 days with interest at 9 percent. (No journal entry is required. Make a notation in the notes payable register.)

18 Borrowed $5,000 from the First National Bank on a 120-day note with interest at 7 percent. The note was discounted at the bank.

20 Purchased two dry-cleaning machines from the Automatic Cleaning Equipment Company and issued a $10,000 90-day note with interest at 9 percent.

30 Borrowed $5,000 from the First National Bank for 60 days with interest at 9 percent payable at maturity.

31 Paid half of the note due the Jackson Equipment Company today and the interest, by Check 331 for $5,150. The payment was authorized by Voucher 12-25. Issued a new note for $5,000 payable in 45 days with interest at 9 percent. (No entry is required in the general journal. Enter Voucher 12-25 in the voucher register. Make a notation of the cash payment and the renewal note opposite the original note in the Remarks column of the notes payable register. Then enter the new note.)

UNIT 21

NOTES RECEIVABLE ANd dRAFTS

Some firms accept promissory notes from customers. For example, a customer may be allowed to use a promissory note to finance a purchase of goods. A note that a firm obtains with a customer's written promise to pay in the future is called a note receivable.

Notes Receivable

A note receivable is usually interest-bearing. However, it can be noninterest-bearing if the parties involved prefer it that way. The methods used to determine maturity dates and interest due on notes receivable are the same as those used for notes payable, which were explained in the previous unit. Of course, the entries needed to record notes receivable on a firm's books are different from those used to record notes payable.

A firm may accept a note receivable from a customer at the time of a sale or when extending credit on a past-due account. The procedures for handling notes receivable can be understood from the following typical example.

Noninterest-Bearing Note Received

Suppose that John Dow has an overdue balance of $300 in his account with the Style Clothing Store. On April 8, 19X2, Dow offers to give the firm a 30-day, noninterest-bearing note to obtain an extension of time in which to pay. The Style Clothing Store agrees to this arrangement because the note provides stronger evidence of the debt in case legal action becomes necessary.

Receipt of the Note

The Style Clothing Store records the receipt of Dow's note in the general journal, as shown below. Notice that a new asset account called Notes Receivable is debited for $300, and Accounts Receivable/John Dow is credited for $300.

19X2				
Apr. 8	Notes Receivable	109	300 00	
	Accounts Receivable/John Dow	111/✓		300 00
	Received a 30-day, noninterest-bearing note in settlement of account.			

381

The credit part of the entry is recorded as Accounts Receivable/John Dow because it must be posted in two places.

1. The Accounts Receivable Control account must be credited in the general ledger.
2. The account with John Dow must be credited in the accounts receivable subsidiary ledger.

As a result of this *double-posting procedure,* the total of the balances in the subsidiary ledger will remain equal to the balance of the Accounts Receivable Control account in the general ledger.

Maturity Date Dow's note, which was issued on April 8, matures on May 8. The maturity date is computed as follows.

Days the note will run in April: 30 − 8 = 22	22 days
Days to maturity in May: 30 − 22 = 8	8 days
Total period of the note	30 days

Collection of the Note When Dow pays the note at maturity, an entry will be made in the cash receipts journal. This entry will consist of a debit to Cash in Bank and a credit to Notes Receivable. Dow's note will then be marked "Paid" and returned to him.

Interest-Bearing Note Received

Most firms are willing to meet customers more than halfway to make sales and to retain goodwill. However, a customer who does not settle a bill within the credit period originally agreed upon can usually expect to pay interest on the amount owed in order to receive an extension of credit. Thus, promissory notes issued under such conditions are normally interest-bearing. Assume that the Style Clothing Store agrees to accept a 60-day, 8 percent note for $400 from Alice Morgan to cover her past-due account. The note is dated April 14, 19X2.

Receipt of the Note When the firm receives the note, Gloria Thompson, the accountant, makes an entry in the general journal. This entry involves a debit to Notes Receivable for $400 and a credit to Accounts Receivable/Alice Morgan for $400.

Maturity Date The maturity date of Morgan's note is June 13. This date is determined as shown below.

Days the note will run in April: 30 − 14 = 16	16 days
Days the note will run in May	31 days
Total days to the end of May	47 days
Days in June to maturity: 60 − 47 = 13	13 days
Total period of the note	60 days

Calculation of Interest The interest on $400 for 60 days at 8 percent is computed as follows by using the standard interest formula.

$$\text{Interest} = \$400 \times 0.08 \times \frac{60}{360}$$

$$\text{Interest} = \$5.33$$

Collection of the Note Morgan's payment of the note on the maturity date should include the $400 face amount of the note plus $5.33 interest. Thus, the maturity value of the note is $405.33. The Style Clothing Store records the collection of the note in the cash receipts journal. This entry contains a debit to Cash in Bank for the total amount, a credit to Notes Receivable for $400, and a credit to Interest Earned for $5.33, as illustrated below. Notice that the entry requires two lines in the cash receipts journal to handle the credits to Notes Receivable and Interest Earned.

CASH RECEIPTS JOURNAL for Month of June 19X2   Page 6

DATE	EXPLANATION	✓	ACCOUNTS RECEIVABLE CR. 111	SALES CR. 401	OTHER ACCOUNTS CREDIT ACCOUNT TITLE	POST. REF.	AMOUNT	CASH IN BANK DR. 101
June 13	Collection of Alice Morgan's note				Notes Receivable Interest Earned	109 491	400 00 5 33	405 33

Partial Collection of a Note Suppose that Alice Morgan offers to pay half her note if the Style Clothing Store will renew the balance for an additional 30 days at 8 percent interest. Ordinarily, any payment made on a note is applied first to the interest due. The remaining amount is then applied to the principal owed. In this case, Morgan is paying the interest to maturity of the original note, $5.33, plus half the principal of the note, $200, for a total of $205.33. The entry to record the $205.33 is made in the cash receipts journal. It consists of a debit to Cash in Bank for the total, a credit to Notes Receivable for $200, and a credit to Interest Earned for $5.33.

CASH RECEIPTS JOURNAL for Month of June 19X2   Page 6

DATE	EXPLANATION	✓	ACCOUNTS RECEIVABLE CR. 111	SALES CR. 401	OTHER ACCOUNTS CREDIT ACCOUNT TITLE	POST. REF.	AMOUNT	CASH IN BANK DR. 101
June 13	Collection of part of Alice Morgan's note				Notes Receivable Interest Earned	109 491	200 00 5 33	205 33

The original note may be endorsed or receipted in part by the Style Clothing Store to reflect the partial payment. Or the firm may cancel the first note and obtain a new note for the remaining balance from Alice Morgan.

Note Not Collected at Maturity

If a note is not paid at maturity, the note is said to be *dishonored*. It is not proper to carry the amount of a dishonored note in the Notes Receivable account. Suppose that Alice Morgan dishonors the note that she issued to the Style Clothing Store. The firm must transfer the balance that she owes so that it is again a part of accounts receivable. This is done by making the general journal entry shown below. Notice that both the Accounts Receivable Control account in the general ledger and Morgan's account in the accounts receivable ledger must be debited. Since Morgan now owes the original balance of $400 plus $5.33 interest on the note, each of these accounts is debited for $405.33. The offsetting credits are to Notes Receivable for the face amount of the note ($400) and to Interest Earned for the interest ($5.33).

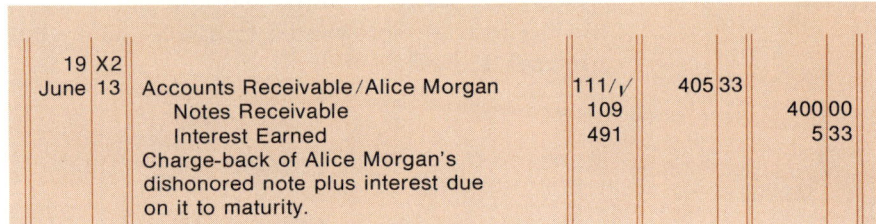

After an interest-bearing note is dishonored, interest continues to run on the note. The interest charged is at a rate specified by law, which in most cases is higher than the original rate shown on the note.

Notes Received at the Time of Sale

The notes from Dow and Morgan were obtained when past-due accounts were extended. The Style Clothing Store does not engage in a type of business in which notes are ordinarily received at the time of sale. If the firm receives an occasional note when a sale is made, the transaction is recorded in the general journal as follows.

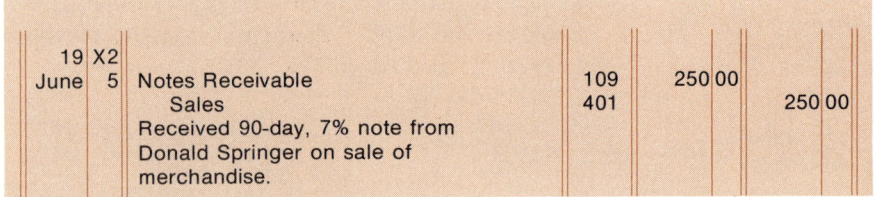

If it is common for a business to receive notes from customers at the time of sale, the accountant will provide a special column in the sales journal for debiting Notes Receivable. In this way, the total of the notes can be posted to the general ledger in one amount at the end of each month.

Discounting a Note Receivable

One of the advantages of a note receivable over an open account is that the holder of the note can borrow on it by discounting it at a bank. The bank takes the note and charges interest on its maturity value at a specified rate for the number of days remaining until maturity. The bank deducts this *discount charge* in advance, and the seller receives the *net proceeds* (the maturity value less the discount charge). The bank usually credits the net proceeds to the firm's checking account.

Noninterest-Bearing Note Discounted

Suppose that the Style Clothing Store has to raise cash to meet an obligation at the end of April. The owners decide to discount a 60-day noninterest-bearing note receivable for $500 that the firm obtained from Peter Ross on April 3. The note is payable on June 2. The Style Clothing Store turns the note over to the City National Bank for discounting on April 18. The bank's discount rate is 9 percent. This transaction must be examined carefully because of new elements involved.

Review of the Record Prior to Discounting

The Style Clothing Store received the note on April 3. The amount of the note ($500) was debited to the asset account Notes Receivable in a general journal entry. Thompson then determined the maturity date, which is June 2.

Calculating the Discount and the Proceeds

The method used to determine the discount and the proceeds on the note receivable is similar to that described for a discounted note payable. The steps are as follows.

1. Determine the maturity value of the note. Since the Style Clothing Store's note is noninterest-bearing, its maturity value is the same as its face amount—$500.
2. Determine the number of days in the discount period (the number of days from the discount date to the maturity date). This number can be computed by working backward from the maturity date to the discount date.

Days the note will run in June to maturity	2 days
Days the note will run in May	31 days
Days the note will run in April: 30 − 18 = 12	12 days
Total discount period	45 days

3. Determine the amount of discount to be charged by the bank. This is found by applying the regular interest formula (Interest = Principal × Rate × Time) as shown below. Notice that the time used is the discount period of 45 days.

    Discount = Maturity Value × Discount Rate × Discount Period

    Discount = $500 × 0.09 × $\frac{45}{360}$

    Discount = $5.63
4. Determine the proceeds—the amount to be received from the bank. This amount is the maturity value of the note less the amount of the discount. $500 − $5.63 = $494.37

Recording the Discounting of the Note

When the computations are completed, the Style Clothing Store records the discounting of the note in its cash receipts journal, as shown in the following illustration.

CASH RECEIPTS JOURNAL for Month of April 19X2   Page 4

DATE	EXPLANATION	ACCOUNTS RECEIVABLE ✓ CR. 111	SALES CR. 401	OTHER ACCOUNTS CREDIT — ACCOUNT TITLE	POST. REF.	AMOUNT	CASH IN BANK DR. 101
Apr. 18	Discounted Peter Ross's note			Notes Receivable Discounted Interest Expense	110 591	500 00 ⟨5 63⟩	494 37

Notice that two debits are involved—one to Cash in Bank for the proceeds ($494.37) and one to Interest Expense for the amount of the discount ($5.63). The debit to Interest Expense is recorded in the cash receipts journal by making a circled entry in the Other Accounts Credit column. Also notice that the principal of the note ($500) is credited to a new account called Notes Receivable Discounted rather than to the Notes Receivable account. This credit entry in Notes Receivable Discounted offsets the amount carried as an asset in the Notes Receivable account.

Notes Receivable Discounted—a Contingent Liability

When a note receivable is discounted, it must be endorsed. If the maker of the note does not pay it at maturity, the holder (the bank) can then obtain payment from the endorser. Hence, the endorser (in this case, the Style Clothing Store) has a possible, or *contingent,* liability. This fact was recorded on the books by crediting Notes Receivable Discounted. On the balance sheet, the balance of Notes Receivable Discounted is deducted from the balance of Notes Receivable. The difference represents the notes receivable still held, which amount to $750 for the Style Clothing Store.

Notes Receivable		$1,250
Less Notes Receivable Discounted	500	$750

Discounted Noninterest-Bearing Note Paid at Maturity

At the maturity date, the holder of the discounted note presents it to the maker for payment. If Peter Ross pays the note when the bank presents it to him, the Style Clothing Store has no further contingent liability. At that time, the firm makes the following general journal entry to remove the liability.

19X2 June	2	Notes Receivable Discounted Notes Receivable Closed out the asset and the contingent liability upon payment by Peter Ross of his note, which we had discounted at the bank.	110 109	500 00	500 00

Discounted Noninterest-Bearing Note Dishonored at Maturity

If Ross dishonors his note by failing to pay it at maturity, the bank may file a formal protest through a notary public. The Style Clothing Store then has to pay the bank the maturity value of the note plus the protest fee charged by the notary public. (Banks often deduct this amount from the firm's checking account and send a debit memorandum with the dishonored note and the protest form.) Assuming that the protest fee is $3 in this case, the resulting entry is a debit to Accounts Receivable/Peter Ross for $503 and a credit to Cash in Bank for $503. Notice that the total of the maturity value and the protest fee ($503)—not merely the amount due on the dishonored note—is charged to the Accounts Receivable Control account in the general ledger and the customer's account in the subsidiary ledger.

One more entry is required to complete the record of this transaction. By paying the dishonored note, the Style Clothing Store has removed the contingent liability that was set up when the note was discounted. To eliminate the liability from the firm's books, an entry must be made in the general journal debiting Notes Receivable Discounted and crediting Notes Receivable.

After paying the dishonored note, the Style Clothing Store would probably turn the note over to an attorney for collection.

Interest-Bearing Note Discounted

The owners of the Style Clothing Store now decide to increase the firm's available cash by discounting a note received from Lois Norman on April 17. The principal is $600, the note runs for 60 days, and the interest rate is 7 percent. The maturity date of the note is June 16.

Review of the Record Prior to Discounting

On April 17, when the Style Clothing Store obtained the note, Thompson debited the Notes Receivable account to record the increase in that asset and credited Accounts Receivable/Lois Norman.

Calculating the Discount

On May 2, the Style Clothing Store arranges to discount Norman's note at the bank at 8 percent. The discount and the proceeds on the note are computed as shown below.

1. Determine the maturity value of the note. Since this is an interest-bearing note, its maturity value is found by adding the face amount ($600) and the interest for 60 days at 7 percent ($7). Thus, the maturity value of the note is $607.
2. Determine the number of days in the discount period. Working back from the maturity date to the discount date, the accountant finds that the discount period is 45 days.

Days the note will run in June to maturity	16 days
Days the note will run in May: 31 − 2 = 29	29 days
Total discount period	45 days

3. Determine the amount of the discount. The bank will levy its charge of 8 percent on the maturity value ($607) for the discount period (45 days).

Putting these figures into the interest formula Discount = Maturity Value × Discount Rate × Discount Period, the accountant finds the discount as follows.

$$\text{Discount} = \$607 \times 0.08 \times \frac{45}{360}$$

Discount = $6.07

4. Determine the proceeds. The amount to be received from the bank is $600.93, the maturity value minus the discount charge ($607 − $6.07).

Recording the Discounting of the Note

The discounting of the note receivable is recorded in the cash receipts journal of the Style Clothing Store. This time the entry consists of a debit to Cash in Bank and two credits—one to Notes Receivable Discounted and the other to Interest Earned.

CASH RECEIPTS JOURNAL for Month of May 19X2 Page 5

DATE	EXPLANATION	✓	ACCOUNTS RECEIVABLE CR. 111	SALES CR. 401	OTHER ACCOUNTS CREDIT ACCOUNT TITLE	POST. REF.	AMOUNT	CASH IN BANK DR. 101
May 2	Discounted Lois Norman's note				Notes Receivable Discounted	110	600 00	
					Interest Earned	491	93	600 93

The credit to Interest Earned of $0.93 represents the $7 total interest determined in computing the maturity value, less the discount of $6.07 charged by the bank. If the proceeds had been less than the face amount of the note, the difference would have been debited to Interest Expense.

Discounted Interest-Bearing Note Paid at Maturity

If Lois Norman pays the note at the maturity date, the Style Clothing Store cancels the contingent liability that was set up at the time the note was discounted. It debits $600 to Notes Receivable Discounted and credits the same amount to Notes Receivable.

Discounted Interest-Bearing Note Dishonored at Maturity

If Lois Norman dishonors the note at the maturity date, the Style Clothing Store must pay the maturity value (the face amount of the note plus the interest) and any protest fee to the bank. The firm charges the entire sum to the Accounts Receivable Control account in the general ledger and Norman's

NOTES RECEIVABLE REGISTER

DATE OF ENTRY	MAKER	WHERE PAYABLE	DATE OF NOTE	TIME TO RUN	MATURITY DATE YEAR	J	F	M	A	M	J	J	A	S	O	N	D
19X2 Apr. 3	Peter Ross	City National Bank	19X2 Apr. 3	60 days	19X2						2						
8	John Dow	First National Bank	8	30 days	19X2					8							
14	Alice Morgan	State Trust Co.	14	60 days	19X2						13						
17	Lois Norman	City National Bank	17	60 days	19X2						16						

account in the subsidiary ledger. An entry is also made to remove the contingent liability by debiting Notes Receivable Discounted and crediting Notes Receivable for the face amount of the note.

Notes Receivable Register

If a firm has many notes receivable, it may be convenient to set up a *notes receivable register*. This record has somewhat the same form as the notes payable register discussed in the previous unit. Information recorded in the notes receivable register includes the date of the note, the maker, where the note is payable, the time it is to run, the maturity date, the face amount, and the rate and amount of interest, if any. Columns are also provided to record the dates on which notes have been discounted and the banks that are holding the notes. The four notes received by the Style Clothing Store during the month of April (used in the previous examples) are shown in the notes receivable register illustrated below.

Notes Receivable and Interest Income on the Statements

The Notes Receivable account is a current asset and appears on the balance sheet, usually just below the accounts for cash items. Interest Earned is shown on the income statement as other (nonoperating) income. It is listed below Net Income From Operations and added to it. The expense that arises from bank charges on discounted notes is shown in the Interest Expense account. This account also appears below the Net Income From Operations but is deducted. The final sections of an income statement for a firm that has received and paid interest might look like this.

Net Income From Operations	$12,500
Other Income	
Interest Earned	125
Total Income	$12,625
Other Expenses	
Interest Expense	200
Net Income	$12,425

Drafts

A *draft* is a written order that requires the person or business firm addressed to pay a stated sum of money to another person or firm or to the bearer. An ordinary check is one form of draft. Two others are bank drafts and commercial drafts.

Page 1

FACE AMOUNT OF NOTE	INTEREST RATE	INTEREST AMOUNT	DISCOUNTED BANK	DISCOUNTED DATE	DATE PAID	REMARKS
500 00	None		City National Bank	Apr. 18		
300 00	None				May 8	
400 00	8%	5 33			June 13	
600 00	7%	7 00	City National Bank	May 2		

389

Bank Drafts   A *bank draft* is a check written by a bank that orders another bank—one in which it has funds on deposit—to pay the indicated amount to a specified person or business firm. Since a bank draft is more readily accepted than an individual's check, a person may use a bank draft to pay a debt to an out-of-town supplier with whom credit has not been established.

Another type of draft is called a *cashier's check*. This form of draft is prepared by a bank official. It orders the bank to pay the specified amount from its own funds. Like a bank draft, a cashier's check offers greater protection to a creditor than an individual's check. For this reason, cashier's checks are sometimes used to pay bills.

At the Style Clothing Store, the purchase of a bank draft or cashier's check is recorded by preparing a voucher. The entry in the voucher register debits the account payable that the draft is intended to settle, debits an expense account for the bank service charge, and credits an account payable with the bank. A check is then issued to the order of the bank and is recorded in the check register. The resulting credit to Cash in Bank is offset by a debit to the account payable with the bank.

For example, suppose that a bill for $525, represented by Voucher 5-08, is to be settled by sending the creditor a bank draft instead of a regular check. The bank imposes a service charge of $0.65 for the draft. The effect of the entries required for the new voucher (6-12) and the payment (Check 479) is shown here in general journal form.

19	X2				
May	15	Accounts Payable (Voucher 5-08)	205	525 00	
		Collection and Exchange Expense	559	65	
		Accounts Payable (Voucher 6-12)	205		525 65
	15	Accounts Payable (Voucher 6-12)	205	525 65	
		Cash in Bank (Check 479)	101		525 65

Commercial Drafts   A *commercial draft* is issued by a person or business firm to order another person or firm to pay a specified sum of money at once or at a determinable later date. This instrument is used to take care of special shipment and collection problems.

A *sight draft* is a commercial draft that is payable on presentation. It is honored by payment. No accounting entry (other than a memorandum notation) is made for the issuance of a sight draft. If the draft is honored, the transaction is recorded as a cash receipt.

Sight drafts may be used for collecting accounts receivable. A draft is usually sent for collection to the customer's bank. If the customer does not honor the draft, his credit standing at the bank may be injured. Thus a debtor is more likely to honor a draft than a collection letter.

It is also possible to ship goods with a sight draft in order to obtain cash on delivery. In this situation, a business paper called a *bill of lading* is sent to a bank near the customer. A sight draft is attached to the bill of lading. The customer must pay the draft to the bank before getting the bill of lading, which is needed to obtain the goods. The collecting bank sends the money, less its collection fee, to the firm that issued the draft. When the funds arrive, the firm records the transaction as a cash sale and debits an expense account for the collection fee.

A *time draft* differs from a sight draft in that a period of time is allowed for payment. The maturity date of a time draft may be stated in several different ways.

1. It may be a date specified in the draft.
2. It may be a specified number of days after the date of the draft.
3. It may be a specified number of days after acceptance of the draft.

A time draft requires no accounting entry (other than a memorandum notation) when it is issued. If the person upon whom the instrument is drawn agrees to honor it at maturity, he indicates his agreement by writing "accepted" on the face of the draft, signing it, and dating it. He then records the accepted draft on his books as a note payable and returns it to the drawer, who enters it on his books as a note receivable.

Trade Acceptances

A *trade acceptance* is a special form of commercial time draft that arises out of the sale of goods and has this fact noted on its face. The original transaction may be recorded in the same manner as a sale on credit. When the draft has been accepted, it is accounted for as a promissory note. Merchants have found that they have fewer credit losses on trade acceptances than on open-account transactions. Trade acceptances can also be discounted. An example of a trade acceptance is shown below.

principles and procedures summary

Notes receivable, like notes payable, may be interest-bearing or noninterest-bearing. Some firms obtain notes receivable when they extend past-due accounts since the notes give more legal protection than open accounts. When a firm receives a note in this situation, it debits Notes Receivable and credits the Accounts Receivable Control account and the individual customer's account. When the note is paid, the firm debits Cash in Bank and credits Notes Receivable. If the note is interest-bearing, the interest received is credited to the Interest Earned account. If the note is dishonored (not paid at maturity), the amount becomes an account receivable again. The face value of the note plus the interest is debited to Accounts Receivable Control and the customer's account. Notes Receivable and Interest Earned are credited.

It is a common practice in certain types of businesses to accept notes at the time sales are made. If a firm has many such transactions, it would probably set up a special column in its sales journal for debits to Notes Receivable.

A note receivable may be discounted at a bank prior to maturity. In this case, the bank will deduct interest at its discount rate for the time remaining to maturity. The firm discounting the note will debit Cash in Bank for the proceeds. Since the note becomes a contingent liability, the amount will be credited to Notes Receivable Discounted. The interest is recorded as a debit to Interest Expense or as a credit to Interest Earned, according to the circumstances.

Bank drafts, commercial drafts, and trade acceptances are other types of negotiable instruments sometimes used in business.

managerial implications

Managers should be aware of the possibilities of using negotiable instruments in connection with sales on credit. These instruments are especially useful when cash is short. Notes due some time in the future can be discounted to raise funds for current operations. In some cases, past-due accounts can be converted into notes receivable. The notes give more legal protection to the creditor and are more likely to be collected.

managerial discussion questions

1. How do negotiable instruments help firms sell goods on credit and obtain important legal safeguards?
2. Why would a seller be concerned about the contingent liability on a customer's discounted note?
3. As a manager, would you consider a note received at the time of sale to be as collectible as a note received in exchange for a further extension of credit? Explain.
4. As a manager, why would you insist that dishonored notes receivable be charged back to the Account Receivable Control account?

5. Suppose that you work in a firm that discounts notes receivable. One of the officers wants to know the meaning of *contingent liability* as it applies to the discounted notes. Explain the meaning of the term in this case.

application of principles

PROBLEM 21-1 The notes received by the Lopez Manufacturing Company during 19X1 are summarized below. Two of the notes were discounted by Lopez at the First National Bank. On February 1 the note dated January 22 was discounted at a rate of 7½ percent, and on October 1 the note dated September 15 was discounted at a rate of 8 percent. (February has 28 days in 19X1.)

LOPEZ MANUFACTURING COMPANY
Summary of Notes Received

Date	Face Amount	Period	Interest Rate
Jan. 22	$ 700	3 months	9%
Mar. 5	3,400	60 days	7%
July 8	1,000	45 days	8%
Sept. 15	2,400	3 months	6%

INSTRUCTIONS
1. Compute the total interest and the maturity value of each note.
2. For the two discounted notes, compute the discount charged by the bank and the net proceeds.
3. Record the discounting of the two notes in general journal form.
4. Make entries in general journal form to record the following transactions.
   a. The receipt of the note on March 5 in settlement of the Adair Company's $3,400 account receivable.
   b. The receipt of payment from the Adair Company on May 4 for the $3,400 note dated March 5 and the interest due on the note.

PROBLEM 21-2 The Barry Lumber Company uses a notes receivable register as a memorandum record to maintain control over the numerous notes it handles. The notes outstanding on March 31, 19X1, are as follows. All the notes are payable at the Republic National Bank unless otherwise specified.

- $2,400, 8 percent, 6-month note from Lucy Adano, dated January 10.
- $2,000, 6 percent, 90-day note from Tram Li, dated January 15. (This note was discounted at the Republic National Bank on February 1, 19X1.)
- $3,000, 8 percent, 90-day note from the Black Construction Company, dated

January 18. (This note was also discounted at the Republic National Bank on February 1, 19X1.)
- $1,350, noninterest-bearing, 60-day note from John Savage, dated February 7, payable at the Madison Bank.
- $2,200, 6 percent, 45-day note from Tomassi Contractors, dated February 25.
- $4,800, 7 percent, 120-day note from Ruiz Home Builders, dated March 20, payable at the Commercial Bank.

The notes receivable transactions listed below took place during April 19X1.

INSTRUCTIONS
1. Enter the notes outstanding on March 31, 19X1, in a notes receivable register like the one shown on pages 388 and 389 of this unit.
2. Using a general journal and a cash receipts journal, record the notes receivable transactions for April. The cash receipts journal should have the same column heads as the journal illustrated on page 388. The required accounts are listed below.
3. Enter data in the notes receivable register where appropriate.

ACCOUNTS
101	Cash in Bank	111	Accounts Receivable
109	Notes Receivable	491	Interest Earned
110	Notes Receivable Discounted	591	Interest Expense

TRANSACTIONS FOR APRIL 19X1

Apr. 2 Accepted a 60-day noninterest-bearing note for $1,800, dated today, from Winston Builders, as an extension of credit on its overdue account receivable. (Record in the general journal and in the notes receivable register.)

5 Discounted Lucy Adano's 6-month note for $2,400 at the Commercial Bank. The note is dated January 10 and is due on July 10. (When the term of the note is specified in months, the maturity date is determined by counting forward in "round" months.) The discount rate set by the bank is 9 percent. (Record in the cash receipts journal.)

8 John Savage's 60-day note dated February 7, 19X1, was due today. He gave a check for $650 and a new note for $700 due in 90 days with interest at 8 percent. (Record the amount received in the cash receipts journal. Make appropriate comments in the Remarks section of the notes receivable register opposite the entry for the original note, and record the new note on the next open line.)

11 Tomassi Contractors dishonored its note for $2,200, dated February 25, 19X1, which was due today with interest at 6 percent. (Charge the note plus the interest to accounts receivable.)

15 Received notice that Tram Li's 90-day, $2,000 note, dated January 15, 19X1, was dishonored today. This note was discounted at the Republic National Bank on February 1, 19X1. The bank charged the checking account of the Barry Lumber Company for $2,035, which represents the maturity value of the note ($2,030) plus a

protest fee ($5). (Record the charge-back by the bank in the general journal. Also record in the general journal the termination of the contingent liability for the discounted note.)

16 Accepted a 90-day, 8 percent note for $2,600 from Sam Gibson as an extension of credit on his past-due account receivable.

18 Received notice from the bank that the Black Construction Company paid its note of January 18, 19X1, which was discounted.

19 Discounted the $4,800 note from Ruiz Home Builders, dated March 20, 19X1, at the First National Bank. The discount rate was 9 percent.

AlterNAte problems

PROBLEM 21-1A The notes received by the Ace Sales Company during 19X1 are summarized below. Ace discounted two of the notes at the Lincoln National Bank. On June 7 the note dated May 18 was discounted at a rate of 7 percent; on August 9 the note dated July 10 was discounted at a rate of 10 percent.

ACE SALES COMPANY
Summary of Notes Received

Date	Face Amount	Period	Interest Rate
Jan. 18	$2,000	90 days	6%
Jan. 30	1,000	1 month	10%
May 18	1,300	90 days	6%
July 10	825	4 months	7%
Oct. 16	425	45 days	7%

INSTRUCTIONS
1. Compute the total interest and the maturity value of each note.
2. For the two discounted notes, compute the discount charged by the bank and the net proceeds.
3. Record the discounting of the two notes in general journal form.
4. Make entries in general journal form to record the following transactions.
   a. The receipt of the note on January 18 in settlement of the Eastern Company's $2,000 account receivable.
   b. Receipt of payment from the Eastern Company on April 18 for the $2,000 note dated January 18 and the interest due on the note.

PROBLEM 21-2A The All-Star Supply Company uses a notes receivable register as a memorandum record to maintain control over its notes. The notes the firm has outstanding on June 30, 19X1, are as follows. All the notes are payable at the First State Bank.

- $9,000, 9 percent, 120-day note from Town Homes, dated March 20. (This note was discounted at the First State Bank on March 30.)

- $1,000, 8 percent, 8-month note from the West Side Construction Company, dated May 8.
- $4,500, 9 percent, 60-day note from the James Company, dated May 14.
- $2,000, noninterest-bearing, 30-day note from Al Walker, dated June 20.

The notes receivable transactions listed below took place during July 19X1.

INSTRUCTIONS

1. Enter the notes outstanding on June 30, 19X1, in a notes receivable register like the one shown on pages 388 and 389 of this unit.
2. Using a general journal and a cash receipts journal, record the notes receivable transactions for July. The cash receipts journal should have the same column heads as the journal illustrated on page 388. The required accounts are listed below.
3. Enter data in the notes receivable register where appropriate.

ACCOUNTS

101	Cash in Bank	111	Accounts Receivable
109	Notes Receivable	491	Interest Earned
110	Notes Receivable Discounted	591	Interest Expense

TRANSACTIONS FOR JULY 19X1

July 2 Accepted a 30-day, 8 percent note for $1,500, dated today, from Rogers Construction Company, as an extension of credit on its overdue account receivable. (Record in the general journal and in the notes receivable register.)

5 Discounted Al Walker's 30-day, $2,000 note at the First State Bank. This note was received on June 20. The discount rate charged by the bank was 8 percent.

13 Received payment from the James Company for its $4,500 note of May 14, plus the interest due.

19 Received notice that Town Homes refused to pay the First State Bank for its note of March 20, which was discounted at the bank on March 30. The bank charged the checking account of the All-Star Supply Company for $9,275, which represents the maturity value of the note ($9,270) plus a protest fee ($5). (Record the charge-back by the bank in the general journal. Also record in the general journal termination of the contingent liability for the discounted note.)

20 Received notice from the First State Bank that Al Walker paid his note of June 20, which was discounted on July 5.

22 Discounted at the First State Bank the $1,000 note from the West Side Construction Company dated May 8. The bank charged a discount rate of 7 percent.

UNIT 22

ACCOUNTS RECEIVABLE AND BAD DEBTS

Whenever there are credit transactions, some people fail to pay their obligations. Businesses try to keep their bad debt losses to a minimum by carefully extending credit and by diligently collecting accounts. However, such losses will occur, and they must be considered an expense of doing business on credit. As you learned in Unit 17, two methods are generally used for recognizing bad debt losses. This unit discusses in detail the valuation or adjustment of receivables to reflect losses that result from customers not paying their bills. It will also examine the special problems arising from installment sales.

Recording Losses When They Occur— The Direct Charge-Off Method

A merchant who extends credit to a customer expects to collect the amount in full. The firm may carry the account on its books until the account has definitely become uncollectible. Then the firm formally recognizes the balance owed as a bad debt loss.

Suppose that Gary Lane, a customer of the Style Clothing Store, has left town without paying his account balance of $75 and that his whereabouts are unknown. After exhausting all possibilities of finding Lane and collecting from him, the Style Clothing Store writes off the account as a bad debt by the general journal entry shown below.

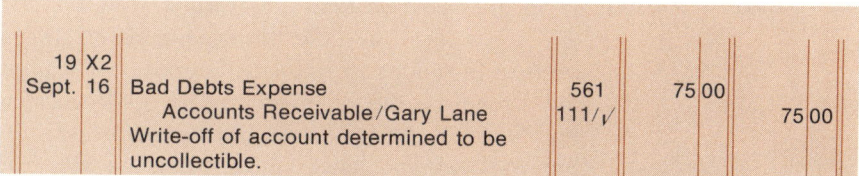

This method of recording bad debts is often referred to as the *direct charge-off method*. The resulting reduction in the value of accounts receivable reflects the current situation. When the new amount is shown on the balance sheet, it represents the total of all accounts receivable except specific accounts that the firm has found to be uncollectible. However, it is likely that other accounts receivable will not be collectible.

Providing for Losses Before They Occur— The Allowance Method

Instead of waiting until a particular account proves uncollectible and then recording the loss, it is possible to anticipate bad debt losses and to provide for them in the period that the sale was made. *By doing so, the seller can match the estimated expense from bad debts against the revenue that the firm has earned during the same accounting period.* This is a logical procedure because the bad debt loss is related to the sales transaction from which the account receivable resulted. The practice of providing for bad debt losses before they occur is often referred to as the *allowance method*.

In order to record bad debts expense and sales revenue in the same accounting period, the accountant has to estimate the losses likely to result from the accounts receivable that have not been collected at the end of the period. There are three common ways of estimating the amount of bad debt losses. These techniques are based on the following procedures.

1. Taking a percentage of the net credit sales for the period.
2. Classifying the accounts receivable into age groups at the end of the period, and taking a percentage of each group.
3. Taking a percentage of the total accounts receivable outstanding at the end of the period.

Percentage of Credit Sales

A business that has been operating for a number of years may be able to determine an average ratio of bad debt losses to credit sales. It can then use this ratio in estimating future bad debt losses. To be accurate, the ratio should be based on net credit sales—total sales on credit minus the sales returns and allowances on these sales. However, when sales returns and allowances are few, businesses usually base their bad debt estimate on total sales on credit because this figure is more easily computed.

In some businesses, it may be difficult to determine the amount of sales on credit. These businesses may need to express the ratio of credit losses on total sales, including cash sales. However, as a general rule, only the credit sales should be used because there is no bad debt loss on cash sales. Since the Style Clothing Store has relatively few sales returns and allowances, its bad debt losses are based on total credit sales.

A new firm may use the experience of other firms in the same line of business in making its estimate. Suppose, for example, that the Style Clothing Store relies on the experience of its predecessor, which was operated for a number of years by Linda Hanson before she formed a partnership with Steven Casey and Janet Miller. Using the data from prior years, Thompson estimates that three-tenths of one percent (0.003) of the firm's credit sales will result in uncollectible accounts. Suppose also that during the partnership's first year of operation $200,000 of sales are made on credit. The store's estimated bad debt loss is determined by applying the percentage to the credit sales (0.003 × $200,000 = $600). The estimated bad debts expense for the period is therefore $600. The entry to record this estimate is shown in general journal form on the next page. (The adjustment is actually entered on the worksheet first and is later recorded in the general journal along with the other adjusting entries.)

19X2 Jan. 31	Bad Debts Expense Allowance for Bad Debts Estimated bad debt losses for the fiscal year, based on 0.3% of credit sales of $200,000.	561 111A	600 00	600 00

The effect of the debit part of the entry is to charge the estimated bad debt loss against the operations of the period. As a result of the credit part of the entry, the Allowance for Bad Debts account (sometimes called Allowance for Uncollectible Accounts) reflects the estimated shrinkage in the asset accounts receivable. This account is called a *valuation account* because it literally revalues or reappraises the accounts receivable in the light of reasonable expectations. It is shown on the balance sheet as a deduction from accounts receivable (as illustrated on page 403).

Note that when the estimate of bad debts is based on sales, the primary emphasis is on charging as an expense the credit losses that apply to the sales of the period. It is through this process that the accounts receivable can be reported at their expected realizable value. However, valuation is of secondary concern. In other words, the matching principle is being emphasized when the bad debts estimate is based on sales.

Aging the Accounts Receivable

A procedure called *aging the accounts receivable* can be used as a guide in estimating probable bad debt losses. This procedure involves setting up a schedule on which each account receivable is listed by name and balance owed. The accountant then analyzes the data in the accounts to determine the age of the various amounts that make up each balance. The column headings of the schedule allow the accountant to classify the amounts according to how long they have been outstanding. The headings may be Current (within the allowed credit period), Past Due 1–30 Days, Past Due 31–60 Days, and Past Due Over 60 days. When a firm breaks down each customer's total debt in this way, it gains a picture of the relative currency of its receivables.

STYLE CLOTHING STORE
Schedule of Accounts Receivable by Age
January 31, 19X2

ACCOUNT WITH	BALANCE	CURRENT	PAST DUE—DAYS		
			1–30	31–60	OVER 60
Lois Adams	125 00	125 00			
Ralph Ames	60 00			45 00	15 00
Irene Ashe	47 50	25 00	22 50		
William Avant	73 00	50 00			23 00
John Zeller	110 00	80 00	30 00		
Totals	12,500 00	9,500 00	1,575 00	850 00	575 00

The longer an account is past due, the less likely it is to be collected. For example, past experience at the Style Clothing Store might indicate that 50 percent of the accounts more than 60 days past due will be uncollectible, whereas the figures for the other age groups are 25 percent for accounts 31–60 days past due, 10 percent for accounts 1–30 days past due, and 1 percent for the current accounts. By applying these percentages to the totals shown on the schedule of accounts receivable by age, the accountant estimates the bad debt loss for the period as follows.

Over 60 days past due	0.50 × $ 575.00 =	$287.50
31–60 days past due	0.25 × 850.00 =	212.50
1–30 days past due	0.10 × 1,575.00 =	157.50
Current	0.01 × 9,500.00 =	95.00
Total estimated bad debt loss		$752.50

The Allowance for Bad Debts account should then be *adjusted to the needed balance* of $752.50. For example, suppose that the Allowance for Bad Debts account has a credit balance of $200 on January 31, prior to adjustment. The account must be credited for $552.50 to bring the balance up to $752.50. The following entry is made in the general journal to record this adjustment.

19 X2				
Jan. 31	Bad Debts Expense	561	552 50	
	Allowance for Bad Debts	111A		552 50
	Adjustment of allowance account to needed balance of $752.50, based on aging of accounts receivable.			

On the other hand, suppose that the Allowance for Bad Debts account has a debit (deficiency) balance of $50 (from writing off specific accounts, as discussed later). It would then be necessary to credit the account for $802.50 ($50 + $752.50) in order to bring the balance up to $752.50. Whatever the amount, the adjusting entry consists of a debit to Bad Debts Expense and a credit to Allowance for Bad Debts, as previously illustrated.

Note that when the provision for bad debts is based on the age of the accounts receivable, the primary concern is the proper valuation of the accounts receivable on the balance sheet. The amount charged as an expense is of secondary concern.

Predetermined Percentage of Accounts Receivable

In some cases, it is possible to estimate the necessary balance of the Allowance for Bad Debts account by applying a single rate, based on past experience, to the total accounts receivable. For example, a firm may estimate that normally one-half of one percent (0.005) of the balance of the Accounts Receivable account will be uncollectible, and it may adjust its Allowance for Bad Debts account to that amount. If this procedure is followed, the emphasis is again on valuation of the accounts receivable on the balance sheet.

Recording Actual Uncollectible Amounts

As you have seen, under the system of providing for bad debt losses before they occur, Bad Debts Expense is debited and Allowance for Bad Debts is credited for the estimated amount of loss. Then, when a particular account proves uncollectible, it is written off. The amount owed is debited to Allowance for Bad Debts. The offsetting credit is to the Accounts Receivable account in the general ledger and the customer's account in the subsidiary ledger. Suppose that the Style Clothing Store determines that the account of Ralph Ames with a balance of $60 is uncollectible. The accountant writes off the account by making the following entry in the general journal.

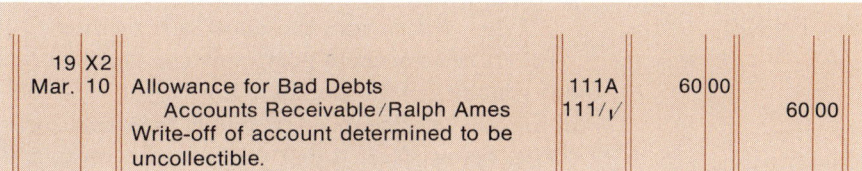

Notice that when bad debt losses are provided for in advance, the write-off of a particular uncollectible account does not involve an entry in the Bad Debts Expense account. The expense has already been recorded by means of the adjustment for estimated bad debt losses made at the end of the period in which the sale took place.

Normally, the Allowance for Bad Debts account will have a credit (excess) balance. However, if the losses written off are greater than those estimated in previous accounting periods, Allowance for Bad Debts may show a debit (deficiency) balance until the current adjustment is recorded. If the amount of the estimated loss is based on sales, the existence of the debit balance will not affect the amount of the adjustment. However, if the estimated loss is based on accounts receivable, it will be necessary to credit the Allowance for Bad Debts account for an amount sufficient to eliminate the debit balance and replace it with the desired credit balance. This means that the adjustment will be greater than the estimated loss from bad debts for the period.

Collecting an Account That Was Written Off

Occasionally, an account written off as uncollectible is later collected, in whole or in part. Remember that Gary Lane's account for $75 was written off under the direct charge-off method by a debit to Bad Debts Expense and a credit to Accounts Receivable/Gary Lane. Suppose that the account is collected in full several months later. In this case, the cash received is recorded in the cash receipts journal by debiting Cash in Bank and crediting Accounts Receivable/Gary Lane. However, since Lane's account has already been written off, a general journal entry must be made to reverse the write-off.

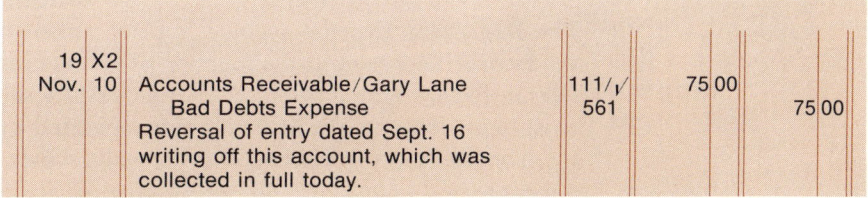

Some accountants prefer to record the amount recovered as a credit to an account called Bad Debts Recovered, especially when the money is received in a later period than the one in which the write-off was made. The debit part of this entry involves the Accounts Receivable account in the general ledger and the customer's account in the subsidiary ledger to make sure that all pertinent facts relating to the customer's debt are recorded and can be used for future credit purposes. The collection of the money is recorded in the cash receipts journal in the usual way as a debit to Cash in Bank and a credit to Accounts Receivable and the customer's account. The Bad Debts Recovered account is shown on the income statement under Other Income.

When a firm uses the allowance method to provide for bad debts, the recovery of an account previously charged off as uncollectible also requires an entry in the general journal to reverse the write-off. For example, the recovery of the $60 balance owed by Ralph Ames is recorded in the general journal as shown below. Notice that Accounts Receivable/Ralph Ames is debited and Allowance for Bad Debts is credited in the reversal process.

19 X2					
June	8	Accounts Receivable/Ralph Ames	111/✓	60 00	
		Allowance for Bad Debts	111A		60 00
		Reversal of entry dated March 10			
		writing off this account, which was			
		collected in full today.			

An entry in the cash receipts journal is then made in the usual way to record the collection of the account receivable.

If the amount recovered represents only part of the balance written off, the reversal entry is used to restore *only the amount actually collected* unless the firm is almost certain that the remainder will be paid. For example, if Ralph Ames pays only $40 on his $60 balance, the reversal entry in the general journal will be for the smaller amount unless the firm is reasonably sure the additional $20 will be paid.

Other Receivables and Bad Debt Losses

Just as accounts receivable may result in bad debt losses, so notes receivable and other receivables may prove uncollectible. Bad debt losses from notes receivable and other receivables may be recorded as they occur, or they may be estimated and provided for ahead of time in the manner previously described for accounts receivable. The same accounts—Bad Debts Expense and Allowance for Bad Debts—can be used for losses from all types of receivables.

Bad Debts Expense on the Income Statement

The Bad Debts Expense account appears among the operating expenses on the income statement. If the function of giving credit and collecting accounts rests in the sales department, it is classified as a selling expense. However, in most businesses, the credit function is separated from the sales function. For these businesses, bad debts expense is usually shown as a general or administrative expense. Some businesses show bad debts expense as a deduction from sales revenue on the income statement.

Allowance for Bad Debts on the Balance Sheet

If an Allowance for Bad Debts account is used, the balance in this account at the end of the period represents the amount of accounts receivable estimated as uncollectible. In preparing the balance sheet, the accountant therefore deducts the balance of the Allowance for Bad Debts account from the balance of the Accounts Receivable account, as shown below. The difference is considered the net value of the asset. In this case, the net value of the firm's accounts receivable is $11,747.50

ASSETS

Current Assets		
Cash in Bank		$10,000.00
Accounts Receivable	$12,500.00	
Less Allowance for Bad Debts	752.50	11,747.50

Recognizing the Effect of Potential Cash Discounts

As explained earlier, cash discounts are sometimes allowed for prompt payment of invoices. If the accounts receivable listed on the balance sheet are subject to cash discounts, the total collected may be somewhat less than the invoice amounts recorded. For example, suppose that a credit sale is recorded by debiting Accounts Receivable for $150. However, if terms such as 2/10, n/30 are allowed, the debt may be settled with the payment of $147 within 10 days.

In some cases, the approximate amount of the discounts that can be taken by customers is shown on the balance sheet so that anyone studying the statement will have fair notice of this possibility. However, in most cases, people using the financial statements are expected to know the normal terms of sale in the industry involved. Therefore, it is usually not considered necessary to list the possible sales discounts.

Installment Sales Procedures

A special type of receivable is found in businesses that sell on an installment basis. Installment sales are common among retailers of furniture, jewelry, and major household appliances. The usual arrangement is for the customer to make a down payment and then pay the balance in installments over the period of time called for in the contract.

Generally accepted accounting principles require installment sales to be recorded exactly like any other sales on credit—except in unusual circumstances. However, some small retailers use an installment basis of accounting for such sales. They do this because the procedure is permitted for tax purposes, and they prefer to have only one set of records for financial accounting and tax accounting purposes. The installment basis of accounting allows the profit on installment sales to be deferred until the cash is actually received.

To see how this accounting procedure works, suppose that on September 1, 19X1, a store sells a color television set on the installment plan to George Lee for a price of $500. Lee pays $50 as a down payment and another $150 in three $50 installments during the first year. He pays the remaining $300 in six installments of $50 each during the second year. The set originally cost the store $300.

1. At the time of the sale on September 1, 19X1, the transaction is recorded by an entry debiting Installment Accounts Receivable—19X1/George Lee for the total obligation ($500), crediting Merchandise Inventory for the cost of the item sold ($300), and crediting Deferred Gross Profit on 19X1 Installment Sales for the deferred income from the transaction ($200). (A 40 percent rate of gross profit is assumed for all installment sales in 19X1.)

19X1					
Sept.	1	Installment Accounts Receivable—19X1/ George Lee	114/✓	500 00	
		Merchandise Inventory	121		300 00
		Deferred Gross Profit on 19X1 Installment Sales	411		200 00
		Made installment sale; deferred income is at 40% rate based on selling price of appliance.			

2. The cash received for the down payment results in a debit to Cash in Bank and a credit to Installment Accounts Receivable—19X1/George Lee. Later receipts are handled in the same way. (For simplicity, the necessary entries are shown here in general journal form.)

19X1					
Sept.	1	Cash in Bank	101	50 00	
		Installment Accounts Receivable— 19X1/George Lee	114/✓		50 00
		Down payment at time of sale.			
Oct.	1	Cash in Bank	101	50 00	
		Installment Accounts Receivable— 19X1/George Lee	114/✓		50 00
		Collections in October.			
Nov.	1	Cash in Bank	101	50 00	
		Installment Accounts Receivable— 19X1/George Lee	114/✓		50 00
		Collections in November.			
Dec.	1	Cash in Bank	101	50 00	
		Installment Accounts Receivable— 19X1/George Lee	114/✓		50 00
		Collections in December.			

3. At the end of the year in which the sale is made, a portion of the deferred income must be recognized. A rate of gross profit is determined for the year and is applied to collections on the installment sales of that year. For example, assuming a 40 percent rate of gross profit, the amount of income to be recognized in 19X1 for the sale to George Lee is $80. Remember that Lee makes four payments of $50 each that year ($50 × 4 × 0.40 = $200 × 0.40 = $80). The journal entry is shown below. Notice that Deferred Gross Profit on 19X1 Installment Sales is debited and an account called Realized Gross Profit on 19X1 Installment Sales is credited.

19X1				
Dec. 31	Deferred Gross Profit on 19X1 Installment Sales	411	80 00	
	Realized Gross Profit on 19X1 Installment Sales	421		80 00
	Realized income of 40% of $200 collections on 19X1 sales.			

4. The rate of gross profit determines the amount of deferred income to be recognized at the end of each year during the period of collection, which may extend over several years. In this instance, the customer made six monthly payments of $50 each to complete the contract in 19X2. Using the 40 percent gross profit rate again, this results in income of $120 to be recognized in 19X2 ($50 × 6 × 0.40 = $300 × 0.40 = $120).

19X2				
Dec. 31	Deferred Gross Profit on 19X1 Installment Sales	411	120 00	
	Realized Gross Profit on 19X1 Installment Sales	421		120 00
	Realized income of 40% of $300 collections on 19X1 sales.			

Recording Defaults on Installment Sales

If a customer defaults on the payments required by an installment contract, the seller may be able to recover the merchandise and put it back into inventory at its current wholesale value. The gain or loss is recognized and recorded at this point. The exact amount to be recorded is determined by the cost and revenue figures in the records. The balance still owed by the customer must, of course, be removed from the Installment Accounts Receivable account. The remaining deferred income must also be removed from the Deferred Gross Profit on Installment Sales account.

Consider again George Lee, who agreed to pay for the $500 television set on an installment basis. Suppose that he made the $50 down payment and the three periodic payments totaling $150 during the first year but failed to make the payments required in the second year. Assume further that the seller repossessed the television set on February 2, 19X2, and appraised its value at $125. The entry to record the repossession is shown below. Deferred Gross Profit on 19X1 Installment Sales is debited for $120 to eliminate the deferred income that will not be realized. Merchandise Inventory—Repossessed Goods is debited for $125, the current wholesale value of the television set. Loss From Defaults is debited for $55, the amount of loss on the sale. These debits are offset by a credit of $300 to Installment Accounts Receivable—19X1/George Lee, which closes out the customer's balance.

19X2					
Feb. 2	Deferred Gross Profit on 19X1 Installment Sales	411	120 00		
	Merch. Inventory—Repossessed Goods	122	125 00		
	Loss From Defaults	461	55 00		
	Installment Accounts Receivable—				
	19X1/George Lee	114/✓		300 00	
	Repossession of appliance and loss on default.				

If the television set had not been recovered, the loss would have been $125 greater, or $180. Thus, it would be necessary to debit Loss From Defaults for $180. The other parts of the final entry would be a debit of $120 to Deferred Gross Profit on 19X1 Installment Sales and a credit of $300 to Installment Accounts Receivable—19X1/George Lee.

19X2					
Feb. 2	Deferred Gross Profit on 19X1 Installment Sales	411	120 00		
	Loss From Defaults	461	180 00		
	Installment Accounts Receivable—				
	19X1/George Lee	114/✓		300 00	
	Default on installment contract; merchandise not repossessed.				

principles and procedures summary

When credit is extended to customers, bad debt losses will inevitably occur. Before receivables can be accurately presented on the balance sheet and net income can be properly measured, the accounts must be studied for possible adjustment to reflect such losses. The losses can be recorded as particular accounts become uncollectible, or an estimate of probable losses can be recorded before they occur.

The estimate of bad debt losses may be determined by taking a certain percentage of credit sales. This percentage is usually based on the firm's past experience. The adjustment for the estimated losses is debited to Bad Debts Expense and credited to Allowance for Bad Debts.

The estimate may also be based on an analysis of the age of the accounts receivable. A different percentage for credit losses is applied to each age group, and the resulting amounts are added together. Then the Allowance for Bad Debts account is adjusted to the proper balance, and the same amount is charged to the Bad Debts Expense account. The adjustment is made in the same way when the estimate of bad debt losses is computed by applying a single rate to the total accounts receivable.

Under the allowance method, when an account actually becomes worthless, it is written off by a debit to Allowance for Bad Debts and a credit to Accounts Receivable and to the customer's account in the subsidiary ledger.

Installment sales usually involve a down payment and additional periodic payments on the balance owed. Special accounts are maintained to record all details. The sales price is usually accounted for in the same way as with other sales on credit. However, some retailers use the installment basis of accounting. In the latter case, profit is recognized only as the accounts are collected. The overall gross profit rate, determined in the year the sale is made, is applied to collections each year to determine the amount of profit recognized.

MANAGERiAL implicATiONS

It is essential that managers keep informed about the losses from bad debts. This enables them to determine the effectiveness of the credit policies used by their firms, especially with regard to profitability. Managers must always weigh the cost of bad debt losses against the effects of tighter credit policies on sales volume.

Managers should insist that estimated losses from bad debts be charged against the revenue of the period in which the sales are made in order to get a proper matching of revenues and expenses. This allows a more accurate determination of net income or net loss.

MANAGERiAL discussioN QUESTiONS

1. How do managers appraise the effectiveness of a firm's credit policies?
2. What are the advantages of using an analysis of the accounts receivable by age as guide in estimating bad debt losses?
3. Why would managers wish to use the allowance method for recording bad debts instead of the direct charge-off method?

4. Why is an account receivable that was charged off as uncollectible reinstated if it is later collected?
5. Why would managers wish to use the installment method of accounting?
6. In the Anchor Company, the credit function is delegated to the sales department. In most cases, the firm's salespeople are authorized to approve credit for customers. Comment on the desirability of this procedure.

application of principles

PROBLEM 22-1 The Abel Tire Company records losses on bad debts as they occur. Selected transactions for 19X1 are described below. The accounts involved in these transactions are Notes Receivable 110, Accounts Receivable 111, and Bad Debts Expense 561.

INSTRUCTIONS Record each transaction in general journal form.

TRANSACTIONS FOR 19X1

Jan. 15 The account receivable of Edith Silver, amounting to $75, is determined to be uncollectible and is to be written off.

Mar. 20 Because of the death of Henry Booker, his note receivable amounting to $250 is considered uncollectible and is to be written off.

June 4 Received $40 from Edith Silver in partial payment of her account, which was written off on January 15. The cash obtained has already been recorded in the cash receipts journal. The balance of Silver's account is not expected to be collected.

July 17 Received $35 from Edith Silver to complete payment of her account, which was written off on January 15. The cash obtained has already been recorded in the cash receipts journal.

Sept. 24 Received $105 from the estate of Henry Booker as part of the settlement of his affairs. This amount is applicable to the note receivable written off on March 20. The cash obtained has already been recorded in the cash receipts journal.

PROBLEM 22-2 The Builders Supply Company sells building materials on credit and records sales in three separate revenue accounts. The company's experience has been that each sales category has a different rate of bad debt losses. Thus the total that the company charges off for bad debts at the end of each accounting period is based on three computations (one computation for each revenue account). The firm uses the percentage of credit sales method.

As of December 31, 19X1, Accounts Receivable 111 has a balance of $234,550 and Allowance for Bad Debts 111A has a credit balance of $2,860.

The following table provides a breakdown of the credit sales for the year 19X1 and the estimated rates of loss.

CREDIT SALES		ESTIMATED RATE OF LOSS
CATEGORY	AMOUNT	
Masonry	$625,000	0.9%
Lumber	470,000	1.4
Hardware	138,000	2.0

INSTRUCTIONS

1. Compute the estimated amount of bad debt loss for each of the three categories of credit sales for the calendar year.
2. Prepare an adjusting entry in general journal form to provide for the bad debt losses before they occur. (Use Bad Debts Expense 561.)
3. Show how the Accounts Receivable and Allowance for Bad Debts accounts should appear on the balance sheet of the Builders Supply Company as of December 31, 19X1.
4. On February 17, 19X2, the account receivable of Roy Bossi, amounting to $344, is determined to be uncollectible and is to be written off. Record this transaction in the general journal.
5. On May 15, 19X2, the attorneys for the Builders Supply Company turned over a check for $344, which they obtained from Roy Bossi in settlement of his account written off on February 17. The money has already been recorded in the cash receipts journal. Make an entry in the general journal to cancel the original write-off.

PROBLEM 22-3 The schedule of accounts receivable by age shown below was prepared for the Bomar Clothing Store at the end of the firm's fiscal year on June 30, 19X2.

BOMAR CLOTHING STORE
Schedule of Accounts Receivable by Age
June 30, 19X2

ACCOUNT WITH	BALANCE	CURRENT	PAST DUE—DAYS		
			1–30	31–60	OVER 60
Armad, John	127 00	63 00	64 00		
Bates, Steven	236 00	111 00	90 00	35 00	
Cline, Judith	98 00	98 00			
Derr, Allen	19 00	19 00			
Everett, Linda	316 00			208 00	108 00
Foley, Ann	74 00	29 00	45 00		
Gorin, Charles	197 00	68 00	92 00		37 00
Hayes, Frank	252 00	114 00	138 00		
Ivan, Thomas	132 00			132 00	
Jones, Ellen	59 00		59 00		
(All Other Accounts)	5,637 00	2,932 00	1,874 00	453 00	378 00
Totals	7,147 00	3,434 00	2,362 00	828 00	523 00

409

INSTRUCTIONS
1. Compute the estimated uncollectible accounts at the end of the fiscal year using these rates.
   Current   1%
   1–30 days past due   4%
   31–60 days past due 10%
   Over 60 days past due 20%
2. On June 30, 19X2, there is a debit balance of $113.50 in Allowance for Bad Debts 111A. Compute the amount of the adjustment for estimated bad debt losses that must be made as part of the adjusting entries.
3. In general journal form, record the adjustment for the estimated bad debt losses. (Use Bad Debts Expense 561.)
4. On July 18, 19X2, the account receivable of Thomas Ivan, amounting to $132, was recognized as uncollectible because of his serious illness. Record this write-off in the general journal. (Use Accounts Receivable 111.)
5. On August 2, 19X2, a check for $100 was received from Jane Scotto to apply on her account, which was written off on April 19, 19X1, as uncollectible. Record the cancellation of the previous write-off in the general journal. The cash obtained has already been entered in the cash receipts journal.
6. Suppose that instead of aging the accounts receivable, the company estimated uncollectible accounts to be simply 5 percent of the total accounts receivable on June 30. Give the journal entry to record the adjustment for estimated bad debt losses. Assume that Allowance for Bad Debts 111A has a credit balance of $62.50 before the adjusting entry.

PROBLEM 22-4

Vargo Appliances is a retail store that sells household appliances and equipment. Small items are sold for cash or on open account to approved credit customers. Major appliances are sometimes sold for cash but are usually sold on the installment plan. On July 2, 19X4, Vargo sells a refrigerator for $1,000 on the installment plan to Alan Koch. The refrigerator cost Vargo $600. Koch agrees to make a down payment of $75 and to pay $25 on the first day of each month thereafter, beginning August 1, 19X4. Vargo's rate of gross profit on installment sales is 40 percent for the year.

INSTRUCTIONS
Prepare in general journal form the entries required to record the following transactions. Use the same account titles used in the text.

1. The sale on July 2, 19X4, of the refrigerator on the installment plan.
2. The receipt of the agreed down payment on the sale date.
3. The receipt on August 2, 19X4, of the agreed monthly payment.
4. Recognition on December 31, 19X4, of that portion of the deferred income that has been earned. Assume that all monthly payments have been received as specified in the contract.
5. Recognition on December 31, 19X5, of that portion of the deferred income that has been earned during the year. Again, assume that all monthly payments have been received.

6. The repossession of the refrigerator by Vargo on March 15, 19X6, and its return, at an appraised value of $180, to inventory. Assume that Koch has failed to make any 19X6 payments.

AlterNate problems

PROBLEM 22-1A

The Rausch Company records losses on bad debts as they occur. Selected transactions for 19X1 are described below. The accounts involved are Notes Receivable 110, Accounts Receivable 111, and Bad Debts Expense 561.

INSTRUCTIONS

Record each transaction in general journal form.

TRANSACTIONS FOR 19X1

Feb. 12 The account receivable of Mary Sweeney, amounting to $85, is determined to be uncollectible and is to be written off.

Mar. 20 Because of the death of Asa Green, his note receivable amounting to $300 is considered uncollectible and is to be written off.

June 4 Received $45 from Mary Sweeney in partial payment of her account, which was written off on February 12. The cash obtained has already been recorded in the cash receipts journal. There is doubt that the balance of Sweeney's account will be collected.

July 9 Received $40 from Mary Sweeney to complete the payment of her account, which was written off on February 12. The cash obtained has already been recorded in the cash receipts journal.

Aug. 14 The account receivable of Arnold Balker amounting to $80 is determined to be uncollectible and is to be written off.

Sept. 18 Received $100 from the estate of Asa Green as part of the settlement of his affairs. This amount is applicable to the note receivable written off on March 20. The cash obtained has already been recorded in the cash receipts journal.

PROBLEM 22-2A

The Sanger Feed Company sells farm supplies at both wholesale and retail. The company has found that there is a higher rate of bad debts from retail credit sales than from wholesale credit sales. The company computes its estimated bad debt loss at the end of each year. The amount is based on the two rates of loss that the firm has developed from experience. Thus, a separate computation must be made for each source of sales. The firm uses the percentage of credit sales method.

As of December 31, 19X1, Accounts Receivable 111 has a balance of $186,700, and Allowance for Bad Debts 111A has a debit balance of $36.20. The following table provides a breakdown of the credit sales for the year 19X1 and the estimated rates of loss.

| CREDIT SALES | | ESTIMATED |
CATEGORY	AMOUNT	RATE OF LOSS
Wholesale	$908,000	0.6%
Retail	274,300	1.1

INSTRUCTIONS
1. Compute the estimated amount of bad debt loss for each of the two categories of credit sales for the calendar year.
2. Prepare an adjusting entry in general journal form to provide for the bad debt losses before they occur. (Use Bad Debts Expense 561.)
3. Show how the Accounts Receivable and Allowance for Bad Debts accounts should appear on the balance sheet of the Sanger Feed Company as of December 31, 19X1.
4. On January 30, 19X2, the account receivable of Anna Schmidt, amounting to $283, is determined to be uncollectible and is to be written off. Record the transaction in the general journal.
5. On June 13, 19X2, the attorneys for the Sanger Feed Company turned over a check for $283, which they obtained from Anna Schmidt in settlement of her account written off on January 30. Record the transaction in the general journal. The money has already been entered in the cash receipts journal. Make an entry in the general journal to cancel the original write-off.

PROBLEM 22-3A The schedule of accounts receivable by age shown below was prepared for the Fall Company at the end of the fiscal year on December 31, 19X1.

FALL COMPANY
Schedule of Accounts Receivable by Age
December 31, 19X1

ACCOUNT WITH	BALANCE	CURRENT	PAST DUE—DAYS		
			1–30	31–60	OVER 60
Anton, Janet	180 00	180 00			
Ardath, Robert	210 00		150 00	60 00	
Aston, Thomas	104 00				104 00
Baltus, Ida	80 00	80 00			
Barton, Leslie	62 00	42 00	20 00		
Bender, Harold	225 00	85 00	100 00	40 00	
Benson, Mary	48 00			32 00	16 00
(All Other Accounts)	10,748 00	9,075 00	1,050 00	360 00	263 00
Totals	11,657 00	9,462 00	1,320 00	492 00	383 00

INSTRUCTIONS
1. Compute the estimated uncollectible accounts at the end of the year using these rates.

    Current   1%
    1–30 days past due   3%
    31–60 days past due   8%
    Over 60 days past due   20%

2. As of December 31, 19X1, there is a debit balance of $64.12 in Allowance

412

for Bad Debts 111A. Compute the amount of the adjustment for estimated bad debt losses that must be made as part of the adjusting entries.

3. In general journal form, record the adjustment for the estimated bad debt losses. (Use Bad Debts Expense 561.)
4. On February 10, 19X2, the account receivable of Joan Gorey amounting to $108 was recognized as uncollectible. Record this write-off in the general journal. (Use Accounts Receivable 111.)
5. On June 12, 19X2, a check for $50 was received from Raymond Garcia to apply on his account, which was written off on November 8, 19X1, as uncollectible. Record the cancellation of the previous write-off in the general journal. The cash obtained has already been entered in the cash receipts journal.
6. Suppose that instead of aging the accounts receivable, the company estimated uncollectible accounts to be simply 3 percent of the total accounts receivable on December 31. Give the journal entry to record the adjustment for estimated bad debt losses. Assume that Allowance for Bad Debts 111A has a debit balance of $31.20 before the adjusting entry.

PROBLEM 22-4A The Audio House is a retail store that deals in stereo equipment. Some of its larger sales are made on the installment plan. The installment sales transactions for the years 19X1 to 19X3 are summarized below and on the next page. The accounts used in connection with these transactions are also listed below. The rate of gross profit on installment sales is $33\frac{1}{3}$ percent.

INSTRUCTIONS Record the transactions in general journal form.

ACCOUNTS

101	Cash in Bank
114	Installment Accounts Receivable—19X1
121	Merchandise Inventory
122	Merchandise Inventory—Repossessed Goods
411	Deferred Gross Profit on 19X1 Installment Sales
421	Realized Gross Profit on 19X1 Installment Sales
461	Loss From Defaults

TRANSACTIONS FOR 19X1

Aug. 15 Sold stereo equipment for $600 on the installment plan to Peter O'Shea. He gave $75 cash as a down payment. The Audio House paid $400 for the equipment.

25 Sold stereo equipment for $420 on the installment plan to Sara Wang. She gave $65 cash as a down payment. The equipment cost the Audio House $280.

Dec. 31 During the remainder of 19X1, O'Shea paid an additional $125 on his installment account and Wang paid an additional $110 on her account. (Record as a combined summary entry on December 31.)

31 Recorded the income realized on collections of 19X1 installment sales.

TRANSACTIONS FOR 19X2

Dec. 31 During 19X2 O'Shea paid $70 on his installment account, and Wang paid $200 on her account.

31 Recorded the income realized in 19X2 on collections of 19X1 installment sales.

TRANSACTIONS FOR 19X3

Jan. 25 O'Shea defaulted on his contract, and his stereo equipment was repossessed. It had a $50 wholesale value on this date.

UNIT 23

VALUATION OF INVENTORY

Information about merchandise inventory must be reported on the financial statements at the end of each accounting period. In Unit 17, you saw how a small business valued its inventory in order to provide the necessary data for the financial statements. Larger firms use more complex methods for inventory valuation. Such methods are discussed in this unit.

Importance of Inventory Valuation

Merchandise Inventory is the one account that appears on both the balance sheet and the income statement. Its valuation is important because in many businesses it represents the asset with the largest dollar value. At the same time, inventory valuation directly affects the amount of net income or net loss reported for the accounting period.

If other items remain the same, the larger the ending inventory valuation, the lower the cost of goods sold and the higher the reported net income (or the lower the reported net loss). The smaller the ending inventory valuation, the higher the cost of goods sold and the lower the reported net income (or the higher the reported net loss). Thus, determining the proper accounting value of inventory is vital.

In most businesses, the merchandise inventory at the end of each accounting period is determined by actually counting the number of units of each type of goods on hand and multiplying that number by the appropriate cost per item. This process is known as *taking a physical inventory*, and it is the approach we will use in this unit. However, in some types of businesses, especially manufacturing businesses, it is desirable to know *at all times* the number of units and the total value of each item. The procedure used to gain this information is known as the *perpetual inventory procedure*. Perpetual inventory records are discussed in Units 42 and 43.

Inventory Costing Methods

In Unit 17, the merchandise inventory of the Modern Cleaning Shop was valued at the purchase cost of the items on hand. In such a small business, the valuation of inventory is a relatively simple matter. The stock of merchandise is limited, and the manager is in direct daily contact with operations. Thus the inventory valuation can be based on the specific identification of merchandise, as shown on the following inventory sheet.

MODERN CLEANING SHOP
Inventory Sheet
Accessories Department

DATE February 28, 19X2

QUANTITY	DESCRIPTION	UNIT COST	TOTAL
600 sets	Assorted hangers, 8 in set	$1.00	$ 600.00
35	Hat racks	2.00	70.00
38	Tie racks	2.50	95.00
20	Shoe racks	3.00	60.00
62	Shoeshine kits	2.25	139.50
18	3-suit garment bags, plastic	.75	13.50
40	2-suit garment bags, plastic	.40	16.00
10	Mothproofing spray cans	.60	6.00
	Total inventory		$1,000.00

Specific Identification Method

As noted previously, it may be possible to keep a record of the purchase price of each item in inventory and therefore to determine the exact cost of the specific merchandise sold. Automobile dealers, art dealers, and merchants who deal with items having a large unit cost or with one-of-a-kind items may account for their inventory by the *specific identification method*. However, this method is not practical for a business such as the Style Clothing Store, where hundreds of similar items of relatively small unit value—such as shirts, blouses, and sweaters—are carried in the inventory. Furthermore, the purchase cost of many types of items may change during the accounting period. Fortunately, accountants can consider several other costing methods in their search for the best one to apply to each business situation.

Average Cost Method

Instead of keeping a record of the cost of each item purchased, it is possible to average the cost of all like items available for sale during the period. This average cost can then be used to value the ending inventory. To understand how the *average cost method* works, study the following analysis of purchases

Explanation	No. of Units	Unit Cost	Total Cost
Beginning Inventory, Feb. 1, 19X1	100	$6.00	$ 600.00
Purchases:			
Feb. 27, 19X1	50	6.50	325.00
April 20, 19X1	100	7.00	700.00
Oct. 15, 19X1	75	7.50	562.50
Jan. 10, 19X2	75	8.00	600.00
Total Merchandise Available for Sale	400		$2,787.50
Average Cost ($2,787.50 ÷ 400)		$6.9688	
Ending Inventory, Jan. 31, 19X2	125	6.9688	871.10
Cost of Goods Sold	275	6.9688	$1,916.40

of a certain brand and quality of shirts during the fiscal year of February 1, 19X1, to January 31, 19X2.

Note that the computation begins with the number of units, unit cost, and total cost of the beginning inventory. To these figures are added the amounts of all purchases made during the period. The sum of the units in the beginning inventory and the units purchased represents the total units available for sale. The total cost of the beginning inventory is added to the total cost of each lot purchased to obtain the total cost of the units available for sale. This total cost, $2,787.50, is then divided by the total number of units available to find the average unit cost ($2,787.50 ÷ 400 = $6.9688). The value of the ending inventory is established by multiplying the number of units on hand by the average unit cost (125 × $6.9688 = $871.10). The cost of goods sold can then be easily determined by subtracting the value of the ending inventory from the total value of the merchandise available for sale ($2,787.50 − $871.10 = $1,916.40).

The average cost method of inventory valuation is relatively simple to use, but it reflects the limitations of any procedure that involves average figures. The unit cost cannot be related to any tangible unit or lot of merchandise, and it does not reveal price changes as clearly as might be desired. In highly competitive businesses that are subject to significant price and style changes, it is desirable to have a more specific and revealing method of cost determination. Two other popular methods of valuation are the first in, first out method and the last in, first out method.

First In, First Out Method

In most businesses, merchants naturally try to sell their oldest items first. Thus the merchandise on hand at any given time is usually the latest bought. The *first in, first out method* of inventory valuation (usually referred to as FIFO) parallels this physical flow of inventory. The cost of the ending inventory is computed by referring to the cost of the latest purchases.

Using the figures from the previous example, the cost of the ending inventory of 125 units is $975 under the FIFO pricing method, as shown below.

EXPLANATION	NO. OF UNITS	UNIT COST	TOTAL COST
From Purchase of Jan. 10, 19X2	75	$8.00	$600.00
From Purchase of Oct. 15, 19X1	50	7.50	375.00
Ending Inventory, Jan. 31, 19X2	125		$975.00

The cost of goods sold is then found by subtracting the value of the ending inventory from the total value of the merchandise available for sale, which was previously computed ($2,787.50 − $975.00 = $1,812.50).

Actually, the FIFO method attempts to approximate the results of the specific identification method, even though large and varied stocks of merchandise are involved. While it does not identify specific items, it does distinguish between recent and earlier purchases of stock so that the inventory valuation will reflect the most recent price levels. This means that the cost of goods sold will reflect the costs applicable to the oldest goods handled during the period. In a time of rising prices, the difference in the cost of goods sold may have a significant impact on the net income to be reported. For example, there is a difference of $103.90 between the average cost method and the FIFO method in the costing of the 275 shirts sold during the period.

Cost of Goods Sold (Average Cost Method)	$1,916.40
Cost of Goods Sold (FIFO Method)	1,812.50
Difference	$ 103.90

Last In, First Out Method

While the FIFO method will result in a more favorable profit picture under the circumstances just discussed, many accountants, owners, and managers hesitate to use it. They believe that the current cost of merchandise should be matched as closely as possible to current sales dollars. They say that failure to do this means ignoring the ultimate day of reckoning, when inventory has to be replaced at higher costs. The system of valuation that they consider more conservative and realistic is the *last in, first out (LIFO) method.*

The LIFO method of inventory pricing assumes that the most current costs of merchandise purchased should be charged to the cost of goods sold. Thus the value assigned to the inventory still on hand is the cost of the oldest merchandise available during the period. Using the figures from the previous example, the value of the 125 shirts on hand at the end of the period is $762.50. That amount is determined as follows.

EXPLANATION	NO. OF UNITS	UNIT COST	TOTAL COST
From Beginning Inventory, Feb. 1, 19X1	100	$6.00	$600.00
From Purchase of Feb. 27, 19X1	25	6.50	162.50
Ending Inventory, Jan. 31, 19X2	125		$762.50

The cost of goods sold is computed by subtracting $762.50 from the previously established value of the merchandise available for sale ($2,787.50 − $762.50 = $2,025.00). It is apparent that in a time of rising prices, the relatively lower inventory valuation under the LIFO method tends to increase the reported cost of goods sold and decrease the reported net income.

Obviously, the LIFO method of determining inventory cost does not match the actual physical flow of merchandise in most businesses. It is merely a procedure developed for charging the current costs of goods against current sales prices.

Comparing the Results of Inventory Costing Methods

The different results obtained from the use of the average cost, FIFO, and LIFO inventory methods can be seen in the following illustration. (The analysis of purchases is the same as the one shown on page 416.)

COMPARISON OF RESULTS OF INVENTORY COSTING METHODS

Explanation	Units	Unit Cost	Total Cost	Inventory Valuation	Cost of Goods Sold
Beginning Inventory, Feb. 1, 19X1	100	$6.00	$ 600.00		
Purchases:					
Feb. 27, 19X1	50	6.50	325.00		
April 20, 19X1	100	7.00	700.00		
Oct. 15, 19X1	75	7.50	562.50		
Jan. 10, 19X2	75	8.00	600.00		
Total Merchandise Available for Sale	400		$2,787.50		
1. Average Cost Method					
Average Cost per Unit		$6.9688			
Valuation of Ending Inventory	125	6.9688		$871.10	
Cost of Goods Sold					$1,916.40
2. First In, First Out Method					
From Purchase of Jan. 10	75	$8.00	$ 600.00		
From Purchase of Oct. 15	50	7.50	375.00		
Valuation of Ending Inventory				$975.00	
Cost of Goods Sold					$1,812.50
3. Last In, First Out Method					
From Beginning Inventory, Feb. 1	100	$6.00	$ 600.00		
From Purchase of Feb. 27	25	6.50	162.50		
Valuation of Ending Inventory				$762.50	
Cost of Goods Sold					$2,025.00

Notice that the ending inventory valuation of the same 125 shirts ranges from a low of $762.50 when the LIFO method is used to a high of $975 when the FIFO method is used. The average cost method gives a figure in between (as is almost always the case) of $871.10. Subtracting the ending inventory valuation in each case from the total cost of merchandise available for sale, $2,787.50, gives a high cost of goods sold of $2,025 with the LIFO method and a low cost of goods sold of $1,812.50 with the FIFO method. The average cost method usually gives a figure in between ($1,916.40 in this situation).

Since price trends are a vital element in any inventory valuation, remember these basic rules. In a period of rising prices, the LIFO method results in a lower reported net income than the FIFO method. In a period of falling prices, the LIFO method results in a higher reported net income than the FIFO method. Whatever direction prices take, the average cost method results in a reported net income somewhere between the amounts obtained with FIFO and LIFO.

A business cannot change its inventory valuation method at will from one period to the next in order to report the amount of net income it prefers. Once the firm adopts a method, it should use that method consistently from one period to the next. If the managers of a business want to change the method of inventory valuation, they should refer to specific authoritative guides that spell out in detail how the change should be treated on the financial statements. These rules are beyond the scope of this text. For federal income tax purposes, a business must obtain permission from the Director of Internal Revenue before making a change in inventory methods.

Cost or Market, Whichever Is Lower

The methods of inventory valuation discussed so far have been based on cost. However, as you learned in Unit 19, accountants generally believe that the asset valuation used on the balance sheet should be conservative and should not overstate the asset values. If the market price of an inventory item declines, the merchant will probably have trouble selling it at the usual increase, or markon, above original cost. If the price decline is especially severe, the merchant may even have to sell the item at a loss. Consequently, accountants prefer to value inventory according to the rule of *cost or market, whichever is lower.* As the name of this rule suggests, when the price of an item is below its original purchase cost, the accountant values it at market price instead of cost in order to reflect the lower current value on the books.

The market price for the purpose of applying the rule can be described as the price at which the item could be bought (at the inventory date) through the usual channels and in the usual quantities. In some cases, current market prices are quoted in trade publications. In other cases, a recent purchase may give a price that is reasonably close to the current market price. In still other circumstances, the firm's regular suppliers can provide quotations for use in valuing the goods. There are two major ways of applying the lower of cost or market rule. The first is to apply it item by item. The second is to use the total cost and the total market value.

Lower of Cost or Market by Items

If the lower of cost or market rule is to be applied item by item, the cost is determined for each item in the inventory according to one of the acceptable methods (specific identification, average cost, FIFO, or LIFO). Current market price is also determined for each item. Then the basis of valuation (the lower figure) is selected. Finally, the quantity on hand of the item is multiplied by the valuation amount to obtain the total value at the lower of cost or market. The lower value figures for all items are added to determine the value of the inventory as a whole. The application of this rule is illustrated below with assumed figures for two stock items (A and B).

Description	Quantity	Unit Price Cost	Unit Price Market	Valuation Basis	Lower of Cost or Market
Item A	100	$1.00	$1.10	Cost	$100.00
Item B	200	1.50	1.20	Market	240.00
Inventory Valuation—Lower of Cost or Market by Items					$340.00

Lower of Total Cost or Total Market

Under another method of applying the rule of lower of cost or market, the accountant determines the total cost and the total market value of the entire inventory. The accountant then uses the lower of these total figures as the inventory valuation.

Description	Quantity	Unit Price Cost	Unit Price Market	Total Cost	Total Market
Item A	100	$1.00	$1.10	$100.00	$110.00
Item B	200	1.50	1.20	300.00	240.00
				$400.00	$350.00
Inventory Valuation—Lower of Total Cost or Total Market					$350.00

This procedure gives a somewhat less conservative inventory valuation than the item-by-item method if the prices of some items have risen while others have declined. However, advocates of this method justify it on the ground that the total inventory figure is the one that should be presented conservatively. If the market value of the inventory as a whole has not declined below cost, then no adjustment is made and the cost value is presented on the statements.

Lower of Cost or Market by Groups

A variation on the method discussed above involves classifying inventory items by groups or departments and determining the lower of total cost or total market according to these classifications. The lower figure (cost or market) for each group is added to the lower figures for the other groups to obtain the total inventory valuation. Assuming that Items A and B in the preceding example make up Group 1 and that Items C and D make up Group 2, the basic computations required for the group total method are as shown below.

Description	Quantity	Unit Price Cost	Unit Price Market	Total Cost	Total Market
Group 1					
Item A	100	$1.00	$1.10	$100.00	$110.00
Item B	200	1.50	1.20	300.00	240.00
Totals—Group 1				$400.00	$350.00°
Group 2					
Item C	30	$ .70	$ .60	$ 21.00	$ 18.00
Item D	150	.60	.80	90.00	120.00
Totals—Group 2				$111.00°	$138.00

° Lower Figures

In this case, market ($350) is the lower basis for valuation of the items in Group 1, and cost ($111) is the lower basis for valuation of the items in Group 2. The combined value of Groups 1 and 2 is $461 ($350 + $111). Compare this valuation with the figures obtained from the two other methods that are shown below.

	Lower of Cost or Market by Items			Lower of Total Cost or Total Market Valued at	
Item	Basis	Valuation	Item	Cost	Market
A	Cost	$100	A	$100	$110
B	Market	240	B	300	240
C	Market	18	C	21	18
D	Cost	90	D	90	120
		$448		$511	$488°

° Lower Figure

Valuation according to lower of total cost or total market by groups is a method that produces middle-of-the-road figures. It does not reflect individual fluctuations, as the lower of cost or market by items method does. But it also does not lump together as many value variations as the grand total cost or market figures do. The final choice of one of the three methods will depend on many factors, including the size and variety of the stock of merchandise, the margin of profit on which the business operates, practices in the industry, and the firm's future plans for expansion. Usually, however, the lower of cost or market by items is used.

Inventory Estimation Procedures

Sometimes a business wants to know the approximate cost of its inventory without taking a physical inventory and applying one of the costing procedures. For example, if a fire occurs, the firm will need to know the cost of goods destroyed in order to provide data for insurance and income tax purposes. Similarly, a department manager in a retail store may be permitted to have only a certain amount of money tied up in inventory. Therefore, the manager must be able to estimate the cost of the department's inventory at any time. Two common techniques for estimating inventory are the gross profit method and the retail method.

Gross Profit Method

The *gross profit method* of estimating inventory assumes that the rate of gross profit on sales is about the same from period to period. It also assumes that the ratio of cost of goods sold to net sales is relatively constant. The procedure can be illustrated as follows. Assume that a company's entire merchandise inventory is destroyed by fire June 26, 19X1, but that its accounting records are preserved. An analysis of the company's income statements for the two preceding years shows that the gross profit rate has been 40 percent of net sales (or that the cost of goods sold has been 60 percent of net sales). The records for the current year provide the following figures.

Inventory (at cost), Jan. 1, 19X1	$ 40,000
Net Purchases (Jan. 1 to June 26, 19X1)	120,000
Net Sales (Jan. 1 to June 26, 19X1)	210,000

The first step is to estimate the cost of goods sold for the period of January 1 to June 26. Since sales were $210,000 and the ratio of cost of goods sold to net sales is assumed to be 60 percent, the estimated cost of goods sold is computed as follows: $0.60 \times \$210,000 = \$126,000$.

The second step is to determine the cost of goods available for sale. This computation is shown below.

Beginning Inventory	$ 40,000
Net Purchases	120,000
Cost of Goods Available for Sale	$160,000

The final step is to compute the estimated ending (destroyed) inventory by subtracting the estimated cost of goods sold ($126,000) from the cost of goods available for sale ($160,000), as shown below.

Cost of Goods Available for Sale	$160,000
Estimated Cost of Goods Sold	126,000
Estimated Ending Inventory	$ 34,000

Retail Method of Inventory Pricing Another method of inventory pricing, one that is widely used by retailers, is called the *retail method*. Under this method, inventory is classified into groups of items that have about the same rate of markon. (*Markon* is the difference between the cost and the initially established retail price of merchandise.)

The beginning inventory is valued both at cost and at retail. At the time merchandise is purchased, it is recorded at cost and its retail value is determined. The retail value of all merchandise available for sale is obtained by adding the retail value of the beginning inventory and the retail value of the new merchandise purchased. Sales are recorded at their retail price in the usual manner. When the total of sales at retail is subtracted from the total retail value of the merchandise available for sale, the difference is the retail value of the ending inventory. This amount is multiplied by the cost ratio (Total Available for Sale at Cost ÷ Total Available for Sale at Retail) to give the approximate cost of the ending inventory. Using assumed figures, the calculations involved in the application of the retail method of inventory pricing are shown below.

	Cost	Retail
Beginning Inventory	$ 4,900	$ 7,500
Merchandise Purchases	60,000	90,000
Freight	100	
Total Merchandise Available for Sale	$65,000	$97,500
Less Sales		79,200
Ending Inventory Priced at Retail		$18,300
Cost Ratio = $\dfrac{\$65,000}{\$97,500} = 66\frac{2}{3}\%$		
Conversion to Approximate Cost:		
Ending Inventory at Retail × Cost Ratio	$18,300 × 0.6667	
Ending Inventory at Cost	$12,200	
Cost of Goods Sold ($65,000 − $12,200)	$52,800	

In practice, the application of the retail method of inventory pricing is not quite as simple as this example suggests. Records must be kept of further price increases—*markups*—above the original markons, as well as of markup cancellations. Records must also be kept of *markdowns* below the original markon and of markdown cancellations. When all this information is assembled, the resulting calculations can yield an inventory valuation that will approximate the lower of cost or market. The requirements of the retail inventory method are discussed in more detail in intermediate-level accounting textbooks.

When there are many merchandise items of small unit value, as is often the case in retail stores, the retail method of inventory pricing permits a firm to determine the approximate cost of its ending inventory from the financial records. Thus the firm does not have to take a physical inventory. In turn, the ease of determining the inventory value makes it possible for the firm to prepare financial statements easily and often.

Many retail stores take a periodic physical inventory at retail values, using the sales prices marked on the merchandise. Then the physical inventory at retail is converted to cost by applying the cost ratio. This is done in the way that the ending retail inventory computed in the previous example was reduced to cost. The Style Clothing Store uses this method of valuation because of its simplicity and because of the firm's need to have inventory values available often.

principles and procedures summary

There are several inventory costing methods. The specific identification method uses the actual purchase price of the specific items in inventory. The average cost method uses the average of the cost of all like items available for sale during the period for valuing the ending inventory. The first in, first out (FIFO) method develops the cost of the ending inventory from the cost of later purchases. The last in, first out (LIFO) method develops the cost of ending inventory from the cost of earlier purchases. In a period of rising prices the LIFO method will result in a lower reported net income than the FIFO method. In a period of falling prices, the LIFO method will result in a higher reported net income. The average cost method will always give a result between the two.

Not all inventory valuation is based on the purchase cost. The rule of cost or market, whichever is lower, is the most conservative method available. It can be applied to individual items in the inventory, to groups of items, or to the inventory as a whole.

The gross profit method of estimating inventory involves estimating the cost of goods sold by applying a historical cost ratio to the sales of the current period. The estimated cost of goods sold is then subtracted from the cost of goods available for sale to arrive at the estimated ending inventory.

The retail method of inventory pricing uses the retail selling price of the items remaining. The retail value of the inventory is multiplied by the cost ratio of the current period to reach the approximate cost. An estimate of the inventory approximating the lower of cost or market can be obtained by fully considering markups, markup cancellations, markdowns, and markdown cancellations.

MANAGERiAl implicATioNS

Because inventory makes up a large part of the assets of most businesses, it must be carefully controlled. The inventory costing method chosen by management must be one that is practical, reliable, and as simple as possible to apply. Inventory valuation is very important in computing federal income tax because the value placed on the inventory determines the net income reported. For example, in times of rising prices, the LIFO method is a means of lowering the income tax by charging off a higher cost of goods sold.

The gross profit method of estimating inventory is an especially valuable tool for approximating the cost of an inventory. It is used in preparing budgets when a physical count cannot be made, and it is used in verifying the reasonableness of the inventory computed under an actual physical count.

Management should consider the retail method of inventory pricing as a means of estimating the cost of goods on hand at any given time. This estimate is especially important in retail businesses where department managers have inventory budgets—specified amounts they are allowed to tie up in inventory. Such managers generally need to know often, sometimes weekly, the amount of inventory they have on hand.

MANAGERIAL DISCUSSION QUESTIONS

1. Why must managers provide for strict control of a firm's inventory?
2. Why do managers instruct their sales staffs to sell the oldest merchandise first?
3. In what special situations are inventory estimation procedures extremely useful?
4. The president of a retail business has suggested that the firm's inventory is too high. He would like to have an estimate of the inventory each week. Outline briefly a plan to develop this estimate without actually counting inventory items.
5. Why would managers be interested in using the LIFO inventory method for federal income tax purposes in a period of inflation?

APPLICATION OF PRINCIPLES

PROBLEM 23-1 The following data concerns inventory and purchases at the Fairfax Company.

Inventory, June 1	150 units at $8.00
Purchases, June 6	200 units at $8.10
June 14	150 units at $8.40
June 24	100 units at $8.50
Inventory, June 30	162 units

INSTRUCTIONS Determine the cost of the ending inventory on June 30 under each of the following methods: (1) average cost method, (2) first in, first out method, and (3) last in, first out method. (When using the average cost method, compute the unit cost to four decimal places.)

PROBLEM 23-2 The following data concerns inventory at the Tamberelli Electronics Corporation.

	Unit Quantity	Cost	Market Value
Magnetic Tape Department			
Stock No. 101	250	$ 3.00	$ 3.20
Stock No. 102	400	4.40	4.20
Stock No. 103	370	2.00	2.10
Tape Recorder Department			
Stock No. 401	4	170.00	182.00
Stock No. 402	2	410.00	400.00
Stock No. 403	5	153.00	144.00

INSTRUCTIONS Determine the amount to be reported as the inventory valuation at cost or market, whichever is lower, under each of these methods.

1. Lower of cost or market for each item separately.
2. Lower of total cost or total market.
3. Lower of total cost or total market by departments.

PROBLEM 23-3 In 19X0 the rate of gross profit on sales at the Decatur Company was 26.2 percent, and in 19X1 the rate was 24.8 percent. At the end of 19X2, the income statement of the company included the following information.

Sales		$820,000
Cost of Goods Sold:		
Inventory, Jan. 1, 19X2	$ 60,000	
Purchases	604,000	
Total Merchandise Available for Sale	$664,000	
Less Inventory, Dec. 31, 19X2	94,000	
Cost of Goods Sold		570,000
Gross Profit on Sales		$250,000

Investigation revealed that employees of the company had not taken an actual physical count of the inventory on December 31, 19X2. Instead, they had merely estimated the inventory.

INSTRUCTIONS Using the gross profit method of inventory estimation, verify the reasonableness (or lack of reasonableness) of the ending inventory shown on the income statement.

PROBLEM 23-4 The January 1 inventory of the J-Star Company had a cost $18,000 and had a retail value of $24,500. During January merchandise was purchased for $8,840 and marked to sell for $11,500. Freight on purchases during January totaled $160. January sales totaled $11,200.

INSTRUCTIONS
1. Estimate the January 31 inventory according to the retail method.
2. Compute the cost of goods sold.

AlteRNAte pRobleMs

PROBLEM 23-1A The following data concerns inventory and purchases at the Tonkin Company.

Inventory, Jan.	1	800 units at $4.00
Purchases, Jan.	8	400 units at $4.20
	Jan. 16	200 units at $4.24
	Jan. 24	400 units at $4.30
Inventory, Jan. 31		820 units

427

INSTRUCTIONS Determine the cost of the ending inventory on January 31 under each of the following methods: (1) average cost method, (2) first in, first out method, and (3) last in, first out method. (When using the average cost method, compute the unit cost to four decimal places.)

PROBLEM 23-2A The following data concerns inventory at Nautical Products Inc.

	Quantity	Unit Cost	Market Value
Boat Department			
Model T	8	$560	$600
Model U	7	840	800
Model W	10	360	380
Motor Department			
Model A	6	380	404
Model B	3	780	760
Model C	5	406	388

INSTRUCTIONS Determine the amount to be reported as the inventory valuation at cost or market, whichever is lower, under each of these methods.

1. Lower of cost or market for each item separately.
2. Lower of total cost or total market.
3. Lower of total cost or total market by departments.

PROBLEM 23-3A In 19X1 the rate of gross profit on sales at the Celeste Company was 39.9 percent, and in 19X2 the rate was 40.1 percent. At the end of 19X3, the auditor found the following data in the records of the company.

Sales		$1,000,000
Cost of Goods Sold:		
Inventory, Jan. 1, 19X3	$120,000	
Purchases	600,000	
Total Merchandise Available for Sale	$720,000	
Less Inventory, Dec. 31, 19X3	190,000	
Cost of Goods Sold		530,000
Gross Profit on Sales		$ 470,000

Inquiry by the auditor revealed that employees of the Celeste Company had estimated the inventory on December 31, 19X3, instead of taking a complete physical count.

INSTRUCTIONS Using the gross profit method of inventory estimation, verify the reasonableness (or lack of reasonableness) of the inventory estimate made by the company's employees.

PROBLEM 23-4A

The Chan Company uses the retail method of inventory pricing. As of December 31, 19X1, the firm's records disclosed the following figures.

	ACTUAL COST	RETAIL SALES PRICE
Beginning Inventory, Jan. 1, 19X1	$ 8,000	$ 11,200
Merchandise Purchases During 19X1	72,640	100,800
Total Merchandise Available for Sale	$80,640	$112,000

Total Sales During 19X1 = $98,000

INSTRUCTIONS

1. Compute the retail value of the ending inventory as of December 31, 19X1.
2. Compute the approximate cost of the ending inventory as of December 31, 19X1.
3. Compute the cost of goods sold during 19X1.

UNIT 24

PROPERTY, PLANT, AND EQUIPMENT

Housing and equipping a modern business enterprise for efficient operation often calls for a large investment in property. This unit explains the accounting procedures and records needed to keep track of the purchase, use, and disposition of property, plant, and equipment—often referred to as fixed assets, *or* long-lived assets.

Classification of Property, Plant, and Equipment

Fixed assets or long-lived assets often include both tangible and intangible property. Tangible property consists of real property and personal property. Among the *real property* holdings of a business are land, buildings, and other structures attached to the land. *Tangible personal property* includes machinery, equipment, furniture, and fixtures. The *intangible personal property* of a business consists of such assets as patents, trademarks, copyrights, organization costs, and goodwill. These assets are classified here in outline form.

  I. Tangible Fixed Assets
    A. Real property
      1. Land
        a. Building sites
        b. Timberland
        c. Mineral land
      2. Buildings and other structures attached to the land
    B. Personal property
      1. Machinery and equipment
      2. Furniture and fixtures
 II. Intangible Fixed Assets
    A. Patents
    B. Trademarks
    C. Copyrights
    D. Organization costs
    E. Goodwill

Acquisition of Property, Plant, and Equipment

Items of property, plant, and equipment are usually acquired by purchase. Under the accounting system used by the Style Clothing Store, a voucher is prepared to authorize payment for a fixed asset. This results in a debit to the appropriate asset account and a credit to Accounts Payable. The voucher is paid in the usual manner, at which time Accounts Payable is debited and Cash in Bank is credited.

The total cost of a fixed asset may actually be made up of several elements, each of which must be debited to the account for that asset. The general rule is that the acquisition cost of an asset includes the net price paid the seller, all transportation and installation costs, and the cost of any adjustments or modifications needed to prepare the asset for use. (A cash discount taken for prompt payment of an invoice for a fixed asset should be credited to the asset account rather than to Purchases Discount. The credit to the asset account can be recorded in the general journal with an offsetting debit to Accounts Payable if a voucher was previously recorded for the gross amount of the invoice.)

Suppose that the Style Clothing Store purchases an office machine at a price of $337.50 *FOB* (*free on board*) the factory (which means that the buyer pays for transportation from the factory). The freight bill is $36.25. When the machine arrives, the firm decides to have extra features installed on it locally, at a net cost of $26.25. At what cost is the machine entered in the Office Equipment account?

The seller's invoice is the first amount to be debited to the Office Equipment account. The transportation charge paid by the Style Clothing Store is part of the cost of the machine and should also be debited to that account. The cost of the changes made to the machine before it is suitable for the intended use is a further charge to the asset account. When all these charges have been posted to the Office Equipment account, the total acquisition cost of the machine will be $400, as shown below.

Net amount paid to seller	$337.50
Freight	36.25
Minor changes in operating features	26.25
Total acquisition cost of machine	$400.00

In the case of land purchased for a building site, the acquisition cost of the land should include the costs of removing unwanted buildings, grading and draining the land, installing permanent walks or roadways, and landscaping. If the land is bought in advance of the time it is to be used, taxes and other carrying charges can be added to the asset value on the books up to the time the property is used for business purposes.

The capitalized costs of intangible assets include only the costs related to acquisition of such assets from outside parties.° (*Capitalized costs* are costs that are recorded in an asset account.) Research and development costs must be charged as expenses when they are incurred, even though they may result in valuable patents or other intangibles.† On the other hand, the cost of a patent purchased from another party is capitalized as an intangible asset.

° "Intangible Assets," *Opinions of the Accounting Principles Board, No. 17* (New York: American Institute of Certified Public Accountants, 1970), par. 24.
† "Accounting for Research and Development Costs," *Statement of Financial Accounting Standards No. 2* (Stamford, Connecticut: Financial Accounting Standards Board, Oct., 1974), par. 12.

Costs of Using Property, Plant, and Equipment

Several obvious costs are incurred in using fixed assets. These costs include repairs, maintenance, insurance, and taxes. However, there are also hidden costs. Assets such as buildings and machines do not last forever. Their inevitable wearing out through use in the firm's operations must be taken into account as an additional expense of doing business. Other types of assets, such as natural resources and patents, are also used up in the course of the firm's operations. Three technical terms are commonly used by accountants to distinguish the nature of the expense involved. They are depreciation, depletion, and amortization.

Depreciation

As explained in Unit 17, *depreciation* is the term used in accounting to describe the periodic transfer of acquisition cost to expense for fixed assets such as buildings, machinery, equipment, furniture, and fixtures (but not land). Four widely used methods of spreading depreciation expense over the useful life of a fixed asset are described later in this unit.

Depletion

Natural resources, such as timber, oil, and minerals, are physically removed from the land in the process of production. Their cost is part of the expense of carrying on such operations. *Depletion* is the term used to describe this expense. Methods for computing depletion are discussed later in this unit.

Amortization

Most intangible assets, such as patents and copyrights, have limited legal and useful lives. Their acquisition cost must be spread over the shorter of the two lives. *Amortization* is the term used in accounting to describe this expense. Methods of accounting for amortization are discussed later in this unit.

Recording Depreciation, Depletion, and Amortization

Assets subject to depreciation or depletion are recorded at acquisition cost. They are generally carried at this figure as long as they remain in use. (Of course, later additions or partial dispositions require an adjustment of the acquisition cost figure.)

At the end of each accounting period, the current depreciation or depletion is debited to an appropriate expense account and credited to an accumulated depreciation or accumulated depletion account. For example, assume that a business has plant buildings that cost $100,000 and that an annual depreciation charge of $5,000 is to be recorded for these buildings. Assume also that the business owns a mineral deposit that cost $200,000 and that depletion on it for the current year is $15,000. These current-year expenses for depreciation and depletion appear on the worksheet as adjustments and are later recorded in the general journal as illustrated below.

Date		Description		Debit	Credit
19X1					
Dec.	31	Depreciation Expense—Plant Buildings	571	5,000 00	
		Accumulated Depr.—Plant Buildings	141A		5,000 00
		Depreciation of plant buildings for the year.			
	31	Depletion Expense—Mineral Deposit	584	15,000 00	
		Accumulated Depl.—Mineral Deposit	154A		15,000 00
		Depletion of mineral deposit for the year.			

Assume that this is the first year of use for both assets. The balance sheet presentation at the end of the year is as follows.

Fixed Assets		
Plant Buildings	$100,000	
Less Accumulated Depreciation	5,000	$ 95,000
Mineral Deposit	$200,000	
Less Accumulated Depletion	15,000	185,000

Because of the importance of depreciation, the following information must be shown on the financial statements or in their accompanying notes.

1. Depreciation expense for the period.
2. Balances of major classes of depreciable assets, by nature or function.
3. Accumulated depreciation.
4. A general description of the method or methods used in computing depreciation.*

The accumulated depreciation or depletion accounts are contra asset accounts. Their credit balances, which are opposite to the normal asset account balances, reflect the amount of acquisition cost that has been transferred to expense. Thus they permit a more accurate representation of the cost applicable to the remaining life of each asset involved. The difference between the acquisition cost shown in the asset account and the balance of the contra account is the book value, or *net book value*, of the asset. In the examples shown above, the plant buildings have a book value of $95,000 and the mineral deposit has a book value of $185,000.

Assets subject to amortization are also recorded at acquisition cost. The periodic amortization is debited to an expense account and, by custom, credited directly to the asset account. The balance in the asset account is thus the book value. For example, assume that a firm has patents with an original cost of $34,000. Of this amount, $2,000 is amortized for the current year. The adjusting entry to record the amortization is shown below.

19 X1				
Dec. 31	Amortization of Patents	538	2,000 00	
	Patents	158		2,000 00
	Amortization of patents for the year.			

The balance sheet will show Patents at the book value of $32,000 ($34,000 − $2,000). If the same amount of amortization is recorded during the second year, the Patents account will be reported at the end of the year at a book value of $30,000.

---

* "Disclosure of Depreciable Assets and Depreciation," *Opinions of the Accounting Principles Board*, No. 12 (New York: American Institute of Certified Public Accountants, 1967), par. 02.

Methods of Accounting for Depreciation

As previously explained, the cost of certain tangible fixed assets is spread over their useful lives through periodic depreciation charges to an expense account and corresponding credits to a contra asset account (commonly referred to as an accumulated depreciation account). The total amount charged to the expense account must not exceed the total cost of the asset less any net salvage value that the asset is expected to have at the end of its useful life. In determining the net salvage value, estimated removal costs are deducted from expected proceeds of sale.

Four widely used methods of depreciation are described here: straight-line, declining-balance, sum-of-the-years'-digits, and units-of-output. Certain other methods are also occasionally used.

Straight-Line Method

The straight-line method (first presented in Unit 17) is, because of its simplicity, the most widely used method of computing depreciation. Under this method, the same amount of depreciation is recorded for each year or other accounting period over the useful life of the asset. To obtain the annual depreciation, the acquisition cost less the expected net salvage value is divided by the expected life in years. This is expressed by the following formula.

$$\frac{\text{Acquisition Cost} - \text{Net Salvage Value}}{\text{Useful Life in Years}} = \text{Annual Depreciation}$$

Suppose that an office machine purchased by the Style Clothing Store at a total cost of $400 is expected to be used for five years and to have a net salvage value of $40 at the end of that time. The result of these figures is the following equation.

$$\frac{\$400 - \$40}{5} = \frac{\$360}{5} = \$72 \text{ Annual Depreciation}$$

If the firm records depreciation at the end of each fiscal year, $72 is debited to Depreciation Expense—Office Equipment and credited to Accumulated Depreciation—Office Equipment. The monthly amount of the depreciation charge on the office equipment is $\frac{1}{12}$ of $72, or $6. Depreciation on a newly acquired asset is usually computed to the nearest month. For example, if the asset had been purchased on September 5, 19X1, depreciation of $30 (5 months × $6) would be recorded for the fiscal year ended January 31, 19X2.

Declining-Balance Method

Under the *declining-balance method* of depreciation, the accountant applies an appropriate percentage to the book value of an asset at the beginning of each year to obtain the depreciation charge for that year. The maximum percentage allowable for income tax purposes on new depreciable personal property (and therefore widely used by business firms) is twice the rate of the straight-line method.

When the straight-line method is applied to the Style Clothing Store's office machine (which has an expected useful life of five years), the yearly depreciation is $\frac{1}{5}$, or 20 percent, of the cost minus the net salvage value. The declining-balance rate allowable on the same item is twice 20 percent, or 40 percent. (Under tax regulations, the salvage value is ignored when the declining-balance method is used. It is also usually ignored in financial accounting.)

In the first year, the acquisition cost of $400 is multiplied by 40 percent to give a depreciation expense of $160 for that year. The book value at the beginning of the second year is $240 ($400 − $160), and the depreciation expense for the second year is $96 (40 percent of $240). The depreciation of the office machine under the declining-balance method for the five years of its useful life can be illustrated as follows.

DEPRECIATION BY DECLINING-BALANCE METHOD

Year	Beginning Book Value	Rate	Depreciation for Year	Depreciation to Date
1	$400.00	40%	$160.00	$160.00
2	240.00	40%	96.00	256.00
3	144.00	40%	57.60	313.60
4	86.40	40%	34.56	348.16
5	51.84	40%	20.74	368.90

Ending Book Value = $31.10

Although no salvage value is used in computing the annual depreciation, there remains at the end of the five years a book value of $31.10—only slightly less than the estimated salvage value of $40 used under the straight-line method.

Sum-of-the-Years'-Digits Method

Under the *sum-of-the-years'-digits method* of depreciation, a fractional part of the depreciable cost of a fixed asset is charged to expense each year. The denominator of the fraction is always the "sum of the years' digits." This amount is found by simply adding together the numbers representing the years of the asset's useful life. For example, the digits for a machine expected to have a useful life of five years are 1, 2, 3, 4, and 5. Thus, the sum of the years' digits is $1 + 2 + 3 + 4 + 5$, or 15. The numerator for any year is the number of years remaining in the useful life of the asset. Thus, for the first year the fraction is $\frac{5}{15}$, for the second year it is $\frac{4}{15}$, and so on. The fraction is applied to the acquisition cost minus the net salvage value. In the example of the office machine discussed before, these amounts are $400 − $40, or $360.

The table on page 436 applies the sum-of-the-years'-digits method to the office machine owned by the Style Clothing Store. The table also compares this method of depreciation with the two methods previously illustrated.

Note that both the declining-balance method and the sum-of-the-years'-digits method give higher depreciation charges in the early years of the asset's life and lower charges in the later years. These two methods are sometimes called *accelerated methods*. For income tax reporting purposes, a change can be made from the declining-balance method to the straight-line method at any time. (The book value at the time of the change, less the estimated salvage value, is depreciated over the estimated remaining useful life.) However, no

	Sum-of-the-Years'-Digits Method			Depreciation by Other Methods	
Year	Fraction	Cost Minus Salvage	Depreciation for Year	Declining Balance	Straight Line
1	$\frac{5}{15}$	$360.00	$120.00	$160.00	$ 72.00
2	$\frac{4}{15}$	360.00	96.00	96.00	72.00
3	$\frac{3}{15}$	360.00	72.00	57.60	72.00
4	$\frac{2}{15}$	360.00	48.00	34.56	72.00
5	$\frac{1}{15}$	360.00	24.00	20.74	72.00
Total Depreciation—5 years			$360.00	$368.90	$360.00
Net Book Value at End of 5 Years			$ 40.00	$ 31.10	$ 40.00

other change in depreciation method can be made without the express permission of the tax authorities.

A business can use several different depreciation methods simultaneously for different assets or different groups of assets. It can also use one depreciation method for tax purposes and another method for financial accounting purposes.

Units-of-Output Method

In some situations, the useful life of a fixed asset is related more directly to units of work performed by the asset than to the passage of time. In such cases, depreciation can be calculated at a certain rate for each unit of output. The expense for any time period is then determined by multiplying the rate for each unit by the number of units produced. This method of computing depreciation is called the *units-of-output method*.

For example, suppose that a firm purchases a metal stamping press for $10,000. The press is expected to have a useful life of 1,000,000 stamping impressions. The rate for each stamping is $10,000 divided by 1,000,000, or $0.01. If 50,000 stampings are produced during a period, the depreciation charge is 50,000 × $0.01, or $500.

Depletion Methods

For accounting purposes, the amount to be charged for depletion of property such as oil, a mineral, or metal is based on cost. However, for income tax purposes, the depletion can also be computed as a percentage of gross income (the sale price) of the asset. (In some cases, income from oil and gas production is not subject to statutory depletion.) The cost depletion and percentage depletion methods are discussed here.

Cost Depletion Method

Depletion based on cost is determined in a manner very similar to depreciation determined by the units-of-output method. The total cost of the mineral deposit is divided by the estimated number of units in the deposit to give the depletion cost for each unit of the mineral extracted. For example, suppose a firm purchases a clay pit that is estimated to contain 500,000 tons of extractable clay suitable for making brick. The firm pays $25,000 for the clay pit. The depletion cost for each ton of clay is $0.05 ($25,000 ÷ 500,000 tons). If the firm extracts 60,000 tons of this clay in a particular year, the depletion cost will be $3,000 (60,000 × $0.05).

Percentage Depletion Method

For income tax purposes, depletion can be calculated as a percentage of the revenue obtained from the sale of the mineral. The amount of depletion calculated in this manner must not be less than the cost depletion would be. Also, it must not be more than 50 percent of the net income from the property before the deduction of depletion.

Assume that the 60,000 tons of clay discussed above bring an average price of $2.50 a ton and that the net income from the operation before the depletion deduction is $40,000. Also assume that the firm applies the percentage depletion rate of $7\frac{1}{2}$ percent that is specified by the tax law to the total sales of $150,000. The result of this computation is the allowable depletion of $11,250. Since this amount is well below the 50 percent limitation on net income before depletion (which is $40,000 × 0.50, or $20,000) and is not less than the cost depletion, the firm assigns the entire $11,250 as the depletion expense for the year.

Over a number of years, the total percentage depletion taken can be well above the total cost of the property. Thus the percentage depletion method can provide a considerable tax advantage. A firm might therefore use this method for income tax purposes but use the cost method for financial accounting purposes.

Amortization of Intangible Assets

There are fewer methods for calculating the amount of amortization of intangible assets than for calculating depreciation. The straight-line method is the one most commonly used, although the units-of-output method is appropriate in some situations. The declining-balance and sum-of-the-years'-digits methods cannot be used.

The *legal life* of a patent is 17 years. The term for a copyright is 28 years, with the possibility of renewing the copyright for another 47 years.[*] The *useful life* is usually much shorter. In computing amortization, the shorter life—legal or useful—should be used. In no case, however, should the amortization period be more than 40 years.

Suppose a company pays $6,000 for a patent that it estimates will have a useful life of 12 years. Annual amortization on the straight-line basis is $500 ($6,000 divided by 12 years). Remember that the entry to record amortization requires a debit to the amortization expense account and a credit to the asset account being amortized.

---

[*] These figures apply only to works copyrighted before January 1, 1978. A new law that went into force on that date specified different copyright periods for works registered after January 1, 1978. The law is complex and cannot be fully explained here. However, for many works, it provides a copyright period that lasts for the author's lifetime plus 50 years after the author's death.

Other types of intangible assets, such as the organization costs incurred in forming a corporation, are examined in later units.

Disposition of an Asset

Fixed assets that are no longer useful to a business are usually disposed of. They may be sold, traded in, or scrapped. Sometimes, useful assets are also sold so the company can purchase better assets. When an asset is disposed of, the following steps are taken to enter the facts in the firm's financial records.

1. The accountant records depreciation to the date of disposition.
2. The accountant closes out the appropriate amounts in the asset account and the related accumulated depreciation account; records the proceeds realized; and determines and records the gain or loss if any.

The accounting entries necessary to record the sale of a fixed asset under various conditions are illustrated by the following example. A firm has a $400 office machine like the one owned by the Style Clothing Store. The firm has recorded depreciation on the straight-line basis for three years at $72 a year, for a total of $216. Six months later ($3\frac{1}{2}$ years after the purchase) management decides to sell the machine. The first thing the accountant must do is record depreciation up to the date of the sale. The amount to be recorded is $36 for the six months following the last year in which depreciation was recorded. This amount is debited to Depreciation Expense—Office Equipment and credited to Accumulated Depreciation—Office Equipment.

The Office Equipment account has a debit balance of $400 representing the acquisition cost. The accumulated depreciation account now has a credit balance of $252 ($216 + $36). The book value is $148 ($400 − $252).

Sale at Book Value

Suppose first that the sale is made on credit for an amount equal to the book value of $148. The accountant must do the following.

1. Record the new account receivable of $148 on the books.
2. Close out the balance of $252 in the accumulated depreciation account.
3. Close out the cost of $400 in the asset account.

In the general journal, all these details can be handled in one compound entry, as shown below.

19 X1				
July 31	Accounts Receivable	111	148 00	
	Accumulated Depr.—Office Equipment	132A	252 00	
	Office Equipment	132		400 00
	Sold machine at book value.			

Since the sale is for the book value, there is no gain or loss to be recorded.

Sale Above Book Value

Suppose that the agreed sales price is $175, which is $27 above the book value. Accounts Receivable is debited for $175. The accumulated depreciation account is debited for $252, and the asset account is credited for $400, as before.

To complete the entry, a new account, called Gain on Sale of Equipment, is credited for $27, as shown below.

19	X1				
July	31	Accounts Receivable	111	175 00	
		Accumulated Depr.—Office Equipment	132A	252 00	
		Office Equipment	132		400 00
		Gain on Sale of Equipment	495		27 00
		Sold machine above book value.			

The $27 gain represents, of course, the difference between the sales price of $175 and the book value of $148. It is shown on the income statement as an item of income, usually under the heading Other Income.

Sale Below Book Value

Suppose that the sales price is $125. Compared with the book value of $148, this price represents a loss of $23. Accounts Receivable is debited for the agreed price of $125. The accumulated depreciation account is debited for its balance of $252, and the asset account is credited for $400, as previously explained. A new account called Loss on Sale of Equipment is debited for $23. This general journal entry appears below.

19	X1				
July	31	Accounts Receivable	111	125 00	
		Accumulated Depr.—Office Equipment	132A	252 00	
		Loss on Sale of Equipment	595	23 00	
		Office Equipment	132		400 00
		Sold machine below book value.			

The loss is shown on the income statement, usually under the heading Other Expenses.

Trade-In of an Asset

Businesses often trade in existing equipment when they purchase new equipment. This type of transaction must be recorded in two steps. First, the accountant records the depreciation on the old asset up to the date of the trade-in. Then the accountant records the trade-in and the purchase.

The Income Tax Method

For many years, the federal tax laws have provided that when an asset used in business is traded in for a similar asset, no gain or loss is to be recorded on the transaction. The cost of the new asset is assumed to be the book value (cost minus accumulated depreciation) of the old asset plus the cash amount paid. This procedure is also required in financial accounting when "productive assets" are exchanged at a gain for similar assets.° (However, a loss resulting from an exchange of productive assets for similar assets must be recognized.)

° "Accounting for Nonmonetary Transactions," *Opinions of the Accounting Principles Board, No. 29* (New York: American Institute of Certified Public Accountants, 1973), par. 21.

Under the income tax method, the accountant must do the following.

1. Credit the asset account for the cost of the old asset traded in.
2. Close out the amount in the accumulated depreciation account that covers the old asset.
3. Record the cash payment to be made (as a credit to Accounts Payable if the voucher system is used).
4. Record the new asset at the sum of the cash to be paid plus the book value of the old asset.

The following example illustrates this procedure. A firm trades in a desk calculator that originally cost $750. Depreciation of $500 was recorded to the date of trade-in, which leaves a book value of $250. The calculator is traded in for a new model having a list price and fair market value of $900. The seller offers an allowance of $300 on the old calculator against the purchase price of the new $900 model. In effect, the trade-in of the old calculator produces a gain of $50 ($300 trade-in allowance less $250 book value) for the purchaser of the new calculator. But that gain is not recognized. Under the procedure outlined above, the accountant must do the following.

1. Remove the cost of the old asset, $750, from the asset account.
2. Remove the applicable depreciation of $500 from the accumulated depreciation account.
3. Record the $600 cash to be paid ($900 cost minus $300 allowance) by crediting Accounts Payable.
4. Record the new calculator on the books at $850, which is the sum of the $600 cash to be paid and the $250 book value of the old calculator traded in ($750 cost minus $500 depreciation to date).

The necessary entry, in general journal form, appears below.

19 X1				
Oct. 31	Office Equipment	132	850 00	
	Accumulated Depr.—Office Equipment	132A	500 00	
	Office Equipment	132		750 00
	Accounts Payable	205		600 00
	Traded in old calculator for new model.			

If the seller of the new equipment had made an allowance of only $150 on the trade-in, the purchaser would have realized a loss of $100 ($250 book value less $150 trade-in allowance received). Under *APB Opinion No. 29*, this kind of loss must be recorded, as shown in the next section. However, for income tax purposes no loss would be recorded; instead the new equipment would have a "tax basis" of $1,000—the total of the book value of the old asset ($250) and the amount of cash paid for the new asset ($750). In spite of the requirements of *APB Opinion No. 29* to record all losses on trade-ins, many businesses continue to use the income tax method. They do so on the ground that such losses are usually immaterial. They also want to avoid duplicate recordkeeping. If the income tax method is used in this case, the exchange is recorded as follows.

	19 X1					
	Oct. 31	Office Equipment	132	1,000 00		
		Accumulated Depr.—Office Equipment	132A	500 00		
		Office Equipment	132		750 00	
		Accounts Payable	205		750 00	
		Traded in old calculator for new model.				

The Fair Market Value Method

As already mentioned, under *APB Opinion No. 29*, if the book value of the old asset exceeds the amount of trade-in allowance received, the new asset should be recognized at its fair market value and the loss should be recognized. The accountant must do the following.

1. Credit the asset account for the cost of the old asset traded in.
2. Close out the amount of depreciation in the accumulated depreciation account that covers the old asset.
3. Record the cash payment to be made.
4. Record the new asset at its fair market value (its cash purchase price).
5. Record a loss equal to the difference between the trade-in allowance received and the book value of the old asset.

Assume that this procedure is followed in the second example given under the income tax method. A trade-in allowance of $150 is received on an old asset with a book value of $250. Thus there is a loss of $100 ($250 book value minus the trade-in allowance of $150). The trade-in is recorded as follows.

	19 X1					
	Oct. 31	Office Equipment	132	900 00		
		Accumulated Depr.—Office Equipment	132A	500 00		
		Loss on Sale of Equipment	595	100 00		
		Office Equipment	132		750 00	
		Accounts Payable	205		750 00	
		Traded in old calculator for new model—allowance below book value of old machine.				

principles and procedures summary

Fixed assets, usually referred to as *property, plant, and equipment,* can be classified as tangible (including real and personal property) or as intangible (including such items as patents, copyrights, trademarks, and goodwill). Depending on the nature of the asset, depreciation, depletion, or amortization must be included as a current cost. Through these charges, the cost of the asset is spread over its useful or legal life.

Four widely used methods of accounting for depreciation are the straight-line method, the declining-balance method, the sum-of-the-years'-digits method, and the units-of-output method. Depletion may be based on cost or, for tax purposes only, on a percentage of revenue obtained. Amortization may be calculated by the straight-line method or, in some cases, by the units-of-output method.

Fixed assets are disposed of in various ways. They may be sold, scrapped, or traded in for other assets. At the time of sale or trade-in, the depreciation to date must be recorded. It is also necessary to remove the cost of the item from the asset account and the total depreciation from the accumulated depreciation account. If a loss results from either a sale or a trade-in, it must be determined and recorded. Gains from sales are, of course, recorded, but gains from trade-ins are not.

MANAGERIAL IMPLICATIONS

Fixed assets involve large sums of money. Managers must therefore keep close watch over them and over the records used in accounting for them. Managers must also understand the various depreciation methods that can be used, particularly the methods that are permissible for income tax purposes. Knowing how the methods work will help managers to evaluate their possible effects and will aid in selecting the method that is most advantageous to the firm. Managers must also study the methods to be used for recording sales or trade-ins of assets, because the results obtained from the different methods affect reported profits and taxes differently.

MANAGERIAL DISCUSSION QUESTIONS

1. Assume that one of the managers of a firm where you work wants to know why, under generally accepted accounting principles, losses on trade-ins of assets for new ones are recognized but gains are not. How would you explain this difference?
2. Explain why a firm might find one method of depreciation more advantageous than another.
3. Why would a firm use the percentage depletion method for tax purposes and the cost depletion method for its financial records? Why not use percentage depletion for both purposes?
4. Why should management insist that a firm's intangible assets, such as patents, be amortized over their useful lives rather than over their legal lives?
5. Under generally accepted accounting principles, all costs incurred for research and development are charged to expense as they are incurred. Suppose that an officer of a company where you are employed is concerned about this requirement. What reasons can you give for it?

application of principles

PROBLEM 24-1   The Hydro Company has purchased a machine at a cost of $6,400. The estimated useful life is five years, and the estimated salvage value is $400.

INSTRUCTIONS
1. Using the straight-line method, compute the annual depreciation charge.
2. Using the declining-balance method, compute the depreciation charge for each year. Also determine both the depreciation to date (the balance in the accumulated depreciation account at the end of each year) and the ending book value.
3. Using the sum-of-the-years'-digits method, compute the depreciation charge for each year and determine both the depreciation to date and the ending book value.
4. Prepare a table showing a comparison of the results obtained under the various methods. Provide columns for Year, Depreciation for Year (one column for each method—Straight-Line, Declining-Balance, Sum-of-the-Years'-Digits), and Depreciation to Date (one column for each method—Straight-Line, Declining-Balance, Sum-of-the-Years'-Digits). Also compute the book values at the end of five years.

PROBLEM 24-2   The Terrace Company purchased four identical machines on January 2, 19X1, paying $555 cash for each. The useful life of each machine is expected to be six years, and the salvage value at the end of that time is estimated to be $75 for each machine. The company uses the straight-line method of depreciation. Selected transactions involving the machines are listed below and on the next page. The necessary accounts for recording these transactions are also given below.

INSTRUCTIONS
1. Record the transactions in general journal form.
2. Assuming that the trade-in of Machine 4 was recorded under the income tax method, give the general journal entry that would be made on July 31, 19X4.

ACCOUNTS

101	Cash in Bank
141	Machinery
141A	Accumulated Depreciation—Machinery
495	Gain on Sale of Machinery
541	Depreciation Expense—Machinery
595	Loss on Sale of Machinery
597	Loss on Stolen Machinery

TRANSACTIONS FOR 19X1
Jan. 2   Paid $555 each, in cash, for four machines.
Dec. 31   Recorded depreciation for the year on the four machines.

TRANSACTIONS FOR 19X2

Mar. 31 Machine 1 was stolen. No insurance was carried.
Dec. 31 Recorded depreciation for the year on the three remaining machines.

TRANSACTIONS FOR 19X3

Sept. 31 Sold Machine 2 for $356 cash.
Dec. 31 Recorded depreciation for the year on the two remaining machines.

TRANSACTIONS FOR 19X4

Apr. 30 Machine 3 was traded in for a similar machine with a list price and fair market value of $610; paid cash, less a $310 trade-in allowance.
July 31 Machine 4 was traded in for a similar machine with a list price and fair market value of $620; paid cash, less a $182 trade-in allowance. (Record the loss on the transaction.)

PROBLEM 24-3

The general ledger of Westex, Inc., on January 1, 19X2, included the accounts shown below.

INSTRUCTIONS

1. Give general journal entries to record the copyright amortization and the depletion expense for 19X2.
2. Assuming that expenses (other than depletion) related to the ore production totaled $220,000 in 19X2, what amount of depletion could the company claim on its federal income tax return during 19X2? Statutory depletion for this type of ore is 10 percent.

ACCOUNTS

154	Copyright
156	Ore Deposits
156A	Accumulated Depletion—Ore Deposits
536	Amortization of Copyright
583	Depletion Expense—Ore Deposits

An analysis of the account balances revealed the following information.

1. The Copyright account contains a debit balance of $20,000. This represents the unamortized cost of a copyright purchased on January 1, 19X1, for $25,000. Management estimated the useful life of the copyright to be five years and charged $5,000 to expense in 19X1, crediting that amount to the Copyright account.
2. The debit balance of the Ore Deposits account is $180,000. The credit balance of the Accumulated Depletion—Ore Deposits account is $30,000. It was estimated that the deposits originally contained 1,000,000 tons of ore. In 19X2, 160,000 tons of ore were produced and sold for $4.20 a ton.

alternate problems

PROBLEM 24-1A   The Vanacek Company has purchased a delivery truck at a cost of $8,800. Its estimated useful life is five years, and its estimated salvage value is $1,200.

INSTRUCTIONS
1. Using the straight-line method, compute the annual depreciation charge.
2. Using the declining-balance method, compute the depreciation charge for each year. Also determine both the depreciation to date (the balance in the accumulated depreciation account at the end of each year) and the ending book value.
3. Using the sum-of-the-years'-digits method, compute the depreciation charge for each year and determine both the depreciation to date and the ending book value.
4. Prepare a table showing a comparison of the results obtained under the three methods. Provide columns for Year, Depreciation for Year (one column for each method—Straight-Line, Declining-Balance, Sum-of-the-Years'-Digits), and Depreciation to Date (one column for each method—Straight-Line, Declining-Balance, Sum-of-the-Years'-Digits). Also compute the book values at the end of five years.

PROBLEM 24-2A   The Arlen Company purchased four identical machines on January 2, 19X1, paying $600 cash for each. The useful life of each machine is expected to be five years, and the salvage value at the end of that time is estimated to be $100 for each machine. The company uses the straight-line method of depreciation. Selected transactions involving the machines are listed below and on the next page. The necessary accounts for recording these transactions are also given below.

INSTRUCTIONS
1. Record the transactions in general journal form.
2. Assuming that the trade-in of Machine 4 was recorded under the income tax method, give the general journal entry that would be made on August 29, 19X4.

ACCOUNTS

101	Cash in Bank
141	Machinery
141A	Accumulated Depreciation—Machinery
495	Gain on Sale of Machinery
541	Depreciation Expense—Machinery
595	Loss on Sale of Machinery
597	Fire Loss on Machinery

TRANSACTIONS FOR 19X1
Jan. 2 Paid $600 each, in cash, for four machines.
Dec. 31 Recorded depreciation for the year on the four machines.

445

TRANSACTIONS FOR 19X2

Apr. 1 Machine 1 was destroyed by fire. No insurance was carried.
Dec. 31 Recorded depreciation for the year on the three remaining machines.

TRANSACTIONS FOR 19X3

Aug. 31 Sold Machine 2 for $400 cash.
Dec. 31 Recorded depreciation for the year on the two remaining machines.

TRANSACTIONS FOR 19X4

June 4 Traded Machine 3 in for a similar machine with a $700 list price and fair market value. A trade-in allowance of $300 was received. The balance was paid in cash.
Aug. 29 Traded Machine 4 in for a similar machine with a $720 list price and fair market value. A trade-in allowance of $150 was received. The balance was paid in cash. (Record the loss on the transaction.)

PROBLEM 24-3A

The general ledger of the Kapoor Development Company on January 1, 19X1, included the accounts shown below.

INSTRUCTIONS

1. Give general journal entries to record the patent amortization and the depletion expense for 19X1.
2. Assuming that expenses (other than depletion) related to the oil production totaled $2,200,000 during the year, what amount of depletion could the company claim on its federal income tax return during 19X1? (Statutory depletion for oil production is at a rate of 22 percent.)

ACCOUNTS

153   Patents
155   Oil Deposits
155A Accumulated Depletion—Oil Deposits
536   Amortization of Patents
584   Depletion Expense—Oil Deposits

An analysis of the account balances revealed the following information.

1. The Patents account contains a debit balance of $13,600. This represents the unamortized cost of a patent purchased on January 2, 19X0, for $17,000. Because of rapid technological changes, management decided to amortize the cost over a period of five years. Consequently, $3,400 was charged to expense in 19X0 and was credited to Patents.
2. The Oil Deposits account contains a balance of $600,000. The Accumulated Depletion—Oil Deposits account contains a credit balance of $200,000. It was estimated that on January 1, 19X1, the remaining content of the deposits was 2,000,000 barrels. In 19X1, 200,000 barrels were produced and sold for $13.50 a barrel.

UNIT 25

BUSINESS TAXES

Most businesses are subject to a variety of taxes. It is therefore necessary for a firm to have orderly procedures to account for taxes, to pay the required amounts on schedule, and to file the proper tax forms with government agencies. In this unit, we examine tax procedures that are used in business.

Types of Business Taxes

One of the costs associated with ownership of assets such as inventory, plant, and equipment is property taxes. These taxes, levied by state and local government units, are based on the value of the assets. In addition to property taxes, a firm may be required to pay a number of other taxes, such as excise taxes, retail license fees, and income taxes. These taxes are discussed in the present unit. The income tax on corporations is also covered more extensively in Unit 33.

In previous units, you learned how a business deducts social security and income taxes from employee earnings and how it accounts for the payroll taxes that it must pay. You also learned how a business adapts its accounting records to keep track of retail sales taxes collected from customers. Because employee tax deductions and the employer's payroll taxes are discussed in detail in Units 15 and 16, they are not covered again here. However, there is a further discussion of sales taxes. In the case of retail sales taxes, a firm's responsibility does not end with collection of the necessary amounts. Proper information must be recorded, tax returns must be prepared and submitted, and the tax money must be sent to the proper government agency at regular intervals. The procedures needed to comply with these additional sales tax requirements are discussed here.

Property Taxes

Property taxes are often called *ad valorem taxes* because they are levied on the value of the property taxed. (*Ad valorem* is a Latin term meaning "according to the value.") The actual amount of tax to be paid depends on two basic factors: the *value* of the property for tax purposes and the tax *rate* applied to that value.

Taxable Property

Some jurisdictions tax only real property; others tax both real and personal property. Real property includes land and buildings or other structures attached to the land. All other property is classified as personal property. It includes such items as machinery and equipment, furniture and fixtures, and intangible assets.

The value of property for tax purposes almost always differs from the value entered in a firm's accounting records. Accounting records typically use cost or cost less depreciation or amortization. The assessed value of property for tax purposes is usually related to the property's current market value on the assessment date. The basis for the assessed value of property for tax purposes can be total market value (100 percent), but more often it is some percentage of market value (for example, 60 percent).

Assessment and Collection of Property Taxes

In some jurisdictions, public officials appraise real property to determine the assessed value for tax purposes. In others, property owners place a value on their own real property. This value is subject to review and change by a public official or board before the tax rate is applied. Personal property values are often assessed by the owner of the items. (Property owners who are required to set the value of their own property should investigate local customs in establishing these values. Substantial inequities can occur in the assessment of property value for tax purposes.)

Tax Rate

The tax rate is often established by the taxing body after the total assessed value of the property subject to tax has been determined. The taxing body estimates the amount of revenue needed from property taxes and then sets a tax rate that will yield the desired amount of tax revenue when applied to the total assessed value.

The same property can be taxed simultaneously by a number of government units (for example, a city, a county, a school district, and a lighting district). Each taxing authority can determine the tax rate required to raise the revenue it needs.

In many cases, each taxing authority assesses property and levies a tax, and the taxpayer must pay each authority separately. In other cases, a single agency levies and usually collects the taxes for all the units and distributes the proper amount to each authority. The illustration on page 449 is of a tax notice that shows real property taxed by several authorities but payment made to only one agency. (A *mill* is a thousandth part of a dollar, or $0.001.)

Assessment and Payment Dates

The assessed value of property is established at a certain date for each tax jurisdiction, often before the tax rate is established. Thus, some time ordinarily elapses between the assessment date and the date on which the tax bills are sent to the taxpayers. Taxes due must then be paid by a specified date. Late payments incur penalties and interest charges. (In some jurisdictions, discounts are allowed for early payment of taxes.)

Accounting for Property Taxes

The accountant in charge of records and procedures for taxes must do the following:

1. Determine the correct amount of tax due and pay it in time to avoid penalties and interest charges.
2. Prepare and file any tax forms that may be required.

```
              COUNTY OF GREENVILLE     TAX NOTICE 19X1         N0 7940
              CITY OF GREENVILLE

              RECEIPT for your taxes for 19X1, as   Ward THREE              ITEMIZED TAXES
              itemized below. In accordance with law.                 TAXPAYERS    HOMESTEAD
              BRYAN CLEMMONS, Sheriff and Ex-       Page No. ___742___ COLUMN      EXEMPTION
              Officio Tax Collector.                                 TAXES PAYABLE  COLUMN
              Per _____ Deputy.          ASSESSED VALUATION  $5,250.00
                                                    State Tax   5.75 Mills   30.19
              NAME AND ADDRESS OF TAXPAYER          *County Tax 28.50 Mills 149.63
                                                    Sewer CS1   1.70 Mills    8.93
                    Vanderbilt Garage Company       Rural Lighting 3.00 Mills 15.75
                    620 Magnolia Avenue             Garbage
                    Greenville, SC 29609            Acreage    2¢ per Acre
                                                    PAY LAST AMOUNT IN   THIS
                                                                        COLUMN
                                                    TOTAL             $204.50
                                                    INTEREST
                    DESCRIPTION OF PROPERTY         PENALTY
                                                    TOTAL
                    Lot 94
                    Magnolia Subdivision
```

3. Enter the tax in the firm's financial records.
4. Charge the tax in the appropriate accounting period or periods as an expense on the income statement. Show the correct amount of tax payable or prepaid on the balance sheet.

Computing the tax liability and completing the appropriate tax returns requires a thorough knowledge of the various tax laws and regulations that apply to the business. Payment of taxes due is handled within the usual disbursement routines used by the business.

As might be supposed, there are several procedures for accounting for taxes, for assigning them as expenses in different accounting periods, and for presenting them on the firm's balance sheet. Generally, however, the most acceptable procedure for recording property taxes is that of a monthly accrual on the firm's books during each fiscal period of the taxing authority that levied the taxes. The books will then show the appropriate accrual or prepayment at any closing date.* The discussion of property tax accounting in the remainder of this unit follows the treatment advocated here.

Retail Licenses States typically require every person or firm doing business as a retailer to obtain a retail license from the state tax commission. In the state where the Style Clothing Store operates, the license must be obtained prior to June 30 for the following fiscal year starting July 1 (or before the opening of any new business). The license fee is $5 for a firm that consists of one retail store.

---

*Committee on Accounting Procedure, *Accounting Research and Terminology Bulletin, Final Edition* (New York: American Institute of Certified Public Accountants, 1961), Chapter 10, sec. A, par. 10.

Higher fees are charged if a firm has additional outlets, with a maximum of $150 for each outlet over 30.

The Style Clothing Store's Tax Situation

The Style Clothing Store is subject to three taxes, which are recorded in an account called Taxes and Licenses 555. The first is the retail license fee. The second is the merchant's stock tax, a personal property tax that is levied on the value of the merchandise inventory. The third is the property tax levied on items not covered by the merchant's stock tax.

To provide complete information about the individual taxes without having a different ledger account for each tax, the firm uses an *analysis ledger sheet*. Notice that the Taxes and Licenses account illustrated below contains separate *analysis columns* to record the details of each type of tax. The three columns on the right (Debit, Credit, and Balance) provide space for the regular postings and the resulting total balance. The columns on the left provide space for entering the individual taxes. Subcode numbers are assigned to each type of tax as follows: Retail License 555.6, Stock Tax 555.7, and Property Tax 555.8. The entry for payment of the retail license fee is given here to show how the columns are used.

RETAIL LICENSE DR. 555.6	STOCK TAX DR. 555.7	PROP. TAX DR. 555.8	DATE	EXPLANATION	POST. REF.	DEBIT	CREDIT	BALANCE	DR. CR.
				Taxes and Licenses				No. 555	
5 00			19 X1 June 30		VR5	5 00		5 00	Dr.

Stock Tax on Merchandise Inventory

Assume that the fiscal year for the stock tax is July 1 to the following June 30. Assume also that the tax is levied on the assessed value of the merchandise inventory on hand on June 30, the last day of the fiscal year. (Many of the technical tax provisions are omitted from the following discussion so that the basic procedural steps are clear. Also keep in mind that procedures vary widely from state to state. Those described here illustrate only one situation.)

In the state where the Style Clothing Store operates, an information return reporting the value of the inventory on June 30 must be filed by each merchant on or before August 31. Then the state tax commission, which administers the stock tax, adjusts the assessed valuation to what it considers necessary, applies the tax rate, and sends a tax bill in December. This bill is payable on or before December 31. If payment is made after that date, there is a penalty.

In the first year of its partnership operations, the Style Clothing Store submits the required information for the stock tax as of June 30. The store starts recording a proportionate amount of this tax each month, beginning July 1 (the start of the state's fiscal year for this tax). However, the firm will not know the exact amount of the tax due until it receives the tax bill in December. To make the monthly accruals prior to receiving the tax bill, the accountant must estimate the total tax due for the year and convert it to monthly amounts.

Assume that the accountant estimates the firm's stock tax for the year as $960, or $80 a month. The accountant then records $80 each month (beginning with July) in a journal entry debiting Taxes and Licenses and crediting Property Taxes Payable. The entry made on July 31 is shown below.

19 X1					
July 31	Taxes and Licenses	555.7	80 00		
	Property Taxes Payable	235.7		80 00	
	Estimated stock tax for month of July.				

Note that the credit entry in the Property Taxes Payable account bears the subcode .7. This number identifies the stock tax. The firm uses an analysis ledger sheet for the liability account so that it can keep the amount of stock tax payable separate from the other property taxes payable that may be credited to the same account later.

A similar entry for the estimated stock tax payable is made each month from July through November. By November the total amount in the Property Taxes Payable account will have increased to $400 (5 months × $80). Suppose that in December the actual tax bill shows a total tax due of $995 ($35 more than the estimate of $960). At this point, the actual tax liability is known and can be recorded. The Property Taxes Payable account is credited for $595 to increase it from its present balance of $400 to the actual liability of $995. Since the $595 applies to December and future months, it is debited to an asset account called Prepaid Taxes. (Note that the term *prepaid* does not, in this case, mean literally "paid in advance." It means that the recorded cost applies to future months. Some accountants prefer to use the title Deferred Property Tax Expense rather than Prepaid Taxes.) The entry for December is shown below.

19 X1					
Dec. 10	Prepaid Taxes	128	595 00		
	Property Taxes Payable	235.7		595 00	
	Balance of stock tax payable as determined on receipt of tax bill.				

At the end of each month, beginning in December and continuing through June, $85 ($595 ÷ 7 months) is transferred to the expense account Taxes and Licenses. By June 30 all the prepaid property tax cost will thus have been charged to expense. The journal entry to be made each month is shown below.

19 X1					
Dec. 31	Taxes and Licenses	555.7	85 00		
	Prepaid Taxes	128		85 00	
	Transfer to expense the December portion of the prepaid stock tax.				

The new asset, Prepaid Taxes, is shown on the balance sheet on December 31 as $510. It represents the tax costs that apply to the future months of January through June (6 months × $85 = $510). When the tax bill is actually paid in January, the payment is debited to Property Taxes Payable. In July the same cycle of entries starts over again—monthly estimates through November, then actual figures for December through June.

Property Tax on Other Property

Suppose that the Style Clothing Store is located in a state where real and personal properties are appraised as of December 31 for the following year. Tax returns are used as the basis for assessment. These returns must be filed by property owners before the end of February. Tax bills are sent out toward the end of the year and are payable on or before December 31. Payments made after that date are subject to penalties.

Since it was not in business and therefore owned no property on December 31 of the year before the start of its operations on February 1, 19X1, the Style Clothing Store pays no property tax for the first 11 months of its business life, February 1 to December 31, 19X1. However, the store must file its first tax return before February 28 of its second year of operations. It is subject to tax for that year and for each succeeding year.

The firm's accountant must make a monthly record of the estimated tax starting in January and continuing until the tax bill is received, usually in December. At that time (since December is the last month of the tax year), the accountant can make a general journal entry to correct both the tax expense and tax liability accounts.

Assume that in January the accountant estimates the property tax for the year to be $240, or $20 a month. This amount is recorded each month by the following entry.

19X2					
Jan. 31	Taxes and Licenses	555.8	20 00		
	Property Taxes Payable	235.8			20 00
	Estimated property taxes for month of January.				

Assume that the tax bill received the following December shows only $210 due. The accountant must then reduce both the tax expense and tax liability balances by $10, since in 11 months the firm has recorded a total of $220 ($20 × 11) in estimated taxes. The general journal entry to make this adjustment debits Property Taxes Payable and credits Taxes and Licenses, both for $10, as illustrated below.

19X2					
Dec. 31	Property Taxes Payable	235.8	10 00		
	Taxes and Licenses	555.8			10 00
	Corrected estimate for prior 11 months for property taxes in order to show actual amount for year listed on tax bill.				

Payment of the tax bill in December results in a debit of $210 to Property Taxes Payable and a credit of $210 to Cash in Bank. The following January the cycle of entries for this tax begins again with the recording of the estimated amount of tax for that month.

Statement Presentation

Let us see how the various tax items that have been discussed appear on the books of the Style Clothing Store at the end of the first year of operations, January 31, 19X2. The three ledger accounts involved are Prepaid Taxes, Property Taxes Payable, and Taxes and Licenses. They are shown below with all entries posted and the balances determined as of January 31.

Prepaid Taxes — No. 128

DATE	EXPLANATION	POST. REF.	DEBIT	CREDIT	BALANCE	DR. CR.
19 X1 Dec. 10		J12	595 00		595 00	Dr.
31		J12		85 00	510 00	Dr.
19 X2 Jan. 31		J1		85 00	425 00	Dr.

Property Taxes Payable — No. 235

STOCK TAX CR. 235.7	PROP. TAX CR. 235.8	DATE	EXPLANATION	POST. REF.	DEBIT	CREDIT	BALANCE	DR. CR.
		19 X1						
80 00		July 31		J7		80 00	80 00	Cr.
80 00		Aug. 31		J8		80 00	160 00	Cr.
80 00		Sept. 30		J9		80 00	240 00	Cr.
80 00		Oct. 31		J10		80 00	320 00	Cr.
80 00		Nov. 30		J11		80 00	400 00	Cr.
595 00		Dec. 10		J12		595 00	995 00	Cr.
(995 00)		31		VR11	995 00		–0–	
		19 X2						
	20 00	Jan. 31		J1		20 00	20 00	Cr.

Taxes and Licenses — No. 555

RETAIL LICENSE DR. 555.6	STOCK TAX DR. 555.7	PROP. TAX DR. 555.8	DATE	EXPLANATION	POST. REF.	DEBIT	CREDIT	BALANCE	DR. CR.
			19 X1						
5 00			June 30		VR5	5 00		5 00	Dr.
	80 00		July 31		J7	80 00		85 00	Dr.
	80 00		Aug. 31		J8	80 00		165 00	Dr.
	80 00		Sept. 30		J9	80 00		245 00	Dr.
	80 00		Oct. 31		J10	80 00		325 00	Dr.
	80 00		Nov. 30		J11	80 00		405 00	Dr.
	85 00		Dec. 31		J12	85 00		490 00	Dr.
			19 X2						
	85 00		Jan. 31		J1	85 00		575 00	Dr.
		20 00	31		J1	20 00		595 00	Dr.
5 00	570 00	20 00							

Balance Sheet. The two tax accounts that appear on the balance sheet as of January 31, 19X2, are Prepaid Taxes (stock tax) of $425 (5 months × $85), which is classified as a current asset, and Property Taxes Payable of $20, which is classified as a current liability.

Income Statement. The tax account that appears on the income statement is Taxes and Licenses, an operating expense of $595 that consists of the following items.

Retail License	$ 5
Stock Tax Estimated, 5 months × $80	400
Stock Tax Adjusted, 2 months × $85	170
Property Tax Estimated, 1 month × $20	20
	$595

Since this is the first year of operations for the Style Clothing Store, taxes shown are for only part of the year. In later years, the income statement will show taxes for the full 12 months.

Sales and Excise Taxes

Sales and excise taxes imposed by city and state governments vary. However, there is sufficient similarity in accounting for them to make a study of the most typical provisions an informative starting point.

City and State Sales Taxes

Many cities and states impose a tax on retail sales. The tax is collected by the merchant making the sales. This type of tax may be levied on all retail sales, but often certain items are exempt. In most cases, the amount of the sales tax is stated separately and then added to the retail price of the merchandise. In previous units you learned how to record sales and sales returns and allowances subject to a sales tax.

The merchant is required to make periodic reports (usually monthly) to the taxing authority and to pay the tax money due at the same time. In some cases, the government allows the merchant to retain part of the tax as compensation for collecting it. The procedures for filing a state sales tax return are discussed in a later section of this unit.

Federal Excise Taxes

The federal government levies an excise tax (which is simply another sales tax) on certain kinds of merchandise, such as automobile tires and petroleum products. This tax is passed on to the consumer by the retailer. Normally, the retailer pays the tax to the manufacturer, who assumes responsibility for preparing quarterly tax returns and sending the tax money to the federal government.

Preparing the State Sales Tax Return

The procedures to be followed at the time a typical sales tax return must be filed are similar to those used by the Style Clothing Store at the end of July 19X1, when it filed the monthly sales tax return with the tax commissioner of the state where it is located. The firm's sales are subject to a 3 percent state sales tax.

At the end of each month, after the accounts have all been posted, the accountant for the Style Clothing Store prepares the state sales tax return. (In some states the sales tax return is filed quarterly rather than monthly.) The information required for the monthly return comes from the accounting data of the current month. Three accounts are involved: Sales Tax Payable, Sales, and Sales Returns and Allowances. To highlight the data needed, only the July postings are shown in the ledger accounts illustrated below.

Sales Tax Payable   No. 231

DATE	EXPLANATION	POST. REF.	DEBIT	CREDIT	BALANCE	DR. CR.
19 X1 July 31		S6		537 00	537 00	Cr.
31		CR6		282 00	819 00	Cr.
31		J7	16 50		802 50	Cr.

Sales   No. 401

DATE	EXPLANATION	POST. REF.	DEBIT	CREDIT	BALANCE	DR. CR.
19 X1 July 31		S6		17,900 00	17,900 00	Cr.
31		CR6		9,400 00	27,300 00	Cr.

Sales Returns and Allowances   No. 452

DATE	EXPLANATION	POST. REF.	DEBIT	CREDIT	BALANCE	DR. CR.
19 X1 July 31		J7	550 00		550 00	Dr.

Using these figures as a basis, the accountant determines the amount of the firm's taxable gross sales for July as follows.

Cash Sales	$ 9,400
Credit Sales	17,900
Total Sales	$27,300
Deduct Sales Returns and Allowances	550
Taxable Gross Sales for July	$26,750

The 3 percent sales tax on the gross sales of $26,750 amounts to $802.50. In the state where the Style Clothing Store is located, a retailer who files the sales tax return on time and who pays the tax when it is due is entitled to a discount. The discount is intended to compensate the retailer, at least in part, for acting as a collection agent for the tax. The discount rate depends on the amount of tax to be paid. On amounts between $100 and $1,000, the rate is 2 percent of the tax due. For the Style Clothing Store in July, the discount amounts to $16.05 (0.02 \times \$802.50)$. With the discount deducted, the net tax due is $786.45 ($802.50 − $16.05), as shown below.

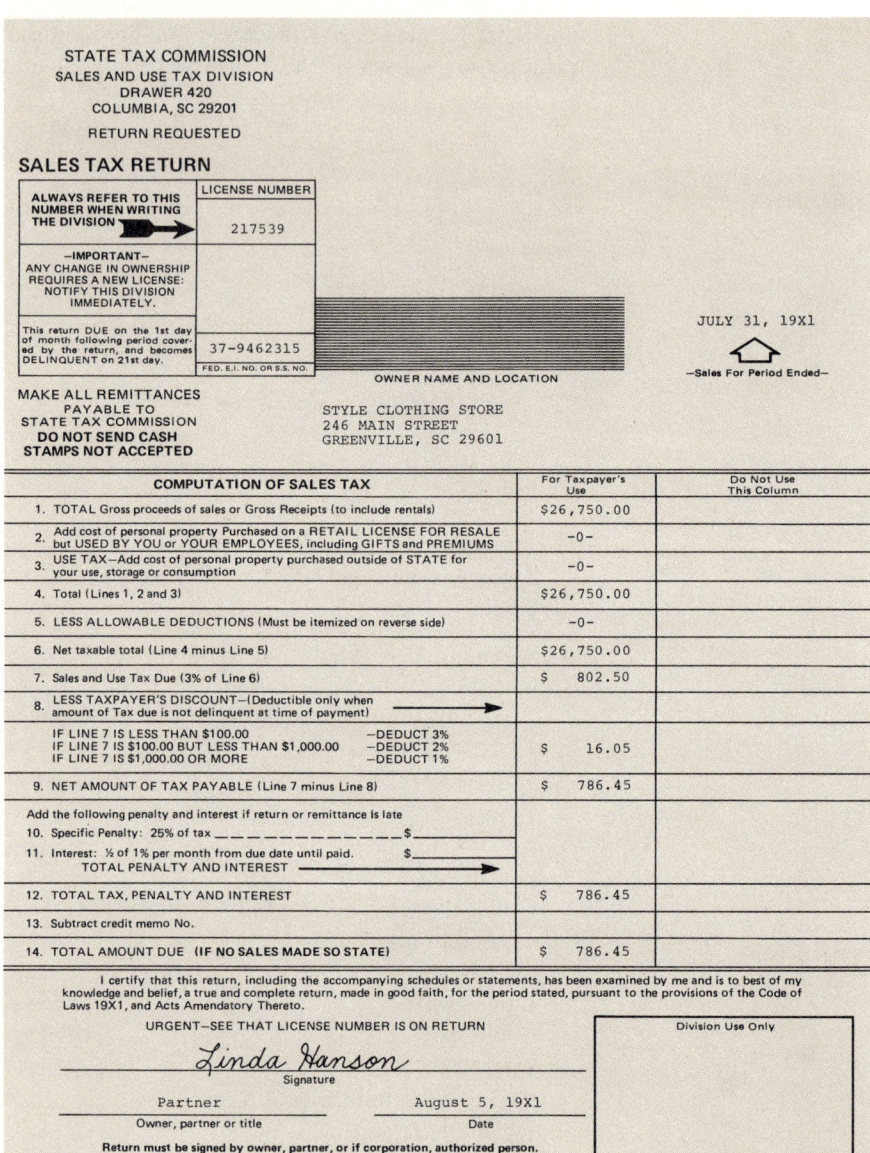

The firm prepares a voucher for the net sales tax due and sends a check with the sales tax return. The voucher calls for a debit to Sales Tax Payable (for $786.45 in this case). After the amount of the payment is posted, the balance in the account should be equal (or very nearly equal) to the discount. In this case it is equal, as shown on the next page. (Slight differences can arise because the tax collected at the time of the sale is determined by a bracket method that can give results slightly more or less than the final computations on the tax return.)

DATE	EXPLANATION	POST. REF.	DEBIT	CREDIT	BALANCE	DR. CR.
Sales Tax Payable						No. 231
19 X1 July 31		S6		537 00	537 00	Cr.
31		CR6		282 00	819 00	Cr.
31		J7	16 50		802 50	Cr.
Aug. 5		VR7	786 45		16 05	Cr.

The remaining balance in the firm's Sales Tax Payable account, $16.05, is transferred to an account called Miscellaneous Income by a general journal entry. This entry consists of a debit to Sales Tax Payable and a credit to Miscellaneous Income, as shown below.

19 X1 Aug. 5	Sales Tax Payable	231	16 05	
	Miscellaneous Income	493		16 05
	Transfer remaining balance in Sales Tax Payable account to the special revenue account.			

Recording Sales Tax in the Sales Account

In some states retailers can credit the entire sales price plus tax to the Sales account. Then, at the end of each month or quarter, they must remove from the Sales account the amount of tax included and transfer that amount to the Sales Tax Payable account.

For example, assume that during January 19X5 a retailer whose sales are all taxable sells merchandise for a total price of $10,920, including a 4 percent tax. The entry to record these sales is summarized in general journal form below.

19 X5 Jan. 31	Accounts Receivable	111	10,920 00	
	Sales	401		10,920 00
	Total sales and sales tax collected during period.			

At the end of the month, the retailer must transfer the sales tax from the Sales account to the Sales Tax Payable account. The first step in the transfer process is to determine the amount of tax involved. The sales tax payable is computed as follows.

$$\text{Sales} + \text{Tax} = \$10{,}920$$
$$100\% \text{ of Sales} + 4\% \text{ of Sales} = \$10{,}920$$
$$104\% \text{ of Sales} = \$10{,}920$$
$$\text{Sales} = \frac{\$10{,}920}{1.04}$$
$$\text{Sales} = \$10{,}500$$
$$\text{Tax} = \$10{,}500 \times 0.04 = \$420$$

The firm then makes the following entry to transfer the liability from the Sales account.

19X5					
Jan. 31	Sales	401	420 00	
	Sales Tax Payable	231		420 00
	Transfer sales tax payable from Sales account to liability account.			

Recording Federal Excise Tax

As previously explained, some businesses are subject to federal excise tax. They account for the excise tax in much the same manner as they account for the state sales tax. A separate column is set up in the cash receipts journal and the sales journal to record the excise tax liability on sales. At the end of each month, the totals of these columns are posted to a liability account called Excise Tax Payable in the general ledger.

A firm that owes more than $100 of federal excise tax in any month must deposit the tax due in an authorized bank on or before the last day of the following month. (If the amount of tax for any calendar month in a calendar quarter exceeds $2,000, the tax due must be deposited twice a month during the next calendar quarter.) The firm prepares a voucher debiting the Excise Tax Payable account and crediting Accounts Payable for the amount due. Finally, the firm issues a check and sends it to the bank with a Tax Deposit Form 504 (a form similar to the one used for social security taxes).

If the tax for the month is $100 or less, it is sent with the Quarterly Federal Excise Tax Return, Form 720. This form must be filed within the month following the end of each calendar quarter. Because retailers usually pay their excise taxes to the manufacturers of the goods, details of the quarterly return are not examined here.

Income Tax Returns for Partnerships

Partnerships are required to file information returns with the federal government on Form 1065. This return indicates the revenues and expenses of each partnership for its tax year and the distribution of the resulting net income or net loss among the partners. The return must be filed on or before the 15th day of the fourth month following the end of the firm's fiscal year. Since the fiscal year of the Style Clothing Store ends on January 31, its information return must be filed by May 15. The firm must also file a similar return with the state. Later, each partner prepares an individual tax return and reports his or her share of the partnership profit whether the profit has actually been distributed or not. The partners pay tax on the profit when they file their individual returns.

Income Tax Returns for Corporations

Every corporation is required to file a federal income tax return on Form 1120. This return is due by the 15th day of the third month following the end of the corporation's fiscal year. Thus, for a corporation using the calendar year, the federal income tax return is due on or before March 15 of the next year. Unlike partnerships, corporations must actually pay federal income taxes on their net income. State or local government units may also levy income taxes on corporations. In addition to the income tax paid by corporations, each corporation's shareholders (owners) must pay income taxes on the dividends they receive. (*Dividends* are distributions of the corporation's profits.) The income tax on corporations is examined further in Unit 33.

Tax Calendar

By now, it has become obvious that there are a considerable number of tax returns to file and tax payments to make. You have studied payroll taxes, sales and excise taxes, and property taxes. You have also seen that in some cases firms must file income tax returns. The accountant must keep up with all these tax responsibilities and must make sure that they are taken care of promptly and correctly. Tax calendars are used to remind accountants of important tax dates throughout the year.

A *tax calendar* should be prepared for each business. It should show the dates before which each tax item must receive attention. It should also indicate the form numbers of any tax returns that must be filed. The calendar should be checked periodically so that required tax information can be assembled carefully without any last-minute rush.

The January and February portion of the tax calendar for the Style Clothing Store is shown below.

STYLE CLOTHING STORE
TAX CALENDAR

Jan. 20 State Sales Tax Return for December; Form ST-3
     31 State Unemployment Tax Return, quarter ended Dec. 31; Form UCE-101
     31 Employer's Annual Federal Unemployment Tax Return (previous year); Form 940
     31 Employer's Quarterly Federal Tax Return, quarter ended Dec. 31; Form 941
     31 Wage and Tax Statements to each employee for previous year; Form W-2
     31 Transmittal of Income and Tax Statements (previous year); Form W-3
Feb. 15 Deposit of FICA Taxes and Income Tax Withheld for January; Form 501
     20 State Sales Tax Return for January; Form ST-3
     28 Property Tax Return; values as of December 31 (previous year)

principles and procedures summary

Property taxes are levied by various state and local government units, including cities, counties, school districts, and lighting districts. The same property can be subject to several taxing authorities. Usually, one agency collects the entire tax and distributes it to the participating units. The accountant's job in connection with property taxes is twofold. First, the accountant must determine the amount of tax due, get it paid on time, and prepare any necessary tax forms. Second, the accountant must record the tax as an expense in the appropriate accounting period and show prepayments or accrued tax liabilities properly on the balance sheet.

Since tax bills are often presented many months after the valuation of the property on which they are based, an estimate of the tax for the year is made. The monthly portion of this estimate is debited to a tax expense account and credited to a tax liability account. When the actual bill is received, the liability and expense accounts must be adjusted to reflect the correct figure, if it is different from the estimate.

Many states and cities impose sales taxes that must be collected by retail merchants from their customers. Although these taxes vary from place to place, they are typically a certain percent of the retail price of each item sold. The total tax collected is sent to the taxing authority, usually monthly or quarterly. In some localities, merchants retain a portion of the sales tax as a commission for acting as collection agents.

Partnerships are required to file tax returns, reporting their revenues, expenses, and net income or net loss, but they do not pay any income tax. Corporations do pay income tax.

managerial implications

Managers should investigate the property tax structure of an area before opening a business there. They must also watch changes in tax structure and rates in order to be able to gauge the effects on the firm's costs and profits. It is especially important that managers be familiar with local property valuation customs to make sure that the firm's property taxes are fair.

Managers of retail businesses must make sure that sales taxes are properly charged to customers and collected. They must also be sure that taxes are accurately entered in the firm's records and promptly sent to the taxing authorities along with any required reports. Sellers are, of course, liable for any undercollection of taxes. This situation can be avoided with an efficient control system.

Tax calendars provide a means of making sure that all tax returns and reports are filed on time.

MANAGERIAL DISCUSSION QUESTIONS

1. How can the managers of a firm help assure that all taxes are paid and all returns filed on or before the due dates?
2. Assume that an officer in a company where you work has suggested that in order to reduce the stock tax on merchandise, the company should reduce its inventory to the lowest possible level on the assessment date. Explain what the officer means.
3. Explain why management might wish to record both sales and sales taxes in the same account.
4. How do various common business taxes affect a firm's costs and profits? What can management do about these taxes?
5. Why can't a taxing authority set the property tax rate at the time it determines the appraised value of the property under its jurisdiction?

APPLICATION OF PRINCIPLES

PROBLEM 25-1 The Won Ho Company estimates its 19X1 property tax on the basis of a proposed property value assessment of $8,000 and a tax rate of 60 mills. The taxing authority operates on a calendar-year basis. The tax bill is usually received in September and must be paid by November 30 to avoid penalty. The entries made during 19X1 in connection with the property tax are listed below.

INSTRUCTIONS In general journal form, record the required entries, using these accounts: Cash in Bank 101, Prepaid Taxes 128, Property Taxes Payable 235, and Property Tax Expense 555.

ENTRIES FOR 19X1

Jan. 31   Recorded the estimated January tax expense.
Feb. 28   Recorded the estimated February tax expense.
Sept. 15 Recorded the tax bill received, $524. (Estimated property taxes were recorded monthly from January through August.)
  30   Recorded the September tax expense.
Nov. 25   Recorded the payment of the tax bill, $524.
  30   Recorded the November tax expense.
Dec. 31   Recorded the December tax expense.

PROBLEM 25-2 The Quality Furniture Store is located in a state that imposes a sales tax. On May 31, 19X1, a study of the sales slips and credit slips revealed the facts shown on the next page about sales, sales returns, and sales tax for May.

INSTRUCTIONS Record each of the facts in general journal form.

1. Credit sales were $155,609.10 for the month of May. There was a 4 percent state sales tax on all these sales.
2. Cash sales for May totaled $3,455.40. There was a 4 percent state sales tax on all these sales.
3. Some goods sold for cash were returned, and the customer was given a cash refund for the amount of the sale, $45.40, plus the 4 percent sales tax.
4. Some goods sold for $890.80 on account were returned, and the customers were given credit for the sales price plus the 4 percent sales tax.

PROBLEM 25-3 During April 19X9 the Home Improvement Center had total sales of $565,400 and sales returns and allowances of $4,600. At the end of April, the Sales Tax Payable account showed a balance of $16,822.18. The sales tax rate is 3 percent. However, the state sales tax agency allows the firm a discount of 3 percent of the gross amount of sales tax due.

INSTRUCTIONS
1. Make the calculations that are required in preparing the sales tax return.
   a. Taxable gross sales for April.
   b. Total sales tax due.
   c. Amount of discount given the firm.
   d. Amount of sales tax to be paid to the state tax agency.
2. Show in general journal form (omitting explanations) the following.
   a. The entry required to record payment of the net sales tax to the state tax agency.
   b. The entry required to transfer the discount to the Miscellaneous Income account and to close the Sales Tax Payable account for April.

PROBLEM 25-4 The LaRue Sporting Goods Store must collect a sales tax on all its sales. The tax, 4 percent of the retail selling price, is credited to the Sales account along with the actual amount of the sale. Similarly, when merchandise is returned by customers, the entire return, both retail selling price and tax, is debited to the Sales Returns and Allowances account. On March 31, 19X1, at the time the quarterly sales tax return is filed, the firm's accounts include the following balances: Sales, $114,240.50, and Sales Returns and Allowances, $1,354.60. The firm is allowed to deduct 3 percent of the sales tax due as a discount to help cover the expense of collecting it.

INSTRUCTIONS
1. Compute the amount of sales tax on the net sales.
2. Prepare a general journal entry to transfer the gross amount of sales tax from the Sales account to the Sales Tax Payable account and from the Sales Returns and Allowances account to the Sales Tax Payable account.
3. Prepare a general journal entry to transfer the discount from the Sales Tax Payable account to the Miscellaneous Income account.
4. Prepare a general journal entry to record payment of the net sales tax due.

alternate problems

PROBLEM 25-1A   The Sanchez Appliance Shop operates on a calendar-year basis. The taxing authority of the city and county in which Sanchez is located operates on a fiscal year that runs from July 1 to June 30. On January 1, 19X2, the Prepaid Taxes account of Sanchez contains a balance of $720, representing the prepaid property taxes through June 30, 19X2. The entries made during 19X2 in connection with the property tax are listed below.

INSTRUCTIONS   In general journal form, record the necessary entries, using these accounts: Cash in Bank 101, Prepaid Taxes 128, Property Taxes Payable 235, and Property Tax Expense 555.

ENTRIES FOR 19X2

Jan. 31   Recorded the January tax expense.
June 30   Recorded the June tax expense. (The tax expense was recorded monthly from January through May.)
July 31   Recorded the estimated July tax expense. The estimate of tax for the taxing authority's fiscal year beginning July 1, 19X2, is based on a proposed assessed value of $40,000 and an assumed tax rate of 36 mills.
Aug. 31   Recorded the estimated August tax expense.
Sept. 10   Recorded the tax bill received for July 1, 19X1, to June 30, 19X2, in the amount of $1,600.
      30   Recorded the September tax expense.
Oct. 16   Recorded the payment of the tax bill of $1,600.
      31   Recorded the October tax expense.

PROBLEM 25-2A   The Bay Hardware Store is located in a state that imposes a sales tax. On June 30, 19X1, a study of the sales slips and credit slips revealed the facts shown below about sales, sales returns, and sales tax for June.

INSTRUCTIONS   Record each of the facts in general journal form.

1. Credit sales for the month of June were $208,790.20. There was a 5 percent state sales tax on all these sales.
2. Cash sales for June totaled $31,820. There was a 5 percent state sales tax on all these sales.
3. Some goods sold for cash were returned, and the customers were given a cash refund of $109 plus the 5 percent sales tax.
4. Some goods sold for $385.70 on account were returned, and the customers were given credit for the sales price plus the 5 percent sales tax.

PROBLEM 25-3A   During January 19X1 the Krueger Jewelry Store had total sales of $364,610.80 and sales returns and allowances of $3,217.40. At the end of January, the Sales

Tax Payable account showed a balance of $18,052.13. The sales tax rate is 5 percent. However, the state sales tax agency allows the firm a discount of 2½ percent of the gross amount of sales tax due.

INSTRUCTIONS
1. Make the calculations that are required in preparing the sales tax return.
   a. Taxable gross sales for January.
   b. Total sales tax due.
   c. Amount of discount given the firm.
   d. Amount of sales tax to be paid to the state tax agency.
2. Show the following in general journal form (omitting explanations).
   a. The entry required to record payment of the net sales tax to the state tax agency.
   b. The entry required to transfer the discount to the Miscellaneous Income account and close the Sales Tax Payable account for January.

PROBLEM 25-4A The Arneson Floor Covering Center must collect a sales tax on all its sales. The tax of 5 percent is added to the retail selling price, and the entire amount (sale plus tax) is credited to the Sales account. Similarly, when merchandise is returned by customers, the entire return, both retail selling price and tax, is debited to the Sales Returns and Allowances account. On March 31, 19X1, at the time the quarterly sales tax return is filed, the firm's accounts include the following balances: Sales, $485,467.28, and Sales Returns and Allowances, $2,855.68. The firm is allowed to deduct 2 percent of the sales tax due as a discount to help cover its collection expenses.

INSTRUCTIONS
1. Compute the amount of sales tax on the net sales.
2. Prepare a general journal entry to transfer the gross amount of sales tax from the Sales account to the Sales Tax Payable account and from the Sales Returns and Allowances account to the Sales Tax Payable account.
3. Prepare a general journal entry to transfer the discount from the Sales Tax Payable account to the Miscellaneous Income account.
4. Prepare a general journal entry to record payment of the net sales tax due.

UNIT 26

ACCRUALS AND deferrals

In previous units you learned that certain adjustments must be made to accounts at the end of each fiscal period so that the income statement will include all revenue and expense items that apply to the current period. In this way, the expenses of the period are matched against the revenues that they helped produce. As you saw in Unit 19, the matching principle is at the heart of financial reporting today.

The Accrual Basis

The procedure that most nearly attains the objective of matching revenues and expenses of specific fiscal periods is called the *accrual basis* of accounting. Under the accrual basis, all revenues and all expenses are recognized on the income statement for the applicable period, regardless of when the cash related to the transactions is received or paid. Revenue is normally recognized when a sale is completed, which is usually when title to the goods passes to the buyer or when the service is provided. This occurs even though accounts receivable resulting from sales on credit are not collected immediately. Purchases are also recorded when they are made—that is, when title to the goods passes to the buyer—regardless of the actual time of payment for the goods.

Transactions involving revenue and expense items often occur before the period to which they actually relate. For example, insurance premiums are normally paid in advance, and supplies may be purchased but remain unused at the end of a period. In other cases, the transaction involving a revenue or expense item may not take place until after the period to which the item applies. For example, the bad debts expense on the sales of a particular fiscal period must be estimated because the specific worthless accounts receivable may not be known until future periods. As another example, employees may work during December but not be paid for this work until January of the next year.

In view of the difference between the time an item is recorded in the accounts and the time it is actually realized or used, each account balance at the end of a fiscal period must be examined to see if it contains amounts of revenues or expenses that should be allocated to other periods. It is impossible to present an accurate picture of the financial position of the business or the results of operations for the period until all pertinent information has been recorded and until the *mixed accounts* (accounts that may contain elements of both assets and expenses) have been analyzed. Adjusting entries may be necessary to ensure that the revenue and expense accounts will contain amounts relating only to the current period and that the asset and liability accounts will reflect amounts properly classified as assets and liabilities.

Preparation of the Worksheet

In this unit you will study various typical adjustments necessary at the end of the fiscal period to get the accounts to reflect actual financial facts at the time. As a basis for the discussion, look at the trial balance of the Style Clothing Store, which has been entered in the first two amount columns of the worksheet on page 467. This worksheet was prepared at the end of the company's second year of operations, January 31, 19X3. (Remember that the company's fiscal year runs from February 1 through January 31.) Note that some accounts have no balances in the Trial Balance columns. Most of these accounts will be used when the adjustments are made.

Additional pairs of Debit and Credit columns with the following headings are provided on the worksheet: Adjustments, Adjusted Trial Balance, Income Statement, and Balance Sheet. (See the complete worksheet illustrated on pages 496 and 497.)

As you learned in Unit 17, the amounts of the adjustments for the accounting period are recorded in the Adjustments section of the worksheet. A letter is used to identify the debit and credit parts of each adjusting entry. After recording all adjustments on the worksheet, the accountant totals the two columns in the Adjustments section to check the equality of the debits and credits. Then the accountant combines the amounts in the Adjustments section with the amounts originally recorded in the Trial Balance section. The resulting figures are entered in the Adjusted Trial Balance section of the worksheet as another verification of equality. Finally, the accountant extends all figures to the proper columns of the Income Statement and Balance Sheet sections and completes the worksheet.

The worksheet is a highly useful device for assembling data about a firm's adjustments.

Recording Bad Debts on the Worksheet

Unit 22 explained how to make an estimate of bad debts at the end of an accounting period so that the expense involved will be matched against the revenues of the same period. The Bad Debts Expense account is debited and the Allowance for Bad Debts account is credited for the estimated bad debts resulting from the current year's sales.

Each firm uses a suitable rate to estimate its bad debt losses. For example, the Style Clothing Store expects that three-tenths of a percent (0.003) of its credit sales will probably become uncollectible. This estimate is based on the past experience of the business operated by Linda Hanson before the present partnership was formed. At the end of the first year of the partnership, the expected rate of loss was applied to the year's total credit sales of $200,000. The resulting $600 was recorded along with the other adjusting entries. The entry consisted of a debit to Bad Debts Expense and a credit to Allowance for Bad Debts to reflect the estimated losses (page 399). Since that time (during the second year of operations), actual uncollectible accounts of $592.94 have

STYLE CLOTHING STORE
Worksheet (Partial)
Year Ended January 31, 19X3

ACCT. NO.	ACCOUNT NAME	TRIAL BALANCE DEBIT	TRIAL BALANCE CREDIT
101	Cash in Bank	14,320 89	
105	Petty Cash Fund	25 00	
106	Change Fund	100 00	
109	Notes Receivable	800 00	
110	Notes Receivable Discounted		
111	Accounts Receivable	28,067 35	
111A	Allowance for Bad Debts		7 06
116	Interest Receivable		
121	Merchandise Inventory (Feb. 1, 19X2)	65,000 00	
126	Prepaid Insurance		
127	Prepaid Interest Expense		
128	Prepaid Taxes	600 00	
129	Store Supplies on Hand		
131	Furniture and Fixtures	4,600 00	
131A	Accum. Depreciation—Furniture and Fixtures		360 00
132	Office Equipment	2,750 00	
132A	Accum. Depreciation—Office Equipment		215 00
201	Notes Payable—Trade		2,000 00
203	Notes Payable—Bank		12,000 00
205	Accounts Payable		5,109 65
216	Interest Payable		
221	Employee Deductions—FICA Taxes		189 80
222	Employee Deductions—Income Tax Withheld		216 00
225	Salaries and Wages Payable		
226	Payroll Taxes Payable		
231	Sales Tax Payable		825 28
235	Property Taxes Payable		
301	Linda Hanson, Capital		29,000 00
302	Linda Hanson, Drawing	7,800 00	
311	Steven Casey, Capital		28,000 00
312	Steven Casey, Drawing	7,800 00	
321	Janet Miller, Capital		28,500 00
322	Janet Miller, Drawing	7,800 00	
401	Sales		359,195 90
452	Sales Returns and Allowances	6,041 25	
491	Interest Earned		226 00
493	Miscellaneous Income		218 60
501	Merchandise Purchases	255,350 00	
506	Freight In	3,590 00	
511	Purchases Returns and Allowances		1,065 00
512	Purchases Discount		5,048 30
521	Sales Salaries Expense	21,400 00	
522	Advertising Expense	6,893 30	
523	Store Supplies and Expense	4,363 75	
529	Cash Short or Over	72 00	
532	Delivery Expense	3,860 00	
536	Insurance Expense	3,390 00	
541	Custodial Wages Expense	5,040 00	
542	Rent Expense	6,000 00	
543	Utilities Expense	1,981 35	
551	Office Salaries Expense	8,400 00	
552	Payroll Tax Expense	2,584 20	
553	Office Supplies and Expense	804 50	
554	Professional Services Expense	775 00	
555	Taxes and Licenses	1,206 00	
561	Bad Debts Expense		
562	Depreciation Expense—Furniture and Fixtures		
563	Depreciation Expense—Office Equipment		
591	Interest Expense	762 00	
	Totals	472,176 59	472,176 59

been debited to Allowance for Bad Debts as they have been charged off. Thus on January 31, 19X3, the end of the second year, there is a credit balance of only $7.06 remaining in the Allowance for Bad Debts account.

The accountant for the Style Clothing Store must now compute the estimated losses arising from the second year's business activities. Assume that an analysis of the Sales account shows that credit sales totaled $223,050. At the expected rate of loss (0.003), the bad debts arising from this year's sales are estimated to be $669.15. The adjustment is recorded on the worksheet below in the Adjustments section as a debit to Bad Debts Expense and a credit to Allowance for Bad Debts. The amounts are marked with the letter a to identify the two parts of the entry.

ACCT. NO.	ACCOUNT NAME	TRIAL BALANCE DEBIT	TRIAL BALANCE CREDIT	ADJUSTMENTS DEBIT	ADJUSTMENTS CREDIT
111A	Allowance for Bad Debts		7 06		(a)669 15
561	Bad Debts Expense			(a)669 15	

Recording Depreciation on the Worksheet

Another familiar adjustment to be made at the end of the accounting period is for depreciation (see Unit 24). The Style Clothing Store owns several types of assets, such as furniture and fixtures and office equipment, for which there must be a gradual, periodic transfer of acquisition cost to expense. Depreciation is recorded on the worksheet at the end of each accounting period by a debit to a depreciation expense account and a credit to an accumulated depreciation account. The Style Clothing Store uses the straight-line method of computing depreciation.

Depreciation of Furniture and Fixtures

The Furniture and Fixtures account shows that these assets cost $4,600. The estimated useful life of the items is 10 years, and there is no estimated salvage value. Depreciation for the year on the furniture and fixtures is therefore computed as follows.

$$\frac{\$4,600 \text{ (cost)} - \$0 \text{ (salvage)}}{10 \text{ years (useful life)}} = \$460 \text{ (yearly depreciation)}$$

The adjustment is shown as Entry b on the partial worksheet on page 469.

Depreciation of Office Equipment

The office equipment, which cost $2,750, is estimated to have a useful life of 10 years and a salvage value of $600. Based on this data, the yearly depreciation is computed as follows.

$$\frac{\$2,750 \text{ (cost)} - \$600 \text{ (salvage)}}{10 \text{ years (useful life)}} = \$215 \text{ (yearly depreciation)}$$

ACCT. NO.	ACCOUNT NAME	TRIAL BALANCE		ADJUSTMENTS	
		DEBIT	CREDIT	DEBIT	CREDIT
131A	Accum. Depr.—Furniture and Fixtures		360 00		(b)460 00
132A	Accum. Depr.—Office Equip.		215 00		(c)215 00
562	Depr. Expense—Furniture and Fixtures			(b)460 00	
563	Depr. Expense—Office Equip.			(c)215 00	

The adjustment for depreciation of the office equipment is recorded on the worksheet as shown above in Entry c.

Recording Accrued and Prepaid Items on the Worksheet

As noted earlier, some transactions related to expense items are recorded in the current period, but the items may not be fully used until a later period. Also, some expense items that pertain to the current period may not have been recorded at all in the day-to-day entries. Therefore, adjustments may be necessary so that the records of the period will show all expenses related to the firm's current operations—no more and no less—before the financial statements are prepared. Similar adjustments may also be required for certain revenue items to make sure that the firm's records accurately reflect the income earned during the period.

Accrued Expenses

Accrued expenses represent items that have been used in the current period but have not yet been paid for. It is necessary in this situation to record both the expense item and the liability. The Style Clothing Store has four accrued expense items that require adjustments on January 31. You are already familiar with the first of these items—accrued property taxes. The other items are accrued salaries and wages, accrued payroll taxes, and accrued interest on notes payable.

Accrued Property Taxes. You learned in Unit 25 that the Style Clothing Store pays its property tax for the calendar year in December of that year. In January, the firm estimates its property tax for the coming year and accrues one-twelfth of the yearly tax as an expense for January. It does so by debiting the Taxes and Licenses account and crediting the Property Taxes Payable account.

The current estimate of a $240 tax for the calendar year 19X3 means that $20 must be accrued at the end of January. Therefore, an entry is made in the Adjustments section of the worksheet. This entry consists of a debit to Taxes and Licenses for $20 and a credit to Property Taxes Payable for the same amount. The elements of the adjustment are identified with the letter d and the subcode .8 to indicate property tax.

ACCT. NO.	ACCOUNT NAME	TRIAL BALANCE		ADJUSTMENTS	
		DEBIT	CREDIT	DEBIT	CREDIT
235	Property Taxes Payable				(d).8–20 00
555	Taxes and Licenses	1,206 00		(d).8–20 00	

Accrued Salaries and Wages. All employees of the Style Clothing Store except the part-time custodian are paid on the 15th and last day of each month. Hence, on the trial balance date, the semimonthly wages for January have been properly charged to expense. However, the part-time custodian is paid weekly, on Friday. Since January 31, 19X3, is a Thursday, his wages for four days (Monday, January 28, through Thursday, January 31) are unpaid and have not yet been recorded on the books. The firm owes $80 for these wages (the custodian earns $20 a day × 4 days). Thus the accountant must debit Custodial Wages Expense and credit Salaries and Wages Payable for $80 so that both the expense and the liability will be properly shown. Entry e on the worksheet below accomplishes this.

ACCT. NO.	ACCOUNT NAME	TRIAL BALANCE		ADJUSTMENTS	
		DEBIT	CREDIT	DEBIT	CREDIT
225	Salaries and Wages Payable				(e)80 00
541	Custodial Wages Expense	5,040 00		(e)80 00	

Accrued Payroll Taxes. The trial balance of the Style Clothing Store lists $2,584.20 on January 31 for Payroll Tax Expense. This figure includes all taxes that apply to salaries and wages for the months of February through December 19X2.

1. FICA tax (recorded when the Employer's Quarterly Federal Tax Return was filed in January 19X3 for the last quarter of 19X2).
2. Federal unemployment tax (recorded when the Employer's Annual Federal Unemployment Tax Return for 19X2 was filed in January 19X3).
3. State unemployment tax (recorded when the quarterly state return was filed in January 19X3 for the last quarter of 19X2).

The payroll tax expense related to January 19X3 earnings has not yet been recorded because the various tax returns covering these earnings have not yet been filed. In order to match revenue and expenses, the payroll taxes that apply to salaries and wages earned in January should be recorded as a January expense and as a liability on January 31. The January earnings of the employees totaled $3,000, including the $80 of accrued wages for the custodian. The assumed applicable tax rates are 6.5 percent for FICA tax, 1.3 percent for state unemployment tax, and 0.7 percent for federal unemployment tax. The accountant applies these rates to the taxable earnings and determines that the total payroll tax expense chargeable to January operations is $255.

FICA Tax	$3,000 × 0.065 =	$195.00
SUTA Tax	$3,000 × 0.013 =	39.00
FUTA Tax	$3,000 × 0.007 =	21.00
Total Payroll Taxes Accrued		$255.00

The accrued expense is entered in the Adjustments section of the worksheet as a debit to Payroll Tax Expense and a credit to Payroll Taxes Payable, as illustrated by Entry f on the partial worksheet shown below. Note that the Style Clothing Store uses a single tax expense account for both FICA tax and the unemployment insurance taxes.

ACCT. NO.	ACCOUNT NAME	TRIAL BALANCE DEBIT	TRIAL BALANCE CREDIT	ADJUSTMENTS DEBIT	ADJUSTMENTS CREDIT
226	Payroll Taxes Payable				(f) 255 00
552	Payroll Tax Expense	2,584 20		(f) 255 00	

Accrued Interest on Notes Payable. The January 31 trial balance (see page 467) shows $2,000 owed on trade notes payable. The files contain a copy of a note dated December 2 for $2,000, payable in 90 days, with interest at 8 percent. In the normal routine, the interest expense is paid at the maturity of the note. However, the interest expense is actually incurred from day to day and should be apportioned to each accounting period involved in order to obtain a complete and accurate picture of expenses.

The amount of interest accrued from December 2 to January 31 must be recorded on the books as an expense and a liability through an adjusting entry. The period is 60 days (31 − 2 = 29 in December plus 31 in January). Applying the interest formula, principal × rate × time, the accrued interest is computed as follows.

$$\$2{,}000 \times \frac{8}{100} \times \frac{60}{360} = \$26.67$$

An entry is then recorded in the Adjustments section of the worksheet by debiting Interest Expense and crediting Interest Payable. This entry is identified with the letter g.

ACCT. NO.	ACCOUNT NAME	TRIAL BALANCE		ADJUSTMENTS	
		DEBIT	CREDIT	DEBIT	CREDIT
216	Interest Payable				(g)26 67
591	Interest Expense	762 00		(g)26 67	

An adjustment for accrued interest expense is made on the worksheet at the end of any month for which financial statements are to be prepared. However, the adjustment is entered in the accounts only at the end of the fiscal year. Hence, the amount of accrued interest expense in the adjustment illustrated is for the entire period from the date of the note to the current date, January 31.

Prepaid Expenses   An expense item that has been recorded in the current period but that pertains in part to a later accounting period should be analyzed to identify the unused element, which should be carried over to the period in which it belongs. In the initial recording of the expense, a debit may have been made directly to the expense account. Thus, if the item is not all used during the current period, the expense account balance is overstated when the period closes. An adjustment should be made to reduce the expense account for the amount of the unused portion and to record the unused portion, or *prepaid* or *deferred expense,* as an asset. The first three prepaid expense items in the accounts of the Style Clothing Store require this type of treatment.

Store Supplies on Hand.   The Style Clothing Store charges office supplies and store supplies to expense accounts as the items are purchased. If any considerable amount of these supplies remains unused at the end of an accounting period, the cost is determined and removed from the expenses of the current period. Assume that the amount of office supplies on hand is too small to justify an adjustment. However, an inventory shows that store supplies costing $110 are on hand.

The $110 cost of supplies on hand is recorded by debiting the asset account Store Supplies on Hand. Since the cost of all store supplies purchased has been charged to the Store Supplies and Expense account, the cost of the items on hand must be removed from that account by a credit of $110 to avoid overstatement of the expense for the year. This procedure is indicated by Entry h on the partial worksheet shown at the top of page 473.

ACCT. NO.	ACCOUNT NAME	TRIAL BALANCE		ADJUSTMENTS	
		DEBIT	CREDIT	DEBIT	CREDIT
129	Store Supplies on Hand			(h)110 00	
523	Store Supplies and Expense	4,363 75			(h)110 00

Unexpired Insurance. Insurance premiums are usually paid in advance. The Style Clothing Store charges all its payments for premiums to the Insurance Expense account during the year. An analysis of the firm's insurance policies indicates that several of them will run into the following period. The appropriate portion of the cost of this protection (prorated on a time basis) should be transferred from the expense account to an asset account. The firm finds that $300 worth of insurance presently charged to expense has not yet expired. The necessary adjustment consists of a debit to an asset account called Prepaid Insurance and a credit to Insurance Expense. This adjustment is shown on the partial worksheet below as Entry i.

ACCT. NO.	ACCOUNT NAME	TRIAL BALANCE		ADJUSTMENTS	
		DEBIT	CREDIT	DEBIT	CREDIT
126	Prepaid Insurance			(i)300 00	
536	Insurance Expense	3,390 00			(i)300 00

Prepaid Interest on Notes Payable. In borrowing funds at the bank, the Style Clothing Store gave its $12,000 note dated December 22, payable in 60 days and bearing interest at 9 percent. The bank deducted $180 interest for the entire period in advance, and this was debited to Interest Expense at the time. On January 31, the note still had 20 days to run until its maturity on February 20. Interest expense for these 20 days has already been recorded, although it should properly appear as an expense for the next period. An adjustment is necessary to get all the facts in the records. First, the usual interest formula (principal × rate × time) is applied to determine the amount of interest prepaid for 20 days.

$$\$12,000 \times \frac{9}{100} \times \frac{20}{360} = \$60$$

Then, in the Adjustments section of the worksheet, an asset account called Prepaid Interest Expense is debited for $60 and Interest Expense is credited for the same amount. The entry is marked j as illustrated on the partial worksheet below.

ACCT. NO.	ACCOUNT NAME	TRIAL BALANCE		ADJUSTMENTS	
		DEBIT	CREDIT	DEBIT	CREDIT
127	Prepaid Interest Expense			(j)60 00	
591	Interest Expense	762 00		(g)26 67	(j)60 00

Alternative Method. In the initial recording procedure for a prepaid expense item, the transaction can be entered as a debit to an asset account. Under this arrangement, any amount that has been used by the end of the period is transferred from the asset account to an appropriate expense account. The Style Clothing Store has one prepaid item that is treated in this way.

As discussed in Unit 25, the Style Clothing Store is subject to a stock tax on its merchandise inventory. For the period of July 1, 19X2, to June 30, 19X3, this tax is payable in December of 19X2. At the time of payment in December, the tax for six months (January 1 to June 30, 19X3) is prepaid and is accordingly debited to the asset account Prepaid Taxes. At the end of January, one-sixth of this amount is transferred to the expense account Taxes and Licenses. On January 31, the Prepaid Taxes account has a balance of $600, representing the prepayment for six months. An adjustment must now be made for one-sixth of this amount, or $100, to record January's share of the prepayment.

The required entry in the Adjustments section of the worksheet consists of a debit to Taxes and Licenses for $100 and a credit to Prepaid Taxes for the same amount. The debit is labeled .7 to identify it as the stock tax. Both parts of the entry are marked with the letter k.

ACCT. NO.	ACCOUNT NAME	TRIAL BALANCE		ADJUSTMENTS	
		DEBIT	CREDIT	DEBIT	CREDIT
128	Prepaid Taxes	600 00			(k)100 00
555	Taxes and Licenses	1,206 00		(d).8– 20 00 (k).7–100 00	

Accrued Income All income that has been earned in the current period should be included in the proper revenue account before the books are closed. If, at the time the trial balance is taken, an item of earned income has not yet been entered in the records, an adjustment is necessary to recognize this *accrued income*. The individual revenue account balance should be increased even though the amount involved has not been actually received or collected. The offsetting debit may represent an increase in assets or a reduction in liabilities. The Style Clothing Store has two accrued income items.

Accrued Interest on Notes Receivable. Interest-bearing notes receivable are ordinarily recorded at face value when received. They are carried in the records at that value until they are collected or written off as uncollectible. The interest income is recorded when it is received, which is usually when the note is settled at maturity. However, the interest is actually earned day by day throughout the period that the note is held. Therefore, at the end of an accounting period, any accrued interest that has been earned but not recorded should be recognized by means of an adjusting entry.

The trial balance prepared at the Style Clothing Store on January 31, 19X3, shows $800 in the Notes Receivable account. This balance represents a 60-day, 9 percent note dated December 17 and signed by Gail Smith. Interest that has accrued on the note as of January 31 is computed as follows.

$$\$800 \times \frac{9}{100} \times \frac{45}{360} = \$9$$

If financial statements had been prepared sometime during the fiscal year, such as on December 31, the accountant would have made a worksheet adjustment for accrued interest on this note and would have shown the appropriate amount on the statements. However, except at the end of the fiscal year, the accountant *would not record* such an adjustment in the journal and the ledger. Consequently, in this case, accrued interest must be determined at the end of January and recorded from the date of the note to the current date.

The facts are entered in the Adjustments section of the worksheet by a debit to Interest Receivable for $9 and a credit to Interest Earned for the same amount. This entry shows that the amount has been earned but not yet received. The adjustment is identified by the letter l on the partial worksheet below.

ACCT. NO.	ACCOUNT NAME	TRIAL BALANCE		ADJUSTMENTS	
		DEBIT	CREDIT	DEBIT	CREDIT
116	Interest Receivable			(l)9 00	
491	Interest Earned		226 00		(l)9 00

The Interest Receivable account is shown on the balance sheet as a current asset.

Accrued Commissions on Sales Tax. In Unit 25, you learned that the Style Clothing Store is entitled to retain a commission on the 3 percent sales tax collected if it files its sales tax return and pays the net amount due promptly.

The commission is 2 percent of the gross sales tax due. At the end of January, the balance shown in the Sales Tax Payable account, $825.28, includes both the amount that will have to be paid to the state tax agency and the amount of the commission to be retained by the Style Clothing Store.

January Sales	$27,550.90
Sales Returns and Allowances	41.25
Taxable Sales for January	$27,509.65
Gross Tax (0.03 × $27,509.65)	$825.29
Commission to Be Retained (0.02 × $825.29)	16.51
Net Tax Liability	$808.78
Balance of Sales Tax Payable Account	$825.28
Net Tax Liability	808.78
Adjustment Necessary for Commission	$ 16.50

The commission is treated as miscellaneous income. An adjustment is needed to transfer the amount of the commission from the liability account to the proper revenue account.

Note that there is a difference of $0.01 between the trial balance figure of $825.28 and the $825.29 amount to be shown as tax due on the sales tax return. Such slight differences often occur because the sales tax collected is determined by the tax bracket method or is computed to the nearest penny on each transaction. The resulting total for the month rarely agrees exactly with the amount calculated as due when the tax rate is applied to the total taxable sales. The procedure is to adjust the Sales Tax Payable account to show the actual correct liability to the taxing authority.

The commission is recorded in the Adjustments section of the worksheet. Sales Tax Payable is debited for $16.50, and Miscellaneous Income is credited for the same amount. This entry in the illustration below is labeled m.

ACCT. NO.	ACCOUNT NAME	TRIAL BALANCE DEBIT	TRIAL BALANCE CREDIT	ADJUSTMENTS DEBIT	ADJUSTMENTS CREDIT
231	Sales Tax Payable		825 28	(m)16 50	
493	Miscellaneous Income		218 60		(m)16 50

Other Accrued Income Items. The Style Clothing Store has no other accrued income items. However, a question is sometimes raised about the treatment of purchases discount. The question is: Should the amount of discount available if payment is made on time (but in the next accounting period) be accrued at the end of the current period in cases where purchases have been recorded at the gross invoice price (the procedure followed by the Style Clothing Store)?

Most accountants would not make an accrual because earning the discount is not yet certain. The invoice must be paid before the discount period expires in order to earn the discount. Accountants generally prefer to wait until a discount has definitely been earned before they record it. The discount is not earned day by day as is the interest on a note receivable. Either it is all earned or none of it is earned when the invoice is paid. Therefore, no adjustment is made for purchases discount.

Unearned Income

Any portion of a firm's income that has been received but not yet fully earned at the end of a period is considered *unearned* or *deferred income* and should not be reported on the income statement until it is earned in the succeeding accounting period. Since there are no unearned income items at the Style Clothing Store, an example from another type of business is presented here.

Unearned Subscription Income for a Publisher. Magazine publishers obtain subscriptions in advance, often several years in advance. The entire subscription may be credited to a revenue account when received. Then, at the end of the year, the publisher must analyze the subscriptions to determine how much of the amount credited to the revenue account has not yet been earned because it applies to future periods. When the amount of income to be deferred is determined, an adjustment is made. Subscription Income is debited, and a liability account called Unearned Subscription Income is credited.

Using assumed amounts for an imaginary publisher, suppose that in the first year a total of $125,000 for subscriptions has been received and credited to Subscription Income. Of this total, $80,000 is for current-year subscriptions and $45,000 is for subscriptions beyond the first year.

The balance in the Subscription Income account at the end of the first year is $125,000. Since only $80,000 has actually been earned in the first year, the amount of the adjustment required to reduce the account to the proper balance is $45,000. This amount is debited to Subscription Income and credited to Unearned Subscription Income, as shown on the partial worksheet below. The credit to Unearned Subscription Income provides a record of the amount applicable to future periods.

ACCT. NO.	ACCOUNT NAME	TRIAL BALANCE DEBIT	TRIAL BALANCE CREDIT	ADJUSTMENTS DEBIT	ADJUSTMENTS CREDIT
241	Unearned Subscription Income				(a)45,000 00
441	Subscription Income		125,000 00	(a)45,000 00	

The Unearned Subscription Income account is classified as a current liability on the balance sheet.

Alternative Method. In the above example, the Subscription Income account was credited when payment was received in advance. However, it is possible to make the initial credit to the Unearned Subscription Income account when the cash is received. Indeed, this may be a more logical and accurate procedure because, at the time of receipt, most subscription revenue is entirely unearned. If the company in the preceding example had used this method of recording receipts from subscriptions, its trial balance at the end of the first year would show Unearned Subscription Income with a credit balance of $125,000, while the Subscription Income account would have no balance. An adjustment would then be needed to transfer the amount earned during the first year, $80,000, to a revenue account. The amount still unearned, $45,000, would remain in the Unearned Subscription Income account. The required journal entry is shown below with the two ledger accounts involved. The account balances reflect the posting of the adjustment.

19 X1				
Dec. 31	Unearned Subscription Income	241	80,000 00	
	Subscription Income	441		80,000 00
	Transfer of income earned from subscriptions during the year.			

Unearned Subscription Income   **No. 241**

DATE	EXPLANATION	POST. REF.	DEBIT	CREDIT	BALANCE	DR. CR.
19 X1						
Dec. 31	Balance	✓			125,000 00	Cr.
31		J12	80,000 00		45,000 00	Cr.

Subscription Income   **No. 441**

DATE	EXPLANATION	POST. REF.	DEBIT	CREDIT	BALANCE	DR. CR.
19 X1						
Dec. 31		J12		80,000 00	80,000 00	Cr.

Results of the Two Methods Compared. The ledger account balances in the two preceding groups of illustrations show the same results after the adjusting entries have been posted. Since the facts are the same, the final outcome must be identical regardless of which method is used. In each case, the Subscription Income account shows an adjusted balance of $80,000, while the Unearned Subscription Income account shows an adjusted balance of $45,000.

Recording the Ending Inventory on the Worksheet

In Unit 17 you learned that accountants must close the beginning merchandise inventory into the Revenue and Expense Summary account and must record the ending merchandise inventory as an asset at the end of a period. Accountants normally have the merchandise inventory information available at the time they make the previously described adjustments on the worksheet. Therefore, they often find it convenient to note the entries for the merchandise inventory on the worksheet at the time they record the adjusting entries. However, since entries for merchandise inventory are not made in the Adjustments section of the worksheet, they are considered in the next unit, along with other closing procedures.

principles and procedures summary

The accrual basis of accounting requires that all revenue and expenses of a period be matched and reported on the income statement of the period to determine the net income. Typically, certain adjustments must be made to the revenue and expense accounts at the end of the period in order to make sure that they correctly reflect amounts that apply to the current period and do not include amounts that pertain to other periods. Provisions for bad debts expense and depreciation expense are common examples of such adjustments. Other typical adjustments of expense accounts involve accrued expenses and prepaid expenses.

Accrued expenses represent expense items that have been incurred or used but not yet paid or recorded. Prepaid, or deferred, expenses represent expense items that have been recorded but not yet incurred or used. A firm may also have adjustments involving accrued income and unearned income. Accrued income is income that has been earned but not yet recorded. Unearned, or deferred, income is income that has not yet been earned but has been received and recorded.

managerial implications

The matching process is necessary if managers are to know the true revenue, expenses, and net income of a period. If accrued and deferred items were not adjusted, the financial statements would be incomplete and misleading. They would then be of no help in evaluating operations. Since adjustments tend to increase or decrease net income, managers should be familiar with the procedures and the underlying assumptions used by their firm's accountant.

managerial discussion questions

1. Assume that you are working as an accountant. Your company received $4,000 income in advance. Your manager is concerned because you

showed part of this as unearned income at the end of the year. He argues that since the cash has been received, the entire amount should be shown as income. Explain why you have not done so.

2. Why should management understand the underlying assumptions used by the firm's accountant in the completion of the financial statements?
3. How can management be sure that the firm's accountant has recognized all accrued and prepaid expenses?
4. Why is the cost of insurance premiums often recorded as prepaid insurance instead of as insurance expense? Does the first method produce financial results different from those that the alternative method would produce?

application of principles

PROBLEM 26-1 An examination of the trial balance of the Hernandez Company at the end of its fiscal year on July 31, 19X3, indicates the need for adjustments. Information about these adjustments is given below and on the next page. The accounts and balances involved are also shown on the next page.

INSTRUCTIONS
1. Prepare a partial worksheet that has a Trial Balance section, an Adjustments section, and an Adjusted Trial Balance section.
2. Enter on the worksheet the accounts and balances given on the next page.
3. Enter on the worksheet the specified adjustments, identifying each with its appropriate letter. (No adjustments have been entered on the books this year.)
4. Combine the amounts that appear in the Trial Balance section and the Adjustments section. Enter the resulting figures in the Adjusted Trial Balance section.

ADJUSTMENTS

a. The estimate of bad debt losses is to be calculated at 0.2 percent of net credit sales for the fiscal year. During the period of July 31, 19X2–July 31, 19X3, the company had net credit sales of $884,000.
b. Depreciation on equipment is to be computed using the straight-line method. The total cost of the equipment is $82,000, and it is estimated to have a useful life of 12 years and a $4,000 net salvage value.
c. Property taxes for the calendar year 19X3 are estimated to be $1,200. They must be accrued at the rate of $100 a month.
d. The salaries earned and recorded in July that were subject to payroll taxes are $6,000. Applicable rates are 6.5 percent (assumed rate) for FICA tax, 2 percent for state unemployment tax, and 0.7 percent for federal unemployment tax. All the necessary payroll taxes through June 30 have been recorded.

e. Notes Payable—Trade consists of a $12,000 note dated May 31, 19X3, and bearing interest at 7 percent.
f. The inventory of supplies on hand as of July 31 is valued at $285.
g. Unexpired insurance on July 31 amounts to $750.

ACCOUNTS AND BALANCES

111A	Allowances for Bad Debts	$ 134.00 Cr.
125	Prepaid Insurance	-0-
127	Supplies Inventory	-0-
131A	Accumulated Depreciation—Equipment	13,950.00 Cr.
216	Interest Payable	-0-
226	Payroll Taxes Payable	-0-
235	Property Taxes Payable	-0-
523	Supplies Expense	2,340.00 Dr.
536	Insurance Expense	4,354.00 Dr.
552	Payroll Tax Expense	3,250.00 Dr.
555	Property Tax Expense	324.00 Dr.
561	Bad Debts Expense	-0-
563	Depreciation Expense—Equipment	-0-
591	Interest Expense	-0-

PROBLEM 26-2 The trial balance shown on page 482 was prepared at the Metro Office Supply Store on December 31, 19X2, the end of the fiscal year. The adjustments that must be made are given below.

INSTRUCTIONS
1. Record the accounts and their balances in the Trial Balance section of a ten-column worksheet. Total the columns.
2. Record the specified adjustments in the Adjustments section of the worksheet, and identify each entry by letter. Show your computations on a separate sheet. Total the columns of the Adjustments section.
3. Save your worksheet for use in Problem 27-1.

ADJUSTMENTS

a. An analysis of the accounts receivable results in an estimate that $286.10 of the accounts will be uncollectible. Adjust the Allowance for Bad Debts account to this balance. (Debit General Operating Expenses 539 for the amount of the adjustment.)
b. Prepaid insurance was $187 as of December 31.
c. Depreciation expense for the year is 10 percent of the cost of the equipment.
d. Rent expense for December of $150 has not been recorded or paid; it was due on December 27. (Credit Accounts Payable 202 for the amount of the adjustment.)
e. Payroll taxes on $700 of December salaries and wages have not been recorded. The rates for these taxes are: FICA tax, 6.5 percent (assumed rate); state unemployment tax, 2.5 percent; and federal unemployment tax, 0.7 percent.

METRO OFFICE SUPPLY STORE
Trial Balance
December 31, 19X2

Acct. No.	Account Name	Debit	Credit
101	Cash in Bank	$ 1,883.46	
111	Accounts Receivable	8,425.00	
111A	Allowance for Bad Debts		$ 31.00
121	Merchandise Inventory	25,000.00	
131	Prepaid Insurance	385.00	
141	Equipment	1,200.00	
141A	Accum. Depr.—Equipment		310.00
202	Accounts Payable		469.00
226	Payroll Taxes Payable		-0-
301	Ann Riley, Capital		15,000.00
302	Ann Riley, Drawing	3,600.00	
311	Mary Gallo, Capital		18,000.00
312	Mary Gallo, Drawing	4,200.00	
401	Sales		124,750.00
501	Merchandise Purchases	84,650.00	
521	Rent Expense	1,650.00	
531	Salaries and Wages Expense	8,125.00	
533	Payroll Tax Expense	720.23	
535	Insurance Expense	525.00	
537	Depr. Expense—Equipment		
539	General Operating Expenses	18,196.31	
	Totals	$158,560.00	$158,560.00

PROBLEM 26-3 The financial records of the Bakilar Company on December 31, 19X6, showed that it had three prepaid expense items.

INSTRUCTIONS

1. Assume that the company follows a policy of charging directly to prepaid expense (asset) accounts certain expenditures made during the year. As of December 31, 19X6, these asset accounts had the following balances before adjustment: Prepaid Insurance, $4,200; Prepaid Interest Expense, $1,850; and Supplies Inventory, $1,420. An analysis on December 31, 19X6, indicates $1,250 of unexpired insurance, $400 of prepaid interest on notes payable outstanding, and $240 of unused supplies on hand.

Show the general journal entry for the adjustment required in each of the accounts as of December 31, 19X6. (Omit explanations.)

2. Assume instead that the company charges expenditures for prepaid expense items directly to the expense accounts involved. As of December 31, 19X6, the expense accounts have the following balances before adjustment: Insurance Expense, $4,200; Interest Expense, $1,850; and Supplies Expense, $1,420. An analysis on December 31, 19X6, indicates $1,250 of

unexpired insurance, $400 of prepaid interest on notes payable outstanding, and $240 of unused supplies on hand.

Show the general journal entry for the adjustment required in each of the accounts as of December 31, 19X6. (Omit explanations.)

PROBLEM 26-4 During its first year of operations, 19X1, the Periodicals Publishing Company received subscriptions in cash totaling $845,600. An analysis as of December 31, 19X1, indicates that $220,500 is applicable to the current year and the remainder is applicable to 19X2 and future years.

INSTRUCTIONS
1. Assuming that the $845,600 was credited to Unearned Subscription Income when it was received, show in general journal form the entry necessary to adjust the books on December 31, 19X1. (Omit the explanation.)
2. Assuming instead that the $845,600 was credited to Subscription Income when it was received, give the necessary adjusting entry on December 31, 19X1. (Omit the explanation.)

alternate problems

PROBLEM 26-1A An examination of the trial balance of the Wallach Company at the end of its fiscal year on September 30, 19X8, indicates the need for adjustments. Information about these adjustments is given below and on the next page. The accounts and balances involved are also shown on the next page.

INSTRUCTIONS
1. Prepare a partial worksheet that has a Trial Balance section, an Adjustments section, and an Adjusted Trial Balance section.
2. Enter on the worksheet the accounts and balances given on the next page.
3. Enter on the worksheet the specified adjustments, identifying each with its appropriate letter. (No adjustments have been entered on the books this year.)
4. Combine the amounts in the Trial Balance section and the Adjustments section. Enter the resulting figures in the Adjusted Trial Balance section.

ADJUSTMENTS

a. The estimate of bad debt losses is to be calculated at 0.5 percent of net credit sales of $150,000 for the fiscal year.
b. Depreciation on the equipment for the fiscal year is to be computed using the straight-line method. The total cost of the equipment amounts to $44,000 as of September 30, 19X8. The equipment is estimated to have a net salvage value of $2,000 and a useful life of 10 years.
c. Property taxes for the calendar year 19X8 are estimated to be $600. They must be accrued at the rate of $50 a month.
d. Salaries earned and recorded in September that were subject to payroll taxes amounted to $3,000. Applicable rates are 6.5 percent (assumed rate) for FICA tax, 1.2 percent for state unemployment tax, and 0.7 percent for

      federal unemployment tax. All payroll taxes through August 31 have been recorded.
- e. Notes Payable—Trade consists of a $10,000 note dated August 31, 19X8, payable in 60 days with interest at 8 percent.
- f. The inventory of supplies on hand as of September 30 is valued at $150.
- g. Unexpired insurance as of September 30 amounts to $860.
- h. Notes Payable—Bank consists of a $25,000 note dated August 1, 19X8, payable in 180 days. The interest at 9 percent was deducted from the proceeds in advance and was debited to Interest Expense.

ACCOUNTS AND BALANCES

111A	Allowance for Bad Debts	$ 14.50 Cr.
126	Prepaid Insurance	-0-
127	Prepaid Interest Expense	-0-
129	Supplies Inventory	-0-
131A	Accumulated Depreciation—Equipment	13,300.00 Cr.
216	Interest Payable	-0-
226	Payroll Taxes Payable	-0-
235	Property Taxes Payable	-0-
523	Supplies Expense	1,320.00 Dr.
536	Insurance Expense	2,870.00 Dr.
552	Payroll Tax Expense	2,126.00 Dr.
555	Property Tax Expense	160.00 Dr.
561	Bad Debts Expense	-0-
563	Depreciation Expense—Equipment	-0-
591	Interest Expense	1,485.00 Dr.

PROBLEM 26-2A

In this problem you are to use the December 31, 19X2, trial balance of the Metro Office Supply Store, given in Problem 26-2 on page 482. The adjustments that must be made are listed below and on the next page.

INSTRUCTIONS
1. Record the accounts and their balances in the Trial Balance section of a ten-column worksheet. Total the columns.
2. Record the specified adjustments in the Adjustments section of the worksheet, and identify each entry by letter. Show your computations on a separate sheet. Total the Adjustments section.
3. Save your worksheet for use in Problem 27-1A.

ADJUSTMENTS

- a. An analysis of the accounts receivable results in an estimate that $249.50 worth of the accounts will be uncollectible. Adjust the Allowance for Bad Debts account for this amount. (Debit General Operating Expenses 539.)
- b. Prepaid insurance was $270 as of December 31.
- c. Depreciation is 8 percent of the cost of the equipment.
- d. Rent expense for December of $150 has not been recorded or paid; it was due December 1. (Credit Accounts Payable 202.)

e. Payroll taxes on $600 of December salaries and wages have not been recorded. The rates are: FICA tax, 6.5 percent; state unemployment tax, 2.7 percent; and federal unemployment tax, 0.7 percent.

PROBLEM 26-3A The financial records of Han Imports Inc. on December 31, 19X2, showed that it had three prepaid expense items.

INSTRUCTIONS
1. Assume that the company follows a policy of charging directly to prepaid expense (asset) accounts certain expenditures made during the year. As of December 31, 19X2, these asset accounts had the following balances before adjustment: Prepaid Insurance, $2,620; Prepaid Interest Expense, $850; and Supplies Inventory, $2,084. An analysis on December 31, 19X2, indicates $450 of unexpired insurance, $180 of prepaid interest on notes payable outstanding, and $356 of unused supplies on hand.

Show the general journal entry for the adjustment required in each of the accounts as of December 31, 19X2. (Omit explanations.)

2. Assume that the company charges expenditures for prepaid expense items directly to the expense accounts involved. As of December 31, 19X2, the expense accounts have the following balances before adjustment: Insurance Expense, $2,620; Interest Expense, $850; and Supplies Expense, $2,084. An analysis on December 31, 19X2, indicates $450 of unexpired insurance, $180 of prepaid interest on notes payable outstanding, and $356 of unused supplies on hand.

Show the general journal entry for the adjustment required in each of the accounts as of December 31, 19X2. (Omit explanations.)

PROBLEM 26-4A During the year 19X1, Gala Publishers received $960,000 revenue from magazine subscriptions. An analysis as of December 31, 19X1, indicates that $500,000 is applicable to the current year and that the remainder is applicable to 19X2 and future years.

INSTRUCTIONS
1. Assuming that the $960,000 was credited to Unearned Subscription Income when it was received, show in general journal form the entry necessary to adjust the books on December 31, 19X1. (Omit the explanation.)
2. Assuming instead that the $960,000 was credited to Subscription Income when it was received, give the necessary adjusting entry on December 31, 19X1. (Omit the explanation.)

UNIT 27

THE WORKSHEET AND THE FINANCIAL STATEMENTS

After determining the end-of-period adjustments and recording them on the worksheet, the accountant must complete the worksheet and prepare the financial statements. These procedures should be carried out as quickly and efficiently as possible because management needs information about the results of operations and the financial position of the business.

Entering Adjustments on the Worksheet

In Unit 26 you saw how the end-of-period adjustments for the Style Clothing Store are made on January 31, 19X3, so that revenues and expenses for the year are properly matched and net income is correctly stated. The twelve adjustments are restated below using the letters corresponding to those on the worksheet. The partial worksheet on page 488 shows how the adjustments are entered in the Adjustments columns and how these columns are then totaled to make sure that the debits and credits are equal. The number of the page on which each adjustment is discussed and illustrated is shown here in parentheses.

a. Estimated bad debts expense for the year (pages 466 and 468).
b. Depreciation of furniture and fixtures (pages 468 and 469).
c. Depreciation of office equipment (pages 468 and 469).
d. Estimated property taxes payable (pages 469 and 470).
e. Accrued salaries and wages (page 470).
f. Payroll taxes payable (pages 470 and 471).
g. Interest payable (pages 471 and 472).
h. Store supplies on hand (pages 472 and 473).
i. Prepaid insurance (page 473).
j. Prepaid interest expense (pages 473 and 474).
k. Prepaid taxes transferred to expense (page 474).
l. Interest receivable (page 475).
m. Commission earned on sales taxes (pages 475 and 476).

Completing the Adjusted Trial Balance Section

The next step in completing the worksheet is to determine the amount to be extended for each account to the Adjusted Trial Balance. This is done by combining the figure (if any) in the Adjustments section with the original trial balance figure for the account. Each item on the partial worksheet illustrated on page 498 will now be traced. You should examine each item closely as it is discussed.

101–109   There are no adjustments related to any of the first four accounts in the original Trial Balance section. The amounts shown are simply moved across the worksheet into the corresponding column of the Adjusted Trial Balance section. Debits in the Trial Balance section are entered in the Debit column of the Adjusted Trial Balance section. Credits in the Trial Balance section are written in the Adjusted Trial Balance Credit column. Each of the first four items is a debit in the Trial Balance section and remains a debit in the Adjusted Trial Balance section.

110   There are no amounts for Notes Receivable Discounted in either the Trial Balance section or the Adjustments section. Hence, no amount is shown on this line in the Adjusted Trial Balance section. (It is customary to enter all ledger accounts except Revenue and Expense Summary on the worksheet even though some of the accounts have no balances.)

111   The debit balance of $28,067.35 for Accounts Receivable is extended unchanged to the Adjusted Trial Balance section.

111A   Allowance for Bad Debts has a credit balance of $7.06 in the Trial Balance section and a credit adjustment of $669.15 (a). The credit amount $676.21 shown in the Adjusted Trial Balance section is the sum of the two credits in the other sections.

116   The next account listed, Interest Receivable, has no balance in the Trial Balance section but has a debit adjustment of $9 (l). Thus, the amount shown in the Adjusted Trial Balance section for this item is a debit of $9.

121   The amount in the Trial Balance section for Merchandise Inventory (beginning) is a debit of $65,000. This amount is extended unchanged to the Adjusted Trial Balance section.

126, 127   Prepaid Insurance and Prepaid Interest Expense have no balances in the Trial Balance section. Their respective debit adjustment figures of $300 (i) and $60 (j) are extended to the Adjusted Trial Balance section.

128   The original debit figure of $600 for Prepaid Taxes in the Trial Balance section is combined with the credit adjustment of $100 (k) to arrive at a $500 debit amount in the Adjusted Trial Balance section.

129   Since there was no amount in the Trial Balance section for Store Supplies on Hand, the $110 debit adjustment (h) is extended to the Adjusted Trial Balance section.

131   The $4,600 debit balance of Furniture and Fixtures is extended unchanged to the Adjusted Trial Balance section.

131A   The $360 credit in the Trial Balance section for Accumulated Depreciation— Furniture and Fixtures is combined with the credit adjustment of $460 (b) to make an $820 credit in the Adjusted Trial Balance section.

132   The $2,750 debit balance of Office Equipment is extended unchanged.

STYLE CLOTHING STORE
Worksheet (Partial)
Year Ended January 31, 19X3

	ACCT. NO.	ACCOUNT NAME	TRIAL BALANCE DEBIT	TRIAL BALANCE CREDIT	ADJUSTMENTS DEBIT	ADJUSTMENTS CREDIT	ADJUSTED TRIAL BALANCE DEBIT	ADJUSTED TRIAL BALANCE CREDIT
1	101	Cash in Bank	14,320 89				14,320 89	
2	105	Petty Cash Fund	25 00				25 00	
3	106	Change Fund	100 00				100 00	
4	109	Notes Receivable	800 00				800 00	
5	110	Notes Receivable Discounted						
6	111	Accounts Receivable	28,067 35				28,067 35	
7	111A	Allowance for Bad Debts		7 06		(a)669 15		676 21
8	116	Interest Receivable			(l)9 00		9 00	
9	121	Merchandise Inventory	65,000 00				65,000 00	
10	126	Prepaid Insurance				(i)300 00	300 00	
11	127	Prepaid Interest Expense				(j)60 00	60 00	
12	128	Prepaid Taxes	600 00			(k)100 00	500 00	
13	129	Store Supplies on Hand				(h)110 00	110 00	
14	131	Furniture and Fixtures	4,600 00				4,600 00	
15	131A	Accum. Depreciation—Furniture and Fixtures		360 00		(b)460 00		820 00
16	132	Office Equipment	2,750 00				2,750 00	
17	132A	Accum. Depreciation—Office Equipment		215 00		(c)215 00		430 00
18	201	Notes Payable—Trade		2,000 00				2,000 00
19	203	Notes Payable—Bank		12,000 00				12,000 00
20	205	Accounts Payable		5,109 65				5,109 65
21	216	Interest Payable				(g)26 67		26 67
22	221	Employee Deductions—FICA Taxes		189 80				189 80
23	222	Employee Deductions—Income Tax Withheld		216 00				216 00
24	225	Salaries and Wages Payable				(e)80 00		80 00
25	226	Payroll Taxes Payable				(f)255 00		255 00
26	231	Sales Tax Payable		825 28	(m)16 50			808 78
27	235	Property Taxes Payable				(d).8–20 00		20 00
28	301	Linda Hanson, Capital		29,000 00				29,000 00
29	302	Linda Hanson, Drawing	7,800 00				7,800 00	
30	311	Steven Casey, Capital		28,000 00				28,000 00
31	312	Steven Casey, Drawing	7,800 00				7,800 00	
32	321	Janet Miller, Capital		28,500 00				28,500 00
33	322	Janet Miller, Drawing	7,800 00				7,800 00	
34	401	Sales		359,195 90				359,195 90
35	452	Sales Returns and Allowances	6,041 25				6,041 25	
36	491	Interest Earned		226 00		(l)9 00		235 00
37	493	Miscellaneous Income		218 60		(m)16 50		235 10
38	501	Merchandise Purchases	255,350 00				255,350 00	
39	506	Freight In	3,590 00				3,590 00	
40	511	Purchases Returns and Allowances		1,065 00				1,065 00
41	512	Purchases Discount		5,048 30				5,048 30
42	521	Sales Salaries Expense	21,400 00				21,400 00	
43	522	Advertising Expense	6,893 30				6,893 30	
44	523	Store Supplies and Expense	4,363 75			(h)110 00	4,253 75	
45	529	Cash Short or Over	72 00				72 00	
46	532	Delivery Expense	3,860 00				3,860 00	
47	536	Insurance Expense	3,390 00			(i)300 00	3,090 00	
48	541	Custodial Wages Expense	5,040 00		(e)80 00		5,120 00	
49	542	Rent Expense	6,000 00				6,000 00	
50	543	Utilities Expense	1,981 35				1,981 35	
51	551	Office Salaries Expense	8,400 00				8,400 00	
52	552	Payroll Tax Expense	2,584 20		(f)255 00		2,839 20	
53	553	Office Supplies and Expense	804 50				804 50	
54	554	Professional Services Expense	775 00				775 00	
55	555	Taxes and Licenses	1,206 00		(d).8– 20 00		1,326 00	
56					(k).7–100 00			
57	561	Bad Debts Expense			(a)669 15		669 15	
58	562	Depr. Expense—Furniture and Fixtures			(b)460 00		460 00	
59	563	Depr. Expense—Office Equipment			(c)215 00		215 00	
60	591	Interest Expense	762 00		(g)26 67	(j)60 00	728 67	
61		Totals	472,176 59	472,176 59	2,321 32	2,321 32	473,911 41	473,911 41

132A	Accumulated Depreciation—Office Equipment had an original credit balance of $215. This figure is combined with the credit adjustment of $215 (c) to make a total credit of $430 in the Adjusted Trial Balance section.
201, 203, and 205	Notes Payable—Trade, Notes Payable—Bank, and Accounts Payable are not adjusted. Their credit balances are extended unchanged to the Adjusted Trial Balance section.
216	The credit adjustment of $26.67 (g) for Interest Payable is extended to the Adjusted Trial Balance section, since there is no balance for this account in the Trial Balance section.
221, 222	The credit balances of Employee Deductions—FICA Taxes and Employee Deductions—Income Tax Withheld are extended from the Trial Balance section to the Adjusted Trial Balance section.
225	The only item for Salaries and Wages Payable is the adjustment of $80 (e) for accrued custodial wages. This $80 credit is extended to the Adjusted Trial Balance section.
226	The adjustment entered for Payroll Taxes Payable, a credit of $255 (f), is extended to the Adjusted Trial Balance section.
231	Sales Tax Payable has a credit balance of $825.28 in the Trial Balance section and a debit of $16.50 (m) in the Adjustments section. The difference of $808.78 is extended as a credit to the Adjusted Trial Balance section.
235	The $20 credit adjustment (d) to Property Taxes Payable is extended to the Adjusted Trial Balance section.
301–322	The balances of all three capital accounts and all three drawing accounts are extended unchanged from the Trial Balance section to the Adjusted Trial Balance section.
401, 452	The credit balance in the Sales account is extended unchanged to the Adjusted Trial Balance section. The debit balance of Sales Returns and Allowances is also extended directly to the Adjusted Trial Balance section.
491	Interest Earned requires the combination of the original credit balance of $226 and the credit adjustment of $9 (1) for a total credit of $235 in the Adjusted Trial Balance section.
493	The credit amount of $235.10 for Miscellaneous Income in the Adjusted Trial Balance section is also determined by the combination of two credit figures—the original balance of $218.60 and the adjustment of $16.50 (m).
501, 506	The original debit balances of Merchandise Purchases and Freight In are extended unchanged to the Adjusted Trial Balance section.
511, 512	Purchases Returns and Allowances requires a simple extension of the original credit balance. The same is true for Purchases Discount.
521, 522	The balances of Sales Salaries Expense and Advertising Expense are extended without change to the Debit column of the Adjusted Trial Balance section.

523	Store Supplies and Expense shows a debit of $4,363.75 in the Trial Balance section and a credit adjustment of $110 (h) for supplies on hand. Subtracting the credit leaves a debit of $4,253.75, which is extended to the Adjusted Trial Balance section.
529, 532	The original debit balances of Cash Short or Over and Delivery Expense are extended without adjustment.
536	The $300 credit adjustment (i) shown for Insurance Expense must be subtracted from the original debit balance of $3,390 to obtain the debit figure of $3,090 recorded in the Adjusted Trial Balance section.
541	Custodial Wages Expense shows an original debit balance of $5,040 in the Trial Balance section. When this figure is combined with the adjustment of $80 (e) for accrued custodial wages on January 31, the result is a final debit balance of $5,120 in the Adjusted Trial Balance section.
542–551	The balances of Rent Expense, Utilities Expense, and Office Salaries Expense can be extended unchanged to the Debit column of the Adjusted Trial Balance section.
552	The original debit balance of $2,584.20 for Payroll Tax Expense is combined with a debit adjustment of $255 (f) to produce a total debit amount of $2,839.20.
553, 554	The balances of Office Supplies and Expense and Professional Services Expense are two more debits that are extended unchanged.
555	Taxes and Licenses has a debit balance of $1,206 in the Trial Balance section and two debit adjustments—one for $20 (d) and one for $100 (k). Adding these three debit items together gives $1,326, which is recorded in the Debit column of the Adjusted Trial Balance section.
561	Bad Debts Expense has a debit adjustment of $669.15 (a). This amount is extended to the Debit column of the Adjusted Trial Balance section.
562	The Depreciation Expense—Furniture and Fixtures account has a debit adjustment of $460 (b), which is extended to the Adjusted Trial Balance section.
563	The adjustment figure $215 (c) listed for Depreciation Expense—Office Equipment is extended to the Debit column in the Adjusted Trial Balance section.
591	The last item, Interest Expense, has a debit of $762 in the Trial Balance section and two adjustments—a debit of $26.67 (g) and a credit of $60 (j). The two debits are added to give a subtotal of $788.67, and then the credit is subtracted. The resulting debit of $728.67 is recorded in the Adjusted Trial Balance section.

Now that all the items in the Trial Balance section have been combined with the related adjustments to complete the Adjusted Trial Balance section, the next step is to add the debit items and the credit items in the Adjusted Trial Balance columns. In this way the accountant can prove the equality of the total debits and the total credits.

Preparing the Balance Sheet Section

After the Adjusted Trial Balance section is completed, the accountant must extend each item to the appropriate financial statement column. The account numbering system is helpful with this task.

In setting up the Style Clothing Store's chart of accounts, Gloria Thompson assigned blocks of numbers to asset, liability, and owners' equity accounts. The numbers used are 100–199 for assets, 200–299 for liabilities, and 300–399 for owners' equity. Since assets, liabilities, and owners' equity appear on the balance sheet, it is known in advance that all accounts through 399 will appear on the balance sheet. The partial worksheet illustrated below shows how the amounts in these accounts are extended to the columns of the Balance Sheet section.

STYLE CLOTHING STORE
Worksheet (Partial)
Year Ended January 31, 19X3

ACCT. NO.	ACCOUNT NAME	ADJUSTED TRIAL BALANCE		BALANCE SHEET	
		DEBIT	CREDIT	DEBIT	CREDIT
101	Cash in Bank	14,320 89		14,320 89	
105	Petty Cash Fund	25 00		25 00	
106	Change Fund	100 00		100 00	
109	Notes Receivable	800 00		800 00	
110	Notes Receivable Discounted				
111	Accounts Receivable	28,067 35		28,067 35	
111A	Allowance for Bad Debts		676 21		676 21
116	Interest Receivable	9 00		9 00	
121	Merchandise Inventory	65,000 00		(n)66,000 00	
126	Prepaid Insurance	300 00		300 00	
127	Prepaid Interest Expense	60 00		60 00	
128	Prepaid Taxes	500 00		500 00	
129	Store Supplies on Hand	110 00		110 00	
131	Furniture and Fixtures	4,600 00		4,600 00	
131A	Accum. Depreciation—Furniture and Fixtures		820 00		820 00
132	Office Equipment	2,750 00		2,750 00	
132A	Accum. Depreciation—Office Equipment		430 00		430 00
201	Notes Payable—Trade		2,000 00		2,000 00
203	Notes Payable—Bank		12,000 00		12,000 00
205	Accounts Payable		5,109 65		5,109 65
216	Interest Payable		26 67		26 67
221	Employee Deductions—FICA Taxes		189 80		189 80
222	Employee Deductions—Income Tax Withheld		216 00		216 00
225	Salaries and Wages Payable		80 00		80 00
226	Payroll Taxes Payable		255 00		255 00
231	Sales Tax Payable		808 78		808 78
235	Property Taxes Payable		20 00		20 00
301	Linda Hanson, Capital		29,000 00		29,000 00
302	Linda Hanson, Drawing	7,800 00		7,800 00	
311	Steven Casey, Capital		28,000 00		28,000 00
312	Steven Casey, Drawing	7,800 00		7,800 00	
321	Janet Miller, Capital		28,500 00		28,500 00
322	Janet Miller, Drawing	7,800 00		7,800 00	

Starting with the first item, Cash in Bank, the debit balance of $14,320.89 shown in the Adjusted Trial Balance section is extended to the Balance Sheet Debit column. The next three items are also debits in the Adjusted Trial Balance section and are therefore extended to the Balance Sheet Debit column. There is no balance in Notes Receivable Discounted at this time. The balance of Accounts Receivable is handled like the other debit balances. The first credit balance in the Adjusted Trial Balance section is $676.21 for Allowance for Bad Debts. This amount is extended to the Balance Sheet Credit column. Interest Receivable is another asset and is treated in the same way as any other account with a debit balance. (Note the basic rule that debit balances are always extended to debit columns and credit balances are always extended to credit columns.)

Next, the Adjusted Trial Balance section shows a debit of $65,000 for Merchandise Inventory, representing the beginning inventory. However, the accountant has been informed that merchandise valued at $66,000 is on hand at the close of business on January 31, 19X3. As you learned previously, the accountant updates the information about merchandise inventory at the end of each accounting period.

a. The beginning inventory must be charged to the cost of goods sold because it is presumed to be the first merchandise sold during the period.
b. The ending inventory must be recorded as an asset.
c. The ending inventory must also be recorded as a reduction in the cost of goods sold.

The accountant achieves these three objectives by means of the following steps. Note that Thompson deals with the ending inventory first.

1. The ending inventory amount, $66,000, is entered in the Balance Sheet Debit column because it is an asset. The entry is identified with the letter n.
2. The ending inventory amount, $66,000, is also extended to the Income Statement Credit column where it represents a reduction in the cost of goods sold during the period. This entry is also identified by the letter n.
3. The beginning inventory figure is disregarded for the moment. As explained shortly, this amount must be extended to the Income Statement Debit column along with other accounts representing the costs of doing business.

The remaining debit balances for asset accounts are extended from the Adjusted Trial Balance section to the Balance Sheet Debit column. The two accumulated depreciation accounts, which have credit balances, are extended from the Adjusted Trial Balance section to the Credit column of the Balance Sheet section. (See the illustration on page 491.)

Each liability account (200–299) has a credit balance in the Adjusted Trial Balance section. The individual balances are extended to the Credit column of the Balance Sheet section. The three capital accounts in the owners' equity group (300–399) also have credit balances in the Adjusted Trial Balance section. Each of these balances must therefore appear in the Credit column of the Balance Sheet section. The three drawing accounts have debit balances in the Adjusted Trial Balance section. Each must therefore be carried over to the Debit column of the Balance Sheet section.

The Balance Sheet section of the worksheet now contains all the amounts that should be extended from the Adjusted Trial Balance section. Note that all but one of the figures in both sections are the same. The ending inventory amount ($66,000) appears in the Balance Sheet section, whereas the beginning merchandise inventory ($65,000) is shown in the Adjusted Trial Balance section.

Preparing the Income Statement Section

The ten-column worksheet includes a pair of Income Statement columns for entering all items that will appear on the income statement. These columns are shown on the partial worksheet illustrated below.

STYLE CLOTHING STORE
Worksheet (Partial)
Year Ended January 31, 19X3

ACCT. NO.	ACCOUNT NAME	ADJUSTED TRIAL BALANCE DEBIT	ADJUSTED TRIAL BALANCE CREDIT	INCOME STATEMENT DEBIT	INCOME STATEMENT CREDIT
121	Merchandise Inventory	65,000 00		(n)65,000 00	(n)66,000 00
401	Sales		359,195 90		359,195 90
452	Sales Returns and Allowances	6,041 25		6,041 25	
491	Interest Earned		235 00		235 00
493	Miscellaneous Income		235 10		235 10
501	Merchandise Purchases	255,350 00		255,350 00	
506	Freight In	3,590 00		3,590 00	
511	Purchases Returns and Allowances		1,065 00		1,065 00
512	Purchases Discount		5,048 30		5,048 30
521	Sales Salaries Expense	21,400 00		21,400 00	
522	Advertising Expense	6,893 30		6,893 30	
523	Store Supplies and Expense	4,253 75		4,253 75	
529	Cash Short or Over	72 00		72 00	
532	Delivery Expense	3,860 00		3,860 00	
536	Insurance Expense	3,090 00		3,090 00	
541	Custodial Wages Expense	5,120 00		5,120 00	
542	Rent Expense	6,000 00		6,000 00	
543	Utilities Expense	1,981 35		1,981 35	
551	Office Salaries Expense	8,400 00		8,400 00	
552	Payroll Tax Expense	2,839 20		2,839 20	
553	Office Supplies and Expense	804 50		804 50	
554	Professional Services Expense	775 00		775 00	
555	Taxes and Licenses	1,326 00		1,326 00	
561	Bad Debts Expense	669 15		669 15	
562	Depr. Expense—Furniture and Fixtures	460 00		460 00	
563	Depr. Expense—Office Equipment	215 00		215 00	
591	Interest Expense	728 67		728 67	

First, the accountant extends the beginning inventory figure of $65,000 in the Merchandise Inventory account from the Adjusted Trial Balance section to the Income Statement Debit column, since it represents one of the major costs of doing business. The letter n is recorded next to this figure to identify it with the merchandise inventory. (As previously pointed out, in actual practice, many accountants enter this figure at the same time they record adjustments on the worksheet.)

Next, the accountant extends the balances of the revenue and expense accounts (numbered from 400 through 599) from the Adjusted Trial Balance section, making sure that each debit balance and credit balance is properly entered in the Debit and Credit columns of the Income Statement section.

Completing the Worksheet

The beginning and ending merchandise inventories, sales, purchases, and other revenue and expense items have now been carried over to the Income Statement columns. It is time to total the debits and credits in the Income Statement columns to determine the net income or net loss for the year.

The items in the Income Statement Debit column are added and found to total $398,869.17, as shown on the completed worksheet on pages 496–497. The credits are likewise added and found to total $431,779.30, as shown. Since the credits exceed the debits, the difference of $32,910.13 represents net income for the period. The net income of $32,910.13 is entered in the Debit column so that the two columns will balance. Then the final total of each column ($431,779.30) is recorded on the worksheet.

Since the net income belongs to the owners and represents an increase in equity, it is also entered in the Credit column of the Balance Sheet section, as explained in Unit 4.

Next, the Balance Sheet Debit and Credit columns are added and the totals are entered above the net income line (to make it easier to find any possible errors). The total of the Debit column is $141,042.24, and the total of the Credit column is $108,132.11. Of course, the difference should equal the net income (or net loss) for the period, which is $32,910.13 in this case.

Then, the final totals of the Balance Sheet columns, including net income, are determined to be $141,042.24 and are entered on the worksheet. The completed ten-column worksheet for the Style Clothing Store for the year ended January 31, 19X3, is shown on pages 496–497.

Preparing the Financial Statements

The next task for the accountant is to prepare financial statements from the information assembled on the worksheet. The figures needed for the income statement are contained in the Income Statement columns of the worksheet. Similarly, the figures needed for the balance sheet are in the Balance Sheet columns. A separate statement of partners' equities can also be prepared, using part of the information in the Balance Sheet columns. This statement is discussed on page 498.

Income Statement

The income statement for the Style Clothing Store, illustrated on page 495, is very much like that for the Modern Cleaning Shop. Note, however, the distribution of the net income to the partners, which is shown at the bottom of the statement. Each partner received one-third of the net income for the year. This arrangement was agreed on when the partnership was established.

STYLE CLOTHING STORE
Income Statement
Year Ended January 31, 19X3

Operating Revenues				
Sales				$359,195.90
Less Sales Returns and Allowances				6,041.25
Net Sales				$353,154.65
Cost of Goods Sold				
Merchandise Inventory, Feb. 1, 19X2			$ 65,000.00	
Purchases		$255,350.00		
Freight In		3,590.00		
Delivered Cost of Purchases		$258,940.00		
Less Purchase Ret. and Allow.	$1,065.00			
Purchases Discount	5,048.30	6,113.30		
Net Delivered Cost of Purchases			252,826.70	
Total Mdse. Available for Sale			$317,826.70	
Less Mdse. Inventory, Jan. 31, 19X3			66,000.00	
Cost of Goods Sold				251,826.70
Gross Profit on Sales				$101,327.95
Operating Expenses				
Selling Expenses				
Sales Salaries Expense		$ 21,400.00		
Advertising Expense		6,893.30		
Store Supplies and Expense		4,253.75		
Cash Short		72.00		
Delivery Expense		3,860.00		
Depr. Expense—Furniture and Fixtures		460.00		
Total Selling Expenses			$ 36,939.05	
General Administrative Expenses				
Insurance Expense		$ 3,090.00		
Custodial Wages Expense		5,120.00		
Rent Expense		6,000.00		
Utilities Expense		1,981.35		
Office Salaries Expense		8,400.00		
Payroll Tax Expense		2,839.20		
Office Supplies and Expense		804.50		
Professional Services Expense		775.00		
Taxes and Licenses		1,326.00		
Bad Debts Expense		669.15		
Depr. Expense—Office Equipment		215.00		
Total Gen. Administrative Expenses			31,220.20	
Total Operating Expenses				68,159.25
Net Income From Operations				$ 33,168.70
Add: Other Income				
Interest Earned		$ 235.00		
Miscellaneous Income		235.10		
Total Other Income			$ 470.10	
Deduct: Other Expense				
Interest Expense			728.67	
Net Nonoperating Expense				$ 258.57
Net Income for Year				$ 32,910.13
Distribution of Net Income				
Linda Hanson				$ 10,970.04
Steven Casey				10,970.04
Janet Miller				10,970.05
Total				$ 32,910.13

STYLE CLOTHING STORE
Worksheet
Year Ended January 31, 19X3

	ACCT. NO.	ACCOUNT NAME	TRIAL BALANCE DEBIT	TRIAL BALANCE CREDIT	ADJUSTMENTS DEBIT	ADJUSTMENTS CREDIT
1	101	Cash in Bank	14,320.89			
2	105	Petty Cash Fund	25.00			
3	106	Change Fund	100.00			
4	109	Notes Receivable	800.00			
5	110	Notes Receivable Discounted				
6	111	Accounts Receivable	28,067.35			
7	111A	Allowance for Bad Debts		7.06		(a) 669.15
8	116	Interest Receivable			(l) 9.00	
9	121	Merchandise Inventory	65,000.00			
10	126	Prepaid Insurance			(i) 300.00	
11	127	Prepaid Interest Expense			(j) 60.00	
12	128	Prepaid Taxes	600.00			(k) 100.00
13	129	Store Supplies on Hand			(h) 110.00	
14	131	Furniture and Fixtures	4,600.00			
15	131A	Accum. Depreciation—Furniture and Fixtures		360.00		(b) 460.00
16	132	Office Equipment	2,750.00			
17	132A	Accum. Depreciation—Office Equipment		215.00		(c) 215.00
18	201	Notes Payable—Trade		2,000.00		
19	203	Notes Payable—Bank		12,000.00		
20	205	Accounts Payable		5,109.65		
21	216	Interest Payable				(g) 26.67
22	221	Employee Deductions—FICA Taxes		189.80		
23	222	Employee Deductions—Income Tax Withheld		216.00		
24	225	Salaries and Wages Payable				(e) 80.00
25	226	Payroll Taxes Payable				(f) 255.00
26	231	Sales Tax Payable		825.28	(m) 16.50	
27	235	Property Taxes Payable				(d) 8-20.00
28	301	Linda Hanson, Capital		29,000.00		
29	302	Linda Hanson, Drawing	7,800.00			
30	311	Steven Casey, Capital		28,000.00		
31	312	Steven Casey, Drawing	7,800.00			
32	321	Janet Miller, Capital		28,500.00		
33	322	Janet Miller, Drawing	7,800.00			
34	401	Sales		359,195.90		
35	452	Sales Returns and Allowances	6,041.25			
36	491	Interest Earned		226.00		(l) 9.00
37	493	Miscellaneous Income		218.60		(m) 16.50
38	501	Merchandise Purchases	255,350.00			
39	506	Freight In	3,590.00			
40	511	Purchases Returns and Allowances		1,065.00		
41	512	Purchases Discount		5,048.30		
42	521	Sales Salaries Expense	21,400.00			
43	522	Advertising Expense	6,893.30			
44	523	Store Supplies and Expense	4,363.75			(h) 110.00
45	529	Cash Short or Over	72.00			
46	532	Delivery Expense	3,860.00			
47	536	Insurance Expense	3,390.00			(i) 300.00
48	541	Custodial Wages Expense	5,040.00		(e) 80.00	
49	542	Rent Expense	6,000.00			
50	543	Utilities Expense	1,981.35			
51	551	Office Salaries Expense	8,400.00			
52	552	Payroll Tax Expense	2,584.20		(f) 255.00	
53	553	Office Supplies and Expense	804.50			
54	554	Professional Services Expense	775.00			
55	555	Taxes and Licenses	1,206.00		(d) 8-20.00	
56					(k) 7-100.00	
57	561	Bad Debts Expense			(a) 669.15	
58	562	Depr. Expense—Furniture and Fixtures			(b) 460.00	
59	563	Depr. Expense—Office Equipment			(c) 215.00	
60	591	Interest Expense	762.00		(g) 26.67	(j) 60.00
61		Totals	472,176.59	472,176.59	2,321.32	2,321.32
62		Net Income				

ADJUSTED TRIAL BALANCE		INCOME STATEMENT		BALANCE SHEET		
DEBIT	CREDIT	DEBIT	CREDIT	DEBIT	CREDIT	
14,320 89				14,320 89		1
25 00				25 00		2
100 00				100 00		3
800 00				800 00		4
						5
28,067 35				28,067 35		6
	676 21				676 21	7
9 00				9 00		8
65,000 00		(n)65,000 00	(n)66,000 00	(n)66,000 00		9
300 00				300 00		10
60 00				60 00		11
500 00				500 00		12
110 00				110 00		13
4,600 00				4,600 00		14
	820 00				820 00	15
2,750 00				2,750 00		16
	430 00				430 00	17
	2,000 00				2,000 00	18
	12,000 00				12,000 00	19
	5,109 65				5,109 65	20
	26 67				26 67	21
	189 80				189 80	22
	216 00				216 00	23
	80 00				80 00	24
	255 00				255 00	25
	808 78				808 78	26
	20 00				20 00	27
	29,000 00				29,000 00	28
7,800 00				7,800 00		29
	28,000 00				28,000 00	30
7,800 00				7,800 00		31
	28,500 00				28,500 00	32
7,800 00				7,800 00		33
	359,195 90		359,195 90			34
6,041 25		6,041 25				35
	235 00		235 00			36
	235 10		235 10			37
255,350 00		255,350 00				38
3,590 00		3,590 00				39
	1,065 00		1,065 00			40
	5,048 30		5,048 30			41
21,400 00		21,400 00				42
6,893 30		6,893 30				43
4,253 75		4,253 75				44
72 00		72 00				45
3,860 00		3,860 00				46
3,090 00		3,090 00				47
5,120 00		5,120 00				48
6,000 00		6,000 00				49
1,981 35		1,981 35				50
8,400 00		8,400 00				51
2,839 20		2,839 20				52
804 50		804 50				53
775 00		775 00				54
1,326 00		1,326 00				55
						56
669 15		669 15				57
460 00		460 00				58
215 00		215 00				59
728 67		728 67				60
473,911 41	473,911 41	398,869 17	431,779 30	141,042 24	108,132 11	61
		32,910 13			32,910 13	62
		431,779 30	431,779 30	141,042 24	141,042 24	63

497

Statement of Partners' Equities

A statement of partners' equities shows the changes that have taken place in the financial interest of the partners during an accounting period. Refer to the statement of partners' equities for the Style Clothing Store, which is illustrated below. There were no new investments made during the year 19X3. The balances of the capital accounts shown on the trial balance and now appearing in the Balance Sheet Credit column of the worksheet are the balances at the beginning of the period. The distribution of net income presented on the income statement shows the amount to be added to each partner's equity. The drawing account balances given in the Balance Sheet Debit column of the worksheet provide the amounts to be deducted for withdrawals.

STYLE CLOTHING STORE
Statement of Partners' Equities
Year Ended January 31, 19X3

	Hanson Capital	Casey Capital	Miller Capital	Total Capital
Capital Balances, Feb. 1, 19X2	$29,000.00	$28,000.00	$28,500.00	$ 85,500.00
Net Income for Year	10,970.04	10,970.04	10,970.05	32,910.13
Totals	$39,970.04	$38,970.04	$39,470.05	$118,410.13
Less Withdrawals	7,800.00	7,800.00	7,800.00	23,400.00
Capital Balances, Jan. 31, 19X3	$32,170.04	$31,170.04	$31,670.05	$ 95,010.13

Note that the statement of partners' equities contains the same information that was shown in the Owner's Equity section of the balance sheet for the Modern Cleaning Shop. However, when there is more than one owner, as in a partnership, showing these details on the balance sheet takes too much space in the Owner's Equity section. Therefore, a separate statement is normally prepared.

Balance Sheet

The balance sheet is prepared in the normal way, using the information in the Balance Sheet columns of the worksheet. Assets are classified as current and fixed. The counterbalancing portion of the statement is usually subdivided into current liabilities, long-term liabilities, and owner's equity. The completed balance sheet for the Style Clothing Store is shown on page 499. There are no long-term liabilities in this instance. Note that the figures shown as the final balances of the partners' capital accounts agree with the amounts that appear on the last line of the statement of partners' equities.

---

principles and procedures summary

As soon as all the adjustments have been entered on the worksheet, the accountant completes the worksheet and prepares the financial statements. The first step is to combine the figures in the Trial Balance section with the adjust-

STYLE CLOTHING STORE
Balance Sheet
January 31, 19X3

Assets

Current Assets
Cash in Bank			$ 14,320.89
Petty Cash Fund			25.00
Change Fund			100.00
Notes Receivable			800.00
Accounts Receivable		$28,067.35	
Less Allowance for Bad Debts		676.21	27,391.14
Interest Receivable			9.00
Merchandise Inventory			66,000.00
Prepaid Expenses			
Prepaid Insurance		$ 300.00	
Prepaid Interest Expense		60.00	
Prepaid Taxes		500.00	
Store Supplies on Hand		110.00	970.00
Total Current Assets			$109,616.03

Fixed Assets
Furniture and Fixtures	$4,600.00		
Less Accumulated Depreciation	820.00	$ 3,780.00	
Office Equipment	$2,750.00		
Less Accumulated Depreciation	430.00	2,320.00	
Total Fixed Assets			6,100.00

Total Assets $115,716.03

Liabilities and Owners' Equity

Current Liabilities
Notes Payable—Trade		$ 2,000.00
Notes Payable—Bank		12,000.00
Accounts Payable		5,109.65
Interest Payable		26.67
Employee Deductions—		
FICA Taxes		189.80
Employee Deductions—		
Income Tax Withheld		216.00
Salaries and Wages Payable		80.00
Payroll Taxes Payable		255.00
Sales Tax Payable		808.78
Property Taxes Payable		20.00
Total Current Liabilities		$ 20,705.90

Owners' Equity
Linda Hanson, Capital	$32,170.04	
Steven Casey, Capital	31,170.04	
Janet Miller, Capital	31,670.05	
Total Owners' Equity		95,010.13

Total Liabilities and Owners' Equity $115,716.03

ing entries to make an adjusted trial balance. Each item is then carried across the worksheet to the appropriate Debit or Credit column corresponding to the financial statement on which it is to appear.

When all items in the Adjusted Trial Balance columns have been extended to the appropriate financial statement sections, the Income Statement columns are totaled and the net income or net loss is determined. The amount of net income or net loss is then entered in the Balance Sheet section. At this point the total debits must equal the total credits in the Balance Sheet columns.

Next, financial statements are prepared from the information on the worksheet. An income statement, a statement of partners' equities, and a balance sheet were prepared for the Style Clothing Store.

MANAGERIAL implications

Managers are keenly interested in receiving timely financial statements, especially periodic income statements showing the results of operations. The worksheet is a very useful device for gathering adjustment data and for preparing the income statement. Managers are also interested in prompt preparation of the balance sheet, since it shows the financial condition of the business. Current statements and supporting schedules provide up-to-date information that managers need to run the business.

Management must carefully study the figures on the financial statements in order to evaluate operations and make decisions. A common technique is to compare the data shown on the current statements with the data from previous statements. This procedure puts the current amounts in perspective and helps management to see trends that have developed.

MANAGERIAL discussion questions

1. What specific information shown on the balance sheet gives managers a better chance of running a successful business?
2. Why is it important to compare the financial statements of the current year with those of prior years?
3. How does the worksheet help the accountant to prepare financial statements more efficiently?
4. How does the classification of expenses on the income statement help managers evaluate the performance of a company and its employees?
5. What specific information shown on the income statement gives managers a better chance of running a successful business?

application of principles

PROBLEM 27-1 This problem is a continuation of Problem 26-2.

INSTRUCTIONS
1. Prepare the Adjusted Trial Balance section of the worksheet for the Metro Office Supply Store that you began in Problem 26-2. Total the columns to prove the equality of the debits and credits.
2. Record the ending merchandise inventory of $24,850, and complete the worksheet. (Save the worksheet for use in Problem 28-3.)
3. Prepare the income statement for the year 19X2, including the Distribution of Net Income section at the bottom. Ann Riley receives 60 percent of net income or net loss. Mary Gallo receives 40 percent.
4. Prepare a statement of partners' equities for the year. There were no additional investments during the year.
5. Prepare a classified balance sheet in report form as of December 31, 19X2.

PROBLEM 27-2 The trial balance of the Suede Shop on December 31, 19X1, is given on page 502. Information about adjustments that must be made is shown below.

INSTRUCTIONS
1. Record the accounts and their balances in the Trial Balance section of a ten-column worksheet. Total the columns.
2. Record the specified adjustments in the Adjustments section of the worksheet, and identify each by letter. On a separate sheet, show the computations for each adjustment. Total the columns of the Adjustments section.
3. Prepare the Adjusted Trial Balance section of the worksheet. Total the columns to prove the equality of the debits and credits.
4. Record the ending merchandise inventory of $20,750, and complete the worksheet.
5. Prepare the income statement for the year 19X1, including the Distribution of Net Income section at the bottom. Net income and net losses are shared equally by Mark Urus and Ralph Mota.
6. Prepare a statement of partners' equities for the year. There were no additional investments during the year.
7. Prepare a balance sheet as of December 31, 19X1.

ADJUSTMENTS

a. Bad debts are estimated at 0.2 percent of sales. (Debit General Operating Expenses 539.)
b. Prepaid insurance is $85.
c. Depreciation is 8 percent of the cost of the office equipment.
d. Rent expense of $100 for December has not yet been paid or recorded. (Credit Accounts Payable 202.)
e. Payroll taxes on $600 of December salaries have not been recorded. The payroll tax rates are FICA tax, 6.5 percent; state unemployment tax, 2.7 percent; and federal unemployment tax, 0.7 percent.

SUEDE SHOP
Trial Balance
December 31, 19X1

Acct. No.	Account Name	Debit	Credit
101	Cash in Bank	$ 12,199.24	
111	Accounts Receivable	15,675.00	
111A	Allowance for Bad Debts		$ 23.00
121	Merchandise Inventory	20,000.00	
131	Prepaid Insurance		
141	Office Equipment	825.00	
141A	Accum. Depr.—Office Equip.		220.00
202	Accounts Payable		275.00
226	Payroll Taxes Payable		
301	Mark Urus, Capital		12,500.00
302	Mark Urus, Drawing	3,000.00	
311	Ralph Mota, Capital		15,500.00
312	Ralph Mota, Drawing	3,600.00	
401	Sales		185,225.00
501	Merchandise Purchases	102,500.00	
521	Rent Expense	1,100.00	
531	Salaries and Wages Expense	6,750.00	
533	Payroll Tax Expense	618.75	
535	Insurance Expense	425.00	
537	Depr. Expense—Office Equip.		
539	General Operating Expenses	47,050.01	
	Totals	$213,743.00	$213,743.00

AlTeRNaTe pRobLems

PROBLEM 27-1A   This problem is a continuation of Problem 26-2A.

INSTRUCTIONS

1. Prepare the Adjusted Trial Balance section of the worksheet for the Metro Office Supply Store that you began in Problem 26-2A. Total the columns to prove the equality of the debits and credits.
2. Record the ending merchandise inventory of $25,400, and complete the worksheet. (Save your worksheet for use in Problem 28-3A.)
3. Prepare the income statement for the year 19X2, including the Distribution of Net Income section at the bottom. Ann Riley and Mary Gallo share net income and net losses equally.
4. Prepare a statement of partners' equities for the year. There were no additional investments during the year.
5. Prepare a classified balance sheet in report form as of December 31, 19X2.

PROBLEM 27-2A In this problem, use the trial balance given for the Suede Shop in Problem 27-2 on page 502. Data about the firm's adjustments is given below.

INSTRUCTIONS
1. Record the accounts and their balances in the Trial Balance section of a ten-column worksheet. Total the columns.
2. Record the specified adjustments in the Adjustments section, and identify each by letter. On a separate sheet, show the computations for each adjustment. Total the columns of the Adjustments section.
3. Prepare the Adjusted Trial Balance section of the worksheet. Total the columns to prove the equality of the debits and credits.
4. Record the ending merchandise inventory of $21,000, and complete the worksheet.
5. Prepare the income statement for the year 19X1, including the Distribution of Net Income section at the bottom. Net income and net losses are shared as follows: 40 percent to Mark Urus and 60 percent to Ralph Mota.
6. Prepare a statement of partners' equities for the year. There were no additional investments during the year.
7. Prepare a balance sheet as of December 31, 19X1.

ADJUSTMENTS

a. Bad debts are estimated at 0.3 percent of sales. (Debit General Operating Expenses 539.)
b. Prepaid insurance is $65.
c. Depreciation is 10 percent of the cost of the office equipment.
d. Rent expense of $100 for December has not yet been paid or recorded. (Credit Accounts Payable 202.)
e. Payroll taxes on $500 of December salaries have not been recorded. The assumed payroll tax rates are FICA tax, 6.5 percent; state unemployment tax, 2.7 percent; and federal unemployment tax, 0.7 percent.

UNIT 28

adjusting and closing procedures

After completing the worksheet and the financial statements, the accountant journalizes and posts the adjusting entries and then closes the books for the period.

Journalizing the Adjusting Entries

As the worksheet was prepared, the accounts to be adjusted and the amounts involved were determined. This information must now be entered in the general journal and posted to the general ledger accounts to complete the written record of events. An entry is required for each worksheet adjustment.

For example, the adjustment for bad debts (Adjustment a), now appearing on the worksheet as a debit to Bad Debts Expense and a credit to Allowance for Bad Debts, is formally recorded in the general journal as shown below.

19 X3	(Adjustment a)			
Jan. 31	Bad Debts Expense	561	669 15	
	Allowance for Bad Debts	111A		669 15
	Estimated bad debt loss for year, based on 0.3% of credit sales of $223,050.			

When the accountant records the adjusting entries in the general journal, it is important that she give complete explanations. The computations made in arriving at the amounts to be debited and credited should be set forth in enough detail so that another person, such as the auditor, can easily understand what was done and why.

The next two adjustments (Adjustments b and c on the worksheet) are both for depreciation, but the accountant made separate computations for furniture and fixtures and for office equipment. In each case, the explanation for the adjusting entry in the journal refers the reader to the schedule on which the computations are based.

Each of the remaining worksheet adjustments is journalized in typical fashion as illustrated on page 505. The identifying letter used on the worksheet is shown above each journal entry. (The ending inventory is recorded in the closing entries, as explained in Unit 18.)

19 X3		(Adjustment b)					
Jan. 31		Depr. Expense—Furniture and Fixtures	562	460	00		
		Accum. Depr.—Furn. and Fixtures	131A			460	00
		Depreciation for year as shown in detail on schedule in file.					
		(Adjustment c)					
31		Depr. Expense—Office Equipment	563	215	00		
		Accum. Depr.— Office Equipment	132A			215	00
		Depreciation for year as shown in detail on schedule in file.					
		(Adjustment d)					
31		Taxes and Licenses—Property Tax	555.8	20	00		
		Property Taxes Payable	235			20	00
		Estimated property tax for January.					
		(Adjustment e)					
31		Custodial Wages Expense	541	80	00		
		Salaries and Wages Payable	225			80	00
		Custodial wages accrued for four days, January 28–31.					
		(Adjustment f)					
31		Payroll Tax Expense	552	255	00		
		Payroll Taxes Payable	226			255	00
		Accrued payroll taxes on January payroll:					
		FICA 6.5% of $3,000 = $195.00					
		SUTA 1.3% of 3,000 = 39.00					
		FUTA 0.7% of 3,000 = 21.00					
		Total $255.00					
		(Adjustment g)					
31		Interest Expense	591	26	67		
		Interest Payable	216			26	67
		Accrued interest on trade note payable dated Dec. 2:					
		$\$2,000 \times \dfrac{8}{100} \times \dfrac{60}{360} = \$26.67$					
		(Adjustment h)					
31		Store Supplies on Hand	129	110	00		
		Store Supplies and Expense	523			110	00
		Ending inventory of store supplies on hand.					
		(Adjustment i)					
31		Prepaid Insurance	126	300	00		
		Insurance Expense	536			300	00
		Unexpired insurance as of January 31.					
		(Adjustment j)					
31		Prepaid Interest Expense	127	60	00		
		Interest Expense	591			60	00
		Interest prepaid on note payable to bank:					
		$\$12,000 \times \dfrac{9}{100} \times \dfrac{20}{360} = \$60$					

			19 X3 Jan. 31	(Adjustment k) Taxes and Licenses—Stock Tax Prepaid Taxes Transferred to expense the amount of prepaid stock tax expired in January.	555.7 128	100 00	100 00
			31	(Adjustment l) Interest Receivable Interest Earned Accrued interest earned on Gail Smith's note dated Dec. 17 for 45 days to Jan. 31: $$\$800 \times \frac{9}{100} \times \frac{45}{360} = \$9$$	116 491	9 00	9 00
			31	(Adjustment m) Sales Tax Payable Miscellaneous Income Commission earned on sales tax for January, computed as follows:	231 493	16 50	16 50

Sales $27,550.90
Returns & Allowances   41.25
Net Sales $27,509.65

Balance of Account 231 = $825.28
Gross tax,
3% × $27,509.65 = $825.29
Commission, 2%   16.51
Net tax due $808.78
Balance of Account 231 $ 16.50

Posting the Adjusting Entries

Next, the adjusting entries must be posted from the general journal to the general ledger accounts. The procedures to be followed are exactly like those described in Unit 18. However, when adjustments are posted to expense analysis accounts, the amounts are recorded in *both* the related individual subdigit expense column and the usual debit or credit column. For example, the postings to the Taxes and Licenses account to record the adjustments for stock tax and property tax are entered on the expense analysis sheet as illustrated below.

Taxes and Licenses   No. 555

RETAIL LICENSE DR. 555.6	STOCK TAX DR. 555.7	PROP. TAX DR. 555.8	DATE	EXPLANATION	POST. REF.	DEBIT	CREDIT	BALANCE	DR. CR.
5 00	1,000 00	201 00 20 00	19 X3 Jan. 1 31	Brought Forward Adjusting	✓ J1	1,206 00 20 00		1,206 00 1,226 00	Dr. Dr.
		100 00	31	Adjusting	J1	100 00		1,326 00	Dr.

When the adjustments have been posted, the ledger account balances should be the same as the amounts shown in the Adjusted Trial Balance section of the worksheet (pages 496 and 497). In the case of Taxes and Licenses, the account balance is $1,326.

Journalizing the Closing Entries

The worksheet is also the source of information for the general journal entries required to close the revenue and expense accounts. Each account balance appearing in the Income Statement columns of the worksheet is closed to the Revenue and Expense Summary account.

The four-step closing procedure is explained in Unit 18. The steps are as follows.

1. Record the ending inventory by debiting Merchandise Inventory for the proper amount. Debit the revenue accounts and other credit items to close their balances. Credit the Revenue and Expense Summary account for the total.
2. Debit the Revenue and Expense Summary account for the total of the beginning inventory, the expense account balances, and other debit items, crediting each account individually.
3. Transfer the resulting balance (the net income or net loss) in the Revenue and Expense Summary account to the owners' capital accounts.
4. Transfer the balance of each owner's drawing account to his or her capital account as the final step in the closing process.

The information for completing Steps 1, 2, and 4 comes directly from the worksheet. The division of net income or net loss is shown at the bottom of the income statement. The closing process is traced step by step in the following sections.

Step 1: Recording Inventory and Closing the Revenue Accounts

Refer to the Credit column in the Income Statement section of the completed worksheet on pages 496 and 497. Six items appear in this column. Each account is debited for the amount shown. This provides a record of the ending inventory of $66,000 and closes each of the other accounts. Revenue and Expense Summary is credited for the total amount transferred, $431,779.30, as shown below.

19 X3					
Jan. 31	Merchandise Inventory	121	66,000 00	
	Sales	401	359,195 90	
	Interest Earned	491	235 00	
	Miscellaneous Income	493	235 10	
	Purchases Returns and Allowances	511	1,065 00	
	Purchases Discount	512	5,048 30	
	Revenue and Expense Summary	399		431,779 30
	Closed the revenue accounts and other credit items and set up the ending merchandise inventory.			

507

Step 2: Closing the Expense Accounts

Next, refer to the Debit column in the Income Statement section of the worksheet on pages 496 and 497. Revenue and Expense Summary is debited for the column subtotal, $398,869.17. Each listed account is credited for the amount shown in the Debit column. This charges the beginning inventory to the current period's cost of operations and closes all the expense accounts and other debit items. The necessary journal entry is illustrated below.

19 X3				
Jan. 31	Revenue and Expense Summary	399	398,869 17	
	Merchandise Inventory	121		65,000 00
	Sales Returns and Allowances	452		6,041 25
	Merchandise Purchases	501		255,350 00
	Freight In	506		3,590 00
	Sales Salaries Expense	521		21,400 00
	Advertising Expense	522		6,893 30
	Store Supplies and Expense	523		4,253 75
	Cash Short or Over	529		72 00
	Delivery Expense	532		3,860 00
	Insurance Expense	536		3,090 00
	Custodial Wages Expense	541		5,120 00
	Rent Expense	542		6,000 00
	Utilities Expense	543		1,981 35
	Office Salaries Expense	551		8,400 00
	Payroll Tax Expense	552		2,839 20
	Office Supplies and Expense	553		804 50
	Professional Services Expense	554		775 00
	Taxes and Licenses	555		1,326 00
	Bad Debts Expense	561		669 15
	Depr. Expense—Furniture and Fixtures	562		460 00
	Depr. Expense—Office Equipment	563		215 00
	Interest Expense	591		728 67
	Closed the beginning merchandise inventory, the expense accounts, and other debit items to Revenue and Expense Summary.			

Step 3: Closing the Revenue and Expense Summary Account

The next step is to close the Revenue and Expense Summary account and divide the net income according to the profit-sharing agreement of the partners (equal shares in this case). The information for this entry is shown at the bottom of the income statement. Since the business has a net income of $32,910.13, the Revenue and Expense Summary account is debited for this amount and the partners' capital accounts are credited to distribute the net income in the agreed manner. The following journal entry is required.

19 X3				
Jan. 31	Revenue and Expense Summary	399	32,910 13	
	Linda Hanson, Capital	301		10,970 04
	Steven Casey, Capital	311		10,970 04
	Janet Miller, Capital	321		10,970 05
	Divided net income for the year equally among the partners.			

Step 4: Closing the Drawing Account

The final step in the closing process is to transfer the balance in each partner's drawing account to the partner's capital account. This can be accomplished in separate entries for each partner or in a single compound entry, as shown below.

19 X3					
Jan. 31	Linda Hanson, Capital	301	7,800 00		
	Steven Casey, Capital	311	7,800 00		
	Janet Miller, Capital	321	7,800 00		
	Linda Hanson, Drawing	302		7,800 00	
	Steven Casey, Drawing	312		7,800 00	
	Janet Miller, Drawing	322		7,800 00	
	Closed partners' drawing accounts.				

Posting the Closing Entries

When the closing entries have been journalized, they are posted to the general ledger accounts in the usual manner. However, the expense analysis accounts require a special posting procedure. In addition to recording entries in the regular money columns, the accountant must make entries in the individual item columns as circled figures. This posting technique is illustrated in the expense analysis ledger sheet for the Taxes and Licenses account below.

Taxes and Licenses — No. 555

RETAIL LICENSE DR. 555.6	STOCK TAX DR. 555.7	PROP. TAX DR. 555.8	DATE	EXPLANATION	POST. REF.	DEBIT	CREDIT	BALANCE	DR. CR.
			19 X3						
5 00	1,000 00	201 00	Jan. 1	Brought Forward	✓	1,206 00		1,206 00	Dr.
		20 00	31	Adjusting	J1	20 00		1,226 00	Dr.
	100 00		31	Adjusting	J1	100 00		1,326 00	Dr.
(5 00)	(1,100 00)	(221 00)	31	Closing	J1		1,326 00	–0–	

Taking a Postclosing Trial Balance

When the adjusting and closing entries have all been posted, a postclosing trial balance is taken of the general ledger to prove that the ledger accounts are in balance at the end of the period. This trial balance should contain the same asset and liability account balances as are shown in the Balance Sheet section of the worksheet. The owners' capital account balances should be the same as those shown on the balance sheet at the end of the period. The postclosing trial balance of the Style Clothing Store as of January 31, 19X3, is illustrated on page 510.

Ruling the Accounts

When the equality of the debits and credits has been demonstrated by the postclosing trial balance, the accounts may be ruled to indicate the point at which the fiscal year has ended. In order to use the balance ledger forms for a

STYLE CLOTHING STORE
Postclosing Trial Balance
January 31, 19X3

ACCT. NO.	ACCOUNT NAME	DEBIT	CREDIT
101	Cash in Bank	14,320.89	
105	Petty Cash Fund	25.00	
106	Change Fund	100.00	
109	Notes Receivable	800.00	
111	Accounts Receivable	28,067.35	
111A	Allowance for Bad Debts		676.21
116	Interest Receivable	9.00	
121	Merchandise Inventory	66,000.00	
126	Prepaid Insurance	300.00	
127	Prepaid Interest Expense	60.00	
128	Prepaid Taxes	500.00	
129	Store Supplies on Hand	110.00	
131	Furniture and Fixtures	4,600.00	
131A	Accum. Depr.—Furniture and Fixtures		820.00
132	Office Equipment	2,750.00	
132A	Accum. Depr.—Office Equipment		430.00
201	Notes Payable—Trade		2,000.00
203	Notes Payable—Bank		12,000.00
205	Accounts Payable		5,109.65
216	Interest Payable		26.67
221	Employee Deductions—FICA Taxes		189.80
222	Employee Deductions—Income Tax Withheld		216.00
225	Salaries and Wages Payable		80.00
226	Payroll Taxes Payable		255.00
231	Sales Tax Payable		808.78
235	Property Taxes Payable		20.00
301	Linda Hanson, Capital		32,170.04
311	Steven Casey, Capital		31,170.04
321	Janet Miller, Capital		31,670.05
	Totals	117,642.24	117,642.24

succeeding year, the revenue and expense accounts should be ruled with double lines across all columns except the Explanation column. If accounts with analysis columns are used, these columns should also be ruled. This ruling procedure is illustrated with the Taxes and Licenses account shown below.

Taxes and Licenses — No. 555

RETAIL LICENSE DR. 555.6	STOCK TAX DR. 555.7	PROP. TAX DR. 555.8	DATE		EXPLANATION	POST. REF.	DEBIT	CREDIT	BALANCE	DR. CR.
			19X3							
5.00	1,000.00	201.00	Jan.	1	Brought Forward	✓	1,206.00		1,206.00	Dr.
		20.00		31	Adjusting	J1	20.00		1,226.00	Dr.
	100.00			31	Adjusting	J1	100.00		1,326.00	Dr.
5.00	1,100.00	221.00		31	Closing	J1		1,326.00	—0—	

Many accountants prefer to set up new ledger account sheets for the revenue and expense items each year. The prior year's ledger sheets are kept in a permanent file. When new ledger account sheets are used each year, the revenue and expense accounts need not be ruled.

No end-of-period ruling is necessary for the balance sheet accounts if balance ledger forms are used. The balances in the accounts at the end of one period simply become the beginning balances for the next period. However, some accountants prefer to rule the accounts even if balance ledger forms are used.

If the balance sheet accounts are to be ruled, the following procedure should be used. (Refer to the Cash in Bank account shown below for an illustration of the necessary steps.) Enter the date and "Carried Forward" on the line following the last entry. On the same line, enter the ending balance in the opposite money column. (Enter a debit balance in the Credit column and a credit balance in the Debit column.) Draw a single line under this figure across the Debit and Credit columns, and total the columns to prove equality. Draw double lines across the Date column, the Posting Reference column, and all three amount columns under the totals. Enter the starting date of the new period and "Brought Forward" on the next line. Enter the balance amount in the appropriate Debit or Credit column and in the Balance column. Put a check mark in the Posting Reference column on both the Carried Forward and Brought Forward lines to show that the amount is not a posted item. This ruling procedure is obviously rather cumbersome and is not normally used.

Cash in Bank   No. 101

DATE		EXPLANATION	POST. REF.	DEBIT	CREDIT	BALANCE	DR. CR.
19 X3 Jan.	1	Brought Forward	✓	13,992 29		13,992 29	Dr.
	31		CR2	34,218 12		48,210 41	Dr.
	31		CP2		33,889 52	14,320 89	Dr.
	31	Carried Forward	✓		14,320 89	-0-	
				48,210 41	48,210 41		
19 X3 Feb.	1	Brought Forward	✓	14,320 89		14,320 89	Dr.

When the accounts have been ruled, the accounting cycle for the current period is essentially completed. However, an experienced accountant knows that certain adjustments made at the end of the current period may lead to recording difficulties in the new period. Adjusting Entry l (page 506) provides a good illustration of a potentially time-consuming problem.

The Need for Reversals

On the worksheet and later in the general journal, Interest Receivable was debited for $9 and Interest Earned was credited for the same amount. This adjustment was made to record 45 days' interest earned but not yet collected on Gail Smith's 60-day, 9 percent note receivable for $800 due February 15.

When this note is collected at maturity, a total of $812 ($800 principal plus $12 interest) will be received. A busy accounting clerk might accidentally overlook the fact that $9 of the interest was accrued as revenue of the prior period by an adjusting entry. Even if the accounting clerk recognizes the item as related to Adjusting Entry l, he or she may not know how to divide the $12 between the two periods without tracing the transaction back to the previous year's records. After determining the proper split, the accounting clerk would have to make a compound entry so that the debit to Cash for $812 is offset by three credits—$800 to Notes Receivable, $9 to Interest Receivable, and $3 to Interest Earned.

Fortunately, there is a much simpler technique for handling this type of situation. Potential complications never occur because a *readjusting entry*, usually called a *reversing entry*, is made before the transactions of the new period are recorded.

An entry made on February 1 that debits Interest Earned for $9 and credits Interest Receivable for $9 guards against any later oversight, eliminates the need for checking old records, and makes it unnecessary to divide the amount of interest when the note and interest are collected. This entry is shown below.

19 X3	(Reversing Entry)			
Feb. 1	Interest Earned	491	9 00	
	Interest Receivable	116		9 00
	Reversed Adjusting Entry I made January 31.			

After the reversing entry has been posted, the asset Interest Receivable is closed out. The debit of $9 in the Interest Earned account will be waiting to offset the credit of $12 to be posted on February 15, when the note and interest are collected. At that time the accounting clerk will simply record the entire $12 amount as a credit to Interest Earned. Then the debit of $9 already in the account will provide the necessary partial counterbalance. The net difference of $3 represents the amount of interest actually earned during February. The two accounts shown below and on page 513 illustrate the reversing entry made on February 1 and the collection of interest on February 15.

Interest Receivable No. 116

DATE	EXPLANATION	POST. REF.	DEBIT	CREDIT	BALANCE	DR. CR.
19 X3						
Jan. 31	Adjusting	J1	9 00		9 00	Dr.
Feb. 1	Reversing	J2		9 00	–0–	

		Interest Earned				No. 491	
DATE		EXPLANATION	POST. REF.	DEBIT	CREDIT	BALANCE	DR. CR.
19 X3 Feb.	1	Reversing	J2	9 00		9 00	Dr.
	15	Collection of note	CR1		12 00	3 00	Cr.

Notice that the entry of February 1 is simply a reversal of the related adjusting entry.

Items Requiring Reversals

Items to be reversed can be determined by the following two simple rules.

1. *Only adjusting entries can possibly be involved.* Thus, only the adjusting entries made at the end of the last period need be considered. (Ending inventory is immediately excluded as a possibility because it is recorded as part of a closing entry.)
2. Not all adjusting entries require reversal. Normally, *only those adjusting entries that put balances in new asset accounts or new liability accounts need be reversed.* ("New" in this situation refers to an asset or liability account that does not contain a balance when the trial balance is taken and does not normally have a balance during the year.)

Locating Reversals

Refer to the completed worksheet (pages 496 and 497) or, better still, to the adjusting journal entries for the period just ended (pages 505 and 506).

Entry a

Adjusting Entry a involved a debit to Bad Debts Expense and a credit to Allowance for Bad Debts. Neither of these items is a new asset or a new liability. Hence, under Rule 2, the entry requires no readjustment.

Entries b and c

Adjusting Entries b and c called for debits to depreciation expense accounts and credits to accumulated depreciation accounts. No new assets or liabilities are involved; hence, no readjustment is necessary.

Entry d

Adjusting Entry d debited Taxes and Licenses and credited Property Taxes Payable. Property Taxes Payable is a liability. Since this account had no balance on the trial balance, a readjustment seems necessary. However, a check of the ledger account shows that no reversal should be made because of an unusual timing element. Property Taxes Payable is actually an old and continuing liability. For 11 months of the year, this account has an end-of-month balance on the trial balance as the amount of tax payable builds up. However, when the annual tax is paid in December the account has a zero balance for a brief interval. An experienced accountant recognizes the exceptional condition of this account in January and therefore does not make a reversing entry.

Entry e

Adjusting Entry e debited Custodial Wages Expense and credited Salaries and Wages Payable for $80 to recognize the unpaid wages for Monday through

Thursday. If no reversing entry is made, when the custodian's paycheck is issued on Friday, it will be necessary to analyze and prorate the $100 payment between the liability account as of January 31 ($80) and the expense account for February ($20). The accountant therefore records a reversing entry to eliminate this problem. The necessary entry is shown below.

19 X3				
Feb. 1	(Reversing Entry)			
	Salaries and Wages Payable	225	80 00	
	Custodial Wages Expense	541		80 00
	Reversed Adjusting Entry e made January 31.			

The debit posting of $80 to the Salaries and Wages Payable account cancels the liability. The $80 credit recorded in the Custodial Wages Expense account offsets the $100 debit that is posted when the full week's wages are paid on February 1. The effect in the expense account is a net charge of $20 ($100 − $80) to the operations of the new period. This amount correctly represents the day's wages earned by the custodian in February. The posting to the two accounts is shown below.

Salaries and Wages Payable   No. 225

DATE	EXPLANATION	POST. REF.	DEBIT	CREDIT	BALANCE	DR. CR.
19 X3						
Jan. 31	Adjusting	J1		80 00	80 00	Cr.
Feb. 1	Reversing	J2	80 00		−0−	

Custodial Wages Expense   No. 541

DATE	EXPLANATION	POST. REF.	DEBIT	CREDIT	BALANCE	DR. CR.
19 X3						
Jan. 18		VR1	100 00		4,940 00	Dr.
25		VR1	100 00		5,040 00	Dr.
31	Adjusting	J1	80 00		5,120 00	Dr.
31	Closing	J1		5,120 00	−0−	
19 X3						
Feb. 1	Reversing	J		80 00	80 00	Cr.
1		VR2	100 00		20 00	Dr.

Entry f   Adjusting Entry f debited Payroll Tax Expense and credited Payroll Taxes Payable. The latter account is a new liability, so no amount is shown on the trial balance or in the ledger account during the year. The adjustment is therefore reversed as shown on the next page.

19 X3		(Reversing Entry)			
Feb. 1		Payroll Taxes Payable	226	255 00	
		Payroll Tax Expense	552		255 00
		Reversed Adjusting Entry f made January 31.			

Entry g   Interest owed on a trade note payable for 60 days was recorded in Adjusting Entry g by a debit to Interest Expense and a credit to Interest Payable. The Interest Payable account represents a new liability. Thus, the entry is reversed as shown below.

19 X3		(Reversing Entry)			
Feb. 1		Interest Payable	216	26 67	
		Interest Expense	591		26 67
		Reversed Adjusting Entry g made January 31.			

Entry h   Adjusting Entry h debited the Store Supplies on Hand account and credited the Store Supplies and Expense account. The asset account is new. For this reason, the adjusting entry used to set up its balance is reversed.

19 X3		(Reversing Entry)			
Feb. 1		Store Supplies and Expense	523	110 00	
		Store Supplies on Hand	129		110 00
		Reversed Adjusting Entry h made January 31.			

Entry i   Adjusting Entry i recognized unexpired insurance by a debit to a new asset account, Prepaid Insurance, and an offsetting credit to the Insurance Expense account. The adjusting entry is reversed as shown below.

19 X3		(Reversing Entry)			
Feb. 1		Insurance Expense	536	300 00	
		Prepaid Insurance	126		300 00
		Reversed Adjusting Entry i made January 31.			

Entry j   Adjusting Entry j recorded prepaid interest on a note payable to the bank. A new asset account called Prepaid Interest Expense was debited, and Interest Expense was credited. Here again, because a new asset account is involved, the adjusting entry is reversed as shown on page 516.

19 X3		(Reversing Entry)			
Feb. 1	Interest Expense		591	60 00	
	Prepaid Interest Expense		127		60 00
	Reversed Adjusting Entry j made				
	January 31.				

Entry k Adjusting Entry k involved a debit to Taxes and Licenses and a credit to Prepaid Taxes for the January share of the prepaid stock tax. No new asset account or new liability account is involved here, and therefore no readjustment is made.

Entry l Adjusting Entry l, debiting Interest Receivable and crediting Interest Earned, was used as the opening example of the readjustment process. The entry clearly qualifies for reversing because it is an adjusting entry and it involves a new asset—Interest Receivable. This reversal was illustrated on pages 512–513.

Entry m Adjusting Entry m consisted of a debit to Sales Tax Payable and a credit to Miscellaneous Income. Sales Tax Payable is a liability account, but it is one that already had a balance (see the trial balance on page 488). The adjusting entry simply reduces the account balance. Since no new liability is set up, no reversing entry is required.

Posting the Reversing Entries

The reversing entries are posted as soon as they have been journalized in order to clear the way for recording the transactions of the new period. The postings are carried out like those for accrued interest on notes receivable and accrued custodial wages, which were illustrated earlier.

After the reversing entries have been posted, the general ledger accounts reflect the following two types of changes.

1. The new asset and liability accounts that were opened by adjusting entries are now closed. The account balances are returned to zero.
2. The revenue and expense accounts involved in the reversing process now contain offset figures recorded in advance so that certain later transactions will not have to be analyzed and divided.

Posting Reversing Entries to Standard Ledger Accounts

The illustration given on page 514 for posting reversing entries involved the balance ledger sheets. If a firm uses the standard ledger form for its general ledger accounts, the reversing entries are entered after the accounts have been balanced and ruled. This is shown on the next page in the Salaries and Wages Payable account and the Custodial Wages Expense account, where the adjustment for accrued custodial wages made on January 31 is reversed. (Salaries and Wages Payable did not require balancing and ruling, because it had only one entry at the end of the accounting period.)

Salaries and Wages Payable — No. 225

DATE	EXPLANATION	POST. REF.	DEBIT	DATE	EXPLANATION	POST. REF.	CREDIT
19 X3 Feb. 1	Reversing	J2	80 00	19 X3 Jan. 31	Adjusting	J1	80 00

Custodial Wages Expense — No. 541

DATE	EXPLANATION	POST. REF.	DEBIT	DATE	EXPLANATION	POST. REF.	CREDIT
19 X3 Jan. 18	Brought Forward	✓	4,840 00	19 X3 Jan. 31	Closing	J1	5,120 00
18		VR1	100 00				
25		VR1	100 00				
			5,040 00				
31	Adjusting	J1	80 00				
			5,120 00				
			5,120 00				5,120 00
Feb. 1		VR2	100 00	Feb. 1	Reversing	J2	80 00
			20.00				

principles and procedures summary

When the year-end worksheet and financial statements have been completed, adjusting and closing entries are made in the general journal and posted to the general ledger. These entries come from the appropriate columns of the worksheet.

After the adjusting entries are journalized and posted, the accountant prepares the closing entries from the Income Statement section of the worksheet. When the closing entries have been posted, the accuracy of the work is verified by taking a postclosing trial balance of the general ledger.

Ledger accounts may be ruled at the end of the year and used in succeeding years. However, some accountants prefer to start the new year's revenue and expense accounts on new sheets and to file the old ledger sheets for future reference.

At the beginning of each new accounting period, certain adjusting entries of the preceding period must be reversed. This is done in order to avoid the necessity of analyzing future entries involving carry-over items.

Only adjusting entries need be considered in the reversing process. Furthermore, only those adjusting entries that set up new asset accounts or new liability accounts should be reversed. The accountant refers to the Adjustments section of the worksheet or to the adjusting entries in the general journal, checking these entries one at a time to locate the items that require reversals.

MANAGERIAL implications

Correct adjusting and closing entries are necessary if all revenue and expense items are to be recorded and matched in the proper period. Managers must be concerned with the adjusting and closing procedures to ensure that the financial records are adequate and correct. Explanations must be sufficiently informative so that future reference to them will be easy. For example, audits of the financial records are greatly speeded up by good adjusting and closing procedures. Also, the sooner the books are closed for the old period, the sooner the recording of transactions for the new period can begin. Any significant lag between the time a transaction occurs and the time it is recorded may lead to serious consequences.

The reversing process has two managerial implications. The first is that it saves time and promotes efficiency by eliminating the need for analyzing future revenue and expense transactions to see what portion applies to past periods and what portion applies to the period in which the transaction occurs. The second managerial implication is that the reversing process helps make sure that revenues and expenses are properly matched in the period to which they apply, thereby improving the accuracy and meaningfulness of the financial statements.

MANAGERIAL discussion questions

1. Why must managers be concerned about a significant time lag between the completion of a transaction and the recording of it?
2. Why should managers insist that the firm's accountant include a complete explanation with each adjusting entry?
3. How do reversing entries minimize confusion and save recording time and effort in a new accounting period?
4. On January 6, 19X2, a firm paid salaries and wages of $8,200. After the amount was posted to the Salaries and Wages Expense account on that date, the account balance was only $5,300. One of the managers asks you, the accountant, whether you have made a mistake. Explain what has happened.
5. Under what circumstances would an accountant reverse an adjusting entry to the Store Supplies Expense account and the Store Supplies Inventory account?

application of principles

PROBLEM 28-1 Adjustment data for the Vortex Company as of December 31, 19X1, is given below.

INSTRUCTIONS
1. Make the adjusting entry required on December 31, 19X1, for each of the items.
2. In general journal form, make the reversing entries that are necessary on January 1, 19X2.

ADJUSTMENTS

a. Unpaid wages on December 31 total $2,850. These wages have not been recorded.
b. The balance of the Prepaid Insurance account is $2,000. This represents the unexpired insurance premium as of January 1, 19X1, on a two-year insurance policy purchased for $2,400 on August 31, 19X0.
c. Interest accrued on notes payable totals $186.
d. The Supplies Expense account has a balance of $3,180. However, a physical count shows that supplies costing $281.50 are on hand on December 31.
e. Depreciation on equipment totals $2,760 for the year.
f. The balance of the Rent Expense account is $6,000. This includes $500 paid in advance for the month of January 19X2.
g. Employer's FICA taxes of 6.5 percent on $700 of accrued wages must be recorded. None of the unpaid wages is subject to unemployment taxes.

PROBLEM 28-2 The completed worksheet of the Northern Retail Company for the year ended December 31, 19X1, is shown on page 520.

INSTRUCTIONS
1. Journalize the adjusting entries for December 31. Omit explanations.
2. Journalize the closing entries on December 31. (Use Revenue and Expense Summary 399.) Omit explanations.
3. Journalize the reversing entries on January 1, 19X2. Omit explanations.

PROBLEM 28-3 This problem is a continuation of Problem 27-1.

INSTRUCTIONS

Refer to the worksheet for the Metro Office Supply Store prepared in Problem 27-1, and carry out the steps given below and on page 521.

1. Open a general ledger, and enter the December 31, 19X2, balance for each account given in the trial balance. Write "Balance" in the Explanation column, and place a check mark in the Posting Reference column in

NORTHERN RETAIL COMPANY
Worksheet
Year Ended December 31, 19X1

ACCT. NO.	ACCOUNT NAME	TRIAL BALANCE DEBIT	TRIAL BALANCE CREDIT	ADJUSTMENTS DEBIT	ADJUSTMENTS CREDIT	ADJUSTED TRIAL BALANCE DEBIT	ADJUSTED TRIAL BALANCE CREDIT	INCOME STATEMENT DEBIT	INCOME STATEMENT CREDIT	BALANCE SHEET DEBIT	BALANCE SHEET CREDIT
101	Cash in Bank	4,800 00				4,800 00				4,800 00	
111	Accounts Receivable	4,200 00				4,200 00				4,200 00	
111A	Allowance for Bad Debts		20 00		(a)305 00		325 00				325 00
121	Merchandise Inventory	9,000 00				9,000 00		(g)9,000 00	(g)10,200 00	(g)10,200 00	
131	Prepaid Insurance	420 00			(b)270 00	150 00				150 00	
132	Supplies	1,280 00			(c)930 00	350 00				350 00	
141	Equipment	9,000 00				9,000 00				9,000 00	
141A	Accum. Depreciation—Equipment		1,800 00		(d)900 00		2,700 00				2,700 00
201	Accounts Payable		1,020 00				1,020 00				1,020 00
202	Salaries and Wages Payable				(e)200 00		200 00				200 00
203	Payroll Taxes Payable				(f)16 00		16 00				16 00
301	Sandra Cox, Capital		12,460 00				12,460 00				12,460 00
302	Sandra Cox, Drawing	3,400 00				3,400 00				3,400 00	
401	Sales		94,060 00				94,060 00		94,060 00		
501	Purchases	60,000 00				60,000 00		60,000 00			
531	Salaries and Wages Expense	6,500 00		(e)200 00		6,700 00		6,700 00			
532	Payroll Tax Expense	510 00		(f)16 00		526 00		526 00			
533	Bad Debts Expense			(a)305 00		305 00		305 00			
534	Supplies Used			(c)930 00		930 00		930 00			
535	Insurance Expense			(b)270 00		270 00		270 00			
537	Depreciation Expense—Equipment			(d)900 00		900 00		900 00			
538	Other Expenses	10,250 00				10,250 00		10,250 00			
	Totals	109,360 00	109,360 00	2,621 00	2,621 00	110,781 00	110,781 00	88,881 00	104,260 00	32,100 00	16,721 00
	Net Income for Year							15,379 00			15,379 00
								104,260 00	104,260 00	32,100 00	32,100 00

each case to show that the amount was not posted from a journal. Also set up an account for Revenue and Expense Summary 399.
2. Journalize the adjusting and closing entries. Omit explanations.
3. Post the adjusting and closing entries to the general ledger accounts.
4. Prepare a postclosing trial balance of the general ledger.
5. Rule the revenue and expense accounts. Do not rule the balance sheet accounts.
6. Record in general journal form the reversing entries necessary on January 1, 19X3. Omit explanations. Reverse the Rent Expense adjustment. (Since Accounts Payable was credited in order to simplify Problem 27-1, it will be necessary to debit Accounts Payable in the reversing entry.)
7. Post the reversing entries to the general ledger accounts.

alternate problems

PROBLEM 28-1A

Adjustment data for the Mathis Clothing Company as of December 31, 19X1, is given below.

INSTRUCTIONS
1. Make the adjusting entry required on December 31, 19X1, for each of the items.
2. In general journal form, make the reversing entries that are necessary on January 1, 19X2.

ADJUSTMENTS

a. Unpaid wages on December 31 total $1,200. These wages have not yet been recorded.
b. The balance of the Prepaid Insurance account is $600. This represents the unexpired insurance premium as of January 1, 19X1, on a three-year insurance policy purchased for $720 on July 1, 19X0.
c. Interest accrued on notes payable totals $110.
d. The Supplies Expense account has a balance of $1,860. However, an actual physical count shows that supplies costing $156.50 are on hand on December 31.
e. Depreciation on equipment totals $2,600 for the year.
f. The balance of the Rent Expense account is $3,900. This figure includes $300 rent paid in advance for January 19X2.
g. Employer's FICA taxes of 6.5 percent on $500 of accrued wages must be recorded. None of the unpaid wages is subject to unemployment taxes.

PROBLEM 28-2A

The completed worksheet of the Renault Retail Company for the year ended December 31, 19X1, is shown on page 522.

INSTRUCTIONS
1. Journalize the adjusting entries for December 31. Omit explanations.
2. Journalize the closing entries on December 31. (Use Revenue and Expense Summary 399.) Omit explanations.
3. Journalize the reversing entries on January 1, 19X2. Omit explanations.

RENAULT RETAIL COMPANY
Worksheet
Year Ended December 31, 19X1

ACCT. NO.	ACCOUNT NAME	TRIAL BALANCE DEBIT	TRIAL BALANCE CREDIT	ADJUSTMENTS DEBIT	ADJUSTMENTS CREDIT	ADJUSTED TRIAL BALANCE DEBIT	ADJUSTED TRIAL BALANCE CREDIT	INCOME STATEMENT DEBIT	INCOME STATEMENT CREDIT	BALANCE SHEET DEBIT	BALANCE SHEET CREDIT
101	Cash in Bank	4,800 00				4,800 00				4,800 00	
111	Accounts Receivable	6,600 00				6,600 00				6,600 00	
111A	Allowance for Bad Debts		150 00		(f)800 00		950 00				950 00
121	Merchandise Inventory	15,500 00				15,500 00		(g)15,500 00	(g)17,000 00	(g)17,000 00	
131	Prepaid Insurance	380 00			(a)130 00	250 00				250 00	
132	Supplies	1,550 00			(b)980 00	570 00				570 00	
141	Equipment	17,000 00				17,000 00				17,000 00	
141A	Accumulated Depr.—Equipment		6,900 00		(c)1,700 00		8,600 00				8,600 00
201	Accounts Payable		3,400 00				3,400 00				3,400 00
202	Salaries and Wages Payable				(d)800 00		800 00				800 00
203	Payroll Taxes Payable		190 00		(e)72 00		262 00				262 00
301	John Renault, Capital		29,000 00				29,000 00				29,000 00
302	John Renault, Drawing	9,600 00				9,600 00				9,600 00	
401	Sales		159,000 00				159,000 00		159,000 00		
501	Purchases	102,300 00				102,300 00		102,300 00			
531	Salaries and Wages Expense	22,600 00		(d)800 00		23,400 00		23,400 00			
532	Payroll Tax Expense	1,810 00		(e)72 00		1,882 00		1,882 00			
533	Bad Debts Expense			(f)800 00		800 00		800 00			
534	Supplies Used			(b)980 00		980 00		980 00			
535	Insurance Expense			(a)130 00		130 00		130 00			
537	Depreciation Expense—Equipment			(c)1,700 00		1,700 00		1,700 00			
538	Other Expenses	16,500 00				16,500 00		16,500 00			
	Totals	198,640 00	198,640 00	4,482 00	4,482 00	202,012 00	202,012 00	163,192 00	176,000 00	55,820 00	43,012 00
	Net Income for Year							12,808 00			12,808 00
								176,000 00	176,000 00	55,820 00	55,820 00

522

PROBLEM 28-3A This problem is a continuation of Problem 27-1A.

INSTRUCTIONS Refer to the worksheet for the Metro Office Supply Store prepared in Problem 27-1A, and carry out the following steps.

1. Open a general ledger, and enter the December 31, 19X1, balance for each account given in the trial balance. Write "Balance" in the Explanation column, and place a check mark in the Posting Reference column in each case to show that the amount was not posted from a journal. Also set up an account for Revenue and Expense Summary 399.
2. Journalize the adjusting and closing entries. Omit explanations.
3. Post the adjusting and closing entries to the general ledger accounts.
4. Prepare a postclosing trial balance of the general ledger.
5. Rule the revenue and expense accounts. Do not rule the balance sheet accounts.
6. Record in general journal form the reversing entries necessary on January 1, 19X2. Omit explanations. Reverse the Rent Expense adjustment. (Since Accounts Payable was credited in order to simplify Problem 27-1A, it will be necessary to debit Accounts Payable in the reversing entry.)
7. Post the reversing entries to the general ledger accounts.

business project 2

THE ACCRUAL basis of ACCOUNTING

In the past several units, you learned how to make adjustments so that the books reflect the accrual basis of accounting. You also learned how to complete a worksheet. You saw how adjusting entries and closing entries are prepared, how financial statements are drawn up, and how reversing entries are made. This project is designed to give you practical experience in carrying out the procedures that you learned in these units.

The Trial Balance

The trial balance of the Style Clothing Store on January 31, 19X4, at the end of the third year of operations, is illustrated on page 525.

Enter this trial balance in the first set of columns of a ten-column worksheet. Use headings that are identical to those on the worksheet shown on pages 496 and 497.

Entering Adjustments

Enter the adjustments on the worksheet and extend the amounts to the Adjusted Trial Balance section. You will need the following data for the adjustments. (Use the letters shown here to identify the adjustments on the worksheet.)

- Entry a—Bad debts expense is estimated at 0.3 percent of credit sales. The records show that the credit sales are $253,200.
- Entry b—Depreciation expense on the furniture and fixtures is $460.
- Entry c—Depreciation expense on the office equipment is $215.
- Entry d—Estimated property taxes for the calendar year 19X4 are $264. One-twelfth of this amount should be accrued as January 19X4 taxes.
- Entry e—Accrued custodial wages are $60.
- Entry f—Employer's payroll taxes to be accrued for January total $266.70.
- Entry g—Interest must be accrued on a trade note payable that has a face value of $2,000. This 9 percent note is dated December 20, 19X3, and has accrued interest for 42 days. The other trade notes payable are noninterest-bearing.
- Entry h—An inventory of store supplies on hand shows that supplies costing $122 are unused.
- Entry i—An analysis of the insurance policies shows that prepaid insurance totals $305.
- Entry j—Prepaid interest on the bank note payable must be recorded. This 60-day, $9,600 note is due on February 25, 19X4. It was discounted at 10

STYLE CLOTHING STORE
Trial Balance
January 31, 19X4

ACCT. NO.	ACCOUNT NAME	DEBIT	CREDIT
101	Cash in Bank	14,110 39	
105	Petty Cash Fund	25 00	
106	Change Fund	100 00	
109	Notes Receivable	1,900 00	
110	Notes Receivable Discounted		
111	Accounts Receivable	27,120 00	
111A	Allowance for Bad Debts	24 00	
116	Interest Receivable		
121	Merchandise Inventory	66,000 00	
126	Prepaid Insurance		
127	Prepaid Interest		
128	Prepaid Taxes	600 00	
129	Store Supplies on Hand		
131	Furniture and Fixtures	4,600 00	
131A	Accumulated Depr.—Furniture and Fixtures		820 00
132	Office Equipment	2,750 00	
132A	Accumulated Depr.—Office Equipment		430 00
201	Notes Payable—Trade		2,150 00
203	Notes Payable—Bank		9,600 00
205	Accounts Payable		5,205 00
216	Interest Payable		
221	Employee Deductions—FICA Taxes		114 66
222	Employee Deductions—Income Tax Withheld		286 65
225	Salaries and Wages Payable		
226	Payroll Taxes Payable		
231	Sales Tax Payable		867 50
235	Property Taxes Payable		
301	Linda Hanson, Capital		30,526 31
302	Linda Hanson, Drawing	7,000 00	
311	Steven Casey, Capital		29,526 31
312	Steven Casey, Drawing	7,000 00	
321	Janet Miller, Capital		30,026 31
322	Janet Miller, Drawing	7,000 00	
401	Sales		383,754 97
452	Sales Returns and Allowances	6,721 35	
491	Interest Earned		200 00
493	Miscellaneous Income		30 00
501	Merchandise Purchases	275,060 90	
506	Freight In	3,775 00	
511	Purchases Returns and Allowances		1,150 00
512	Purchases Discount		5,195 00
521	Sales Salaries Expense	21,970 00	
522	Advertising Expense	7,650 00	
523	Store Supplies and Expense	6,456 00	
529	Cash Short or Over	51 00	
532	Delivery Expense	4,162 27	
536	Insurance Expense	3,960 00	
541	Custodial Wages Expense	6,292 00	
542	Rent Expense	7,000 00	
543	Utilities Expense	3,169 85	
551	Office Salaries Expense	8,670 00	
552	Employer's Payroll Tax Expense	2,927 95	
553	Office Supplies and Expense	955 00	
554	Professional Services Expense	875 00	
555	Taxes and Licenses	1,208 00	
561	Bad Debts Expense		
562	Depr. Expense—Furniture and Fixtures		
563	Depr. Expense—Office Equipment		
591	Interest Expense	749 00	
	Totals	499,882 71	499,882 71

percent on December 27, 19X3, and the discount of $160 was charged to Interest Expense. Record the prepaid interest for 25 days.
- Entry k—The Prepaid Taxes account represents the $600 stock tax for the period of January 1, 19X4, through June 30, 19X4, paid in advance in December 19X3. The amount to be transferred to expense in January is $100.
- Entry l—Interest must be accrued on one 9 percent, $1,600 note receivable dated January 1, 19X4. The other notes receivable are noninterest-bearing.
- Entry m—Net taxable sales for January are $28,916.70, and this amount is subject to the 3 percent state sales tax. The Style Clothing Store is entitled to a commission of 2 percent on the tax due. Record this commission by debiting Sales Tax Payable and crediting Miscellaneous Income.

Completing the Worksheet

Complete the worksheet. The January 31, 19X4, merchandise inventory is $67,500. The January 31, 19X3, inventory was $66,000.

Preparing the Financial Statements

Prepare the following financial statements.

1. A classified income statement for the year, similar to that on page 495, with the distribution of net income or net loss at the bottom. (The partners share net income and net losses equally.)
2. A statement of partners' equities.
3. A balance sheet as of January 31, 19X4.

Completing the Cycle

Complete the remaining steps in the accounting cycle.

1. Journalize the adjusting entries. Before each entry, record the letter corresponding to the adjustment on the worksheet. (Use the adjusting journal entry on page 504 of the text as a model.) Number the journal page *12*.
2. Journalize the closing entries.
3. Journalize the reversing entries that will be necessary on February 1, 19X4.

(**Note:** You are not required by these instructions to open general ledger accounts and post to them. Your instructor may, however, require that you do so.)

UNIT 29

PARTNERSHIP ORGANIZATION

In the last several units, you have become familiar with the financial records of the Style Clothing Store, a partnership. You have seen that the routine accounting procedures for a partnership differ very little from those of a sole proprietorship. In this unit and the next unit, you will learn more about the accounting procedures that must be followed when a partnership is formed and when changes in the partners' capital accounts take place.

Formation of a Partnership

Linda Hanson had owned and operated a clothing store for a number of years. Her business had prospered, but success had also brought some problems. For one thing, competition had increased and customers were demanding a larger assortment of merchandise. For the Style Clothing Store to maintain its competitive position in the rapidly expanding community, Hanson would have to expand the store and carry a bigger and more varied stock. This would, however, require a large sum of money.

Hanson was borrowing all the funds the bank would lend her. Even with this help, however, she was finding it difficult to keep up with bills while adding to her stock and offering liberal credit terms to her customers. As her accountant and her banker explained, the Style Clothing Store needed more *working capital*. (The current assets of a business are its working capital. However, sometimes this term is used to refer to what is more exactly termed *net working capital*—the excess of current assets over current liabilities.)

Hanson decided to remedy her lack of capital by seeking to form a partnership with another person. In the words of the Uniform Partnership Act adopted by most states, "A partnership is an association of two or more persons to carry on, as co-owners, a business for profit." By forming a partnership with a person who would contribute financial resources, Hanson could carry out her plans for expansion. Furthermore, she knew that a good partner would also assume a substantial share of the growing managerial responsibility. For example, the new person might take charge of purchasing and selling while she concentrated on administration and financial management.

Hanson learned that an acquaintance, Steven Casey, was interested in owning a business. Casey had been employed as a salesperson for a clothing store in another city. He had recently inherited some money, and he wanted to use it to go into business for himself. Hanson and Casey arranged a meeting to explore the possibility of pooling their resources.

Hanson prepared a balance sheet to show the assets, liabilities, and owner's equity of her business as of the date set for the meeting with Casey. This balance sheet is shown below. (For the sake of brevity, many firms do not use the word *Control* in the account title for Accounts Receivable or Accounts Payable. The shorter title is used in this illustration and throughout the rest of the book.)

After their discussion, Hanson and Casey agreed to form a partnership. They decided that a partnership would be a mutually profitable arrangement.

Determining the Value of Net Assets

Linda Hanson offered to contribute the assets of the Style Clothing Store (other than the small cash balance) to the new partnership, which would also assume the liabilities of her firm. Steven Casey agreed to invest cash equal to the value of Hanson's contribution—that is, to the value of the net assets (assets minus liabilities) of the Style Clothing Store. However, the determination of the exact value of Hanson's net assets raised certain questions that had to be resolved. For example, Casey pointed out that some of the accounts receivable might not be collectible. Any resulting loss should be borne by Hanson, not by the partnership. On the other hand, Hanson noted that the inventory was worth more than the amount shown on the books because prices had gone up since the goods were acquired. Obviously, any gain under these circumstances should belong entirely to Hanson. The prospective partners decided to seek professional advice from a public accountant and from their personal lawyers.

The public accountant examined the records of the Style Clothing Store to make an independent verification of the values shown on the firm's balance sheet. He recommended that $800 of the accounts receivable be regarded as uncollectible, rather than the $300 shown on the January 31 balance sheet. This meant that the customers' accounts transferred to the partnership should be valued at $10,000 instead of $10,500. The accountant also checked the inventory and recommended that the book value be increased by $1,000 to reflect higher current prices. The merchandise inventory should thus be valued at $40,000 instead of $39,000 when the transfer takes place.

STYLE CLOTHING STORE
Balance Sheet
January 31, 19X1

Assets			Liabilities and Owner's Equity		
Cash in Bank		350 00	Liabilities		
Accounts Receivable	10,800 00		Notes Payable—Bank	20,000 00	
Less Allow. for Bad Debts	300 00	10,500 00	Accounts Payable	3,000 00	
Merchandise Inventory		39,000 00	Total Liabilities		23,000 00
			Owner's Equity		
			Linda Hanson, Capital		26,850 00
			Total Liabilities and		
Total Assets		49,850 00	Owner's Equity		49,850 00

Further examination of the books by the accountant revealed that the liabilities were properly recorded. Accounts payable amounted to $3,000 and notes payable to the bank amounted to $20,000. One note for $10,000 at 6 percent had 60 days to run. The other note, for $10,000 at 9 percent, had 90 days to run. By special arrangement with the bank, the Style Clothing Store's interest on both notes had been paid up to the date on which the balance sheet was prepared.

Adjustments on Proprietorship Books

Since the assets of the Style Clothing Store were to be transferred to the new partnership at amounts different from those shown on the balance sheet on page 528, it became necessary to adjust the book value of Linda Hanson's equity in the business.

Two entries were made in the general journal to record the adjustment of the asset accounts involved. At that time, the Allowance for Bad Debts account contained a balance of $300, showing that this amount was considered uncollectible. However, the balance had to be increased to $800 to reflect the valuation given by the accountant. Hanson had to bear the loss by having her owner's equity reduced by the difference ($500).

In the second adjustment, the inventory was increased by $1,000, and Hanson received the benefit of the gain. This adjustment required a debit to the Merchandise Inventory account and a credit to the Linda Hanson, Capital account. The two entries to revalue the assets are made in the general journal as shown below.

19 X1					
Jan. 31	Linda Hanson, Capital	301	500 00		
	Allowance for Bad Debts	111A		500 00	
	Increased allowance and charged additional estimated bad debts to Hanson prior to transferring accounts to the new partnership.				
31	Merchandise Inventory	121	1,000 00		
	Linda Hanson, Capital	301		1,000 00	
	Increased valuation of merchandise inventory before transferring it to the new partnership.				

Notice that since the books had already been closed, these adjustments were made directly to the Linda Hanson, Capital account rather than to revenue and expense accounts. The withdrawal of the cash balance by Hanson and the resulting decrease in her equity were recorded by a debit to her capital account and a credit to Cash in Bank. After these journal entries were posted to the general ledger accounts, a trial balance contained the amounts shown on page 530.

Observe that the balance of the Linda Hanson, Capital account is now $27,000. This reflects the adjustments that were made to revalue the assets of the firm and to withdraw the cash.

STYLE CLOTHING STORE
Trial Balance
January 31, 19X1

Accounts Receivable	$10,800	
Allowance for Bad Debts		$ 800
Merchandise Inventory	40,000	
Notes Payable—Bank		20,000
Accounts Payable		3,000
Linda Hanson, Capital		27,000
Totals	$50,800	$50,800

The Partnership Agreement

To avoid any future misunderstanding about the terms of their arrangement, Hanson and Casey had their lawyers draw up a written contract, called a *partnership agreement* or *articles of copartnership*. Both partners signed the agreement, and each received a signed copy. Another copy was provided for the partnership records. The major provisions of the partnership agreement were as follows.

Name, Location, and Nature of the Business

The name of the new business was to be the Style Clothing Store. It was to be located in rented premises at the address specified in the agreement. The store would sell men's and women's clothing at retail and would specialize in sportswear and casual clothes.

Starting Date of Agreement

The agreement was to be effective on February 1, 19X1, at which time the store would open for business in its new location. The agreement was to run until the partnership was terminated either by the death of one of the partners or by mutual consent. (The lawyers explained that a partnership has a limited life. It ends with the death or withdrawal of any partner.)

Fiscal Year

The partners agreed that their fiscal year would begin on February 1 and end on the following January 31. This date was chosen not only because the partnership was to begin on February 1 but also because January 31 was a time of low inventory and light business activity. This meant it would be easy to take a physical inventory and close the books then.

Names of the Partners

The partners were Linda Hanson and Steven Casey. Both were residents of Greenville, South Carolina. (Another partner, Janet Miller, was admitted to the firm later, as you will learn in Unit 30.)

Amounts of Capital to Be Contributed

Hanson was to contribute the assets and liabilities of her sole proprietorship business. She was to receive credit for the amount of her net capital, $27,000, as shown previously on the trial balance. Casey was to contribute $27,000 in cash.

Rights and Duties of Each Partner

Each partner is to devote his or her full time to the operation of the business. Hanson will concentrate on administration, financial management, and advertising. Casey will handle purchasing and selling. Their lawyers explained that a legal characteristic of any partnership is known as *mutual agency*. This means that either partner can make valid contracts for the business and can otherwise conduct its affairs.

Method of Distributing Profits and Losses	The agreement specifies exactly how the profits and losses of the firm will be divided between the partners. (This aspect of the agreement is discussed in the next unit.)	
Accounting Records	The agreement provides that Hanson is to be in charge of the accounting records. She is to keep records on the accrual basis according to generally accepted accounting principles.	
Drawings by the Partners	In order to have the funds needed to meet living expenses, each partner can withdraw a limited amount from the business each month as part of his or her share of the expected profits for the year.	
Dissolution or Liquidation	If one of the partners should die, the books must be closed at the end of that month and the firm's profits to that date must be distributed. The surviving partner can, at his or her option, either pay the amount of the deceased partner's investment to the person's estate and continue the business or liquidate the business and pay the balance of the deceased partner's capital account to the estate. If the partners decide to liquidate the business at the end of the five-year term of the original agreement, Hanson will be in charge of the liquidation process.	
Other Provisions	The partners could have included any other items pertinent to the business operation at the time they drew up their contract.	

Dissolving the Sole Proprietorship

Once a definite legal and financial understanding had been reached between Hanson and Casey, it was time to terminate the affairs of the Style Clothing Store as a sole proprietorship. Only one entry was needed to close out the adjusted balances of all the accounts in the proprietorship's general ledger. This entry is shown below. Note that it debited the Allowance for Bad Debts account, all the liability accounts, and the Linda Hanson, Capital account; and it credited all the asset accounts.

19X1				
Jan. 31	Allowance for Bad Debts	111A	800 00	
	Notes Payable—Bank	203	20,000 00	
	Accounts Payable	205	3,000 00	
	Linda Hanson, Capital	301	27,000 00	
	Accounts Receivable	111		10,800 00
	Merchandise Inventory	121		40,000 00
	Closed all accounts to record dissolution of the proprietorship business.			

The general ledger accounts of the proprietorship are illustrated on pages 532 and 533. The first balances shown are those that appear on the balance sheet prepared on January 31, 19X1 (see page 528). The journal entries to adjust the asset accounts, the entry for the withdrawal of cash, and the final entry closing out all the account balances were posted to these accounts. This completed the work on the proprietorship records.

Cash in Bank — No. 101

DATE	EXPLANATION	POST. REF.	DEBIT	CREDIT	BALANCE	DR. CR.
19 X1 Jan. 31	Balance	✓			350 00	Dr.
31		CP3		350 00	-0-	

Accounts Receivable — No. 111

DATE	EXPLANATION	POST. REF.	DEBIT	CREDIT	BALANCE	DR. CR.
19 X1 Jan. 31	Balance	✓			10,800 00	Dr.
31		J1		10,800 00	-0-	

Allowance for Bad Debts — No. 111A

DATE	EXPLANATION	POST. REF.	DEBIT	CREDIT	BALANCE	DR. CR.
19 X1 Jan. 31	Balance	✓			300 00	Cr.
31		J1		500 00	800 00	Cr.
31		J1	800 00		-0-	

Merchandise Inventory — No. 121

DATE	EXPLANATION	POST. REF.	DEBIT	CREDIT	BALANCE	DR. CR.
19 X1 Jan. 31	Balance	✓			39,000 00	Dr.
31		J1	1,000 00		40,000 00	Dr.
31		J1		40,000 00	-0-	

Notes Payable—Bank — No. 203

DATE	EXPLANATION	POST. REF.	DEBIT	CREDIT	BALANCE	DR. CR.
19 X1 Jan. 31	Balance	✓			20,000 00	Cr.
31		J1	20,000 00		-0-	

Accounts Payable — No. 205

DATE	EXPLANATION	POST. REF.	DEBIT	CREDIT	BALANCE	DR. CR.
19 X1 Jan. 31	Balance	✓			3,000 00	Cr.
31		J1	3,000 00		-0-	

		Linda Hanson, Capital				No. 301	
DATE		EXPLANATION	POST. REF.	DEBIT	CREDIT	BALANCE	DR. CR.
19 X1 Jan.	31	Balance	✓			26,850 00	Cr.
	31		J1	500 00		26,350 00	Cr.
	31		J1		1,000 00	27,350 00	Cr.
	31		CP3	350 00		27,000 00	Cr.
	31		J1	27,000 00		–0–	

Opening the Partnership Books

A new set of books covering the operations of the partnership was then opened. In setting up books for a new business, the accountant should record a *memorandum entry* in the general journal. This entry should indicate the name of the business, the name of the proprietor or partners, and any other pertinent introductory information. The memorandum entry to set up the books for Hanson and Casey's partnership is shown below.

19 X1 Feb.	1	On this date, a partnership was formed between Linda Hanson and Steven Casey to carry on a retail clothing business under the name of the Style Clothing Store, according to the terms of the partnership agreement effective this date.			

Notice the reference to the partnership agreement. The accountant needs to consult this document from time to time. It provides guidance on questions about the partners' original investments, the division of profits, and other matters.

Investment of Hanson

Linda Hanson's investment consisted of her equity in her former business. The partnership assumed the revalued assets and the liabilities. Hanson's capital account was credited for the difference between the two amounts. The facts were recorded in the general journal of the new partnership, as shown below.

19 X1 Feb.	1	Accounts Receivable	111	10,800 00	
		Merchandise Inventory	121	40,000 00	
		Allowance for Bad Debts	111A		800 00
		Notes Payable—Bank	203		20,000 00
		Accounts Payable	205		3,000 00
		Linda Hanson, Capital	301		27,000 00
		Investment of Linda Hanson.			

Note that the gross balances of both the Accounts Receivable account and the Allowance for Bad Debts account were recorded on the partnership books. This was necessary because all the individual customers' balances in the accounts receivable subsidiary ledger were transferred to the partnership. Since the Accounts Receivable account in the general ledger must agree with the subsidiary ledger, the total gross amount must be entered in the control account. The Allowance for Bad Debts account was transferred to the partnership at its revised balance of $800. Thus, the net value of accounts receivable on the partnership books was $10,000 ($10,800 − $800), the amount agreed on.

However, when a sole proprietorship transfers items of plant and equipment to a partnership, only the net agreed-on value of these assets is recorded in the partnership accounts. The accumulated depreciation accounts begin with a zero balance in the partnership.

Investment of Casey

Steven Casey's investment consisted of cash in the same amount as Hanson's equity. The receipt of the $27,000 was recorded in the cash receipts journal.

CASH RECEIPTS JOURNAL for Month of February 19X1   Page 1

DATE	EXPLANATION	OTHER ACCOUNTS CREDIT			CASH IN BANK DR. 101
		ACCOUNT TITLE	POST. REF.	AMOUNT	
Feb. 1	Investment of Steven Casey	Steven Casey, Capital	311	27,000 00	27,000 00

Opening Balance Sheet

The accountant immediately posted the opening entries to record the investments made by the two partners. Of course, the debit to Cash in Bank to record Casey's investment was posted only at the end of the month as part of the Cash in Bank column of the cash receipts journal.

Linda Hanson, Capital   No. 301

DATE	EXPLANATION	POST. REF.	DEBIT	CREDIT	BALANCE	DR. CR.
19 X1 Feb. 1	Beginning investment	J1		27,000 00	27,000 00	Cr.

Steven Casey, Capital   No. 311

DATE	EXPLANATION	POST. REF.	DEBIT	CREDIT	BALANCE	DR. CR.
19 X1 Feb. 1	Beginning investment	CR1		27,000 00	27,000 00	Cr.

The accountant prepared a balance sheet at this time to reflect the status of the assets, liabilities, and owners' equity at the start of the new partnership venture. This balance sheet is illustrated on page 535.

As you have already learned, the balance sheet of a partnership is in the same form as that for a sole proprietorship except that each partner's equity is shown in a separate capital account in the Owners' Equity section.

With these initial entries and postings, the books of the Style Clothing Store as a partnership were formally opened.

STYLE CLOTHING STORE
Balance Sheet
February 1, 19X1

Assets			Liabilities and Owners' Equity		
Cash in Bank		27,000.00	Liabilities		
Accounts Receivable	10,800.00		Notes Payable—Bank	20,000.00	
Less Allow. for Bad Debts	800.00	10,000.00	Accounts Payable	3,000.00	
Merchandise Inventory		40,000.00	Total Liabilities		23,000.00
			Owners' Equity		
			Linda Hanson, Capital	27,000.00	
			Steven Casey, Capital	27,000.00	
			Total Owners' Equity		54,000.00
Total Assets		77,000.00	Total Liabilities and Owners' Equity		77,000.00

principles and procedures summary

It is important that the agreement about a partnership's operation be in writing. This will mean fewer chances for possible misunderstanding later. Partnership agreements typically provide for the amounts of capital to be contributed, the rights and duties of each partner, the method of distributing profits and losses, the accounting methods, and the fiscal year to be used. In the case of the partnership of Hanson and Casey, one partner contributed the assets and liabilities of her business and received credit for the difference. The other partner contributed cash equal to the first partner's investment.

The value at which contributed assets are to be recorded on the partnership books is a matter of agreement between the partners. If the values agreed on are different from those shown on the books of the prior business, the books of the prior business are adjusted before being finally closed.

The books of the new partnership are opened with a memorandum entry in the general journal. Then the partners' investments are entered in their capital accounts.

managerial implications

The partnership form of business offers many advantages to the sole proprietor who needs more capital, managerial assistance, or technical help. It is extremely important, however, that individuals who enter into a partnership have a clear understanding about the duties, obligations, rights, and responsibilities of each partner. These points must be clearly and thoroughly covered in a written partnership agreement. Consultation with a lawyer and an accountant is advisable at every stage of the negotiations.

managerial discussion questions

1. What specific duties, rights, and obligations of partners may have a significant effect on managerial efficiency?
2. If Hanson's accountant has been competent and accurate, why should the exact value of the balance sheet items be questioned by Casey?
3. What guidance does the partnership agreement give the accountant?
4. How is the net value of Hanson's assets determined before their transfer to the new partnership's books?
5. Why should partners insist that their agreement be in writing?

application of principles

PROBLEM 29-1 Ahmed Almassi operates the AA Electronics Center, a small retail store that sells calculators, radios, cassette players, and other electronic products. His postclosing trial balance on December 31, 19X1, is given on page 537. Almassi reached an agreement with Thomas Brown to form a partnership, effective January 1, 19X2. Profits and losses will be shared equally, and each partner is to devote at least 90 percent of his time to the business. The arrangement is to continue for five years. The new name of the store will be A & B Electronics.

Almassi is to transfer the assets of his firm to the partnership at agreed values as follows: Cash, as shown on books; Accounts Receivable (net), $8,200; Merchandise Inventory, $43,600; and Delivery Truck, $6,600. The partnership is to assume Almassi's liabilities. He is to receive credit for his net investment as adjusted. Brown will invest cash that is equal to Almassi's net investment.

INSTRUCTIONS
1. Adjust and close the books of the AA Electronics Center on December 31, 19X1, as follows.
   a. Prepare general journal entries adjusting the assets to the agreed values. (The entry to revalue the delivery truck should be made by crediting the accumulated depreciation account.)
   b. Prepare a general journal entry dissolving the sole proprietorship.
2. Record the following in general journal form.
   a. The opening memorandum entry for the partnership.
   b. Almassi's investment in the partnership.
   c. Brown's investment in the partnership.
3. Prepare a balance sheet for the partnership (A & B Electronics) on January 1, 19X2, at the beginning of its operations.

PROBLEM 29-2 Daniel Roberts operates a small shoe store. His postclosing trial balance as of December 31, 19X1, is given on page 537. Roberts has agreed to enter into a

AA ELECTRONICS CENTER
Postclosing Trial Balance
December 31, 19X1

Acct. No.	Account Name	Debit	Credit
101	Cash in Bank	$ 900	
111	Accounts Receivable	8,400	
111A	Allowance for Bad Debts		$ 400
121	Merchandise Inventory	42,000	
141	Delivery Truck	7,600	
141A	Accumulated Depreciation		600
202	Accounts Payable		2,200
301	Ahmed Almassi, Capital		55,700
	Totals	$58,900	$58,900

partnership with Sharon Moore, effective January 1, 19X2. The new firm will be called the Family Shoe Center. Profits and losses are to be shared equally. Roberts will transfer the assets and liabilities of his store to the partnership at agreed values. These values are Accounts Receivable (net), $6,200; Merchandise Inventory (net), $22,400; and Furniture and Equipment (net), $5,600. Roberts will receive credit for his net investment as adjusted. Moore is to invest cash that is equal to Roberts' net investment.

INSTRUCTIONS

1. Give the general journal entries to revalue the assets of the Roberts Shoe Store and to close out the accounts on December 31, 19X1.
2. Give the memorandum entry in the general journal to record formation of the partnership that will operate the Family Shoe Center.
3. Give the general journal entry to record Roberts' investment in the partnership on January 1, 19X2.
4. Give the general journal entry to record Moore's investment in the partnership on January 1, 19X2.

ROBERTS SHOE STORE
Postclosing Trial Balance
December 31, 19X1

Acct. No.	Account Name	Debit	Credit
101	Cash in Bank	$ 1,500	
111	Accounts Receivable	7,000	
111A	Allowance for Bad Debts		$ 500
121	Merchandise Inventory	21,500	
141	Furniture and Equipment	13,500	
141A	Accumulated Depreciation		10,000
202	Accounts Payable		2,000
301	Daniel Roberts, Capital		31,000
	Totals	$43,500	$43,500

alternate problems

PROBLEM 29-1A   Alicia Delapena owns a small fabric shop with a growing clientele. In order to obtain additional capital needed for expansion, she entered into a partnership agreement with Marion Roth effective January 1, 19X2, for the operation of the Fashion Fabric Shop. The partnership agreement is to continue indefinitely. Profits and losses will be divided equally. Each partner is to devote full time to the business, except for an annual three-week vacation. Delapena has rented the building, furniture, and fixtures. Her postclosing trial balance as of December 31, 19X1, is shown below.

Delapena will transfer the assets of her business. However, one $50 account receivable is thought to be uncollectible, and the partners agreed to set up an Allowance for Bad Debts account for this amount. The merchandise inventory is to be transferred at an agreed-on value of $9,000. The partnership will take over Delapena's liabilities, and she is to receive credit for her net investment as adjusted. Roth will invest cash that is equal to Delapena's net investment.

INSTRUCTIONS

1. Adjust and close the books of the Delapena Fabric Shop on December 31, 19X1, as follows.
   a. Prepare general journal entries adjusting the assets to the agreed values.
   b. Prepare a general journal entry to dissolve the sole proprietorship.
2. In general journal form, record the following.
   a. The opening memorandum entry for the partnership.
   b. Delapena's investment in the partnership.
   c. Roth's investment in the partnership.
3. Prepare a balance sheet for the partnership (the Fashion Fabric Shop) at the beginning of its operations on January 1, 19X2.

DELAPENA FABRIC SHOP
Postclosing Trial Balance
December 31, 19X1

Acct. No.	Account Name	Debit	Credit
101	Cash in Bank	$ 600	
111	Accounts Receivable	2,600	
121	Merchandise Inventory	10,000	
202	Accounts Payable		$ 800
301	Alicia Delapena, Capital		12,400
	Totals	$13,200	$13,200

PROBLEM 29-2A   Rita Mann operates a laundry that provides services to restaurants, hotels, and motels. Financial data for the firm as of December 31, 19X1, is given on page 539. Mann has agreed to enter into a partnership with Thomas Ott effective January 1, 19X2. The new firm is to be called the Ajax Commercial Laundry. Profits and losses will be shared equally.

Mann is to transfer the assets and liabilities of her firm to the partnership, at the values agreed on. Ott will invest cash that is equal to Mann's investment after revaluation.

INSTRUCTIONS
1. Give the general journal entries to revalue the assets of the Mann Commercial Laundry and to close out the accounts on December 31, 19X1.
2. Give the memorandum entry in the general journal to record formation of the partnership that will operate the Ajax Commercial Laundry.
3. Give the general journal entry to record Mann's investment in the partnership on January 1, 19X2.
4. Give the general journal entry to record Ott's investment in the partnership on January 1, 19X2.

		Balances Shown on Mann's Books	Value Agreed on by Partners
Assets Transferred			
Cash		$ 800	$ 800
Accounts Receivable	$500		
Allowance for Bad Debts	50	450	400
Laundry Equipment	$10,000		
Accumulated Depreciation	3,000	7,000	6,000
Building	$12,000		
Accumulated Depreciation	2,000	10,000	8,000
Land		1,000	6,700
Total Assets		$19,250	$21,900
Liabilities and Owner's Equity Transferred			
Accounts Payable		1,000	1,000
Rita Mann, Capital		$18,250	$20,900

539

UNIT 30

PARTNERSHIPS: PROFIT DIVISION AND EQUITY ACCOUNTING

The accountant who keeps the books of a partnership must develop a system of records in which the equity of each of the co-owners is clearly identified and in which all changes are promptly and properly recorded. The most efficient arrangement in accounting for partnership equity is to set up two accounts for each partner, a capital account and a drawing account.

Partner's Capital Account

You learned about the initial contribution of cash or other assets by a partner in Unit 29. If a partner makes additional investments at a later date, these amounts are credited to the partner's capital account. Withdrawals that are intended to reduce the invested capital permanently are recorded directly as debits to the partner's capital account.

Partner's Drawing Account

Owners and partners of businesses need funds with which to pay their living expenses. They can obtain these funds from their businesses by making current withdrawals against anticipated profits. A drawing account is set up for each partner to record such withdrawals.

The partnership agreement for the Style Clothing Store specified that Linda Hanson could withdraw up to $600 each month and Steven Casey up to $575 each month. The withdrawals are recorded in the cash payments journal by a credit to Cash in Bank and a debit to the drawing accounts. The debits are then posted individually from the Other Accounts Debit section of the journal to each partner's drawing account in the general ledger. Thus, if Hanson and Casey withdraw the specified amounts each month for 12 months, on January 31, 19X2, Hanson's drawing account will have a debit balance of $7,200 and Casey's will have a debit balance of $6,900.

Instead of withdrawing a lump sum periodically, a partner may have the accountant for the business pay personal bills with business checks. This is not a sound practice because it leads to confusion between business transactions and personal ones. If the practice is followed, however, each check written to pay a personal bill must be charged to the partner's drawing account by an entry in the cash payments journal. If such entries occur often, special columns may be set up in the cash payments journal for the drawing accounts. Under this system only one posting to each drawing account will be required at the end of the month.

Although a partner's current withdrawals are not subject to payroll taxes or income tax withholding, they are sometimes called salary. The term *salary* is not completely accurate, but it will be used in this book to conform to common practice. Nonetheless, such withdrawals should *not* be considered expenses of the partnership. Furthermore, they do not represent withdrawals of invested capital. Therefore, they should not be debited directly to the capital accounts of the partners involved but should instead be charged to the drawing accounts.

Division of Partnership Profits

Once the net income or net loss from the operations of the period is determined, it is transferred from the Revenue and Expense Summary account to the partners' capital accounts. If no other method for the division of net income and net loss is specified, it is divided equally between the partners. For example, if the net income of $19,800 earned by the Style Clothing Store in the first year of operations is to be divided equally, the credit balance in the Revenue and Expense Summary account is transferred to the partners' capital accounts by the following general journal entry.

19 X2				
Jan. 31	Revenue and Expense Summary	399	19,800 00	
	Linda Hanson, Capital	301		9,900 00
	Steven Casey, Capital	311		9,900 00
	Distributed net income for the year equally.			

At the end of each fiscal year, the drawing accounts are closed into the partners' capital accounts. Assume that Hanson's drawing account contains a debit balance of $7,200 and Casey's drawing account contains a debit balance of $6,900 at the end of the first year's operations. The following general journal entries are made to close the two partners' drawing accounts into their capital accounts on January 31, 19X2.

19 X2				
Jan. 31	Linda Hanson, Capital	301	7,200 00	
	Linda Hanson, Drawing	302		7,200 00
	Closed drawing account.			
31	Steven Casey, Capital	311	6,900 00	
	Steven Casey, Drawing	312		6,900 00
	Closed drawing account.			

Note that the closing procedure illustrated is almost the same as for a sole proprietorship. The single difference is that there are two drawing accounts and two capital accounts, one for each partner.

Again assume that Hanson and Casey agreed to divide net income and net losses equally. However, suppose that the store experiences a net loss of

$15,000 instead of a net income of $19,800 from the year's operations. The entries to transfer the balances of the Revenue and Expense Summary account and the drawing accounts to the capital accounts are shown below.

19X2					
Jan. 31	Linda Hanson, Capital	301	7,500 00		
	Steven Casey, Capital	311	7,500 00		
	Revenue and Expense Summary	399		15,000 00	
	Distributed net loss for the year equally.				
31	Linda Hanson, Capital	301	7,200 00		
	Linda Hanson, Drawing	302		7,200 00	
	Closed drawing account.				
31	Steven Casey, Capital	311	6,900 00		
	Steven Casey, Drawing	312		6,900 00	
	Closed drawing account.				

Notice that in the preceding examples there was *no connection* between the partners' drawings and the division of net income. Each partner withdrew the maximum amount permitted under the agreement. The net income or net loss was then divided equally. It is important to remember that the withdrawals of cash are *not of themselves a division of net income.* They are instead drawings in anticipation of net income that will be divided according to the profit sharing agreement.

Profit Sharing Agreement

Hanson and Casey discussed the question of profit sharing when they were outlining the provisions to be included in their partnership agreement. They did not feel that an equal division of the net income was satisfactory for their particular circumstances. They sought the advice of their lawyers and their accountant to help them work out a fair arrangement.

Hanson and Casey agreed that each would devote full time to the business. Hanson felt that her longer experience in the trade should entitle her to a larger share of the profits. Casey acknowledged Hanson's superior skill and ability, and he conceded that the new business would greatly benefit from Hanson's good reputation and established clientele.

Casey's primary concern was for his capital investment. He planned to leave his entire original capital invested indefinitely and thought he might even add to it. Thus, if Hanson made any permanent withdrawals of capital, Casey wanted to be sure that his proportionately larger investment would be considered in the division of net income.

The consultants recommended a combination plan for profit distribution. They pointed out that both partners' interests would be fairly protected if the partnership agreement stated that net income or net losses would be distributed as follows.

1. Salary allowances will be $7,200 a year to Hanson and $6,900 a year to Casey.

2. Interest at 9 percent will be allowed to each partner on the balance of his or her capital account at the beginning of the year.
3. The remainder of the net income will be distributed in the ratio of 75 percent to Hanson and 25 percent to Casey.

The partners agreed to accept this plan, with the understanding that it might later be changed. Let us analyze each part of the plan to identify the purpose and effect on the partners' interests.

Salary Allowance   The salary allowance provision gave a slight advantage to Hanson to compensate for her greater experience in store operation. The difference was small because both partners were to devote full time to the firm and because Casey too had considerable experience in the clothing business. (Under other conditions, there might have been a greater difference in the salary allowance provision.)

There is no necessary connection between the salary allowance (as a step in the distribution of net income) and the limit on withdrawals of cash for the partners' current living expenses during the year. However, the two are often the same (as they were in the Hanson and Casey agreement), although there are *vital differences in the purpose and the recording of the items*. The entry for the salary allowance is made regardless of the amount of net income or net loss for the period.

Interest on Capital   Payment of interest at 9 percent on the balance of each partner's capital account at the beginning of the year gives special consideration to the partner who maintains the larger permanent balance in his or her capital account. The interest allowance is also recorded regardless of the amount of net income earned or net loss incurred during the period.

Distribution Ratio for Remainder   The ratio of 75 percent to Hanson and 25 percent to Casey was intended to compensate Hanson for the value of her outstanding reputation in the community and the established clientele of the Style Clothing Store.

Putting the Plan Into Operation

Now let us see how the combination plan works, taking one section at a time. Remember that the profit division is made at the end of the year. It transfers the balance of the Revenue and Expense Summary account to the partners' capital accounts. Assume that the drawing accounts have been debited month by month during the year for the cash withdrawals made by the partners and that they total $7,200 for Hanson and $6,900 for Casey.

Salary Allowance   The first step in dividing net income or net loss is to record the salary allowances of $7,200 to Hanson and $6,900 to Casey. The general journal entry to record these allowances is shown below.

19 X2					
Jan. 31	Revenue and Expense Summary	399	14,100 00		
	Linda Hanson, Capital	301		7,200	00
	Steven Casey, Capital	311		6,900	00
	Agreed salary allowances.				

543

Interest on Capital

The partners' capital accounts at the beginning of the fiscal year (when the business was established) were: Linda Hanson, Capital, $27,000; Steven Casey, Capital, $27,000. At 9 percent interest on each account for the year, the interest allowance is $2,430 ($27,000 × 0.09) for each partner. This allowance is recorded in the general journal as follows.

19X2				
Jan. 31	Revenue and Expense Summary	399	4,860 00	
	Linda Hanson, Capital	301		2,430 00
	Steven Casey, Capital	311		2,430 00
	Agreed interest allowance of 9% on beginning capital balances.			

Distribution of Remainder

After the entries to record salary and interest allowances have been posted, the balance remaining in the Revenue and Expense Summary account will be distributed in the agreed ratio to the partners' drawing accounts. The procedures followed at this point depend on whether there was a net income or a net loss and on its amount. These procedures are illustrated in the following paragraphs.

Profit Greater Than Salaries and Interest. Assume that at the end of the fiscal year, the Revenue and Expense Summary account shows a net income of $19,800 after all revenues and expenses are transferred to it. Then the entries are made for the salary allowances ($14,100) and the interest allowances ($4,860). These entries reduce the balance of the Revenue and Expense Summary account to $840, as shown below.

Revenue and Expense Summary   No. 399

DATE	EXPLANATION	POST. REF.	DEBIT	CREDIT	BALANCE	DR. CR.
19X2 Jan. 31	Net Income	✓			19,800 00	Cr.
31	Salary Allowances	J1	14,100 00		5,700 00	Cr.
31	Interest Allowances	J1	4,860 00		840 00	Cr.

The credit balance of $840 is divided in the ratio of 75 to 25 between Hanson and Casey, as specified in the partnership agreement. The entry to close the Revenue and Expense Summary account transfers $630 as a credit to Hanson's capital account and transfers $210 as a credit to Casey's capital account, as shown below.

19X2				
Jan. 31	Revenue and Expense Summary	399	840 00	
	Linda Hanson, Capital	301		630 00
	Steven Casey, Capital	311		210 00
	Distributed balance of Revenue and Expense Summary 75% to Hanson and 25% to Casey.			

After this journal entry is posted, the Revenue and Expense Summary account is closed. This account and the partners' capital accounts are shown below.

Revenue and Expense Summary   **No. 399**

DATE	EXPLANATION	POST. REF.	DEBIT	CREDIT	BALANCE	DR. CR.
19 X2						
Jan. 31	Net Income	✓			19,800 00	Cr.
31	Salary Allowances	J1	14,100 00		5,700 00	Cr.
31	Interest Allowances	J1	4,860 00		840 00	Cr.
31	Bal. 75%: 25% to Partners	J1	840 00		–0–	

Linda Hanson, Capital   **No. 301**

DATE	EXPLANATION	POST. REF.	DEBIT	CREDIT	BALANCE	DR. CR.
19 X2						
Jan. 31	Balance	✓			27,000 00	Cr.
31	Salary Allowance	J1		7,200 00	34,200 00	Cr.
31	Interest Allowance	J1		2,430 00	36,630 00	Cr.
31	75% of Bal. of R & E Summary	J1		630 00	37,260 00	Cr.

Steven Casey, Capital   **No. 311**

DATE	EXPLANATION	POST. REF.	DEBIT	CREDIT	BALANCE	DR. CR.
19 X2						
Jan. 31	Balance	✓			27,000 00	Cr.
31	Salary Allowance	J1		6,900 00	33,900 00	Cr.
31	Interest Allowance	J1		2,430 00	36,330 00	Cr.
31	25% of Bal. of R & E Summary	J1		210 00	36,540 00	Cr.

The final step is to close the balances of the partners' drawing accounts into their permanent capital accounts. The necessary journal entries are illustrated below.

19 X2				
Jan. 31	Linda Hanson, Capital	301	7,200 00	
	Linda Hanson, Drawing	302		7,200 00
	Closed drawing account.			
31	Steven Casey, Capital	311	6,900 00	
	Steven Casey, Drawing	312		6,900 00
	Closed drawing account.			

Operating Loss. Now assume the opposite situation—that the Style Clothing Store suffers a net loss of $15,000 for the first year's operation. The Revenue and Expense Summary account shows this amount as a debit balance after all revenues and expenses have been transferred into it. Even though a loss has occurred, the allowances for salaries and interest must still be made in accordance with the partnership agreement, as in the previous example. The debits of $14,100 for the salary allowances and $4,860 for the interest allowances increase the debit balance of the summary account to $33,960, as shown below.

\	Revenue and Expense Summary					No. 399
DATE	EXPLANATION	POST. REF.	DEBIT	CREDIT	BALANCE	DR. CR.
19 X2 Jan. 31	Net Loss	✓			15,000 00	Dr.
31	Salary Allowances	J1	14,100 00		29,100 00	Dr.
31	Interest Allowances	J1	4,860 00		33,960 00	Dr.

The debit balance of $33,960 must be divided between Hanson and Casey according to the 75 to 25 ratio specified in the partnership agreement. The entry to close the Revenue and Expense Summary account thus results in a debit of $25,470 to Hanson's capital account and a debit of $8,490 to Casey's capital account. The journal entry to close the summary account is given below.

19 X2 Jan. 31	Linda Hanson, Capital	301	25,470 00	
	Steven Casey, Capital	311	8,490 00	
	Revenue and Expense Summary	399		33,960 00
	Closed debit balance of Revenue and Expense Summary to partners' capital accounts in ratio of 75:25.			

After this entry is posted, the Revenue and Expense Summary account and the partners' capital accounts appear as shown below and on page 547.

\	Revenue and Expense Summary					No. 399
DATE	EXPLANATION	POST. REF.	DEBIT	CREDIT	BALANCE	DR. CR.
19 X2 Jan. 31	Net Loss	✓			15,000 00	Dr.
31	Salary Allowances	J1	14,100 00		29,100 00	Dr.
31	Interest Allowances	J1	4,860 00		33,960 00	Dr.
31	Bal. 75%: 25% to Partners	J1		33,960 00	-0-	

Linda Hanson, Capital — No. 301

DATE	EXPLANATION	POST. REF.	DEBIT	CREDIT	BALANCE	DR. CR.
19 X2 Jan. 31	Balance	✓			27,000 00	Cr.
31	Salary Allowance	J1		7,200 00	34,200 00	Cr.
31	Interest Allowance	J1		2,430 00	36,630 00	Cr.
31	75% of Bal. of R & E Summary	J1	25,470 00		11,160 00	Cr.

Steven Casey, Capital — No. 311

DATE	EXPLANATION	POST. REF.	DEBIT	CREDIT	BALANCE	DR. CR.
19 X2 Jan. 31	Balance	✓			27,000 00	Cr.
31	Salary Allowance	J1		6,900 00	33,900 00	Cr.
31	Interest Allowance	J1		2,430 00	36,330 00	Cr.
31	25% of Bal. of R & E Summary	J1	8,490 00		27,840 00	Cr.

The drawing account balances are then closed into the permanent capital accounts, as follows.

19 X2 Jan. 31	Linda Hanson, Capital		301	7,200 00	
	Linda Hanson, Drawing		302		7,200 00
	Closed drawing account.				
31	Steven Casey, Capital		311	6,900 00	
	Steven Casey, Drawing		312		6,900 00
	Closed drawing account.				

Profit Less Than Salary and Interest Allowances. Now assume that the operations of the Style Clothing Store for the year resulted in a net income of only $5,000. The net income appears as a credit balance in the Revenue and Expense Summary account after all the revenues and expenses have been closed into it. The later debits of $14,100 for salary allowances and $4,860 for interest, totaling $18,960, change the balance in the Revenue and Expense Summary account to a debit of $13,960 ($18,960 − $5,000). Distributing this in the 75 to 25 ratio results in a debit to Hanson's capital account of $10,470 and a debit to Casey's capital account of $3,490, with an offsetting credit to the Revenue and Expense Summary account. When the journal entry is posted to the permanent capital accounts, there is a resulting decrease in each partner's equity. The drawing accounts are closed into the capital accounts in the normal way.

547

Partnership Equity on the Statements

Showing Profit Distribution on the Income Statement

Once the net income or net loss distribution is completed, the financial statements can be prepared. The firm's accountant should present complete financial information but should not clutter the statements with too many details.

The final figure on the income statement of a sole proprietorship is the amount of net income or net loss. On the income statement for a partnership, a schedule is added below this final figure to show the distribution of the net income or net loss to the partners. This portion of the income statement for the Style Clothing Store appears as follows, assuming a net income of $19,800 for the year.

Net Income for Year			$19,800
DISTRIBUTION OF NET INCOME	HANSON	CASEY	TOTAL
Salary Allowance	$ 7,200	$6,900	$14,100
Interest Allowance	2,430	2,430	4,860
Remainder in 75:25 Ratio	630	210	840
Totals	$10,260	$9,540	$19,800

Showing the Results on the Balance Sheet

As a general rule, only the final balances of the partners' capital accounts are shown on the balance sheet. A separate statement of partners' equities summarizes the changes that have taken place in the capital accounts during the year. As shown in the illustration on page 498, the statement of partners' equities contains the beginning capital of each partner, additional investments during the year, each partner's share of the net income or net loss, withdrawals, and ending capital.

Admitting a New Partner

Existing partners may decide to take in a new partner. When a new partner is admitted, a new partnership results and the old one is dissolved. (The dissolution of a partnership is a legal and financial matter and may have no noticeable effect on the operations of the business.)

Before the admission of the new partner is recorded on the books, two steps should be taken.

1. The books should be closed as of the date preceding the new partnership, and the net income or net loss of the period should be recorded and transferred to the partners' capital accounts in the usual manner.
2. Assets and liabilities should be revalued between the old partners and the incoming partners, as agreed upon. This is done in the same way that the values of sole proprietorship accounts are adjusted when they are transferred to a partnership. The gain or loss resulting from revaluation is allocated to the capital accounts of the old partners in their profit and loss ratio. Then the admission of the new partner is recorded.

The procedures for recording the admission of a new partner can be illustrated as follows. Assume that Hanson and Casey have decided to admit a third partner, Janet Miller, as of August 1, 19X1. Following are the capital balances of Hanson and Casey as of July 31, 19X1, after the books have been closed. Assets and liabilities have been revalued as agreed upon with Miller, and the resulting gain or loss has been allocated to the capital accounts.

    Linda Hanson, Capital $28,500
    Steven Casey, Capital $27,500

Purchase of an Interest

One way to join an existing partnership is to buy a portion of an old partner's share for an agreed sum. (Of course, the prospective partner must have the approval of the old partners.) The money or other consideration passes directly from the purchaser to the old partner and does not appear on the partnership books.

Suppose that Hanson sells half her interest in the business to Miller for $15,000. The $15,000 is paid by Miller directly to Hanson. On the partnership's books, the transfer of half of Hanson's capital account balance to Miller is recorded by a debit to Hanson's capital account for $14,250 and a credit to Miller's capital account for the same amount.

The amount paid by the new partner is not necessarily the same as the amount credited to that person's capital account. In the case of the Style Clothing Store, Miller paid $15,000 but was credited with only $14,250. The price paid is a matter of bargaining between the parties, because the value of the interest is a matter of opinion and because circumstances affect the willingness of the buyer and seller to trade at any particular price.

With the admission of the new partner, the old partnership comes to an end and a new one comes into being. The partners should therefore draw up a new partnership agreement that covers all the usual topics.

Investment of Assets by a New Partner

A prospective partner may invest money or other property to obtain admission to the partnership while the old partners continue to participate. The new partner's investment, share of the business, and share of the net income or net losses are matters for agreement among the partners. They are specified in the partnership contract for the new organization.

Instead of buying part of Hanson's interest, suppose that Miller invests cash in the business. There are several different methods for recording her investment in the partnership.

New Partner Given Credit for Amount Invested. Assume that Hanson, Casey, and Miller agreed that Miller would receive a one-third interest in the capital of the store on investing cash in an amount equal to one-third of the total capital in the new partnership. Hanson and Casey, whose capital amounts totaled $56,000 ($28,500 + $27,500), owned two-thirds of the business. Therefore, Miller's one-third must equal $28,000 ($56,000 ÷ 2 = $28,000 = $\frac{1}{3}$ interest). Miller invested $28,000, and her capital account was credited for this amount.

The partners further agreed that all future profits and losses would be split equally among them and that there would be no salary or interest allowances.

Miller received credit for the amount of cash she invested in the business. However, a new partner can invest more or less than book value for a share of ownership. (The *book value* is the person's share of the total owners' equity after investment.)

Bonus to Old Partners. Suppose Miller had agreed to invest $34,000 in cash for a one-third interest. The $34,000 investment would first be recorded in the regular way by a debit to Cash in Bank and a credit to Janet Miller, Capital.

After the recording of Miller's investment, the total owners' equity would amount to $90,000 (Hanson, $28,500; Casey, $27,500; Miller, $34,000). Although Miller would receive credit for only one-third of the total equity, $30,000, she would have paid more than this amount. One method of adjusting Miller's capital account would be to allow a bonus to the old partners. In this case Miller's capital would be reduced to $30,000 by a debit of $4,000. The $4,000 difference would be credited to the capital accounts of Hanson and Casey in the old 75 to 25 profit ratio. After the posting of this entry, Miller's capital account balance would reflect one-third of the total owners' equity, as agreed ($\frac{1}{3} \times \$90,000 = \$30,000$). Hanson's capital account would show $31,500 ($28,500 + $3,000), and Casey's capital account would show $28,500 ($27,500 + $1,000).

Goodwill to Old Partners. Miller may be reluctant to receive credit for less than she actually invested. Another way of treating Miller's investment involves the recording of goodwill.

Miller's investment of $34,000 cash is recorded in the usual way. If Miller's capital account balance is to remain at $34,000, the total equity of the partnership must be three times that amount, or $102,000. The $12,000 difference ($102,000 − $90,000) is recorded on the books as an intangible asset called *goodwill*. The amount is allocated between the old partners in the 75 to 25 ratio by the following entry.

19 X1					
Aug.	1	Goodwill	191	12,000 00	
		Linda Hanson, Capital	301		9,000 00
		Steven Casey, Capital	311		3,000 00
		Set up goodwill on admission of new partner.			

After this entry is posted, the total equity will be $102,000 (Hanson, $37,500; Casey, $30,500; Miller, $34,000). Miller's capital account reflects her one-third share, as agreed.

Bonus to New Partner. The incoming partner may also invest less than the book value of his or her interest. For example, Miller may be given a one-third interest for investing only $25,000. After the $25,000 investment is recorded in the usual way, the new total of the owners' equity is $81,000 ($56,000 + $25,000). Miller's $25,000 investment is less than one-third of $81,000. A bonus of $2,000 can be credited to the new partner to increase her capital account to one-third of $81,000, or $27,000. The credit to the Janet Miller, Capital account for $2,000 is offset by debits to the old partners' capital accounts, allocated in the profit and loss ratio of the old partnership. The effect of this procedure on the capital account balances is as follows.

	PREVIOUS BALANCE	CHANGE			NEW BALANCE
Linda Hanson, Capital	$28,500	−	$1,500	=	$27,000
Steven Casey, Capital	27,500	−	500	=	27,000
Janet Miller, Capital	25,000	+	2,000	=	27,000
Total Owners' Equity	$81,000	+	–0–	=	$81,000

Goodwill to New Partner. Suppose the old partners are reluctant to have their capital accounts reduced under the bonus method. In this case, their agreement to give Miller a one-third share can be satisfied by increasing her capital balance by the appropriate amount and by debiting Goodwill. The combined capital of the old partners, $56,000, is equal to two-thirds of the total equity of the new partnership. Thus, $28,000 must be the value of a one-third share. The difference between Miller's cash contribution and the $28,000 ($28,000 − $25,000 = $3,000) is recorded as goodwill in a journal entry, as shown below.

19X1					
Aug.	1	Goodwill	191	3,000 00	
		Janet Miller, Capital	321		3,000 00
		Set up goodwill and increased new partner's capital to one-third of total owners' equity.			

After this entry is posted, the total equity is $84,000 (Hanson, $28,500; Casey, $27,500; Miller, $28,000). Miller's capital account shows a one-third interest, as agreed.

principles and procedures summary

Investments by a partner are credited to the partner's capital account. Permanent withdrawals of capital are charged to this account. Temporary withdrawals are debited to a drawing account. At the end of the period, the Revenue and Expense Summary account is closed into the capital accounts; and the drawing accounts are also closed into the capital accounts.

Division of partnership profits or losses can be arranged in any manner agreed on by the partners. Allowances such as salaries and interest are made whether the partnership has a profit or a loss. Any balance remaining in the Revenue and Expense Summary account is then divided as agreed.

A new partner is admitted into an established partnership in either of two ways. The new partner may purchase an interest from an old partner, in which case no cash comes into the business. Or the new partner may invest cash or other property, in which case the person may put in more or less than the share of equity agreed to. If the new partner puts in more, a bonus may be allowed to the old partners, or goodwill may be recorded and credited to their capital accounts. A new partner who puts in less than the agreed share of total equity may receive credit for a bonus from the capital accounts of the old partners or may have goodwill credited to his or her capital account.

MANAGERIAL IMPLICATIONS

Partners must give serious consideration to the profit and loss distribution formula to make sure that each pertinent factor is properly considered. Before admitting new partners, the old partners must carefully study the advantages and disadvantages of the bonus and goodwill methods. The new profit and loss agreement that results may produce long-term effects different from those expected or intended.

MANAGERIAL DISCUSSION QUESTIONS

1. Why does the sale of a share of capital interest by one partner not affect the capital accounts of any of the other original partners?
2. What factors must be weighed when prospective partners attempt to devise a fair profit sharing agreement?
3. The partnership agreement between two partners specifies that one partner shall be allowed a monthly "drawing" of $1,000 and the other a monthly "drawing" of $600. The agreement does not mention salary allowances for the partners. At the end of the year, one partner maintains that a "drawing" is the same as a salary allowance. Comment on this.
4. Why do partners usually make periodic withdrawals of funds against anticipated profits?
5. Under what circumstances would the members of an existing partnership offer a bonus to a prospective new partner in the firm? Why would a prospective new partner be required to offer a bonus to the old partners in order to obtain admission to the firm?

APPLICATION OF PRINCIPLES

PROBLEM 30-1 Century Metal Fabricators is a sheet metal shop organized as a partnership by Robert Moka and John Terry. The partners have agreed that Moka can withdraw $1,000 a month and Terry $600 a month in anticipation of profits. Net income and net losses are to be shared 60 percent to Moka and 40 percent to

Terry. For the year ended December 31, 19X1, the partnership has earned a net income of $18,600. The drawing accounts of the partners indicate that each withdrew the maximum amount authorized.

INSTRUCTIONS
1. In general journal form, give the entry required to transfer the net income to the capital account of each partner.
2. Give the general journal entries required to close each partner's drawing account to his capital account.

PROBLEM 30-2 The partnership agreement of Ellen Tosti and Roy Crane provides for (a) salary allowances of $18,000 for Tosti and $14,000 for Crane and (b) interest of 8 percent on each partner's invested capital at the beginning of the year. The remainder of the net income is to be distributed 40 percent to Tosti and 60 percent to Crane. On January 1, 19X1, the capital account balances were: Tosti, $80,000; and Crane, $100,000. The net income for 19X1 was $68,000.

INSTRUCTIONS
1. Prepare the general journal entry dated December 31, 19X1 to record the agreed allowances for salaries.
2. Prepare the general journal entry to record the agreed allowance for interest.
3. Prepare the general journal entry to record distribution of the remaining balance of the net income.
4. Prepare the general journal entries to close the drawing accounts into the capital accounts, assuming that Tosti had drawings of $18,000 and Crane had drawings of $15,000 during the year.
5. Prepare a schedule showing the distribution of net income as it would appear on the income statement of Tosti and Crane.
6. Prepare a statement of partners' equities showing the changes that took place in the partners' capital accounts during the year, assuming no additional investments were made during that period.

PROBLEM 30-3 The partnership agreement of Greta Weil and Alicia Warren provides that net income and net losses for the year are to be divided as follows.

	WEIL	WARREN
Monthly salary	$700	$600
Interest on beginning capital balance	7%	7%
Ratio for division of balance	70%	30%

The balances of the capital accounts as of January 1, 19X1 were $40,000 for Weil and $50,000 for Warren. During 19X1 both partners withdrew their monthly salary allowances, and the withdrawals were charged to the drawing accounts.

INSTRUCTIONS Give the general journal entries on December 31, 19X1, necessary to record the net income or net loss distribution and to close the drawing accounts into the partners' capital accounts if:

1. The net income for the year is $48,000, as shown by the balance in the Revenue and Expense Summary account after all revenues and expenses have been closed into it.
2. The net income for the year is $4,000.
3. The net loss for the year is $6,000.

PROBLEM 30-4 On January 1, 19X2, the capital accounts of partners James Black and Walter Vollney show balances of $20,000 and $10,000, respectively. On that date the partners agree to admit Ralph Rabb as a partner in the business. Rabb is to pay $10,000 under the conditions described below. The profit (or loss) ratio is Black $\frac{2}{3}$, Vollney $\frac{1}{3}$.

INSTRUCTIONS In general journal form, give separate entries to record the admission of Rabb into the partnership on January 1, 19X2, under each of the following independent conditions.

a. Rabb pays Black for one-half of Black's interest.
b. Rabb receives credit for the actual amount invested in the firm.
c. Rabb acquires a one-third interest in the equity, a bonus being allowed.
d. Rabb acquires a one-third interest in the equity, goodwill being recorded.
e. Rabb acquires a one-fifth interest in the equity, a bonus being allowed.
f. Rabb acquires a one-fifth interest in the equity, goodwill being recorded.

Alternate problems

PROBLEM 30-1A The partnership of Alan Rubino and Bruce Meng has earned a net income of $30,000 for the year ended December 31, 19X2. Under the terms of the partnership agreement, Rubino is authorized to withdraw $1,000 a month and Meng $800 a month, in anticipation of profits. Each has withdrawn the maximum amount, which has been charged to his drawing account. By agreement, net income is to be shared two-thirds to Rubino and one-third to Meng.

INSTRUCTIONS
1. In general journal form, record the entry to transfer the net income to the capital accounts of the partners.
2. Give the general journal entries needed to close each partner's drawing account to his capital account.

PROBLEM 30-2A The partnership agreement of Jane Molina and David Morton provides for (a) allowances for salaries of $12,000 a year for Molina and $9,600 for Morton and (b) interest of 8 percent on each partner's invested capital at the beginning of the year. The remainder of the net income is to be distributed equally between the two partners. On January 1, 19X1, the capital account balances were: Molina, $24,000; and Morton, $56,000. The net income for 19X1 was $46,000.

INSTRUCTIONS
1. Prepare the general journal entry dated December 31, 19X1, to record the agreed allowances for salaries.
2. Prepare the general journal entry to record the agreed allowance for interest.
3. Prepare the general journal entry to record distribution of the remaining balance of the net income.
4. Prepare the general journal entries to close the drawing accounts into the capital accounts, assuming that the allowed salaries were withdrawn during the year.
5. Prepare a schedule showing the distribution of net income as it would appear on the income statement of Molina and Morton.
6. Prepare a statement of partners' equities showing the changes that took place in the partners' capital accounts during the year.

PROBLEM 30-3A

The partnership agreement of Maria Valdez and Irene Cruz provides that net income and net losses for the year are to be divided as follows.

	VALDEZ	CRUZ
Monthly salary	$1,000	$800
Interest on beginning capital balance	6%	6%
Ratio for division of balance	60%	40%

The balances of the capital accounts as of January 1, 19X1, were $100,000 for Valdez and $80,000 for Cruz. During 19X1 both partners withdrew their monthly salary allowances, and the withdrawals were charged to the drawing accounts.

INSTRUCTIONS
Give the general journal entries on December 31, 19X1, necessary to record the net income or net loss distribution and to close the drawing accounts into the partners' capital accounts if:

1. The net income for the year is $81,600, as shown by the balance in the Revenue and Expense Summary account after all revenues and expenses have been closed into it.
2. The net income for the year is $2,800.
3. The net loss for the year is $8,000.

PROBLEM 30-4A

Ray Martinez and Fred Simpson own the Rand Dry Cleaning Service. They are interested in expanding their operations into suburban areas and, in anticipation of this, have offered John Forbes an interest in the partnership for a payment by Forbes of $30,000 in cash. The capital account balances for

Martinez and Simpson on January 1, 19X1 are: Martinez, $45,000; Simpson, $35,000. Net income or net loss is shared equally.

INSTRUCTIONS Give the entries in general journal form to record the admission of Forbes to the partnership on January 1, 19X1, under each of the following independent conditions.

    a. Forbes pays Martinez for one-half of Martinez's interest in the partnership.
    b. Forbes receives credit for the actual amount invested in the firm.
    c. Forbes acquires a one-fourth interest, a bonus being allowed.
    d. Forbes acquires a one-fourth interest, goodwill being recorded.
    e. Forbes acquires a one-third interest, a bonus being allowed.
    f. Forbes acquires a one-third interest, goodwill being recorded.

UNIT 31
CHARACTERISTICS AND FORMATION OF A CORPORATION

Up to this point, you have studied the operations of two different types of businesses—a sole proprietorship and a partnership. Now we turn to another important form of business organization—the corporation. This unit discusses the basic characteristics of the corporation and explains how corporations are formed. Later units cover various aspects of corporate operations and the accounting procedures connected with them.

Legal Aspects of a Corporation

The organization and operation of a sole proprietorship form of business was explained in the discussion of the Modern Cleaning Shop and the Kent Novelty Company. The partnership form was covered in the presentation of the Style Clothing Store. Thousands of sole proprietorships and partnerships operate successfully, but these popular forms of organization do not meet the needs of all businesses. James Duncan is an example of a person who must explore other possible forms of business organization to solve his problems.

Duncan has been operating the Duncan Woodworking Shop for a number of years on a rather modest scale as a sole proprietorship. He has decided to concentrate his efforts on producing a high-quality wooden chair. He wants to increase the output of his shop in order to obtain greater economy in manufacturing and more efficiency in selling. To achieve these goals, Duncan needs more operating capital to buy new machinery, to build up larger inventories, and to extend more credit to customers.

Several of Duncan's friends are willing to invest as partners in his business, but he has put off a decision because he has some doubts about this arrangement. Although he wants the extra funds, he does not want to share operating control of the firm with people who know nothing about the business. Also, he does not wish to go further in debt.

Duncan's prospective backers have some doubts, too. They don't mind risking the money they invest, but they don't want to be responsible for other debts of the business. Although they don't mind letting Duncan run the business, they do want to have some voice in general policy. They would also like to be assured of a reasonable and regular return on their money.

After several exploratory discussions, Duncan and his friends decide to consult a lawyer who specializes in business law and taxation. The lawyer suggests that the group consider forming a *corporation* to carry on the expanded business operations.

Structure of a Corporation

Under the corporate plan, a *corporate charter* must be obtained from the state. As a corporation, the firm would be a legal entity separate from its owners. In exchange for their investment, the owners of the firm—known as *shareholders* or *stockholders*—would receive *shares of stock*. The owners could then participate in stockholders' meetings, elect a board of directors, and vote on certain questions of basic corporate policy.

The directors would formulate general operating policies and be responsible for seeing that the activities of the corporation were carried on. They would select officers and other top management personnel to handle everyday operations. The officers would hire employees and would make the day-to-day decisions necessary to operate the business.

The top management of a corporation might consist of the president, one or more vice presidents, a secretary, and a treasurer. (The top accounting official might be called the controller, or might be given some other title.) As the firm grows, there might be a need for several layers of management, including division managers, plant managers, department heads, and supervisors. The levels would depend on the nature and complexity of the firm's operations.

Characteristics of a Corporation

The lawyer points out to Duncan and his friends that the corporate form of organization—unlike the partnership form—would overcome their objections to investing and would provide other important advantages.

Limited Liability of Owners

As stockholders Duncan and his associates would have no personal liability for the corporation's debts. In the event of liquidation, the corporation's creditors must look to the assets of the firm to satisfy their claims, not to the owners' personal property. (Often, however, lending institutions require major stockholders in small corporations personally to guarantee repayment of loans made to the corporation.)

Owners Are Not Agents

The stockholders of a corporation are not empowered to act for the firm. Instead, the board of directors controls the corporation, and the corporate officers are in direct charge of operations. If Duncan were elected president by the board, he would have full responsibility for and control of operations. The other stockholders could, however, express their views at stockholders' meetings and might elect one or more of their number to membership on the board.

Continuous Existence

Potential investors are interested in knowing that operations continue indefinitely. The life of a corporation is not affected by the death, disability, or withdrawal of individual stockholders. (Any of these events would terminate a sole proprietorship or partnership.)

Transferability of Ownership Rights

The owners can sell their shares of stock without consulting or obtaining the consent of other stockholders. Thus Duncan's friends would be free to shift their investments if a better opportunity came along, provided they could find buyers for their shares.

Legal Basis The corporation is a special form of organization created by law. As previously mentioned, it is a legal entity separate from its stockholders. It can own property, be a party to contracts, sue and be sued in the courts, and otherwise carry on the business activities defined in its charter. Thus, the corporate form of organization allows the owners to do anything they may reasonably wish to do as individuals and yet gives them personal immunities, such as limited liability, not obtainable in a sole proprietorship or a partnership.

Corporate Income Tax Since the corporation is a creation of law, it is subject to certain formalities, regulations, and taxes that are not applied to partnerships and sole proprietorships. For instance, a corporation's profits are subject to federal income taxes. Profits paid to stockholders in the form of dividends are taxed a second time as part of the personal income of the recipients. (Under certain conditions and where there are relatively few stockholders, a corporation can choose not to pay the corporate income tax but instead be treated for tax purposes in much the same way as a partnership.)

State and local governments can also levy an income tax on corporations. In addition, most states require corporations to pay an annual *franchise tax* for the privilege of carrying on business in the state.

Forming a Corporation

When Duncan and his friends express their desire to organize a corporation, the lawyer explains the steps to be taken. (Requirements and procedures differ from state to state, but those listed below are typical.)

1. Three or more persons must apply to the designated state officer (usually the secretary of state) for a charter permitting the proposed corporation to do business.
2. When issued, the charter specifies the exact name, length of life (state laws often provide for unlimited life), rights and duties, and scope of operations of the corporation. The charter also sets forth the class and number of shares of stock that can be issued in exchange for money, property, or services.
3. The stockholders elect a board of directors. The board then selects officers, who hire employees and begin operating the business.
4. The capital stock issued by the corporation appears on its balance sheet as part of the owners' equity, which is usually called *stockholders' equity*.

Types of Stock

The decision about the classes of stock and number of shares must be made before the charter application can be filed. The lawyer for Duncan and his friends therefore suggests that the parties consider the various possibilities.

If there is only one class of stock, each share carries the same rights and privileges. In general, these rights are as follows.

One Class
1. The right to attend stockholders' meetings.
2. The right to vote in the election of directors and on certain other matters.
3. The right to receive dividends as declared by the board of directors.

4. The right to inspect the corporation's books and records for proper purposes at certain times and places.
5. The right to purchase a proportionate amount of any new stock issued at a later date.

Common Stock

When several classes of stock exist, one class is usually designated *common stock*. This stock normally has all the general rights and privileges, although other classes of stock may enjoy certain preferences over it.

Preferred Stock

One or more classes of stock may have certain preferred claims on the corporation's profits or on its assets in case of liquidation, or they may convey other special preferences that set them apart from the common stock. This kind of stock is known as *preferred stock*. In receiving special preferences, the owners of preferred stock may lose some of their general rights, such as the right to vote.

Liquidation Preferences on Preferred Stock. The terms of issue of preferred stock usually provide that in case of liquidation the preferred stockholders have a prior claim on assets. Often a *liquidation value* is assigned to the preferred stock. This means that after the creditors have been paid their claims, the preferred stockholders are paid the specified liquidation value for each share before any assets are distributed to common stockholders. The liquidation value of preferred stock is extended to include any cumulative dividends that may not have been paid. (Cumulative dividends are explained in the next section.) Because of its importance to users of financial statements, the total amount of liquidation preference on all preferred stock should be shown in the Stockholders' Equity section of the balance sheet.°

Dividends to Stockholders

The right to receive a share in the distribution of the corporation's profits is obviously one of the major incentives for investment. Therefore, Duncan's associates give careful thought to their positions under different types of dividend privileges. Stockholders receive part of a corporation's profits in the form of dividends only when the board of directors declares a dividend. The board has almost complete discretion, especially on common stock, in deciding whether to declare a dividend and how much it will be.

Dividends on Preferred Stock

One of the preferences often accorded preferred stock is a priority with respect to dividends. The exact nature of the priority is established by the preferred stock contract for each issue.

1. If the preferred stock is *cumulative* as to dividends, its owners must receive the stated dividend for both the current year and any prior years in which the stated dividend was not paid before the common stockholders can receive any dividends.
2. If the preferred stock is *noncumulative*, its stated dividend for a particular year must be paid in that year before dividends can be paid to common

---

° "Liquidation Preferences of Preferred Stock," *Opinions of the Accounting Principles Board, No. 10* (New York: American Institute of Certified Public Accountants, 1966), pars. 10 and 11.

stockholders. However, if no dividends are declared in one year, the next year represents a fresh start. This type of stock has no continuing rights to dividends for the year in which none were declared.
3. Preferred stock is *nonparticipating* unless otherwise stated on the stock certificate. When the stock is nonparticipating, the preferred stockholders receive only the dividend amount specified on the stock certificate.
4. Preferred stock may be *participating*, in which case preferred stockholders receive the regular preferred dividend and may also participate in additional dividends with the common stockholders.

Dividends on Common Stock

Dividends on common stock are paid only after dividend requirements for preferred stock have been met. The fewer the dividend privileges enjoyed by the preferred stockholders, the greater the dividends that the common stockholders can receive, especially in prosperous years.

Values of Capital Stock

Any experienced lawyer or financial adviser would quickly point out that a purely theoretical consideration of the pros and cons of different types of dividends has only limited usefulness. Even percentage rates (such as 6 percent) or stated dollar amounts of dividends (such as $6 a share) have little significance unless the amount invested or the value of the stock is known. A number of different terms are used in referring to the value of capital stock. These terms are discussed below.

Par Value

Par value is a figure selected by the organizers of the corporation to be assigned to each share of stock for accounting purposes. The par value, if any, is specified in the charter. It is often $100 or $50, but it may be any amount, such as $5, $1, or even less than $1 a share. Thus, when a $100 par value preferred stock (without specified extra privileges) is said to have a 10 percent dividend rate, a return of $10 a year is meant.

Stated Value

Laws in many states permit stock to be issued without par value. This type of stock is called *no-par value* stock. In this case the board of directors of the corporation may assign a *stated value* to the stock. When a stated value is established for no-par value stock, this figure is the amount credited to the capital stock account for each share issued. The stated value serves much the same purpose as par value. The practice of stating the amount of the annual dividend on preferred stock in dollars (such as $6 a share) is expedient with no-par value stock because there is no practical basis for applying a percentage rate to compute the dividend. When no-par value stock does not have a stated value, it is customary to credit the entire proceeds from the sale of the stock to the capital stock account.

Capital Stock on the Balance Sheet

As shown on page 562, the Stockholders' Equity section of the corporate balance sheet usually includes information that identifies the classes of stock, the number of shares authorized and issued for each class, their par value, and any special privileges carried by the stock.

Stockholders' Equity

Preferred Stock (8%, cumulative, participating, $100 par value, 1,000 shares authorized) At Par Value (500 shares issued)	$50,000
Common Stock (no-par value, with stated value $25, 4,000 shares authorized) At Stated Value (1,000 shares issued)	25,000
Total Stockholders' Equity	$75,000

Comparison of Dividend Provisions

Having supplied the basic background information about corporate stock financing to Duncan and his associates, the lawyer explains the effects of the various plans, privileges, and values of stock, using specific figures for each of the alternatives.

Plan A— Only Common Stock Issued

Assume that a corporation has only one class of stock—common stock. Assume also that 2,500 shares at $100 par value were authorized and that all 2,500 shares authorized were issued and remain outstanding.

Situation 1. The dividend declared by the board of directors depends on the corporate earnings and the need to keep profits (called *retained earnings*) for use in the business. A 6 percent dividend would amount to $15,000 a year (2,500 shares × $100 par value × 0.06).

Situation 2. Of course, the board has the right to *pass* the dividend (not pay it) or to declare a smaller dividend if conditions so warrant ($7,500, or 3 percent, instead of $15,000, for instance). If the board does declare a smaller dividend, the stockholders have to be content with the amount. Similarly, stockholders may be fortunate enough to receive a larger dividend if the directors see fit to declare one.

Plan B—Common and Preferred Stock Issued

The uncertainty of dividends described in Plan A is a risk of stock ownership that cannot be entirely avoided. However, preferred stock offers advantages that are attractive to certain types of investors. Assume that a corporation has both preferred and common stock issued and outstanding as follows.

Preferred Stock (8%, $100 par value, 500 shares)	$ 50,000
Common Stock (no-par value, stated value $50, 4,000 shares)	200,000
Total Capital Stock	$250,000

Situation 1. If the board of directors decides to distribute $15,000, the preferred stockholders will get first consideration. The owners of the 500 shares outstanding will receive a total of $4,000 (500 shares × $100 par value × 0.08), or $8 a share. This will leave $11,000 ($15,000 − $4,000) to be distributed to the common stockholders, who will receive $2.75 a share ($11,000 ÷ 4,000 shares).

Situation 2. If there is only $7,500 to distribute, the preferred stockholders will receive their full 8 percent, or $4,000, and the remaining $3,500 will allow a return of only $0.875 a share on the common stock ($3,500 ÷ 4,000 shares).

Situation 3. If there is only $2,000 to distribute, the preferred stockholders will receive it all—$4 a share ($2,000 ÷ 500). The remaining amount of dividends owed on the preferred stock ($4 a share) will not be paid since the stock is noncumulative. The common stockholders will receive nothing.

Plan C—Common and Cumulative Preferred Stock Issued

When business conditions are poor, preferred stockholders have a better chance for a return than do common stockholders. However, the preferred stockholders' chances can be further improved if the preferred stock is cumulative. Under this privilege, the $4 balance owed on each share of the 8 percent dividend remaining unpaid (discussed in the last paragraph) will be carried forward as a continuing claim into future periods.

Situation 1. Thus, if the board of directors has $7,000 to distribute in the next year and the preferred stock is cumulative, the preferred stockholders collect the $2,000 (500 × $4) in arrears, plus the regular dividend of $4,000 (500 × $100 × 0.08). This leaves only $1,000, or $0.25 a share, for the common stockholders.

In preparing financial statements, the total and the per-share amounts of cumulative preferred dividends not previously paid should be shown either on the face of the balance sheet or in footnotes to the statements.°

Situation 2. Of course, in good years, the common stockholders may enjoy very substantial gains. This time, suppose that the directors decide to distribute $34,000. If there is no balance owed to the preferred stockholders because of the cumulative privilege and if their stock is not participating, they will receive only the regular $4,000 (500 × $100 × 0.08). The balance of $30,000 will be divided among the common stockholders. The result will be a dividend of $7.50 a share ($30,000 ÷ 4,000)—a return of 15 percent on the $50 stated value, far greater than the return received by the preferred stockholders.

Plan D—Common and Cumulative Participating Preferred Stock Issued

Investors may be induced to purchase preferred stock in a company, even if present earnings and dividends are low, through the use of participating preferred stock. Under this plan the preferred stockholder receives the regular specified dividend and then shares in any additional dividends with the common stockholders, as provided by the terms of the preferred stock contract.

The exact terms of participation vary, but one common arrangement calls for the preferred stockholders to receive a dividend rate equal to that provided to the common stockholders. The preferred stockholders are first paid their regular preference dividend. Then common stockholders are paid a dividend at the same rate as the preference rate on the preferred stock. Any remaining dividends to be distributed will be allocated between the two classes of stockholders so that each receives the same rate.

° Ibid.

Suppose that in the preceding example the 500 shares of preferred stock carried the participating privilege (8 percent, $100 par value, cumulative, participating preferred). In order to distribute $30,000 or 15 percent to the owners of the 4,000 shares of common stock, as just described in Situation 2 of Plan C, provision must be made for a 15 percent return to the preferred stockholders. The latter will receive a regular 8 percent dividend and a further participating dividend of 7 percent, totaling $3,500, as follows.

To Preferred Stock	
8% Contract Rate (500 shares × $100 par value × 0.08)	$ 4,000
7% Participation (500 shares × $100 par value × 0.07)	3,500
15% Total to Preferred	$ 7,500
To Common Stock	
15% (4,000 × $50 stated value × 0.15)	30,000
Total Dividends Paid	$37,500

Thus, for the common stockholders to receive $30,000, a total dividend of $37,500 would have to be declared in order to meet the contractual demand that preferred stockholders receive the same dividend rate as common stockholders.

Other types of participation formulas for preferred stock are also used by some corporations.

Financing With Bonds

Besides obtaining funds through issuing common and preferred stock, corporations can obtain part of their funds by issuing bonds. Bonds are long-term liabilities of the corporation rather than stockholders' equity. They ordinarily carry a fixed rate of interest that may be somewhat lower than the dividend rate for preferred stock. In addition, interest paid on bonds is deductible in computing the federal income tax, while dividends are not deductible.

In practice, the funds for investment in corporate assets are raised through varying combinations of common stock, preferred stock, and bonds. Let us see how a typical combination financial structure might affect the rate of return earned on common stock under circumstances comparable to Situation 2 of Plan C. Suppose that total capital of $250,000 has been raised by the sale of the following securities.

100 Bonds (7% interest, $1,000 par value)	$100,000
500 Shares Preferred Stock (8%, $100 par value)	50,000
2,000 Shares Common Stock (no-par value, stated value $50)	100,000
Total Capital	$250,000

Assume that the company had profits of $52,000 before bond interest and before income taxes and that the company plans to distribute all profits. The amount available for distribution to stockholders, $36,000, is computed as shown on page 565. (Assume a hypothetical income tax rate of 20 percent.)

Net Income Before Income Taxes	$52,000
Less Bond Interest (7% × $100,000)	7,000
Net Income Before Income Taxes	$45,000
Less Income Taxes (assumed rate of 20%)	9,000
Net Income After Income Taxes	$36,000

If the company plans to distribute all available profits to stockholders, the $36,000 is allocated as follows.

To Preferred Stock	
500 Shares, 8% Contract Rate (500 × $100 par value × 0.08)	$ 4,000
To Common Stock	
2,000 Shares, Balance ($36,000 − $4,000)	32,000
	$36,000

The common stockholders in this combination now enjoy a return of $16 a share, or 32 percent, on the $50 stated value. The favorable outcome is due to the fact that the company's profits are higher than the contract rate of interest on the bonds and the rate paid as dividends on the preferred stock. This situation is called *trading on the equity.* In lean years such financing may be dangerous from the investors' standpoint because the prior fixed claim of bond interest expense may leave little or nothing for dividends to the stockholders. Moreover, even when the firm operates at a loss, the bondholders' interest must be paid in full.

Incorporating a Sole Proprietorship

Now that Duncan and his associates have a knowledge of the usual alternatives in corporate financing, they devise a capital structure to meet their specific needs. Based on capital requirements of $350,000, the prospective owners decide to use two classes of stock, preferred and common, as shown below.

Preferred Stock (8%, $100 par value,	
noncumulative and nonparticipating, 1,000 shares)	$100,000
Common Stock (no-par value, stated	
value $50, 5,000 shares)	250,000
Total Capital Stock	$350,000

Stock will be issued to Duncan in payment for the net assets of the Duncan Woodworking Shop. Stock will also be sold to Duncan's friends who have agreed to go into the venture with him. Duncan will be president of the new corporation.

The lawyer completes the application for a corporate charter for the new corporation, to be known as the Duncan Manufacturing Corporation. On December 31, 19X1, when the charter is received, the accounting records are set up and a memorandum entry is made in the general journal. This entry, shown on page 566, gives the details of the authorized capital stock.

19X1 Dec. 31	The Duncan Manufacturing Corp. has been organized to manufacture and market furniture and to carry on all necessary and convenient related activities. It is authorized to issue 5,000 shares of no-par value common stock ($50 stated value) and 1,000 shares of $100 par value 8% preferred stock that is noncumulative and nonparticipating.					

For permanent reference, the data relating to each authorized class of stock is entered on a separate ledger sheet. The information for the Duncan Manufacturing Corporation might be entered at the top of the ledger sheets as shown below.

Common Stock
No-Par Value
($50 Stated Value), 5,000 Shares Authorized   **No. 301**

DATE	EXPLANATION	POST. REF.	DEBIT	CREDIT	BALANCE	DR. CR.

Preferred Stock
8% Noncumulative, Nonparticipating
$100 Par Value, 1,000 Shares Authorized   **No. 311**

DATE	EXPLANATION	POST. REF.	DEBIT	CREDIT	BALANCE	DR. CR.

The books of the new corporation are now ready for transactions, including stock issues, to be recorded as they occur. However, before the Duncan Manufacturing Corporation can take over the assets and liabilities of the Duncan Woodworking Shop, the values shown on the shop's books must be examined and possibly adjusted to reflect the true current value of each item owned by the sole proprietorship. The situation is similar to that of a sole proprietor revaluing assets before entering into a partnership (see Unit 29).

Revaluation of Assets   The postclosing trial balance as of December 31, 19X1—the date the proprietorship is being terminated—serves as the starting point for the revaluation process. Duncan is interested in getting as much for his business as he can. The corporation wants to be sure that it is getting true value for its payment. Consequently, both parties will examine every account balance with extreme care in an effort to establish complete and fair values.

DUNCAN WOODWORKING SHOP
Postclosing Trial Balance
December 31, 19X1

ACCT. NO.	ACCOUNT NAME	DEBIT	CREDIT
101	Cash in Bank	2,500 00	
111	Accounts Receivable	4,500 00	
121	Inventory	6,000 00	
140	Land	5,000 00	
141	Building	20,000 00	
141A	Accumulated Depreciation—Building		4,000 00
142	Equipment	10,000 00	
142A	Accumulated Depreciation—Equipment		3,000 00
202	Accounts Payable		4,800 00
301	James Duncan, Capital		36,200 00
	Totals	48,000 00	48,000 00

At this stage, any gain or loss resulting from an adjustment or revaluation of assets will cause a corresponding increase or decrease in Duncan's capital. (If the business being incorporated were a partnership, the same procedures would be followed, except that the gain or loss resulting from the revaluation of the assets would be divided among the partners in their profit sharing ratio.)

Accounts Receivable

The first asset about which there are some reasonable doubts is accounts receivable. Duncan has previously used the direct charge-off method, so there is no Allowance for Bad Debts account in his general ledger. It is estimated that only $4,000 of the $4,500 shown in the Accounts Receivable account will be collected. The revised estimate of the value of the account indicates an expected loss of $500. This loss is charged to a new account called Gain or Loss on Asset Revaluation. A corresponding credit is made to Allowance for Bad Debts, since it is not known at this time just which accounts may prove uncollectible. The revaluation is formally recorded in the general journal of the Duncan Woodworking Shop, as shown below.

19 X1 Dec. 31	Gain or Loss on Asset Revaluation	409	500 00		
	Allowance for Bad Debts	111A		500 00	
	Reduced book value of accounts receivable by setting up an allowance for bad debts.				

Of course, the gain or loss resulting from revaluing each asset could be entered directly in the owner's capital account, as illustrated in Unit 29. However, when a number of revaluations are to be recorded, it is easier to use a Gain or Loss on Asset Revaluation account to assemble and summarize the changes. The net gain or loss is then transferred to the capital account of the

Inventory

owner of a sole proprietorship or is divided among the co-owners of a partnership according to the profit and loss ratio.

Some of the items carried in the inventory will not be useful in the operations of the new corporation and will have to be sold for less than their original cost. The merchandise is restated at its estimated value of $5,000 on the books of the proprietorship by a general journal entry debiting Gain or Loss on Asset Revaluation and crediting Inventory for $1,000, the amount of the expected loss.

Land

The value of land has generally risen in the area in which the Duncan property is located. Expert appraisers estimate that the current market value of Duncan's land is $7,500, rather than the $5,000 shown on the books. A general journal entry is made debiting Land for $2,500 and crediting Gain or Loss on Asset Revaluation for that amount.

Building

Building costs have also risen, and the current market value of the Duncan building is appraised at $18,000. The proprietorship records show that the building cost $20,000 and that the Accumulated Depreciation—Building account has a balance of $4,000. This leaves a book value of only $16,000. To increase the book value to the appraised value of $18,000, the Building account is debited for $2,000 and the Gain or Loss on Asset Revaluation account is credited for that amount. The necessary general journal entry is given below.

Date	Description	Post. Ref.	Debit	Credit
19 X1 Dec. 31	Building	141	2,000 00	
	Gain or Loss on Asset Revaluation	409		2,000 00
	Increased book value of building to estimated current market value.			

Equipment

It is further estimated that the equipment will be worth $7,000 to the new corporation. The books show a cost of $10,000 and accumulated depreciation of $3,000, which leaves a book value of $7,000. Thus, no adjustment is required in the value of the equipment.

Revaluation Account

When the four revaluation entries have been posted, the Gain or Loss on Asset Revaluation account has a credit balance of $3,000, as shown below.

Gain or Loss on Asset Revaluation No. 409

DATE	EXPLANATION	POST. REF.	DEBIT	CREDIT	BALANCE	DR. CR.
19 X1 Dec. 31		J12	500 00		500 00	Dr.
31		J12	1,000 00		1,500 00	Dr.
31		J12		2,500 00	1,000 00	Cr.
31		J12		2,000 00	3,000 00	Cr.

Since the Duncan Woodworking Shop is a sole proprietorship, the entire gain or loss on asset revaluation belongs to the owner, James Duncan. Therefore, the net gain of $3,000 is now transferred to his capital account by a general journal entry debiting Gain or Loss on Asset Revaluation and crediting James Duncan, Capital. The balance of Duncan's capital account is now $39,200. This figure represents the net assets after revaluation (assets, $44,000, minus liabilities, $4,800, equals capital, $39,200).

If the Duncan Woodworking Shop had been a partnership, the balance of the Gain or Loss on Asset Revaluation account would have been apportioned to the partners in their profit sharing ratio.

Transfer of Assets and Liabilities to the Corporation

Once the asset revaluations are recorded on the proprietorship books and the resulting gain or loss is transferred to the owner's capital account, the next step is to transfer the assets and liabilities to the corporation. This is done by making a compound entry in the general journal, as shown below. The entry debits an account receivable from the new corporation for the net value of the assets; debits Allowance for Bad Debts, the accumulated depreciation accounts, and Accounts Payable; and credits the asset accounts.

19X1				
Dec. 31	Receivable From Duncan Mfg. Corp.	112	39,200 00	
	Allowance for Bad Debts	111A	500 00	
	Accumulated Depreciation—Building	141A	4,000 00	
	Accumulated Depreciation—Equipment	142A	3,000 00	
	Accounts Payable	202	4,800 00	
	Cash in Bank	101		2,500 00
	Accounts Receivable	111		4,500 00
	Inventory	121		5,000 00
	Land	140		7,500 00
	Building	141		22,000 00
	Equipment	142		10,000 00
	Transferred proprietorship assets and liability to the new corporation.			

Receipt of Stock From the Corporation

The new Duncan Manufacturing Corporation proposes to issue shares of its stock for the revalued net assets of the Duncan Woodworking Shop, and Duncan has agreed to accept such stock in payment. Preferred stock is issued at par for $20,000 of the assets (200 shares of stock at $100 par value). An additional 384 shares of no-par value common stock with a stated value of $50 a share are issued for the balance of the assets, $19,200. The entry for the receipt of this stock on the books of the proprietorship is shown on page 570.

Distribution of Stock to the Proprietor

At this point all but three of the proprietorship's accounts have been closed. The remaining open accounts are the two asset accounts representing the two kinds of stock received from the corporation and the James Duncan, Capital

	19 X1				
	Dec. 31	Common Stock of Duncan Mfg. Corp.	113	19,200 00	
		Preferred Stock of Duncan Mfg. Corp.	114	20,000 00	
		Receivable From Duncan Mfg. Corp.	112		39,200 00
		Received 384 shares of common stock (at $50 a share) and 200 shares of preferred stock at par ($100 a share) in payment for net assets of Duncan Woodworking Shop.			

account. The final entry, shown below, records the distribution of stock to Duncan and closes all remaining accounts. This entry brings the proprietorship business to an end.

	19 X1				
	Dec. 31	James Duncan, Capital	301	39,200 00	
		Common Stock of Duncan Mfg. Corp.	113		19,200 00
		Preferred Stock of Duncan Mfg. Corp.	114		20,000 00
		Distributed to Duncan the stock received in payment for the net assets of the Duncan Woodworking Shop, completing the liquidation of the proprietorship.			

Acquisition of Assets and Liabilities by the Corporation

The acquisition of the assets and liabilities of the Duncan Woodworking Shop is now recorded on the books of the Duncan Manufacturing Corporation, and a record is made of the stock issued in payment. Identical account titles are used in setting up these acquisitions on the corporation's books, and the same amounts are used—with two exceptions. The former accumulated depreciation accounts are not entered in the corporation's books. Instead, the related assets are recorded at their book value. The following two accounts are affected.

1. Building, recorded at $18,000 ($22,000 cost − $4,000 accumulated depreciation).
2. Equipment, recorded at $7,000 ($10,000 cost − $3,000 accumulated depreciation).

However, note that Accounts Receivable (a control account) and the Allowance for Bad Debts account are both shown on the corporation's books. The balance of Accounts Receivable must be recorded in full because it is not yet known which customers' accounts will prove to be uncollectible and all the individual accounts in the subsidiary ledger have been transferred to the corporation. The control account balance must agree with the total of the balances in the accounts receivable subsidiary ledger. The Allowance for Bad Debts account continues to reflect the estimate that $500 of the accounts receivable will not be paid.

  The entry made in the general journal of the new corporation records the assets and liabilities taken over and acknowledges a liability to the proprietorship for the amount of the net assets. This record, which is shown below, follows the memorandum opening entry that was explained previously.

19X1 Dec. 31	Cash in Bank	101	2,500 00	
	Accounts Receivable	111	4,500 00	
	Inventory	121	5,000 00	
	Land	140	7,500 00	
	Building	141	18,000 00	
	Equipment	142	7,000 00	
	Allowance for Bad Debts	111A		500 00
	Accounts Payable	202		4,800 00
	Due to Duncan Woodworking Shop	203		39,200 00
	Recorded the assets and liability taken over from the Duncan Woodworking Shop, for which capital stock is to be issued.			

Issuance of Stock

To complete the purchase of the Duncan Woodworking Shop, stock is issued as agreed—384 shares of common stock at $50 a share and 200 shares of preferred stock at par, $100 a share. This entry is made in the general journal, as shown below.

19X1 Dec. 31	Due to Duncan Woodworking Shop	203	39,200 00	
	Common Stock	301		19,200 00
	Preferred Stock	311		20,000 00
	Issued stock in payment for net assets of the Duncan Woodworking Shop: 384 shares of common stock at $50 a share; 200 shares of preferred stock at par ($100).			

Organization Costs

Bringing a new corporation into existence involves a variety of expenses, such as legal fees, charter fees to the state, and the costs of preparing stock certificates. These expenses are ordinarily paid soon after the corporation receives its charter. They are charged to an intangible asset account, usually called Organization Costs. This account is set up initially as an asset because it is a necessary cost of bringing the corporation into existence, rather than an operating expense.

It has often been argued that since organization costs are incurred to benefit the corporation over its entire life, they should be carried indefinitely on the balance sheet as an intangible asset and should be charged off only when the corporation is liquidated. However, since organization costs would have no sales value if the corporation were to liquidate, accountants follow the conservative practice of charging the amount off to expense over a period of several years.

Generally accepted accounting principles permit organization costs to be amortized over a period of up to 40 years.* However, these costs are often charged off over a 5-year period. This period is commonly used because, for federal income tax purposes, organization costs can be amortized over a period of not less than 60 months (5 years). The procedure is illustrated in Unit 33.

Suppose that the Duncan Manufacturing Corporation incurred organization costs totaling $500. Suppose also that these costs were paid on December 31, immediately after the corporation acquired the assets and liabilities of the proprietorship business. In general journal form, this transaction would be recorded as shown below.

19X1				
Dec. 31	Organization Costs	191	500 00	
	Cash in Bank	101		500 00
	Recorded payment of legal fees, charter fee, and engraving cost of stock certificates to get corporation organized.			

Balance Sheet Immediately After Organization

Immediately following the organization of the Duncan Manufacturing Corporation, a balance sheet can be prepared. This balance sheet will reflect the acquisition of the Duncan Woodworking Shop by the issuance of stock and the payment of organization costs. The statement on page 573 summarizes the firm's status before operations begin and will serve as a valuable basis for later comparisons.

principles and procedures summary

A corporation is organized under state law to carry on activities permitted by its charter. Ownership is evidenced by shares of stock. Stockholders owning voting stock elect a board of directors, which selects officers who hire employees and direct the operations of the business.

Stocks may have a par value specified in the charter. If they do not have a specified par value, they are called no-par value stock. The directors may assign to no-par stock a stated value, which is used for accounting purposes. Preferred stockholders enjoy certain privileges, often including priority in distribution of dividends. Cumulative and participating provisions may give further advantage to the preferred stockholders.

---

*"Accounting for Intangible Assets," *Opinions of the Accounting Principles Board*, No. 17 (New York: American Institute of Certified Public Accountants, 1970), pars. 28 and 29.

DUNCAN MANUFACTURING CORPORATION
Balance Sheet
December 31, 19X1

Assets

Current Assets
  Cash $ 2,000
  Accounts Receivable $ 4,500
  Less Allowance for Bad Debts   500   4,000
  Inventory   5,000
    Total Current Assets $11,000
Fixed Assets
  Land $ 7,500
  Building   18,000
  Equipment   7,000
    Total Fixed Assets   32,500
Intangible Assets
  Organization Costs   500
Total Assets $44,000

Liabilities and Stockholders' Equity

Current Liabilities
  Accounts Payable $ 4,800
Stockholders' Equity
  Preferred Stock (8%, $100 par value,
    1,000 shares authorized)
  At Par Value (200 shares issued) $20,000
  Common Stock (no-par value, stated value $50,
    5,000 shares authorized)
  At Stated Value (384 shares issued)   19,200
    Total Stockholders' Equity   39,200
Total Liabilities and Stockholders' Equity $44,000

Corporate assets can be bought with funds obtained from the sale of bonds as well as the sale of various types of stock. Common stockholders may benefit when preferred stock or bonds are issued and profits are greater than required for paying the interest on the bonds or the dividends on the preferred shares.

When a new corporation receives its charter, a memorandum entry is usually made in the general journal setting forth the details relating to each class of authorized stock. In turn, separate general ledger accounts are set up for each class of stock authorized, and the data pertaining to each is recorded in the general ledger for future reference.

When a partnership or proprietorship is to incorporate, the accountant's first step is to adjust and close the books of the old business. Asset accounts are adjusted to reflect current values. The gain or loss resulting from asset revaluations is transferred to the owner's capital account or to the capital accounts of the partners in their profit sharing ratio.

If an existing business is being purchased by the new corporation, the values of the assets and liabilities being assumed are recorded in the corporation's general journal. The excess of the assets over the liabilities represents the amount that the corporation owes to the former owner or owners. This balance can be paid in stock, in cash, or in other property.

Certain costs are usually incurred in organizing a corporation. These organization costs are ordinarily paid by the corporation. They are charged to an intangible asset account and amortized to expense over a few years' time.

MANAGERiAl implicATioNs

It is essential that managers have a clear idea of the nature of a corporation, its rights and limitations, and how the corporation differs from other forms of business organization in order to make a rational selection of the business form to be used. For example, managers should know that the corporation is a separate legal entity apart from its owners, that it has continuous existence regardless of changes in ownership, and that owners have limited liability and are free to dispose of their stock without consulting other stockholders. Managers should also understand the corporation's potential obligations with reference to the payment of taxes and the regulation of operations. High taxes and stringent regulations may make it unprofitable, if not impossible, to operate as intended.

Gains and losses on assets being transferred to a corporation should be recognized on the books of the sole proprietorship or partnership from which the assets are being transferred. These gains or losses rightly belong to the proprietor or to the partners in proportion to their profit sharing ratio. It is also essential to corporate management that assets be realistically valued so that the true measure of their worth can be made and so that the corporation's profitability can be properly computed and evaluated.

MANAGERiAl discussioN quesTioNs

1. What legal characteristics and limitations of a corporation are of special significance to its management?
2. Would management generally expect to pay a higher rate or a lower rate of dividends on preferred stock than the rate of interest necessary on bonds? Explain.
3. Why would management be interested in issuing no-par value stock?
4. A group of individuals are interested in forming a corporation. Explain in general terms the usual steps necessary to do this.
5. Explain the difference between preferred stock and common stock. Why is this difference important to management?

6. Why should the management of a corporation be concerned about the realistic valuation of assets transferred to the firm?
7. Why didn't the Duncan Manufacturing Corporation pick up the accumulated depreciation accounts from the books of the sole proprietorship? Was this a management decision?
8. Why would the accountant urge the Duncan Manufacturing Corporation to charge off its organization costs over a period of several years?

application of principles

PROBLEM 31-1 The Delta Corporation has issued and has outstanding 10,000 shares of $50 par value common stock and 1,000 shares of $100 par value 9 percent preferred stock. The board of directors voted to distribute $4,000 as dividends in 19X1, $12,000 in 19X2, and $60,000 in 19X3.

INSTRUCTIONS Compute the total dividend and the dividend for each share paid to preferred stockholders and common stockholders each year under the following assumed situations.

Case A: The preferred stock is nonparticipating and noncumulative.
Case B: The preferred stock is cumulative and nonparticipating.
Case C: The preferred stock is participating and noncumulative. Under terms of the preferred stock contract, in any one year the regular 9 percent dividend is paid to preferred stockholders. Then common stockholders are paid a 9 percent dividend. Finally, all remaining dividends are shared on a proportionate basis between preferred and common stockholders.

PROBLEM 31-2 This problem consists of two parts.
A. A portion of the Stockholders' Equity section of the Wayne Corporation's balance sheet as of December 31, 19X5, appears below. Dividends have not been paid for the years 19X3 and 19X4. There has been no change in the number of shares of stock issued and outstanding during these years. Assume that the board of directors of the Wayne Corporation declares a dividend of $11,900 after completing operations for the year 19X5.

> Stockholders' Equity
> Preferred Stock (8%, cumulative, $100 par value, 1,000
>   shares authorized)
>   At Par Value (700 shares issued) $ 70,000
> Common Stock (no-par value, with stated value of $50,
>   5,000 shares authorized)
>   At Stated Value (3,000 shares issued)   150,000

INSTRUCTIONS 1. Compute the total amount of the dividend to be distributed to the preferred stockholders.

2. Compute the amount of the dividend to be paid on each share of preferred stock.
3. Compute the total amount of the dividend available to be distributed to the common stockholders.
4. Compute the amount of the dividend to be paid on each share of common stock.
5. Compute the amount of dividends in arrears (if any) that the preferred stockholders may expect from future declarations of dividends.
6. Compute the amount of dividends in arrears (if any) that the common stockholders may expect from future declarations of dividends.

B. Assume that the board of directors of the Wayne Corporation declares a dividend of $28,800 instead of $11,900 after operations of the year 19X5 are completed. Use the information given in Part A in solving this part.

INSTRUCTIONS
1. Compute the total amount of the dividend to be distributed to the preferred stockholders.
2. Compute the amount of the dividend to be paid on each share of preferred stock.
3. Compute the total amount of the dividend available to be distributed to the common stockholders.
4. Compute the amount of the dividend to be paid on each share of common stock.
5. Compute the amount of dividends in arrears (if any) that the preferred stockholders may expect from future declarations of dividends.
6. Compute the amount of dividends in arrears (if any) that the common stockholders may expect from future declarations of dividends.

PROBLEM 31-3 The Firth Corporation is organized for the purpose of producing fire extinguishers. Authorization has been granted for the issuance of 10,000 shares of 9 percent preferred, noncumulative, nonparticipating stock with a par value of $50 and 30,000 shares of no-par value common stock with a stated value of $35.

INSTRUCTIONS Prepare the Stockholders' Equity section of the corporation's balance sheet as it would appear after issuance of 7,500 shares of the preferred stock and 20,000 shares of the common stock. Assume that the preferred stock was sold at par value and the common stock at stated value.

PROBLEM 31-4 A group of individuals is forming a corporation. Two possible financing structures are being considered.

1. The issuance of 3,000 shares of no-par value common stock at $100 a share, which will bring in $300,000.
2. The issuance of 2,000 shares of no-par value common stock for $200,000 and the issuance of 8 percent bonds payable at a par value of $100,000.

INSTRUCTIONS Assume an income tax rate of 20 percent. Compute the net income or net loss for each share of common stock under each financing method if the net income, before interest and taxes, for the first year is:

1. $36,000
2. $4,000

PROBLEM 31-5 Anthony Coda and Paul Wilson are equal partners in C and W Motors, which sells used cars and operates an automobile repair service. Net income and losses are shared equally. Wilson expresses a desire to retire from the business. Therefore, Coda joins with Harold Mason, Frank Mason, and Sharon Neimer to form a corporation to be known as Economy Motors Corporation, for the purpose of continuing the business activities.

The new corporation is authorized to issue 1,000 shares of $100 par value 9 percent preferred stock that is noncumulative and nonparticipating and 2,000 shares of no-par value common stock with a stated value of $50 a share. It is mutually agreed that the books of C and W Motors will be closed on December 31, 19X1, that Coda and Wilson will each be permitted to withdraw $10,000 in cash, that certain assets will be revalued, and that Economy Motors Corporation will then take over all remaining assets and assume all liabilities. In payment for the business, Economy Motors Corporation will issue 200 shares of preferred stock to Coda and 200 shares of preferred stock to Wilson, plus a sufficient number of shares of common stock to each partner to equal the balance of his capital account. Any amount of less than $50 that remains in either account will be paid in cash. The balance sheet accounts of C and W Motors as of December 31, 19X1, are shown on the postclosing trial balance given below.

C AND W MOTORS
Postclosing Trial Balance
December 31, 19X1

Acct. No.	Account Name	Debit	Credit
101	Cash in Bank	$ 24,050	
111	Accounts Receivable	12,720	
111A	Allowance for Bad Debts		$ 2,120
121	Parts and Accessories Inventory	12,750	
122	Used Car Inventory	22,700	
140	Land	12,000	
141	Building	33,000	
141A	Accumulated Depr.—Building		13,870
142	Repair Equipment	8,720	
142A	Accumulated Depr.—Repair Equipment		2,170
202	Accounts Payable		17,860
301	Anthony Coda, Capital		44,960
302	Paul Wilson, Capital		44,960
	Totals	$125,940	$125,940

INSTRUCTIONS
1. Open general ledger accounts for C and W Motors, and record the December 31, 19X1, balances.
2. Record in general journal form the withdrawal in cash of $10,000 each by Coda and Wilson. Begin the entries for this problem on journal page 12. As each entry is recorded, post it to the appropriate general ledger accounts.
3. Record the following revaluations of assets. Open a Gain or Loss on Asset Revaluation 409 account to reflect all changes in values.
   a. The accounts receivable are estimated to have a book value of $8,600.
   b. The parts and accessories inventory has a current value of $10,950.
   c. The land has an appraised value of $20,000.
   d. The building is appraised at $24,000.
   e. The repair equipment has an appraised value of $7,100.
4. Record the entry to transfer the net gain or loss to the partners' capital accounts. Divide it equally between the accounts.
5. Record the withdrawal of equal amounts of cash by Coda and Wilson to round off their capital accounts so that they can be closed by the receipt of stock as agreed.
6. Record the entry to transfer the assets and liabilities of C and W Motors to the corporation. Open a new account—Receivable From Economy Motors Corporation 112.
7. Record receipt of the number of shares of preferred and common stock required to pay for C and W Motors under the terms of the agreement. Open accounts for Common Stock of Economy Motors Corporation 113 and Preferred Stock of Economy Motors Corporation 114.
8. Record the distribution of the shares of preferred and common stock to the partners. After this entry is posted, all C and W Motors accounts should be closed.
9. In the corporation's general journal, record a memorandum entry describing the corporation's formation on December 31, 19X1.
10. Record general journal entries as of December 31 to show the takeover of the assets and liabilities of the partnership and the issuance of stock in payment to Coda (Certificates C-2 and P-2) and Wilson (Certificates C-1 and P-1). Use the same account titles that the partnership used for assets and liabilities. Also use the following new account titles: Due to C and W Motors 203, Common Stock 301, and Preferred Stock 311. (Save your working papers for use in Problem 31-6.)

PROBLEM 31-6 This is a continuation of Problem 31-5. In addition to the transactions of the Economy Motors Corporation that you recorded in Problem 31-5, the transactions shown on page 579 took place on December 31, 19X1.

INSTRUCTIONS
1. Prepare the general journal entries to record the given transactions.
2. Prepare the opening balance sheet as of January 1, 19X2, for the Economy Motors Corporation.

TRANSACTIONS ON DECEMBER 31, 19X1

1. Cash was received as follows from purchasers of capital stock, and the stock was issued. (Use a separate entry for the dealings with each investor.)

    Harold Mason, 50 shares of preferred stock at $100 a share and 100 shares of common stock at $50 a share.

    Frank Mason, 50 shares of preferred stock at $100 a share and 100 shares of common stock at $50 a share.

    Sharon Neimer, 200 shares of preferred stock at $100 a share.

2. Organization expenses of $1,500 were paid in cash. (Debit Organization Costs 191.)

PROBLEM 31-7

A group of investors recently formed the Oregon Corporation, which manufactures paper products.

INSTRUCTIONS

1. Record in general journal form the selected transactions shown below that occurred during the first month of the Oregon Corporation's existence.
2. What disposition should be made of the balance in the Organization Costs account of the Oregon Corporation?

TRANSACTIONS FOR JANUARY 19X1

Jan. 4 Issued 80 shares of $100 par value common stock to the promoters for their work in forming the corporation.

9 Issued 14 shares of $100 par value common stock to an attorney for his work in organizing the corporation.

13 Paid the secretary of state $25 as a fee to secure the corporation's charter.

Alternate problems

PROBLEM 31-1A

The West Corporation has issued and has outstanding 2,000 shares of $75 par value common stock and 2,000 shares of $50 par value 8 percent preferred stock. The board of directors voted to distribute $3,000 as dividends in 19X1, $10,000 in 19X2, and $51,000 in 19X3.

INSTRUCTIONS

Compute the total dividend and the dividend for each share paid to preferred stockholders and common stockholders each year under the following assumed situations.

Case A: The preferred stock is nonparticipating and noncumulative.
Case B: The preferred stock is cumulative and nonparticipating.
Case C: The preferred stock is participating and noncumulative. Under terms of the preferred stock contract, in any one year the regular 8 percent dividend is paid to preferred stockholders. Then common stockholders are paid an 8 percent dividend. Finally, all remaining dividends are shared on a proportionate basis between preferred and common stockholders.

PROBLEM 31-2A This problem consists of two parts.

A. A portion of the Stockholders' Equity section of the Mineda Corporation's balance sheet as of December 31, 19X2, appears below. Dividends have not been paid for the year 19X1. There has been no change in the number of shares of stock issued and outstanding during 19X1 or 19X2. Assume that the board of directors of the corporation declared a dividend of $13,000 after completing operations for the year 19X2.

Stockholders' Equity
Preferred Stock (8%, cumulative, $50 par value,
    10,000 shares authorized)
    At Par Value (4,000 shares issued) $200,000
Common Stock (par value $25 per share, 15,000
    shares authorized)
    At Par Value (10,000 shares issued)   250,000

INSTRUCTIONS
1. Compute the total amount of the dividend to be distributed to the preferred stockholders.
2. Compute the amount of the dividend to be paid on each share of preferred stock.
3. Compute the total amount of the dividend available to be distributed to the common stockholders.
4. Compute the amount of the dividend to be paid on each share of common stock.
5. Compute the amount of dividends in arrears (if any) that the preferred stockholders may expect from future declarations of dividends.
6. Compute the amount of dividends in arrears (if any) that the common stockholders may expect from future declarations of dividends.

B. Assume that after operations for 19X2 are completed, the board of directors declares a dividend of $74,000 instead of $13,000. Use the information given in Part A in solving this part.

INSTRUCTIONS
1. Compute the total amount of the dividend to be distributed to the preferred stockholders.
2. Compute the amount of the dividend to be paid on each share of preferred stock.
3. Compute the total amount of the dividend available to be distributed to the common stockholders.
4. Compute the amount of the dividend to be paid on each share of common stock.
5. Compute the amount of dividends in arrears (if any) that the preferred stockholders may expect from future declarations of dividends.
6. Compute the amount of dividends in arrears (if any) that the common stockholders may expect from future declarations of dividends.

PROBLEM 31-3A City Corporation has been authorized to issue 20,000 shares of 10 percent noncumulative, nonparticipating preferred stock with a par value of $100 and 50,000 shares of no-par value common stock with a stated value of $50.

INSTRUCTIONS Prepare the Stockholders' Equity section of the corporation's balance sheet as it will appear after issuance of 12,000 shares of the preferred stock and 18,000 shares of the common stock. Assume that the preferred stock was sold at par value and the common stock at stated value.

PROBLEM 31-4A The Emery Corporation earned net income (after taxes) of $25,000 in 19X1. Its capital structure on December 31, 19X1, is shown in part below. The corporation has an expansion plan costing $120,000. It is considering raising funds through (a) issuing 1,000 additional shares of common stock at $120 a share or (b) issuing $120,000 of 8 percent bonds payable. Assume that additional corporate income will be taxed at a rate of 30 percent and that the bond interest can be deducted in computing the income tax.

> Stockholders' Equity
> Common Stock ($100 par value, 5,000 shares authorized)
>   At Par Value (4,000 shares outstanding) $400,000

INSTRUCTIONS
1. Assume that the plant expansion would result in increased revenue (before taxes) of $30,000. Show the effects on net income per share of common stock if the financing is carried out under each of the proposed methods.
2. Assume that the expansion would result in increased revenue (before taxes) of only $10,000. Show the effects on net income per share of common stock if the financing is carried out under each of the methods.

PROBLEM 31-5A Randall Stone has been operating the Stone Supply Store as a sole proprietorship. The postclosing trial balance shown below was prepared after the books were closed at the end of the firm's fiscal year on December 31, 19X1.

Stone and three friends have decided to form the Stone Corporation and take over the operation of the Stone Supply Store on December 31, 19X1. The Accounts Receivable account is to be revalued at $4,400, Merchandise Inventory at $30,000, and Equipment at $2,100. Stone is to receive 200 shares of Stone Corporation preferred stock at par value ($100) and sufficient $50 par value common shares to cover his adjusted net investment.

STONE SUPPLY STORE
Postclosing Trial Balance
December 31, 19X1

Acct. No.	Account Name	Debit	Credit
101	Cash in Bank	$ 6,000	
111	Accounts Receivable	4,750	
111A	Allowance for Bad Debts		$ 250
121	Merchandise Inventory	31,000	
131	Equipment	2,900	
131A	Accumulated Depreciation—Equipment		1,100
202	Accounts Payable		3,300
301	Randall Stone, Capital		40,000
	Totals	$44,650	$44,650

INSTRUCTIONS
1. Open general ledger accounts for the Stone Supply Store, and record the December 31 balances.
2. Give the general journal entries necessary to record the following events. As each entry is made, post it to the appropriate accounts.
   a. Revaluing the accounts on the books and transferring the net gain or loss on asset revaluation to the Randall Stone, Capital account. Use an account called Gain or Loss on Asset Revaluation 409. Begin entries on journal page 12.
   b. Transferring the proprietorship's revalued assets and liabilities to the corporation. Set up an account called Receivable From Stone Corporation 112.
   c. Receiving stock from the Stone Corporation: 200 shares of $100 par value preferred at par and common stock of $50 par value to settle the Receivable From Stone Corporation account. Set up the accounts Common Stock of Stone Corporation 113 and Preferred Stock of Stone Corporation 114.
   d. Distributing stock to Randall Stone. (After this entry is posted, all the proprietorship accounts should be closed.)
3. In the corporation's general journal, record a memorandum entry describing the formation of the corporation on December 31, 19X1. The corporation is authorized to issue 2,000 shares of $50 par value common stock and 1,000 shares of $100 par value 7 percent preferred stock that is noncumulative and nonparticipating.
4. Record general journal entries as of December 31 to show the takeover of the assets and liabilities of the proprietorship and the issuance of stock in payment to Randall Stone (Certificates C-1 and P-1). Use the same account titles that the proprietorship used for assets and liabilities. Also use the following new account titles: Due to Stone Supply Store 202, Common Stock 301, and Preferred Stock 311.

(**Note:** Save your working papers for use in Problem 31-6A.)

PROBLEM 31-6A

This problem is a continuation of Problem 31-5A. In addition to the transactions of the Stone Corporation that you recorded in Problem 31-5A, the transactions shown below took place on December 31, 19X1.

INSTRUCTIONS
1. Prepare the general journal entries to record the given transactions.
2. Prepare the opening balance sheet as of January 1, 19X2, for the Stone Corporation.

TRANSACTIONS FOR DECEMBER 31, 19X1
1. Cash was received from John Arroyo for the purchase of capital stock, and the stock was issued as follows:
   Common stock, 100 shares at $50 a share.
   Preferred stock, 70 shares at $100 a share.
2. Randall Stone was issued 15 shares of common stock to pay for his services in organizing the corporation. It was agreed that $750 is a fair value for his services. (Debit Organization Costs 191.)

PROBLEM 31-7A

The Kansas Corporation was formed by a group of investors.

INSTRUCTIONS

1. Record in general journal form the selected transactions shown below that occurred during the first month of the Kansas Corporation's existence.
2. What disposition should be made of the balance in the Organization Costs account of the Kansas Corporation?

TRANSACTIONS FOR JANUARY 19X2

Jan. 5 Issued 100 shares of $20 par value common stock to the promoters for their work in forming the corporation.

8 Issued 30 shares of $20 par value common stock to an attorney for his work in organizing the corporation.

8 Paid the secretary of state $50 as a fee to secure the corporation's charter.

UNIT 32

CAPITAL STOCK TRANSACTIONS; CORPORATE RECORDS

The records needed by a business vary with the nature of its activities and the form of its organization. The accounting records of a typical corporation include most of the accounts, journals, and ledgers that you have been studying. However, corporations must keep some additional records. These records are discussed in the present unit.

Corporate Records

The type of owners' equity (stockholders' equity) that a corporation has requires more elaborate recording than that needed for owner's equity in a sole proprietorship or partnership. Not only does the corporation have to keep detailed records of the stockholders' equity, but it must also keep special corporate records such as minutes of meetings of stockholders and directors, corporate bylaws, stock certificate books, stock ledgers, and stock transfer records. These corporate records and procedures will be explained by tracing the various steps of stock issuance followed by the newly organized Duncan Manufacturing Corporation.

Articles of Incorporation

A number of provisions in the approved articles of incorporation (corporate charter) relate to the firm's capital structure. It is apparent that the nature and extent of the owners' equity will be directly affected by the authority granted or limitations imposed with regard to the following items.

1. The nature and amount of capital stock authorized.
2. The nature of the business.
3. The property to be acquired.
4. The powers of the corporation.
5. The names, addresses, and investment pledges of incorporators.

The articles of incorporation of the Duncan Manufacturing Corporation include the following provisions concerning each of the above.

1. Capital stock authorized. Total authorized capital stock consists of 5,000 shares of no-par value common stock with a stated value of $50, and 1,000 shares of $100 par value 8 percent preferred stock, noncumulative and nonparticipating.

2. Nature of the business. The firm is to manufacture and market furniture.
3. Property to be acquired. The corporation may acquire whatever property is necessary or convenient for carrying out corporate purposes.
4. Powers of the corporation. The corporation is granted power to do whatever is appropriate in conducting the stated business activities and purposes. No length of life is specified.
5. Incorporators. The incorporators and the number of shares they agree to purchase (common stock at $50, preferred stock at par value) are shown below.

	COMMON STOCK	PREFERRED STOCK
James Duncan	400 shares	200 shares
Ralph East	100 shares	100 shares
Mary Fields	100 shares	100 shares

Issuing Stock to the Incorporators

The first stock issued by the corporation includes the 384 shares of common and 200 shares of preferred allowed to James Duncan in payment for the assets and liabilities of the Duncan Woodworking Shop. Now Duncan must buy 16 more shares of common stock at $50 a share to fulfill his agreement as one of the original incorporators.

Suppose he purchases the remaining 16 shares on January 2, 19X2, paying cash. This receipt would ordinarily be recorded in the corporation's cash receipts journal. However, to simplify the illustration, we will show the issuance of stock through general journal entries. The original stock issue entry from December 31, 19X1, is repeated first for reference. It is followed by the entry for issuing the 16 additional shares on January 2.

19X1					
Dec. 31	Due to Duncan Woodworking Shop	203	39,200 00		
	Common Stock (384 shares)	301		19,200 00	
	Preferred Stock (200 shares)	311		20,000 00	
	Issued stock in payment for net assets of Duncan Woodworking Shop: common stock at $50 a share and preferred stock at par ($100).				

19X2					
Jan. 2	Cash in Bank	101	800 00		
	Common Stock (16 shares)	301		800 00	
	Issued stock to James Duncan at $50 a share—balance of purchase agreed to as original incorporator.				

The other two incorporators, Ralph East and Mary Fields, have each agreed to purchase 100 shares of common stock at $50 a share and 100 shares of preferred stock at par value, $100 a share. On January 2, 19X2, they pay the corporation the agreed amounts. The stock issued to them is shown in general journal form in the following entries.

	19	X2				
	Jan.	2	Cash in Bank	101	15,000 00	
			Common Stock (100 shares)	301		5,000 00
			Preferred Stock (100 shares)	311		10,000 00
			Issued stock to Ralph East, one of the original incorporators: common stock at $50 a share and preferred stock at par ($100).			
		2	Cash in Bank	101	15,000 00	
			Common Stock (100 shares)	301		5,000 00
			Preferred Stock (100 shares)	311		10,000 00
			Issued stock to Mary Fields, one of the original incorporators: common stock at $50 a share and preferred stock at par ($100).			

Issuing Additional Stock

Two other people interested in the new corporation, John Valdez and Alice Hill, agreed to buy 50 shares of common stock apiece at $50 a share. Valdez comes to the company office on January 2 with checks to cover both pledges. The two blocks of stock are issued, as shown in the following general journal entries.

	19	X2				
	Jan.	2	Cash in Bank	101	2,500 00	
			Common Stock (50 shares)	301		2,500 00
			Issued common stock to John Valdez at $50 a share.			
			Cash in Bank	101	2,500 00	
			Common Stock (50 shares)	301		2,500 00
			Issued common stock to Alice Hill at $50 a share.			

Meeting of the Stockholders

Immediately following the issuance of stock on January 2, the first stockholders' meeting is held. The stockholders present and the number of shares of voting stock owned are shown on the next page. Only common stockholders have voting rights in this corporation.

Note that although Alice Hill is not present in person, she is able to vote her stock by executing a proxy and giving it to John Valdez. A *proxy* is an authorization to someone else of the right to vote. Particularly in large corporations, it is common practice for stockholders who cannot attend stockholders' meetings to give their proxy to someone who will be present. The man-

DUNCAN MANUFACTURING CORPORATION
(STOCKHOLDERS)

NAME	SHARES
James Duncan	400
Ralph East	100
Mary Fields	100
John Valdez	50
Proxy from Alice Hill to John Valdez	50

agement of a corporation often obtains enough proxies to control the vote in the stockholders' meeting. Occasionally, rival factions will each seek proxies and a *proxy fight* develops to decide which slate of directors will be elected.

Adoption of Bylaws The first act of the stockholders is the adoption of a proposed set of *bylaws* to serve as guides for the general operation of the corporation. Bylaws must be consistent with the corporation's charter. They usually include provisions that define the following items.

1. The time, place, and nature of the meetings of stockholders and directors.
2. The number of directors and officers and the method of electing them.
3. The duties of directors, officers, and committees.
4. The rules and procedures governing the conduct of meetings and other activities.
5. The fiscal year to be used by the corporation.
6. The method for changing the bylaws.

The bylaws of the Duncan Manufacturing Corporation include the following initial provisions.

1. A five-member board of directors is to be elected at the first meeting of the stockholders and annually thereafter on the third Saturday in February. Vacancies occurring between annual elections are to be filled by vote of the remaining members of the board.
2. Each director's compensation for attending a regular or special meeting of the board is $100. No additional payment will be made for meetings of the executive committee, which is composed of the president, vice president, and secretary-treasurer.
3. The officers of the corporation are to be a president, a vice president, and a secretary-treasurer.
4. Additional common stock may be issued at not less than $50 a share, with a stated value of $50 a share.
5. Additional preferred stock may be issued at not less than $100 (par value) a share.
6. The fiscal year is the calendar year, ending December 31.

Election of Board of Directors The five initial stockholders are unanimously elected to serve as the first board of directors.

Meeting of the Board of Directors

As soon as the stockholders' meeting is adjourned, the four directors present hold the first meeting of the new board of directors. The board unanimously elects the following officers.

OFFICERS OF
DUNCAN MANUFACTURING CORPORATION

President	James Duncan
Vice President	Ralph East
Secretary-Treasurer	Mary Fields

Annual salaries are set for the officers, who are expected to devote full time to the business: Duncan, president, $18,000; East, vice president, $12,500; and Fields, secretary-treasurer, $12,500. (Salaries are purposely being kept low at this point in order to control expenses and provide maximum funds for other needs.) The board now instructs the officers to purchase materials and additional equipment for the manufacturing operations, hire workers, and start production.

Minute Book

To keep accurate and complete records of all meetings of stockholders and directors, the corporation maintains a minute book. In the *minute book*, actions taken, directives issued, directors elected, officers elected, and all other matters discussed are formally reported. The chief accountant should study the minutes of each meeting to determine if any of the actions taken concern records and payments for which the accountant is responsible. Decisions noted in the minute book about salaries to officers, authorizations to purchase assets, and declarations of dividends may affect accounting records and procedures.

Stock Certificate Books

Capital stock issued by a corporation is in the form of a stock certificate. A separate series of stock certificates must be prepared for each class of stock. Therefore, the Duncan Manufacturing Corporation has one series for common stock and one for preferred stock.

A corporation that expects to issue relatively few stock certificates may have them prepared in books. Each certificate is numbered consecutively and attached to a stub from which it is separated at the time of issuance. The certificate indicates the class of stock and the number of shares. If the stock is preferred, the essence of the preferred stock contract is printed on the certificate itself. Certificates become valid when they are properly signed by corporate officers and have the corporate seal affixed to them.

Certificate and Stub Illustrated

The first common stock certificate of the Duncan Manufacturing Corporation is issued to James Duncan for 384 shares. The illustration on the next page shows the certificate and stub as they appear just before the certificate is detached. (The lower section of the stub is used when stock is transferred. This procedure is explained and illustrated shortly.)

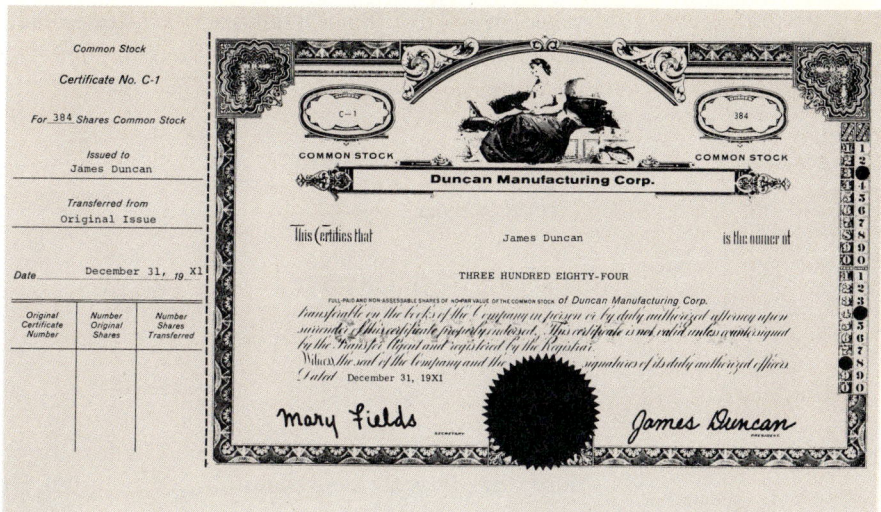

Stubs for Other Issues of Common Stock

As each additional block of shares of common stock is issued, the pertinent information is first recorded on the prenumbered stub. Then a certificate is filled out, detached, and delivered to the purchaser. Certificates C-2 through C-6 are issued to Duncan, East, Fields, Valdez, and Hill for the shares previously described. The stubs have the necessary information filled in.

Stubs for Issues of Preferred Stock

Three blocks of preferred stock are issued to the three incorporators. A separate set of stock certificates is used for the preferred stock. These certificates are also bound in a stock certificate book, and each certificate is attached to a prenumbered stub. The procedures for issuing preferred stock are the same as those for issuing common stock. The stub is completed first. Then the certificate is filled in and detached.

Capital Stock Ledger and Procedures

It is important for the corporation or for an agent acting in its behalf to keep careful records of the number of shares of stock issued and of the names and addresses of the stockholders. This information is needed when dividend checks are mailed, when official notices of stockholders' meetings are sent out, when proxies are solicited, and at other times. The record also serves as a check against the possibility of issuing more stock than is authorized by the corporation's charter.

In order to maintain the required information about stockholders, the corporation or its agent sets up a *capital stock ledger,* or *stockholders' ledger,* for each class of stock issued. Within this ledger there is a sheet for each stockholder with the person's name and address, the dates of transactions affecting his or her stock holdings, the certificate numbers, and the number of shares involved in each transaction. The balance shows the number of shares held. The same ledger sheets may also include a record of dividend payments. The ledger sheet set up for the Duncan Manufacturing Corporation preferred stock owned by James Duncan is illustrated below. Similar capital stock ledger sheets are maintained for the common stockholders.

CAPITAL STOCK LEDGER—PREFERRED

Sheet No. 1 **Name:** James Duncan **Address:** 714 Oak Lane, Greenville, SC 29609

DIVIDENDS PAID			TRANSFERRED FROM OR TO		POST. REF.	CERT. NOS.	RECORD OF SHARES		
DATE	CHECK NO.	AMOUNT	DATE	NAME			SHARES ISSUED	SHARES SURREND.	BALANCE
			19X1 Dec. 31	Original Issue	J12	P-1	200		200

In all the transactions illustrated so far, the stockholders have acquired their stock directly from the issuing corporation. However, once a quantity of stock has been issued, new stockholders are likely to obtain their shares by purchasing them from an owner who wants to sell all or part of his or her holdings. The corporation receives no money in such a transaction. The buyer pays the seller, and the stock is transferred to the new owner on the corporation's books. The corporation needs a special record of such stock transfers to be sure that they are properly recorded in the stockholders' ledger. The *capital stock transfer journal* is the record used for this purpose. One of these journals is maintained for each class of stock issued by the corporation, and all transfers involving that class of stock are recorded in it. (This journal is illustrated in a later section of this unit.)

Stock Assignment Form

In order to transfer ownership of shares of stock an *assignment* must be made in proper legal form, and the stock certificate must be surrendered for cancellation. For convenience, an assignment form is usually printed on the back of each stock certificate. Suppose James Duncan agrees to sell 100 shares of his preferred stock to Tina Serrano on February 15, 19X2. He completes the assignment form on the reverse side of his stock certificate, P-1, as shown below.

For value received I *hereby sell, assign and transfer unto*
Tina Serrano
179 Laurel Street, Greenville, SC 29609
———— ONE HUNDRED ———— *Shares of the Capital Stock represented by the within Certificate, and do hereby irrevocably constitute and appoint* Mary Fields *Attorney to transfer the said stock on the books of the within named Company with full power of substitution in the premises.*
Dated February 15, 19X2
In Presence of:
Peter Smith   James Duncan

Capital Stock Transfer Journal Entry

When Certificate P-1 with the completed stock assignment form is presented to the corporation, a new certificate is issued to James Duncan for the 100 shares (of the original 200 shares) he still retains. A new certificate is issued to Tina Serrano for the 100 shares she has purchased from him. However, before the new certificates are issued, an entry is made in the preferred stock transfer journal of the Duncan Manufacturing Corporation, as shown in the illustration below.

PREFERRED STOCK TRANSFER JOURNAL								Page 1
DATE	SURREND. BY	√	CERT. NO.	NO. OF SHARES	TRANSFER. TO	√	CERT. NO.	NO. OF SHARES
19 X2 Feb. 15	James Duncan	√	P-1	200	James Duncan	√	P-4	100
					Tina Serrano	√	P-5	100

Issuance of New Certificates

The surrendered Certificate P-1 is canceled. The stock certificate stub may have this fact noted on it, or the canceled certificate may be permanently attached to the stub. New certificates for this preferred stock are issued, and the appropriate information is entered on their stubs, as shown in the illustrations below.

```
Preferred Stock

Certificate No. P-4

For  100  Shares Preferred Stock

Issued to
James Duncan

Transferred from
James Duncan

Date        February 15,  19 X2

Original         Number        Number
Certificate      Original      Shares
Number           Shares        Transferred

P-1              200           100
```

```
Preferred Stock

Certificate No. P-5

For  100  Shares Preferred Stock

Issued to
Tina Serrano

Transferred from
James Duncan

Date        February 15,  19 X2

Original         Number        Number
Certificate      Original      Shares
Number           Shares        Transferred

P-1              200           100
```

Posting to the Capital Stock Ledger

From the information entered in the preferred stock transfer journal, postings are made to the capital stock ledger sheets that are affected. A new sheet is established for Tina Serrano because she is a new shareholder. Then a record of the cancellation of Certificate P-1 and the issuance of new Certificate P-4 is noted on the ledger sheet for James Duncan. After these postings are made, the sheets for Serrano and Duncan in the corporation's capital stock ledger appear as illustrated on page 592.

CAPITAL STOCK LEDGER—PREFERRED

Sheet No. 1   Name: James Duncan   Address: 714 Oak Lane, Greenville, SC 29609

DIVIDENDS PAID			TRANSFERRED FROM OR TO		POST. REF.	CERT. NOS.	RECORD OF SHARES		
DATE	CHECK NO.	AMOUNT	DATE	NAME			SHARES ISSUED	SHARES SURREND.	BALANCE
			19 X1 Dec. 31	Original Issue	J12	P-1	200		200
			19 X2 Feb. 15	Tina Serrano	PST1	P-1		200	–0–
			Feb. 15	James Duncan	PST1	P-4	100		100

CAPITAL STOCK LEDGER—PREFERRED

Sheet No. 4   Name: Tina Serrano   Address: 179 Laurel Street, Greenville, SC 29609

DIVIDENDS PAID			TRANSFERRED FROM OR TO		POST. REF.	CERT. NOS.	RECORD OF SHARES		
DATE	CHECK NO.	AMOUNT	DATE	NAME			SHARES ISSUED	SHARES SURREND.	BALANCE
			19 X2 Feb. 15	James Duncan	PST1	P-5	100		100

Transfer Agent and Registrar

The directors of the Duncan Manufacturing Corporation expect the firm to have relatively few stockholders and only infrequent transactions affecting its capital stock. They decide, therefore, that the business will keep its own stock records.

However, corporations whose stock is widely held and actively traded ordinarily do not keep their own stockholder records. Instead, they turn the responsibility for these records over to a transfer agent and a registrar. The bank that is to serve as a transfer agent is often chosen because of its nearness to the stock exchange or the market in which the corporation's stock is expected to be traded. The same bank may also be appointed registrar.

Transfer Agent

The *transfer agent* receives the stock certificates being surrendered with the assignment forms indicating to whom new certificates are to be issued. The agent cancels the old certificates, issues the new ones, and makes the necessary entries in the capital stock ledger. When required to do so by the corporation, the agent also prepares lists of stockholders who should receive dividend payments, notices, and other items. The agent may also prepare and mail the dividend checks.

Registrar

The *registrar* accounts for all the stock issued by the corporation and makes sure that the corporation does not issue more shares than are authorized. The registrar receives from the transfer agent all the canceled certificates and all the new certificates issued. The new certificates must be countersigned by the registrar before they are valid.

Issuing Stock at a Premium

Once the business is launched and its relative success and prospects can be evaluated, investors may feel that its stock is actually worth more or less than par value. For example, if the corporation produces very attractive profits even in the early stages of operations, investors may understandably be willing to pay more than par value to become stockholders. Similarly, if the dividend rate on an issue of preferred stock is higher than the rate that could be earned on other investments with similar risk, investors may be willing to pay more than par value for the preferred stock. The amount paid in excess of par value for securities is called a *premium*.

Suppose that Linda Levy offers to pay a premium of $10 a share, or $110 a share, for 100 shares of the 8 percent $100 par value preferred stock of the Duncan Manufacturing Corporation. Suppose also that the corporation accepts her offer. Here is how the transaction would be recorded in general journal form.

19 X2				
Mar. 2	Cash in Bank	101	11,000 00	
	Preferred Stock (100 shares)	311		10,000 00
	Paid-in Capital in Excess of Par Value of Preferred Stock	315		1,000 00
	Issued preferred stock to Linda Levy for $110 a share.			

In the Stockholders' Equity section of the balance sheet shown below, the amount of the new account, called Paid-in Capital in Excess of Par Value of Preferred Stock, is added to the par value of the shares issued to show the total paid in by that class of stockholder. (The account title might also be Premium on Preferred Stock or some other name.)

Stockholders' Equity
   Preferred Stock (8%, $100 par value,
     1,000 shares authorized)
     At Par Value (500 shares issued) $50,000
     Paid-in Capital in Excess of Par Value   1,000 $51,000

Issuing Stock at a Discount

Although most states prohibit the issuance of stock at a *discount,* or less than par value, this procedure is permitted in a few states. Corporations sometimes sell their stock at a discount as an inducement to hesitant investors. The technique for recording the sale of stock at a discount is illustrated on page 594. In this example, 50 shares of $100 par value common stock are issued for $90 a share.

In presenting items in the Stockholders' Equity section of the balance sheet, the discount is shown as a deduction from the amount credited to the

	19 X5					
	May	6	Cash in Bank	101	4,500 00	
			Discount on Common Stock	306	500 00	
			Common Stock	301		5,000 00
			Issued 50 shares of $100 par value common stock at $90 a share.			

related stock account. The difference indicates the amount paid in by that class of stockholder. If both premiums and discounts occur in sales of the same class of stock, the premiums are added and the discounts deducted separately. The two figures are not combined. For example, assume that the corporation in the above example had already issued 350 shares of common stock at a total premium of $2,000. The Stockholders' Equity section of the balance sheet after issue of the 50 shares at a discount would appear as follows.

Stockholders' Equity
   Common Stock ($100 par value,
      1,000 shares authorized)
      At Par Value (400 shares issued) $40,000
      Paid-in Capital in Excess of Par Value   2,000
                                              $42,000
      Less Discount on Common Stock   500 $41,500

In states where stock can be issued at a discount, the stockholder may have a *contingent liability* to pay the amount of the discount if the corporation needs it to pay its creditors.

Stated Value for No-Par Value Stock

No-par value stock provides several theoretical advantages over stock with par value, such as:

1. No-par value stock can be issued for whatever it will bring, without considering premium or discount. This eliminates the contingent liability that might exist if the stock were sold at a discount.
2. The stock buyer is not misled into thinking that a par value amount represents the actual value of the stock. For no-par value stock, the purchaser must be the judge of its worth.
3. The value of no-par stock issued for property is determined according to the market value of the property received, not according to the par value of the stock issued in payment. This reduces the possibility of issuing stock with a recorded value of more than property received. Stock issued in excess of the value of property received is sometimes called *watered stock*.

Despite these theoretical advantages, no-par value stock has not proved popular. In most cases, a stated value is set by the board of directors, and this stated value has come to be treated as though it were par value. The stated value is credited to the capital stock account, and any excess received over stated value is treated as a premium.

Issuing No-Par Value Stock Above Stated Value

As you know, the board of directors of the Duncan Manufacturing Corporation set a stated value of $50 a share for the no-par value common stock at the time the firm was organized. Assume that the firm's prospects appear bright and that a new investor pays $52 a share for 200 shares of common stock. This transaction would be recorded in general journal form as follows.

19X2				
Mar. 8	Cash in Bank	101	10,400 00	
	Common Stock (200 shares)	301		10,000 00
	Paid-in Capital in Excess of Stated Value of Common Stock	305		400 00
	Issued 200 shares of common stock to Susan Lang at $52 a share (stated value $50 a share).			

Note the credit of $400 to the Paid-in Capital in Excess of Stated Value of Common Stock account (200 shares × $2 a share). On the balance sheet, this item is added to the amount in the Common Stock account to show the total paid by common stockholders.

Subscriptions for Capital Stock

Some prospective stockholders may not be able to pay immediately for the securities they want to buy. These investors are asked to sign a subscription contract in which they agree to buy the stock at a certain price, to pay for it in accordance with a fixed plan, and to receive the stock when payment is completed. The payment may be due in a single amount at a future date or may be payable in installments. Such an arrangement gives the corporation a receivable from the subscriber and an obligation to hold enough stock to issue when the subscription is paid in full.

Receipt of Subscriptions

Suppose the Duncan Manufacturing Corporation receives a subscription from Doris Martin to purchase 100 shares of common stock at $50 a share (the stated value) and a subscription from Lewis Nichols to buy 100 shares of preferred stock at $110 a share. These subscriptions are recorded as follows.

19X2				
Apr. 1	Subscriptions Receivable—Common	114	5,000 00	
	Common Stock Subscribed (100 shares)	302		5,000 00
	Subscription from Doris Martin to buy 100 shares of common stock at stated value of $50 a share.			
1	Subscriptions Receivable—Preferred	115	11,000 00	
	Preferred Stock Subscribed (100 shares)	312		10,000 00
	Paid-in Capital in Excess of Par Value of Preferred Stock	315		1,000 00
	Subscription from Lewis Nichols to buy 100 shares of $100 par value preferred stock at $110 a share.			

Notice that separate subscriptions receivable accounts are used for each class of stock. It is convenient to use the separate accounts in this case because the subscription contract for each type of stock may call for a different payment plan. In the example given here, the common stock is to be paid for in full on the first of the following month. The preferred stock subscription is payable in five monthly installments, beginning on the first day of the following month. Both receivables are shown as current assets on the balance sheet.

Separate accounts must also be kept for the subscribed stock because the corporation has agreed to hold enough stock to issue to the subscribers when they have paid their contracts in full. Until this time the subscribed accounts are presented in the Stockholders' Equity section of the balance sheet as additions to the same class of stock issued. For example, immediately after the receipt of Nichols' stock subscription, the preferred stock listing in the Stockholders' Equity section appears as shown below.

Stockholders' Equity
Preferred Stock (8%, $100 par value,
   1,000 shares authorized)
    At Par Value (500 shares issued) $50,000
    Subscribed (100 shares)   10,000
    Paid-in Capital in Excess of Par Value   2,000 $62,000

Collection of Subscriptions and Issuance of Stock

The collection of subscriptions and the issuance of stock under these two plans works out as follows.

Single Cash Payment. When Martin pays her $5,000 subscription in full on May 1, 19X2, 100 shares of common stock are issued to her. The cash received for this transaction is normally recorded in the cash receipts journal. However, for illustrative purposes, the transaction is shown below in general journal form, followed by an entry to record the issuance of the stock.

19 X2					
May	1	Cash in Bank	101	5,000 00	
		Subscriptions Receivable—Common	114		5,000 00
		Received Doris Martin's subscription in full.			
	1	Common Stock Subscribed (100 shares)	302	5,000 00	
		Common Stock (100 shares)	301		5,000 00
		Issued 100 shares of common stock to Doris Martin.			

When these entries have been posted, the Subscriptions Receivable—Common account with Doris Martin is closed and the Common Stock Subscribed account is also closed. The net effect of this series of transactions is to increase the corporation's Cash in Bank account by $5,000 and to increase its Common Stock account by the same amount.

Installment Payments. Nichols agreed to pay his preferred stock subscription in five monthly installments. If he lives up to his contract, he will pay $2,200 in cash each month for five months, beginning May 1. Each collection will be debited to Cash in Bank and credited to Nichols' Subscriptions Receivable—Preferred account. When he makes his final payment, the stock will be issued to him. In general journal form, the collection of the final installment and the issuance of the stock would be recorded as shown below.

19X2				
Sept. 1	Cash in Bank	101	2,200 00	
	Subscriptions Receivable—Preferred	115		2,200 00
	Collected final installment from Lewis Nichols on his stock subscription.			
1	Preferred Stock Subscribed (100 shares)	312	10,000 00	
	Preferred Stock (100 shares)	311		10,000 00
	Issued 100 shares of preferred stock to Lewis Nichols.			

With the posting of these last entries, the Subscriptions Receivable—Preferred account with Nichols and the Preferred Stock Subscribed account are closed. This series of transactions has resulted in an increase in Cash in Bank of $11,000. This amount is offset by a $10,000 increase in the Preferred Stock account for 100 shares sold to Nichols and a $1,000 increase in the Paid-in Capital in Excess of Par Value of Preferred Stock account.

Treatment of Defaults on Stock Subscriptions

Not every stock subscriber pays in full according to the contract. What is done about subscriptions that are paid only in part? The answer depends on the action permitted under state law and on the corporation's policy. Among the procedures that may be used are the following.

1. Issuing the amount of stock actually paid for and canceling the balance of the subscription.
2. Retaining the amount paid but issuing no stock, canceling the balance of the subscription, and canceling the entire subscribed stock amount.
3. Refunding the entire amount paid by the subscriber, canceling the entire subscription, and canceling the entire subscribed stock amount.
4. Reselling the subscribed stock to another person and refunding the amount paid to the original subscriber after subtracting any costs or losses on the resale.

Each of these default procedures has a significantly different effect on the interests of the corporation and the subscriber. The specifics of defaults are beyond the scope of this course. They are examined in intermediate accounting textbooks.

Records of Stock Subscriptions

The corporation needs two special records to keep track of stock subscriptions: the subscription book and the subscribers' ledger.

Subscription Book

The *subscription book* is a listing of stock subscriptions that have been received. This book is used to record the names and addresses of the subscribers, the number of shares they have agreed to buy, and the amounts and times of payment. The subscription book may consist of the actual stock subscription contracts.

Subscribers' Ledger

A separate subsidiary ledger, the subscribers' ledger, is maintained. The *subscribers' ledger* contains an account receivable record for each subscriber. The accounts are debited for the total amount of the original subscription and credited as payments are made by the subscriber to the corporation. No new principles are involved here. The balances of the individual subscriber accounts are summarized by a subscriptions receivable control account in the general ledger.

Treasury Stock

Treasury stock is a corporation's own capital stock that has been reacquired. The reacquired stock must have been previously paid for in full and issued to a stockholder in order to be considered treasury stock. Any class or type of stock can be reacquired as treasury stock. No dividends, voting rights, or liquidation preferences apply to this stock.

Reacquisition of a corporation's own capital stock can occur in several different ways. For example:

1. Donation of the stock to the corporation by a stockholder.
2. Receipt of the stock by the corporation in settlement of a debt that is owed to it.
3. Purchase of the stock by the corporation in exchange for cash or property. (Some states limit the purchase of treasury stock to a total purchase price not in excess of retained earnings.)

There are a number of special accounting procedures involved in the purchase and resale of treasury stock by the corporation. These procedures are explained below and on pages 599–601.

Purchased Treasury Stock—Cost Basis

When a corporation purchases its own stock, which will probably be reissued at a later date, the transaction is usually recorded at cost. Treasury Stock is debited for the amount paid, and Cash in Bank or some other asset account, or a liability account, is credited for the entire amount involved. For example, a preferred share reacquired at $105 after being issued at $100 par value is recorded by a debit to Treasury Stock—Preferred and a credit to Cash in Bank, both for $105. (Separate treasury stock accounts are set up as needed for each class of stock.) On the balance sheet, the cost of the reacquired stock is deducted from the sum of all items in the Stockholders' Equity section, as illustrated on the next page.

Stockholders' Equity
 Preferred Stock (9%, $100 par value, 10,000 shares authorized)
  At Par Value (200 shares issued, of which one share has
   been reacquired as treasury stock) ... $ 20,000
 Common Stock ($20 par value, 5,000 shares authorized)
  At Par Value (2,000 shares issued) ... 40,000
                                          $ 60,000
 Retained Earnings ... 42,000
                       $102,000
 Deduct Treasury Stock, Preferred (one share at cost) ... 105
  Total Stockholders' Equity ... $101,895

Suppose the share of stock reacquired at $105 is later sold for $108. The entry at the time of sale would be recorded as shown below.

19 X1				
Nov. 1	Cash in Bank	101	108 00	
	Treasury Stock—Preferred	319		105 00
	Paid-in Capital From Treasury Stock			
	Transactions—Preferred	317		3 00
	Sale at $108 of a share of preferred treasury stock purchased at $105.			

Assume that another share of treasury stock previously reacquired at $105 was later sold for only $90. Assume further that this is a share of $100 par value preferred stock originally issued at a premium of $10 a share. The entry required to record the sale includes a number of elements, as shown below.

19 X1				
Nov. 2	Cash in Bank	101	90 00	
	Paid-in Capital From Treasury Stock			
	Transactions—Preferred	317	3 00	
	Paid-in Capital in Excess of Par Value			
	of Preferred Stock	315	10 00	
	Retained Earnings	381	2 00	
	Treasury Stock—Preferred	319		105 00
	Sale at $90 of a share of preferred treasury stock purchased at $105 that had been issued originally at $110.			

Note that Cash in Bank is debited for the amount received ($90) and Treasury Stock—Preferred is credited for the amount paid ($105). The difference is absorbed to the extent that credit balances are available. First, Paid-in Capital From Treasury Stock Transactions—Preferred is debited for any amount up to the balance of the account. Second, Paid-in Capital in Excess of Par Value of Preferred Stock is debited up to the amount of the premium received on the issuance of that particular share of stock—in this case, $10. Third, the remaining balance is debited to Retained Earnings.

It is usually impossible to determine the exact original issue price for a specific share of stock. In that case, the Paid-in Capital in Excess of Par Value of Preferred Stock account is debited for the average amount that applies to each share of outstanding preferred stock being reacquired.

For the example just given, if there had been a large enough balance in the Paid-in Capital From Treasury Stock Transactions—Preferred account to absorb the $15 loss on the resale of the treasury stock (purchased at $105, sold at $90), the entire loss would have been debited to that account. In this case, no debits would have been made to Paid-in Capital in Excess of Par Value of Preferred Stock or to Retained Earnings.

Donated Treasury Stock

A corporation may reacquire shares of its own stock by donation under various circumstances. Since the treasury stock in this case is obtained without cost, no entry in dollar amounts is made at the time of acquisition. Only a memorandum entry is made in an appropriate treasury stock account to record the number of shares donated. If the donated treasury stock is later sold, the amount received is debited to Cash in Bank and credited to Donated Capital From Treasury Stock Transactions.

Redemption of Preferred Stock

The terms of a preferred stock issue may give the corporation the right to "call" the stock for redemption and retirement. The *call price* may be a single specified amount for each share, or it may vary depending on the length of time the stock has been outstanding. Also, the corporation may purchase its own preferred stock on the open market with the intent of permanently retiring the shares. Historically, there has been a great deal of argument among accountants over the appropriate way to account for the retirement of preferred stock. However, *Opinion No. 6* of the Accounting Principles Board clarifies the practices to be followed in accounting for the retirement of either preferred or common stock. The practices are summarized here.°

1. If the repurchase price is less than the par value or stated value, the excess should be credited to a paid-in capital account (such as Paid-in Capital From Retirement of Preferred Stock). The stock account is then debited for the par value or stated value.
2. Any excess may be charged first against any previous paid-in capital arising from previous retirements and from net "gains" on sales of treasury stock of the same issue.
3. Any remaining excess may next be charged on an average-per-share basis against other paid-in capital in excess of par value accounts for the same issue.
4. Any remaining balance would be charged against Retained Earnings.

As an alternative, *Opinion No. 6* provides that the entire excess of repurchase price over par value may be charged against Retained Earnings in rec-

---

° "Status of Accounting Research Bulletins," *Opinions of the Accounting Principles Board, No. 6* (New York: American Institute of Certified Public Accountants, 1965), par. 12.

ognition of the fact that a corporation can always capitalize retained earnings for such purposes. For example, if a $75 par value preferred share originally issued at $80 is redeemed for $85, the following entry can be used to record the transaction.

19X1				
Oct. 1	Preferred Stock (1 share)	311	75 00	
	Paid-in Capital in Excess of Par Value of Preferred Stock	315	5 00	
	Retained Earnings	381	5 00	
	Cash in Bank	101		85 00
	Redeemed one share of $75 par value preferred stock originally issued at $80.			

principles and procedures summary

The accounting records of a typical corporation include the usual journals and ledgers kept by any firm. In addition, however, corporations must keep special records. These records include minute books, stockholders' ledgers, stock certificate books, and stock transfer records.

The corporation charter specifies the amounts and types of capital stock authorized. The bylaws serve as guides for the general operations of the firm, which must be consistent with the charter provisions.

When capital stock is transferred, the seller completes the assignment form printed on the back of each stock certificate and surrenders the certificate for cancellation. New certificates are issued to the persons to whom the stock is transferred. A capital stock transfer journal is used to record the transactions, which are posted to the appropriate stockholders' capital stock ledger sheets. A corporation whose stock is more actively traded will usually employ a bank as its transfer agent (to keep the records of stock transfers) and its registrar (to account for all the stock issued by the corporation).

When stock is issued at a premium (more than par value), Cash in Bank is debited for the total amount received, the capital stock account is credited for the par value, and the premium is credited to Paid-in Capital in Excess of Par Value or a similar account.

In a few states, stock may also be issued at a discount (less than par value) although most state laws prohibit this. Again, Cash in Bank is debited for the total, the stock account is credited for par value, and the discount is debited to a discount on stock account. No-par value stock is often given a stated value, which serves the same purpose in accounting as does a par value.

Stock can be paid for and issued in a single transaction. It can also be subscribed for first, then paid for and issued at a later date. To record stock subscriptions, a corporation sets up a special subsidiary ledger, called a subscribers' ledger, with a separate account receivable for each subscriber. The individual accounts receivable are controlled by a Subscriptions Receivable account in the general ledger. The stock is issued when the subscription price has been fully paid. Sometimes subscribers fail to pay all the necessary installments on their subscriptions. Those who default on their payments may be treated in various ways according to state law and the policy of the corporation.

Treasury stock is stock that has been fully paid for, issued, and then reacquired by the corporation. Normally, treasury stock that has been purchased is recorded at cost.

Preferred stock may sometimes be redeemed and canceled by the issuing corporation. The capital stock account is debited for the par value, Cash in Bank is credited for the amount paid, and some other stockholders' equity account or accounts will be debited or credited for the difference.

MANAGERIAL implications

Corporate management must be certain that it has adequate records to comply with legal requirements and to keep track of stockholder transactions. The bylaws and charter provisions of the corporation must be carefully followed, and minutes must be kept of all meetings of directors and stockholders. Actions of the board of directors, as reported in the corporate minutes, often have accounting effects that must be recognized and acted upon.

Management must be sure that capital stock issues are properly accounted for. State laws regarding the issuance of stock at a discount must be carefully observed. Management must also be fully informed about state laws concerning stock subscriptions and defaults and must be sure that the accounting records fully reflect all information relating to such transactions. The accounting records must also provide full data on treasury stock because of the detailed laws in most states that relate to such stock.

MANAGERIAL discussion questions

1. How can management be sure that the accounting effects of actions recorded in the corporate minute book receive proper attention?
2. In what ways is a corporation's capital structure affected by the provisions of its articles of incorporation?
3. What roles do the incorporators of a corporation assume in the management of the new business?
4. Why would the management of a corporation seek to control votes at the stockholders' meeting?

5. Why must the management and directors of a corporation be fully informed about laws and regulations affecting corporations? How can they find out what they need to know?
6. How do you think the directors of the Duncan Manufacturing Corporation reached their decision to set the stated value of the no-par value common stock at $50?
7. Why would the management of a corporation be willing to sell its stock on a subscription basis, considering all the recordkeeping involved?
8. Why would the management of a corporation consider using corporate funds to purchase the firm's own outstanding stock?
9. Why would both management and stock subscribers be interested in the state laws that deal with defaulting subscribers?
10. The management of the O'Riley Corporation wishes to know why its common stock held as treasury stock should not be shown on the balance sheet as an asset since the stock has a ready market value. Explain.

application of principles

PROBLEM 32-1 The Alamo Corporation was formed to take over the operations of Rudy Gomez on June 1, 19X1. The assets and liabilities to be transferred to the corporation by Gomez are as follows.

Cash in Bank	$ 3,000
Accounts Receivable	16,000
Merchandise Inventory	14,000
Equipment	3,000
Notes Payable	1,000
Accounts Payable	5,000

The corporation is to issue sufficient shares of $50 par value 9 percent preferred stock to cover the cash that Gomez transferred. The corporation will issue sufficient shares of $20 par value common stock to cover the remainder of the net assets transferred. The directors feel that Gomez's work and expenses in organizing the corporation are worth $800 and that he should therefore receive 40 shares of common stock as reimbursement.

INSTRUCTIONS In general journal form, record the following transactions of the corporation on June 1, 19X1.

1. The acquisition of the assets and liabilities by the corporation and the liability to Gomez.
2. The issuance of shares to Gomez for the net assets transferred.
3. The issuance of 40 shares of common stock to Gomez for organizing the corporation.

PROBLEM 32-2 Cook Manufacturing Inc. has been formed for the purpose of manufacturing electrical parts. It has been authorized to issue 20,000 shares of no-par value common stock with a stated value of $10 a share and 10,000 shares of 8 percent noncumulative and nonparticipating preferred stock with a par value of $100 a share. The shares of stock sold for cash are shown below.

STOCK SOLD FOR CASH

COMMON STOCK ISSUED AT $10
6,000 shares—Walter Cook (Certificate C-1)
3,000 shares—Roberta Hess (Certificate C-2)
3,000 shares—James Monroe (Certificate C-3)
3,000 shares—Morgan Roper (Certificate C-4)

PREFERRED STOCK ISSUED AT $100
2,000 shares—Walter Cook (Certificate P-1)
1,000 shares—Roberta Hess (Certificate P-2)
1,000 shares—James Monroe (Certificate P-3)
1,000 shares—Morgan Roper (Certificate P-4)

INSTRUCTIONS
1. Record in general journal form the receipt of cash in payment for the shares of stock listed above and the issuance of the stock on March 1, 19X1. Use a single entry.
2. Prepare the common and preferred capital stock ledger sheets for the individual stockholders, and post the above entry to the sheets. (Save all papers for use in Problem 32-3.)

PROBLEM 32-3 This is a continuation of Problem 32-2. The same data applies. Use the capital stock ledger sheets already prepared.

INSTRUCTIONS
1. Prepare a common stock transfer journal, and record the transfer required by the sale of 1,000 shares of common stock by Walter Cook (Certificate C-1) to Sarah Markham on June 15, 19X1. Certificate C-5 was issued to Cook and Certificate C-6 to Markham. Open an account for Markham. Post to the capital stock ledger.
2. Prepare the general journal entry required to record the issuance on July 1, 19X1 of 500 shares of common stock, paid in cash at stated value, to James Monroe. Post to the capital stock ledger.
3. Prepare a preferred stock transfer journal, and record the transfer of 500 shares of the preferred stock issued to Morgan Roper (Certificate P-4) to Alice Roper on August 1, 19X1. Certificate P-5 was issued to Morgan Roper and Certificate P-6 to Alice Roper. Open an account for Alice Roper. Post to the capital stock ledger.
4. Prepare the general journal entry required to record the issuance on August 15, 19X1, of 250 shares of preferred stock to Carl Walker, paid in cash at par value. Post to the capital stock ledger.
5. From the capital stock ledgers, prepare a list of the common stockholders and a list of the preferred stockholders and show the number of shares of each type of stock owned by each stockholder.

PROBLEM 32-4 The Metroplex Supply Company, Inc., was organized on July 1, 19X1. It is authorized to issue 2,000 shares of $50 par value common stock and 2,000 shares of $100 par value 9 percent preferred stock that is nonparticipating and noncumulative. Selected transactions that took place during July 19X1 are shown below.

INSTRUCTIONS
1. Set up the following general ledger accounts. Use balance ledger sheets.

   101 Cash in Bank
   114 Subscriptions Receivable—Common Stock
   115 Subscriptions Receivable—Preferred Stock
   301 Common Stock
   302 Common Stock Subscribed
   305 Paid-in Capital in Excess of Par Value—Common
   311 Preferred Stock
   312 Preferred Stock Subscribed
   315 Paid-in Capital in Excess of Par Value—Preferred

2. Record the transactions listed below in general journal form, and post them to the general ledger accounts.
3. Prepare the Shareholders' Equity section of a balance sheet for the Metroplex Supply Company, Inc., as of July 31, 19X1.

TRANSACTIONS FOR JULY 19X1

July 1 The corporation received its charter. (Make a memorandum entry.)
   1 Issued 300 shares of common stock for cash, $50 a share, to Fern Campbell (Certificate C-1).
   2 Issued 250 shares of preferred stock for cash at par value to Louis Berg (Certificate P-1).
   5 Issued 150 shares of common stock for cash at $52 to Elmo Pena (Certificate C-2).
   10 Received a subscription for 200 shares of common stock at $53 a share from Susan Adams, payable in two installments due in 10 and 20 days.
   12 Received a subscription for 100 shares of preferred stock at $103 a share from George Moore, payable in two installments due in 15 and 30 days.
   20 Received payment of a stock subscription installment due from Susan Adams (one-half of the purchase price—see July 10 transaction).
   27 Received payment of a stock subscription installment due from George Moore (one-half of the purchase price—see July 12 transaction).
   30 Received the balance due on the stock subscription of July 10 from Susan Adams. Issued the stock (Certificate C-3).

PROBLEM 32-5 As of December 31, 19X1, the stockholders' equity of the Drake Corporation consisted of common stock ($20 stated value, 2,000 shares authorized), 600 shares issued ($12,000), and preferred stock (8 percent, noncumulative, nonparticipating, $100 par value, 2,000 shares authorized), 800 shares issued ($80,000). Selected stock transactions that took place during 19X2 are listed below.

INSTRUCTIONS
1. Analyze each of the selected stock transactions, and record it in general journal form. Use account titles similar to those in the text.
2. Open a general ledger for the accounts listed in the general journal entries. Use balance-form ledger sheets. Enter the December 31, 19X1, balances given.
3. Post the general journal entries to the general ledger.
4. Prepare the Stockholders' Equity section of the balance sheet of the Drake Corporation as of June 30, 19X2.

TRANSACTIONS FOR 19X2

Jan. 20 Received cash from Karen Baker for 100 shares of preferred stock at par and issued the stock.
Feb. 12 Received cash from Joseph Kraus for 100 shares of common stock at $21 a share and issued the stock.
Mar. 10 Received cash from James Heilman for 200 shares of preferred stock at $98 a share and issued the stock.
Apr. 1   Louis Erwin subscribed to 50 shares of preferred stock at $101 a share, paying $2,000 in cash today. The balance is to be paid in cash on July 1.
May 15   Morris Fisher subscribed to 200 shares of common stock at $19 a share, paying $1,800 in cash today. The balance is to be paid in cash on July 15.
June 5   The corporation purchased 10 shares of its own preferred stock for cash from Ella Green at $100 a share. The stock was originally sold and issued at par. (Record the purchase on the cost basis.)
     30 The corporation purchased 20 shares of its own common stock for cash from John Harris at $20 a share. The stock was originally sold and issued at $21 a share. (Record the purchase on the cost basis, and use the Treasury Stock—Common 309 account.)

PROBLEM 32-6 Golden Brothers Inc. has 2,000 shares of 8 percent $100 par value preferred stock and 5,000 shares of $50 par value common stock outstanding on January 1, 19X1. The common stock was issued at par. The preferred stock was issued at $102 a share. Selected transactions that took place during 19X1 are listed on the next page.

INSTRUCTIONS
1. Give the entries in general journal form to record the listed transactions. Use the cost method to record all treasury stock transactions. (Omit explanations to save time.)
2. Prepare the Stockholders' Equity section of the balance sheet after the transaction of September 19. (The corporation is authorized to issue 10,000 shares of preferred stock and 10,000 shares of common stock.) Assume that the ending balance of Retained Earnings is $417,500.

TRANSACTIONS FOR 19X1

Feb. 5 The corporation repurchased on the open market 30 shares of its own common stock at $80 a share, to be held as treasury stock.

May 4 The corporation repurchased on the open market 70 shares of its own common stock at $82 a share, to be held as treasury stock.

July 2 The corporation paid $103 a share to redeem and retire 25 shares of its own preferred stock.

Aug. 21 The corporation sold for $92 a share the treasury stock that was acquired on February 5.

Sept. 19 The corporation sold 20 shares, at $81 a share, of the treasury stock acquired on May 4.

alternate problems

PROBLEM 32-1A

Belmont Appliances, Inc., was formed to take over the operations of Alicia Rossi on January 2, 19X2. Assets and liabilities to be transferred to the corporation by Rossi are as follows.

Cash in Bank	$ 800
Accounts Receivable	9,500
Merchandise Inventory	12,000
Furniture and Equipment	6,000
Notes Payable	2,000
Accounts Payable	4,000

The corporation is to issue to Rossi sufficient shares of $20 par value 8 percent preferred stock to cover the amount of cash and accounts receivable transferred. The corporation is also to issue sufficient shares of no-par value, $50 stated value common stock to cover the remainder of the net assets transferred. Rossi is to be issued 10 shares of common stock in payment for her $500 fee for organizing the corporation.

INSTRUCTIONS In general journal form, record the following transactions of the corporation on January 2, 19X2.

1. The acquisition of the assets and liabilities by the corporation and the liability to Rossi.
2. The issuance of preferred and common shares to Rossi for the net assets transferred.
3. The issuance of 10 shares of common stock to Rossi for organizing the corporation.

PROBLEM 32-2A

Ruiz Hardware Inc. has been authorized to issue 10,000 shares of no-par value common stock with a stated value of $25 a share and 5,000 shares of 7 percent noncumulative and nonparticipating preferred stock with a par value of $50 a share. The shares of stock sold for cash are shown on the next page.

STOCK SOLD FOR CASH

COMMON STOCK ISSUED AT $25
800 shares—Barry Brown (Certificate C-1)
1,700 shares—Tom Howard (Certificate C-2)
2,000 shares—Kim Lee (Certificate C-3)
1,500 shares—John Ruiz (Certificate C-4)

PREFERRED STOCK ISSUED AT $50
500 shares—Janet Ames (Certificate P-1)
800 shares—Ann Burke (Certificate P-2)
1,500 shares—Barry Brown (Certificate P-3)
1,000 shares—Floyd Tarr (Certificate P-4)

INSTRUCTIONS
1. Record in general journal form the receipt of cash in payment for the shares of stock listed above and the issuance of the stock on January 2, 19X1. Use a single entry.
2. Prepare the common and preferred capital stock ledger sheets for the individual stockholders, and post the above entry to the sheets. (Save all papers for use in Problem 32-3A.)

PROBLEM 32-3A This is a continuation of Problem 32-2A. The same data applies. Use the capital stock ledger sheets already prepared.

INSTRUCTIONS
1. Prepare a common stock transfer journal, and record the transfer required by the sale of 850 shares of common stock by Tom Howard (Certificate C-2) to Joseph Dunn on March 14, 19X1. Certificate C-5 was issued to Howard and Certificate C-6 to Dunn. Open an account for Dunn. Post to the capital stock ledger.
2. Prepare the general journal entry required to record the issuance on June 8, 19X1, of 300 shares of common stock, paid in cash at stated value, to Joseph Dunn. Post to the capital stock ledger.
3. Prepare a preferred stock transfer journal, and record the transfer of 200 shares of the preferred stock issued to Ann Burke (Certificate P-2) to Donna Harris on June 18, 19X1. Certificate P-5 was issued to Burke and Certificate P-6 to Harris. Open an account for Harris. Post to the capital stock ledger.
4. Prepare the general journal entry on July 16, 19X1, to record the issuance of 200 shares of preferred stock to Floyd Tarr, paid in cash at par value. Post to the capital stock ledger.
5. From the capital stock ledgers, prepare a list of the common stockholders and a list of the preferred stockholders and show the number of shares of each type of stock owned by each stockholder.

PROBLEM 32-4A Antonelli Movers, Inc., was organized on January 2, 19X1. It is authorized to issue 10,000 shares of $20 par value common stock and 4,000 shares of $50 par value 9 percent preferred stock. The preferred stock is noncumulative and nonparticipating. Selected transactions that took place during January 19X1 are shown below.

INSTRUCTIONS

1. Set up the following ledger accounts. Use balance ledger sheets.

   - 101 Cash in Bank
   - 114 Subscriptions Receivable—Common Stock
   - 115 Subscriptions Receivable—Preferred Stock
   - 301 Common Stock
   - 302 Common Stock Subscribed
   - 305 Paid-in Capital in Excess of Par Value—Common
   - 311 Preferred Stock
   - 312 Preferred Stock Subscribed
   - 315 Paid-in Capital in Excess of Par Value—Preferred

2. Record the transactions listed below in general journal form, and post them to the ledger accounts.
3. Prepare the Shareholders' Equity section of a balance sheet for Antonelli Movers, Inc., as of January 31, 19X1.

TRANSACTIONS FOR JANUARY 19X1

Jan. 2 The corporation received its corporate charter. (Make a memorandum entry.)

3 Issued 1,000 shares of common stock for cash, $20 a share, to Ralph Antonelli (Certificate C-1).

3 Issued 500 shares of preferred stock for cash, $50 a share, to Rita Harrison (Certificate P-1).

10 Issued 200 shares of common stock at $21 a share to Alex LeFebre for cash (Certificate C-2).

10 Received a subscription for 500 shares of common stock at $21 a share from Jack Starling, payable in two installments due in 5 and 15 days.

14 Received a subscription for 400 shares of preferred stock at $52 a share from Jack Lindsay, payable in two installments due in 10 and 20 days.

15 Received payment of a stock subscription installment due from Jack Starling (one-half of purchase price—see the January 10 transaction).

24 Received payment of a stock subscription installment due from Jack Lindsay (one-half of purchase price—see the January 14 transaction).

25 Received the balance due on the stock subscription of January 10 from Jack Starling. Issued the stock (Certificate C-3).

PROBLEM 32-5A As of December 31, 19X1, the stockholders' equity of Bailey Home Furnishings Inc. consisted of common stock (no-par value, $50 stated value, 20,000 shares authorized), 4,000 shares issued ($200,000), and preferred stock (9 percent cumulative, nonparticipating, $20 par value, 25,000 shares authorized), 4,000 shares issued ($80,000). Selected stock transactions that took place during 19X2 are shown below.

INSTRUCTIONS
1. Analyze each of the selected stock transactions, and record it in general journal form. Use account titles similar to those in the text.
2. Open a general ledger for the accounts listed in the general journal entries. Use balance ledger sheets. Enter the December 31, 19X1, balances given.
3. Post the general journal entries to the general ledger.
4. Prepare the Stockholders' Equity section of the balance sheet for the corporation as of April 30, 19X2.

TRANSACTIONS FOR 19X2

Jan. 15 Received cash from Ruth Eddy for 200 shares of common stock at $52 a share and issued the stock.

Mar. 3 Received cash from Frank Carter for 500 shares of preferred stock at $23 a share and issued the stock.

Apr. 15 Ruth Heilig subscribed to 1,000 shares of preferred stock at $24 a share, paying $12,000 in cash today. The balance is to be paid in cash on May 15.

18 Richard Roberts subscribed to 400 shares of common stock at $53 a share, paying $10,600 in cash today. The balance is to be paid on May 18.

25 The corporation purchased from Frank Carter, at $23.50 a share, 50 shares of its own preferred stock for cash. The stock was originally issued at $23 a share. Record the purchase on the cost basis. (Use the Treasury Stock—Preferred 319 account.)

29 The corporation purchased 100 shares of its own common stock for $54 a share, in cash, from Ruth Eddy. The stock was originally issued at $52 a share. Record the purchase on the cost basis. (Use the Treasury Stock—Common 309 account.)

PROBLEM 32-6A Lansing & Sons, Inc., has 6,000 shares of 9 percent, $50 par value preferred stock and 8,000 shares of $50 par value common stock outstanding on January 1, 19X2. Preferred stock was issued at $52 a share and common stock at $55 a share. Selected transactions that took place during 19X2 are shown on the next page.

INSTRUCTIONS
1. Give the entries in general journal form to record the transactions listed. Use the cost method to record all treasury stock transactions. (Omit explanations to save time.)
2. Prepare the Stockholders' Equity section of the balance sheet after the transaction of October 13. (The corporation is authorized to issue 8,000 shares of preferred stock and 10,000 shares of common stock.) Assume that the ending balance of Retained Earnings is $285,600.

TRANSACTIONS FOR 19X2

Jan. 17 The corporation repurchased on the open market 100 shares of its own common stock at $56 a share to be held as treasury stock.

Apr. 12 The corporation repurchased on the open market 150 shares of its own common stock at $57 a share to be held as treasury stock.

May 23 The corporation repurchased 200 shares of its own preferred stock at $55 a share and retired them.

July 26 The corporation sold, at $57 a share, the treasury stock that was acquired on January 17.

Oct. 13 The corporation sold 50 shares, for $56.50 a share, of the treasury stock acquired on April 12.

UNIT 33

CORPORATION EARNINGS AND CAPITAL TRANSACTIONS

The successful operation of a corporation is of vital concern to a number of groups—stockholders, managers and employees, creditors, and the community where the firm is located. For example, the stockholders hope that profits will justify the declaration of dividends or result in an increased value for their stock. Various governmental units are also interested because the corporation's income represents a potential source of revenue through taxes. This unit explains how accountants determine the corporation's net income, record estimated income taxes due, show the results on the statements, and distribute profits to stockholders.

Determining Corporate Net Income

The matching of normal and recurring expenses with revenues by time periods, preferably on the accrual basis, is handled on the corporate books according to the same principles and procedures used for other types of businesses. The net income or net loss is determined by subtracting expenses from revenue. Ultimately, the results of operations are described in summary form on the firm's periodic income statements. Certain items of revenue or expense require special consideration. These are known as *extraordinary, nonrecurring items*.

Current Operating Concept

Some accountants argue that judgment must be used in selecting the items to present on the income statement. They say significant amounts representing *prior period adjustments* (primarily corrections of errors of previous periods), gains or losses on the sale of assets not held for resale, and losses from casualties such as fire might mislead statement users if these items are included on the income statement. This view, called the *current operating* concept, holds that only normally recurring items of profit and loss should appear on the income statement. Nonrecurring gains and losses should be credited or debited directly to the Retained Earnings account. (This procedure is illustrated later in the present unit.) However, the current operating concept has little authoritative support today.

The All-Inclusive Concept

Some accountants maintain that *every item* of profit or loss—for example, even corrections of prior years' errors—should be included on the income statement. This view is known as the *historical* or *all-inclusive* concept. The generally accepted position today is a modified all-inclusive approach which holds that almost all items of profit and loss should be reported on the income statement but that in some cases the income statement should be divided into two distinct parts. The first part of the income statement should report the income arising from ordinary, recurring operations. The second part should report gains (or losses) arising from extraordinary, nonrecurring items. These gains or losses are added to (or subtracted from) the net income from operations in order to arrive at the final net income figure.

However, very few items meet the requirements specified in *Opinion No. 30* of the Accounting Principles Board to qualify as extraordinary items. Those requirements are as follows.

> Extraordinary items are events and transactions that are distinguished by their unusual nature *and* by the infrequency of their occurrence. Thus, *both* of the following criteria should be met to classify an event or transaction as an extraordinary item:
> (a) *Unusual nature*—the underlying event or transaction should possess a high degree of abnormality and be of a type clearly unrelated to, or only incidentally related to, the ordinary and typical activities of the entity, taking into account the environment in which the entity operates.
> (b) *Infrequency of occurrence*—the underlying event or transaction should be of a type that would not reasonably be expected to recur in the foreseeable future, taking into account the environment in which the entity operates.°

Under this concept, almost no gains or losses are entered directly in the Retained Earnings account. The major items affecting profit and loss to be entered in the Retained Earnings account are prior period adjustments—principally corrections of errors made in prior periods.† However, settlement in the current period of lawsuits or other litigation initiated in a prior period is not a prior period correction and is therefore not treated as an adjustment of Retained Earnings.‡

A hypothetical income statement reflecting extraordinary gains and losses is illustrated on page 614. Note that the gross amount of each extraordinary item of gain or loss is shown and the related effect on income taxes is offset against it so that the item is reported "net of taxes." Some accountants prefer to show only the net amount and to indicate the gross amount and the tax effect in a parenthetical note.

Net Income and Income Taxes

A worksheet is used to assemble the information for corporation financial statements in much the same manner as for proprietorships and partnerships. First, the accountant takes a trial balance of the general ledger and enters the figures in the first two money columns of the worksheet. Then the accountant makes necessary adjustments and determines the amounts for the Adjusted

---

° "Reporting the Results of Operations," *Opinions of the Accounting Principles Board*, No. 30 (New York: American Institute of Certified Public Accountants, 1973), par. 20.

† "Reporting the Results of Operations," *Opinions of the Accounting Principles Board*, No. 9 (New York: American Institute of Certified Public Accountants, 1966), par. 23.

‡ "Prior Period Adjustments," *Statement of Financial Accounting Standards*, No. 16 (Stamford, Conn.: Financial Accounting Standards Board, 1977), par. 10.

BRISTOL CORPORATION
Income Statement
Year Ended December 31, 19X1

Revenues			
Sales		$1,738,730	
Interest, Discount, and Other Revenues		9,670	
Total Revenues			$1,748,400
Costs and Expenses			
Cost of Goods Sold		$ 766,480	
Research and Development Expense		45,650	
Depreciation Expense		42,420	
Branch Expense and Commissions		430,330	
Selling, Advertising, General, and			
Administrative Expenses		184,140	
Interest Expense		1,160	
Total Costs and Expenses			1,470,180
Income From Operations Before Income Taxes			$ 278,220
Income Taxes Applicable to Operating Income			131,552
Net Income From Operations After Taxes			$ 146,668
Extraordinary Gains and Losses			
Add Gain on Condemnation of			
Land by City	$10,000		
Less Federal Taxes on Gain	3,000	$ 7,000	
Deduct Tornado Loss on Building	$ 8,000		
Less Federal Tax Reduction	3,840	4,160	
Excess of Extraordinary Gains Over Losses			2,840
Net Income for Year			$ 149,508

Trial Balance section. Next, these adjusted amounts are extended into the Income Statement and Balance Sheet sections. At this point, the total debits and total credits in the Income Statement columns are determined as before. Then the income tax on the net difference is estimated and recorded along with the net income remaining after the tax.

Estimating the Income Tax

The amount of income tax due is estimated so that the completion of the corporation's financial statements will not be delayed at the end of the period.

Tax Rates

Under federal laws, the net income of a corporation is subject to a federal income tax. Income taxes are also imposed by some state and local governments. Federal tax rates are subject to changes by Congress. At the time of this writing, the federal rates for corporate income tax are 17 percent on the first $25,000 of net taxable income, 20 percent on the next $25,000, 30 percent on the next $25,000, 40 percent on the next $25,000, and 46 percent on all net taxable income in excess of $100,000. Certain types of income receive special treatment. For example, gains on the sale of some assets (such as investments in securities, land, and buildings) may be taxed at a rate of only 28 percent if the assets are held more than 12 months. Interest received on state and local bonds held for investment is not taxed at all. Because of these categories of taxable and nontaxable income, the net income reported in the tax return is often not the same as that reported in financial statements.

Recording the Estimated Tax on the Worksheet

The amount of the estimated tax is entered on the worksheet as a debit in the Income Statement section and a credit in the Balance Sheet section. The self-explanatory title, Provision for Income Taxes, is noted in the Account Name column. Then, the net income after income taxes is entered in the same columns, and the worksheet is completed. The illustration below shows how the last step would appear on the worksheet of the Duncan Manufacturing Corporation at the end of its first year of operations. It assumes that Duncan's accountant estimated the income tax liability at $6,700.

ACCOUNT NAME	INCOME STATEMENT		BALANCE SHEET	
	DEBIT	CREDIT	DEBIT	CREDIT
	214,679 18	247,326 54	188,942 36	156,295 00
Provision for Income Taxes	6,700 00			6,700 00
Net Income After Income Taxes	25,947 36			25,947 36
	247,326 54	247,326 54	188,942 36	188,942 36

Statement Presentation

A corporation's financial statements ordinarily include an income statement, a balance sheet, and a statement of retained earnings. The income and income tax items affect each statement. Other types of presentations can be made, but the methods described and illustrated below are typical.

Income Statement

Income taxes are usually deducted at the bottom of the income statement from the figure entitled Net Income Before Income Taxes. This deduction is illustrated below for the Duncan Manufacturing Corporation.

Net Income Before Income Taxes	$32,647.36
Provision for Income Taxes	6,700.00
Net Income After Income Taxes	$25,947.36

As you saw in the income statement on the previous page, any income tax reduction or addition resulting from extraordinary gains or losses should be matched with the gain or loss to which it applies. Only the income tax that applies to operating income should be deducted from the operating income figure. Sometimes income taxes are listed with operating expenses such as salaries, depreciation, and other routine items.

Balance Sheet

On the balance sheet on page 616, the provision for income taxes figure ($6,700) is listed as a current liability called Estimated Income Taxes Payable.

(Some accountants use Accrued Income Taxes or a similar title for this item.) The amount of retained earnings appearing on the balance sheet is ordinarily the balance in the Retained Earnings account after all adjusting and closing entries have been posted. This is also the final amount shown on the statement of retained earnings on page 623.

Liabilities and Stockholders' Equity

Current Liabilities			
Accounts Payable		$18,000.00	
Dividends Payable—Preferred		5,600.00	
Dividends Payable—Common		4,000.00	
Accrued Expenses Payable		1,300.00	
Estimated Income Taxes Payable		6,700.00	
Total Liabilities			$ 35,600.00
Stockholders' Equity			
Preferred Stock (8%, $100 par value, 1,000 shares authorized)			
At Par Value (700 shares issued)	$70,000.00		
Paid-in Capital in Excess of Par Value	3,000.00	$73,000.00	
Common Stock (no-par value, stated value $50, 5,000 shares authorized)			
At Stated Value (1,000 shares issued)	$50,000.00		
Paid-in Capital in Excess of Stated Value	400.00	50,400.00	
Retained Earnings		16,347.36	
Total Stockholders' Equity			139,747.36
Total Liabilities and Stockholders' Equity			$175,347.36

Statement of Retained Earnings

The statement of retained earnings starts with the balance of the Retained Earnings account at the beginning of the period and shows all the changes that have taken place during the period. In the case of the Duncan Manufacturing Corporation, one of these changes is the addition of the $25,947.36 net income figure previously illustrated. The statement of retained earnings prepared for the Duncan Manufacturing Corporation is presented in detail later in this unit.

Entering Income Taxes and Transferring Net Income

After the adjusting entries have been recorded and posted, the closing entries are prepared for the corporation from the information assembled on the worksheet. The recording procedure is the same as that used for the Style Clothing Store, except for the last entry. The final closing entry for the corporation closes out the balance of the Revenue and Expense Summary account, sets up the liability for Estimated Income Taxes Payable, and transfers the net income after income taxes to Retained Earnings.

    The partial worksheet illustrated on page 615 would call for the final closing entry shown on the next page.

	19	X2							
	Dec.	31	Revenue and Expense Summary	399	32,647	36			
			Estimated Income Taxes Payable	219			6,700	00	
			Retained Earnings	381			25,947	36	
			Set up estimated income taxes and closed net income after income taxes to Retained Earnings.						

Formal Tax Return

The precise amount of income tax due is determined when the formal tax return is completed. The calculation of taxable income and of the resulting income tax due is a technical problem beyond the scope of this book. However, it should be noted that certain transactions can be reported one way for purposes of determining income for the financial statements and another way in determining taxable income. The accountant is required to explain or reconcile all such differences in preparing the tax return.

Charge-Off of Intangible Assets

As pointed out in Unit 24, intangible assets—such as organization costs and goodwill—should be amortized, or charged off, to expense over a period not to exceed 40 years. Most accountants prefer to charge them off over a much shorter period, often only five years. The organization costs of $500 incurred by the Duncan Manufacturing Corporation are to be written off in a five-year period because this is the minimum time for charging off organization costs on the federal income tax return. The entry required each year is shown below.

	19	X2							
	Dec.	31	Organization Costs Written Off	691	100	00			
			Organization Costs	191			100	00	
			Amortization of organization costs for year ($500 ÷ 5 years).						

Organization Costs Written Off (or Amortization of Organization Costs) is shown on the income statement as an administrative expense or under Other Expenses.

Prior Period Adjustments

This unit explained earlier that today an all-inclusive concept is used to determine corporate net income. Under the "pure" all-inclusive concept, no direct entries are made in Retained Earnings for any items of gain or loss recognized during the year. The only entries made in the Retained Earnings account are for the transfer of the net income or net loss after income taxes at the end of the year, for dividends declared, and for setting up and closing out reserves of retained earnings. (In older terminology, this was called the *clean surplus* concept.) As you have learned, however, authoritative bodies today favor a modified version of the all-inclusive concept. Under this version, a very limited number of items, primarily prior period adjustments, can be entered directly in the Retained Earnings account.

617

The procedure for handling prior period adjustments can be illustrated with an example of a correction relating to a prior period. Suppose a used truck having an estimated life of five years and a salvage value of $500 was purchased on January 2, 19X1, for $3,500. Its purchase was erroneously charged to Delivery Expense instead of Delivery Equipment. The error was discovered at the end of October of the current year, 19X2. How should it be corrected?

Actually, there are two errors involved. One is the charge of $3,500 to the Delivery Expense account on January 2, 19X1, instead of the correct charge to the Delivery Equipment account (overstating expenses and understating assets). The second error is that no depreciation was taken on the truck in 19X1, since the entire cost was written off as an expense when the truck was purchased. Thus expenses were overstated in one respect and understated in another.

If the amount to be corrected is substantial, it should be entered in the Retained Earnings account. The procedure calls for the following steps.

1. Recording the original cost of the truck in the proper asset account.
2. Crediting Accumulated Depreciation—Delivery Equipment for the amount that should have been entered in 19X1.
3. Entering the difference as a direct adjustment to Retained Earnings.

In the journal entry shown below, straight-line depreciation is assumed. Depreciation for 19X2 will be recorded among the usual end-of-year adjustments.

19X2				
Oct. 31	Delivery Equipment	146	3,500 00	
	Accumulated Depreciation—Delivery Equipment	146A		600 00
	Retained Earnings	381		2,900 00
	Correction of error made January 2, 19X1, when truck was charged to Delivery Expense instead of Delivery Equipment; and credit to Accumulated Depreciation for last year's depreciation on straight-line basis, 5-year life, $500 salvage value.			
	$\dfrac{\$3{,}500 - \$500}{5} = \$600$ per year			

If the prior period error to be corrected is not substantial and is therefore to be shown on the income statement, the accountant records the facts by using this procedure.

1. Recording the asset at original cost by debiting the asset account.
2. Crediting a special revenue account called Gain From Correction of Prior Year's Delivery Expense for the cost of the asset.

The accountant then corrects the depreciation omission for the prior year (19X1) by doing the following.

1. Debiting a special expense account called Correction of Prior Year's Depreciation Expense—Delivery Equipment for $600, the amount of depreciation not recorded in 19X1. (Alternatively, the prior year's depreciation could have been debited to the current year's depreciation expense account.)
2. Crediting Accumulated Depreciation—Delivery Equipment for the amount that should have been entered in 19X1.

The illustration below shows how these corrections would be recorded in one compound entry.

19X2 Oct. 31	Delivery Equipment	146	3,500 00	
	Correction of Prior Year's Depreciation Expense—Delivery Equipment	646	600 00	
	Accumulated Depreciation—Delivery Equipment	146A		600 00
	Gain From Correction of Prior Year's Delivery Expense	432		3,500 00
	Correction of error made when January 2, 19X1 purchase of truck was charged to Delivery Expense.			

Depreciation for the current year (19X2) will be recorded in the usual manner at the close of the period. Over the two-year interval, the total depreciation expense will be found by adding together the amounts in the Depreciation Expense—Delivery Equipment account and the Correction of Prior Year's Depreciation Expense—Delivery Equipment account.

Appropriations of Retained Earnings

The amount in the Retained Earnings account provides one indication of a corporation's ability to pay dividends because ordinary dividends to stockholders are generally distributions of retained earnings. However, all or part of retained earnings is usually reinvested in fixed assets or working capital rather than distributed as dividends. In some cases, distribution of dividends may be restricted by contract—for example, in connection with a bond issue. How can these limitations be indicated on the financial statements?

One way of presenting such information is by adding a footnote to the balance sheet. The footnote states that management's plans or contractual obligations will probably affect the dividends that will be declared. A more formal way for the board of directors to show this intention is to *appropriate* part of the retained earnings by resolution at a formal meeting.

Suppose, for example, that after several years of successful operations, the directors of the Duncan Manufacturing Corporation foresee the need to build a storage shed costing $25,000 within the next five years. Construction of the new shed will put a financial strain on the corporation. The directors therefore wish to restrict dividend payments and to notify the stockholders that the shed is to be built and that dividends are to be restricted. A resolution is passed at a board meeting in November 19X4 to order the transfer of $5,000 from Retained Earnings to a Retained Earnings Appropriated for Plant Expansion account. Similar appropriations will be made during each of the next four years. (Appropriations of retained earnings are sometimes called *reserves*. For example, an account showing appropriated amounts might be called Reserve for Plant Expansion.)

The resolution appropriating $5,000 in 19X4 for the storage shed would be recorded in the minutes and would serve as the accountant's authorization to make the general journal entry shown below. A similar entry is made during each of the succeeding four years.

19X4				
Nov. 5	Retained Earnings	381	5,000.00	
	Retained Earnings Appropriated for Plant Expansion	382		5,000.00
	Set up appropriation for plant expansion as ordered by board of directors in meeting of November 5.			

The balance sheet presentation of Retained Earnings indicates the amounts appropriated and unappropriated. The specific reserves are listed under the Appropriated heading. Assume that Retained Earnings for the Duncan Manufacturing Corporation amounted to $67,645.25 before the first appropriation was made. The following illustration shows how the figures would appear on a balance sheet prepared immediately thereafter.

    Retained Earnings
      Appropriated
        Appropriated for Plant Expansion   5,000.00
      Unappropriated $62,645.25
        Total Retained Earnings $67,645.25

Notice that the Total Retained Earnings figure is the same as before, but it is now divided into two parts—the appropriated portion from which dividends cannot, for the moment at least, be declared and the unappropriated balance available for any purpose. Remember, however, that retained earnings do not represent cash balances. Nor does reserving retained earnings provide the cash for any desired purpose. The availability of cash therefore influences the timing of the actual work of plant expansion.

Assume that cash is available and that the previously mentioned plant expansion project is completed in 19X9 at a cost of $25,000. The effect of the project has been to increase plant assets by $25,000 and to decrease Cash in Bank by that amount. (The balance in the Retained Earnings Appropriated for Plant Expansion account has not been affected.) Now that the project is finished, the board of directors can pass another resolution to return the amount of the reserve to unappropriated retained earnings. When such a resolution has been adopted, the entry shown on the next page is made in the general journal.

	19	X9								
	Aug.	7	Retained Earnings Appropriated for							
			Plant Expansion		382		25,000	00		
			Retained Earnings		381				25,000	00
			Returned to Retained Earnings the balance in Retained Earnings Appropriated for Plant Expansion as ordered by board of directors in its meeting of August 7, following completion of the new construction.							

The board can use the reserve technique to notify stockholders of its intention to undertake virtually any type of activity that will affect the amount and probability of dividends. When the purpose for which retained earnings have been appropriated is attained, the board can direct that the reserve be closed and that the amount be transferred back to Retained Earnings.

The board of directors of a large corporation that has many geographically scattered and uninformed stockholders may regard appropriations of retained earnings as an extremely important precaution. These appropriations may not be so necessary in a small corporation whose few stockholders are fully informed about daily operations.

Dividends The board of directors of a corporation has broad powers in declaring and paying dividends (which are ordinarily distributions of earnings). The board must weigh two basic considerations in connection with ordinary dividends—their legality and their financial feasibility.

Legality   State laws differ with respect to the conditions under which a board of directors can declare a dividend. In some states, the corporation must have accumulated earnings. In other states, dividends can be declared out of contributed capital or other nonoperating sources of stockholders' equity. Laws limiting the payment of dividends to stockholders generally are intended to protect the corporation's creditors by preventing an impairment of the corporation's capital.

Financial Feasibility   Even if a corporation has accumulated earnings, the earnings may have been invested in plant and equipment, inventories, or other assets. Although payment of dividends is sometimes made in other property or obligations of the corporation, dividend payments usually require cash. Ordinarily, the board of directors examines the corporation's position and does not declare a dividend that would lead to financial difficulties.

Dividend Policy   In some corporations, the board of directors tries to establish a policy of regular dividend distributions to stockholders, perhaps at the same amount per share each year. In years when net income is large, some of the earnings are retained for use in the corporation or for distribution as dividends in years when net income is small. A regular dividend policy tends to make the stock more attractive to investors and may help avoid sharp fluctuations in the stock's market price.

Declaration of a Cash Dividend

Three dates are involved in declaring dividends. The first is the *declaration date*—the date of the board of directors' meeting at which formal action is taken to declare the dividend. The dividend declaration and other actions taken by the board are recorded in the corporation's minute book. Once notice of the board action in declaring a dividend has been given to the stockholders (for example, by an announcement in the newspapers), the corporation has a liability to the stockholders for the amount of the declared dividend. If statements are prepared before the dividend is paid, the amount appears on the balance sheet as a current liability.

The second date is the *record date*. This is the date on which the stockholders' ledger is closed and a list is made of the stockholders (called *stockholders of record*) to whom dividends will be paid on a still later date, the *payment date*.

Suppose that the board of directors of the Duncan Manufacturing Corporation meets on December 1, 19X2, after 11 months of operation. The accounting records and interim financial reports indicate that the corporation will show a comfortable profit for its first year. Therefore, the board declares cash dividends of 8 percent on the preferred stock and $4 a share on the common stock. The dividends are payable the following January 15 to stockholders of record on December 31. On the declaration date (December 1, 19X2), there are 700 shares of preferred stock and 1,000 shares of common stock outstanding. The dividend liability is recorded as shown below.

19 X2 Dec.	1	Retained Earnings	381	5,600 00	
		Dividends Payable—Preferred	208		5,600 00
		Dividend payable on Jan. 15 to preferred stockholders of record Dec. 31 (700 shares of $100 par value at 8%).			
	1	Retained Earnings	381	4,000 00	
		Dividends Payable—Common	209		4,000 00
		Dividend payable on Jan. 15 to common stockholders of record Dec. 31 (1,000 shares at $4 a share).			

Notice that Retained Earnings is debited and that separate liability accounts are credited for the dividends payable to each class of stockholders. The dividends payable accounts will appear on the balance sheet as current liabilities on December 31, as shown on page 616. The statement of retained earnings for the Duncan Manufacturing Corporation for its first year is illustrated on the next page.

DUNCAN MANUFACTURING CORPORATION
Statement of Retained Earnings
Year Ended December 31, 19X2

Balance, Jan. 1		$ –0–
Additions		
Net Income After Income Taxes		25,947.36
Deductions		
Dividend on Preferred Stock	$5,600.00	
Dividend on Common Stock	4,000.00	
Total Deductions		9,600.00
Balance, Dec. 31		$16,347.36

Since this is the first year of operations, there is no opening balance for retained earnings and there are no prior period adjustments. The net income after taxes for the current year is the only source of retained earnings. The declared dividends reduce the retained earnings, leaving the balance shown on the statement.

Payment of a Cash Dividend

On the record date, December 31, the stockholders' ledger accounts are analyzed, and a list is made of the stockholders on that date and the number of shares each holds. Then the amount of the dividend due each investor is computed. These computations are shown in the table below.

STOCKHOLDERS AS OF DECEMBER 31, 19X2, AND DIVIDENDS PAYABLE

STOCKHOLDER	NO. SHARES	DIVIDEND RATE	DIVIDEND AMOUNT
Preferred Stock ($100 par value)			
James Duncan	100	$8 a share	$ 800.00
Ralph East	100	$8 a share	800.00
Kenneth Riley	100	$8 a share	800.00
Total Preferred Dividend Payable	700		$5,600.00
Common Stock (no-par value)			
James Duncan	400	$4 a share	$1,600.00
Ralph East	100	$4 a share	400.00
Doris Martin	100	$4 a share	400.00
Total Common Dividend Payable	1,000		$4,000.00

On January 15, the payment date, the dividend checks are issued to the stockholders on the list. Large corporations with many stockholders may set up a separate bank account for dividend payments, or they may have a transfer agent make the payments from funds provided by the corporation. The Duncan Manufacturing Corporation issues its own dividend checks, drawn on its regular bank account. The total effect of these checks is shown below.

19X3						
Jan.	15	Dividends Payable—Preferred	208	5,600	00	
		Dividends Payable—Common	209	4,000	00	
		Cash in Bank	101			9,600 00
		Paid dividends declared Dec. 1 to stockholders of record on Dec. 31.				

Stock Dividends

A corporation that has accumulated profits may actually be short of cash or may prefer to reinvest earnings permanently in the business. In this case, the board of directors may reward stockholders by declaring a *stock dividend,* which is a distribution of the corporation's own stock on a pro rata basis. The following paragraph contains an example of a pro rata distribution of stock.

Suppose that in the second year of its operations, the Duncan Manufacturing Corporation continues to be profitable and that on December 3, 19X3, the board of directors declares an 8 percent dividend payable to the preferred stockholders in cash. (The corporation would make entries similar to those just illustrated.) Suppose also that at the same meeting, the board declares a stock dividend payable the following January 20 to common stockholders of record on December 28, at the rate of one new share of common stock for each ten shares held. There are presently 1,000 shares outstanding, so 100 additional shares will be issued.

When a stock dividend is declared, the total amount charged to Retained Earnings is the estimated market value of the shares to be issued.° Assuming that each share of Duncan stock is expected to have a market value of $54, a total of $5,400 would be charged against Retained Earnings. The stated value of the shares, $5,000, is credited to a new account entitled Common Stock Dividend Distributable. The $400 excess of the market value over the stated value is credited to a new account that is called Paid-in Capital From Stock Dividends, or some similar title. The entry that records the corporation's obligation to issue the new shares of common stock is shown below.

19X3						
Dec.	3	Retained Earnings	381	5,400	00	
		Common Stock Dividend Distributable	310			5,000 00
		Paid-in Capital From Stock Dividends	307			400 00
		Common stock dividend distributable Jan. 20 to common stockholders of record on Dec. 28 at the rate of one share for each ten held (100 shares at stated value of $50 a share). Expected market value, $54 a share.				

° "Restatement and Revision of Accounting Research Bulletins Nos. 1-42," *Accounting Research Bulletin, No. 43* (New York: American Institute of Certified Public Accountants, 1953), Chapter 7, par. 10.

The balance in the new Common Stock Dividend Distributable account appears on the December 31 balance sheet. It is shown not as a current liability (as was the case with the cash dividends payable), but in the Stockholders' Equity section with the common stock.

On December 28 the stockholders' ledger is closed, and the stockholders' names are listed with the number of shares they hold and the number of shares each is to receive as the stock dividend. For example, James Duncan, who owns 400 shares of common stock, will receive 40 new shares as his stock dividend.

On January 20, stock certificates are prepared for each stockholder on the list, and the 100 shares are distributed as a stock dividend. This issue of stock is recorded by the general journal entry shown below.

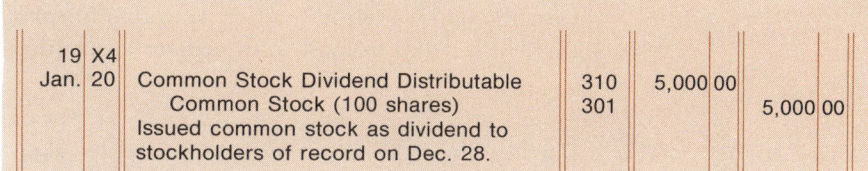

The effect of issuing a stock dividend is to convert a portion of the firm's retained earnings to permanent capital. Since no assets leave the corporation or enter the corporation, the total book value belonging to the stockholders is the same as it was before. However, the book value of each share is less because there are now more shares of stock outstanding. Each stockholder has the same total book value after the stock dividend as before, but each owns more shares of stock.

Other Stockholders' Equity Accounts

Many of the account titles used in the Stockholders' Equity section of the balance sheet are of relatively recent origin. They are the result of continuing professional efforts to make accounting terminology more descriptive, precise, and functional.

On a typical corporate balance sheet a quarter of a century ago, the Stockholders' Equity section was commonly called Net Worth. It consisted of two principal elements—capital stock and surplus. The capital stock was identified according to type—common and preferred—as is done today. The surplus element was subdivided into three categories.

1. Appraisal Surplus, arising from the upward revaluation of fixed assets.
2. Paid-in Surplus, obtained from a variety of sources, such as premium on stock issued.
3. Earned Surplus, the accumulated net income from operations that is called retained earnings in this text.

The American Institute of Certified Public Accountants has urged that the terminology be clarified and that in accounting for stockholders' equity, corporations emphasize the distinctions among (1) legal capital, (2) capital in excess of legal capital, and (3) undivided net income. The term *retained earnings* has already been used to describe what was formerly called earned surplus.

Equity Increase From Appraisal

Before 1940 corporations commonly revalued their fixed assets upward or downward to reflect substantial changes in price levels. In the 1920s, upward revaluations were common. In the 1930s downward revaluations were generally made. Most accountants no longer consider it proper to increase the value of assets. Many feel that corporations whose books still reflect the results of earlier revaluations or corporations on whose books revaluations are currently made should use a more informative account title. For example, Appraisal Capital, Appraisal Increase, or Excess of Appraisal Value of Fixed Assets Over Cost should be used instead of Appraisal Surplus. This complex problem is treated in detail in most intermediate accounting textbooks.

Additional Paid-In Capital

The heading Paid-in Surplus has been replaced on the balance sheet by more descriptive headings, such as Additional Paid-in Capital. It is also considered good practice to identify the sources of the capital in the titles of the separate accounts used for each type of capital. Examples of such titles are discussed in the following sections.

Premium on Capital Stock

It has already been explained how capital stock can be issued at a premium above par value or at an amount above stated value. The descriptive titles of the accounts credited for premium on capital stock issued by the Duncan Manufacturing Corporation are consistent with modern trends in terminology. The specific account names used are Paid-in Capital in Excess of Par Value of Preferred Stock for the preferred stock and Paid-in Capital in Excess of Stated Value of Common Stock for the no-par value common stock. The amounts in these accounts are shown on the balance sheet as additions to the credits in the Preferred Stock account and the Common Stock account. (Many corporate balance sheets use the titles Premium on Common Stock and Premium on Preferred Stock.)

Treasury Stock

Another source of paid-in capital is gain on treasury stock transactions. These gains might arise from selling donated treasury stock or from selling purchased treasury stock for more than it cost. The account titles Donated Capital From Treasury Stock Transactions and Paid-in Capital From Treasury Stock Transactions are typical of titles now used. On the balance sheet, the amounts relating to each class of stock are grouped with and added to the credits in the respective capital stock accounts.

Stock Dividends

This unit has shown that when stock dividends are declared, an amount equal to the estimated market value of the new shares should be transferred from Retained Earnings to Paid-in Capital. The excess of market value over stated value (or over par value) is credited to Paid-in Capital From Stock Dividends, another part of Paid-in Capital.

Redemption of Stock Below Issue Price

Unit 32 indicated that preferred stock can be redeemed at a price below the issue price. For example, a share of $100 par value preferred stock originally issued at par might be repurchased in the open market at $94 and canceled. The general journal entry to record this transaction is shown below.

19X1					
May 19	Preferred Stock (1 share)	311	100 00		
	Cash in Bank	101		94 00	
	Paid-in Capital From Redemption of Preferred Stock	318		6 00	
	Redeemed a share for $94; issue price $100.				

Notice that the $6 difference between the issue price of the stock redeemed and canceled and the amount paid for it is credited to the Paid-in Capital From Redemption of Preferred Stock account. This treatment follows the suggestion of the American Institute of Certified Public Accountants to avoid the use of the term *surplus*. Instead, the account title used is one that effectively describes the source of the paid-in capital. In the Stockholders' Equity section of the balance sheet, this account is grouped with the preferred stock and items related to it.

Property Acquired by Gift

Another source of paid-in capital is the receipt of a gift of valuable property. For example, a community that wishes to attract new industry may offer a plant site as an inducement for a corporation to move there. This gift of property is recorded on the books at its estimated or appraised current value. The offsetting credit is made to a paid-in capital account, which may be called Donated Capital. On the balance sheet, Donated Capital is shown as an addition to paid-in capital. The general journal entry below shows how a gift of a plant site valued at $25,000 is recorded on a corporation's books.

19X1				
June 2	Land	140	25,000 00	
	Donated Capital	371		25,000 00
	Recorded appraised value of plant site donated to corporation by city.			

Sometimes stockholders also donate assets to a corporation. These assets should be recorded on the firm's books at the fair market value on the date of the gift.

principles and procedures summary

It is now generally accepted that all items of profit and loss except prior period adjustments should be included on the income statement. However, a few unusual and nonrecurring items of profit or loss may be shown separately in a section of the income statement called Extraordinary Items. This section separates the unusual and nonrecurring items from the normal recurring operating items.

Corporate income is subject to federal income tax and to the income taxes of many states. The estimated taxes are credited to an account such as Estimated Income Taxes Payable. Net income after income taxes is credited to Retained Earnings in the final closing entry when the Revenue and Expense Summary account is closed. Net income is distributed to stockholders as dividends at the discretion of the board of directors.

Retained earnings reflect the accumulated, undistributed profits of the corporation. The board of directors may transfer amounts from the Retained Earnings account to appropriated retained earnings accounts (sometimes referred to as reserve accounts) to indicate restrictions on the distribution of retained earnings as dividends. Retained Earnings and the various appropriated accounts do not represent cash on hand. Thus, when the purpose for which an appropriation of retained earnings was originally set up has been fulfilled, the directors may transfer the balance of the appropriated account back to Retained Earnings.

Paid-in capital represents capital arising from contributions for shares or from other dealings with stockholders.

MANAGERIAL implications

Managers must understand just what enters into corporate net income—especially the difference between the all-inclusive and the current operating concepts of income reporting. Otherwise, managers may not interpret the statement figures correctly and may make unwise decisions.

Managers must also be thoroughly familiar with the provisions of law and the principles of accounting that relate to dividends. It is especially important that they understand the nature of stock dividends since such dividends permit the business to retain its cash for operations and to invest a portion of the retained earnings in the firm's permanent capital.

Managers should know about the use of appropriated accounts to inform stockholders about restrictions on retained earnings. At the same time, they should realize that the mere appropriation of retained earnings does not in any way guarantee that the necessary cash will be on hand.

MANAGERIAL discussion questions

1. Why would managers be interested in establishing a policy of regular dividend payments?

2. Why might a lack of understanding about how corporate net income is calculated lead to unwise decisions?
3. Explain what powers a board of directors has to declare dividends.
4. Why might a board of directors want to declare a stock dividend for the preferred stockholders in the early stages of the corporation's development?
5. Some members of the board of directors have asked you, the controller of the company, how the firm can have a large balance in the Retained Earnings account but no cash with which to pay dividends. Explain.
6. How can management indicate that it intends to reinvest some of the firm's retained earnings in fixed assets?
7. A director has asked you how an appropriation of retained earnings will help the corporation accumulate funds to achieve a specific purpose. Explain this to the director.

application of principles

PROBLEM 33-1 The Newton Corporation has been authorized to issue 3,000 shares of 7 percent noncumulative, nonparticipating preferred stock with a par value of $100 a share and 200,000 shares of common stock with a par value of $10 a share. As of December 31, 19X1, 800 shares of preferred stock and 28,600 shares of common stock have been issued. A condensed trial balance as of December 31, 19X1, is provided on page 630. Assume that all necessary adjusting entries, except those given in the instructions, have been made.

INSTRUCTIONS
1. Prepare a condensed ten-column worksheet as of December 31, 19X1. Enter the trial balance accounts and amounts shown. (Provide three lines for the Retained Earnings account.) Total and rule the Trial Balance columns.
2. On the worksheet record the results of the board of directors' action in declaring the following dividends payable on January 31, 19X2, to stockholders of record on December 31, 19X1. (Debit Retained Earnings for these amounts.)
   a. The normal annual 7 percent dividend on the preferred stock (Adjustment a).
   b. A cash dividend of $0.20 a share on the common stock (Adjustment b).
   c. An additional common stock dividend of 1 share for each 20 shares owned. The current market value of the common stock is $10 a share (Adjustment c).
3. Extend the combined Trial Balance and Adjustments figures into the Adjusted Trial Balance columns. Then total and balance these columns.
4. Extend the Adjusted Trial Balance figures into the appropriate columns of the Income Statement and Balance Sheet sections. Then total both sections. The company uses the all-inclusive concept of income reporting.

629

NEWTON CORPORATION
Trial Balance (Condensed)
December 31, 19X1

Account Name	Debit	Credit
Cash in Bank	$ 11,745	
Notes Receivable	2,500	
Accounts Receivable	35,200	
Allowance for Bad Debts		$ 460
Receivable From Insurance Company	171,400	
Land	50,000	
Buildings	250,000	
Accumulated Depreciation—Buildings		25,000
Equipment	125,000	
Accumulated Depreciation—Equipment		20,000
Notes Payable		20,000
Accounts Payable		24,900
Accrued Expenses Payable		7,110
Dividends Payable—Preferred		
Dividends Payable—Common		
Stock Dividend Payable on Common		
Common Stock		286,000
Preferred Stock—7%		80,000
Paid-in Capital in Excess of Par Value—Preferred		8,000
Retained Earnings		50,000
Sales (Net Total)		560,275
Expenses (Total)	431,400	
Loss From Earthquake Damage	8,000	
Gain on Sale of Securities		3,500
	$1,085,245	$1,085,245

5. Enter the provision for income taxes, which the accountant estimates to be $49,200.
6. Determine and enter the amount of net income after income taxes, total and balance all columns, and rule the columns.
7. Prepare a condensed income statement for the year, using the all-inclusive concept of reporting. The gain on the sale of securities resulted in an income tax of $1,050, while the loss from earthquake damage resulted in a tax reduction of $3,800. (Both items are deemed to be unusual and non-recurring and are to be classified as extraordinary gains and losses.)
8. Prepare a statement of retained earnings for the year, assuming that no entries were made in the Retained Earnings account during the year.
9. Prepare a balance sheet as of December 31, 19X1.

PROBLEM 33-2 The stockholders' equity accounts of Pacer Shoes, Inc., on January 1, 19X1, contained the balances shown on the next page.

Preferred Stock (10%, $50 par value, 2,000 shares authorized)		
At Par Value (600 shares issued)	$30,000	
Paid-in Capital in Excess of Par Value	1,200	$ 31,200
Common Stock ($20 par value, 10,000 shares authorized)		
At Par Value (5,000 shares issued)		100,000
		$131,200
Retained Earnings		320,000
Total Stockholders' Equity		$451,200

The corporation's transactions affecting stockholders' equity during 19X1 are shown below. The worksheet that the accountant prepared at the end of 19X1 showed estimated income taxes of $9,400 and net income after taxes of $35,600.

INSTRUCTIONS

1. Set up a ledger account for Retained Earnings 381, and record the January 1, 19X1, balance.
2. Record the transactions given below in general journal form. Use the account titles illustrated in the textbook. Post these entries to the Retained Earnings account only.
3. Give the general journal entry as of December 31, 19X1, to record the income tax liability and close the balance of the Revenue and Expense Summary account to the Retained Earnings account. Post to the Retained Earnings account.
4. Analyze the Retained Earnings account, and prepare a statement of retained earnings for the year 19X1.

TRANSACTIONS FOR 19X1

June 15   Declared a semiannual dividend of 5 percent on the preferred stock, payable on July 15 to stockholders of record on July 1.

July 15   Paid the dividend on the preferred stock.

Dec. 15   Declared a semiannual dividend of 5 percent on the preferred stock, payable on January 15, 19X2, to stockholders of record on December 31, 19X1.

     15   Declared a 12 percent common stock dividend on the common stock. The new shares are to be issued on January 15, 19X2, to stockholders of record on December 31, 19X1. A market price of $30 a share is expected for the new shares that the corporation will issue.

PROBLEM 33-3   The Stockholders' Equity section of the Ranger Corporation's balance sheet on December 31, 19X2, is given on page 632.

Stockholders' Equity
Preferred Stock (9%, $100 par value,
    2,000 shares authorized)
    At Par Value (1,200 shares issued) $120,000
    Paid-in Capital in Excess of Par Value   2,400 $122,400
Common Stock (no-par value, stated value $20,
    10,000 shares authorized)
    At Stated Value (7,000 shares issued) $140,000
    Paid-in Capital in Excess of Stated Value   21,000   161,000
Retained Earnings   135,000
Total Stockholders' Equity $418,400

Some of the corporation's transactions that took place during 19X3 are given below and on the next page.

INSTRUCTIONS

1. Set up general ledger accounts for the stockholders' equity items, and enter the given balances. Use the account titles and numbers illustrated in the text.
2. Record the transactions listed below in general journal form.
3. Post the general journal entries to the stockholders' equity accounts only. (Set up new accounts as required.)
4. Prepare the Stockholders' Equity section of the Ranger Corporation's balance sheet as of December 31, 19X3.

TRANSACTIONS FOR 19X3

Jan. 3   The corporation received land valued at $10,000 for location of a new plant as a gift from a group of citizens.

Feb. 8   The corporation reacquired 100 shares of preferred stock, paying $105 a share.

Mar. 13   Sold, for $106 a share, 30 shares of preferred treasury stock.

Apr. 19   Paid $105.50 a share to redeem and cancel 50 shares of preferred stock.

May 30   Sold, for $102 a share, 20 shares of preferred treasury stock.

July 18   Discovered that office equipment purchased on January 5, 19X2, costing $2,000, was incorrectly charged to Office Supplies and Expense 681 instead of to Office Equipment 136. The equipment was estimated to have a useful life of 8 years from the date of purchase and no salvage value. The corporation uses the straight-line method of depreciation. (Make the necessary corrections for 19X2, recording the correction through retained earnings.)

Dec. 10   The board of directors declared an annual 9 percent cash dividend on the outstanding preferred stock and a $2 a share cash dividend on the outstanding common stock. Both dividends are payable on January 20, 19X4, to stockholders of record on December 31.

    31   The board of directors voted that $25,000 of retained earnings be appropriated for plant expansion.

    31   The accountant was instructed to amortize $500 of goodwill (debit Goodwill Written Off 690, credit Goodwill 190) and $300 of organi-

zation costs. The amortization is to appear on the income statement.

31 The worksheet prepared at the end of the year shows estimated income taxes of $6,980 and net income of $27,020 after income taxes. (Make the appropriate closing entry.)

PROBLEM 33-4 On December 31, 19X1, the ledger accounts of Black Star Inc. included the balances shown below. The corporation is authorized to issue 20,000 shares of $20 par value, 9 percent cumulative preferred stock and 10,000 shares of $100 par value common stock. Dividends are in arrears for two years on the preferred shares.

INSTRUCTIONS Prepare the Stockholders' Equity section of the balance sheet as of December 31, 19X1, using the cost basis to account for treasury stock.

ACCOUNTS	BALANCES
Retained Earnings Appropriated for Contingencies	$ 20,000
Paid-in Capital From Treasury Stock Transactions	6,000
Retained Earnings—Unappropriated	49,250
Accumulated Depreciation—Buildings	3,600
Preferred Stock Subscribed (1,200 shares)	24,000
Subscriptions Receivable on Preferred Stock	16,000
Preferred Stock	164,000
Treasury Stock—Preferred (200 shares at cost)	3,200
Common Stock	400,000
Treasury Stock—Common (100 shares at cost)	10,000
Common Stock Subscribed (1,000 shares)	100,000
Paid-in Capital in Excess of Par Value—Common Stock	12,000
Subscriptions Receivable on Common Stock	40,000
Organization Costs	4,560
Paid-in Capital in Excess of Par Value—Preferred Stock	2,000
Retained Earnings Appropriated for Treasury Stock—Common	10,000
Retained Earnings Appropriated for Treasury Stock—Preferred	3,200

AlternAte problems

PROBLEM 33-1A The Krauss Corporation has been authorized to issue 5,000 shares of 9 percent noncumulative, nonparticipating preferred stock with a par value of $100 a share and 5,000 shares of common stock with a stated value of $100 a share. As of December 31, 19X1, 400 shares of preferred stock and 200 shares of common stock have been issued. A condensed trial balance as of December 31, 19X1, is provided on page 634. Assume that all necessary adjusting entries, except those given in the instructions, have been made.

INSTRUCTIONS 1. Prepare a condensed ten-column worksheet as of December 31, 19X1. Enter the trial balance accounts and amounts shown. (Provide three lines for the Retained Earnings account.) Total and rule the Trial Balance columns.

KRAUSS CORPORATION
Trial Balance (Condensed)
December 31, 19X1

Account Name	Debit	Credit
Cash in Bank	$ 10,265	
Notes Receivable	12,460	
Accounts Receivable (Net)	27,130	
Land	18,000	
Building	44,000	
Accumulated Depreciation—Building		$ 4,000
Equipment	39,000	
Accumulated Depreciation—Equipment		11,000
Notes Payable		5,000
Accounts Payable		6,325
Dividends Payable—Preferred		
Dividends Payable—Common		
Common Stock Dividends Distributable		
Common Stock		20,000
Paid-in Capital in Excess of Stated Value—Common		1,000
Discount on Common Stock	400	
Preferred Stock—9%		40,000
Paid-in Capital in Excess of Par Value—Preferred		3,000
Paid-in Capital From Treasury Stock Transactions—Preferred		600
Retained Earnings		26,225
Sales (Net Total)		206,840
Expenses (Total)	173,185	
Gain on Sales of Securities		2,400
Loss on Condemnation of Building	3,200	
Refund on Prior Year's Income Tax		1,250
Totals	$327,640	$327,640

2. On the worksheet record the results of the board of directors' action in declaring the following dividends payable on January 31, 19X2, to stockholders of record on December 31, 19X1. (Debit the Retained Earnings account for these amounts.)
    a. The normal annual 9 percent dividend on the preferred stock (Adjustment a).
    b. A cash dividend of $5 a share on the common stock (Adjustment b).
    c. An additional common stock dividend of one share for each four shares held. The current market value of the common stock is $100 a share (Adjustment c).
3. Extend the combined Trial Balance and Adjustments figures into the Adjusted Trial Balance columns. Then total and balance these columns.
4. Extend the Adjusted Trial Balance figures into the appropriate columns of the Income Statement and Balance Sheet sections. Then total both sec-

tions. The company uses the all-inclusive concept of income reporting. The tax refund is to be included on the income statement.
5. Enter the provision for income taxes, estimated to be $8,280.
6. Determine and enter the amount of net income after income taxes, total and balance all columns, and rule the columns.
7. Prepare a condensed income statement for the year. The tax refund is to be included on the income statement. The gain on the sale of securities resulted in an income tax of $528, while the loss on condemnation of the building resulted in a tax saving of $704. (Both of these items are nonrecurring and unusual and are to be considered as extraordinary gains and losses.) The income tax applicable to operating income was $8,456.
8. Prepare a statement of retained earnings for the year, assuming that no entries were made in the Retained Earnings account during the year.
9. Prepare a balance sheet as of December 31, 19X1.

PROBLEM 33-2A The Retained Earnings account of the Kelly Corporation had a credit balance of $16,800 before closing entries were made on December 31, 19X1. The worksheet prepared at the end of 19X1 showed estimated income taxes of $5,200 and net income after income taxes of $19,800. The worksheet prepared at the end of 19X2 showed estimated income taxes of $6,100 and net income after income taxes of $23,500. The selected transactions shown below and on page 636 took place during 19X2.

INSTRUCTIONS
1. Set up a ledger account for Retained Earnings 381, and record the December 31, 19X1, balance.
2. Give the general journal entry as of December 31, 19X1, to set up the income tax liability and close the balance of Revenue and Expense Summary to the Retained Earnings account.
3. Record the transactions shown below in general journal form. Use the account titles illustrated in the textbook. Post these entries to the Retained Earnings account only.
4. Give the general journal entry as of December 31, 19X2, to record the income tax liability and close the balance of Revenue and Expense Summary to the Retained Earnings account. Post to the Retained Earnings account.
5. Analyze the Retained Earnings account, and prepare a statement of retained earnings for the year 19X2.

TRANSACTIONS FOR 19X2

Nov. 15 The board of directors declared an annual 7 percent cash dividend on 500 shares of $100 par value preferred stock and a cash dividend of $3 a share on 2,000 shares of no-par value common stock, with a stated value of $50. Both dividends are payable December 15 to stockholders of record on December 1. (Use a compound entry.)

15 The board of directors declared a 10 percent common stock dividend to be distributed on December 20 to common stockholders of record on December 1. The common stock is expected to have a market value of $58 a share when issued.

Dec. 15 Paid the cash dividends declared on November 15.
20 Issued common stock for the stock dividend declared on November 15.

PROBLEM 33-3A The Stockholders' Equity section of the Shakiba Corporation's balance sheet on December 31, 19X1, is given below.

Stockholders' Equity		
Preferred Stock (10%, $50 par value, 1,000 shares authorized)		
At Par Value (500 shares issued)	$25,000	
Paid-in Capital in Excess of Par Value	2,000	$ 27,000
Common Stock (no-par value, stated value $50, 1,000 shares authorized)		
At Stated Value (900 shares issued)	$45,000	
Paid-in Capital in Excess of Stated Value	1,500	46,500
Retained Earnings		32,475
Total Stockholders' Equity		$105,975

Some of the corporation's transactions that took place during 19X2 are shown below and on the next page.

INSTRUCTIONS
1. Set up general ledger accounts for the stockholders' equity items, and enter the given balances. Use the account titles and numbers illustrated in the text.
2. Record the transactions listed below and on the next page in general journal form.
3. Post the general journal entries to the stockholders' equity accounts only. (Set up new accounts as required.)
4. Prepare the Stockholders' Equity section of the Shakiba Corporation's balance sheet as of December 31, 19X2.

TRANSACTIONS FOR 19X2

Jan. 15 Received land valued at $7,000 as a gift from a neighboring city. The corporation has agreed to build a new factory in this location.
Feb. 6 The corporation reacquired 60 shares of preferred stock, paying $56 a share. (Record at cost.)
Mar. 12 Sold, for $58 a share, 10 shares of the corporation's preferred treasury stock.

Apr. 19   Paid $54 a share to redeem and cancel 30 shares of the corporation's preferred stock.

May 28   Sold, for $47 a share, 10 shares of the corporation's preferred treasury stock.

June 10   Store fixtures costing $600 and paid for on January 2, 19X1, were charged in error to Store Supplies and Expense 523 rather than to Store Fixtures 153. The fixtures are expected to have a useful life of 10 years and no salvage value. The corporation uses the straight-line method of depreciation for all of its store fixtures. (Make the necessary correction for 19X1. Record the correction through retained earnings.)

Nov. 20   The board of directors declared an annual 10 percent cash dividend on preferred stock issued and outstanding and a $4 a share cash dividend on common stock issued and outstanding. Both dividends are payable January 15, 19X3, to stockholders of record on December 20.

Dec. 31   The corporation's board of directors instructed that $14,000 be appropriated from Retained Earnings. This appropriation is for an expansion of the firm's warehouse that is needed.

31   The accountant is instructed to amortize $400 of goodwill (debit Goodwill Written Off 690, credit Goodwill 190) and $200 of organization costs.

31   The worksheet prepared at the end of the year shows estimated income taxes of $5,400 and net income after income taxes of $22,750. (Make the appropriate closing entry in the general journal.)

PROBLEM 33-4A

On December 31, 19X1, the general ledger accounts of the Steinberg Corporation included the balances shown on the next page. According to its charter, the corporation is authorized to issue 10,000 shares of $10 par value, 9 percent cumulative preferred stock and 5,000 shares of $50 par value common stock. Dividends are in arrears for two years on the preferred shares.

INSTRUCTIONS   Prepare the Stockholders' Equity section of the balance sheet as of December 31, 19X1.

ACCOUNTS	BALANCES
Retained Earnings Appropriated for Contingencies	$ 10,000
Paid-in Capital From Treasury Stock Transactions	3,000
Retained Earnings—Unappropriated	524,625
Accumulated Depreciation—Buildings	1,800
Preferred Stock Subscribed (1,200 shares)	12,000
Subscriptions Receivable on Preferred Stock	8,000
Preferred Stock	82,000
Treasury Stock—Preferred (200 shares at cost)	1,600
Common Stock	200,000
Treasury Stock—Common (100 shares at cost)	5,000
Common Stock Subscribed (1,000 shares)	50,000
Paid-in Capital in Excess of Par Value—Common Stock	6,000
Subscriptions Receivable on Common Stock	20,000
Organization Costs	2,280
Paid-in Capital in Excess of Par Value—Preferred Stock	1,000
Retained Earnings Appropriated for Treasury Stock—Common	5,000
Retained Earnings Appropriated for Treasury Stock—Preferred	1,600

UNIT 34
bonds and other long-term liabilities

As you have seen, corporations may obtain needed funds by selling stock. However, there are also other ways for a corporation to obtain the money it requires for expansion and other purposes. In this unit we will discuss the use of bonds as a means of raising additional funds.

The Need to Borrow Money

Suppose that after several years, the operations of the Duncan Manufacturing Corporation have been successful and that a minimum of $100,000 is now needed to expand the business. The directors wonder how best to raise the additional money. They can, of course, issue more stock. However, James Duncan and the other stockholders are not in a position to buy more stock themselves. They are also reluctant to sell stock to outsiders because it might mean sharing managerial control of the business with the new stockholders.

The finance committee discusses the problem with the firm's banker, who suggests that it would be wise to borrow the needed funds. The company could probably borrow money at a rate of interest lower than the rate of return it could earn by using the funds. Furthermore, the banker points out that interest on the loan would be deductible for income tax purposes. Thus the government would, in effect, pay part of the cost of the borrowed money. The banker then outlines various ways to obtain credit.

Short-Term and Long-Term Credit

The manner of borrowing depends somewhat on the length of time for which credit is required.

Short-Term Notes

The procedure for discounting a note payable was discussed in Unit 20. The bank lends the face amount of the note, less interest. The note is paid in full at maturity, which is usually a few months after the issue date.

Banks and other lending agencies may also advance sums that are secured by a pledge of inventories or accounts receivable. Control of the inventories, such as goods stored in a public warehouse, may be transferred to the lender for collection. Although these arrangements may continue over fairly long periods of time, they are classified as short-term credit.

Long-Term Notes   Loans for what might be called an intermediate period (two to five years) can sometimes be obtained with long-term notes. The accounting procedures for such notes may differ from those used for the ordinary short-term bank note because the interest is often paid periodically over the life of the note instead of being deducted in advance. A special problem may arise if a noninterest-bearing note is issued for assets other than cash. This problem is discussed later in the present unit.

Mortgage Loans   Loans for periods of five or more years are often secured by a mortgage on property—land, buildings, equipment, or even trucks. The mortgage ordinarily gives the lender the right to seize and sell the property pledged as security if either the principal or the current interest is not paid when due. Interest may be payable annually, but it is usually paid at shorter intervals over the life of the loan. Repayment of the principal may be in a lump sum at a future date or in installments over the life of the loan.

Bonds   Corporations may also borrow for a long term by issuing bonds, which are written promises to pay the principal borrowed at a specified future date. Interest is due at a fixed rate that is payable annually or at shorter intervals over the life of the bond.

Types of Bonds

Since borrowing by issuing bonds seems to be the best method for the Duncan Manufacturing Corporation, the banker supplies information on the various types of bonds: secured, unsecured, registered, and coupon.

Secured Bonds   Bonds are called *secured* when property of value is pledged for the benefit of the bondholders. A *bond contract*, or *bond indenture*, is prepared with a trustee who acts to protect the bondholders' interest when necessary. In the case of default, for example, the trustee takes legal steps to sell the pledged property and pay off the bonds. The bonds may be identified according to the nature of the property pledged and the year of maturity—for example, First Mortgage 8 Percent Real Estate Bonds Payable, 19X5; or Collateral Trust 9 Percent Bonds Payable, 19X2. A *collateral trust* involves the pledge of securities, such as stocks or bonds of other companies.

Unsecured Bonds   Bonds issued on the general credit of the corporation (often called *debenture* bonds) are *unsecured*. They involve no pledge of specific property that the bondholders can seize to satisfy their claims. However, the bondholders do have some protection in case of liquidation because the claims of creditors, including the bondholders, rank above those of stockholders. Creditors must be paid in full before stockholders can receive anything.

Registered Bonds   Bonds issued to a particular individual whose name is listed in the corporation's records are *registered* bonds. Ownership is transferred by completing an assignment form and having the change of ownership noted in the corporation's records. Interest is paid by check to each registered bondholder. The corporation must maintain a detailed subsidiary ledger, similar to the stockholders' ledger, for registered bonds. This ledger lets the corporation know at all times who owns the bonds and is therefore entitled to receive interest payments.

Coupon Bonds Some bonds are issued with individual coupons attached for each interest payment. These coupons are in the form of a check payable to the bearer. On or after each interest date, the bondholder detaches the coupon from the bond and presents it to a bank for payment. *Coupon* bonds are transferred by delivery, and no record of the owner's identity is kept by the corporation.

Other Characteristics of Bonds Bonds are issued in various denominations. A face value of $1,000 is typical. Some bonds offer special privileges, such as convertibility into common stock at the option of the bondholder under specified conditions. These privileges are discussed in most intermediate accounting textbooks.

Entries for Bond Issue and Interest

Suppose that the finance committee of the Duncan Manufacturing Corporation recommends the authorization of $100,000 of 8 percent bonds, maturing in 10 years, with interest payment dates on April 1 and October 1. Suppose also that the board of directors approves the plan. The bonds are duly registered with the Securities and Exchange Commission so they can be sold outside the state in which they are issued. Half the authorized bonds are to be sold immediately. The remainder are to be held for possible future needs. The bonds are in coupon form and are unsecured.

Bonds Issued at Par On April 1, 19Y1, the issue date, Duncan sells $50,000 of the above bonds at par value for cash. The corporation records this transaction by debiting Cash in Bank and crediting 8% Bonds Payable, 19Z1 (indicating the maturity date 10 years later). The ledger account for the bonds is shown below as it would appear after the entry is posted.

8% Bonds Payable, 19Z1
(Authorized $100,000; Interest April 1, October 1)   No. 261

DATE	EXPLANATION	POST. REF.	DEBIT	CREDIT	BALANCE	DR. CR.
19 Y1 Apr. 1		J4		50,000 00	50,000 00	Cr.

Notice that the amount of bonds authorized is recorded as a memorandum item in the ledger account. On financial statements, the bonds payable are listed as long-term liabilities. Both the amount authorized and the amount issued are shown. One of two methods is generally used to present the bonds on the balance sheet.

1. The par value of the bonds authorized is shown. The amount unissued is deducted to arrive at the par value of the bonds issued. This presentation is illustrated in the section of the balance sheet shown on page 642.

Long-Term Liabilities
  8% Bonds Payable, due April 1, 19Z1
    Authorized $100,000
    Less Unissued   50,000
    Issued $50,000

2. The par value of the bonds authorized is shown as a parenthetical note. Only the par value of the bonds issued is extended.

Long-Term Liabilities
  8% Bonds Payable, due April 1, 19Z1. (Bonds with a par value of $100,000 are authorized, of which bonds with a par value of $50,000 are unissued) $50,000

The second method of presentation is the one more commonly used.

Payment of Interest

On October 1 the interest for six months at 8 percent becomes due on the $50,000 of bonds issued. Since some interest coupons may not be presented promptly by the bondholders, it is convenient to transfer the amount of cash needed to pay the interest to a special account in the bank. The entry to record this transfer of funds is illustrated in general journal form below.

19Y1				
Oct. 1	Bond Interest Expense	692	2,000 00	
	Cash in Bank	101		2,000 00
	Transferred funds to special account to pay semiannual interest on $50,000 bonds issued.			

Accrual of Interest

On December 31, when the fiscal year ends for the Duncan Manufacturing Corporation, bond interest of $1,000 has accrued for three months ($50,000 × 0.08 × 3/12). An adjusting entry is made debiting Bond Interest Expense and crediting Bond Interest Payable.

When the adjusting entry has been posted, the Bond Interest Expense account has a balance of $3,000 ($2,000 + $1,000)—the correct amount of interest for the nine months since the bonds have been issued. (The Bond Interest Expense account is listed under nonoperating expenses on the income statement.)

Entries for Interest—Second Year

Assuming that the same bonds remained outstanding during all of the second year, 19Y2, the following entries would be required to record bond interest transactions.

1. January 1: Reverse the $1,000 entry for accrued interest made on December 31. Record a reversing entry in the general journal, debiting Bond Interest Payable and crediting Bond Interest Expense.
2. April 1: Record the payment of interest for six months, $2,000, by debiting Bond Interest Expense and crediting Cash in Bank.

3. October 1: Record the payment of interest for six months, $2,000, by debiting Bond Interest Expense and crediting Cash in Bank.
4. December 31: Record accrued interest for three months, $1,000, by debiting Bond Interest Expense and crediting Bond Interest Payable. After these four entries have been posted, the Bond Interest Expense account will look like this.

_____	Bond Interest Expense				No. 692	
DATE	EXPLANATION	POST. REF.	DEBIT	CREDIT	BALANCE	DR. CR.
19 Y2						
Jan. 1	Reversing Entry	J1		1,000 00	1,000 00	Cr.
Apr. 1		J4	2,000 00		1,000 00	Dr.
Oct. 1		J10	2,000 00		3,000 00	Dr.
Dec. 31	Adjusting Entry	J12	1,000 00		4,000 00	Dr.

Notice that the balance in the Bond Interest Expense account on December 31 is $4,000, which is the correct amount of interest incurred for one year on the $50,000 of bonds issued.

Bonds Issued at a Premium

Two years after the first bonds were sold, the Duncan Manufacturing Corporation decides to issue another $20,000 of the $100,000 authorized. Although interest rates have fallen in the two years since the first bonds were issued, the bond interest remains fixed at 8 percent. Each $1,000 bond will therefore earn $80 a year interest. Bondholders will naturally be attracted by the favorable interest rate offered and will probably be willing to pay more than $1,000 for each bond. Under these conditions, the $20,000 of bonds are sold on April 1, 19Y3, at a market quotation of 104 ($1,040 each: 104 percent of $1,000 par), yielding $20,800 in cash. The $800 above the face amount of the bonds is a premium paid by investors because the contract rate of interest on the bonds is above the market rate of interest at the time they are sold. This transaction is recorded in general journal form as shown below.

19 Y3				
Apr. 1	Cash in Bank	101	20,800 00	
	Premium on Bonds Payable	251		800 00
	8% Bonds Payable, 19Z1	261		20,000 00
	Sold bonds at 104.			

Amortization of Bond Premium

On the books of the issuing corporation, the premium paid by the bond purchaser is written off, or amortized, over the period from the issue date to maturity. In this case, the bonds are ten-year bonds sold two years after their issue date, leaving an eight-year period over which to amortize the premium. On a straight-line basis, the amortization amounts to $100 a year, or $8.333 a month ($100 ÷ 12). A commonly used method of handling the amortization is to write off a proportionate amount with each interest payment. Using this method, the October 1 entries to record the interest on the $70,000 of bonds outstanding and the amortization of the premium on $20,000 of these bonds are as shown below. Bond interest expense is $2,800 ($70,000 × 0.08 × 6/12).

19 Y3					
Oct. 1	Bond Interest Expense	692	2,800 00		
	Cash in Bank	101		2,800 00	
	Paid semiannual interest on $70,000 bonds issued.				
1	Premium on Bonds Payable	251	50 00		
	Bond Interest Expense	692		50 00	
	Amortized premium for 6 months on $20,000 bonds.				

The bond interest paid includes $2,000 for the $50,000 of bonds first issued and $800 for the $20,000 issued two years later. The $50 amortization of bond premium is for six months at $8.333 a month.

Adjusting and Reversing Entries

On December 31 an adjusting entry is required for three months' interest on $70,000 of bonds and for amortization of the three months' premium on $20,000 of bonds. Interest payable on the $70,000 of bonds is $1,400 ($70,000 × 0.08 × 3/12). The amortization of the premium amounts to $25 ($8.333 × 3). In the entry shown below, Premium on Bonds Payable is debited for $25 and Bond Interest Payable is credited for $1,400. The difference of $1,375 is charged to Bond Interest Expense.

19 Y3					
Dec. 31	Bond Interest Expense	692	1,375 00		
	Premium on Bonds Payable	251	25 00		
	Bond Interest Payable	232		1,400 00	
	Accrued interest on $70,000 bonds issued, and amortized premium on $20,000 for 3 months.				

On January 1 of the following year, this adjusting entry would be reversed. The entries on April 1 and October 1 for interest and amortization would be the same as the one previously illustrated for October 1, 19Y3. The adjusting and reversing entries would be repeated at the end of each year.

Bonds Issued at a Discount

Suppose that the Duncan Manufacturing Corporation decides to issue another $20,000 of bonds on April 1, 19Y4, a year after the preceding issue. If the prevailing interest rates on other investments have risen since the last sale of bonds, investors will no longer be willing to pay a premium for an investment paying only 8 percent. In fact, they may not be interested in buying the bonds at par value either. Instead, they may offer only $972, or 97.2, for a $1,000, 8 percent bond. Assuming that the Duncan Manufacturing Corporation sells the bonds at 97.2, the cash it receives for the $20,000 par value bonds is $19,440 and there is a $560 discount as shown by the general journal entry below.

19Y4				
Apr. 1	Cash in Bank	101	19,440.00	
	Discount on Bonds Payable	151	560.00	
	8% Bonds Payable, 19Z1	261		20,000.00
	Sold bonds at 97.2.			

Amortization of Bond Discount

The bonds in question have seven years to run, and the $560 discount must be amortized over this period. On a straight-line basis, the amortization will thus be $80 a year ($560 ÷ 7). The October 1 interest payment will be made on the $90,000 of bonds outstanding for a total of $3,600 cash. The premium on the bonds issued in 19Y3 will be amortized as previously illustrated. A new entry is required to amortize $40 of the discount for half a year. This entry debits Bond Interest Expense (since the discount increases the actual cost of borrowing) and credits Discount on Bonds Payable.

Adjusting and Reversing Entries

On December 31 an adjusting entry is made to accrue interest payable for three months on $90,000 of bonds at 8 percent, or $1,800. Bond discount amortized for three months, $20 (3/12 × $80), is added, and bond premium amortized for three months, $25, is subtracted from this figure. What remains is a debit of $1,795 to Bond Interest Expense. The adjusting entry is illustrated below.

19Y4				
Dec. 31	Bond Interest Expense	692	1,795.00	
	Premium on Bonds Payable	251	25.00	
	Discount on Bonds Payable	151		20.00
	Bond Interest Payable	232		1,800.00
	Recorded interest on $90,000 bonds issued, amortized premium on $20,000, and amortized discount on $20,000 for 3 months.			

This entry is, of course, reversed on the first day of the following year.

Balance Sheet Presentation of Premium and Discount

The Premium on Bonds Payable account has a credit balance that should be shown on the balance sheet under the heading Long-Term Liabilities, as an addition to the par value of bonds payable. The Discount on Bonds Payable account has a debit balance that should be subtracted from the par value of the bonds payable. If there are both a discount and a premium on a bond issue, the two are combined and shown on the balance sheet as a single net figure. The method of reporting bonds payable and the related discount or premium on the balance sheet is illustrated on the next page for the Duncan Manufacturing Corporation on December 31, 19Y4.

```
            Long-Term Liabilities
              8% Bonds Payable, due April 1, 19Z1
                 (Authorized $100,000 par value, less
                 $10,000 par value unissued)            $90,000
              Net Premium on Bonds
                 Payable                                    125
              Net Liability                                         $90,125
```

The amount of the Bonds Payable account plus that of the Premium on Bonds Payable account (or minus that of the Discount on Bonds Payable account) is referred to as the *book value* or the *carrying value* of the bonds.

Bonds Issued Between Interest Dates

The preceding examples were for bonds that were issued on interest dates. In practice, however, bonds are often issued between interest dates. The new owner is nevertheless entitled to be paid for the entire interest period when he or she cashes the interest coupon on the interest payment date. Consequently, when bonds are sold between interest dates, the purchaser pays the seller for the interest accrued to the day of purchase.

Recording Issuance of the Bonds

Suppose that the Duncan Manufacturing Corporation sells its remaining $10,000 par value bonds on July 1, 19Y5. At this time the prevailing interest rate has again changed. Purchasers of the bonds are now willing to pay face value for the bonds, $10,000, plus accrued interest from April 1 to July 1, 19Y5—a period of three months. Interest for three months at 8 percent on $10,000 is $200, and the total cash actually collected is $10,200. The required entry is presented in general journal form below.

```
19 Y5
July  1  Cash in Bank                              101   10,200 00
            Bond Interest Expense                  692              200 00
            8% Bonds Payable, 19Z1                 261           10,000 00
         Sold bonds at par plus accrued
         interest for 3 months.
```

Notice that the $200 received for accrued interest is credited to the Bond Interest Expense account. When the interest is paid in October, the purchasers of these $10,000 of bonds will receive $400. Of this amount, $200 is a return of what they paid for accrued interest and the remaining $200 is interest actually earned for the three months (July, August, and September) during which they have owned the bonds. On the corporation's books the final result is a net interest expense of $200 on these bonds.

Amortization of Discount or Premium

If bonds are issued at a discount or premium between interest dates, the discount or premium is amortized over the time remaining from the date of issue to the date of maturity. Suppose, for example, that on March 1, 19X4, a corporation issues $100,000 par value, 9 percent, 10-year bonds, dated January 1, 19X1, and maturing January 1, 19Y1, with interest payments due on January 1 and July 1 of each year. The bonds are issued at 102.5, plus accrued interest. The entry to record the issue is shown below.

19X4 Mar. 1	Cash in Bank	101	104,000 00	
	Bond Interest Expense ($100,000 × 9% × 2/12)	692		1,500 00
	9% Bonds Payable, 19Y1	261		100,000 00
	Premium on Bonds Payable	251		2,500 00
	Issued $100,000 of 9% bonds at 102.5 plus accrued interest for 2 months.			

On July 1, 19X4, the date of the first interest payment, the amount of the bond premium to amortize is $121.95, computed as follows.

Total premium	$2,500
Number of months from date of issue to date of maturity (March 1, 19X4, to January 1, 19Y1)	82
Amortization each month = $2,500 ÷ 82 =	$30.488
Amortization from March 1, 19X4, to July 1, 19X4 = $30.488 × 4 =	$121.95

The entry to record payment of the interest and amortization of the premium on July 1, 19X4, is shown below.

19X4 July 1	Bond Interest Expense	692	4,378 05	
	Premium on Bonds Payable	251	121 95	
	Cash in Bank	101		4,500 00
	Paid semiannual interest on 9% bonds and amortized bond premium for 4 months.			

Bond Sinking Fund and Appropriation of Retained Earnings

At the maturity of the bond issue on April 1, 19Z1, the Duncan Manufacturing Corporation will have to pay bondholders the face amount of their bonds, a total of $100,000 in cash. (The premium and discount are completely amortized with the last interest payment on April 1, 19Z1.) Careful planning is needed to make sure that the required cash will be available on the maturity date. In order to ensure the availability of cash, the corporation may voluntarily set up a *bond sinking fund* or it may be required to do so by contract with the bondholders. Here is how the plan might work.

Bond Sinking Fund

Suppose that the corporation is to accumulate $20,000 a year in the bond sinking fund for each of the last five years the bonds are outstanding. The cash put into the fund will be invested, and the net earnings of the fund will reduce the amount that the corporation will have to add each year after the first. For example, the bond sinking fund is started on April 1, 19Y6, by transferring $20,000 in cash to it. This $20,000 is immediately invested to earn interest. During the next year $950 is earned on the investments made by the sinking fund, and a $50 expense is incurred in operating the fund. This leaves net earnings of $900 for the year. On April 1 of the second year, only $19,100 need be added to the fund. At the end of the fifth year, the fund should have accumulated the $100,000 needed to pay off the bonds.

Entries for the first two transfers to the fund, the first year's net earnings, and the final retirement of the bonds at the end of the fifth year are given in general journal form below.

19 Y6				
Apr. 1	Bond Sinking Fund	138	20,000 00	
	Cash in Bank	101		20,000 00
	Transferred first of five annual installments to bond sinking fund.			
19 Y7				
Apr. 1	Bond Sinking Fund	138	900 00	
	Income From Sinking Fund Investments	493		900 00
	Recorded net income earned by bond sinking fund during the year.			
1	Bond Sinking Fund	138	19,100 00	
	Cash in Bank	101		19,100 00
	Transferred second annual installment to bond sinking fund, $20,000 less $900 net earned on fund investments during the year.			
19 Z1				
Apr. 1	8% Bonds Payable, 19Z1	261	100,000 00	
	Bond Sinking Fund	138		100,000 00
	Paid bonds with cash from bond sinking fund.			

In order to simplify the illustration, it is assumed that the sinking fund is handled by an outside trustee, who makes the necessary detailed entries to record the fund transactions. If the corporation handled the bond sinking fund itself, additional entries would be required to show the investment of the fund's cash, the receipt of earnings, and the payment of fund expenses.

The bond sinking fund is reported as an investment in the Assets section of the balance sheet.

Retained Earnings Appropriated for Bond Retirement

As further protection for the bondholders and as a clear indication to the stockholders that retained earnings are being held in the business to pay the bonds at maturity, the bond indenture may require that dividend payments be restricted by appropriations of retained earnings while the bonds are outstanding. Even if the bond indenture does not require the appropriation, retained earnings may be appropriated by order of the board of directors.

If such an appropriation is decided on, an entry might be made to appropriate $20,000 a year during each of the last five years of the life of the bonds.

The firm might also adopt some other "schedule of appropriations." When the bonds have been paid off, the appropriated retained earnings are returned to the Retained Earnings account. The entries shown below are to make an appropriation on April 1, 19Y6 (similar entries would be made each year for the next four years), and to remove the appropriation when the bonds have been paid. The Retained Earnings Appropriated for Bond Retirement account would be shown under the heading Appropriated Retained Earnings on the balance sheet.

19Y6				
Apr. 1	Retained Earnings	381	20,000 00	
	Retained Earnings Appropriated for Bond Retirement	383		20,000 00
	Set up appropriation for bond sinking fund.			
19Z1				
Apr. 1	Retained Earnings Appropriated for Bond Retirement	383	100,000 00	
	Retained Earnings	381		100,000 00
	Closed out appropriation for bond sinking fund.			

The Retained Earnings Appropriated for Bond Retirement account is sometimes referred to as the Reserve for Bond Sinking Fund, even though the account has nothing to do with a sinking fund.

Retirement of Bonds

There are several different ways that corporations can retire the bonds they issue.

Retirement on Due Date

The retirement of Duncan's bonds by payment from the sinking fund illustrates one method of bond retirement. Of course, if there had been no bond sinking fund, the corporation would have recorded the retirement on the maturity date by debiting 8% Bonds Payable, 19Z1, and crediting Cash in Bank.

Early Retirement

Under certain circumstances a corporation may retire some or all of its bonds before maturity by purchasing them on the open market. This may be done because the corporation has surplus cash, because it wants to save interest costs, because it expects interest rates to decrease, or for other reasons. When bonds are retired prior to maturity, the bondholders are paid the agreed-upon price for the bonds plus the accrued interest to the date of purchase. The following steps are taken to record the purchase and retirement.

1. The corporation records the amortization of the discount or premium from the date of the last amortization to the current date on the bonds being retired.
2. The corporation removes the par value of the bonds from the Bonds Payable account and removes the unamortized discount or premium applicable to the retired bonds from the Bond Discount account or the Bond Premium account. The purchase price is credited to Cash in Bank (or Accounts Payable), and the difference between the purchase price and the

book value of the bonds is recorded as a gain or loss. Interest Expense is debited and Cash in Bank is credited for the accrued interest paid.

On the income statement, any significant gain or loss on early retirement of bonds is always shown as an extraordinary gain or loss.*

To illustrate the early retirement of bonds, we will assume that on January 1, 19X1, the Drake Corporation issued $1,000,000 par value of its 10 percent, 20-year bonds payable, maturing January 1, 19Z1, with interest payable on January 1 and July 1 of each year. The bonds were issued at 102.4, so a premium of $24,000 was recorded. The premium is being amortized on a straight-line basis of $100 a month ($600 for each interest payment period).

On July 1, 19X6, after the interest was paid and the premium was amortized, the account balances related to the bonds were as follows: 10% Bonds Payable, 19Z1, $1,000,000; Premium on Bonds Payable, $17,400 ($24,000 − $6,600).

On September 1, 19X6, the corporation decided to purchase on the open market at 101 plus accrued interest $300,000 par value of the bonds—30 percent of the total outstanding.

On that date the bondholders were paid $303,000 for the bonds, plus $5,000 accrued interest for two months, and the bonds were retired. The necessary entries are as follows.

1. The amortization on the bonds being retired is recorded as shown in the general journal entry below.

19 X6					
Sept. 1	Premium on Bonds Payable (30% × $100 × 2)	251		60 00	
	Bond Interest Expense	692			60 00
	Amortized premium for 2 months on bonds being retired.				

$$\$24{,}000 \times \frac{\$300{,}000}{\$1{,}000{,}000} \times \frac{2 \text{ mos.}}{240 \text{ mos.}} = \$60$$

2. The par value and unamortized premium are removed. The cash payment for the bonds and the accrued interest are recorded. The unamortized premium is computed as follows.

Unamortized premium after July 1, 19X6, amortization:	
30% × $17,400	$5,220
Less Amortization for July and August	60
Balance	$5,160

---

*"Reporting Gains and Losses From Extinguishment of Debt," *Statement of Financial Accounting Standards*, No. 4 (Stamford, Conn.: Financial Accounting Standards Board, 1975), par. 8.

The entry to record the retirement of the bonds is shown in general journal form below.

19 X6 Sept. 1	10% Bonds Payable, 19Z1
	Premium on Bonds Payable
	Bond Interest Expense ($300,000
	    × 10% × 2/12)
	    Cash in Bank
	    Gain on Early Retirement of Bonds
	Retired bonds at 101 plus accrued
	interest and wrote off unamortized premium.
		261
		251
		
		692
		101
		496
			300,000 00
			5,160 00
			
			5,000 00
				
				308,000 00
				2,160 00

$$\$24{,}000 \times \frac{\$300{,}000}{\$1{,}000{,}000} \times \frac{172 \text{ mos.}}{240 \text{ mos.}} = \$5{,}160.$$

On the income statement, the gain of $2,160 less the related income tax is shown as an extraordinary gain.

Mortgage Liabilities

If long-term borrowing is arranged through a mortgage loan instead of by issuing bonds, the following entries are required.

1. When cash is received, debit Cash in Bank and credit Mortgage Payable. Ordinarily no premium or discount is involved on a mortgage loan.
2. When interest payments are made, debit Mortgage Interest Expense and credit Cash in Bank. Payments on the principal are of course debited to Mortgage Payable. Payments are usually made in equal installments. A schedule of amortization shows what part of each payment is applied to interest and what part is applied to principal.
3. Accrue interest at the end of each year, and reverse the adjustment at the beginning of the next year.
4. When the mortgage is paid at maturity, debit Mortgage Payable and credit Cash in Bank.

Issuance of Noninterest-Bearing Notes for Noncash Assets

Although most notes payable bear interest, and almost invariably notes issued in return for cash do so, sometimes noninterest-bearing notes are issued to obtain assets other than cash. For example, a person may purchase land for $50,000, giving the seller a two-year noninterest-bearing note for $50,000. A transaction such as this suggests that the land is "overpriced" and that in reality the purchaser is paying less than $50,000 for the property. The difference between $50,000 and the true value of the property is considered the interest charge. (If interest is specified but the rate is unreasonably low, there may be a presumption that the face value of the note does not reflect the true purchase price of the asset.)

Generally accepted accounting principles require that if the fair market value of the acquired property is known, the asset should be recorded at its fair market value. The Notes Payable account should then be credited for the face value of the note, and the difference should be debited to the Discount on

Notes Payable account. For example, the acquisition of land with a fair market value of $40,000 by the issuance of a two-year noninterest-bearing note payable for $50,000 is recorded as shown below.

19 X1				
May 1	Land	141	40,000 00	
	Discount on Notes Payable	251A	10,000 00	
	Notes Payable	251		50,000 00
	Issued a 2-year noninterest-bearing note for $50,000 to purchase land with a fair market value of $40,000.			

If the value of the asset acquired cannot be determined, its present value must be imputed. This is done by computing the present value of the note, using an interest rate that seems reasonable under the circumstances, given the financial condition of the debtor.[*]

For example, assume that the debtor issues a $100,000 noninterest-bearing note in return for used machinery whose market value cannot be determined. Assume also that an interest rate of 10 percent is reasonable under the circumstances. By referring to a "present value" table, you would find that the "present value of $1" due two years from now is 0.82645. This means that $0.82645 would have to be invested today to accumulate $1 two years from now if the amount invested today were to earn interest of 10 percent a year, compounded annually. Thus, the present value of $100,000 due two years from now is $82,645. The entry to record the purchase in the general journal is shown below.

19 X1				
June 1	Machinery and Equipment	131	82,645 00	
	Discount on Notes Payable	251A	17,355 00	
	Notes Payable	251		100,000 00
	Issued a 2-year noninterest-bearing note for $100,000 to purchase machinery. Present value of $100,000 at 10% discount rate used to establish value.			

The amount shown in the Discount on Notes Payable account would be subtracted from the face value of the long-term notes payable on the balance sheet. The account would be amortized over the period to maturity in much the same way as discounts on bonds payable are amortized. There are special rules governing the computation of the amount to be amortized each period. However, since such amounts are usually relatively immaterial, the straight-line method is commonly used to record amortization.

---

[*] "Interest on Receivables and Payables," *Opinions of the Accounting Principles Board, No. 21* (New York: American Institute of Certified Public Accountants, 1971), pars. 12–13.

principles and procedures summary

Long-term borrowing may be accomplished through the issuance of bonds. A bond is a written promise to repay a certain sum at a future date. It bears interest that is usually payable annually or semiannually at a specified rate. Bonds may be secured or unsecured and may be registered or may be bearer bonds with interest coupons attached.

Bonds may be issued at par, at a premium, or at a discount. Premium and discount are amortized over the life of the bonds as an adjustment of the interest expense. When bond interest dates do not coincide with the fiscal year, an adjustment is made for accrued bond interest at the end of the year. The adjustment is reversed at the beginning of the next year. When bonds are issued between interest dates, the purchaser pays for the accrued interest to the date of purchase.

A bond sinking fund may be used to accumulate the cash required to pay bonds at maturity. In addition, an appropriation of retained earnings for bond retirement may be established by transfers from retained earnings. This appropriation indicates that the earnings are not available for dividends because of the need to accumulate funds with which to pay the bonds.

When bonds are retired prior to maturity, a gain or loss results if the repurchase price differs from the book value of the bonds. The gain or loss is shown as an extraordinary item on the income statement.

If noninterest-bearing notes are issued for assets other than cash, it may be appropriate to record the assets at fair market value or imputed value, giving rise to a discount on the notes payable.

managerial implications

Managers should be aware of the possibility of using bonds as a means of obtaining long-term financing. They should understand the different types of bonds and bond retirement funds, the provisions relating to interest, and the appropriations of retained earnings. Managers should also appreciate and understand the advantages and disadvantages of using bonds so that they can raise capital under terms and conditions most favorable to the firm.

managerial discussion questions

1. Under what circumstance would it be wise for corporate management to borrow needed long-term funds instead of selling stock?

2. Which type of bonds would give management greater flexibility in formulating and controlling the corporation's financial affairs?
3. If registered bonds are safer than coupon bonds, why are coupon bonds still in common use?
4. Over what period of time must a premium on bonds payable be amortized? What impact does this premium have on the effective cost of borrowing?

application of principles

PROBLEM 34-1 The Schulman Company obtains authorization from its board of directors to issue $800,000 of 9 percent bonds dated May 1, 19X1. The bonds will mature in 19Y1. Interest is payable on May 1 and November 1. The bond transactions shown below occurred in 19X1 and 19X2.

INSTRUCTIONS Record the given transactions in general journal form. (Use the account titles illustrated in the textbook.)

TRANSACTIONS FOR 19X1
May 1 Issued $300,000 of bonds at par value for cash.
Nov. 1 Paid semiannual bond interest on the outstanding bonds.
Dec. 31 Recorded the adjusting entry to accrue interest on the bonds issued.
     31 Closed the Bond Interest Expense account to the Revenue and Expense Summary account.

TRANSACTIONS FOR 19X2
Jan. 1 Reversed the adjusting entry of December 31, 19X1.
May 1 Paid semiannual bond interest.
Nov. 1 Paid semiannual bond interest.
     1 Issued $50,000 of bonds at par value.
Dec. 31 Recorded the adjusting entry to accrue interest on the bonds.
     31 Closed the Bond Interest Expense account to the Revenue and Expense Summary account.

PROBLEM 34-2 Johansen Contractors Inc. obtained authorization from its board of directors to issue $600,000 of 7 percent bonds. Each bond has a face value of $1,000 and is in registered form. The bonds mature in 10 years from the issue date (May 1, 19X1). Because the funds to be raised were not immediately needed, no bonds were issued until 19X3. The transactions that occurred in 19X3 and 19X4 are shown on the next page. (Interest was payable on May 1 and November 1.)

INSTRUCTIONS 1. Record the given transactions in general journal form. (Use the account titles illustrated in the textbook.)

2. Prepare the Long-Term Liabilities section of the corporation's balance sheet on December 31, 19X3.

TRANSACTIONS FOR 19X3

Feb. 1   Issued $50,000 of bonds at par value, plus accrued interest, for cash.
May   1   Paid semiannual interest on the bonds issued.
      1   The corporation issued $100,000 of bonds at 102 for cash.
Nov. 1   Paid semiannual interest on the bonds.
      1   Recorded amortization of the premium on the bonds sold on May 1.
Dec. 31   Recorded the adjusting entry to accrue interest on the bonds issued and to amortize the premium for two months.
     31   Closed the Bond Interest Expense account to the Revenue and Expense Summary account.

TRANSACTIONS FOR 19X4

Jan. 1   Reversed the adjusting entry of December 31, 19X3.

PROBLEM 34-3 The Plains Company obtained authorization from its board of directors to issue $500,000 of 8 percent bonds. The bonds mature 10 years from their issue date of May 1, 19X1. Interest is payable on May 1 and November 1. Because the funds were not immediately needed, no bonds were issued until 19X4. The transactions that occurred in 19X4 and 19X5 are shown below.

INSTRUCTIONS
1. Record the given transactions in general journal form. (Use the account titles illustrated in the textbook.)
2. Prepare the Long-Term Liabilities section of the corporation's balance sheet on December 31, 19X4.

TRANSACTIONS FOR 19X4

May   1   Issued $100,000 of bonds at 98 for cash.
Nov. 1   Paid semiannual bond interest.
      1   Made the entry to amortize the discount on the bonds issued.
Dec. 31   Recorded the adjusting entry to accrue interest on the bonds issued and to amortize the discount for two months.
     31   Made the entry to close the Bond Interest Expense account to the Revenue and Expense Summary account.

TRANSACTIONS FOR 19X5

Jan. 1   Reversed the adjusting entry of December 31, 19X4.

PROBLEM 34-4 Overhill Drugs Inc. has outstanding $6,000,000 of 8 percent bonds payable dated January 1, 19X1, and maturing January 1, 19Y3, 12 years later. The corporation is required under the bond indenture to transfer $410,000 each year to a sinking fund. The directors have also voted to restrict retained earnings by transferring $500,000 each year to a Retained Earnings Appropriated for Bond Retirement account. On January 1, 19X6, the pertinent account balances are as follows: Bond Sinking Fund, $2,210,000; Retained Earnings Appropriated for Bond Retirement, $2,500,000. Transactions that took place at the end of 19X6 are given below.

TRANSACTIONS FOR 19X6

Dec. 31 The annual bond sinking fund deposit was made.
    31 The annual appropriation of retained earnings was recorded.
    31 The bond sinking fund trustee reported a net income of $208,400 on the sinking fund investments for the year.

INSTRUCTIONS
1. Prepare entries in general journal form to record the end-of-year transactions.
2. Show how the Bond Sinking Fund account and the Retained Earnings Appropriated for Bond Retirement account would appear on the balance sheet as of December 31, 19X6. (Assume that the ending balance of Retained Earnings—Unappropriated was $8,495,670.)
3. Assuming that the Bond Sinking Fund account had a balance of $6,000,000 on January 1, 19Y3, give the entry in general journal form to record payment of the amount due and the retirement of the bonds.

PROBLEM 34-5 On April 1, 19X1, the Bruzzi Company, Inc., issued $1,000,000 par value, 8 percent bonds at 98.8. The bonds have a life of 20 years. The discount was to be amortized on each interest payment date. Interest is payable on April 1 and October 1. On March 1, 19X6, the company purchased one-half of the outstanding bonds from the bondholders and retired them. The purchase price was 99.2, plus accrued interest for five months.

INSTRUCTIONS Give the entries in general journal form for the following.

1. To amortize the discount on the bonds being retired (five months' amortization).
2. To record the repurchase and retirement of the bonds. (Use the Loss on Early Retirement of Bonds 693 account.)

alternate problems

PROBLEM 34-1A The HPT Corporation's board of directors authorizes the issuance of $300,000 par value, 10-year, 10 percent bonds dated April 1, 19X1, and maturing on April 1, 19Y1. Interest is payable semiannually on April 1 and October 1. The HPT Corporation uses the calendar year as its fiscal year. The bond transactions that occurred in 19X1 and 19X2 are shown on the next page.

INSTRUCTIONS Record the given transactions in general journal form. (Use the account titles illustrated in the textbook.)

TRANSACTIONS FOR 19X1

Apr. 1 Issued $80,000 of bonds at par value.
Oct. 1 Paid semiannual interest on the bonds issued.
Dec. 31 Recorded the accrued bond interest.
     31 Closed the Bond Interest Expense account to the Revenue and Expense Summary account.

TRANSACTIONS FOR 19X2

Jan. 1 Reversed the adjusting entry made on December 31, 19X1.
Apr. 1 Issued $20,000 of bonds at par value.
     1 Paid interest for six months on the bonds previously issued.
Oct. 1 Paid interest for six months on the outstanding bonds.
Dec. 31 Recorded the accrued bond interest.
     31 Closed the Bond Interest Expense account to the Revenue and Expense Summary account.

PROBLEM 34-2A The Cleary Corporation is authorized by its board of directors to issue $700,000 of 10-year, 7 percent bonds dated April 1, 19X1, and maturing on April 1, 19Y1. Interest is payable semiannually on April 1 and October 1. The corporation does not immediately issue the bonds because funds are not currently needed. The transactions that take place in 19X3 and 19X4 are shown below.

INSTRUCTIONS
1. Record the given transactions in general journal form. (Use the account titles illustrated in the textbook.)
2. Prepare the Long-Term Liabilities section of the corporation's balance sheet on December 31, 19X3.

TRANSACTIONS FOR 19X3

Feb. 1 Issued $20,000 par value bonds for $20,196, plus accrued interest.
Apr. 1 Paid semiannual interest on the outstanding bonds and amortized the bond premium. (Make two entries.)
Oct. 1 Paid semiannual interest on the outstanding bonds and amortized the bond premium.
Dec. 31 Recorded accrued interest and amortized the bond premium for three months. (Make one entry.)
     31 Closed the Bond Interest Expense account to the Revenue and Expense Summary account.

TRANSACTIONS FOR 19X4

Jan. 1 Reversed the adjusting entry made on December 31, 19X3.

PROBLEM 34-3A The Kuhn Corporation's board of directors authorized issuance of $400,000 par value, 10-year, 7 percent bonds, dated March 1, 19X1, and maturing on March 1, 19Y1. Interest is payable semiannually on September 1 and March 1. The transactions that occurred in 19X1 and 19X2 are shown on page 658.

INSTRUCTIONS
1. Record the given transactions in general journal form. (Use the account titles illustrated in the textbook.)
2. Prepare the Long-Term Liabilities section of the corporation's balance sheet on December 31, 19X1.

TRANSACTIONS FOR 19X1

May 1 Issued bonds with a par value of $200,000 for $195,280, plus accrued interest.
Sept. 1 Paid semiannual bond interest and amortized the discount for four months. (Make two entries.)
Dec. 31 Recorded an adjusting entry to accrue interest and to amortize the discount. (Make one entry.)
  31 Closed the Bond Interest Expense account to the Revenue and Expense Summary account.

TRANSACTIONS FOR 19X2

Jan. 1 Reversed the adjusting entry made on December 31, 19X1.
Mar. 1 Paid semiannual bond interest and amortized the discount on the outstanding bonds.

PROBLEM 34-4A The Martinelli Company has outstanding $1,000,000 of 8 percent bonds payable, dated January 1, 19X1, and maturing on January 1, 19Z1, 20 years later. The corporation is required under the bond indenture to transfer $37,400 to a sinking fund each year. The directors have also voted to restrict retained earnings by transferring $50,000 each year to a Retained Earnings Appropriated for Bond Retirement account. The pertinent account balances on January 1, 19X5, are as follows: Bond Sinking Fund, $158,500; Retained Earnings Appropriated for Bond Retirement, $200,000. Transactions that took place at the end of 19X5 are shown below.

INSTRUCTIONS
1. Prepare entries in general journal form to record the end-of-year transactions.
2. Show how the Bond Sinking Fund account and the Retained Earnings Appropriated for Bond Retirement account would be presented on the balance sheet as of December 31, 19X5. (Assume that the ending balance of the Unappropriated Retained Earnings account was $455,720.)
3. Assuming that the Bond Sinking Fund account had a balance of $1,000,000 on January 1, 19Z1, give the entry in general journal form to record payment of the amount due and the retirement of the bonds.

TRANSACTIONS FOR 19X5

Dec. 31 The annual bond sinking fund deposit was made.
  31 The annual appropriation of retained earnings was recorded.
  31 The bond sinking fund trustee reported $6,820 of net income on the sinking fund investments for the year.

PROBLEM 34-5A On February 1, 19X1, the Farrell Corporation issued $600,000 par value, 9 percent bonds at 98.2. The bonds were to have a life of 20 years. The discount was to be amortized on each interest payment date. Interest is payable on February 1 and August 1. On September 1, 19X4, the corporation purchased $300,000 par value of the bonds from the bondholders and retired them. The purchase price was 98.

INSTRUCTIONS Give the entries in general journal form for the following.

1. To amortize on September 1 the discount on the bonds being retired.
2. To record the repurchase and retirement of the bonds. (Use the Gain on Early Retirement of Bonds 496 account.)

UNIT 35

TEMPORARY AND LONG-TERM INVESTMENTS

The last several units showed that corporate capital can be obtained by issuing stocks and bonds. Each of the corporation's transactions involved someone who was willing to buy the stocks or bonds as an investment. However, investors are not always individuals. Corporations too may invest part of their funds in the stocks and bonds of other firms. This unit details the accounting entries needed to record investment transactions by a business.

Investments by Business Firms

Investments by business firms can be broadly divided into two classes—temporary and long-term. Some firms have enough invested capital to meet their busy-season needs and therefore have idle funds in the slack season. They may invest these funds in government bonds, U.S. Treasury certificates of indebtedness, or other obligations that will earn them interest and that they can easily sell when they again need cash.

Other firms have funds in excess of all current needs and can invest them for a longer term. In this situation, a corporation may purchase stock in another corporation (if it is permitted to do so by state law and by its own charter) and receive dividend income. It may even purchase enough voting stock to control the second corporation. The purchaser of a majority of another company's voting stock is called the *parent company*, or *holding company*. The corporation whose stock is purchased is called the *subsidiary company*. A corporation may also buy another company's bonds for long-term investment.

Assets—such as land, buildings, and machinery—that are owned but not used in business operations are also considered investments. Similarly, funds such as the bond sinking fund described in the preceding unit are classified as investments.

Temporary Investments

In order to be classified as *temporary*, an investment must be easily marketable. The firm must also intend to convert the investment into cash within one year from the balance sheet date. Temporary investments can be made in either bonds or stocks.

Bonds as a Temporary Investment

Because they are easily marketable and safe, government bonds are a popular investment for funds that are temporarily available. Suppose that the Duncan

Manufacturing Corporation finds itself with idle funds available for temporary investment. The board of directors authorizes the treasurer to buy U.S. government bonds. On August 1, $10,000 face value 8 percent bonds are purchased at 92. Interest is payable on May 1 and on November 1. A broker's fee of $45 is paid in making the purchase. The broker's fee and any other acquisition costs are considered part of the cost of the securities, as shown below.

Price of $10,000 bonds at 92	$9,200
Plus broker's fee	45
Total cost of bonds	$9,245
Plus accrued interest (May 1 to August 1 = $10,000 × 0.08 × 3/12)	200
Total cash paid	$9,445

These facts are now recorded in a compound entry that debits U.S. 8% Bonds, 19Z4, for $9,245, debits Interest Earned for $200, and credits Cash in Bank for $9,445. The accrued interest is debited to the Interest Earned account so that when the interest payment check representing interest for May 1 to November 1 is received on November 1, the entire amount can be credited to the Interest Earned account.

Recording Interest Income Received. On November 1, the Duncan Manufacturing Corporation receives interest for six months, amounting to $400 ($10,000 × 0.08 × 6/12). The firm debits Cash in Bank and credits Interest Earned. The $400 credit to Interest Earned is partially offset by the $200 debit to Interest Earned for accrued interest that was recorded at the time of purchase. This leaves a net credit of $200, the amount of interest earned for the three months that the bonds have been owned.

Accrued Interest Income at the End of the Year. When the corporation's fiscal year ends on a date other than an interest date for the bonds it holds, accrued interest income will have to be recorded by an adjusting entry. Thus, when Duncan closes its books on December 31, interest of $133.33 has accrued for two months. The adjusting entry debits Interest Receivable and credits Interest Earned, as shown below.

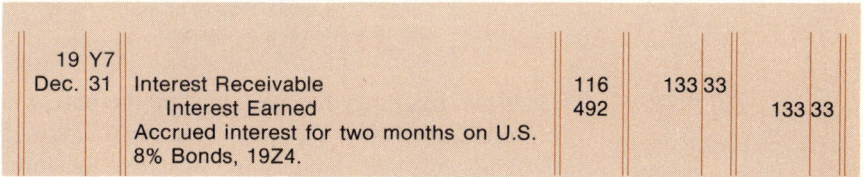

19 Y7						
Dec. 31	Interest Receivable		116	133 33		
	Interest Earned		492			133 33
	Accrued interest for two months on U.S. 8% Bonds, 19Z4.					

Statement Presentation. The Interest Receivable of $133.33 is shown as a current asset on the balance sheet. The cost of the bonds, including the broker's fee, also appears as a current asset. If the market price changes materially by the balance sheet date, it can be noted in parentheses after the account title on the statement. If the price has fallen and the decline is expected to be permanent, many accountants would reduce the figure shown on the balance sheet to the market price. Accountants who handle the situation this way are following the lower of cost or market concept discussed in connection with inventory valuation.* (However, this loss is not deductible by the corporation for income tax purposes until the bonds are sold.)

The $333.33 balance of Interest Earned is shown near the bottom of the income statement as nonoperating income.

Reversing Entry for Accrued Interest. On January 1, a reversing entry is made debiting Interest Earned and crediting Interest Receivable. This entry makes it possible to record the receipt of interest on the next interest date (May 1) as it was handled on November 1. Cash in Bank is debited and Interest Earned is credited for the entire $400 received.

Sale of Temporary Investment. Suppose that shortly after the first of the year, the Duncan Manufacturing Corporation's busy season begins and the treasurer is instructed to sell the temporary investments in order to raise extra funds. On February 1, the $10,000 bonds are sold at 93 plus accrued interest, less a broker's fee of $46. The transaction is analyzed below.

Price of $10,000 bonds at 93	$9,300
Less broker's fee	46
Net proceeds from sale of bonds	$9,254
Accrued interest (Nov. 1 to Feb. 1—	
$10,000 × 0.08 × 3/12)	200
Total cash received	$9,454

The gain on the sale of the bonds is determined by comparing the net proceeds (excluding interest) of $9,254 with the cost of $9,245, which is shown in the ledger account. The gain is $9, as shown below in general journal form.

19 Y8					
Feb. 1	Cash in Bank	101	9,454 00		
	U.S. 8% Bonds, 19Z4	119		9,245 00
	Interest Earned	492		200 00
	Gain or Loss on Sale of Investments	495		9 00
	Sold bonds at 93 plus accrued interest and less broker's fee of $46.			

When this entry has been posted, the bond investment account is closed. Interest Earned shows a balance of $66.67 ($200 less $133.33 debited in the reversing entry on January 1), which is the interest for one month in the current year. The gain realized on the sale is reflected in the Gain or Loss on Sale of Investments account, which is reported on the income statement as a

---

*Committee on Accounting Procedure, "Restatement and Revision of Accounting Research Bulletins," *Accounting Research Bulletin, No. 43* (New York: American Institute of Certified Public Accountants, 1953), Chapter 3A, par. 9.

nonoperating income item. If a loss had been incurred, the account would have shown a debit balance and would have appeared as a nonoperating expense on the income statement.

Although the example given above illustrates the accounting for an investment in government bonds, temporary investments in bonds of corporations are accounted for in exactly the same manner.

Equity Securities (Stock) as a Temporary Investment

Because temporary investments should have easy marketability and low risk, most corporations prefer to invest temporarily idle funds in U.S. government bonds and corporate bonds. However, a corporation may wish to make temporary investments in equity securities (shares of stock of other corporations) in order to take advantage of a favorable market. If the firm intends to convert the investment into cash within one year of the balance sheet date, the investment is classified as a temporary (or short-term) investment.

Recording a Purchase of Stock. All costs incurred in purchasing shares of stock are treated as part of the asset's cost. This cost includes the purchase price, the broker's fee, transfer taxes, and any other incidental acquisition cost. For example, assume that on June 12, 19Y5, the Duncan Manufacturing Corporation purchases 200 shares of the 100,000 shares of outstanding common stock of the Harpool Corporation at a price of $60 a share. The broker's fee and transfer taxes are $200. The recording of the transaction is shown below.

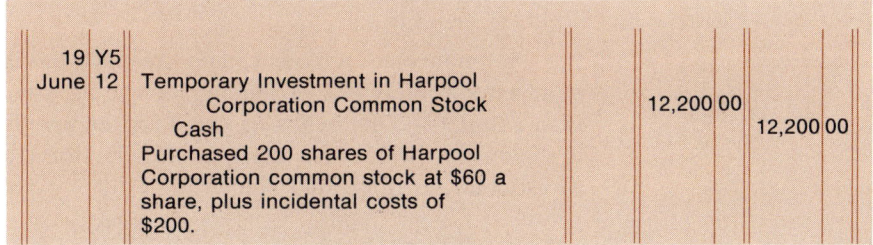

Recording a Decline in Market Value. Under generally accepted accounting principles, a portfolio of temporary investments in marketable equity securities should be reported on the balance sheet at the lower of its aggregate (total) cost or its aggregate market value as of the balance sheet date. When aggregate market value falls below aggregate cost, a valuation account (with a credit balance) is set up to reduce the total carrying value of the portfolio to its total market value.* Any amount that must be credited to the allowance account in order to reduce the carrying value of the securities is debited to an "unrealized loss" account, which appears on the income statement for the period. Assume, for example, that on December 31, 19Y5, the Duncan Manufacturing Corporation owns the temporary investments in common stock shown on page 664. The market value on December 31, 19Y5 and the original cost are also shown.

---

*"Accounting for Certain Marketable Securities," *Statement of Financial Accounting Standards, No. 12* (Stamford, Conn.: Financial Accounting Standards Board, 1975).

Security	Cost	Market Value December 31, 19Y5
200 shares, Harpool Corp. common stock	$12,200	$11,600
100 shares, Dane Corp. common stock	8,700	8,800
Aggregate (total)	$20,900	$20,400

Excess of cost over market value: $500

On December 31, 19Y5, the Duncan Manufacturing Corporation must provide an allowance account of $500. The necessary entry is shown below in general journal form.

19Y5				
Dec. 31	Unrealized Loss on Valuation of Temporary Investment in Equity Securities		500 00	
	Allowance to Reduce Temporary Investment in Equity Securities to Market Value			500 00
	Reduced carrying value of marketable short-term securities to market value.			

On the income statement, the unrealized loss is shown as an ordinary loss or an extraordinary loss, depending on whether or not the holding of securities is an unusual and nonrecurring event for the investor. The allowance account is shown on the balance sheet as a deduction from the cost of temporary investments, as illustrated below.

Temporary Investments
    Investment in Marketable Equity Securities, at Cost $20,900
        Less Allowance to Reduce Securities to
            Market Value   500
    Marketable Securities at Lower of Cost or Market $20,400

Subsequent Recovery of Market Value. Assume that at the next balance sheet date the allowance necessary to reduce the carrying value of Duncan's temporary investment in equity securities from cost to market value is less than $500. In this situation, the allowance account is debited to reduce it, and the amount of the necessary adjustment is credited as unrealized income. For example, suppose that Duncan still holds both the Dane Corporation stock and the Harpool Corporation stock on December 31, 19Y6 (even though it had been management's plan to sell the stock prior to this date), and the shares are still classified as temporary investments. Suppose further that the market price of the Harpool stock is $60 a share and the market price of the Dane stock is $86 a share. The necessary balance in the allowance account is thus $300, as shown on the next page.

Security	Cost	Market Value December 31, 19Y6
200 shares, Harpool Corp. common stock	$12,200	$12,000
100 shares, Dane Corp. common stock	8,700	8,600
Aggregate (total)	$20,900	$20,600

Excess of cost over market value: $300

The adjusting entry to reduce the allowance account to the desired balance is shown here.

19Y6 Dec. 31	Allowance to Reduce Temporary Investment in Equity Securities to Market Value	200 00	
	Unrealized Gain on Recovery in Market Value of Temporary Investment in Equity Securities		200 00
	Reduced allowance account to required balance		

The unrealized gain is shown on the income statement as other income (or, if nonrecurring and unusual, as an extraordinary gain).

An unrealized gain resulting from recovery of market value is recorded only to the point that the allowance account is reduced to zero. In other words, the investment carrying value is never more than aggregate cost. If the aggregate market value of the Harpool Corporation stock and the Dane Corporation stock on December 3, 19Y6, had been $30,000, the allowance account would have been eliminated and an unrealized gain of only $500 would have been recorded.

Sale of Temporary Investments in Equity Securities. When temporary investments in marketable equity securities are sold, the difference between the amount realized from the sale and the *recorded cost* of the securities is recorded as a gain or loss. For example, assume that on January 3, 19Y7, the Duncan Manufacturing Corporation sells 50 shares of Dane Corporation stock for $4,225. The entry to record the sale is shown below in general journal form.

19Y7 Jan. 3	Cash in Bank	4,225 00	
	Loss on Sale of Marketable Securities	125 00	
	Temporary Investment in Dane Corporation Common Stock		4,350 00
	Sold Dane Corporation common stock at a loss.		

Obviously, the sale of the Dane Corporation stock will affect the amount that must be in the allowance account on the next balance sheet date. However, this will be taken care of automatically in the routine entry made to adjust the allowance account to the proper balance at that time.

Cash Dividends on Stock. Under the lower of cost or market method of recording investments in equity securities, the investor does *not* record its share of the net income reported by the corporations that issued the securities. Only when dividends are declared or paid by these corporations does the investor record income. For example, if at the end of 19Y5 the Dane Corporation reports net income of $1,000,000, the Duncan Manufacturing Corporation will make no entry. If, however, on January 10, 19Y6, Dane declares a dividend of $1 a share, payable on February 10 to stockholders of record on January 25, Duncan will make the entry shown below.

19Y6			
Jan. 10	Dividend Receivable—Dane Corporation	100 00	
	Dividend Income		100 00
	Recorded declaration of dividend by Dane Corporation of $1 a share (100 shares).		

Duncan makes no entry on January 25, the date of record of the Dane dividend. When it receives cash in payment of the dividend, it will record the facts as shown below in general journal form.

19Y6			
Feb. 10	Cash in Bank	100 00	
	Dividend Receivable—Dane Corporation		100 00
	Received dividend from Dane Corporation.		

Many investors prefer to make no entry on the declaration date of a dividend. Instead they wait until they receive the cash, at which time they debit Cash in Bank and credit Dividend Income for the amount received.

Long-Term Investments

Long-term investments are investments that are expected to be held for more than one year from the balance sheet date. As in the case of temporary investments, such investments can be made either in bonds or in the stock of other corporations.

Bonds as Long-Term Investments

Bonds purchased for long-term investment are recorded at cost. However, when such bonds are purchased at a price that is more or less than the face value, the premium or discount is amortized over the remaining life of the bonds. (In the case of a short-term investment, the discount or premium is not amortized because the buyer does not intend to hold the bonds until maturity.)

Purchasing Bonds at a Discount. On May 1, 19Z1, the Duncan Manufacturing Corporation buys bonds with a face value of $20,000 and pays a $60 broker's fee. The bonds are the Wayne Corporation's 7 percent bonds, which are priced at 96.5 plus accrued interest. These bonds are to mature on September 1, 19Z9, eight years and four months later. Interest on them is payable March 1 and September 1. The amount of cash to be paid for the bonds is analyzed below.

Wayne Corporation bonds: $20,000 at 96.5	$19,300.00
Broker's fee	60.00
Total cost of bonds	$19,360.00
Accrued interest ($20,000 × 0.07 × 2/12)	233.33
Total cash paid out	$19,593.33

The entry required is shown below in general journal form.

19Z1					
May	1	Wayne Corporation 7% Bonds, 19Z9	132	19,360 00	
		Interest Earned	492	233 33	
		Cash in Bank	101		19,593 33
		Purchased $20,000 of bonds at 96.5			
		plus accrued interest for two months.			

Recording Interest Income Received. On September 1, the $700 interest on the bonds for six months is received by the Duncan Manufacturing Corporation. This amount is recorded by a debit to Cash in Bank and a credit to Interest Earned. With the $233.33 debit to Interest Earned at the time of purchase, this account now shows a net credit balance of $466.67, the interest actually earned on the bonds for four months.

Amortizing the Discount. The bonds were purchased at a discount that must be amortized over the remaining life of the investment. They mature eight years and four months (100 months) after the purchase date, and the amount of their discount is $640 ($20,000 face value − $19,360 cost). On a straight-line basis, the amount to be amortized is $6.40 a month ($640 ÷ 100). For the four months from May 1 to September 1, the amount to be amortized is $25.60 ($6.40 × 4).

The bond investment account is debited and Interest Earned is credited because the discount is assumed to be an adjustment of the face rate of interest on the bonds to the market rate. The periodic debits will gradually increase the investment account to $20,000 (the face amount of the bonds) by the maturity date. The two entries required to record the receipt of interest and the amortization of the discount are shown on page 668 in general journal form.

Accrued Interest Income at the End of the Year. On December 31, interest must be accrued on the bonds for the four months since September 1, and the discount must be amortized for the same period, as shown on page 668.

	19	Z1						
	Sept.	1	Cash in Bank	101	700	00		
			Interest Earned	492			700	00
			Received interest on Wayne Corporation 7% bonds for six months.					
		1	Wayne Corporation 7% Bonds, 19Z9	132	25	60		
			Interest Earned	492			25	60
			Amortized discount on bonds at $6.40 a month for four months.					

	19	Z1						
	Dec.	31	Interest Receivable	116	466	67		
			Wayne Corporation 7% Bonds, 19Z9	132	25	60		
			Interest Earned	492			492	27
			Accrued interest and amortized discount for four months.					

Statement Presentation. Interest Receivable appears on the balance sheet as a current asset. The account Wayne Corporation 7% Bonds, 19Z9, is shown under Investments at $19,411.20, the original cost plus the amount of discount amortized ($19,360 + $51.20). Interest Earned appears as a nonoperating income item on the income statement.

Reversing Entry for Accrued Interest. The adjusting entry is completely reversed on January 1. Then, on March 1, when the full six-month interest payment is received, Cash in Bank is debited and Interest Earned is credited for $700, as was done on September 1. The accountant also makes another entry to amortize the six months' discount. This entry debits Wayne Corporation 7% Bonds, 19Z9, and credits Interest Earned for $38.40 ($6.40 × 6).

Interest and amortization entries similar to these are made each year as long as the bonds are held. At maturity, the asset account will have a balance of $20,000. This balance will be credited and closed out when the bonds are paid off by the Wayne Corporation and the Duncan Manufacturing Corporation receives the face value in cash.

Sale of Long-Term Bond Investment. Suppose that four years and one month after purchasing the Wayne Corporation bonds (June 1, 19Z5), the Duncan Manufacturing Corporation sells them at 99 plus accrued interest and pays a $65 broker's fee. The first step in recording this transaction is to amortize the

	19	Z5						
	June	1	Wayne Corporation 7% Bonds, 19Z9	132	19	20		
			Interest Earned	492			19	20
			Amortized discount for three months at $6.40 a month to date of sale of bonds.					

discount from the last interest date, March 1, to the date of sale—a period of three months. This amounts to $19.20 ($6.40 × 3). The entry is shown at the bottom of page 668.

When the amortization is brought up to date, the Wayne Corporation 7% Bonds, 19Z9 account has a debit balance of $19,673.60, which is explained below.

Cost recorded on date of purchase	$19,360.00
Discount amortized: 49 months at $6.40 each month	313.60
Balance of asset account	$19,673.60

The next step is to compute accrued interest on these bonds for a period of three months (March 1 to June 1). The interest amounts to $350 ($20,000 × 0.07 × 3/12). Finally, the sale is analyzed, as illustrated below.

Price of $20,000 bonds at 99	$19,800
Less broker's fee	65
Net proceeds from sale of bonds	$19,735
Accrued interest for 3 months	350
Total cash received	$20,085

The previous entries and calculations now make it possible to determine the gain or loss. In this instance, the gain on the sale is $61.40. It is determined by comparing the net proceeds from the sale of the bonds with the book value shown in the asset account ($19,735.00 − $19,673.60). The entry to record the sale of this bond investment is given below in general journal form.

19 Z5					
June	1	Cash in Bank	101	20,085 00	
		Wayne Corporation 7% Bonds, 19Z9	132		19,673 60
		Interest Earned	492		350 00
		Gain or Loss on Sale of Investments	495		61 40
		Sold bonds at 99 plus accrued interest for three months less $65 broker's fee.			

Purchasing Bonds at a Premium. If a long-term investment in bonds is made at a premium, the purchase is recorded at full cost, including broker's fees. Interest is recorded in the usual manner. The premium is amortized over the remaining life of the bonds. The principles and computations are the same as those applied to investments purchased at a discount. However, the effect of the premium amortization is to reduce interest income. This reduction is accomplished by a periodic debit to Interest Earned and a credit to the bond investment asset account for the amortization. By maturity, the balance of the asset account is reduced to the face value of the bonds. This amount is also the amount of cash to be received when the bonds are redeemed by the issuing corporation.

Equity Securities (Stock) as Long-Term Investments

Investors purchase the stock of other corporations for a variety of reasons. In some cases, the purchase is made solely for investment purposes—for the stock's dividends or for its expected appreciation in value. In other cases, the purchase is made for "political" reasons—for example, to gain a measure of control over a corporation that is a source of supply or is a major customer of the investor. The proper accounting for a long-term investment in the stock of another corporation depends on whether the investor exercises "significant influence" over the investee (the company that issued the stock).*

Accounting for a Long-Term Investment in Stock When Investor Does Not Exercise Significant Influence Over Investee. In general, if the investor owns less than 20 percent of the voting stock of the investee, the investor is presumed to be incapable of exercising significant influence over the investee. In that event, the long-term investment in the stock is accounted for at the lower of cost or market value. The method is much the same as that used for short-term investments in stock.

Recording a Stock Purchase. The entry to record the purchase of a long-term investment in stock is almost identical to that previously illustrated for short-term investments. The only difference is that the account indicates a long-term investment.

Recording a Decline in Value. If at a balance sheet date the aggregate market value of long-term investments in stock is less than the aggregate cost, an allowance account is set up to reduce the carrying value to market price. This is done in much the same way as previously illustrated for short-term investments. However, for long-term investments, adjustments to the allowance account are not reported on the income statement. Instead, they are accumulated in an account that is shown in the Stockholders' Equity section of the balance sheet.†

This procedure can be illustrated as follows. Assume that on December 31, 19Y5, the portfolio of long-term investments in marketable equity securities of the Duncan Manufacturing Corporation includes the stocks shown below. All have been purchased during 19Y5.

Security	Cost	Market Value Dec. 31, 19Y5
300 shares, Glenn Corp. common stock	$44,000	$36,000
200 shares, Klammer Corp. common stock	30,000	33,000
Aggregate (total)	$74,000	$69,000

Excess of cost over market value: $5,000

---

* "The Equity Method of Accounting for Investments in Common Stock," *Opinions of the Accounting Principles Board, No. 18* (New York: American Institute of Certified Public Accountants, 1971).

† "Accounting for Certain Marketable Securities," *Statement of Financial Accounting Standards, No. 12* (Stamford, Conn.: Financial Accounting Standards Board, 1975).

No allowance account to reduce the carrying value has previously been set up. The entry to record the decline in market value and establish the allowance account on December 31, 19Y5, is shown below.

19Y5 Dec. 31	Cumulative Unrealized Net Loss on Long-Term Equity Securities	5,000 00	
	Allowance to Reduce Long-Term Equity Securities to Market Value		5,000 00
	Allowance account established for decline in market value of long-term equity securities.		

On the December 31, 19Y5, balance sheet, the allowance account is offset against the long-term investments as shown below.

Long-Term Investments		
Marketable Equity Securities, at Cost		$74,000
Less Allowance to Reduce Equity Securities to Market Value		5,000
Marketable Equity Securities at the Lower of Cost or Market Value		$69,000

The Cumulative Unrealized Net Loss account is shown in the Stockholders' Equity section below.

Stockholders' Equity		
Common Stock		$200,000
Retained Earnings		250,000
		$450,000
Less Cumulative Unrealized Net Loss on Long-Term Equity Securities		5,000
Total Stockholders' Equity		$445,000

Recovery of Market Value. At the time a balance sheet is prepared, a comparison is made of the cost and the market value of the portfolio of long-term equity securities. Suppose that the comparison reveals that all or part of the allowance account previously established is no longer needed. In this situation, the allowance account is reduced to the appropriate balance. The entry required is a debit to the allowance account and a credit to the Cumulative Unrealized Net Loss account. For example, assume that the market value of Duncan's portfolio of long-term investments in equity securities on December 31, 19Y6, is as shown on page 672.

The recovery is recorded by a $2,000 debit to the Allowance to Reduce Long-Term Equity Securities to Market Value account and a $2,000 credit to the Cumulative Unrealized Net Loss on Long-Term Equity Securities account.

Security	Cost	Market Value December 31, 19Y6
300 shares, Glenn Corp. common stock	$44,000	$36,000
200 shares, Klammer Corp. common stock	30,000	35,000
Aggregate (total)	$74,000	$71,000

Excess of cost over market value: $3,000

Sale of Stock. The sale of shares of stock held for long-term investment and accounted for at the lower of cost or market value is handled in the same way as the sale of shares held for temporary investment. The difference between the amount realized from the sale and the original cost of the shares is recorded as a realized gain or loss (see pages 665–666).

Cash Dividends. Cash dividends on long-term investments in marketable equity securities accounted for at the lower of cost or market value are handled in the same way as those on short-term investments in equity securities (see page 666).

Accounting for Long-Term Investments in Equity Securities When Investor Exercises Significant Influence Over the Investee. If the investor owns 20 percent or more of the voting stock of the issuing company (the *investee*), the investor is considered to be capable of exercising significant influence over the investee. (Significant influence can also be exercised in other ways. Interlocking members of boards of directors and long-term purchase or sales contracts, for example, are considered to have such influence.) The investor is generally required to show the economic results of this influence by recording the investment using the *equity method* of accounting. Under this method, the investor records in each period its proportionate share of the net income or net loss reported by the investee. The following procedures illustrate this method of accounting for stock investments.

Recording a Stock Purchase. As with other methods of accounting, the stock investment is initially recorded at total cost. This cost includes purchase price, brokers' fees, transfer taxes, and other incidental acquisition costs.

Recording a Share of the Investee's Net Income. If the investee reports net income at the end of the fiscal year, the investor records its proportionate share under the equity method of accounting. It does so by debiting the investment account and crediting a revenue account.

For example, suppose that on January 12, 19Y5, the Duncan Manufacturing Corporation purchases 10,000 shares of the 40,000 shares of outstanding common stock of the Newmont Manufacturing Company. Duncan pays a total of $245,000 for the stock and charges this amount to an account called Long-Term Investment in Newmont Manufacturing Company Common Stock. At the end of 19Y5, Newmont reports net income of $120,000. Since Duncan owns 25 percent of the common stock of Newmont, Duncan records $30,000 of Newmont's net income. The entry is shown on the next page.

	19Y5			
	Dec. 31	Long-Term Investment in Newmont Manufacturing Company Common Stock	30,000 00	
		Income From Investment in Newmont Manufacturing Company Common Stock		30,000 00
		Recorded share of investee's income for year.		

Recording Dividends Under the Equity Method. Under the equity method of accounting for investments in stock, cash dividends are treated as a reduction of the investment account. In effect, the dividends represent a return of part of the investment's cost. For example, suppose that on February 10, 19Y6, Newmont pays a cash dividend of $1 a share, and Duncan receives $10,000. The dividend is recorded by the entry shown below, assuming that Duncan records dividends only when they are received.

	19Y6			
	Feb. 10	Cash in Bank	10,000 00	
		Long-Term Investment in Newmont Manufacturing Company Common Stock		10,000 00
		Received dividend on Newmont stock.		

Recording a Share of the Investee's Net Loss. If the investee reports a net loss for the period, the investor using the equity method records its proportionate share of the loss. For example, if at the end of 19Y6, Newmont reports a net loss of $50,000, Duncan records its 25 percent share of the loss as shown below.

	19Y6			
	Dec. 31	Loss From Investment in Newmont Manufacturing Company Common Stock	12,500 00	
		Long-Term Investment in Newmont Manufacturing Company Common Stock		12,500 00
		Recorded 25 percent of loss reported by Newmont Manufacturing Company.		

Carrying Value of Investment. Under the equity method, the investment in common stock is carried at its original cost plus the investor's share of cumulative net income or less the investor's share of cumulative net loss and less the dividends received by the investor. The Long-Term Investment in Newmont Manufacturing Company Common Stock account as it appears on Duncan's books on December 31, 19Y6 is shown on page 674.

\multicolumn{6}{c}{Long-Term Investment in Newmont Manufacturing Company Common Stock No. 136}					
DATE	EXPLANATION	POST. REF.	DEBIT	CREDIT	BALANCE / DR. CR.
19 Y5 Jan. 12		J1	245,000 00		245,000 00 Dr.
Dec. 31		J12	30,000 00		275,000 00 Dr.
19 Y6 Feb. 10		J2		10,000 00	265,000 00 Dr.
Dec. 31		J12		12,500 00	252,500 00 Dr.

Amortization of Goodwill Under the Equity Method. Under the equity method, any amount by which the cost of the stock investment exceeds the investor's share of the value of the investee's net assets (the fair market value of the total assets minus the total liabilities) at the date the stock is purchased is considered to be attributable to the unrecorded intangible asset of goodwill. Like all intangibles, the goodwill cost is amortized over its useful life, which cannot exceed 40 years.

Using a highly simplified illustration, assume that on January 2, 19X4, an investor purchases 30 percent of the outstanding stock of an investee for $600,000. At that time, the book value and the fair market value of the investee's assets are $2,500,000 and its liabilities are $700,000. Its net assets, therefore, are $1,800,000. The purchase price of $600,000 is thus $60,000 more than the actual value of the net assets purchased, as shown below.

Purchase price of 30 percent interest	$600,000
Value of 30 percent of net assets (0.30 × $1,800,000)	540,000
Excess	$ 60,000

Assume also that the investor decides that the $60,000 should be amortized over a period of 20 years. The amount paid for goodwill is included in the investment account. Therefore, the entry shown below is made by the investor on December 31, 19X4, to amortize the goodwill for that year.

19 X4 Dec. 31	Income From Investment in Investee		3,000 00	
	Investment in Investee			3,000 00
	Amortized goodwill included in purchase price of stock of investee ($60,000 ÷ 20 years).			

Sale of Stock. No unusual problems arise from the sale of stock under the equity method of accounting. The portion of the investment account balance that applies to the shares sold is removed from the account by a credit. Cash in Bank is debited for the amount realized from the sale, and the difference is recorded as a gain or loss.

Stock Dividends. The procedures to be followed when the investor receives a stock dividend are the same no matter which method of accounting for the investment is used.

When a stock dividend is received, only a memorandum entry is made in the general journal. A notation is also made in the investment account. It shows the number of shares received as a dividend and the total number of shares now held. The cost of the original shares is assumed to apply to all shares owned, including those received as a dividend. If shares are later sold, the cost of each share to be removed from the investment account is found by dividing the total shares (both old and new) into the total cost. For example, assume that on January 3, 19X1, the Felton Company purchases 1,000 shares of Acme Unlimited common stock for a total purchase price of $7,040. In July Acme Unlimited declares and issues a 10 percent stock dividend, and Felton receives 100 shares of common stock. The memorandum entry to be made is shown below.

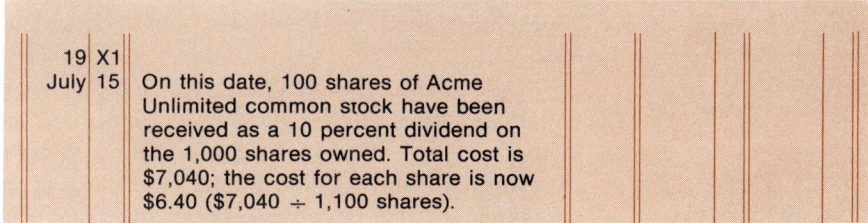

When a stock investment is sold, the gain or loss is determined by comparing the net proceeds with the recorded cost. If Felton later sells Acme's common stock for $9 a share, the recognized gain to be reported is $2.60 a share ($9 selling price — $6.40). This gain is shown as a nonoperating income item on the income statement. If a loss is incurred, it will appear as a nonoperating expense on the same statement.

principles and procedures summary

Short-term or temporary investments (classified on the balance sheet as current assets) are often made to use temporarily idle funds. If bonds are purchased as temporary investments, they are recorded at cost. Interest income is recorded when it is received, and it is accrued at the end of the fiscal year. Short-term investments in stock are recorded at cost initially, but if the aggregate (total) market value on the balance sheet date is less than the aggregate cost, an allowance account is used to reduce the carrying value to the market value. On the income statement, declines in aggregate market value to below cost are shown as unrealized losses and recoveries of previous declines in aggregate market value are shown as unrealized income. The difference between the amount realized from the sale of stock and the original cost of the shares is recognized as a realized gain or loss.

Long-term investments in bonds usually involve a discount or premium. Interest is recorded as it is received, and it is accrued at the end of each fiscal year. The original cost of the bonds is adjusted at the time of each interest entry to amortize the premium or discount over the remaining life of the investment. The adjusted cost is shown in the investment section of the balance sheet. Interest Receivable is a current asset. Bonds can, of course, be sold at a gain or loss before maturity. The discount or premium must be amortized up to the date of sale.

Long-term investments in stock are accounted for on the basis of the lower of cost or market value if the investor owns less than 20 percent of the investee's voting stock. An allowance account is used to reduce the carrying value to the market value. Under this method, declines in market value to below cost and recoveries of previous declines in value are recorded as adjustments of a Cumulative Unrealized Net Loss account. This account does not appear on the income statement, but it is a deduction from stockholders' equity.

If the investor owns 20 percent or more of the investee's voting stock, the investment is usually accounted for under the equity method. Using this method, the investor debits its share of the investee's net income to the investment account and credits it to a revenue account. Similarly, the investor charges its share of the investee's net losses to a loss account and credits them to the investment account. It also credits any dividends to the investment account.

Stock dividends distributed do not represent income under either method of accounting for stock investments. The new shares are added to the old shares, and their total is divided into the balance of the investment account to get the cost for each share.

MANAGERIAL implications

Corporate managers must be alert to the possibility of investing idle funds for short periods of time in order to earn income until the money is required in business operations. In addition, managers may want to make investments for long periods of time to gain long-term earnings or fixed income, to acquire an interest in another business, or to establish goodwill with a supplier or customer.

Managers must keep a close watch over investments in securities by appraising any changes in market conditions. Such changes may require prompt action. Managers must also be sure that all of the firm's investment transactions are properly accounted for. Income must be accurately recorded. Gains and losses must be carefully recognized on sales of investments for both financial and tax reporting purposes.

MANAGERIAL discussion QUESTIONS

1. For what reasons would managers choose to make a long-term investment in another company instead of using the funds to expand their own business?
2. Why would directors consider a short-term bond investment for the use of excess funds when they know that the bonds are subject to market fluctuations?
3. One of the directors of a corporation asks why a stock dividend on the firm's long-term stock investment was not entered as an increase in the investment account. How would you explain the recording procedure?
4. Why would a corporation buy bonds at a premium for a long-term investment, knowing that the premium will have to be amortized?
5. A corporation's balance sheet shows its long-term investment in marketable equity securities at cost even though the market value far exceeds cost. A manager wants to know why the securities are not shown at their market value. Explain this situation.

application of principles

PROBLEM 35-1 The Perfecto Company has idle funds that it decides to invest temporarily in marketable securities. Selected transactions for 19X1 are given below.

INSTRUCTIONS Record each of the transactions in general journal form. (Use the account titles shown in the related textbook illustrations.)

TRANSACTIONS FOR 19X1

Feb. 1 Purchased $40,000 face value U.S. Treasury 7 percent bonds, maturing Oct. 1, 19Y1, at 101 plus accrued interest. Interest is payable on Apr. 1 and Oct. 1. The broker's fee was $210.

Apr. 1 Received a check for the semiannual interest on the U.S. Treasury bonds.

May 1 Purchased 50 University Corporation 8 percent, $1,000 bonds, maturing Mar. 1, 19Y1, at 101.6 plus accrued interest. Interest is payable on Mar. 1 and Sept. 1. The broker's fee was $205.

Sept. 1 Received a check for the semiannual interest on the 8 percent University Corporation bonds.

Oct. 1 Received a check for the semiannual interest on the U.S. Treasury bonds.

Nov. 1 Sold all the U.S. Treasury bonds at 100.9 plus accrued interest. The broker's fee was $150.

Dec. 1 Sold the University Corporation bonds at 102 plus accrued interest. The broker's fee was $165.

PROBLEM 35-2 The transactions shown below are for the Richie Corporation. They relate to the firm's temporary investments in common stock in 19X1 and 19X2.

INSTRUCTIONS
1. Record each of the transactions in general journal form.
2. Show how the short-term investments will appear on the balance sheet as of December 31, 19X1.

TRANSACTIONS FOR 19X1
Nov. 12 Purchased 500 shares of Appleton Corporation common stock for $26 a share plus brokerage fees of $220.
     19 Purchased 300 shares of Belmo Corporation common stock for $38 a share plus brokerage fees of $210.
Dec. 31 On this date, the market values of the stock investments were Appleton Corporation, $24 a share; Belmo Corporation, $39 a share.

TRANSACTIONS FOR 19X2
Apr. 17 The Appleton Corporation declared a cash dividend of $1 a share, payable on May 15 to stockholders of record as of April 30. (Richie records dividend income when dividends are declared.)
May 15   Received a cash dividend on the Appleton Corporation stock.
Dec. 31 On this date, the market values of the stock investments were Appleton Corporation, $25 a share; Belmo Corporation, $39 a share.

PROBLEM 35-3 The Thornton Corporation makes long-term investments. The selected transactions shown below and on page 679 took place during 19X1 and 19X2.

INSTRUCTIONS Record the transactions in general journal form.

TRANSACTIONS FOR 19X1
Jan. 1   As a long-term investment, purchased $25,000 par value Martin Corporation 9 percent bonds at a price of $23,870 for the bonds, plus accrued interest and a brokerage fee of $200. The bonds pay interest semiannually on Mar. 31 and Sept. 30. They mature on Sept. 30, 19X8.
Mar. 31   Received interest on the Martin Corporation bonds. Amortized the discount for three months.
Sept. 30 Received interest on the Martin Corporation bonds. Amortized the discount for six months.
Dec. 31   Made an adjusting entry for accrued interest on the Martin Corporation bonds. Amortized the discount for three months. Made an entry to close Interest Earned to Revenue and Expense Summary.

TRANSACTIONS FOR 19X2
Jan. 1   Reversed the adjusting entry prepared on Dec. 31.
Mar. 31 Received interest on the Martin Corporation bonds. Amortized the discount for six months.

Sept. 30 Received interest on the Martin Corporation bonds. Amortized the discount for six months.

Nov. 30 Because cash was needed for an unexpected plant retooling, sold the Martin Corporation bonds for $24,400 plus accrued interest, less a brokerage fee of $135. (Amortize the discount for two months. Then determine and record the gain or loss on the sale.)

Dec. 31 Closed the Interest Earned and Gain or Loss on Sale of Investments accounts to Revenue and Expense Summary.

PROBLEM 35-4

The 19X1 and 19X2 data relating to long-term investments in stock by the Camus Company is shown below.

INSTRUCTIONS
1. Record all the transactions in general journal form.
2. Show how the investments will appear on the balance sheet as of December 31, 19X1.
3. Show how the Cumulative Unrealized Net Loss account will be reported on the balance sheet as of December 31, 19X1.

TRANSACTIONS FOR 19X1

June 8 Purchased 1,500 shares of Dentex Corporation common stock for $20 a share, plus a brokerage fee of $360. Dentex Corporation has outstanding 60,000 shares of common stock.

Sept. 10 Received 150 shares of Dentex Corporation common stock, representing a 10 percent dividend on the 1,500 shares owned.

Oct. 18 Purchased 400 shares of Ervin Corporation common stock for $62 a share, plus a brokerage fee of $312.

Dec. 31 On this date, the values of the shares held for investment were Dentex Corporation, $20 a share; Ervin Corporation, $49 a share.

TRANSACTIONS FOR 19X2

Apr. 12 Sold 200 shares of Dentex Corporation common stock for $19 a share, less a brokerage fee of $85.

Dec. 31 On this date, the values of the shares held for investment were Dentex Corporation, $20 a share; Ervin Corporation, $53 a share.

PROBLEM 35-5

Selected transactions relating to long-term investments of the Fuji Corporation are given below and on page 680.

INSTRUCTIONS Record all the transactions in general journal form.

TRANSACTIONS FOR 19X1

Feb. 10 Purchased 2,000 of the 8,000 outstanding common shares of the Gestic Corporation for $49.75 a share, plus brokerage fees of $500.

Dec. 31 The Gestic Corporation reported net income of $56,000 for the year ended Dec. 31, 19X1.

TRANSACTIONS FOR 19X2

July 5   Received $4,000 representing a cash dividend of $2 a share on the outstanding common stock of the Gestic Corporation.

Dec. 31   The Gestic Corporation reported a net loss of $8,000 for the year ended Dec. 31, 19X2.

TRANSACTIONS FOR 19X3

Mar. 8   Received 200 shares of Gestic Corporation common stock, representing a 10 percent common stock dividend distributed by Gestic. (Compute the new cost for each share to the nearest tenth of a cent.)

June 8   Sold the 200 shares of Gestic Corporation common stock received as a stock dividend on Mar. 8. The stock was sold for $49.50 a share less transfer taxes of $49.50.

alternate problems

PROBLEM 35-1A

The Boulder Realty Corporation has excess cash on hand between development projects and decides to invest the funds temporarily. Selected transactions for 19X1 are shown below.

INSTRUCTIONS   Record each of the transactions in general journal form. (Use the account titles given in the related textbook illustrations.)

TRANSACTIONS FOR 19X1

Jan. 1   Purchased $100,000 face value U.S. Treasury 8 percent bonds, maturing in 19Y1, at 97. Interest is payable on Apr. 1 and Oct. 1. The brokerage fee amounted to $500.

Mar. 1   Purchased 25 City National Bank Company 10 percent, $1,000 bonds, maturing in 19Y1, at 99. Interest is payable on Jan. 1 and July 1. The brokerage fee amounted to $215.

Apr. 1   Received a check for the semiannual interest on the government bonds.

July 1   Received a check for the semiannual interest on the bank bonds.

Oct. 1   Received a check for the semiannual interest on the government bonds.

Nov. 1   Sold the 25 City National Bank Company bonds at 98 plus accrued interest. Paid a brokerage fee of $200.

Dec. 1   Sold all the government bonds at 98 plus accrued interest. Paid a brokerage fee of $375.

PROBLEM 35-2A

The transactions shown on the next page are for the Ginsberg Company. They relate to its temporary investments in common stock in 19X1 and 19X2.

INSTRUCTIONS
1. Record each of the transactions in general journal form.
2. Show how the short-term investments will appear on the balance sheet as of December 31, 19X1.

TRANSACTIONS FOR 19X1

Nov. 1 Purchased 100 shares of Zeno Corporation common stock for $42 a share, plus brokerage fees of $120.
Nov. 8 Purchased 200 shares of Bay Corporation common stock for $36 a share, plus brokerage fees of $190.
Dec. 31 On this date, the market values of the stock investments owned by the Ginsberg Company were as follows: Zeno Corporation, $43 a share; Bay Corporation, $32 a share.

TRANSACTIONS FOR 19X2

June 18 The Zeno Corporation declared a cash dividend of $1 a share payable on July 10 to stockholders of record as of June 30. (The Ginsberg Company records dividend income when dividends are declared.)
July 10 Received a cash dividend on the Zeno Corporation stock.
Dec. 31 On this date, the market values of the stock investments owned by the Ginsberg Company were as follows: Zeno Corporation, $43 a share; Bay Corporation, $41 a share.

PROBLEM 35-3A The Earle Corporation makes certain long-term investments to earn income. The selected transactions shown below and on page 682 took place during the years 19X1 and 19X2.

INSTRUCTIONS Record the transactions in general journal form.

TRANSACTIONS FOR 19X1

Jan. 1 Purchased as a long-term investment $30,000 par value AB Corporation 7 percent bonds at a price of $30,795 for the bonds, plus accrued interest and a brokerage fee of $25. The bonds pay interest semiannually on Apr. 30 and Oct. 31. They mature on Oct. 31, 19X7.
Apr. 30 Received interest on the AB Corporation bonds. Amortized the premium for four months. (Use one compound entry.)
Oct. 31 Received interest on the AB Corporation bonds. Amortized the premium for six months. (Use a compound entry.)
Dec. 31 Made an adjusting entry for accrued interest on the AB Corporation bonds. Amortized the premium for two months. (Use a compound entry.) Made an entry to close Interest Earned to Revenue and Expense Summary.

TRANSACTIONS FOR 19X2

Jan. 1 Reversed the adjusting entry prepared on Dec. 31.
Apr. 30 Received interest on the AB Corporation bonds. Amortized the premium for six months. (Use a compound entry.)
Oct. 31 Received interest on the AB Corporation bonds. Amortized the premium for six months. (Use a compound entry.)
Nov. 30 Because cash was needed for unexpected repairs, sold the AB Cor-

poration bonds for $30,300 less a brokerage fee of $150 plus accrued interest. (Amortize the premium for one month. Then determine and record the gain or loss on the sale of the AB Corporation bonds.)

Dec. 31 Closed the Interest Earned and Gain or Loss on Sale of Investments accounts to Revenue and Expense Summary.

PROBLEM 35-4A The data shown below relates to long-term investments in stock made by the Craig Corporation in 19X1 and 19X2.

INSTRUCTIONS
1. Record all transactions in general journal form.
2. Show how the investments will appear on the balance sheet as of December 31, 19X1.
3. Show how the Cumulative Unrealized Net Loss account will be reported on the balance sheet as of December 31, 19X1.

TRANSACTIONS FOR 19X1

July 10 Purchased 2,000 shares of Welt Company common stock for $11.75 a share plus a brokerage fee of $500. The Welt Company has outstanding 50,000 shares of common stock.

Aug. 30 Received 200 shares of Welt Company common stock, representing a 10 percent dividend on the 2,000 shares owned.

Sept. 18 Purchased 500 shares of Veno Corporation common stock for $42 a share plus a brokerage fee of $300.

Dec. 31 On this date, the values of the shares held for investment by the Craig Corporation were as follows: Welt Company, $10 a share; Veno Corporation, $40 a share.

TRANSACTIONS FOR 19X2

June 10 Sold 1,100 shares of Welt Company common stock for $13.50 a share, less a brokerage fee of $230.

Dec. 31 On this date, the values of the shares held as an investment by the Craig Corporation were as follows: Welt Company, $12 a share; Veno Corporation, $40 a share.

PROBLEM 35-5A Selected transactions relating to long-term investments of the Urus Company are given below and on the next page.

INSTRUCTIONS Record all the transactions in general journal form.

TRANSACTIONS FOR 19X1

Jan. 6 Purchased 1,000 of the 3,000 outstanding common shares of the Thiro Corporation for $22 a share plus a brokerage fee of $440.

Dec. 31 The Thiro Corporation reported net income of $12,000 for the year ended Dec. 31, 19X1.

TRANSACTIONS FOR 19X2

June 10   Received $1,000 representing a cash dividend of $1 a share on the outstanding common stock of the Thiro Corporation.

Dec. 31   The Thiro Corporation reported a net loss of $6,000 for the year ended Dec. 31, 19X2.

TRANSACTIONS FOR 19X3

Feb. 10   Received 100 shares of Thiro Corporation common stock, representing a 10 percent common stock dividend distributed by that corporation.

Mar. 20   Sold the 100 shares of Thiro Corporation common stock received as a dividend on Feb. 10. The stock was sold for $21.50 a share less a brokerage fee of $65.

index

Accountants, 2–3
Accounting, *def.*, 2
Accounting principles, 352–367
  accrual basis, 358
  consistency, 358
  cost basis, 356
  full disclosure, 358
  matching costs with revenue, 357
  modifying conventions, 360–361
    conservatism, 360–361
    industry practice, 361
    materiality, 360
  need for, 352
  realization, 356–357
  sources of, 352–355
    FASB and predecessors, 353–355
    other organizations, 355
    SEC and, 353
  underlying assumptions, 358–360
    going concern, 359
    objectivity, 359
    periodicity of income, 360
    separate entity, 358–359
    stable monetary unit, 359
Accounting Principles Board (APB)
  Opinions, 353, 440–441, 613
  Statements, 353–354
Accounting Series Releases, 353
Accounts, 19–37; *def.*, 19 (*see also specific types of accounts*)
  asset, 20 (*see also* Assets)
  chart of accounts, 30, 83, 305–306
  double-entry system, 29–30
  expense, 25–28 (*see also* Expenses)
  finding the balance of, 52–55
  liability, 21–22 (*see also* Liabilities)
  owner's equity, 21 (*see also* Owner's Equity)
  permanent, 30–31
  revenue, 23–25 (*see also* Revenue)
  rules of debit and credit, 29
  temporary, 31
Accounts payable, *def.*, 5
  schedule of, 214; *illus.*, 214
Accounts Payable Control account, 214
Accounts payable ledger, 205–220
  accounts with individual creditors and, 208
    posting a payment to, 209–210
    posting a purchase to, 208–209
    posting a purchase return or allowance to, 210
  control account and, 214
  proving, 214
  routine for posting, 210–213
  schedule of accounts payable and, 214; *illus.*, 214
Accounts receivable, *def.*, 9
  collecting, 9–10
  from credit card company sales, 182–184

Accounts receivable (*continued*)
  schedule of, 181–182; *illus.*, 181
  schedule of accounts receivable by age, 399–400; *illus.*, 399
  writing off as uncollectible, 397–400
Accounts Receivable Control account, 182
Accounts receivable ledger, 169–190
  accounts for individual credit customers and, 171–172
    posting a receipt to, 173–174
    posting a sale to, 172–173
    posting a sales return or allowance to, 175–176
  aging of, 399–400; *illus.*, 399
  bad debts and (*see* Bad debts)
  control account and, 182
  credit card company sales and, 182–184
  proving, 181–182
  routine for posting, 176–177, 180–181
  schedule of accounts receivable and, 181–182; *illus.*, 181
  schedule of accounts receivable by age and, 399–400; *illus.*, 399
Accrual basis of accounting, 358, 465–466, 524–526; *def.*, 358, 465
Accruals, 465–485
  adjustments for, on worksheet, 465–485
  recording accrued expenses, 469–472
    interest on notes payable, 471–472; *illus.*, 472
    payroll taxes, 470–471; *illus.*, 471
    property taxes, 469–470; *illus.*, 470
    salaries and wages, 470; *illus.*, 470
  recording accrued income, 474–477
    commissions on sales tax, 475–476; *illus.*, 476
    interest on notes receivable, 475; *illus.*, 475
    other income items, 476–477
  recording bad debts, 467–468; *illus.*, 468
  recording depreciation, 468–469
  recording prepaid expenses, 472–474
    prepaid interest on notes payable, 473–474; *illus.*, 474
    store supplies on hand, 472; *illus.*, 473
    unexpired insurance, 473; *illus.*, 473
  recording unearned income, 477–478
    subscription income for a publisher, 477; *illus.*, 477

Adjusted trial balance, 312, 486–491; *illus.*, 312, 488
Adjusting and closing procedures, 307–312, 324–334, 504–523
  journalizing the adjusting entries, 324–325, 504; *illus.*, 324–325, 504–506
  journalizing the closing entries, 68–77, 325–330, 507–509; *illus.*, 69–70, 72, 326–327, 329–330, 507–509
    closing the drawing accounts, 330, 509
    closing the expense accounts, 70–72, 326–327, 508
    closing the revenue accounts, 69, 326, 507
    closing the Revenue and Expense Summary account, 72, 329–330, 508
  posting the adjusting entries, 325, 506–507; *illus.*, 506
  posting the closing entries, 71–72, 327–330, 509
  reversing entries, 511–517; *illus.*, 512
    items requiring, 513
    locating, 513–516; *illus.*, 514–516
    posting, 516; *illus.*, 517
  ruling the accounts, 74–77, 509–511; *illus.*, 74–77, 510–511
  taking a postclosing trial balance, 77, 331, 509; *illus.*, 77, 331, 510
Ad valorem taxes, 447
After-closing trial balance, 77; *illus.*, 77 (*see also* Postclosing trial balance)
Aging the accounts receivable, 399–400; *illus.*, 399
Allowance method for charge-off of bad debts, 398–400
American Accounting Association, 354–355, 359
American Institute of Certified Public Accountants (AICPA), 353–354, 359, 362
Amortization, *def.*, 432
  of bond discount, 645–647
  of bond premium, 643–644, 646–647
  of intangible assets, 437–438
  recording, 432–433
Analysis ledger sheet, 450; *illus.*, 450
Articles of copartnership, 530–531
Articles of incorporation, 584–585
Assets, *def.*, 6
  accounts for, 20; *def.*, 20; *illus.*, 21
  contra asset, 310
    debit and credit rules for, 29
    making entries in, 21
  acquisition of, by a corporation, 570–571

Assets (*continued*)
   charge-off of intangible, 617
   current, 334–337
   determining the value of, for partnerships, 528–529; *illus.*, 529
   fixed (*see* Assets, plant and equipment)
   plant and equipment, 337 (*see also* Property, plant, and equipment)
   revaluation of, 566–568
   transfer of, to a corporation, 569
Average cost inventory valuation, 416–417; *illus.*, 416

Bad debts, 310–312, 397–414
   anticipating, 310–312
   on the balance sheet, 403
   charging off, 312
     allowance method, 398–400
     direct method, 397; *illus.*, 397
     collecting an account that was written off, 401–402; *illus.*, 401, 402
   credit policy and, 155–156
   estimating, 398–400
   on the income statement, 402–403
   installment sales procedures and, 403–405; *illus.*, 404, 405
     recording defaults, 405–406
   other receivables and, 402
   providing for losses before they occur, 398–400
     aging the accounts receivable method, 399–400; *illus.*, 399, 400
     percentage of credit sales method, 398–399; *illus.*, 399
     predetermined percentage of accounts receivable method, 400
     valuation account and, 399
   recording losses, 310–311, 397–401
     actual uncollectible amounts, 397, 401; *illus.*, 397, 401
     estimated amount, 398–400; *illus.*, 399–400
   worksheet adjustment for, 311, 467–468
Balance ledger form, 92–93; *illus.*, 93
Balance sheet, 13–14; *def.*, 6, 11; *illus.*, 6, 13, 19, 22, 28, 73, 324, 335, 499, 573
   classified, 334–338; *illus.*, 335, 499
   for a corporation, 572; *illus.*, 573
   fundamental accounting equation and, 7
   for a partnership, 499, 535
   preparing, 6–7, 498; *illus.*, 6, 499
   report form, 334; *illus.*, 335
   taxes and, 454, 615–616; *illus.*, 616

Balance sheet (*continued*)
   worksheet and, 58–61, 491–493, 498; *illus.*, 60–61, 491, 499
Bank credit cards, 157–159
Bank draft, 390
Bank reconciliation, 137–143; *def.*, 137; *illus.*, 137, 138, 142
   adjusting the records and, 143
   bank statement and, 136, 139; *illus.*, 139
   book balance of cash and, 139–140
   deposit in transit and, 137
   outstanding checks and, 137
   reconciliation statement and, 137–138, 142–143; *illus.*, 137–138, 142
   steps in, 140–143
Banking procedures, 129–148
   bank reconciliation (*see* Bank reconciliation)
   bank statement and, 136
   cash controls and, 129
   checks and (*see* Checks)
   deposits and, 129–132
Bill of lading, 390–391
Blank endorsement, 131
Bonds, 564–565, 639–659
   balance sheet presentation of premium and discount, 645–646
   book value of, 646
   carrying value of, 646
   coupon, 641
   interest and, 641–643
     accrual of interest, 642
     payment of interest, 642
   as investment
     long-term, 666–669
     temporary, 660–663
   issued at a discount, 644–645
     adjusting and reversing entries, 645
     amortization of bond discount, 645
   issued at a premium, 643–644
     adjusting and reversing entries, 644
     amortization of bond premium, 643–644
   issued between interest dates, 646–647
     amortization of discount or premium, 646–647
     recording, 646
   registered, 640–641
   retirement of, 648–651
     on due date, 649
     early, 649–651
     retained earnings for, 648–649
   secured, 640
   sinking fund, 647–648; *illus.*, 648
   unsecured, 640
Book of final entry, 42

Book of original entry, 39
Book value
   of bonds, 646
   of fixed assets, 310, 433; *def.*, 310
   sale of assets and, 438–439
Borrowing money, 639
   bonds, 640 (*see also* Bonds)
   long-term notes, 640
   mortgage loans, 640, 651
   short-term notes, 639
Business credit cards, 156–157
Business entity, 4; *def.*, 2
Business taxes, 447–464
   federal excise, 454, 458
   franchise tax, 559
   income tax (*see also* Corporation earnings, income tax)
     for corporations, 459, 559
     for partnerships, 458–459
   payroll taxes (*see* Payroll taxes)
   property taxes, 447–449, 452–453
     accounting for, 448–449, 452–453
     assessment of, 448
     collection of, 448
     notice of, *illus.*, 449
     payment dates, 448
     tax rate, 448
     taxable property, 447–448
   retail licenses and, 449–450
   statement presentation, 453–454
   stock tax on merchandise inventory, 450–452; *illus.*, 451
   sales (*see* Sales tax)
   tax calendar, 459
   types of, 447
Business transactions, analyzing, 2–18
   balance sheet and, 13–14
   collecting receivables, 9–10
   effects of revenue and expenses, 7–8
   fundamental accounting equation and, 7
   income statement and, 11–13
   investment by owner, 3–4
   paying a creditor, 5–6
   paying expenses, 10–11
   purchasing business property, 4–5
   selling services, 8–9

Capital, *def.*, 3
   interest on, 543, 544
Capital account, owner's, 20–21
Capital account, partner's, 529, 540
   division of profits and, 541–542
Capital stock ledger, 589–592; *illus.*, 590, 592
Capital stock transactions, 584–611
   issuing new certificates, 591; *illus.*, 591
   issuing stock
     additional, 586

Capital stock transactions, issuing
    stock (*continued*)
  at a discount, 593–594
  to the incorporators, 585–586
  no-par value, 595
  at a premium, 593
  subscriptions and, 596–597
  no-par value stock
    issuing, above stated value, 595
    stated value for, 594
  posting to capital stock ledger,
    589–592; *illus.*, 590, 592
  premium on, 626
  recording in capital stock transfer
    journal, 590–591; *illus.*, 591
  redemption of preferred stock,
    600–601
  registrar and, 592–593
  stock assignment form, 590; *illus.*,
    590
  stock certificate books, 588–589;
    illus., 589
  subscriptions, 595–598
    collection of, and issuance of
      stock, 596–597
    defaults on, 597
    receipt of, 595–596
    records of, 597–598
    subscribers' ledger, 598
    subscription book, 598
  transfer agent and, 592
  treasury stock, 598–600; *def.*, 598
  watered stock, 594
Capital stock transfer journal, 590–
  591; *illus.*, 591
Capitalized costs, 431
Carrying value of bonds, 646
Carrying value of fixed assets, 310
Cash discounts, recording
  on purchases, 116
  on sales, 94–95
  statement presentation, 338; *illus.*,
    339
Cash discounts lost, recording, 243–
  244
Cash payments
  internal control over, 116–117
    petty cash fund and, 120
    voucher system and, 117
  recording, 107–116
Cash payments journal, 107–121
  multicolumn, 111; *illus.*, 111
    advantages of, 112–113
    posting from, 112
    recording entries in, 108, 111,
      114–116
      cash discount on purchases, 116
      cash purchase of assets, 108, 111
      payment on account, 108, 111
      payment of expenses, 108, 111
      payment of notes and interest,
        115–116

Cash payments journal, recording
    entries in (*continued*)
    payment of sales taxes, 114–115
    withdrawals by owner, 114
  single column, 108; *illus.*, 108
  posting from, 109–111
Cash receipts
  cash short or over, 99–100
  internal control over, 98, 129
    change fund and, 99
  recording, 87–97
Cash receipts journal, 87–106
  multicolumn, 90–91; *illus.*, 91
    advantages of, 92
    posting from, 91–92
    recording entries in, 88–91, 94–97
      cash discounts on sales, 94–95
      cash received on account, 88, 91
      cash sales, 88, 91
      investment by the owner, 95
      notes receivable collection, 95–97
      sales tax, 93–94
  single column, 88–89; *illus.*, 88
    posting from, 89–90
Cash short or over, 99–100
Cashier's check, 390
Change fund, 99
Charge account, *def.*, 5
Charge account sales, 156–157 (*see
    also* Sales on credit)
Chart of accounts, 30, 83, 305; *def.*,
    30; *illus.*, 30, 83, 232, 305–306
Check register, 236–239; *illus.*, 237
Checks, *def.*, 133; *illus.*, 134, 136
  ABA identification number on, 131
  cashier's, 390
  deposit slips and, 131
  dishonored, 132, 141
  endorsements of, 131; *illus.*, 131
  magnetic character readers and,
    135
  making payments by, 133–136
  NSF, 132, 141
  outstanding, 137
  postdated, 132–133
  signature cards and, 133
  stubs of, 134–135; *illus.*, 134
Clearing account, 198
Closing the books, 68–86, 325–330,
    507–511; *def.*, 68 (*see also* Ad-
    justing and closing procedures)
COD sales, 161
Combined journal, 221–230; *illus.*,
    224
  designing, 221–222
  merchandising business and, 226
  postings from, 224, 226
  professional offices and, 226
  proving, 224; *illus.*, 225
  recording transactions in, 222–224;
    illus., 224
  service business and, 226

Commercial draft, 390–391
Common stock, *def.*, 560 (*see also*
    Stock)
  dividends on, 561
Compensation record, 268
Conservatism, 360–361
Consistency, 358
Contingent liability, 386, 594
Continuity of existence, 359
Contra asset accounts, *def.*, 310
Control account
  for accounts payable, 214
  for accounts receivable, 182
Copyrights, 437
Corporate charter, 558
Corporate records
  capital stock ledger, 589–592
  capital stock transfer journal, 590–
    591
  corporate charter, 558
  minute book, 588
  stock certificate books, 588–589
  stockholders' ledger, 589
  subscribers' ledger, 598
  subscription book, 598
Corporation earnings, 612–638
  appropriations of retained earnings,
    619–621, 626
  dividends, 560–561, 621–625
    cash, 622–623
    on common stock, 561
    declaration of, 622–623
    declaration date, 622
    legality, 621
    payment of cash, 623–624
    payment date, 622
    on preferred stock, 560–561
    record date, 622
    stock, 624–625, 626
  income tax
    balance sheet and, 615–616
    estimating, 614–615
    formal tax return, 617
    income statement and, 615
    net income and, 613–614
    recording on the worksheet, 615
    statement of retained earnings
      and, 616
    tax rates and, 614–615
    transferring net income and,
      616–617
  net income, *illus.*, 614
    all-inclusive concept, 612–613,
      617–618
    clean surplus concept, 617
    current operating concept, 612
    determining, 612–613
    extraordinary, nonrecurring items
      and, 612
    income taxes and, 613–614, 616–
      617
    prior period adjustments and, 612

Corporation earnings, net income (*continued*)
   transferring, 616–617
   prior period adjustments, 617–619; *illus.*, 618, 619
   retained earnings, 616, 619–621, 625–626 (*see also* Retained earnings)
Corporations, 557–583
  assets and liabilities and
   acquisition of, 570–571
   transfer of, 569
  balance sheet for, 572; *illus.*, 573
  characteristics of, 558–559
   continuous existence, 558
   corporate income tax, 559
   legal basis, 559
   limited liability of owners, 558
   owners are not agents, 558
   transferability of ownership rights, 558
  comparison of dividend provisions, 562–564
  distribution of stock, 569–570
  dividends to stockholders, 560–561
  financing with bonds, 564–565
  formation of, 559
  income tax returns for, 459, 559
  incorporating a sole proprietorship, 565–566
  issuance of stock to the proprietorship, 571
  legal aspects of, 557
  organization costs, 571–572
  organizing, 559–572
  records for (*see* Corporate records)
  structure of, 558
  types of stock, 559–560
   common stock, 560
   preferred stock, 560
  values of capital stock, 561
   par value, 561
   stated value, 561
Cost of goods sold, 313–314, 323, 338; *illus.*, 323, 339, 495
  accounting for, 313–314
Cost or market method of inventory valuation, 420–422
Credit, 155–161 (*see also* Purchases on credit; Sales on credit)
  bad debts and, 155–156
  charge account sales, 156–157
  COD sales, 161
  credit cards (*see* Credit cards)
  granting of, 155
  layaway, 160–161
  open-account, 156
  policies, 155–156
Credit balance, 53–54; *illus.*, 54
Credit cards
  accounts payable and, 214
  bank, 157–159

Credit cards (*continued*)
  business, 156–157
  credit card companies and, 159–160
   accounts receivable from, 182–184
  purchases by, 197–198
  sales slips for, 156, 157, 159; *illus.*, 157
Credit customers, accounts for (*see* Accounts receivable ledger)
Credit purchases (*see* Purchases on credit)
Credit sales (*see* Sales on credit)
Creditors, *def.*, 5
  accounts for (*see* Accounts payable ledger)
Current assets, 334–337
Current liabilities, 337

Debit balance, *def.*, 52; *illus.*, 53
Debit and credit rules, 29
Declining-balance method of depreciation, 434–435
Departmental accounting
  income statement for, 338; *illus.*, 339
Depletion, *def.*, 432
  cost method, 436–437
  percentage method, 437
  recording, 432–433
Deposit slip, 129–132
Deposits, bank
  delivering, 132
  receipt for, 132
  in transit, 137
Depreciation, 307–310; *def.*, 307, 432
  adjusting journal entries for, 307, 324, 504; *illus.*, 324, 505
  determining, 308
  methods of accounting for, 432–436
   declining-balance, 434–435
   straight-line, 307, 434
   sum-of-the-years'-digits, 435–436
   units-of-output, 436
  recording, 309, 432–433
  schedule of equipment and, 308
  worksheet adjustments for, 309–310, 468–469; *illus.*, 309, 469
Direct charge-off method, for bad debts, 397
Discount, issuing stock at a, 593–594
Discounting
  notes payable, 373–374
  notes receivable, 384–389
Discounts
  for bank credit card sales, 157–159
  cash, 94–95, 116
   paying invoices less, 238
   recording lost cash discounts, 243–244

Discounts (*continued*)
   statement presentation of cash discounts, 338; *illus.*, 339
  trade, 154–155
Dishonored notes receivable, 384
Dividends, 560–561, 621–625; *def.*, 459 (*see also* Corporation earnings, dividends)
  on common stock, 561
  comparison of, 562–564
  on preferred stock, 560–561
Dollar signs in financial records, 78
Double-entry system, *def.*, 29–30
Double-posting procedure, 382
Drafts, 389–391; *def.*, 389
  bank, 390
  commercial, 390–391
  sight, 390–391
  time, 391
Drawee of checks, 133
Drawer of checks, 131, 133
Drawing account, owner's, 114
Drawing account, partner's, 540–541

Earnings, corporation, 612–638
Economic entity, *def.*, 2
Employer's Annual Federal Unemployment Tax Return, Form 940, 292–294; *illus.*, 293
Employer's Quarterly Federal Tax Return, Form 941, 283–286; *illus.*, 285
Endorsements of checks, 131
Equity, *def.*, 3 (*see also* Owner's equity; Partners' equity; Stockholders' equity)
  trading on the, 565
Excise tax, federal, 454, 458
Expenses, *def.*, 8
  accounts for, 25–28
  administrative, 340
  closing expense accounts, 70–72, 326–327, 508
  operating, 338, 340
  other (nonoperating), 341
  paying, 10–11
  plant, 340
  selling, 340
  types of, 338, 340
Experience-rating system, for unemployment insurance, 290

Face value, of notes, 369
Fair Labor Standards Act, 253
Fair market value, 441
Federal income tax withholding, 256–260
  computing, 257, 260; *illus.*, 259
  deposits of, 279–283

Federal income tax withholding (continued)
  exemptions and allowances, 257; illus., 258
Federal Insurance Contributions Act (FICA) tax, 252, 255–256, 263
  deposits of, 279–283
  employee's, 255–256
  employer's, 280
Federal Tax Deposit
  Form 501, 279; illus., 281
  Form 508, 291–292; illus., 292
Federal Unemployment Tax Act (FUTA) tax, 252, 289–294
  deposit of, 291–292, 294
  payment of, 294
Federal unemployment tax return, 292–294; illus., 293
Financial Accounting Standards Board (FASB), 353–355
Financial statements, 11–14, 322–324, 334–341, 494–498 (see also specific statements)
  balance sheet, 13–14, 323–324, 334–338, 489, 572; illus., 13, 324, 335, 499, 573
    for a corporation, 572; illus., 573
    for a partnership, 498; illus., 499
    for a sole proprietorship, 13–14, 61, 323–324, 334–338; illus., 13, 61, 324, 335
  classified balance sheet, 334–338; illus., 335
  classified income statement, 338–341; illus., 339
  income statement, 11–13, 322–323, 494; illus., 12, 61, 322–323, 495
    for a departmental business, 338; illus., 339
    for a partnership, 494; illus., 495
    for a sole proprietorship, 11–13, 322–323; illus., 12, 61, 322–323
  statement of partners' equities, 498; illus., 498
  statement of retained earnings, 616; illus., 623
First in, first out inventory valuation (FIFO), 417
  compared to other methods, 419
Fixed assets (see Property, plant, and equipment)
Footings, 53
Franchise tax, 559
Free on board (FOB), def., 431
Freight in, 192–193
Full disclosure, 358
Full endorsement, 131
Fundamental accounting equation, 7, 20

General journal, 38–42; def., 38; illus., 38, 41

General journal (continued)
  entries in, 39–42
    for cash payments, 107–108
    for cash receipts, 87–88
    compound, 41–42; illus., 42
    posting of, to the ledger, 43–46
    for purchases on credit, 192–194
    for sales on credit, 149
General ledger, 42–43; def., 42
  analysis ledger form for, 450; illus., 450
  balance ledger form for, 92–93; illus., 93
  balancing, 52–55
  postclosing trial balance for, 77
  posting to, 43–46
  proving, 52, 55–56, 77
  ruling the accounts, 74–77, 509–511; illus., 74–77, 510–511
  standard ledger form for, 42; illus., 42
  trial balance for, 52, 55–56
Generally accepted accounting principles (see Accounting principles)
Going concern, 359
Gross profit inventory estimation, 422–423; illus., 423

Historical cost framework of accounting, 356
Holding company, 660
Hourly-paid employees (see Payroll accounting)

Income, def., 8 (see also Revenue)
  periodicity of, 360
Income and Expense Summary account, 68 (see also Revenue and Expense Summary account)
Income statement, 11–13, 322–323, 494; def., 11–12; illus., 12, 61, 322–323, 495
  classified, 338, 340–341; illus., 339, 495
  for a departmental business, 338; illus., 339
  for a partnership, 494; illus., 495
  preparing, 11–13, 322–323, 494
  for a sole proprietorship, 11–13, 322–323; illus., 12, 61, 322–323
  taxes and, 454, 615
  worksheet and, 58–61, 493–494; illus., 60–61, 493, 495
Income Summary account, 68 (see also Revenue and Expense Summary account)
Income taxes (see also Corporation earnings, income tax; Payroll taxes)
  for corporations, 559
  returns, 459

Income taxes (continued)
  returns for partnerships, 458–459
Individual earnings record, 268–269
  proving, 270–271
Installment sales, 403–407
Intangible personal property, 430
Interest
  on bonds, 641–643
    accrual of interest, 642
    issued at par, 641–642
    payment of interest, 642
  on notes payable, 369–372
    calculation of, 371–372
    financial statements and, 375
    payment of the note and, 372
    purchase of an asset and, 369–370
  on notes receivable, 382–383
    calculation of, 383
    collection of note, 383
    discounting, 387–389
    maturity date, 382
    receipt of note, 382
Internal control system, 97–100 (see also Voucher system)
  cash payments and, 116–117
    petty cash fund and (see Petty cash fund)
    voucher system and, 117
  cash receipts and, 98
    cash short or over and, 99–100
    change fund and, 99
    controls for, 129
  general principles of, 97–98
  purchases and, 197
Inventory, 313–314
  beginning merchandise, 331–334
  ending merchandise, 313–314
  estimation procedures
    for gross profit method, 422–423
    for retail method, 423–424
  stock tax on, 450–452; illus., 451
  valuation of, 415–422 (see also Valuation of inventory)
Inventory sheet, 313; illus., 313
Investments, 660–675 (see also Long-term investments; Temporary investments)

Journals (see specific journals)
Journalizing, 39

Last in, first out inventory valuation (LIFO), 418
  compared to other methods, 419
Layaway sale, 160–161
Ledger (see Accounts payable ledger; Accounts receivable ledger; General ledger)
Ledger sheet, 42, 92–93, 450
Legal life, 437

Liabilities, *def.*, 6
  accounts for, 21–22; *illus.*, 22
    debit and credit rules for, 29
  contingent, 386, 594
  current, 337
  long-term, 337–338
Liquidation value, 560
List price, 154–155
Long-term investments, 666–675; *def.*, 666
  bonds as, 666–669
    accrued interest on, 667–668
    amortizing the discount, 667
    purchase of, at a discount, 667
    purchase of, at a premium, 669
    sale of, 668–669
    statement presentation, 668
  stock as, 670–675
    accounting for, when investor exercises significant influence, 672–674
    accounting for, when investor has no significant influence, 670–672
    amortization of goodwill under equity method, 674
    carrying value of investment, 673–674
    cash dividends from, 672
    recording a decline in value, 670–671
    recording dividends under equity method, 673
    recording a share of the investee's net income, 672–673
    recording a share of the investee's net loss, 673
    recording a stock purchase, 670, 672
    recovery of market value, 671–672
    sale of, 672, 674
    stock dividends, 675
Long-term liabilities, 337–338
Long-term notes, 640

Matching costs with revenue, 307, 357
Materiality, 360
Maturity date, of notes, 369–370
Maturity value, of notes, *def.*, 369
Memorandum entry, 533; *illus.*, 533
Merchandise on hand, 313–314, 331–334
  cost of goods sold and, 314, 331–334
  taking an inventory, 313
  tax on, 450–452; *illus.*, 451
  worksheet and, 313–314, 331–334
Merit-rating system, 290
Minute book, for corporations, 588
Mixed accounts, 465

Mortgage loans, 640, 651

Negotiable instruments, 368 (*see also* Bank draft; Checks; Commercial draft; Notes payable; Notes receivable)
Net book value, 433
Net of discount, 243
Net income, *def.*, 12
  transferring to owner's equity, 72–73
Net loss, *def.*, 12
  transferring to owner's equity, 72–73
Net price, *def.*, 154
Net working capital, *def.*, 527
Net worth (*see* Owner's equity)
No-par value stock, 594–595
Nominal accounts, 31
Notes
  long-term, 640
  noninterest-bearing, 381–382, 385–387, 651–652
  payable, 369–380
  receivable, 381–396
  short-term, 639
Notes and interest, payment of, 115–116
Notes payable, 369–380; *def.*, 369; *illus.*, 368
  discounting of, at the bank, 373–374
    paying the note, 374
    recording the note, 373–374
  financial statements and, 375
  given in purchase of an asset, 369–370
  interest on, 369–372
  payment of, 372, 374
    partial, 372–373
  register, 374–375
  renewing, 373
  schedule of, 374
Notes payable register, 374–375; *illus.*, 374
Notes receivable, 381–396; *def.*, 381
  collection, 95–97
    of interest-bearing note, 383
    of noninterest-bearing note, 382
    not collected at maturity, 384
    partial, 383
  discounting, 384–389
    contingent liability, 386
    dishonored at maturity and, 387–389
    interest-bearing notes, 387–389
    noninterest-bearing notes, 385–386
    paid at maturity and, 386, 388
  dishonored, 387, 388–389
  financial statements and, 389
  interest-bearing, 382–383

Notes receivable, interest bearing (*continued*)
    calculation of interest, 383
    collection of note, 383
    discounting, 387–389
    maturity date, 382
    receipt of note, 382
  noninterest-bearing, 381–382
    collection of note, 382
    discounting, 385–387
    maturity date, 382
    receipt of note, 381–382
  register, 389
  at time of sale, 384
Notes receivable register, 389; *illus.*, 389
NSF check, 132, 141

Objectivity, 359
Open-account credit, 156; *def.*, 5 (*see also* Sales on credit)
Owner's equity, *def.*, 6 (*see also* Partners' equity; Stockholders' equity)
  capital, 21
  debit and credit rules for, 29
  drawing, 114
  expense, 25–27
  revenue, 23–25

Paid-in capital, 626–627
Parent company, 660
Partners' equity
  accounts for, 231–232, 540–541
  statement of, 498; *illus.*, 498
Partnerships, 527–529
  admitting a new partner, 548–551
  conversion of a sole proprietorship to a partnership, 529–535
  division of profits, 541–547
  financial statements for
    balance sheet, 498; *illus.*, 499, 535
    income statement, 494; *illus.*, 495
    statement of partners' equities, 498; *illus.*, 498
  formation of, 527–528
  income tax returns for, 458–459
  interest on capital, 543–544
  opening the partnership books, 533–534; *illus.*, 533–535
  partner's capital account, 540
  partner's drawing account, 540–541
    salary and, 541
  partnership agreement, 530–531
  partnership equity on the statements, 548
  profit sharing agreement, 542–543
  salary allowance, 543
Patents, 437

691

Payee, 131, 133–134
Payment voucher, 232–234; *illus.*, 234
Payor, 131
Payroll accounting, 252–272, 279–295
  accounting entries for payroll
    posted to ledger accounts, 269–270, 282
    recorded in journals, 265–266, 267–268, 272, 281, 286
  deductions from gross pay, 255–263
    not required by law, 260, 262
    required by law, 255–260
  Employee's Withholding Allowance Certificate, Form W-4, 257; *illus.*, 258–259
  federal income tax withholding, 256–260, 263
    tax tables for, 257, 260; *illus.*, 261–262, 264
  FICA tax, 255–256
  hourly-rate employees, *def.*, 254
    determining gross pay of, 254–255
  individual earnings records, 268–269; *illus.*, 268, 270, 283
    proving, 270–271
  liability for unpaid wages, 271–272
  paying the payroll, 266–267
  payroll register, 263, 265; *illus.*, 266–267
  recording gross pay and deductions, 263, 265; *illus.*, 266–267
  salaried employees, 254, 263; *def.*, 254
    determining gross pay of, 263
    recording gross pay and deductions for, 267–268
  tax-exempt wages, 255
Payroll register, 263, 265; *illus.*, 266–267
Payroll taxes, 279–295
  changes in tax rates and bases and, 279
  deposits of taxes, 279–283, 291–292, 294
  Employer's Quarterly Federal Tax Return, 283–286; *illus.*, 285
  Employer's Tax Guide (Circular E), 256, 267
  federal income tax withholding, 256–260, 263
    computing, 257, 260
    exemptions and allowances, 257; *illus.*, 258–259
    tax tables, 257, 260; *illus.*, 261–262, 264
  Transmittal of Income and Tax Statements, 288; *illus.*, 288
  unemployment insurance, 288–294 (*see also* Unemployment insurance)
  Wage and Tax Statements to employees, 286–287; *illus.*, 287

Payroll taxes (*continued*)
  worker's compensation insurance, 294–295
Percentage-of-completion basis, for income realization, 357
Periodicity of income, 360
Permanent accounts, *def.*, 30–31
Petty cash book, 118
Petty cash fund, 117–120
  analysis sheet, 118–120; *illus.*, 119
  establishing, 117–118
  internal control of, 120
  making payments from, 118
  replenishing, 119–120
Petty cash voucher, 118; *illus.*, 118
Physical inventory, 415
  taking a, 313
Postclosing trial balance, 77, 331, 509; *illus.*, 77, 331, 510
Posting, 43–46; *def.*, 43
  to accounts payable ledger, 208–210
  to accounts receivable ledger, 173–176
  adjusting entries, 325, 506–507
  from cash payments journal
    multicolumn, 112
    single column, 109–111
  from cash receipts journal, 100
    multicolumn, 91–92
    single column, 89–90
  closing entries, 71–72, 327–330, 509
  from combined journal, 224, 226
  from general journal, 43–46
  to general ledger, 43–46
  from purchases journal, 194–195
  from sales journal, 151
  voucher system and, 235–236, 238–239
Preferred stock, 560–561 (*see also* Stock, preferred)
Premium, issuing stock at a, 593
Prepaid taxes, 451–453, 474
Principal, of a note, 369
Profit and loss statement (*see* Income statement)
Promissory notes, 95–97 (*see also* Notes payable; Notes receivable)
Property, plant, and equipment, 430–446
  acquisition of, 430–431
  amortization of, *def.*, 432
    of intangible assets, 437–438
    recording, 432–433
  classification of, 430
  costs of using, 431
  depletion of, *def.*, 432
    cost method of, 436–437
    percentage method of, 437
    recording, 432–433
  depreciation of, *def.*, 432
    accelerated methods of, 435
    declining-balance method of, 434–435

Property, plant, and equipment, depreciation of, (*continued*)
    recording, 432–433
    straight-line method of, 434
    sum-of-the-years'-digits method of, 435–436
    units-of-output method of, 436
  disposition of an asset, 438–439
    sale above book value, 438–439
    sale at book value, 438
    sale below book value, 439
  intangible personal property, 430
  real property, 430
  tangible personal property, 430
  trade-in of an asset, 439–441
    fair market value method, 441
    income tax method, 439–441
Property taxes, 447–449, 452–453 (*see also* Business taxes, property taxes)
Proprietorship (*see* Owner's equity)
Proxy, 586–587
Purchases discount, 116, 338
Purchases journal, 191–204; *illus.*, 194, 196
  advantages of, 195
  credit cards and, 197–198
  internal control of purchases and, 197
  multicolumn, 196; *illus.*, 196
  posting from, 194–195
  recording entries in, 194, 205–206
  recording freight in, 195–196
  single column, 194; *illus.*, 194
Purchases on credit
  internal control of, 197
  recording, 191–198, 205–214
Purchases returns and allowances, 196
  accounts payable ledger and, 210
  statement presentation, 338; *illus.*, 339
  voucher system and, 242–243

Readjusting entry, 512 (*see also* Reversing entries)
Real accounts, 30–31
Real property, 430 (*see also* Property, plant, and equipment)
Realization of revenue, 356–357; *def.*, 356
Receivables, collecting, 9–10
Registrar, for corporate stock, 592–593
Reserves, 620
Restrictive endorsement, 131
Retail licenses, 449–450
Retail method of inventory estimation, 423–424; *illus.*, 424
Retailers, *def.*, 154
Retained earnings, 625–626
  appropriations of, 619–621, 648–649
  statement of, 616; *illus.*, 623

Returns and allowances
   purchases, 196, 210, 242–243
   sales, 153–154, 174–176
Revaluation account, 568–569
Revenue, *def.*, 8
   accounts for, 23–25
   closing revenue accounts, 69, 326, 507
   matching costs with, 357
   operating, 338
   other (nonoperating) income, 341
   realization of, 356–357; *def.*, 356
Revenue and Expense Summary account, 68–73, 326–330, 507–508
   closing of, 71–72, 329–330, 508
   transferring expense balances to, 70–72, 326–327, 508
   transferring revenue balances to, 69, 326, 507
Reversing entries, 511–517; *illus.*, 512
   items requiring, 513
   locating, 513–516; *illus.*, 515–516
   posting, 516; *illus.*, 517
Ruling ledger accounts, 74–77, 509–511, 516; *illus.*, 74–77, 510, 511

Safeguarding receipts, 97
Salaried employees, 254, 263 (*see also* Payroll accounting)
Salary, 541
   allowance for partnership, 543
Sales discount, 94–95
Sales journal, 149–168; *illus.*, 150, 152
   advantages of, 151–152
   multicolumn, 152; *illus.*, 152
   posting from, 151, 173
   recording entries in, 150–152
   sales tax and, 152–154
   single column, 150–151; *illus.*, 150
Sales on credit, 155–161
   recording, 149–161, 169–184
Sales returns and allowances, 153–154; *def.*, 153
   accounts receivable ledger and, 174–175
   sales journal and, 153
   sales tax and, 154
   statement presentation, 338; *illus.*, 339
Sales returns and allowances journal, 176; *illus.*, 176
Sales tax
   city and state, 454
   preparing returns, 454–457; *illus.*, 455–457
   recording, 93–94
      payment of, 114–115
      in Sales account, 457–458; *illus.*, 457, 458
      sales journal and, 152–154
Schedule of accounts payable, 214; *illus.*, 214
Schedule of accounts receivable, 181–182; *illus.*, 181
   by age, 399–400; *illus.*, 399
Schedule of equipment, 308; *illus.*, 308
Securities and Exchange Commission (SEC), 353
Selling expenses, 340
Separate entity, 358–359
Shareholders, 558 (*see also* Stockholders)
Short-term notes, 639
Sight draft, 390–391
Signature card, 133; *illus.*, 133
Sinking fund, bond, 647–648; *illus.*, 648
Social entity, *def.*, 2
Social security system, 252–253
Sole proprietorship, 97, 231
   conversion to a partnership, 529–535
   incorporating, 565–566
Special journals, 87 (*see also specific journals*)
Specific identification inventory valuation, 416
Stable monetary unit, 359
State unemployment insurance, 289–291
State unemployment tax return, 290–291
Statement of income and expenses (*see* Income statement)
Statement of partners' equities, 498; *illus.*, 498
Statement of retained earnings, 616; *illus.*, 623
Statements of Financial Accounting Standards, 354
Stock (*see also* Capital stock transactions)
   on the balance sheet, 561–562, 593–594, 596
   common, *def.*, 560
      dividends on, 561
   distribution of, 569–570
   dividend provisions, 562–564
   dividends, 560–561, 624–625 (*see also* Dividends)
   as investment
      long-term, 670–675
      temporary, 663–666
   no-par value, 561
   one class, 559–560
   par value of, 561
   preferred, *def.*, 560
      cumulative, 560
      dividends on, 560–561
      liquidation preferences on, 560
      noncumulative, 560–561
      nonparticipating, 561
      participating, 561
   redemption of, 600–601

Stock (*continued*)
   stated value of, 561
   types of, 559–560
Stockholders, 558
   meeting of, 586–587
   of record, 622
Stockholders' equity, 625–626
   on balance sheet, 561–562, 593–594, 596
   capital stock, 560–564, 585–586, 593–596, 598–601
   retained earnings, 625–626 (*see also* Retained earnings)
Stockholders ledger, 589
Straight-line depreciation, 307, 434
Subsidiary company, 660
Subsidiary ledgers, 178–180, 211–212 (*see also* Accounts payable ledger; Accounts receivable ledger)
   proving, 181–182, 214
Sum-of-the-years'-digits depreciation, 435–436

T account, *def.*, 20; *illus.*, 20
Tangible personal property, 430
Tax calendar, 459
Taxes
   business (*see* Business taxes)
   depreciation and, 435–436
   inventory valuation and, 420
   payroll (*see* Payroll taxes)
   sales, 93–94, 114–115, 152–154
Temporary accounts, 31 (*see also* Drawing account; Expenses, accounts for; Revenue, accounts for; Revenue and Expense Summary account)
Temporary investments, 660–666; *def.*, 660
   bonds as, 660–663
   stocks as, 663–666
Time-and-a-half pay, 253
Time draft, 391
Trade acceptance, 391
Trade discounts, 154, 155
Trading on the equity, 565
Transfer agent, for corporate stock, 592
Transmittal of Income and Tax Statements, Form W-3, 288; *illus.*, 288
Treasury stock, 598–600; *def.*, 598
   donated, 600
   as paid-in capital, 626
   purchased, 598–600
Trial balance, 52; *illus.*, 53, 55
   adjusted, 312, 486–491
   finding the balance of an account and, 52–55
   finding errors in, 56

Trial balance (continued)
  postclosing (see Postclosing trial balance)
  preparing, 55
  purpose of, 56
  section of worksheet, 57

Uncollectible accounts (see Bad debts)
Unemployment insurance, 288–290
  experience rating and, 290
  federal unemployment insurance, 288–294
    Annual Federal Unemployment Tax Return, Form 940, and, 291–294; illus., 293
    computing credit and, 293
    computing taxable wages and, 294
    deposit of FUTA taxes and, 291–292, 294
    Federal Tax Deposit, Form 508, 291–292; illus., 292
    payment of FUTA taxes and, 294
  legislation concerning, 289
  merit rating and, 290
  state unemployment insurance, 289–291
    payment of taxes and, 290–291
    tax return for, 290–291
    taxable wages and, 290
Uniform Commercial Code, 368
Units-of-output depreciation, 436
Useful life, 437

Valuation account, 399
Valuation of inventory, 415–429
  cost or market, whichever is lower, 420–422
    by groups, 421–422
    by items, 420
    total cost or total market, 421
  costing methods, 415–420
    average cost, 416–417
    comparing results of, 418–420
    first in, first out, 417
    last in, first out, 418
    specific identification, 416
  estimation procedures, 422–424
    gross profit method, 422–423
    retail method, 423–424
  physical inventory and, 415
Verification stamp, 234; illus., 233
Voucher system, 117, 231–244
  check register and, 236–237; illus., 237
  internal control and, 231–232
  paying an invoice less discount, 238
  payment voucher and, 232–234; illus., 234
  petty cash and, 118
  preparing and approving the voucher, 234–235
  proving the accounts payable balance and, 239–240
  recording purchase discounts lost, 243–244
  schedule of unpaid vouchers and, 240

Voucher system (continued)
  transactions requiring special treatment, 240–243
    notes payable, 241–242
    partial payments, 240–241
    purchases returns and allowances, 242–243
  voucher register and, 235; illus., 236–237

Wage and Tax Statement, Form W-2, 286–287; illus., 287
Watered stock, 594
Will-call sale, 160–161
Worker's compensation insurance, 254, 294–295
Working capital, def., 527
Worksheet, 56–60, 309, 311, 314, 466–479, 486–494; illus., 57–60, 68, 316, 496–497
  adjusted trial balance columns, 312, 486–491; illus., 312, 488
  adjustments on, 307–312, 465–479
  balance sheet and, 61
  balance sheet columns, 57–58
  income statement and, 61
  income statement columns, 57–58
  inventory and, 313–314, 331–334, 478, 492–494; illus., 315, 333, 491, 493
  recording estimated tax on, 615; illus., 615
  trial balance columns, 57